500FISH
& SHELLFISH

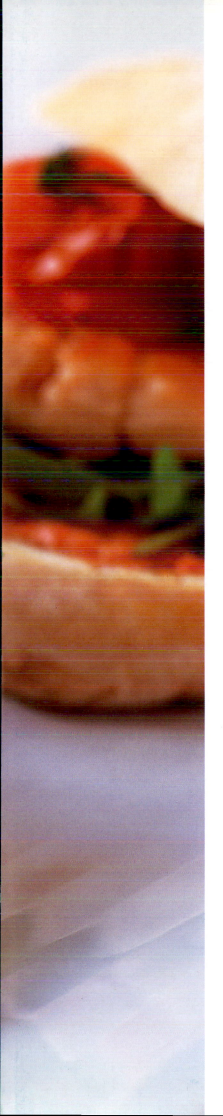

500 FISH
& SHELLFISH

A fabulous collection of classic recipes featuring salmon, trout, tuna, sole, sardines, crab, lobster, squid and more, shown in 500 glorious photographs

EDITED BY ANNE HILDYARD

LORENZ BOOKS

This edition is published by Lorenz Books,
an imprint of Anness Publishing Ltd,
Blaby Road, Wigston,
Leicestershire LE18 4SE

Email: info@anness.com

Web: www.lorenzbooks.com; www.annesspublishing.com

If you like the images in this book and would like to investigate using them for publishing, promotions or advertising, please visit our website www.practicalpictures.com for more information.

Publisher: Joanna Lorenz
Editor: Anne Hildyard
Jacket Design: Nigel Partridge
Production Controller: Wendy Lawson
Design: Ian Sandom

ETHICAL TRADING POLICY
At Anness Publishing we believe that business should be conducted in an ethical and ecologically sustainable way, with respect for the environment and a proper regard to the replacement of the natural resources we employ.
As a publisher, we use a lot of wood pulp to make high-quality paper for printing, and that wood commonly comes from spruce trees. We are therefore currently growing more than 750,000 trees in three Scottish forest plantations: Berrymoss (130 hectares/ 320 acres), West Touxhill (125 hectares/305 acres) and Deveron Forest (75 hectares/185 acres). The forests we manage contain more than 3.5 times the number of trees employed each year in making paper for the books we manufacture.
Because of this ongoing ecological investment programme, you, as our customer, can have the pleasure and reassurance of knowing that a tree is being cultivated on your behalf to naturally replace the materials used to make the book you are holding.
Our forestry programme is run in accordance with the UK Woodland Assurance Scheme (UKWAS) and will be certified by the internationally recognized Forest Stewardship Council (FSC). The FSC is a non-government organization dedicated to promoting responsible management of the world's forests. Certification ensures forests are managed in an environmentally sustainable and socially responsible way. For further information about this scheme, go to www.annesspublishing.com/trees

© Anness Publishing Ltd 2012

A CIP catalogue record for this book is available from the British Library.

Recipes in this book have previously appeared in other books published by Lorenz Books.

PUBLISHER'S NOTE
Although the advice and information in this book are believed to be accurate and true at the time of going to press, neither the authors nor the publisher can accept any legal responsibility or liability for any errors or omissions that may be made nor for any inaccuracies nor for any harm or injury that comes about from following instructions or advice in this book.

Notes

Bracketed terms are intended for American readers.

For all recipes, quantities are given in both metric and imperial measures and, where appropriate, in standard cups and spoons. Follow one set of measures, but not a mixture, because they are not interchangeable.

Standard spoon and cup measures are level. 1 tsp = 5ml, 1 tbsp = 15ml, 1 cup = 250ml/8fl oz. Australian standard tablespoons are 20ml. Australian readers should use 3 tsp in place of 1 tbsp for measuring small quantities.

American pints are 16fl oz/2 cups. American readers should use 20fl oz/2.5 cups in place of 1 pint when measuring liquids.

Electric oven temperatures in this book are for conventional ovens. When using a fan oven, the temperature will probably need to be reduced by about 10–20°C/20–40°F. Since ovens vary, you should check with your manufacturer's instruction book for guidance.

The nutritional analysis given for each recipe is calculated per portion (i.e. serving or item), unless otherwise stated. If the recipe gives a range, such as Serves 4–6, then the nutritional analysis will be for the smaller portion size, i.e. 6 servings. Measurements for sodium do not include salt added to taste. Medium (US large) eggs are used unless otherwise stated.

Main front cover image shows Salmon with Lemon and Tofu Sauce – for recipe, see page 181.

Contents

Introduction

Fish is one of healthiest proteins available; it is low in fat and cholesterol, and high in minerals and vitamins. Eating one portion of oily fish each week is said to be enough to contribute to the well being of your heart by lowering cholesterol levels and helping to clear blocked arteries. However, aside from the benefits to health, fish, when prepared properly, is one of the most delicious foods possible. The infinite variety of fish and shellfish in markets and stores is matched

by the many ways of cooking and preparing this most delightful of foods. However, there is not an infinite supply, and to ensure that sustainable sources of fish are available, schemes such as that of the Marine Stewardship Council (MSC), recognize and reward the fisheries that meet the required environmental standard to secure fish stocks for the future.

For many years fish seemed to fall out of favour, perhaps owing to the prevalence of fast food, or because traditionally fish was eaten only on fast days. However, fish has made a comeback and doctors recommend it as part of a healthy diet. Oily fish in particular may have benefits for heart health. The busy pace of life can mean that people do not have time to cook or prepare fish, but most fishmongers will help by filleting and cleaning the fish, and prepared packs are available at supermarkets. In fact, fish is quicker and easier to cook than foods such as meat, which require some knowledge and judgement to cook correctly.

Fish and shellfish can be used for every type of savoury dish, from appetizers and main courses to salads and soups. Fish lends itself to robust spicy flavours as well as delicate creamy sauces and tangy dressings. Each type of fish has a unique flavour that can be enhanced by cooking it with complementary flavours and ingredients.

This book provides a fantastic resource for cooking any type of fish or shellfish. All the classic dishes are here: Bouillabaisse, Ceviche, Tuna Salad Niçoise, Halibut Steaks with Lemon Butter and Classic Fish Pie. There is also a wide selection of unusual international dishes from Mexico, Africa, the Caribbean, China, Japan, Thailand, Russia, Norway, Spain, France and many other international cuisines. Enjoy the best of fish and shellfish cooking with Fried Squid with Salt and Pepper; Chilli Crab Cakes; Chopped Herring Salad; Crispy Egg Noodle Pancake with Prawns, Scallops and Squid, and Paella Valenciana. Scandinavia has a rich tradition of cooking fish and seafood, and there are recipes for Salt Cod with Mustard Sauce, Fried Eel with Potatoes in Cream Sauce and Anchovy Terrine.

The seafood that is covered in the recipes in this book includes sole, carp, trout, salmon, grouper, mackerel, pike, catfish, cuttlefish, octopus, lobster, clams, cockles and whelks.

The recipes are divided into eight sections: Soups; Appetizers; Salads; Pasta, Rice and Noodles; Poached, Grilled and Steamed; Fried and Baked; Pies, Gratins and Bakes, and Stews, Casseroles and Curries, so it is easy to find the perfect dish for any occasion. Whether you are looking for a family midweek dish, a tasty lunch or an elegant dinner party menu, you will find a recipe that your family or guests will enjoy.

There are 500 tempting recipes, with clearly explained steps, attractive photographs to show what you are aiming for, and nutritional information for each dish to help you plan a balanced meal. With so many dishes to choose from, and a wide range of fish and shellfish available, there is sure to be a dish here to tempt every palate, for every occasion and season.

Bouillabaisse

Perhaps the most famous of all Mediterranean fish soups, this recipe, originating from Marseilles in the south of France, is a rich and colourful mixture of fish and shellfish, flavoured with tomatoes, saffron and orange.

Serves 4–6

1.3–1.6kg/3–3½lb mixed fish and shellfish, such as red mullet, John Dory, monkfish, large prawns (shrimp) and clams
1.2 litres/2 pints/5 cups water
225g/8oz tomatoes
pinch of saffron threads
90ml/6 tbsp olive oil
1 onion, sliced
1 leek, sliced
1 celery stick, sliced
2 garlic cloves, crushed
bouquet garni
1 strip pared orange rind
2.5ml/½ tsp fennel seeds
15ml/1 tbsp tomato
  purée (paste)
10ml/2 tsp Pernod
4–6 thick slices French bread
45ml/3 tbsp chopped
  fresh parsley
salt and ground black pepper

1 Remove the heads, tails and fins from the fish and put in a large pan, with the water. Bring to the boil, and simmer for 15 minutes. Strain, and reserve the liquid. Cut the fish into large chunks. Leave the shellfish in their shells.

2 Scald the tomatoes, then drain and refresh in cold water. Peel and chop them. Soak the saffron in 15–30ml/1–2 tbsp hot water. Heat the oil in the cleaned pan, add the onion, leek and celery and cook until softened. Add the garlic, bouquet garni, orange rind, fennel seeds and tomatoes, then stir in the saffron and liquid and the fish stock. Season with salt and pepper, then bring to the boil and simmer for 30–40 minutes.

3 Add the shellfish and boil for 6 minutes. Discard any clams that remain closed. Add the fish and cook for a further 6–8 minutes. Using a slotted spoon, transfer the fish to a warmed serving platter. Keep the liquid boiling and add the tomato purée and Pernod, then check the seasoning.

4 Place a slice of bread in each soup bowl, pour the broth over and serve the fish separately, sprinkled with the parsley.

Mediterranean Leek and Fish Soup

This chunky soup, which is almost a stew, makes a robust meal in a bowl. Serve it with garlic croûtes.

Serves 4

30ml/2 tbsp olive oil
2 large thick leeks, white and green parts separated
5ml/1 tsp crushed coriander seeds
pinch of dried red chilli flakes
300g/11oz small salad potatoes, thickly sliced
200g/7oz can chopped tomatoes
600ml/1 pint/2½ cups fish stock
150ml/¼ pint/⅔ cup white wine
1 fresh bay leaf
1 star anise
1 strip pared orange rind
good pinch of saffron threads
450g/1lb white fish fillets, such as sea bass, monkfish, cod or haddock, skinned
450g/1lb small squid, cleaned
250g/9oz uncooked peeled prawns (shrimp)
30–45ml/2–3 tbsp chopped fresh parsley
salt and ground black pepper

For the garlic croûtes
1 short French loaf, sliced and toasted
spicy garlic mayonnaise

1 Gently heat the olive oil in a pan, then thinly slice the green part of the leeks. Add with the crushed coriander seeds and the chilli flakes, and cook for 5 minutes, stirring occasionally.

2 Add the sliced potatoes and chopped tomatoes and pour in the fish stock and white wine. Add the bay leaf, star anise, pared orange rind and saffron threads to the pan and stir well.

3 Bring to the boil, reduce the heat and partly cover the pan. Simmer for 20 minutes until the potatoes are tender.

4 Cut the fish into chunks. Cut the squid sacs into rectangles and lightly score a criss-cross pattern into them. Add the fish to the soup and cook for 4 minutes.

5 Add the prawns and cook for 1 minute. Add the squid and the thinly sliced white part of the leek and cook, stirring, for 2 minutes.

6 Stir in the chopped parsley and serve with the toasted croûtes topped with spicy garlic mayonnaise.

Bouillabaise Energy 338Kcal/1418kJ; Protein 42.2g; Carbohydrate 12.8g, of which sugars 3.8g; Fat 13.2g, of which saturates 1.9g; Cholesterol 100mg; Calcium 55mg; Fibre 1.6g; Sodium 239mg.
Leek and Fish Soup Energy 383Kcal/1615kJ; Protein 52g; Carbohydrate 17.8g, of which sugars 4.7g; Fat 9.4g, of which saturates 1.6g; Cholesterol 427mg; Calcium 107mg; Fibre 3.2g; Sodium 326mg.

Fish Soup with Orange

This soup is good served post-Christmas, when bitter Seville oranges are in season.

Serves 6

1kg/2¼lb small hake or whiting, whole but cleaned and filleted
1.2 litres/2 pints/5 cups water
4 bitter oranges or 4 sweet oranges and 2 lemons
30ml/2 tbsp olive oil

5 garlic cloves, unpeeled
1 large onion, finely chopped
1 tomato, peeled, seeded and chopped
4 small potatoes, cut into rounds
5ml/1 tsp paprika
salt and ground black pepper
15–30ml/1–2 tbsp finely chopped fresh parsley, to garnish

1 Cut each fillet into three, reserving all the trimmings. Put the fillets on a plate, salt lightly and chill. Put the trimmings in a pan, add the water and a spiral of orange rind. Bring to a simmer, skim, then cover and cook gently for 30 minutes.

2 Heat the oil in a large flameproof casserole over a high heat. Crush the garlic cloves with the flat of a knife and fry until they are well-coloured. Discard them and turn down the heat. Fry the onion gently until it is softened, adding the tomato halfway through.

3 Strain in the hot fish stock and bring back to the boil. Add the potatoes to the pan and cook them for about 5 minutes.

4 Add the fish pieces to the soup, a few at a time, without letting it go off the boil. Cook for about 15 minutes. Add the orange juice and lemon juice, if using, and the paprika, with salt and pepper to taste. Serve in bowls, garnished with parsley.

> **Cook's Tip**
> To make fish stock, place 450g/1lb white fish trimmings in a large pan. Add a chopped onion, carrot, bay leaf, parsley sprig, 6 peppercorns and a 5cm/2in piece of pared lemon rind. Add 1.2 litres/2 pints/5 cups water, bring to the boil, then simmer gently for 25–30 minutes. Strain through muslin.

Provençal Fish Soup

The rice makes this a substantial main meal soup.

Serves 4–6

450g/1lb fresh mussels
250ml/8fl oz/1 cup white wine
675–900g/1½–2lb mixed white fish fillets such as plaice or cod
6 large scallops
30ml/2 tbsp olive oil
3 leeks, chopped
1 garlic clove, crushed
1 red pepper, seeded and cut into 2.5cm/1in pieces
1 yellow pepper, seeded and cut into 2.5cm/1in pieces

175g/6oz fennel, cut into 4cm/1½in pieces
400g/14oz can chopped tomatoes
about 1.2 litres/2 pints/5 cups well-flavoured fish stock
pinch of saffron threads, soaked in 15ml/1 tbsp hot water
175g/6oz/scant 1 cup basmati rice, soaked
8 large raw prawns, peeled and deveined
salt and freshly ground black pepper
30–45ml/2–3 tbsp fresh dill, to garnish
crusty bread, to serve (optional)

1 Discard any mussels that do not close when tapped with a knife. Place them in a heavy-based pan. Add 90ml/6 tbsp of the wine, cover, bring to the boil and cook for 3 minutes or until all the mussels have opened. Strain, reserving the liquid. Set aside half the mussels in their shells for the garnish; shell the rest and put them in a bowl. Discard any mussels that have not opened.

2 Cut the fish into 2.5cm/1in cubes. Detach the corals from the scallops and slice the white flesh into three or four pieces. Add the scallops to the fish and the corals to the mussels.

3 Heat the oil in a saucepan and fry the leeks and garlic for 3–4 minutes. Add the peppers and fennel and fry for 2 minutes.

4 Add the tomatoes, stock, saffron water, reserved mussel liquid and the remaining wine. Season and cook for 5 minutes. Drain the rice, add to the mixture, cover and simmer for 10 minutes.

5 Add the white fish and cook for 5 minutes. Add the prawns, cook for 2 minutes then add the scallop corals and mussels and cook for 2–3 minutes more. Spoon into soup dishes, top with the mussels in their shells and sprinkle with the dill.

Soup with Orange Energy 223kcal/937kJ; Protein 18.3g; Carbohydrate 25.2g, of which sugars 11.7g; Fat 6.1g, of which saturates 0.9g; Cholesterol 19mg; Calcium 86mg; Fibre 3.5g; Sodium 103mg.
Provençal Soup Energy 568kcal/2385kJ; Protein 59.9g; Carbohydrate 50.5g, of which sugars 12.9g; Fat 9.7g, of which saturates 1.6g; Cholesterol 163mg; Calcium 182mg; Fibre 5.9g; Sodium 418mg.

Mediterranean Seafood Soup with Saffron Rouille

Choose firm fish that will not fall apart while cooking.

Serves 4
450g/1lb fresh clams, scrubbed
120ml/4fl oz/½ cup white wine
15ml/1 tbsp olive oil
4 garlic cloves, crushed
5ml/1 tsp fennel seeds
pinch of dried chilli flakes
1 fennel bulb, halved and sliced
1 red pepper, seeded and sliced
8 plum tomatoes, halved
1 onion, cut into thin wedges
225g/8oz waxy potatoes, sliced

1 bay leaf
1 sprig fresh thyme
600ml/1 pint/2½ cups fish stock
1 mini French stick
225g/8oz monkfish fillet, sliced
350g/12oz red mullet, scaled,
    filleted and cut into wide strips
45ml/3 tbsp Pernod
salt and ground black pepper
fennel fronds, to garnish

For the rouille
a few saffron threads
150ml/¼ pint/⅔ cup mayonnaise
dash of Tabasco

1 Discard any open clams that do not shut when tapped. Place the rest in a pan with the wine. Cover and cook over a high heat for 4 minutes, until the shells have opened. Drain, strain, and reserve the cooking liquid. Discard any unopened shells and reserve 8 clams in their shells. Shell the remaining clams.

2 Heat the oil and add the garlic, fennel seeds and chilli flakes and cook for about 2 minutes. Add the fennel, pepper, tomatoes, onion and cooking liquid. Cover and simmer for 10 minutes. Stir in the potatoes, bay leaf and thyme, then pour in the fish stock. Cover and cook for 15–20 minutes.

3 Meanwhile, make the saffron rouille. Pound the saffron to a powder, then beat it into the mayonnaise with the Tabasco. Cut the French stick into eight thin slices and toast on both sides. Add the fish and Pernod to the soup and cook for 3–4 minutes.

4 Add all the clams and heat for 30 seconds. Remove the bay leaf and thyme sprigs, and season well. Spoon the rouille on to the toasts. Ladle the soup into bowls, garnish each with a frond of fennel and serve with the toasts.

Seafood Chowder

This filling fish soup is infinitely adaptable according to the availability of fresh fish and shellfish.

Serves 4–6
50g/2oz/¼ cup butter
1 large onion, chopped
115g/4oz bacon, rind
    removed, diced
4 celery sticks, diced
2 large potatoes, diced
400g/14oz can chopped tomatoes

450ml/¾ pint/2 cups fish stock
450g/1lb white fish fillets, such as
    cod, plaice, or haddock, skinned
    and cut into small chunks
225g/8oz shellfish, such as
    prawns (shrimp), scallops
    or mussels
300ml/½ pint/1¼ cups milk
25g/1oz/¼ cup cornflour
    (cornstarch)
sea salt and ground black pepper
lightly whipped cream and
    chopped parsley, to garnish

1 Melt the butter in a pan, add the onion, bacon, celery and potatoes, cover and sweat over gentle heat for 5–10 minutes. Meanwhile purée the tomatoes in a blender, and sieve them to remove any skin and pips. Add the tomato purée and fish stock to the pan. Bring to the boil, cover and simmer gently until the potatoes are tender, skimming the top occasionally.

2 Prepare the prawns by plunging them briefly in a pan of boiling water. Remove from the pan as the water boils. Cool and peel. If using mussels, scrub the shells and discard any that do not open when tapped. Put the mussels into a shallow, heavy pan, without adding any liquid. Cover and cook over a high heat for a few minutes, shaking , until all the mussels have opened. Discard any that fail to open.

3 Remove the cooked mussels from their shells. Raw shelled scallops can be left whole. Add the shellfish to the soup. Blend the milk and cornflour together in a small jug (pitcher), stir into the soup and bring to the boil again. Reduce the heat, and cover and simmer for a few minutes until the fish is just tender.

4 Adjust the texture with milk or stock if necessary and season to taste with sea salt, if required, and freshly ground black pepper. Serve in warm soup bowls, garnished with a swirl of cream and some parsley.

Seafood Soup Energy 728Kcal/3048kJ; Protein 50.2g; Carbohydrate 40g, of which sugars 10.9g; Fat 37.1g, of which saturates 5.4g; Cholesterol 111mg; Calcium 238mg; Fibre 4.7g; Sodium 1200mg.
Seafood Chowder Energy 488Kcal/2050kJ; Protein 46g; Carbohydrate 36.2g, of which sugars 11.3g; Fat 18.7g, of which saturates 9.6g; Cholesterol 127mg; Calcium 163mg; Fibre 3.5g; Sodium 771mg.

Fish Soup with Salted Cucumber and Capers

This fish dish is considered to be the queen of Russian soups. Its lovely, rich flavour is accentuated by the salty additions of capers, salted cucumbers and olives.

Serves 4

2 onions
2–3 carrots
1 parsnip
200g/7oz salted cucumbers
30–45ml/2–3 tbsp rapeseed
    (canola) oil
15ml/1 tbsp tomato
    purée (paste)
1 bay leaf
4–5 black peppercorns
1 litre/1¾ pints/4 cups home-
    made or good quality fish stock
400–500g/14oz–1¼lb salmon,
    halibut and turbot
    fillets, skinned
8 green olives
8 black olives
30ml/2 tbsp capers plus
    5ml/1 tsp juice from the jar
4 thin lemon slices
60ml/4 tbsp smetana or
    crème fraîche
45ml/3 tbsp chopped fresh dill,
    to garnish

1 Finely chop the onions. Dice the carrots, parsnip and finely dice the cucumbers. Heat the oil in a large pan, add the onions and fry over a medium heat for 2–3 minutes, until softened. Add the carrots and parsnip and fry over a medium heat, stirring all the time, for 5 minutes.

2 Add the cucumbers, tomato purée, bay leaf and peppercorns to the pan and fry for a further 2–3 minutes. Add half of the stock, cover and bring to the boil. Reduce the heat and simmer for 10 minutes.

3 Meanwhile, cut the fish into 2cm/¾in cubes. Add the remaining stock, green and black olives, the capers and the caper juice to the pan. Return to the boil and add the fish cubes. Reduce the heat and simmer for 5 minutes, until the fish is just tender, being careful not to overcook the fish.

4 To serve, spoon the soup into warmed bowls, add a slice of lemon, a spoonful of smetana or crème fraîche and garnish with chopped dill.

Seafood Soup

Whenever you prepare a dish with prawns or fillet fish, save the heads and bones and freeze them until you have enough to make a flavoursome stock, such as the one used in this recipe.

Serves 6

60ml/4 tbsp olive oil
2kg/4½lb prawn (shrimp) heads
    and fish bones
1kg/2¼lb mixed onions, carrots,
    leek, and garlic, chopped
1 bay leaf
6 black peppercorns
105ml/7 tbsp dry white wine
1 green and 1 red (bell) pepper,
    seeded and finely diced
1 onion, chopped
2 ripe tomatoes, peeled and diced
1 garlic clove, chopped
15ml/1 tbsp chopped fresh thyme
185g/6½oz live clams, scrubbed
125g/4¼oz prepared squid
300g/11oz white fish fillet, cut
    into chunks
12 prawns (shrimp), peeled
chopped fresh coriander (cilantro),
    to garnish

1 Heat 30ml/2 tbsp of the olive oil in a large pan. Add the prawn heads and cook over a low heat for 5 minutes.

2 Add the mixed vegetables, bay leaf and peppercorns and cook for a further 5 minutes, mashing the prawn heads with a wooden spoon.

3 Pour in the wine and 2 litres/3½ pints/8¾ cups water. Bring to the boil, then lower the heat and simmer gently for 1 hour.

4 Add the fish bones and bring back to the boil. Lower the heat and simmer very gently for 20 minutes. Remove the pan from the heat and strain the stock into a bowl.

5 Heat the remaining olive oil in a clean pan. Add the green and red peppers, onion and tomatoes, and cook over a low heat, stirring occasionally, for 5 minutes, until softened. Add the garlic and thyme, pour in the stock and bring just to the boil.

6 Add the clams and squid and cook for 2–3 minutes, until the clams have opened. Add the fish and prawns and cook for 5 minutes more, until the fish is opaque. Sprinkle with the coriander and serve immediately.

Fish Soup Energy 389kcal/1613kJ; Protein 24.5g; Carbohydrate 9.1g, of which sugars 7.2g; Fat 28.5g, of which saturates 7.7g; Cholesterol 73mg; Calcium 74mg; Fibre 3.1g; Sodium 361mg.
Seafood Soup Energy 267kcal/1112kJ; Protein 20.1g; Carbohydrate 25.2g, of which sugars 18.7g; Fat 9g, of which saturates 1.3g; Cholesterol 96mg; Calcium 96mg; Fibre 4.8g; Sodium 262mg.

Ancona Fish Soup

Although the diminutive name used locally to describe this Italian dish would make you think you were getting a simple soup, it is actually a chunky and substantial stew. Traditionally, 13 different varieties of fish are used in brodetto, which is symbolic of the great port of Ancona. Among these you would always find scorpion fish, gurnard, eel, sea cricket and red mullet. Because the fish are added whole, bones and all, you need plenty of time to leisurely wade through the process of removing the fish from the bone, then enjoy the fish juices with some crusty bread. There are no other ingredients of any note, so the freshness and variety of the fish are the most important elements of the dish.

Serves 4–6

60ml/4 tbsp extra virgin olive oil
1 onion, chopped
1 garlic clove, chopped
90ml/6 tbsp white or red
   wine vinegar
300g/11oz canned tomatoes,
   sieved (strained) or
   coarsely chopped
900g/2lb mixed whole fish, such
   as small monkfish, red mullet,
   whiting or scorpion fish
sea salt and ground black pepper
crusty bread, to serve

1 Put the oil in a very large pan, add the onion and garlic, and fry over medium heat for 5 minutes, or until soft.

2 Gradually add the vinegar, stirring constantly, until the sharp vinegar smell has disappeared.

3 Add the canned tomatoes, stir and simmer for 10 minutes. Gradually add the fish, one at a time, starting with the largest.

4 Cook, stirring gently, for 30 minutes, until the fish is cooked through. Serve with crusty bread.

> **Cook's Tip**
> When choosing your fish, avoid strongly flavoured oily fish, such as mackerel, as this could overpower more delicate fish.

Chilca-style Fish Soup

A small town to the south of Lima called Chilca has contributed the chilcano to Peruvian cooking, a fish soup enriched with lime and chilli. Sometimes it is made with the heads of the fish (an economical version once almost compulsory for students), at other times with the whole fish or with shellfish. For the soup to be a genuine chilcano it is important to make it with only one kind of fish.

Serves 6

2 litres/3½ pints/8 cups water
2 medium white fish, such as sea
   bass, about 1kg/2¼lb total
   weight, cleaned and gutted
2 garlic cloves, very finely chopped
1 small red onion, finely chopped
1 spring onion (scallion),
   finely chopped
1 red chilli, seeded and finely
   chopped
30ml/2 tbsp finely chopped
   parsley
salt and ground black pepper
1 lime, sliced, to serve

1 Bring the water to the boil in a large pan with the garlic, red onion, and half the spring onion, chilli and parsley. When it bubbles, lay the fish in the pan. Season. Return to the boil, reduce the heat, cover and simmer for 10 minutes.

2 Lift out the fish and leave the soup simmering, uncovered, for a further 15–20 minutes to reduce and concentrate the flavour.

3 Meanwhile, remove the heads and tails from the fish, take off the fillets and divide into individual portions. Keep warm.

4 Strain the soup and adjust the seasoning to taste. Divide the pieces of fish among hot bowls, pour over the soup, garnish with the reserved spring onion, chilli and parsley, and serve with slices of lime.

> **Cook's Tip**
> Although only one type of fish is used, this can vary from the traditional corvina to any firm white fish. It can also be made with prawns (shrimps), crabs, or mussels, depending on the ingredients to hand.

Ancona Soup Energy 389kcal/1627kJ; Protein 27.4g; Carbohydrate 29g, of which sugars 4.8g; Fat 18.9g, of which saturates 2.8g; Cholesterol 68mg; Calcium 46mg; Fibre 2.7g; Sodium 207mg.
Chilca Soup Energy 145kcal/610kJ; Protein 31g; Carbohydrate 1.1g, of which sugars 0.8g; Fat 1.9g, of which saturates 0.7g; Cholesterol 87mg; Calcium 63mg; Fibre 0.6g; Sodium 164mg.

Grecian Fish Soup

Fish soup in Greece makes a complete meal. The liquid soup is served first, followed by a platter of the fish and vegetables from the pot. In Greece, the fish would be the Mediterranean scorpion fish.

Serves 4

1.5 litres/2½ pints/6¼ cups
    water or fish stock
75–90ml/5–6 tbsp extra virgin
    olive oil
2kg/4½lb whole fish, cleaned
    and scaled
8 small potatoes, peeled and
    left whole
8 small onions, peeled and
    left whole
2 carrots, peeled and cut into
    5cm/2in lengths
1–2 celery sticks and leaves
2 courgettes (zucchini), quartered
    lengthways
juice of 1 lemon
salt and ground black pepper
extra virgin olive oil, juice of 1
    lemon and a pinch of dried
    oregano, to serve

1 Mix the water or stock and olive oil in a large pan. Bring to the boil, and boil rapidly for about 4 minutes in order to emulsify the liquid. Add the fish to the pan, with salt and pepper. Slowly let the liquid return to the boil and, using a slotted spoon, carefully skim the surface until it is clear.

2 Add the potatoes, onions, carrots, celery sticks and leaves and courgettes to the pan with more hot water, if needed, to cover.

3 Put a lid on the pan and cook over a medium heat until the fish is cooked and the flesh flakes when tested with the tip of a sharp knife. Large fish will take up to 35 minutes; smaller ones a little less. Make sure that the fish does not disintegrate.

4 Carefully lift the fish out of the pan and place it on a warm platter. Scoop out the hot vegetables with a draining spoon and arrange them around the fish. Cover and keep hot.

5 Stir the lemon juice into the soup. Serve it first, then bring out the platter of fish and vegetables. Invite guests to help themselves to a piece of fish and a selection of vegetables. Quickly whisk the olive oil with the lemon juice and oregano. This makes an excellent dressing for the fish and vegetables.

Hot and Sour Filipino Fish Soup

Chunky, filling and satisfying, Filipino fish soups are meals in themselves. There are many variations on the theme, depending on the region and the local fish, but most are packed with shellfish, flavoured with sour tamarind combined with hot chilli, and served with coconut vinegar flavoured with garlic.

Serves 4–6

2 litres/3½ pints/8 cups
    fish stock
250ml/8fl oz/1 cup white wine
15–30ml/1–2 tbsp
    tamarind paste
30–45ml/2–3 tbsp patis (Filipino
    fish sauce)
30ml/2 tbsp palm sugar (jaggery)
50g/2oz fresh root ginger, grated
2–3 fresh red or green chillies,
    seeded and finely sliced
2 tomatoes, skinned, seeded and
    cut into wedges
350g/12oz fresh fish, such as
    trout, sea bass, swordfish or
    cod, cut into bitesize chunks
12–16 fresh prawns (shrimp),
    in their shells
1 bunch fresh basil leaves,
    roughly chopped
1 bunch fresh flat leaf parsley,
    roughly chopped
salt and ground black pepper

For the spiked suka

60–90ml/4–6 tbsp suka (Filipino
    coconut vinegar)
1–2 garlic cloves, finely chopped
1–2 limes, cut into wedges
2 fresh red or green chillies,
    seeded and quartered
    lengthways

1 In a wok or large pan, bring the stock and wine to the boil. Stir in the tamarind paste, patis, sugar, ginger and chillies. Reduce the heat and simmer for 15–20 minutes. Add the tomatoes to the broth and season with salt and pepper.

2 Add the chunks of fish and the prawns and simmer for a further 5 minutes, until the fish is cooked and flakes easily. Meanwhile, in a bowl, quickly mix together the suka and garlic for serving and put aside.

3 Stir half the basil and half the parsley into the broth and ladle into bowls. Garnish with the remaining basil and parsley and serve immediately, with the spiked suka to splash on top, the lime wedges to squeeze into the soup, and the chillies to chew on for those who like extra heat.

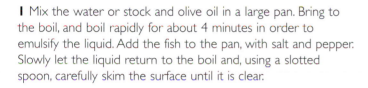

Grecian Soup Energy 454kcal/1895kJ; Protein 53.8g; Carbohydrate 17g, of which sugars 6.4g; Fat 19.3g, of which saturates 3.1g; Cholesterol 135mg; Calcium 138mg; Fibre 2.5g; Sodium 345mg.
Filipino Soup Energy 137kcal/576kJ; Protein 17.7g; Carbohydrate 8.1g, of which sugars 8g; Fat 1g, of which saturates 0.1g; Cholesterol 92mg; Calcium 76mg; Fibre 1.3g; Sodium 644mg.

Spicy Tamarind Fish Soup

This is the Malay version of the hot and sour fish soup found throughout south-east Asia. The sour notes are from tamarind; the hot flavourings are from rempah.

Serves 4

30ml/2 tbsp vegetable oil
15–30ml/1–2 tbsp tamarind paste
115g/4oz snake beans (long beans), trimmed
450g/1lb fish cutlets (such as trout, cod, sea perch, pike), about 2.5cm/1in thick

fresh coriander (cilantro) leaves, to garnish
rice or bread, to serve

For the rempah
8 dried red chillies, soaked in warm water until soft, drained and seeded
8 shallots, chopped
4 garlic cloves, chopped
2 lemon grass stalks, trimmed and sliced
25g/1oz fresh galangal, chopped
25g/1oz fresh turmeric, chopped
5ml/1 tsp shrimp paste

1 To make the rempah, grind all the ingredients to a paste, using a mortar and pestle or food processor.

2 Heat the oil in a wok or heavy pan, and stir in the rempah. Fry it until it is fragrant and begins to change colour. Stir in the tamarind paste and add the snake beans, tossing them around the wok until they are coated in the spice mixture.

3 Pour in 900ml/1½ pints/3¾ cups water and bring to the boil. Reduce the heat and simmer for 5 minutes. Season with salt and pepper, then add the fish cutlets. Cook gently for 2–3 minutes until cooked through, then ladle the soup into bowls. Garnish with coriander and serve with steamed rice or chunks of fresh bread.

> **Cook's Tip**
> *You can adjust the balance of hot and sour by adding more chilli or tamarind to taste. Enjoyed as a meal in itself, the soup is usually served with plain steamed rice, but in Saigon it is served with chunks of fresh baguette, to soak up the sauce.*

Hot and Sour Fish Soup

This unusual tangy soup can be found throughout South-east Asia. Chillies provide the heat and tamarind produces the tartness.

Serves 4

1 catfish, sea bass or red snapper, about 1kg/2¼lb, filleted
25g/1oz dried squid, soaked in water for 30 minutes
15ml/1 tbsp vegetable oil
2 spring onions (scallions), sliced
2 shallots, sliced
4cm/1½in fresh root ginger, peeled and chopped
2–3 lemon grass stalks, cut into strips and crushed
30ml/2 tbsp tamarind paste
2–3 Thai chillies, seeded and sliced

15ml/1 tbsp sugar
30–45ml/2–3 tbsp nuoc mam
225g/8oz fresh pineapple, peeled and diced
3 tomatoes, skinned, seeded and roughly chopped
50g/2oz canned sliced bamboo shoots, drained
1 small bunch of fresh coriander (cilantro), stalks removed, leaves finely chopped
salt and ground black pepper
115g/4oz/½cup beansprouts and 1 bunch of dill, fronds roughly chopped, to garnish
1 lime, cut into quarters, to serve

For the marinade
30ml/2 tbsp nuoc mam
2 garlic cloves, finely chopped

1 Cut the fish into bitesize pieces. Reserve the head, tail and bones for the stock. In a bowl, mix the marinade ingredients and add the fish. Set aside. Drain and rinse the squid.

2 Heat the oil in a deep pan and stir in the spring onions, shallots, ginger, lemon grass and squid. Add the reserved fish head, tail and bones, and sauté them gently for 2 minutes. Pour in 1.2 litres/2 pints/5 cups water and bring to the boil. Reduce the heat and simmer for 30 minutes.

3 Strain the stock into another pan and bring to the boil. Add the tamarind paste, chillies, sugar and nuoc mam and simmer for 2–3 minutes. Add the pineapple, tomatoes and bamboo shoots and simmer for 2–3 minutes. Stir in the fish pieces and the coriander, and cook until the fish turns opaque.

4 Season and ladle the soup into hot bowls. Garnish with beansprouts and dill, and serve with the lime quarters.

Spicy Soup Energy 164Kcal/686kJ; Protein 21.7g; Carbohydrate 4.9g, of which sugars 3.5g; Fat 6.5g, of which saturates 0.8g; Cholesterol 52mg; Calcium 33mg; Fibre 1.3g; Sodium 69mg.
Hot and Sour Soup Energy 335Kcal/1415kJ; Protein 44g; Carbohydrate 24g, of which sugars 19g; Fat 7g, of which saturates 1g; Cholesterol 108mg; Calcium 138mg; Fibre 2.3g; Sodium 1.2mg.

Chinese Fish Ball Soup

This light Chinese soup can be found in coffee shops and at the tze char stalls, where the food is ordered from the menu and cooked on the spot. Often eaten as a snack or light lunch, the soup is garnished with spring onions and fresh chillies, and the Malays often add an extra drizzle of chilli sauce or a spoonful of chilli sambal.

Serves 4–6

For the fish balls
450g/1lb fresh fish fillets (such as haddock, cod, whiting or bream), boned and flaked

15–30ml/1–2 tbsp rice flour
salt and ground black pepper

For the soup
1.5 litres/2½ pints/6¼ cups fish or chicken stock
15–30ml/1–2 tbsp light soy sauce
4–6 mustard green leaves, shredded
90g/3½oz mung bean thread noodles, soaked in hot water until soft

For the garnish
2 spring onions (scallions), trimmed and finely sliced
1 red chilli, seeded and sliced
fresh coriander (cilantro) leaves, finely chopped

1 To make the fish balls, grind the flaked fish fillets to a paste, using a mortar and pestle or a food processor. Season with salt and pepper and stir in 60ml/4 tbsp water. Add enough rice flour to form a paste. Roll small portions into balls.

2 Bring the stock to the boil and season to taste with soy sauce. Drop in the fish balls and simmer for 5 minutes. Add the shredded mustard greens and cook for 1 minute.

3 Divide the noodles among four to six bowls. Using a slotted spoon, add the fish balls and greens to the noodles, then ladle over the hot stock. Garnish with the spring onions and chilli and sprinkle the chopped coriander over the top.

Cook's Tip
Sambals are chilli-based sauces, which are often used instead of fresh chillies. They can be extremely hot.

Dogfish Soup

Dogfish, a member of the shark family, is found along the Alentejo coast, where this soup is very popular. This fish is also known as huss, flake, tope and rock salmon. This recipe is sufficient for a meal-in-a-bowl soup for four or, alternatively, a first course for eight.

Serves 4–8
4 dogfish fillets, about 4cm/1½in thick, or about 150g/5oz each

75ml/5 tbsp olive oil
2 garlic cloves, chopped
1 bunch of fresh coriander (cilantro), chopped
1 bay leaf
50ml/2fl oz/¼ cup white wine vinegar
15ml/1 tbsp plain (all-purpose) flour
salt

For the marinade
1 bay leaf
50ml/2fl oz white wine vinegar
salt

1 First, make the marinade by combining all the ingredients with 500ml/7fl oz/2 cups water in a jug (pitcher). Place the fish fillets in a dish and pour the marinade over them. Leave to marinate for at least 2 hours, then rinse in water.

2 Heat the olive oil in a large pan. Add the garlic and coriander and cook, stirring, for a few minutes. Pour in 1 litre/1¾ pints/4 cups water, add the fish and the bay leaf, and season with salt. Bring to the boil, then lower the heat and simmer for 10 minutes. Reserve the fish and discard the bay leaf.

3 Mix together the vinegar and flour and blend into the soup. Simmer for about 10 minutes, stirring until the flour is combined, and add more water if necessary. Add the fish and serve immediately.

Cook's Tips
This soup can also be made with swordfish or shark fillets. Dogfish is a firm fish with a fairly pronounced flavour. In the UK it is often referred to as 'rock salmon', and baking or frying are recommended cooking methods.

Fish Ball Soup Energy 127Kcal/533kJ; Protein 14.9g; Carbohydrate 14.8g, of which sugars 0.5g; Fat 0.6g, of which saturates 0.1g; Cholesterol 35mg; Calcium 17mg; Fibre 0.2g; Sodium 408mg.
Dogfish Soup Energy 174kcal/724kJ; Protein 18.8g; Carbohydrate 2.2g, of which sugars 0.2g; Fat 10g, of which saturates 1.4g; Cholesterol 46mg; Calcium 29mg; Fibre 0.5g; Sodium 63mg.

Mullet and Fennel Soup

Olives and tomato toasts are delicious in this soup.

Serves 4
25ml/1½ tbsp olive oil
1 onion, chopped
3 garlic cloves, chopped
2 fennel bulbs, thinly sliced
4 tomatoes, chopped
1 bay leaf
sprig of fresh thyme
1.2 litres/2 pints/5 cups fish stock
675g/1½lb red mullet or
   snapper, scaled and filleted
salt and ground black pepper

For the toasts
8 slices baguette, toasted
1 garlic clove
30ml/2 tbsp tomato
   purée (paste)
12 black olives, stoned (pitted)
   and quartered
fresh fennel fronds, to garnish

For the aioli
2 egg yolks
1–2 garlic cloves, crushed
10ml/2 tsp lemon juice
300ml/½ pint/1¼ cups extra
   virgin olive oil

1 Heat the olive oil in a large, heavy pan. Add the onion and garlic and cook for 5 minutes, until soften. Add the fennel and cook for 2–3 minutes. Stir in the tomatoes, bay leaf, thyme and stock. Boil, reduce the heat, cover and simmer for 30 minutes.

2 Meanwhile, make the aioli in a large bowl. Whisk the egg yolks, garlic, lemon juice and seasoning together. Whisk in the oil, drop by drop. As the mixture begins to thicken, add the oil in a slow trickle. Transfer to a large bowl and set aside.

3 Cut each mullet fillet into two or three pieces, then add them to the soup and cook gently for 5 minutes. Use a slotted spoon to remove the mullet and set aside.

4 Strain the cooking liquid, pressing the vegetables well. Whisk a ladleful of soup into the aioli, then whisk in the remaining soup in one go. Return the soup to a clean pan and cook very gently, whisking continuously, until the mixture is very slightly thickened. Add the mullet to the soup.

5 Rub the toasted baguette with garlic, spread with tomato purée and top with olives. Serve the soup topped with the toasts and garnished with fennel.

Smoked Haddock Chowder with Sweet Thai Basil

Based on a traditional Scottish recipe, this soup has American-style sweetness from the sweet potatoes and butternut squash, and is flavoured with a hint of Thai basil.

Serves 4
400g/14oz sweet potatoes (pink-
   fleshed variety), cut into small
   bite-size pieces
225g/8oz peeled butternut
   squash, cut into 1cm/½in slices
50g/2oz/¼ cup butter
1 onion, chopped
450g/1lb Finnan haddock fillets,
   skinned
300ml/½ pint/1¼ cups water
600ml/1 pint/2½ cups milk
small handful of Thai basil leaves
60ml/4 tbsp double cream
salt and ground black pepper

1 Cook the sweet potatoes and butternut squash separately in boiling salted water for 15 minutes or until just tender. Drain both well.

2 Meanwhile, melt half the butter in a large, heavy-based saucepan. Add the onion and cook for 4–5 minutes, until softened but not browned. Add the haddock fillets and water. 3 Bring to the boil, reduce the heat and simmer for 10 minutes, until the fish is cooked. Use a draining spoon to lift the fish out of the pan and leave to cool. Set the cooking liquid aside.

3 When cool enough to handle, carefully break the flesh into large flakes, discarding the skin and bones. Set the fish aside.

4 Press the sweet potatoes through a sieve and beat in the remaining butter with seasoning to taste. Strain the reserved fish cooking liquid and return it to the rinsed-out pan, then whisk in the sweet potato. Stir in the milk and bring to the boil. Simmer for about 2–3 minutes.

5 Stir in the butternut squash, fish, Thai basil leaves and cream. Season the soup to taste and heat through without boiling. Ladle the soup into six warmed soup bowls and serve immediately.

Mullet Soup Energy 492kcal/2079kJ; Protein 41.2g; Carbohydrate 53.6g, of which sugars 10g; Fat 14.1g, of which saturates 1.2g; Cholesterol 0mg; Calcium 256mg; Fibre 6.1g; Sodium 965mg.
Haddock Chowder Energy 258kcal/1196kJ; Protein 19.1g; Carbohydrate 20.7g, of which sugars 9.9g; Fat 14.7g, of which saturates 8.9g; Cholesterol 64mg; Calcium 166mg; Fibre 2.1g; Sodium 173mg.

Pad Thai Red Monkfish Soup

This light and creamy coconut soup provides a base for a colourful fusion of red-curried monkfish and pad Thai, the classic stir-fried noodle dish of Thailand.

Serves 4
175g/6oz flat rice noodles
30ml/2 tbsp vegetable oil
2 garlic cloves, chopped
15ml/1 tbsp red curry paste
450g/1lb monkfish tail, cut into
   bite-size pieces
300ml/½ pint/1¼ cups
   coconut cream

750ml/1¼ pints/3 cups hot
   chicken stock
45ml/3 tbsp Thai fish sauce
   (nam pla)
15ml/1 tbsp palm sugar (jaggery)
60ml/4 tbsp roughly chopped
   roasted peanuts
4 spring onions (scallions),
   shredded lengthways
50g/2oz beansprouts
large handful of fresh Thai
   basil leaves
salt and ground black pepper
1 red chilli, seeded and cut
   lengthways into slivers,
   to garnish

1 Soak the noodles in boiling water for 10 minutes, or according to the packet instructions. Drain.

2 Heat the oil in a wok or saucepan over a high heat. Add the garlic and cook for 2 minutes. Stir in the curry paste and cook for 1 minute until fragrant.

3 Add the monkfish and stir-fry over a high heat for 4–5 minutes, until just tender. Pour in the coconut cream and stock.

4 Stir in the fish sauce and sugar, and bring just to the boil. Add the drained noodles and cook over a medium heat for 1–2 minutes, until tender.

5 Stir in half the peanuts, half the spring onions, half the beansprouts, the basil and seasoning.

6 Ladle the soup into deep individual bowls and sprinkle over the remaining peanuts. Garnish with the remaining spring onions, beansprouts and the slivers of red chilli.

Salmon Chowder

Dill is the perfect partner for salmon in this creamy soup from the USA. It takes its inspiration from the satisfying soups that are typical of the eastern seaboard of the United States and is best served immediately after cooking, when the salmon is just tender.

Serves 4
20g/¾oz/1½ tbsp butter
1 onion, finely chopped
1 leek, finely chopped

1 small fennel bulb, finely
   chopped
25g/1oz/¼ cup plain
   (all-purpose) flour
1.75 litres/3 pints/7 cups
   fish stock
2 medium potatoes, cut in
   1cm/½in cubes
450g/1lb salmon fillet, skinned
   and cut into 2cm/¾in cubes
175ml/6fl oz/¾ cup milk
120ml/4fl oz/½ cup
   whipping cream
30ml/2 tbsp chopped fresh dill
salt and ground black pepper

1 Melt the butter in a large pan. Add the onion, leek and chopped fennel and cook for 6 minutes. Stir in the flour. Reduce the heat to low and cook for 3 minutes, stirring occasionally.

2 Add the fish stock and potatoes to the mixture in the pan. Season with a little salt and ground black pepper. Bring to the boil, then reduce the heat, cover and simmer gently for about 20 minutes or until the potatoes are tender.

3 Add the cubed salmon fillet and simmer gently for 3–5 minutes until it is just cooked.

4 Stir the milk, cream, and chopped dill into the contents of the pan. Cook until just warmed through, but do not allow to boil. Adjust the seasoning to taste, then serve.

Variation
Fresh mackerel fillets are good in this recipe, which has lots of vegetables. Add a crushed garlic clove, and use tarragon instead of dill. For a zesty flavour, add the grated rind of 1 lemon.

Monkfish Soup Energy 379kcal/1589kJ; Protein 25.5g; Carbohydrate 41.2g, of which sugars 4.7g; Fat 12g, of which saturates 2g; Cholesterol 18mg; Calcium 49mg; Fibre 0.9g; Sodium 111mg.
Chowder Energy 301kcal/1253kJ; Protein 18.3g; Carbohydrate 13g, of which sugars 3.8g; Fat 19.9g, of which saturates 8.6g; Cholesterol 67mg; Calcium 83mg; Fibre 1.5g; Sodium 78mg.

Rocket Soup with Kiln-Smoked Salmon

Kiln-smoked salmon has actually been "cooked" during the smoking process, producing a delicious flaky texture. This is in contrast to traditional cold-smoked salmon, which is not actually cooked but does not spoil because it has been preserved first in brine.

Serves 4
15ml/1 tbsp olive oil
1 small onion, sliced
1 garlic clove, crushed
150ml/¼ pint/⅔ cup double (heavy) cream
350ml/12fl oz/1½ cups vegetable stock
350g/12oz rocket (arugula)
4 fresh basil leaves
salt and ground black pepper
flaked kiln-smoked salmon, to garnish

1 Put the olive oil in a high-sided pan over a medium heat and allow to heat up. Add the sliced onion and sweat for a few minutes, stirring continuously. Add the garlic and continue to sweat gently until soft and transparent, although you should not allow the onion to colour.

2 Add the cream and stock, stir in gently and bring slowly to the boil. Allow to simmer gently for about 5 minutes. Add the rocket, reserving a few leaves to garnish, and the basil. Return briefly to the boil and turn off the heat. Add a little cold water and allow to cool for a few minutes.

3 Purée in a blender until smooth, adding a little salt and pepper to taste. When ready to serve, reheat gently but do not allow to boil. Serve in warmed bowls with a few flakes of salmon, a leaf or two of rocket and a drizzle of virgin olive oil.

> **Variation**
> Cold-smoked salmon is also very good with this soup, and can be used if you can't find the kiln-smoked variety. Simply cut a few slices into medium to thick strips and add to the hot soup.

Salmon Soup with Salsa and Rouille

Tangy sorrel goes well with salmon but dill or fennel are delicious alternatives.

Serves 4
90ml/6 tbsp olive oil
1 onion, chopped
1 leek, chopped
1 celery stick, chopped
1 fennel bulb, roughly chopped
1 red pepper, seeded and sliced
3 garlic cloves, chopped
grated rind and juice of 2 oranges
1 bay leaf
400g/14oz can chopped tomatoes
1.2 litres/2 pints/5 cups fish stock
pinch of cayenne pepper

800g/1¾lb salmon fillet, skinned
300ml/½ pint/1¼ cups double (heavy) cream
salt and ground black pepper
4 thin slices baguette, to serve

For the ruby salsa
2 tomatoes, peeled, seeded and diced
½ small red onion, very finely chopped
15ml/1 tbsp cod's roe
15ml/1 tbsp chopped fresh sorrel

For the rouille
120ml/4fl oz/½ cup mayonnaise
1 garlic clove, crushed
5ml/1 tsp sun-dried tomato paste

1 Heat the oil in a large pan. Add the onion, leek, celery, fennel, pepper and garlic. Cover and cook gently for 20 minutes.

2 Add the orange rind and juice, bay leaf and tomatoes. Cover and cook for 4–5 minutes, stirring occasionally. Add the stock and cayenne, cover the pan and simmer for 30 minutes.

3 Add the salmon and poach it for 8–10 minutes, until just cooked. Lift out the fish and flake it coarsely, discarding bones.

4 Mix all the salsa ingredients and set aside. For the rouille, mix the mayonnaise with the garlic and the sun-dried tomato paste. Toast the baguette slices on both sides and set aside.

5 Purée the soup and sieve it back into the rinsed pan. Stir in the cream, seasoning and salmon. Heat gently but do not boil.

6 To serve, ladle the soup into bowls. Top the baguette slices with rouille, float on the soup and spoon over the salsa. Serve immediately.

Curried Salmon Soup

A hint of mild curry paste really enhances the flavour of this soup, without making it too spicy. Grated creamed coconut adds a luxury touch, while helping to amalgamate the flavours. Served with chunks of warm bread, this soup makes a very satisfying appetizer.

Serves 4

50g/2oz/¼ cup butter
2 onions, roughly chopped
10ml/2 tsp mild curry paste
475ml/16fl oz/2 cups water
150ml/¼ pint/⅔ cup white wine
300ml/½ pint/1¼ cups double (heavy) cream
50g/2oz/½ cup creamed coconut, grated or 120ml/4fl oz/½ cup coconut cream
2 potatoes, about 350g/12oz, cubed
450g/1lb salmon fillet, skinned and cut into bitesize pieces
60ml/4 tbsp chopped fresh flat-leaf parsley
salt and ground black pepper

1 Melt the butter in a large pan, add the onions and cook for about 3–4 minutes until beginning to soften. Stir in the curry paste. Cook for 1 minute more.

2 Add the water, wine, cream and creamed coconut or coconut cream, with seasoning. Bring to the boil, stirring until the coconut has dissolved.

3 Add the potatoes to the pan. Simmer, covered, for about 15 minutes or until they are almost tender. Do not allow them to break down into the mixture.

4 Add the fish gently so as not to break it up. Simmer for 2–3 minutes until just cooked. Add the parsley and adjust the seasoning. Serve immediately.

Cook's Tip
There is a wide choice of curry pastes available. Select a concentrated paste for this recipe, rather than a 'cook-in-sauce' type of paste. If you cannot find a suitable paste, cook a little curry powder in melted butter over low heat and use instead.

Noodle, Pak Choi and Seared Salmon Ramen

Ramen is a Japanese noodle soup for which a good stock is essential. Here, the lightly spiced broth is enhanced by slices of fresh salmon and crisp vegetables.

Serves 4

1.5 litres/2½ pints/6¼ cups good vegetable stock
2.5cm/1in piece fresh root ginger, finely sliced
2 garlic cloves, crushed
6 spring onions (scallions), sliced
45ml/3 tbsp soy sauce
45ml/3 tbsp sake
450g/1lb salmon fillet, skinned and boned
5ml/1 tsp groundnut oil
350g/12oz ramen or udon noodles
4 small heads pak choi
1 red chilli, seeded and sliced
50g/2oz/¼ cup beansprouts
salt and ground black pepper

1 Pour the stock into a large saucepan and add the ginger, garlic, and a third of the spring onions. Add the soy sauce and sake. Bring to the boil, then reduce the heat; simmer for 30 minutes.

2 Meanwhile, remove any pin bones from the salmon using tweezers, then cut the salmon on the slant into 12 slices, using a very sharp knife.

3 Brush a ridged griddle or frying pan with the oil and heat until very hot. Sear the salmon slices for 1–2 minutes on each side until tender and marked by the ridges of the pan. Set aside.

4 Cook the ramen or udon noodles in boiling water for 4–5 minutes or according to the packet instructions. Drain well and refresh under cold running water. Drain again and set aside.

5 Strain the broth into a clean pan and season to taste, then bring to the boil. Break the pak choi into leaves and add to the pan. Using a fork, twist the noodles into four nests and put these into deep bowls. Add three slices of salmon to each bowl. Divide the remaining spring onions, the chilli and beansprouts among the bowls, then ladle the steaming broth around the ingredients.

Salmon Soup Energy 837kcal/3466kJ; Protein 26.3g; Carbohydrate 16.6g, of which sugars 3.6g; Fat 71.8g, of which saturates 41.2g; Cholesterol 186mg; Calcium 74mg; Fibre 0.9g; Sodium 158mg.
Noodle and Salmon Energy 572kcal/2406kJ; Protein 34.1g; Carbohydrate 65.2g, of which sugars 3.1g; Fat 21.2g, of which saturates 4.6g; Cholesterol 83mg; Calcium 150mg; Fibre 4g; Sodium 826mg.

Trout Bisque

A bisque is a thick, rich, velvety soup, usually containing fish or shellfish. This wonderfully coloured pale pink version has a deliciously creamy texture with a hint of spiciness. Serve it with crusty bread and unsalted butter.

Serves 4
15ml/1 tbsp olive oil
1 onion, chopped
1 red (bell) pepper, finely chopped
1 garlic clove, crushed
1 medium potato, diced
2 tomatoes, skinned and chopped
300ml/½ pint/1¼ cups fish stock
225g/8oz trout fillet, skinned
  and diced
1.5ml/¼ tsp chilli powder
15ml/1 tbsp chopped
  fresh tarragon
300ml/½ pint/1¼ cups milk
30ml/2 tbsp dry sherry
150ml/¼ pint/⅔ cup double
  (heavy) cream
salt and ground black pepper
sprigs of watercress or rocket
  (arugula), to garnish

1 Heat the olive oil in a large pan, add the onion, pepper, garlic and potato. Fry gently for 5 minutes, stirring constantly, until the onion has just softened.

2 Add the tomatoes and fish stock to the pan, increase the heat and bring to the boil. Then reduce the heat and leave to simmer for about 10 minutes or until the vegetables are just tender when tested with a knife.

3 Add the trout, chilli powder and chopped tarragon. Simmer gently for a further 5 minutes or until the fish is just cooked and is starting to flake when tested with a fork.

4 Remove the pan from the heat, and stir in half the milk. Set aside for 20–30 minutes to allow the contents to cool.

5 Pour the fish and vegetable mixture into a food processor and blend until smooth. Scrape into a clean pan and stir in the sherry and cream, with the remaining milk.

6 Heat the soup gently, stirring, until piping hot. Season to taste, then divide among soup bowls, garnish with the watercress or rocket and serve.

Soup Niçoise with Seared Tuna

Ingredients for the famous salad from Nice in the South of France are transformed into a simple, yet elegant, soup by adding a hot garlic-infused stock.

Serves 4
12 drained bottled anchovy fillets
30ml/2 tbsp milk
115g/4oz French beans, halved
4 plum tomatoes, peeled, halved
  and seeded
16 black olives, stoned
1 litre/1¾ pints/4 cups good
  vegetable stock
3 garlic cloves, crushed
30ml/2 tbsp lemon juice
15ml/1 tbsp olive oil
4 tuna steaks, about
  75g/3oz each
small bunch of spring onions
  (scallions), shredded lengthways
handful of fresh basil leaves,
  shredded
salt and ground black pepper
fresh crusty bread, to serve

1 Soak the anchovies in the milk for 10 minutes. Drain well and dry on kitchen paper. Cook the French beans in boiling salted water for 2–3 minutes. Drain, refresh under cold running water and drain. Split any thick beans diagonally lengthways. Cut the tomatoes into thin wedges. Wash the olives to remove any oil, then cut into quarters. Set all the prepared ingredients aside.

2 Bring the stock to the boil in a large, heavy-based saucepan. Add the garlic, reduce the heat and simmer for 10 minutes. Season the stock well and add the lemon juice.

3 Meanwhile, brush a griddle pan or frying pan with the oil and heat until very hot. Season the tuna and cook for about 2 minutes each side. Do not overcook the tuna or it will become dry.

4 Gently toss together the French beans, tomatoes, spring onions, anchovies, black olives and shredded basil leaves.

5 Put the seared tuna steaks into four bowls and pile the vegetable mixture on top. Carefully ladle the hot garlic stock around the ingredients. Serve at once, with crusty bread.

Trout Bisque Energy 355kcal/1475 kJ; Protein 14g; Carbohydrate 14g, of which sugars 7g; Fat 27g, of which saturates 14g; Cholesterol 89mg; Calcium 50mg; Fibre 2g; Sodium 192mg.
Niçoise Energy 578kcal/2408kJ; Protein 46.4g; Carbohydrate 15g, of which sugars 10.6g; Fat 37.5g, of which saturates 7.1g; Cholesterol 235mg; Calcium 127mg; Fibre 4.7g; Sodium 585mg.

Salt Cod and Okra Soup with Creamed Yam

Inspired by the ingredients of the Caribbean, this chunky soup is served in deep bowls around a chive-flavoured sweet yam mash.

Serves 6

200g/7oz salt cod, soaked for
   24 hours, changing the water
   several times
15ml/1 tbsp olive oil
1 garlic clove, chopped
1 onion, chopped
1 green chilli, seeded and
   chopped
6 plum tomatoes, peeled and
   chopped

250ml/8fl oz/1 cup white wine
2 bay leaves
225g/8oz okra, trimmed and cut
   into chunks
225g/8oz callaloo or spinach
30ml/2 tbsp chopped
   fresh parsley
salt and ground black pepper

For the creamed yam

675g/1½lb yam, peeled and cut
   into chunks
juice of 1 lemon
50g/2oz/¼ cup butter
30ml/2 tbsp double
   (heavy) cream
15ml/1 tbsp chopped fresh chives

1 Drain and skin the cod, then rinse it under cold running water. Cut into bitesize pieces, removing bones, and set aside. Heat the oil in a pan. Add the garlic, onion and chilli. Cook for 4–5 minutes until soft. Add the cod and cook for 3–4 minutes, until it begins to colour. Stir in the tomatoes, wine and bay leaves. Pour in 900ml/1⅓ pints/3¾ cups water, bring to the boil, reduce the heat and simmer for 10 minutes.

2 Add the okra and cook for 10 minutes. Stir in the callaloo or spinach and cook for 5 minutes, until the okra is tender.

3 Prepare the creamed yam. Place the yam in a pan with the lemon juice and add cold water to cover. Bring to the boil and cook for 15–20 minutes, until tender. Drain well, return to the pan and dry it out over the heat for a few seconds. Mash with the butter and cream, and season well. Stir in the chives.

4 Season the soup and stir in the parsley. To serve, divide the creamed yam between six bowls and ladle the soup around it.

Cauliflower Soup with Prawns

Considered the most elegant member of the cabbage family, cauliflower is much appreciated in Denmark. Along with its rustic cabbage cousins, it is a favourite in Danish kitchen gardens. In this simple, old-fashioned recipe, cauliflower is elevated into an elegant, creamy soup prettily garnished with sweet, pink prawns.

Serves 6

1 large cauliflower (about 800g/
   1¾lb trimmed and chopped)
5ml/1 tsp salt, or to taste
25g/1oz/2 tbsp butter
35g/1¼oz/¼ cup plain
   (all-purpose) flour
250ml/8fl oz/1 cup
   whipping cream
1 egg yolk, beaten
salt and ground white pepper
225g/8oz cooked small prawns
   (shrimp), to garnish

1 Put the cauliflower into a large pan and add 1.5 litres/2½ pints/6¼ cups water and the salt. Bring to the boil and cook over a medium heat for 12–15 minutes until tender. Remove 475ml/16fl oz/2 cups of the cooking liquid and reserve. Cover the pan and keep warm.

2 Melt the butter in a separate pan, and stir in the flour to make a smooth paste. Cook, stirring constantly, for 3–5 minutes until the roux is pale beige. Slowly stir in the cream. Remove from the heat and stir in the egg yolk.

3 Stir the reserved cauliflower water into the roux and cook over a low heat, stirring constantly, until the mixture thickens. Do not allow it to boil or it will curdle.

4 Add the cream mixture to the cauliflower. Season with salt and pepper. Divide the soup among six soup plates and garnish with a few prawns. Serve immediately.

Cook's Tip
Season the cream mixture with 5ml/1 tsp curry powder. Purée the cauliflower before adding the cream mixture for a smooth soup.

Cod and Okra Energy 322kcal/1352kJ; Protein 10.7g; Carbohydrate 36.7g, of which sugars 5.3g; Fat 12.8g, of which saturates 6.6g; Cholesterol 40mg; Calcium 159mg; Fibre 4.6g; Sodium 137mg.
Cauliflower Soup Energy 294kcal/1217kJ; Protein 13.3g; Carbohydrate 9.7g, of which sugars 4.6g; Fat 22.6g, of which saturates 13.3g; Cholesterol 159mg; Calcium 95mg; Fibre 2.6g; Sodium 121mg.

Tomato and Peach Jus with Butterfly Prawns

American-style soups, made from the clear juices extracted from vegetables or fruits are called 'water' soups by chefs, and provide the inspiration for this dish.

Serves 6
1.5kg/3–3½ lb ripe peaches, peeled, stoned and chopped
1.2kg/2½ lb beef tomatoes, peeled and cut into chunks
30ml/2 tbsp white wine vinegar
1 lemon grass stalk, crushed and chopped
2.5cm/1in fresh root ginger, grated
1 bay leaf
150ml/¼ pint/⅔ cup water
18 tiger prawns, shelled with tails on and deveined
olive oil, for brushing
salt and ground black pepper
handful of fresh coriander leaves and 2 vine-ripened tomatoes, peeled, seeded and diced, to garnish

1 Purée the peaches and tomatoes in a food processor. Stir in the vinegar and seasoning. Line a large bowl with muslin. Pour the purée into the bowl, gather up the ends of the muslin and tie tightly. Suspend over the bowl and leave at room temperature for 3 hours or until about 1.2 litres/2 pints/5 cups juice have drained through.

2 Meanwhile, put the lemon grass, ginger and bay leaf into a saucepan with the water, and simmer for 5–6 minutes. Set aside to cool. Strain the mixture into the tomato and peach juice and chill for at least 4 hours.

3 Using a sharp knife, slit the prawns down their curved sides, cutting about three-quarters of the way through and keeping their tails intact. Open them out flat.

4 Heat a griddle or frying pan and brush with a little oil. Sear the prawns for 1–2 minutes on each side, until tender and slightly charred. Pat dry on kitchen paper to remove any remaining oil. Cool, but do not chill.

5 Ladle the soup into bowls and place three prawns in each. Add torn coriander leaves and diced tomato to each bowl.

Chunky Prawn Chupe

Chowders, known as chupes in South America, are a meal in themselves. Potatoes are always included, but the other ingredients vary. This is a seafood version.

Serves 6
500g/1¼ lb raw king prawns (jumbo shrimp)
750ml/1¼ pints/3 cups fish stock
1 carrot, finely chopped
2 celery sticks, thinly sliced
45ml/3 tbsp annatto (achiote) oil
1 large onion, finely chopped
1 red (bell) pepper, seeded and diced
2 garlic cloves, crushed
2 fresh red chillies, seeded and chopped
5ml/1 tsp turmeric
1 large tomato, peeled and chopped
675g/1½ lb potatoes, peeled and cut into 2.5cm/1in cubes
115g/4oz/1 cup fresh or frozen peas
15ml/1 tbsp chopped fresh mint
15ml/1 tbsp chopped fresh coriander (cilantro)
salt

1 Peel the prawns and set them aside. Place the shells in a large, heavy saucepan with the fish stock, chopped carrot and celery sticks. Bring to the boil, then simmer over a low heat for 20 minutes. Strain into a bowl or jug (pitcher) and set the stock aside.

2 Heat the oil in a large heavy sauce an over a low heat. Stir in the onion and red pepper and sauté for 5 minutes. Stir in the garlic, chillies and turmeric and cook for a further 2 minutes.

3 Add the chopped tomato and potatoes to the pan, season to taste with salt and cook for about 10 minutes, allowing the tomato to break down slightly and the potatoes to absorb the flavours of the other ingredients.

4 Pour in the strained stock and bring to the boil. Lower the heat and simmer for 15 minutes, or until the potatoes are cooked through.

5 Stir the prawns and peas into the soup and simmer for 4–5 minutes, or until the prawns become opaque. Finally, stir in the mint and coriander, and serve in warmed bowls.

Tomato and Peach Jus Energy 188kcal/797kJ; Protein 12.7g; Carbohydrate 25.2g, of which sugars 25.2g; Fat 4.8g, of which saturates 0.8g; Cholesterol 98mg; Calcium 71mg; Fibre 5.8g; Sodium 116mg.
Prawn Chupe Energy 175kcal/742kJ; Protein 18.9g; Carbohydrate 23.2g, of which sugars 4.3g; Fat 1.4g, of which saturates 0.3g; Cholesterol 163mg; Calcium 100mg; Fibre 2.7g; Sodium 175mg.

Prawn Wonton Soup

The light stock for this wonton soup derives its richness from dried fish like sprats or anchovies. While Chinese stores sell instant wonton soup stock, it is easier – and more satisfying – to make your own. Extra flavour comes from the wontons, which are filled with a delicious seafood mixture.

Serves 4

60g/2oz dried sprats or anchovies
750ml/1¼ pints/3 cups water
15ml/1 tbsp light soy sauce
chopped spring onions (scallions),
*   to garnish*

For the wontons

300g/11oz raw prawns (shrimp),
*   peeled and deveined*
15ml/1 tbsp light soy sauce
15ml/1 tbsp sesame oil
2.5ml/½ tsp ground black pepper
15ml/1 tbsp cornflour
*   (cornstarch)*
16 wonton wrappers

1 Start by preparing the wonton filling. Chop the prawns finely to make a coarse paste. This can be done in a food processor, but make sure you use the pulse button, or the prawns will become rubbery.

2 Scrape the chopped prawns into a bowl and add the soy sauce, sesame oil, pepper and cornflour. Mix thoroughly. Place about 5ml/1 tsp of the mixture in the centre of a wonton wrapper, bring the edges together so that they meet at the top, and pinch the neck to seal. Fill the remaining wontons in the same way.

3 Bring a small pan of water to the boil. Add the wontons and cook them for 5 minutes. Drain in a colander; transfer to a bowl and toss with a light dribble of oil to prevent them from sticking together.

4 Put the dried sprats or anchovies in a large pan. Pour in the water; add the soy sauce and bring to the boil. Cook for 5 minutes. Taste and add more soy sauce if needed. Strain the soup, return it to the pan and heat through. Place four wontons in each soup bowl, add the soup and garnish with spring onions.

Singapore Hot and Sour Pineapple Prawn Broth

This simple Nonya dish is served as an appetite enhancer because of its hot and sour flavour. The broth may be served in a hollowed-out pineapple.

Serves 4

30ml/2 tbsp vegetable oil
15–30ml/1–2 tbsp tamarind paste
15ml/1 tbsp sugar
450g/1lb fresh prawns (shrimp),
*   peeled and deveined*
4 thick fresh pineapple slices, cored
*   and cut into bitesize chunks*

salt and ground black pepper
fresh coriander (cilantro) and
*   mint leaves, to garnish*
steamed rice or plain noodles,
*   to serve*

For the spice paste

4 shallots, chopped
4 red chillies, chopped
25g/1oz fresh root ginger, peeled
*   and chopped*
1 lemon grass stalk, trimmed
*   and chopped*
5ml/1 tsp shrimp paste

1 Make the spice paste. Using a mortar and pestle or a food processor, grind the shallots, chillies, ginger and lemon grass together until a smooth paste is reached. Add the shrimp paste and mix well.

2 Heat the oil in a wok or heavy pan. Stir in the spice paste and fry until fragrant. Stir in the tamarind paste and the sugar, then pour in 1.2 litres/2 pints/5 cups water. Mix well and bring to the boil. Reduce the heat and simmer for 10 minutes. Season the broth with salt and pepper.

3 Add the prawns and pineapple to the broth and simmer for 4–5 minutes, or until the prawns are cooked. Using a slotted spoon, lift the prawns and pineapple out of the broth and divide them among four warmed bowls.

4 Ladle over some of the broth and garnish with coriander and mint leaves. The rest of the broth can be served separately as a drink, or spooned over steamed rice or plain noodles, if you want to transform this broth into a slightly more substantial dish.

Prawn Wonton Energy 178kcal/748kJ; Protein 19g; Carbohydrate 15.2g, of which sugars 0.8g; Fat 4.9g, of which saturates 0.8g; Cholesterol 156mg; Calcium 132mg; Fibre 0.6g; Sodium 1267mg.
Prawn Broth Energy 192Kcal/808kJ; Protein 20.4g; Carbohydrate 14.2g, of which sugars 13.9g; Fat 6.4g, of which saturates 0.8g; Cholesterol 219mg; Calcium 111mg; Fibre 1.3g; Sodium 216mg.

Hokkein Prawn Noodle Soup

As most of the Chinese population of Singapore is Hokkein, this is a very popular dish. Traditionally, prawn noodle soup is served with crispy cubes of pork fat, but in this recipe, crispy bacon is used instead.

Serves 4–6

For the stock
45ml/3 tbsp dried shrimp
1 dried red chilli
50g/2oz fresh root ginger, peeled
*   and sliced*
2 onions, quartered
4 cloves garlic, bruised
2 lemon grass stalks, bruised

2.5ml/½ tsp black peppercorns
30–45ml/2–3 tbsp dark
soy sauce
700g/1lb 10oz pork and
*   chicken bones*

For the soup
15ml/1 tbsp sugar
6 rashers (strips) streaky (fatty)
*   bacon, sliced*
150g/5oz fresh egg noodles
20 fresh, large prawns (shrimp),
*   peeled (add the shells to*
*   the stock)*
90g/3½oz beansprouts
2 spring onions (scallions),
*   trimmed and finely sliced*
salt and ground black pepper

1 Put all the stock ingredients into a deep pan along with the prawn shells. Pour in 2 litres/3½ pints/7¾ cups water and bring to the boil. Reduce the heat and simmer gently, uncovered, for about 2 hours, until the stock has reduced by half.

2 Strain the stock into a clean pan and put it over a low heat to keep hot. Season with salt and pepper to taste.

3 In a small pan heat the sugar with 15ml/1 tbsp water, until it turns a rich brown. Add it to the stock and mix well. In a heavy pan, dry-fry the bacon until it turns crispy and golden. Drain on kitchen paper and set aside.

4 Using a perforated ladle or sieve (strainer), plunge the noodles into the hot stock for 1 minute to heat through, then divide them among four bowls. Add the prawns to the stock, heat for 1 minute, remove with a slotted spoon and add to the bowls. Add the beansprouts to the prawns and noodles and ladle the hot stock into the bowls. Scatter the crispy bacon and spring onions over the top and serve immediately.

Crayfish and Corn Soup

This is one of the most special of all Peruvian dishes. The word 'chupe' can be translated as 'chowder', and it means a hearty soup containing meat or fish, eggs, potatoes, vegetables and rice or noodles; a complete meal in one dish. In many parts of the world fishmongers sell crayfish live, in which case they are quickly immersed in boiling water, before being cleaned. However, they are available in brine, if you cannot find them live.

Serves 6

1kg/2¼lb fresh crayfish or
*   Red Sea king prawns*
*   (jumbo shrimp)*
75ml/5 tbsp vegetable oil
1 large tomato, diced
1 litre/1¾ pints/4 cups stock
*   or water*
6 medium floury potatoes, peeled
*   and cut into chunks*
250g/9oz butternut squash,
*   cut into cubes*
250g/9oz/1½ cups shelled and
*   skinned broad (fava) beans*
100g/3¾oz/½ cup long
*   grain rice*
2 corn cobs, cut into chunks
7.5ml/1½ tsp salt
6 eggs
350ml/12fl oz evaporated milk

1 If the crayfish are living, bring a large pan of water to the boil. Add the crayfish or prawns to the water and boil for 3–5 minutes until they change colour. Remove from the pan, reserving the stock, dry with kitchen paper, devein them, and set aside.

2 Heat the oil in a large pan over high heat and add the tomato. Cook for 2 minutes, stirring, then add 1 litre/1¾ pints/ 4 cups of crayfish stock, or water.

3 Add the potato, butternut squash, beans, rice, corn and salt to the pan. Bring to the boil, then lower the heat and simmer for 15 minutes, until the potatoes are almost cooked.

4 Break the eggs into the hot soup, taking care that each one stays separate from the others. Simmer for 10–15 minutes, then remove from the heat. Stir in the milk and serve, distributing the crayfish evenly and adding a poached egg to each bowl.

Prawn Noodle Energy 257Kcal/1082kJ; Protein 18.7g; Carbohydrate 27.1g, of which sugars 6.9g; Fat 9g, of which saturates 2.8g; Cholesterol 94mg; Calcium 145mg; Fibre 3g; Sodium 1080mg.
Crayfish Soup Energy 466kcal/1956kJ; Protein 38.2g; Carbohydrate 41.5g, of which sugars 5.9g; Fat 17.1g, of which saturates 2.9g; Cholesterol 365mg; Calcium 119mg; Fibre 4.4g; Sodium 426mg.

Lobster and Tomato Soup

This luxurious lobster soup is for special occasions. The Norwegian lobster is smaller than those caught in the US, but its flesh is just as delicious. The soup can also be made with prawns, if you are feeling less extravagant, and is equally good. It is important to keep the shells as well as the flesh because they are used to provide additional flavour to the soup.

Serves 4

1 large cooked lobster or
   500g/1¼lb/3 cups cooked
   prawns (shrimp)
25g/1oz/2 tbsp butter
30ml/2 tbsp finely
   chopped shallot
2 red (bell) peppers, seeded
   and chopped
2.5cm/1in fresh root ginger,
   finely chopped
1 clove garlic, finely chopped
60ml/4 tbsp brandy
30ml/2 tbsp tomato
   purée (paste)
1.25 litres/2¼ pints/5½
   cups water
15ml/1 tbsp sherry vinegar
15ml/1 tbsp sugar
4 ripe tomatoes, skinned, seeded
   and chopped, or 400g/14oz
   can tomatoes
juice of 1 lime
salt and ground black pepper
chopped fresh dill, to garnish

1 Remove the lobster or prawn meat from their shells, reserving the shells. Set the meat aside. Melt the butter in a pan, add the shallots, peppers, ginger and garlic and cook for 5 minutes. Add the shells and cook gently for a further 10 minutes.

2 Add the brandy to the pan and set alight. Stir in the tomato purée. Add the water, season lightly with salt and pepper, and bring slowly to the boil. Lower the heat and simmer very gently for 40 minutes.

3 Strain the mixture into a clean pan. Add the vinegar, sugar, tomatoes and lime juice to taste, and check the seasonings, adding salt and pepper only if necessary.

4 Divide the lobster or prawn meat between four individual serving bowls. Bring the soup to the boil then pour over the shellfish. Serve garnished with chopped dill.

Creamy Crayfish Soup

Crayfish are delicate and delicious and the sweetness of the meat gives a distinctive taste to the creamy soup. Paprika and lemon juice contrast well with the crayfish, and the remaining ingredients highlight the flavour of the shellfish rather than competing with or disguising it.

Serves 4

50g/2oz/¼ cup unsalted
   (sweet) butter
50g/2oz/1 cup plain
   (all-purpose) flour
700ml/1 pint 3½fl oz/scant
   3 cups fish or
   chicken stock
5ml/1 tsp paprika
1 egg yolk
120ml/4fl oz/½ cup double
   (heavy) cream
250g/9oz cooked
   crayfish meat
15ml/1 tbsp lemon juice
salt and ground
   black pepper
15ml/1 tbsp chopped fresh dill,
   to garnish

1 Melt the butter in a large heavy saucepan, stir in the flour to make a roux and cook gently over a low heat for 30 seconds, without colouring. Remove from the heat and gradually stir in the fish or chicken stock to form a smooth sauce. Return the pan to the heat and, stirring all the time, cook until the sauce boils and thickens. Add the paprika and season to taste with salt and pepper.

2 In a small bowl, mix the egg yolk and cream together, then stir into the soup and heat gently, taking care not to let the mixture boil or the soup will curdle.

3 Add the crayfish and lemon juice to the soup and heat gently. Pour the soup into individual serving bowls and serve hot, garnished with chopped dill.

> **Variation**
> Since the flavour of crayfish is rather similar to that of lobster, you can use lobster in this dish instead. Like crayfish, lobsters also turn red on cooking.

Crayfish Soup Energy 348kcal/1444kJ; Protein 12.2g; Carbohydrate 10.9g, of which sugars 0.8g; Fat 28.8g, of which saturates 17g; Cholesterol 184mg; Calcium 65mg; Fibre 0.4g; Sodium 383mg.
Lobster and Tomato Energy 275kcal/1155kJ; Protein 29.6g; Carbohydrate 14.1g, of which sugars 13.5g; Fat 7.8g, of which saturates 3.7g; Cholesterol 151mg; Calcium 99mg; Fibre 2.6g; Sodium 479mg.

Shore Crab Soup

Ideally, this soup should be made with the little velvety-shelled crabs that are mostly caught off the west coast of Scotland, but common or brown crabs can be used instead.

Serves 4

1kg/2¼lb shore or velvet crabs
50g/2oz/¼ cup butter

50g/2oz leek, chopped
50g/2oz carrot, chopped
30ml/2 tbsp brandy
225g/8oz ripe tomatoes, chopped
15ml/1 tbsp tomato purée (paste)
120ml/4fl oz/½ cup dry
    white wine
1.5 litres/2½ pints/6¼ cups
    fish stock
sprig of fresh tarragon
60ml/4 tbsp double (heavy) cream
lemon juice

1 Bring a large pan of water to a rolling boil and plunge the live crabs into it. They will be killed very quickly. Once the crabs are dead – a couple of minutes at most – take them out of the water, place in a large bowl and break them up. This can be done with either a wooden mallet or the end of a rolling pin.

2 Melt the butter in a heavy pan, add the leek and carrot and cook gently until soft but not coloured.

3 Add the crabs and when very hot pour in the brandy, stirring to allow the flavour to pervade the whole pan. Add the tomatoes, tomato purée, wine, stock and tarragon. Bring to the boil and simmer gently for 30 minutes.

4 Strain the soup through a metal sieve, forcing as much of the tomato mixture through as possible. (If you like you could remove the big claws and purée the remains in a blender.)

5 Return to the heat, simmer for a few minutes then season to taste. Add the cream and lemon juice, and serve.

Cook's Tips
If you don't have fish stock then water will do, or you could use some of the water used to boil the crabs initially.

Devon Crab Soup

Locals will tell you that crab caught around the coastline of Devon, in England, UK, is especially sweet. Although crab is available all the year round, it is at its best and is least expensive during the summer months – the perfect time to make this lovely creamy soup.

Serves 4–6

25g/1oz/2 tbsp butter
1 medium onion, finely chopped
1 celery stick, finely chopped
1 garlic clove, crushed
25ml/1½ tbsp flour
225g/8oz cooked crab meat, half
    dark and half white
1.2 litres/2 pints/5 cups fish stock
150ml/¼ pint/⅔ cup double
    (heavy) cream
30ml/2 tbsp dry sherry
salt and ground black pepper

1 Melt the butter in a pan and add the onion, celery and garlic. Cook over a medium heat for about 5 minutes, stirring frequently, until the vegetables are soft but not browned.

2 Remove from the heat and quickly stir in the flour, then the brown crab meat. Gradually stir in the stock.

3 Bring the mixture just to the boil, then reduce the heat and simmer for about 30 minutes. Process or blend the soup and return it to the cleaned pan. Season to taste with salt and pepper.

4 Chop the white crab meat, leaving some shreds whole, and stir it into the pan with the cream and sherry. Reheat the soup and serve immediately.

Cook's Tips
If you prefer the white meat, just replace the brown meat with the white. Large crabs, such as king crabs or snow crabs are extremely meaty, and cooked legs are available frozen. The meat is of excellent quality with delicious, sweet flesh.

Shore Crab Soup Energy 419kcal/1741kJ; Protein 35.1g; Carbohydrate 3.8g, of which sugars 3.6g; Fat 25.7g, of which saturates 15.1g; Cholesterol 196mg; Calcium 252mg; Fibre 1.1g; Sodium 1122mg.
Devon Crab Soup Energy 209kcal/867kJ; Protein 7.8g; Carbohydrate 4.6g, of which sugars 1.2g; Fat 17.3g, of which saturates 10.6g; Cholesterol 70mg; Calcium 69mg; Fibre 0.3g; Sodium 241mg.

Corn and Crab Soup

This dish is believed to have originated in Java, where at some time it was copied from the Chinese immigrants. It is now a well-loved soup throughout the islands, eaten whenever corn and crab are plentiful. It makes a delicious appetizer, or a light lunch with rice or bread. A dash of vinegar adds piquancy to the richness of the egg and crab meat.

Serves 4
750ml/1¼ pints/3 cups water
1 seafood stock cube
450g/1lb can creamed corn
5ml/1 tsp salt
15ml/1 tbsp sesame oil
250g/9oz crab meat
2 eggs
2 spring onions (scallions), trimmed and sliced, to garnish
black vinegar, to serve

1 Combine the water, stock cube, creamed corn, salt and sesame oil in a large, heavy saucepan and bring the mixture to the boil.

2 Simmer for 5 minutes, then shred the crab meat and add to the pan. Gently cook for about 3 minutes.

3 Lightly beat the eggs and add to the barely simmering soup, stirring quickly to distribute the egg evenly and thicken the soup.

4 Adjust the seasoning and serve garnished with spring onions, with a dish of black vinegar on the side.

Cook's Tips
• *Nothing quite matches the flavour of fresh crab, but Scandinavian canned crab or frozen crab are acceptable substitutes when the fresh variety is not available.*
• *Use regular corn and add a dash of cream or coconut cream if you cannot obtain creamed corn.*
• *Black vinegar is made from fermented rice, millet, wheat, sorghum and barley. Its flavour varies from region to region.*

Crab and Asparagus Soup with Nuoc Cham

In this delicious soup, the recipe has been adapted from the classic French asparagus velouté to produce a meatier version that has more texture, and nuoc cham has been added.

Serves 4
15ml/1 tbsp vegetable oil
2 shallots, finely chopped
2 garlic cloves, finely chopped
15ml/1 tbsp rice flour or cornflour (cornstarch)
225g/8oz/1⅓ cups cooked crab meat, chopped into small pieces

450g/1lb preserved asparagus, finely chopped or 450g/1lb fresh asparagus, trimmed and steamed
salt and ground black pepper
basil and coriander (cilantro) leaves, to garnish
nuoc cham, to serve

For the stock
1 meaty chicken carcass
25g/1oz dried shrimp, soaked in water for 30 minutes, rinsed and drained
2 onions, peeled and quartered
2 garlic cloves, crushed
15ml/1 tbsp nuoc mam
6 black peppercorns
sea salt

1 To make the stock, put the chicken carcass into a deep pan. Add all the other stock ingredients, except the salt, and pour in 2 litres/3½ pints/8 cups water. Bring to the boil, boil for a few minutes, skim off any foam, reduce the heat then simmer, covered for 1½–2 hours. Remove the lid and simmer for a further 30 minutes to reduce the stock. Skim off any fat, season with salt, strain and measure out 1.5 litres/2½ pints/6¼ cups.

2 Heat the oil in a wok. Stir in the shallots and garlic, until they begin to colour. Remove from the heat, stir in the flour, and then the stock. Return to the heat and bring to the boil, stirring constantly, until smooth.

3 Add the crab meat and asparagus, reduce the heat and simmer for 15–20 minutes. Season, then serve, garnished with basil and coriander, and a splash of nuoc cham.

Corn and Crab Energy 279kcal/1173kJ; Protein 18.6g; Carbohydrate 29.9g, of which sugars 10.8g; Fat 10.3g, of which saturates 1.9g; Cholesterol 140mg; Calcium 19mg; Fibre 1.6g; Sodium 1093mg.
Crab and Asparagus Energy 143Kcal/593kJ; Protein 45g; Carbohydrate 4g, of which sugars 2g; Fat 7g, of which saturates 1g; Cholesterol 41mg; Calcium 29mg; Fibre 3.5g; Sodium 0.8g.

Crab and Chilli Soup with Fresh Coriander Relish

Prepared fresh crab is readily available, high quality and convenient – perfect for creating an exotic soup in minutes. Here it is accompanied by a hot coriander and chilli relish.

Serves 4

45ml/3 tbsp olive oil
1 red onion, finely chopped
2 red chillies, seeded and chopped
1 garlic clove, finely chopped
450g/1lb fresh white crab meat
30ml/2 tbsp chopped fresh parsley
30ml/2 tbsp chopped
  fresh coriander
juice of 2 lemons

1 lemon grass stalk
1 litre/1¾ pints/4 cups good fish
  or chicken stock
15ml/1 tbsp Thai fish sauce
  (nam pla)
150g/5oz vermicelli or angel hair
  pasta, broken into
  5–7.5cm/2–3in lengths
salt and ground black pepper

For the coriander relish

50g/2oz/1 cup fresh
  coriander leaves
1 green chilli, seeded and chopped
15ml/1 tbsp sunflower oil
25ml/1½ tbsp lemon juice
2.5ml/½ tsp ground roasted
  cumin seeds

1 Heat the oil in a pan and add the onion, chillies and garlic. Cook over a gentle heat for 10 minutes until the onion is soft. Transfer to a bowl and stir in the crab meat, parsley, coriander and lemon juice, then set aside.

2 Crush the lemon grass with a rolling pin. Pour the stock and fish sauce into a pan. Add the lemon grass and bring to the boil, then add the pasta. Simmer, uncovered, for 3–4 minutes or according to the packet instructions, until the pasta is just tender.

3 Meanwhile, make the coriander relish. Place the fresh coriander, chilli, oil, lemon juice and cumin in a food processor or blender and process to form a coarse paste. Season to taste.

4 Remove and discard the lemon grass. Stir the chilli and crab mixture into the soup and season. Bring to the boil, reduce the heat and simmer for 2 minutes. Ladle the soup into four bowls and put a spoonful of the relish in each. Serve at once.

Crab, Coconut and Coriander Soup

Quick and easy to prepare, this soup has all the flavours associated with the Bahia region of Brazil: creamy coconut, palm oil, fragrant coriander and, of course, fresh chilli.

Serves 4

30ml/2 tbsp olive oil
1 onion, finely chopped
1 celery stick, finely chopped
2 garlic cloves, crushed
1 fresh red chilli, seeded
  and chopped

1 large tomato, peeled
  and chopped
45ml/3 tbsp chopped fresh
  coriander (cilantro)
1 litre/1¾ pints/4 cups fresh crab
  or fish stock
500g/1¼lb crab meat
250ml/8fl oz/1 cup coconut milk
30ml/2 tbsp palm oil
juice of 1 lime
salt
hot chilli oil and lime wedges,
  to serve

1 Heat the olive oil in a pan over a low heat. Stir in the onion and celery, and sauté gently for 5 minutes, until softened and translucent. Stir in the garlic and chilli and cook for a further 2 minutes.

2 Add the tomato and half the coriander and increase the heat. Cook, stirring, for 3 minutes, then add the stock. Bring to the boil, then simmer for 5 minutes.

3 Stir the crab, coconut milk and palm oil into the pan and simmer over a very low heat for a further 5 minutes. The consistency should be thick, but not stew-like, so add some water if needed.

4 Stir in the lime juice and remaining coriander, then season with salt to taste. Serve in heated bowls with the chilli oil and lime wedges on the side.

> **Variation**
> *If crab meat is not available, or you would like a change, try using chunks of white fish instead.*

Crab and Chilli Energy 425kcal/1773kJ; Protein 26.7g; Carbohydrate 50.7g, of which sugars 1.4g; Fat 12.6g, of which saturates 1.6g; Cholesterol 81mg; Calcium 198mg; Fibre 1.1g; Sodium 767mg.
Crab Soup Energy 228kcal/951kJ; Protein 23.6g; Carbohydrate 5.4g, of which sugars 5g; Fat 12.6g, of which saturates 3.7g; Cholesterol 90mg; Calcium 199mg; Fibre 1.1g; Sodium 767mg.

Blue Crab Casserole

Blue crabs are not always available but European crab can be used instead.

Serves 4

2 live blue crabs
7.5ml/1½ tsp sesame oil
15ml/1 tbsp Korean chilli powder
2 garlic cloves, crushed
300g/11oz Chinese white radish, peeled and diced
300g/11oz courgette (zucchini), thinly sliced
50g/2oz green chilli, seeded and sliced
20g/³⁄₄oz red chilli, seeded and sliced
5ml/1 tsp light soy sauce
5ml/1 tsp dark soy sauce
5ml/1 tsp each salt and sugar
275g/10oz leeks, roughly sliced
50g/2oz chrysanthemum leaves
50g/2oz watercress
15ml/1 tbsp doenjang soya bean paste
15ml/1 tbsp sake

1 Put the crabs in iced water for at least 5 minutes to stun them. Remove their top shells and small legs (set these aside). Remove the entrails, gills and mouth parts. Slit the crabs down the middle, using a heavy knife and a meat mallet.

2 Place the shells and legs in a large pan. Pour in 1.5 litres/2½ pints/6¼ cups water and bring to the boil. Reduce the heat and simmer for 1 hour, removing any scum, if necessary. Strain the stock, discarding the shells and legs.

3 Heat a large pan over a low heat and add 50ml/2fl oz/¼ cup of the crab stock. Stir in the sesame oil, half the chilli powder and the garlic. Bring to the boil, then reduce the heat and simmer the mixture briefly. Add the rest of the stock and mix it with the chilli-flavoured stock. Add the radish. Bring back to the boil, then reduce the heat and simmer for 10 minutes.

4 Add the crabs, courgette and green and red chillies, and boil for a further 10 minutes, until the crab turns bright orange. Add the remaining chilli powder, the light and dark soy sauces, salt and sugar. Bring the soup back to the boil.

5 Add the leeks, chrysanthemum leaves, watercress, doenjang soya bean paste and sake. Remove the pan from the heat and cover it, then leave to stand for 2 minutes before serving.

Seafood Rice Soup

Aguadito is the name given to a rice soup, usually flavoured with coriander, in which the main ingredient may be meat, poultry or seafood. It comes from the north of Peru.

Serves 6

12 New Zealand greenshell mussels in half shells, fresh or frozen
12 clams
12 whole raw king prawns (jumbo shrimp)
12 small scallops
12 small squid, cleaned
45ml/3 tbsp vegetable oil
1 medium red onion, chopped
2 large red (bell) peppers, sliced lengthways
250g/9oz/2 cups shelled peas
large bunch of coriander (cilantro), chopped
1 whole chilli
4 litres/7 pints/16 cups water
250g/9oz/1¼ cups long grain rice, washed and drained
salt

1 If using fresh mussels, scrub and rinse in three changes of cold water. Scrub and rinse the clams in the same way. Discard any that are open and do not close when tapped. Remove the heads of the prawns and devein them, but leave any roe intact.

2 Clean the scallops by removing the elastic part around the shell and the brown part around the scallop; it is better to keep them in their shells. Slice the squid into rings.

3 Heat the oil in a large, deep pan and fry the onion for 10 minutes until it softens and browns, add the red pepper, drained rice and peas and stir. Place the whole chilli in the pan.

4 Add the water to the pan and bring to the boil. If you are using fresh mussels, add them to the pan with the clams. Add the coriander. Season with salt, bring back to the boil and simmer for 10–12 minutes, until the clams and mussels have opened and the rice has cooked. Finally, add the squid, scallops and prawns to the pan and fold into the rice, with the mussels if using frozen. Simmer for another 3 minutes.

5 Serve immediately, while piping hot, dividing the seafood among the bowls. Discard mussels or clams which have not opened.

Blue Crab Energy 168kcal/700kJ; Protein 20.5g; Carbohydrate 7g, of which sugars 6.3g; Fat 6.4g, of which saturates 0.9g; Cholesterol 63mg; Calcium 57mg; Fibre 3.4g; Sodium 1055mg.
Seafood Soup Energy 329kcal/1374kJ; Protein 20.7g; Carbohydrate 43.8g, of which sugars 5.3g; Fat 7.9g, of which saturates 1g; Cholesterol 135mg; Calcium 83mg; Fibre 3.5g; Sodium 193mg.

Coconut and Seafood Soup with Garlic Chives

The long list of ingredients in this Thai-inspired recipe could mislead you into thinking that this soup is complicated. In fact, it is very easy to put together.

Serves 4

600ml/1 pint/2½ cups fish stock
5 thin slices fresh root ginger
2 lemon grass stalks, chopped
3 kaffir lime leaves, shredded
25g/1oz garlic chives
  (1 bunch), chopped
15g/½oz fresh coriander (cilantro)

15ml/1 tbsp vegetable oil
4 shallots, chopped
400ml/14fl oz can coconut milk
30–45ml/2–3 tbsp Thai
  fish sauce
45–60ml/3–4 tbsp Thai green
  curry paste
450g/1lb uncooked large prawns
  (jumbo shrimp), peeled
  and deveined
450g/1lb prepared squid
a little lime juice (optional)
salt and ground black pepper
60ml/4 tbsp fried shallot slices,
  to serve

1 Pour the stock into a pan and add the slices of fresh ginger, the chopped lemon grass and half the lime leaves. Add half the chopped chives to the pan with the coriander stalks. Bring to the boil, then reduce the heat. Cover the pan, then simmer gently for 20 minutes. Strain the stock.

2 Rinse the pan, then add the oil and shallots. Cook over a medium heat for 5–10 minutes, stirring occasionally, until the shallots are just beginning to brown.

3 Stir in the stock, coconut milk, the remaining lime leaves and half the fish sauce. Heat gently until the soup is just simmering and cook over a low heat for 5–10 minutes.

4 Stir in the curry paste and the peeled prawns and cook for 3 minutes. Add the squid, cook for a further 2 minutes. Add the lime juice, if using, and season.

5 Stir in the remaining fish sauce, chopped chives and the chopped coriander leaves. Ladle in to warmed bowls and serve sprinkled with fried shallots.

Vermouth Soup with Seared Scallops, Rocket Oil and Caviar

Seared scallops form an elegant tower in the centre of this crème de la crème of fine soups. The caviar garnish is an attractive and delicious addition.

Serves 4

25g/1oz/2 tbsp butter
5 shallots, sliced
300ml/½ pint/1¼ cups dry
  white wine
300ml/½ pint/1¼ cups vermouth
900ml/1½ pints/3¾ cups
  fish stock

300ml/½ pint/1¼ cups
  double cream
300ml/½ pint/1¼ cups
  single cream
15ml/1 tbsp olive oil
12 large scallops
salt and ground black pepper
15ml/1 tbsp caviar and snipped
  chives, to garnish

For the rocket oil
115g/4oz rocket leaves
120ml/4fl oz/½ cup olive oil

1 Prepare the rocket oil first. Process the rocket leaves and olive oil in a food processor or blender for 1–2 minutes to give a paste. Line a bowl with muslin and add the paste. Squeeze the muslin to extract the rocket-flavoured oil. Set aside.

2 Melt the butter in a large saucepan. Add the shallots and cook over a gentle heat for 8–10 minutes, until they are soft but not browned. Add the wine and vermouth and boil for 8–10 minutes, until reduced to about a quarter of the volume.

3 Add the stock and bring back to the boil. Boil until reduced by half. Pour in the double and single creams, and return to the boil. Reduce the heat and simmer for 12–15 minutes, until the soup is just thick enough to coat the back of a spoon. Strain the soup through a sieve into the rinsed-out pan, and set aside.

4 Heat a frying pan. Brush the scallops with oil, and sear for 1–2 minutes on each side. Reheat the soup, taste and season. Arrange three scallops in the centre of each of four soup plates. Ladle the soup around the scallops and top with a little caviar. Drizzle rocket oil over the soup, then sprinkle with chives.

Seafood Soup Energy 282Kcal/1185kJ; Protein 37.9g; Carbohydrate 7.7g, of which sugars 6g; Fat 11.3g, of which saturates 1.9g; Cholesterol 473mg; Calcium 156mg; Fibre 0.7g; Sodium 451mg.
Scallop Soup Energy 999kcal/4129kJ; Protein 26g; Carbohydrate 10g, of which sugars 6g; Fat 95g, of which saturates 43g; Cholesterol 213mg; Calcium 149 mg; Fibre 1g; Sodium 635mg.

Lemon and Pumpkin Moules Marinière

This mussel soup is based on the classic French shellfish dish.

Serves 4

1kg/2¼lb fresh mussels
300ml/½ pint/1¼ cups dry
  white wine
1 large lemon
1 bay leaf
15ml/1 tbsp olive oil
1 onion, chopped
1 garlic clove, crushed
675g/1½lb pumpkin or squash,
  seeded, peeled and chopped
900ml/1½ pints/3¾ cups
  vegetable stock
30ml/2 tbsp chopped fresh dill
salt and ground black pepper
lemon wedges, to serve

1 Scrub the mussels in cold water and remove the dark hairy beards. Discard any open mussels that do not shut when tapped sharply, and put the rest into a large pan. Add the wine.

2 Pare large pieces of rind from the lemon and squeeze the juice, then add both to the mussels with the bay leaf. Cover and bring to the boil, then cook for 4–5 minutes, shaking the pan until all the mussels have opened. Drain in a colander over a bowl. Reserve the liquid and the mussels. Discard the lemon rind and bay leaf, and any mussel shells that have not opened.

3 When all the mussels are cool enough to handle, set aside a few in their shells for the garnish. Remove the remaining mussels from their shells. Strain the reserved cooking liquid through a muslin-lined sieve to remove any sand or grit.

4 Heat the oil in a pan. Add the onion and garlic and cook for 4–5 minutes. Add the pumpkin and the mussel cooking liquid. Bring to the boil and simmer, uncovered, for 5–6 minutes. Pour in the vegetable stock and cook for a further 25–30 minutes.

5 Cool slightly, then process it in a food processor or blender until smooth. Return the soup to the rinsed-out saucepan and season well. Stir in the chopped dill and the shelled mussels, then bring just to the boil. Ladle into soup plates and garnish with the mussels in their shells. Serve lemon wedges with the soup.

Saffron-Flavoured Mussel Soup

There's a fragrant taste of the sea from the Spanish coast in this creamy soup filled with the jet black shells of plump mussels.

Serves 4

1.5kg/3–3½lb fresh mussels
600 ml/1 pint /2½ cups
  white wine
few fresh parsley stalks
50g/2oz/¼ cup butter
2 leeks, finely chopped
2 celery sticks,
  finely chopped
1 carrot, chopped
2 garlic cloves, chopped
large pinch of saffron threads
600ml/1 pint/2½ cups
  double cream
3 tomatoes, peeled, seeded
  and chopped
salt and ground black pepper
30 ml/2 tbsp chopped fresh
  chives, to garnish

1 Scrub the mussels and pull away the beards that protrude from the shells. Put them into a large saucepan with the wine and parsley stalks. Cover, bring to the boil and cook for 4–5 minutes, shaking the pan occasionally, until the mussels have opened. Discard the stalks and any mussels that refuse to open.

2 Drain the mussels over a large bowl, reserving the cooking liquid. When they are cool enough to handle, remove about half of the cooked mussels from their shells. Set aside with the remaining mussels in their shells.

3 Melt the butter in a large saucepan and add the leeks, celery, carrot and garlic, and cook for 5 minutes until softened. Strain the reserved mussel cooking liquid through a fine sieve or muslin to remove any grit. Add to the pan and cook over a high heat for 8–10 minutes to reduce slightly. Strain again into a clean saucepan, add the saffron strands and cook for about another minute.

4 Add the cream and bring back to the boil. Season well. Add all the mussels and the tomatoes and heat gently to warm through. Ladle the soup into four warmed shallow soup bowls, then scatter with the chopped chives and serve immediately.

Mussel with Pumpkin Energy 126kcal/532kJ; Protein 13g; Carbohydrate 7.5g, of which sugars 4g; Fat 5g, of which saturates 0.8g; Cholesterol 40mg; Calcium 113mg; Fibre 2.5g; Sodium 245mg.
Saffron Mussel Soup Energy 441kcal/1825kJ; Protein 9.6g; Carbohydrate 3.1g, of which sugars 3.1g; Fat 39.1g, of which saturates 23.9g; Cholesterol 116mg; Calcium 137mg; Fibre 0.6g; Sodium 156mg.

Mussel and Fennel Bree

'Bree' is the Scots word for a soup or broth, most often associated with shellfish rather like a bisque or bouillabaisse. Mussels partner particularly well with the anise flavour of Pernod or Ricard. Try to get the native Scottish mussels that are smaller and have a good flavour. You will need two pans for this dish, one to cook the mussels and one for the bree.

Serves 4

1kg/2¼lb fresh mussels
1 fennel bulb
120ml/4fl oz/½ cup dry
   white wine
1 leek, finely sliced
olive oil
25g/1oz/2 tbsp butter
splash of Pernod or Ricard
150ml/¼ pint/⅔ cup double
   (heavy) cream
25g/1oz fresh parsley, chopped

1 Clean the mussels thoroughly, removing any beards and scraping off any barnacles. Discard any that are broken or open, or do not close when sharply tapped.

2 Strip off the outer leaves of the fennel and roughly chop them. Set to one side. Then take the central core of the fennel and chop it very finely. Set it aside in a separate dish or bowl.

3 Place the roughly chopped fennel leaves, the mussels and the wine in a large pan, cover and cook gently until all the mussels open, about 5 minutes. Discard any that remain closed.

4 In a second pan sweat the leek and finely chopped core of the fennel gently in the oil and butter until soft.

5 Meanwhile remove the mussels from the first pan and either leave in the shell or remove. Set aside.

6 Strain the liquor on to the leek mixture and bring to the boil. Add a little water and the pastis, and simmer for a few minutes. Add the cream and parsley and bring back to the boil.

7 Place the mussels in a serving tureen and pour over the soup. Serve with crusty bread for mopping up the juices.

Spinach and Clam Soup

The leafy flavour of the fresh spinach marries perfectly with the nutty taste of the doenjang soya bean paste to make this mouthwatering soup with clams.

Serves 3

9 clams
90g/3½oz spinach
2 spring onions (scallions)
40g/1½oz/scant ¼ cup minced
   (ground) beef
15ml/1 tbsp doenjang soya
   bean paste
15ml/1 tbsp crushed garlic
salt

1 Scrub the clams in cold water, and rinse the spinach. Cut the spring onions lengthways and then into 5cm/2in strips.

2 Place the beef and soya bean paste in a saucepan. Cook over a medium heat stirring occasionally until the beef is cooked.

3 Pour in 750ml/1½ pints/3 cups water and bring to the boil. Add the clams and spinach and simmer for 5 minutes.

4 When the clams have opened, add the spring onions and garlic. Discard any clams that remain closed. Season and serve.

> **Cook's Tip**
> Doenjang soybean paste is a Korean fermented soybean paste. It is similar to miso but slightly milder. Miso, available from wholefood and healthfood stores as well as Asian supermarkets, can be used instead.

> **Variations**
> • Use fish stock instead of water and omit the beef.
> • Use shredded pak choi (bok choy) instead of the spinach.
> • For a vegetarian soup, omit the beef and use vegetable stock. Add tofu instead of the clams.

Mussel Bree Energy 392kcal/1624kJ; Protein 13.4g; Carbohydrate 5.7g, of which sugars 3g; Fat 33g, of which saturates 16.9g; Cholesterol 105mg; Calcium 95mg; Fibre 2.8g; Sodium 297mg.
Spinach and Clam Energy 90kcal/377kJ; Protein 11.1g; Carbohydrate 4.7g, of which sugars 3.8g; Fat 3.1g, of which saturates 1.1g; Cholesterol 30mg; Calcium 119mg; Fibre 2.2g; Sodium 1471mg.

Chilli Clam Broth

This soup of succulent clams in a tasty stock could not be easier to prepare. Popular in coastal areas of Colombia, it makes the perfect lunch on a hot summer's day.

Serves 6
30ml/2 tbsp olive oil
1 onion, finely chopped
3 garlic cloves, crushed
2 fresh red chillies, seeded and finely chopped
250ml/8fl oz/1 cup dry white wine
400ml/14fl oz can plum tomatoes, drained
1 large potato, about 250g/9oz, peeled and diced
400ml/14fl oz/1²/₃ cups fish stock
1.3kg/3lb fresh clams
15ml/1 tbsp chopped fresh coriander (cilantro)
15ml/1 tbsp chopped fresh flat leaf parsley
salt
lime wedges, to garnish

1 Heat the oil in a pan. Add the onion and sauté for 5 minutes over a low heat. Stir in the garlic and chillies and cook for a further 2 minutes. Pour in the wine and bring to the boil, then simmer for 2 minutes.

2 Add the tomatoes, diced potato and stock. Bring to the boil, cover and lower the heat so that the soup simmers.

3 Season with salt and cook for 15 minutes, until the potatoes are beginning to break up and the tomatoes have made a rich sauce.

4 Meanwhile, wash the clams thoroughly under cold running water. Gently tap any that are open, and discard them if they do not close.

5 Add the clams to the soup, cover the pan and cook for about 3–4 minutes, or until the clams have opened, then stir in the chopped herbs. Season with salt to taste.

6 Check over the clams and throw away any that have failed to open. Ladle the soup into warmed bowls. Offer the lime wedges separately, to be squeezed over the soup before eating.

Corn Soup with Cockles

The basis of this soup is coarse cornmeal, which is left over after fine cornmeal has been produced. Poor people used to collect these "leftovers" from the miller, and would mix them with whatever seafood they could find along the shore. This traditional recipe is from the Algarve, in the south of Portugal. Coarse cornmeal is also used in other regions, but usually in combination with meat, or even as a dessert mixed with sugar and egg yolks.

Serves 4
300g/11oz live cockles
1 litre/1³/₄ pints/4 cups water or light chicken stock
50ml/2fl oz/¼ cup olive oil
1 onion, finely chopped
150g/5oz/1¼ cups coarse cornmeal or semolina
30ml/2 tbsp chopped fresh parsley

1 Wash the cockles thoroughly and discard any with broken shells. Bring the water or stock to the boil, add the cockles and cook for about 4–5 minutes until they open.

2 Discard any cockles that remain closed. Strain the cooking liquid through a fine sieve (strainer) into a bowl and reserve. Set the cockles aside.

3 Heat the olive oil in a large pan, add the onion and cook over a low heat, stirring occasionally, for 5 minutes, until softened.

4 Add the reserved cooking liquid to the pan and sprinkle in the cornmeal or semolina, stirring constantly.

5 Simmer for 5 minutes, add the cockles and parsley and heat through briefly. Pour into a tureen and serve immediately.

> **Cook's Tip**
> Buy cockles from a reputable supplier and cook them on the day of purchase. It is unwise to collect them from the beach because of the high risk of pollution.

Chilli Clam Energy 290kcal/1217kJ; Protein 36.2g; Carbohydrate 14.1g, of which sugars 3.5g; Fat 7.2g, of which saturates 1.3g; Cholesterol 145mg; Calcium 184mg; Fibre 1.5g; Sodium 151mg.
Corn Soup Energy 240kcal/999kJ; Protein 8.4g; Carbohydrate 28.8g, of which sugars 1g; Fat 9.8g, of which saturates 1.3g; Cholesterol 20mg; Calcium 52mg; Fibre 1.4g; Sodium 186mg.

Marinated Smoked Haddock Fillets

This simple dish is also excellent made with kipper fillets.

Serves 6
450g/1lb undyed smoked
   haddock fillet, skinned
1 onion, very thinly sliced
   into rings
5–10ml/1–2 tsp Dijon mustard
30ml/2 tbsp lemon juice
90ml/6 tbsp olive oil
45ml/3 tbsp dark rum
12 small new potatoes, scrubbed
30ml/2 tbsp chopped fresh dill,
   plus 6 sprigs to garnish
ground black pepper

1 Cut the fish fillet in half lengthways. Check for and remove any bones by pressing gently with your fingertips and thumb all the way down. Arrange the pieces in a single layer in a shallow non-metallic dish. Sprinkle the onion rings evenly over the top.

2 Whisk together the mustard, lemon juice and some ground black pepper. Add the oil gradually, whisking continuously. Pour two-thirds of the dressing over the fish. Cover the dish with clear film (plastic wrap) and leave the fish to marinate for 2 hours in a cool place. Sprinkle with the rum and leave for 1 hour more.

3 Cook the potatoes in boiling salted water until tender. Drain, cut in half and place in a bowl. Cool a little, then toss in the remaining dressing. Stir in the dill, cover and set aside.

4 Slice the haddock thinly, as for smoked salmon, or leave whole if you like. Arrange on small plates and spoon over some marinade and onion rings. Pile the potato halves on one side of each plate and garnish each portion with a sprig of dill. Serve chilled or at room temperature.

> **Cook's Tip**
> *A large, thick haddock fillet is best. If all you can find are small pieces, serve the pieces whole instead of slicing them. In some parts of Scotland, whisky is used instead of rum. A good whisky with a subtle flavour would be best for this delicate dish.*

Sussex Smokies

England's smokehouses produce some fine products. The flavour and colour of this Sussex dish is best when made with pale, undyed smoked haddock rather than the bright yellow artificially dyed variety. Follow this filling appetizer with a light main course or serve it with crusty bread as a light meal or snack.

Serves 4
350g/12oz smoked haddock
450ml/¾ pint/scant
   2 cups milk
25g/1oz/2 tbsp butter
25g/1oz/4 tbsp flour
115g/4oz mature Cheddar
   cheese, grated
60ml/4 tbsp fresh
   breadcrumbs
salt and ground black pepper
crusty bread, to serve

1 Remove and discard all skin and bones from the haddock and cut the fish into strips.

2 Put the milk, butter, flour and seasoning into a pan. Over a medium heat and whisking constantly, bring to the boil and bubble gently for 2–3 minutes until thick and smooth.

3 Add the haddock and half the cheese to the hot sauce and bring it just back to the boil to melt the cheese.

4 Divide the mixture between individual flameproof dishes or ramekins. Toss together the remaining cheese and the breadcrumbs and sprinkle the mixture over the top of each filled dish.

5 Put the dishes under a hot grill (broiler) until bubbling and golden. Serve immediately with crusty bread.

> **Cook's Tip**
> *It helps to use a pair of tweezers when removing bones from the smoked haddock fillets. Run your fingers over the fillet to feel for the bones and then pull them out with the tweezers.*

Smoked Haddock Energy 212kcal/884kJ; Protein 15.3g; Carbohydrate 7.7g, of which sugars 1.3g; Fat 11.7g, of which saturates 1.7g; Cholesterol 27mg; Calcium 37mg; Fibre 0.9g; Sodium 577mg.
Sussex Smokies Energy 363kcal/1525kJ; Protein 30.1g; Carbohydrate 21.8g, of which sugars 5.8g; Fat 17.4g, of which saturates 10.8g; Cholesterol 79mg; Calcium 396mg; Fibre 0.5g; Sodium 1073mg.

Smoked Haddock Pâté

Arbroath smokies are small haddock that are beheaded and gutted but not split before being salted and hot-smoked. You can also use kippers or any smoked fish for this recipe.

Serves 6
butter for greasing
3 large Arbroath smokies, approximately 225g/8oz each

275g/10oz/1¼ cups soft white (farmer's) cheese
3 eggs, beaten
30–45ml/2–3 tbsp lemon juice
ground black pepper
chervil sprigs, to garnish
lettuce leaves and lemon wedges, to serve

1 Preheat the oven to 160°C/325°F/Gas 3. Butter six ramekin dishes. Lay the smokies in a baking dish and heat through in the oven for 10 minutes.

2 Remove the fish from the oven, carefully remove the skin and bones then flake the flesh into a bowl.

3 Mash the fish with a fork then work in the cheese, then the eggs. Add lemon juice and pepper to taste.

4 Divide the fish mixture among the ramekins and place in a roasting pan. Pour hot water into the roasting pan to come halfway up the dishes. Bake for 30 minutes, until just set.

5 Allow to cool for 2–3 minutes, then run a knife pint around the edge of each dish and invert on to a warmed plate. Garnish with chervil sprigs and serve with the lettuce and lemon wedges.

> **Cook's Tip**
> The traditional method of smoking haddock has earned it the Protected Geographical Indication status, granted by the European Commission. The name 'Arbroath smokie' can only be used to describe the genuine article, made within an 8km/ 5-mile radius of Arbroath.

Fried Plaice Fillet with Remoulade

A tangy, creamy mayonnaise-based relish with pickles, similar to tartare sauce, remoulade is eaten with seafood, open sandwiches and frikadeller (Danish meatballs), and used as a garnish or a spread. It is superb as a garnish for fried plaice.

Serves 4
1 egg
50g/2oz/½ cup fine breadcrumbs
225g/8oz plaice fillets
40g/1½oz/3 tbsp salted butter, softened

2 slices crusty white bread
2 round (butterhead) lettuce leaves
4 lemon slices and 4 fresh dill sprigs

For the remoulade
250ml/8fl oz/1 cup mayonnaise
120ml/4fl oz/½ cup chopped sweet dill pickles or relish
15ml/1 tbsp mustard powder
15ml/1 tbsp finely chopped fresh dill
30ml/2 tbsp chopped parsley
30ml/2 tbsp diced onion
2.5ml/½ tsp lemon juice
15ml/1 tbsp capers (optional)

1 First make the remoulade. Put the mayonnaise in a bowl and stir in the dill pickles or relish, mustard powder, dill, parsley, onion, lemon juice and capers (if using) until well blended. Cover and refrigerate until needed.

2 Briefly whisk the egg with 5ml/1 tsp water in a shallow dish. Place the breadcrumbs in another shallow dish. If required, cut the fillet into four 10–15cm/ 4–6in pieces. Dip the plaice fillet in the egg, then into the breadcrumbs, to evenly coat both sides.

3 Melt 15g/½oz/1 tbsp of the butter in a pan over a medium heat, and cook the fillets for about 6 minutes, turning once, until golden brown on each side. Drain on kitchen paper and leave to cool.

4 Spread the slices of bread to the edges with the remaining butter. Place a lettuce leaf on each slice and cut the slices in half. Leaving one curl of lettuce showing on each sandwich, arrange the fish over the lettuce, dividing the pieces evenly. Garnish each sandwich with a spoonful of remoulade, a lemon slice and a sprig of dill.

Haddock Pâté Energy 206kcal/859kJ; Protein 25.3g; Carbohydrate 1.7g, of which sugars 0.1g; Fat 11g, of which saturates 5.8g; Cholesterol 153mg; Calcium 82mg; Fibre 0g; Sodium 940mg.
Fried Plaice Energy 667kcal/2762kJ; Protein 15.6g; Carbohydrate 19.1g, of which sugars 2.3g; Fat 59.9g, of which saturates 12.9g; Cholesterol 140mg; Calcium 89mg; Fibre 0.7g; Sodium 593mg.

Fish and Chermoula Mini Pies

These filling of these savoury pies is flavoured with chermoula, a mixture of spices, fresh coriander and flat leaf parsley. The chermoula may be stored in the refrigerator for a few days.

Serves 8
500g/1¼lb firm white fish fillets
225g/8oz uncooked king prawns (jumbo shrimp)
16 sheets of ouarka or filo pastry
60–75ml/4–5 tbsp sunflower oil

1 egg yolk, mixed with a few drops of water
salt

For the chermoula
75ml/5 tbsp olive oil
juice of 1 lemon
5ml/1 tsp ground cumin
5–10ml/1–2 tsp paprika
2–3 garlic cloves, crushed
1 red chilli, seeded and chopped
large bunch of fresh flat leaf parsley, chopped
large bunch of fresh coriander (cilantro), chopped

1 Prepare the chermoula. Mix all the ingredients in a bowl and set aside. Place the fish in a frying pan and add just enough water to cover the fillets. Season the fish with salt and heat until just simmering, then cook gently for 3 minutes, until the fish just begins to flake. Remove the fish from the liquid and break it up, taking care to remove all bones as you do so.

2 Poach the prawns in the fish liquor for 10 minutes, until they turn pink, then drain and shell them. Gently toss the prawns and fish in the chermoula, cover and set aside for 1 hour.

3 Preheat the oven to 180°C/350°F/Gas 4 and grease two baking sheets. To make the pies, lay the filo pastry under a damp cloth. Take two sheets of filo: brush one with oil, lay the second one on top, then brush it with oil. Place some of the fish mixture in the middle of the length of the sheet but to one side of its width. Fold the edge of the pastry over the filling, then fold the long side over to cover the filling.

4 Wrap the ends of the pastry around the filling to make a neat package with the edges tucked in. Brush with egg yolk. Continue with the rest of the fish and chermoula mixture. Bake for 20 minutes, until the pastry is golden. Serve hot or warm.

Three Fish Mousse

This rich and creamy mousse is flavoured with lemon and dill.

Serves 6–8
15ml/1 tbsp oil
450g/1lb cod fillet, skinned
1 bay leaf
1 slice lemon
6 black peppercorns
275g/10oz thinly sliced smoked trout
60ml/4 tbsp cold water

15g/½oz powdered gelatine
175g/6oz cooked peeled prawns (shrimp), halved
300ml/½ pint/1¼ cups sour cream
225g/8oz/1 cup cream cheese
30ml/2 tbsp chopped fresh dill
juice of 1 lemon
3 drops Tabasco sauce
salt and ground black pepper
sprigs of fresh herbs, such as parsley or dill, and 6–8 lemon wedges, to garnish

1 Brush a 1.2 litre/2 pint/5 cup ring mould with the oil. Place the cod, bay leaf, lemon and peppercorns in a pan. Cover with cold water and bring to simmering point. Poach for 10–15 minutes, or until the fish flakes when tested with a fork.

2 Line the oiled ring mould with overlapping slices of smoked trout, leaving plenty hanging over the edge.

3 Remove the cod from the pan with a fish slice (metal spatula). Chop the cod into chunks and put it in a large bowl. Place the measured cold water in a small heatproof bowl and sprinkle the gelatine over the surface. Leave for 5 minutes, until spongy, then place the bowl over a pan of hot water. Stir until the gelatine has dissolved. Leave to cool slightly.

4 Add the prawns, sour cream, cream cheese and dill to the cod. Add the lemon juice and Tabasco sauce. Mash all together. Season to taste. Fold the gelatine into the fish mixture, then spoon into the ring mould and smooth the top with a spoon.

5 Fold the overhanging edges of the trout over the mousse. Cover and chill in the refrigerator for 2 hours. Run a round-bladed knife around the edge of the mousse, invert a plate on top and turn both over. Shake together until the mousse drops out on to the plate. Garnish with the herbs and lemon and serve.

Mini Pies Energy 236Kcal/984kJ; Protein 18.2g; Carbohydrate 10g, of which sugars 0.4g; Fat 13.9g, of which saturates 2g; Cholesterol 109mg; Calcium 67mg; Fibre 0.9g; Sodium 96mg.
Fish Mousse Energy 334kcal/1386kJ; Protein 25g; Carbohydrate 2g, of which sugars 2g; Fat 25g, of which saturates 14g; Cholesterol 161mg; Calcium 101mg; Fibre 0g; Sodium 506mg.

Three-fish Terrine

This striped terrine uses haddock, salmon and turbot and is slowly baked in the oven. Serve with a small salad, brown bread or Melba toast and butter.

Serves 8–10

450g/1lb spinach
350–450g/12oz–1lb haddock, cod or other white fish, skinned and chopped
3 eggs
115g/4oz/2 cups fresh breadcrumbs
300ml/½ pint/1¼ cups fromage blanc or low-fat cream cheese
a little freshly grated nutmeg
350–450g/12oz–1lb salmon fillet
350–450g/12oz–1lb fresh turbot fillet, or other flat fish
oil, for greasing
salt and ground black pepper
lemon wedges and rocket (arugula), to serve

1 Preheat the oven to 160°C/325°F/Gas 3. Remove the stalks from the spinach and cook the leaves briskly in a pan without any added water, shaking the pan occasionally, until the spinach is just tender. Drain and squeeze out the water.

2 Put the spinach into a food processor or blender with the haddock or other white fish, eggs, breadcrumbs, fromage blanc or cream cheese, salt, pepper and nutmeg to taste. Process until smooth. Skin and bone the salmon fillet and cut into long thin strips. Repeat with the turbot.

3 Oil a 900g/2lb loaf tin (pan) and line the base with baking parchment or foil. Make layers from the spinach mixture and the strips of salmon and turbot, starting and finishing with spinach.

4 Press down carefully and cover with oiled baking parchment. Prick a few holes in it, then put the terrine into a roasting tin and pour boiling water around it to come two-thirds of the way up the sides.

5 Bake in the preheated oven for 1–1½ hours, or until risen, firm and set. Leave to cool, then chill well before serving.

6 To serve, ease a sharp knife down the sides to loosen the terrine and turn out on to a flat serving dish. Slice the terrine and serve with lemon wedges and fresh rocket.

Striped Fish Terrine

Serve this tasty terrine cold or just warm, with a hollandaise sauce if you like.

Serves 8

15ml/1 tbsp sunflower oil
450g/1lb salmon fillet, skinned
450g/1lb sole fillets, skinned
3 egg whites
105ml/7 tbsp double (heavy) cream
15ml/1 tbsp fresh chives, chopped
juice of 1 lemon
115g/4oz/scant 1 cup fresh or frozen peas, cooked
5ml/1 tsp chopped fresh mint leaves
salt, ground white pepper and freshly grated nutmeg
thinly sliced cucumber, salad or land cress and chives, to garnish

1 Grease a 1 litre/1¾ pint/4 cup loaf pan or terrine with the oil. Slice the salmon thinly; cut it and the sole into long strips, 2.5cm/1in wide. Preheat the oven to 200°C/400°F/Gas 6. Line the terrine with alternate slices of salmon and sole, so the ends hang over the edge, leaving a third of the salmon and half the sole.

2 Beat the egg whites with a pinch of salt until they form soft peaks. Purée the remaining sole in a food processor. Spoon into a mixing bowl, season, then fold in two-thirds of the egg whites, followed by two-thirds of the cream. Put half the mixture into a second bowl; stir in the chives. Add nutmeg to the first bowl.

3 Purée the remaining salmon, scrape it into a bowl and add the lemon juice. Fold in the remaining whites and cream. Purée the peas with the mint. Season the mixture and spread it on the base of the terrine. Smooth the surface. Spoon over the sole and chive mixture and spread evenly. Add the salmon mixture, then the sole and nutmeg mixture. Cover with the overhanging fish fillets then oiled foil. Stand the terrine in a roasting pan and pour in enough boiling water to come halfway up the sides.

4 Bake for 15–20 minutes, until the top fillets are just cooked and the mousse is springy. Remove the foil, lay a wire rack over the terrine and invert both on to a lipped baking sheet to catch the cooking juices. Leave to stand for 15 minutes, then turn out by inverting it on to a serving dish and lifting off the pan. Serve warm or chilled. Garnish with cucumber, salad or land cress and chives.

Three-fish terrine Energy 290Kcal/1216kJ; Protein 32.5g; Carbohydrate 13.7g, of which sugars 2.8g; Fat 12.1g, of which saturates 3.9g; Cholesterol 112mg; Calcium 203mg; Fibre 1.5g; Sodium 306mg.
Striped Terrine Energy 248kcal/1030kJ; Protein 24g; Carbohydrate 2.2g, of which sugars 0.6g; Fat 15.9g, of which saturates 5.7g; Cholesterol 74mg; Calcium 51mg; Fibre 0.7g; Sodium 108mg.

Smoked Salmon Terrine

This melt-in-the-mouth
smoked salmon terrine
makes a spectacular first
course for a special dinner.

Serves 6
4 sheets leaf gelatine
60ml/4 tbsp water

400g/14oz smoked salmon, sliced
300g/11oz/scant 1½ cups
    cream cheese
120ml/4fl oz/½ cup crème
    fraîche
30ml/2 tbsp dill mustard
juice of 1 lime
2 lemons, to garnish

1 Soak the gelatine in the water in a small bowl until softened.
Meanwhile, line a 450g/1lb loaf pan with clear film (plastic
wrap). Use some of the smoked salmon to line the pan, laying
the slices widthways across the base and up the sides and
leaving enough hanging over the edge to fold over the top
of the filling.

2 Set aside enough of the remaining smoked salmon to make
a middle layer the length of the pan. Chop the rest finely by
hand or in a food processor. Take care not to over-process
the salmon; it must not form a paste.

3 In a bowl, beat the cream cheese, crème fraiche and dill
mustard until well combined. Scrape in the chopped salmon
and mix with a rubber spatula or a spoon until well combined.

4 Squeeze out the gelatine and put the sheets in a small, heavy
pan. Add the lime juice. Place over a low heat until the gelatine
has melted, cool slightly, then stir into the salmon mixture.

5 Spoon half the mixture into the lined pan. Lay the reserved
smoked salmon slices on the mixture along the length of the
pan, then spoon on the rest of the filling and smooth the top.

6 Tap the pan on the surface to expel any trapped air. Fold over
the overhanging salmon slices to cover the top. Cover the
whole pan with clear film and place in the refrigerator to chill
for at least 4 hours, preferably 6–8 hours.

7 Serve, garnished with lemon slices.

Salmon and Pike Mousse

When sliced, this light-
textured Russian mousse
loaf, Pate iz Shchuki, reveals
a pretty layer of pink
salmon. For a special
occasion, serve topped with
red salmon roe.

Serves 8
10ml/2 tsp oil
225g/8oz salmon fillet, skinned

600ml/1 pint/2½ cups fish stock
finely grated rind and juice of
    ½ lemon
900g/2lb pike fillets, skinned
4 egg whites
475ml/16fl oz/2 cups double
    (heavy) cream
30ml/2 tbsp chopped fresh dill
salt and ground black pepper
red salmon roe or a fresh dill
    sprig, to garnish (optional)

1 Preheat the oven to 180°C/350°F/Gas 4. Brush a 900g/2lb
loaf pan with oil and line with baking parchment.

2 Cut the salmon into 5cm/2in strips. Pour the stock and lemon
juice into a pan and bring to the boil, then turn off the heat.
Add the salmon strips, cover and leave for 2 minutes. Remove
with a slotted spoon.

3 Cut the pike into cubes and process in a food processor or
blender until smooth. Lightly whisk the egg whites with a fork.
With the motor of the food processor or blender running,
slowly pour in the egg whites, then the cream through the
feeder tube or lid. Finally, add the lemon rind and dill. Taste the
mixture and add a little salt and pepper if you think more
seasoning is needed.

4 Spoon half of the pike mixture into the prepared loaf pan.
Arrange the poached salmon strips on top, then carefully spoon
in the remaining pike mixture.

5 Cover the loaf pan with foil and put in a roasting pan. Add
enough boiling water to come halfway up the sides of the loaf
pan. Bake for 45–50 minutes, or until firm.

6 Leave on a wire rack to cool, then chill for at least 3 hours.
Invert on to a serving plate and remove the lining paper. Serve
the mousse in slices. Garnish with red salmon roe and fresh dill.

Salmon Terrine Energy 406kcal/1683kJ; Protein 21g; Carbohydrate 1g, of which sugars 1g; Fat 35g, of which saturates 21g; Cholesterol 93mg; Calcium 84mg; Fibre 0g; Sodium 1611mg.
Salmon Mousse Energy 477kcal/1977kJ; Protein 27.8g; Carbohydrate 1g, of which sugars 1g; Fat 40.3g, of which saturates 21.4g; Cholesterol 171mg; Calcium 89mg; Fibre 0g; Sodium 105mg.

Smoked Salmon and Herb Roulade

Make the most of a small amount of smoked salmon by using it in the filling for this delicately flavoured roulade. Make the roulade in advance to give it time to cool, but don't put it in the refrigerator or it will lose its light texture.

Serves 6–8 as part of a buffet

25g/1oz/2 tbsp butter
25g/1oz/1/4 cup plain
   (all-purpose) flour
175ml/6fl oz/3/4 cup milk, warm
3 large eggs, separated
50g/2oz/2/3 cup freshly grated
   Parmesan cheese
60ml/4 tbsp chopped fresh dill
30ml/2 tbsp chopped
   fresh parsley
150ml/1/4 pint/2/3 cup full fat
   crème fraîche or sour cream
115g/4oz smoked salmon
salt and ground black pepper
lamb's lettuce, to garnish

1 Melt the butter in a heavy pan, stir in the flour and cook over a low heat to a thick paste. Gradually add the milk, whisking constantly until the sauce boils and thickens, then cook for 1–2 minutes more. Stir in the egg yolks, two-thirds of the Parmesan cheese, the parsley and half the dill. Add salt and ground black pepper to taste.

2 Prepare a 33 x 28cm/13 x 11in Swiss roll tin (jelly roll pan) and preheat the oven to 180°C/350°F/Gas 4. Whisk the egg whites and fold into the yolk mixture, then pour into the tin or pan and bake for 12–15 minutes. Cover with baking parchment and set aside for 10–15 minutes, then tip out on to another sheet of parchment, this time sprinkled with a little Parmesan. Leave to cool.

3 Coarsely chop the smoked salmon, then mix it in a bowl with the crème fraîche or sour cream and remaining chopped dill. Stir gently but thoroughly, then taste and add salt and pepper as needed.

4 Peel off the lining paper from the roulade, spread the filling evenly over the surface and roll up, then leave to firm up in a cold place. Sprinkle with the rest of the Parmesan and garnish with the lamb's lettuce.

Smoked Salmon Pâté

This pâté is made in individual ramekins lined with smoked salmon enclosing a tasty salmon pâté. Taste the mousse and add more lemon juice and seasoning if necessary.

Serves 4

350g/12oz thinly sliced
   smoked salmon
150ml/1/4 pint/2/3 cup double
   (heavy) cream
finely grated rind and juice of
   1 lemon
salt and ground black pepper
Melba toast, to serve

1 Line four small ramekins with clear film (plastic wrap). Line the dishes with 115g/4oz of the smoked salmon, cut into strips long enough to flop over the edges.

2 Put the remaining smoked salmon into a food processor and add the cream, lemon rind and three-quarters of the lemon juice. Process until smooth, then taste and add more salt and ground black pepper. If the salmon was quite oily, it may also be necessary to add a little more lemon juice.

3 Pack the lined ramekins with the smoked salmon pâté. Bring over the loose strips of salmon to cover the pâté completely. Cover and chill for at least 30 minutes, then turn out of the moulds, lift off and discard the clear film, and serve with the Melba toast.

Cook's Tips
To make Melba toast, simply toast a slice of bread, cut off the crusts and slice in half horizontally, then brown the untoasted sides. Process the salmon in short bursts until it is just smooth. Don't over-process the pâté or it will thicken too much and the texture will be compromised.
• Try this with smoked trout, which has a lovely rosy colour and a more delicate flavour than smoked salmon.
• A little horseradish cream makes a good addition to the pate, but don't overdo it, or you won't be able to taste the smoked fish.

Salmon Roulade Energy 200kcal/829kJ; Protein 10g; Carbohydrate 4g, of which sugars 2g; Fat 16g, of which saturates 9g; Cholesterol 129mg; Calcium 126mg; Fibre 0g; Sodium 383mg.
Salmon Pâté Energy 311kcal/1293kJ; Protein 22.9g; Carbohydrate 0.8g, of which sugars 0.8g; Fat 24.1g, of which saturates 13.2g; Cholesterol 82mg; Calcium 36mg; Fibre 0g; Sodium 1654mg.

Sea Trout Mousse

This deliciously creamy mousse makes a little sea trout go a long way. It is equally good made with salmon instead of sea trout.

Serves 6
250g/9oz sea trout fillet
120ml/4fl oz/½ cup fish stock
2 gelatine leaves or 15ml/1 tbsp
   powdered gelatine
juice of ½ lemon
30ml/2 tbsp dry sherry or
   dry vermouth

30ml/2 tbsp freshly grated
   Parmesan
300ml/½ pint/1¼ cups
   whipping cream
2 egg whites
15ml/1 tbsp sunflower oil
salt and ground white pepper

For the garnish
5cm/2in piece cucumber, with
   peel, thinly sliced
6 small sprigs fresh dill or chervil,
   plus extra, chopped

1 Place the sea trout fillet in a shallow pan. Pour in the fish stock and heat to simmering point. Poach the fish for about 3–4 minutes, until lightly cooked. Lift the trout out and set it aside to cool slightly. Strain the stock into a jug (pitcher), then add the gelatine to the hot stock and stir until dissolved. Cool.

2 Remove the skin from the trout and flake the flesh. Pour the stock into a food processor. Process briefly, then gradually add the trout, lemon juice, sherry or vermouth and Parmesan through the feeder tube and process the mixture until smooth. Scrape into a large bowl and leave to cool completely.

3 Lightly whip the cream then fold it into the cold trout mixture. Season to taste, then cover with clear film (plastic wrap) and chill until the mousse is beginning to set.

4 Beat the egg whites with a pinch of salt until softly peaking. Stir one-third into the trout mixture to lighten it, then fold in the rest.

5 Lightly grease six ramekin dishes with the oil. Divide the mousse among the ramekins and level the surface. Place in the refrigerator for 2–3 hours, until set. Arrange slices of cucumber and a herb sprig on each mousse with chopped dill or chervil.

Fish Patties with Parsley and Oatmeal

Well-made fishcakes are always a treat, and they can be made with salmon or any fresh or smoked white fish. This dish makes a little fish go a long way, but do not stretch it beyond equal quantities of fish and potato. Parsley sauce is the traditional accompaniment.

Serves 4
450g/1lb fresh salmon or smoked
   white fish

wedge of lemon
small bay leaf and a few fresh
   parsley stalks
25g/1oz/2 tbsp butter
1 onion, finely chopped
450g/1lb potatoes, cooked
   and mashed
30ml/2 tbsp chopped
   fresh parsley
pinhead oatmeal, to coat
butter and oil, for frying
ground black pepper
watercress, to garnish

1 Cut the fish into medium-size pieces. Put it into a pan with the lemon, bay leaf and parsley stalks and cold water to cover. Bring slowly to the boil, reduce the heat and simmer gently for 5–7 minutes. Remove the fish and drain.

2 When cool, flake the flesh and discard the skin and bones. Melt the butter in a large pan, add the onion and cook gently for a few minutes until softened but not coloured. Add the flaked fish, potato and parsley. Season to taste with pepper.

3 Turn the mixture on to a work surface covered with pinhead oatmeal. Divide the mixture in half, and then quarter each piece. Form into eight cakes and coat them with the oatmeal.

4 Heat a little butter and an equal quantity of oil in a frying pan, add the fishcakes and fry until golden. Drain and serve.

> **Cook's Tip**
> *Any fresh white or hot-smoked fish is suitable; smoked cod and haddock are particularly good.*

Sea Trout Mousse Energy 286kcal/1181kJ; Protein 12g; Carbohydrate 1.5g, of which sugars 1.5g; Fat 25.2g, of which saturates 13.9g; Cholesterol 58mg; Calcium 94mg; Fibre 0g; Sodium 111mg.
Fish Patties Energy 380Kcal/1584kJ; Protein 25.3g; Carbohydrate 20.5g, of which sugars 3.3g; Fat 22.4g, of which saturates 8.6g; Cholesterol 83mg; Calcium 49mg; Fibre 1.8g; Sodium 138mg.

Grilled Oysters with Highland Heather Honey

Heather honey is very fragrant, the pollen gathered by bees late in the season when the heather on the moors is in full flower. Beekeepers in Scotland will take their hives up to the hills once the spring and early summer blossoms are over, so the flavour is more intense.

Serves 4

1 bunch spring onions
  (scallions), washed
20ml/4 tsp heather honey
10ml/2 tsp soy sauce
16 fresh oysters
lemon wedges, to serve

1 Preheat the grill (broiler) to medium. Chop the spring onions finely, removing any coarser outer leaves.

2 Place the heather honey and soy sauce in a bowl and mix. Then add the finely chopped spring onions and mix them in thoroughly.

3 Open the oysters with an oyster knife or a small, sharp knife, taking care to catch the liquid in a small bowl. Leave the oysters attached to one side of the shell. Strain the liquid to remove any pieces of broken shell, and set aside.

4 Place a large teaspoon of the honey and spring onion mixture on top of each oyster.

5 Place under the preheated grill until the mixture bubbles, which will take about 5 minutes. Take care when removing the oysters from the grill as the shells retain the heat. Make sure that you don't lose any of the sauce from inside the oyster shells.

6 Allow the oysters to cool slightly before serving with slices of bread to soak up the juices. Add a squeeze of lemon juice, and either tip them straight into your mouth or lift them out with a spoon or fork.

Dressed Crab with Asparagus

Crab is the juiciest and most flavoursome seafood, possibly better even than lobster and considerably cheaper. This dish is a mix of two excellent ingredients: crab as the king of seafood and asparagus as a prince among vegetables.

Serves 4

24 asparagus spears
4 dressed crabs
30ml/2 tbsp mayonnaise
15ml/1 tbsp chopped fresh
  parsley

1 Cook the asparagus, and when just tender plunge the stems into iced water to stop them from cooking further. Drain them when cold and pat dry with kitchen paper.

2 Scoop out the white crab meat from the shells and claws and place it in a bowl. If you can't find fresh crabs, you can use the same amount of canned or frozen white crab meat.

3 Add the mayonnaise and chopped fresh parsley and combine with a fork. Place the mixture into the crab shells and add six asparagus spears per serving. Serve with crusty bread.

> **Cook's Tip**
> *Choose asparagus that is bright green with firm stalks and tight tips. When preparing asparagus, cut off any tough ends and peel off the outer layer at the ends of the stalks. Wash the stalks well before cooking. The best way to cook asparagus is to have the ends in boiling water and the tips in steam, so either tie the asparagus in a bundle and stand in a special asparagus pan in boiling salted water, or place flat in a large frying pan.*

> **Cook's Tips**
> *If you buy cooked crabs, choose ones that feel fairly heavy, indicating that the crabs are mature and have plenty of meat in the shell and claws.*

Grilled Oysters Energy 81kcal/343kJ; Protein 9.2g; Carbohydrate 9.1g, of which sugars 6.9g; Fat 1.2g, of which saturates 0.2g; Cholesterol 46mg; Calcium 121mg; Fibre 0.3g; Sodium 588mg.
Crab with Asparagus Energy 207kcal/859kJ; Protein 19.5g; Carbohydrate 3g, of which sugars 2.8g; Fat 13g, of which saturates 1.9g; Cholesterol 72mg; Calcium 157mg; Fibre 2.6g; Sodium 540mg.

Salmon Puffs

Canned salmon is convenient and easy to use. The flavour and texture are perfectly acceptable in dishes such as this one.

Serves 6–8
65g/2¹/₂oz/9 tbsp plain (all-purpose) flour
50g/2oz/¹/₄ cup butter
150ml/¹/₄ pint/²/₃ cup water
2 eggs, beaten

For the filling
200g/7oz can red salmon, drained, or 175g/6oz poached salmon
60ml/4 tbsp mayonnaise
50g/2oz/¹/₃ cup sun-dried tomatoes in oil, drained and finely chopped
grated rind and juice of ¹/₂ lemon
30ml/2 tbsp freshly chopped parsley
salt and ground black pepper
salad leaves and halved cherry tomatoes, to serve

1 Sift the flour. Heat the butter and water gently until the butter melts. Bring to the boil and remove from the heat.

2 Immediately pour in all the flour and beat with a wooden spoon until the mixture forms a smooth, glossy paste. Leave the paste in a warm room to cool slightly for 5 minutes.

3 Meanwhile, make the filling. Flake the salmon into a bowl. Add the mayonnaise, sun-dried tomatoes, lemon rind and juice. Stir in the parsley, with salt and pepper to taste. Cover and chill.

4 Add the egg gradually to the cooled paste, stirring well after each addition to prevent curdling. Stir in just enough egg to produce a smooth, shiny mixture that is thick enough to hold its shape. Set the choux pastry aside.

5 Preheat the oven to 190°C/375°F/Gas 5. Grease a large baking sheet. Carefully spoon the choux pastry into a piping (pastry) bag fitted with a 1cm/1/2in plain round nozzle. Pipe the pastry on to the baking sheet to make about 24 small rounds, spaced well apart. Bake for 20–25 minutes until browned.

6 Remove the puffs from the oven and split them horizontally in half. Leave to cool on a wire rack. Fill each puff with some salmon mixture. Serve with salad leaves and halved tomatoes.

Smoked Trout Tartlets

Golden filo pastry tartlets made with layers of filo and filled with a tasty trout and cheesy filling make a tempting appetizer. The crisp pastry is a good contrast with the creamy trout and three-cheese filling.

Serves 4
8 x 15cm/6in squares filo pastry
50g/2oz/¹/₄ cup butter, melted
50g/2oz Gruyère cheese, grated
115g/4oz/¹/₂ cup mascarpone cheese
50g/2oz Parmesan cheese, grated
45ml/3 tbsp milk
75g/3oz smoked trout
8 cherry tomatoes, halved
salt and ground black pepper
fresh flat leaf parsley and salad leaves, to garnish

1 Preheat the oven to 180°C/350°F/Gas 4. For each tartlet, place two squares of filo pastry on top of each other at angles to form a star shape. Brush the pastry with melted butter and place, buttered side down, in an individual Yorkshire pudding pan or 10cm/4in tartlet pan. Repeat with the remaining filo.

2 Support the pans on a baking sheet and brush the pastry with a little more butter. Bake for 5 minutes or until the tartlets are crisp and light golden brown in colour. Remove the tartlets from the oven but leave the oven on.

3 In a large bowl, combine the three cheeses and milk. Season generously with salt and pepper and mix well.

4 Cut the smoked trout into bitesize pieces using kitchen scissors or a knife. Arrange the halved tomatoes and trout in the pastry cases.

5 Spoon the cheese mixture into the cooked pastry cases, gently pressing it down with the back of a spoon. Return the tartlets to the oven and bake for 10–15 minutes more, until the cheese is bubbling and golden brown. Serve immediately divided among individual plates, garnished with the parsley and a few salad leaves.

Salmon Puffs Energy 206kcal/855kJ; Protein 8g; Carbohydrate 7g, of which sugars 0g; Fat 16g, of which saturates 5g; Cholesterol 86mg; Calcium 46mg; Fibre 0g; Sodium 232mg.
Trout Tartlets Energy 469kcal/1953kJ; Protein 17g; Carbohydrate 25g, of which sugars 4 g; Fat 33g, of which saturates 21g; Cholesterol 94mg; Calcium 298mg; Fibre 0g; Sodium 515mg.

Goat's Cheese and Trout Toasties

These little rounds are packed full of flavour – the goat's cheese and trout combine beautifully to make a delicious snack suitable for any time of the day.

Serves 4
8 thick slices of white bread

30ml/2 tbsp olive oil
5ml/1 tsp fresh thyme leaves
20ml/4 tsp pesto
50g/2oz smoked trout slices
4 round goat's cheese slices, each about 50g/2oz
salt and ground black pepper
cherry tomatoes and fresh basil, to serve

1 Preheat the oven to 200°C/400°F/Gas 6. Using a pastry cutter that is slightly larger than the goat's cheese rounds, cut a circle from each slice of bread.

2 Brush the bread rounds with a little olive oil, scatter with a few thyme leaves and season well. Place the bread rounds on a baking sheet and bake for 5 minutes or until crisp and a light golden colour.

3 Remove the bread from the oven and spread 5ml/1 tsp pesto over half the rounds. Divide the smoked trout among the pesto-topped bread, top with the cheese rounds and season well with black pepper. Top the cheese with the remaining bread circles.

4 Bake the toasties in the oven for 5 minutes more, until the cheese has just started to soften. Remove from the oven and serve immediately with the cherry tomatoes and basil leaves.

Cook's Tips
The easiest way to crumb a small quantity of bread is with a hand-held grater. Rub the bread down the coarsest side, in the same way as grating cheese. Fresh breadcrumbs can be stored in the freezer until you need them.
• Thyme goes particularly well with goat's cheese but other strong herbs can be substituted. Try oregano, marjoram or sage for a completely different taste.

Smoked Salmon with Dill and Lemon

Smoked salmon is a delicacy in Denmark. Thin slices of the succulent pink fish are a favourite smørrebrød topping. The crusts are left on the bread, and a drizzle of mustard sauce with dill and lemon slices are the traditional garnishes.

Makes 4
25g/1oz/2 tbsp salted butter, softened
2 slices crusty white bread
2 round (butterhead) lettuce leaves

4 (100g/3–4 oz) slices smoked salmon
2 lemon slices
4 dill sprigs

For the mustard sauce
15ml/1 tbsp distilled white vinegar
25g/1oz/2 tbsp sugar
90ml/6 tbsp Dijon mustard
1 egg yolk (optional)
50ml/2fl oz/1/4 cup vegetable oil
7.5ml/1 1/2 tsp chopped fresh dill
salt and ground black pepper

1 First make the mustard sauce. In a small bowl, mix together the vinegar, sugar, mustard, egg yolk (if using) and oil. Stir in 7.5ml/1 1/2 tsp chopped dill, and season.

2 Butter the slices of bread to the edges, top with the lettuce leaves and cut each slice in half. Leaving one curl of lettuce visible on each slice, arrange a slice of salmon on each sandwich, folding or rolling the edges to fit.

3 Spoon 5ml/1 tsp mustard sauce down the middle of each sandwich. Cut each lemon slice in half, twist and place in the middle of the salmon. Tuck a dill sprig under each lemon twist.

Variations
A layer of thinly sliced cucumber can be substituted for the lettuce leaves. If you don't have lemons, use lime twists instead and wholegrain mustard rather then smooth mustard.

Trout Toasties Energy 349kcal/1467kJ; Protein 13g; Carbohydrate 41g, of which sugars 3 g; Fat 16g, of which saturates 4g; Cholesterol 22mg; Calcium 249mg; Fibre 3g; Sodium 629mg.
Salmon with Dill Energy 249kcal/1037kJ; Protein 9.3g; Carbohydrate 15.7g, of which sugars 8.9g; Fat 17g, of which saturates 6.2g; Cholesterol 30mg; Calcium 44mg; Fibre 0.3g; Sodium 1265mg.

Lemon-marinated Salmon with Horseradish

For a celebratory meal there's no finer fish than salmon. Curing it yourself in a blanket of salt and sugar – the preparation known as gravad lax – is simple and makes a tasty appetizer.

Serves 8–10
1kg/2¼lb fresh salmon fillet, skin on
75g/3oz/⅓ cup coarse salt
25g/1oz/2 tbsp sugar
10ml/2 tsp ground white pepper
30ml/2 tbsp fresh lemon juice
105ml/7 tbsp chopped fresh dill
½ lemon, thinly sliced, plus extra to garnish

For the dressing
250ml/8fl oz/1 cup sour cream
30ml/2 tbsp double (heavy) cream
45ml/3 tbsp prepared creamed horseradish sauce, or to taste
45ml/3 tbsp chopped fresh dill
salt and ground white pepper
fresh dill sprigs, to garnish

1 Line a baking tin (pan) with foil, leaving the ends overlapping. Remove any bones from the salmon. Nick the skin to allow the salt and seasonings to penetrate, then cut the fillet in half.

2 Mix the salt, sugar and pepper in a bowl. Place one piece of salmon skin side down in the lined dish. Drizzle with lemon juice, rub evenly with half the salt mixture and sprinkle with half the dill. Arrange the lemon slices over the fish. Place the second fillet on a board and rub the flesh evenly with the remaining salt mixture, then sprinkle with the remaining dill. Carefully lift the second fillet and place it over the fillet in the dish, turning it skin side up to make a 'sandwich'.

3 Wrap tightly in the foil and weight with a heavy pot or board. Refrigerate for 48 hours, turning the fish twice daily. The salmon will be cured when it turns a deep, bright red and the edges are slightly white from the salt. To serve, cut the salmon into very thin slices. Arrange on a serving plate; discard the skin.

4 For the dressing, mix the sour cream, double cream, horseradish, dill, salt and pepper. Serve with the salmon, garnished with dill sprigs.

Smoked Wicklow Trout with Cucumber

Rainbow trout is farmed in the Wicklow Hills and the smoked trout fillets are widely available in vacuum packs. They need no further cooking or preparation except for any accompanying salad or sauce, making them an excellent fresh convenience food and a deservedly popular cold first course or light meal. Allow one or two fillets per person.

Serves 4
1 small cucumber
4–8 smoked trout fillets
sprigs of dill, to garnish
brown bread and butter, to serve

For the dressing
90ml/6 tbsp extra virgin olive oil
30ml/2 tbsp white wine vinegar
15ml/1 tbsp chopped fresh dill
sea salt and ground black pepper

1 To make the dressing, whisk the olive oil and vinegar together vigorously. Alternatively, mix in a screw-top jar and shake until combined.

2 Add the chopped fresh dill to the oil and vinegar and blend in with the whisk, or by shaking the jar. Season with salt and ground black pepper to taste.

3 Peel the cucumber, if you prefer. You can peel off strips, if you like, to give the slices a decorative, ridged effect. Cut the cucumber into slices as thin as possible.

4 Arrange the smoked trout fillets on four serving plates. Place an equal amount of cucumber slices beside the trout. Sprinkle the fish and cucumber with the dressing, and garnish with sprigs of dill. Serve with brown bread and butter.

Cook's Tip
The cucumber salad can be made up beforehand, if you prefer, allowing the cucumber slices to marinate in the dressing.

Salmon with Horseradish Energy 479kcal/1981kJ; Protein 26.2g; Carbohydrate 0.4g, of which sugars 0.3g; Fat 40.4g, of which saturates 6.4g; Cholesterol 113mg; Calcium 35mg; Fibre 0g; Sodium 169mg.
Smoked Trout Energy 467Kcal/1943kJ; Protein 55g; Carbohydrate 0.7g, of which sugars 0.6g; Fat 27g, of which saturates 4.7g; Cholesterol 226mg; Calcium 92mg; Fibre 0.3g; Sodium 206mg.

Chilli and Salt-cured Salmon

Buy very fresh fish from a reputable source for this delicious alternative to smoked salmon. Even though the fish is raw, the process of marinating it and curing it in a mixture of salt, sugar and chilli powder acts in a similar way to cold-smoking of raw salmon. It also results in a delicious flavour.

Serves 10

50g/2oz/¼ cup sea salt
45ml/3 tbsp caster
 (superfine) sugar
5ml/1 tsp chilli powder
5ml/1 tsp ground black pepper
45ml/3 tbsp chopped fresh
 coriander (cilantro)
2 salmon fillets, about 250g/
 9oz each
fresh flat leaf parsley,
 to garnish
garlic mayonnaise, to serve

1 In a bowl, mix together the sea salt, sugar, chilli powder, pepper and chopped fresh coriander. Rub the mixture into the salmon flesh.

2 Place one of the fillets, skin side down, in a shallow glass dish. Place the other fillet on top, with the skin side up. Cover with foil or clear film (plastic wrap), then place a weight on top.

3 Chill for 48 hours, turning the fish every 8 hours or so and basting it thoroughly with the liquid that forms in the dish.

4 Drain the salmon well, pat dry with kitchen paper and transfer to a board. Using a sharp knife, slice it diagonally into wafer-thin slices. Arrange on plates and garnish with sprigs of parsley. Serve with garlic mayonnaise.

Cook's Tip
Don't discard the fish skin, use it as a garnish for the salt-cured salmon. Scrape any remaining fish off the skin. Cut the skin into 1cm/½in wide strips and fry for about 1 minute in hot oil until crisp. Drain and cool on kitchen paper.

Smoked Salmon with Warm Potato Cakes

Although the ingredients are timeless, this combination makes an excellent modern dish, which is deservedly popular as a first course or as a substantial canapé to serve with drinks. It also makes a perfect brunch dish, served with lightly scrambled eggs and freshly squeezed orange juice. Choose wild salmon if possible.

Serves 6

450g/1lb potatoes,
 cooked and mashed
75g/3oz/⅔ cup plain
 (all-purpose) flour
2 eggs, beaten
2 spring onions (scallions),
 chopped
a little freshly grated nutmeg
50g/2oz/¼ cup butter, melted
150ml/¼ pint/⅔ cup
 sour cream
12 slices of smoked salmon
salt and ground black pepper
chopped fresh chives, to garnish

1 Put the potatoes, flour, eggs and spring onions into a large bowl. Season with salt, pepper and a little nutmeg, and add half the butter. Mix thoroughly and shape into 12 small potato cakes.

2 Heat the remaining butter in a non-stick pan and cook the potato cakes until browned on both sides.

3 To serve, mix the sour cream with some salt and pepper. Fold a piece of smoked salmon and place on top of each potato cake. Top with the cream and chives and serve immediately.

Cook's Tip
If it is more convenient, you can make the potato cakes in advance and keep them overnight in the refrigerator. When required, warm them through in a hot oven 15 minutes before serving and assembling. Top the potato cakes with smoked mackerel and a squeeze of lemon juice, if you like.

Chilli Salmon Energy 108kcal/451kJ; Protein 10g; Carbohydrate 5g, of which sugars 5g; Fat 6g, of which saturates 1g; Cholesterol 25mg; Calcium 25mg; Fibre 0g; Sodium 1961mg.
Salmon with Potato Cakes Energy 326Kcal/1365kJ; Protein 21.9g; Carbohydrate 22.9g, of which sugars 2.3g; Fat 17g, of which saturates 8.6g; Cholesterol 119mg; Calcium 70mg; Fibre 1.2g; Sodium 1315mg.

Smoked Fish Platter with Honey Dressing

A wide variety of smoked fish is available – trout, salmon and mackerel feature in this simple appetizer – but any smoked fish can be used. Ask your fishmonger or inquire at the fish counter at the supermarket for the best buys.

Serves 4
1/2 Charentais melon
1/2 cantaloupe melon
50g/2oz rocket (arugula)
75g/3oz hot-smoked trout fillets
75g/3oz smoked salmon
75g/3oz smoked mackerel
   with peppercorns

For the dressing
75ml/5 tbsp extra virgin olive oil
15ml/1 tbsp white wine vinegar
5ml/1 tsp wholegrain mustard
5ml/1 tsp clear honey
salt and ground black pepper

1 Scoop out and discard the seeds from the melons and cut each melon into four or eight slices, leaving the skin on. Divide the melon slices among four small serving plates. Add a quarter of the rocket leaves to each plate.

2 Make the dressing by combining all the ingredients in a small jug (pitcher). Add salt and black pepper and whisk with a fork.

3 Divide the smoked fish into four portions, breaking or cutting the trout fillets and smoked salmon into bitesize pieces. Peel the skin from the mackerel, then break up the flesh. Arrange the trout fillets, smoked salmon and mackerel over the rocket and melon on each platter. Drizzle the dressing over and serve.

Cook's Tips
Among the more unusual types of smoked fish available are smoked halibut and smoked sturgeon. Smoked halibut has translucent white flesh and would make a good addition to the fish platter. Smoked sturgeon is a luxury fish, comparable with the finest smoked salmon, it is best served solo, so its rich flavour and succulent texture can be fully appreciated.

Salmon and Trout Canapés

These tiny little bites are ideal for serving with a glass of chilled sparkling wine or as part of a finger buffet.

Makes 44
**For the salmon and dill
   squares**
15ml/1 tbsp olive oil
175g/6oz salmon fillet, skinned
500g/1 1/2lb sliced
   pumpernickel bread
mayonnaise, for spreading
1 small cucumber, thinly sliced

60ml/4 tbsp sour cream
30ml/2 tbsp chopped fresh dill
10ml/2 tsp lemon juice
1/2 red (bell) pepper, seeded and
   finely chopped
salt and ground black pepper

For the smoked trout squares
5 thin slices white bread, toasted
75g/3oz/scant 1/2 cup cream
   cheese with garlic and herbs
75g/3oz smoked trout, skinned
finely grated rind of 2 lemons
lemon wedges, to garnish

1 Heat the oil in a griddle pan. Season the salmon fillet well on both sides and fry for 5–8 minutes or until the flesh is opaque. Remove from the pan and leave to cool.

2 Using a fluted 5cm/2in cutter, cut out 24 squares from the sliced pumpernickel. Spread a little mayonnaise on each bread square and top with a cucumber slice.

3 Flake the salmon into bitesize pieces and remove any remaining bones. Put the fish in a bowl and mix with the sour cream, dill and lemon juice. Season with salt and pepper to taste. Spread a little of the mixture on each pumpernickel square and top with pieces of red pepper.

4 Make the smoked trout squares. Trim the crusts from the toast and spread a fifth of the cheese on each slice. Cut each slice into four squares. Cut the smoked trout into pieces and divide among the toast squares.

5 Sprinkle the lemon rind over the trout and season with plenty of black pepper.

6 Arrange the canapés on a serving platter or separate plates and garnish with the lemon wedges. Chill until ready to serve.

Smoked Fish Platter Energy 312kcal/1298kJ; Protein 14.8g; Carbohydrate 15.2g, of which sugars 15.2g; Fat 21.7g, of which saturates 3.5g; Cholesterol 33mg; Calcium 66mg; Fibre 1.3g; Sodium 961mg.
Salmon Canapés Energy 71kcal/294kJ; Protein 2g; Carbohydrate 6g, of which sugars 1g; Fat 5g, of which saturates 1g; Cholesterol 6mg; Calcium 13mg; Fibre 1g; Sodium 29mg.

Salmon Ceviche with Gin and Lime

Marinating raw salmon in a mixture of gin and lime juice changes the texture of the fish, effectively "cooking" it. The flavour is superb.

Serves 4 as part of a buffet
675g/1½lb salmon fillet, skinned
1 small red onion, thinly sliced

6 chives
6 fennel sprigs
3 fresh parsley sprigs
2 limes
30ml/2 tbsp gin
45ml/3 tbsp olive oil
sea salt and ground
    black pepper
salad leaves, to serve

1 Cut the salmon fillet into thin slices, removing any remaining bones with tweezers. Lay the pieces in a wide, shallow non-metallic dish.

2 Sprinkle over the onion slices and strew with the chives, fennel and parsley sprigs. Using a canelle knife, remove a few fine strips of rind from the limes and reserve for the garnish. Cut off the remaining rind, avoiding the pith, and slice it roughly.

3 Squeeze the lime juice into a jug (pitcher). Add the roughly sliced rind, with the gin and olive oil. Stir in sea salt and black pepper to taste. Pour the mixture over the fish and stir gently to coat each piece thoroughly.

4 Cover the dish and chill for 4 hours, stirring occasionally. To serve, arrange the slices of marinated fish on a platter, with the salad leaves. Sprinkle over the reserved strips of lime rind.

Cook's Tips
• When preparing salmon in this way, it is vital to use very fresh fish from a reputable source. Tell the fishmonger you intend making ceviche, explaining that the fish will not be cooked in the conventional way, but that the texture will be altered by marinating it in lime juice, gin and olive oil.
• Serve the ceviche on the day you prepare it. It needs to be chilled for 4 hours, but do not leave it for much longer before serving.

Spicy Fried Mackerel

This tasty appetizer goes down very well with chilled Japanese lager beer. Called Saba Tatsuta Agge, it is also excellent cold and is very good served with salad. Dipping the fish fillets in cornflour produces a crispy coating when the fish is deep-fried.

Serves 4
675g/1½lb mackerel, filleted
60ml/4 tbsp shoyu
60ml/4 tbsp sake
60ml/4 tbsp caster
    (superfine) sugar
1 garlic clove, crushed
2cm/¾in piece fresh root ginger,
    peeled and finely grated
2–3 shiso leaves, chopped into
    thin strips (optional)
cornflour (cornstarch), for dusting
vegetable oil, for deep-frying
1 lime, cut into thick wedges

1 Using a pair of tweezers, remove any remaining bones from the mackerel. Cut the fillets in half lengthways, then slice diagonally crossways into bitesize pieces.

2 Mix the shoyu, sake, sugar, garlic, grated ginger and shiso leaves, if using, in a mixing bowl. Add the mackerel and leave to marinate for 20 minutes.

3 Drain and pat gently with kitchen paper. Dust the fillets all over with cornflour.

4 Heat plenty of oil in a wok or a deep-fryer. The temperature must be kept around 180°C/350°F. Deep-fry the fillets, a few pieces at a time, until they are a shiny brown colour. Drain on kitchen paper. Serve at once with the lime wedges.

Variations
• This recipe would lend itself to most fish, if you cannot find mackerel, or prefer another type of fish, sea bass, sea bream or monkfish would work equally well.
• If shiso leaves are difficult to find, substitute flat-leaf parsley or fresh coriander leaves instead.

Ceviche Energy 335kcal/1397kJ; Protein 35g; Carbohydrate 3g, of which sugars 2g; Fat 19g, of which saturates 3g; Cholesterol 84mg; Calcium 48mg; Fibre 1g; Sodium 77mg.
Fried Mackerel Energy 580kcal/2414kJ; Protein 32.2g; Carbohydrate 24g, of which sugars 17g; Fat 38.2g, of which saturates 6.9g; Cholesterol 91mg; Calcium 31mg; Fibre 0g; Sodium 1181mg.

Salmon and Rice Triangles

In Japan, where these originated, they are often used for packed lunches or picnics, but would also make elegant party pieces. They are great fun to make and look marvellous.

Serves 4 as part of a buffet

I salmon steak
15ml/1 tbsp salt
450g/1lb/4 cups freshly cooked Japanese short grain rice
4 umeboshi (plum pickles)
½ sheet yaki-nori seaweed, cut into four equal strips
white and black sesame seeds, for sprinkling

I Grill (broil) the salmon steak for 4–5 minutes on each side, until the flesh flakes easily when it is tested with the tip of a sharp knife. Set aside to cool.

2 Put the salt in a bowl. Spoon a quarter of the warm cooked rice into a small rice bowl. Make a hole in the middle and put in one umeboshi. Smooth the rice carefully over to cover it.

3 Wet the palms of both hands with cold water, then rub the salt evenly on to your palms. Empty the rice and umeboshi from the bowl on to one hand. Use both hands to shape the rice into a triangular shape, using firm but not heavy pressure. Make three more rice triangles in the same way.

4 Flake the salmon, discarding any skin and any bones. Mix the flaked salmon into the remaining rice, then shape it into triangles as before.

5 Wrap a strip of yaki-nori around each of the umeboshi triangles. Sprinkle sesame seeds on the salmon triangles. Serve immediately or cool completely, then wrap each in foil or clear film (plastic wrap).

Cook's Tips
Always use warm rice to make triangles as it makes it much easier to mould.

Simple Rolled Sushi

Salmon makes a superb filling for these simple rolls, which make good canapés.

Makes 12 rolls or 72 slices
400g/14oz/2 cups Japanese short grain rice, soaked for 20 minutes in water to cover
550ml/18fl oz/2¼ cups cold water
55ml/3½ tbsp rice vinegar
15ml/1 tbsp sugar

10ml/2 tsp salt
6 sheets yaki-nori
200g/7oz very fresh salmon fillet
200g/7oz very fresh tuna, in one piece
wasabi paste
½ cucumber, quartered lengthways and seeded
salmon roe and pickled ginger, to garnish (optional)
shoyu (Japanese soy sauce), to serve

I Drain the rice, then put it in a pan with the measured water. Bring to the boil, then lower the heat, cover and simmer for 20 minutes, or until all the liquid has been absorbed. Meanwhile, heat the vinegar, sugar and salt in a pan, stir well and cool. Fold into the hot rice, then remove the pan from the heat, cover and leave to stand for 20 minutes.

2 Cut the yaki-nori sheets in half. Cut the salmon and tuna into sticks the length of the long side of the yaki-nori and 1cm/½in square if viewed end-on. Place a sheet of yaki-nori, shiny side down, on a bamboo mat. Divide the rice into 12 portions. Spread one portion over the yaki-nori, leaving a 1cm/½in clear space around the edges.

3 Spread a little wasabi paste in a horizontal line along the middle of the rice and lay one or two sticks of tuna lengthways on this, so that when rolled, the tuna will form a filling. Holding the mat and the edge of the yaki-nori nearest to you, roll up the yaki-nori and rice into a cylinder with the tuna in the middle. Use the mat as a guide. Roll the rice tightly so that it sticks together. Carefully roll the sushi off the mat.

4 Make 11 more rolls in the same way, four for each filling ingredient, but do not use wasabi with the cucumber. Use a wet knife to cut each roll into six slices. Garnish the sushi with salmon roe and pickled ginger, if you wish, and serve with shoyu.

Salmon Triangles Energy 342kcal/1427kJ; Protein 10.5g; Carbohydrate 29.8g, of which sugars 1.9g; Fat 20.7g, of which saturates 7.8g; Cholesterol 37mg; Calcium 140mg; Fibre 1.1g; Sodium 38mg.
Simple Sushi Energy 32kcal/134kJ; Protein 2g; Carbohydrate 5g, of which sugars 0g; Fat 1g, of which saturates 0g; Cholesterol 2mg; Calcium 6mg; Fibre 0g; Sodium 66mg.

Salt Cod Fritters with Aioli

Bitesize fish cakes, dipped into creamy, garlicky aioli, are good as an appetizer.

Serves six
450g/1lb salt cod
500g/1¼lb floury potatoes, cooked
300ml/½ pint/1¼ cups milk
6 spring onions (scallions), chopped
30ml/2 tbsp extra virgin olive oil
30ml/2 tbsp chopped fresh parsley
juice of ½ lemon
2 eggs, beaten

plain (all-purpose) flour, for dusting
90g/3½oz/1¼ cups dried white
    breadcrumbs
olive oil, for shallow frying
lemon wedges and salad leaves,
    to serve
salt and ground black pepper

For the aioli
2 large garlic cloves, finely chopped
2 egg yolks
300ml/½ pint/1¼ cups olive oil
juice of ½ lemon, to taste

1 Rehydrate the salt cod in cold water for at least 24 hours, changing the water two or three times. It should not taste too salty when fully rehydrated. Drain and pat dry with kitchen paper.

2 Mash the potatoes. Pour the milk into a pan, add half the spring onions and bring to a simmer. Add the cod and poach gently for 10–15 minutes, or until it flakes easily. Remove and flake it with a fork into a bowl, discarding bones and skin. Add 60ml/4 tbsp potato to the cod and beat together. Work in the olive oil, then gradually add the remaining mashed potato. Beat in the remaining spring onions with the parsley.

3 Season with lemon juice and pepper to taste. Add one egg to the mixture and beat in until well combined, then chill until firm. Shape the fish mixture into 12–18 balls, then flatten into round cakes. Coat each in flour, then dip in the remaining egg and coat with dried breadcrumbs. Chill until ready to fry.

4 Make the aioli. Pound the garlic and a pinch of salt to a paste. Beat in the egg yolks, then half the olive oil, a drop at a time. When the sauce is thick, beat in 5ml/1tsp lemon juice. Add oil until the aioli is thick. Season, adding more lemon juice if you wish.

5 Fry the fritters in oil for 4 minutes on each side, until crisp and golden. Drain, then serve with the aioli, lemon and leaves.

Brandade of Salt Cod

There are many versions of this creamy French salt cod purée: some contain mashed potatoes, others truffles. Serve the brandade with warmed crispbread or crusty bread for a really tasty starter, or for a light lunch serve the brandade with a tomato and basil salad and bread. You can omit the garlic from the brandade, if you prefer, and serve toasted slices of French bread rubbed with garlic instead.

Serves six
200g/7oz salt cod
250ml/8fl oz/1 cup extra virgin
    olive oil
4 garlic cloves, crushed
250ml/8fl oz/1 cup double
    (heavy) or whipping cream

1 Soak the fish in cold water for 24 hours, changing the water frequently. Drain the fish well. Cut the fish into pieces, place in a shallow pan and pour in enough cold water to cover. Heat the water until it is simmering and poach the fish for 8 minutes, until it is just cooked. Drain the fish, then remove the skin and bones.

2 Combine the extra virgin olive oil and crushed garlic cloves in a small pan and heat gently. In another pan, heat the double cream until it just starts to simmer.

3 Put the cod into a food processor, process it briefly, then gradually add alternate amounts of the garlic-flavoured olive oil and cream, while continuing to process the mixture. The aim is to create a purée with the consistency of mashed potato.

4 Season to taste with freshly ground black pepper, then scoop the brandade into a serving bowl or on to individual serving plates and serve with crispbread or crusty bread.

> **Cook's Tips**
> When buying salt cod, the best pieces are from the middle of the fish rather than the tail end. Look for pieces that are already the size you require, as it is very difficult to cut up.

Fritters Energy 653kcal/2721kJ; Protein 32.7g; Carbohydrate 28.1g, of which sugars 4.2g; Fat 46.4g, of which saturates 7.6g; Cholesterol 178mg; Calcium 123mg; Fibre 1.4g; Sodium 472mg.
Brandade Energy 467kcal/1927kJ; Protein 11.7g; Carbohydrate 1.1g, of which sugars 1.1g; Fat 46.2g, of which saturates 14.8g; Cholesterol 63mg; Calcium 32mg; Fibre 0g; Sodium 144mg.

Cod with Chickpeas

Fresh coriander is used in many dishes in southern Portugal. In this region, salt cod is often served almost raw, although it is first thoroughly soaked to remove the salt, then accompanied only by some olive oil and vinegar. However, in this recipe, you can cook the fish to your taste first.

Serves 6
1 tomato
250g/9oz salt cod, soaked
500g/1¼lb canned chickpeas, drained and rinsed
1 small onion, chopped
1 small bunch of coriander (cilantro), chopped
75–105ml/5–7 tbsp olive oil
30–45 ml/2–3 tbsp white wine vinegar

1 Cut the tomato into quarters, scoop out the seeds and dice the flesh. Place the cod in boiling water and let it stand away from the heat for 5 minutes. Then drain the water and slice the fish (cleaned of skin and bones).

2 Put the cod, chickpeas, onion and coriander in a serving dish and mix gently. Add olive oil and vinegar to taste and toss lightly. Sprinkle the salad with the diced tomato.

Cook's Tips
Depending on which country it comes from, salt cod is known by different names: bacalhau (Portugal), baccalà (Italy), and stockfish (northern Europe, Scandinavia, The Caribbean and Africa). Whichever type you buy, it needs lengthy soaking in water to rehydrate it before cooking.

Cook's Tips
You can also make this salad with cubes of raw tuna loin fillet. Cut 350g/12oz of fresh tuna into cubes and marinate in some red wine vinegar with a good twist of black pepper and a little Worcestershire sauce for half hour, and combine it with the other ingredients.

Fish Roe with Marinated Peppers

Fresh fish roe is considered to be a real delicacy in Portugal, along with some other southern European countries, although it has rather gone out of favour elsewhere. Despite this, smoked and preserved roe are still widely available. This cheap ingredient is a Portuguese favourite that is used in a number of traditional dishes. For this recipe, you will require fresh hard roe, preferably from hake or cod.

Serves 6
1 bunch of parsley
1 bay leaf
2 garlic cloves
75ml/5 tbsp white wine vinegar
600g/1lb 6oz fresh hard roe
75ml/5 tbsp olive oil
2 marinated (bell) peppers, drained
sea salt

1 Chop the most tender parsley leaves and reserve the stalks and any remaining leaves. Place the reserved parsley leaves and stalks, the bay leaf, garlic, 15ml/1 tbsp of the vinegar and a pinch of sea salt in a large, shallow pan.

2 Add the roe to the pan, and enough water to cover. Bring just to the boil, then lower the heat until the water is barely simmering. Gently poach the roe for 10–15 minutes, until firm. Remove with a slotted spatula and leave to cool.

3 Whisk together the olive oil, the remaining vinegar and the chopped parsley in a bowl. Cut the marinated peppers into strips, if necessary, and then cut the roe into 1cm/½in slices.

4 Add the pepper strips and slices of roe to the vinaigrette and toss gently. Transfer to individual plates and serve immediately.

Cook's Tips
• To serve fresh roe as a main course, place it in an ovenproof dish, drizzle generously with olive oil and sprinkle with salt. Bake in a preheated oven at 180°C/350°F/Gas 4 for 10–15 minutes. Serve with cabbage and potatoes.

Cod with Chickpeas Energy 245kcal/1028kJ; Protein 20g; Carbohydrate 15g, of which sugars 1.6g; Fat 12.1g, of which saturates 1.7g; Cholesterol 25mg; Calcium 65mg; Fibre 4.1g; Sodium 355mg.
Fish Roe Energy 207kcal/862kJ; Protein 22.4g; Carbohydrate 3.9g, of which sugars 3.7g; Fat 11.4g, of which saturates 1.8g; Cholesterol 330mg; Calcium 24mg; Fibre 1.1g; Sodium 114mg.

Olive and Anchovy Bites

These little melt-in-the-mouth morsels are made from two ingredients that are forever associated with tapas – olives and anchovies. The reason for this is that both contain salt, which helps to stimulate thirst and therefore drinking.

Makes 40–45
115g/4oz/1 cup plain (all-purpose) flour

115g/4oz/1/2 cup chilled butter, diced
115g/4oz/1 cup finely grated Manchego, mature (sharp) Cheddar or Gruyère cheese
50g/2oz can anchovy fillets in oil, drained and roughly chopped
50g/2oz/1/2 cup pitted black olives, roughly chopped
2.5ml/1/2 tsp cayenne pepper
sea salt, to serve

1 Place the flour, butter, cheese, anchovies, olives and cayenne pepper in a food processor and pulse until the mixture forms a firm dough.

2 Wrap the dough loosely in clear film (plastic wrap). Chill for 20 minutes.

3 Preheat the oven to 200°C/400°F/Gas 6. Roll out the dough thinly on a lightly floured surface.

4 Cut the dough into 5cm/2in wide strips, then cut across each strip in alternate directions, to make triangles. Transfer to baking sheets and bake for 8–10 minutes until golden. Cool on a wire rack. Sprinkle with sea salt.

Cook's Tips
• To add a little extra spice, dust the olive and anchovy bites lightly with cayenne pepper before baking.
• Crisp little nibbles set off most drinks. Serve these bites alongside little bowls of seeds and nuts such as sunflower seeds and pistachios. These come in the shell, the opening of which provides a diversion while gossiping. Toasted chickpeas are another popular tapas snack.

Anchovy Terrine

This dish is based on a traditional Swedish recipe called Old Man's Mix. Just like the English speciality, Gentleman's Relish, it uses anchovies as the main ingredient, in this case the sweet, Swedish variety that are flavoured with cinnamon, cloves and allspice.

Serves 6–8
5 hard-boiled eggs
100g/3½oz can Swedish or matjes anchovies

2 gelatine leaves
200ml/7fl oz/scant 1 cup sour cream
1/2 red onion, chopped
1 bunch fresh dill, chopped
15ml/1 tbsp Swedish or German mustard
salt and ground black pepper
peeled prawns (shrimp) or lumpfish roe and dill fronds, to garnish
Melba toast or rye bread, to serve

1 Line a 20cm/8in terrine with clear film (plastic wrap). Mash the hard-boiled eggs in a bowl. Drain the juice from the anchovy can and add to the eggs. In a large, separate bowl, mash the anchovies.

2 Prepare the gelatine as directed on the packet and stir in to the mashed eggs with the sour cream, mashed anchovies, chopped onion, dill and mustard. Season with salt and ground black pepper to taste and stir thoroughly together. Pour the mixture into the prepared terrine and chill in the refrigerator for about 2 hours.

3 To serve, turn out the terrine and garnish with freshly peeled prawns or lumpfish roe and dill fronds. Serve with Melba toast or rye bread.

Cook's Tips
If you have neither Swedish nor matjes anchovies, simply soak normal, salted canned anchovies in milk for about 2–3 hours before you use them, adding a final sprinkling of ground cinnamon and cloves. Then proceed with the recipe.

Anchovy Terrine Energy 127kcal/529kJ; Protein 8.1g, Carbohydrate 1.8g, of which sugars 1.6g; Fat 9.9g, of which saturates 4.3g; Cholesterol 142mg; Calcium 88mg; Fibre 0.3g; Sodium 602mg.
Anchovy Bites Energy 42kcal/173kJ; Protein 1.2g; Carbohydrate 2g, of which sugars 0.1g; Fat 3.2g, of which saturates 1.9g; Cholesterol 9mg; Calcium 27mg; Fibre 0.1g; Sodium 103mg.

Anchovy Fritters

Make the batter for this recipe in a large bowl, and be sure to use only your hands to beat the batter in order to make it really tacky and light. The fritters make a lovely tasty snack, especially when served with plenty of dry white wine.

Serves 12

1kg/2¼lb/9 cups plain
    (all-purpose) flour
120ml/4fl oz/½ cup
    hand-hot water
50g/2oz fresh (compressed) yeast
1.5ml/¼ tsp salt
300g/11oz salted anchovies,
    rinsed, boned and dried
sunflower oil or light olive oil,
    for deep-frying

1 Put the flour into a bowl and make a well in the centre.

2 Pour the water into a cup and crumble in the yeast. Pour the mixture into the well in the flour. Using your hands, mix the water into the flour, adding more water if required to make a sticky, stringy mass. Be careful not to add too much liquid.

3 Knead the batter by beating with your hands in a circular motion for about 30 minutes. Beat in the salt. Cover the bowl with a cloth and leave the batter to rise at warm room temperature for 3–4 hours. Meanwhile, roughly chop the anchovies.

4 Heat the oil in a large pan to 180°C/350°F or until a small cube of bread, dropped into the oil, browns in about 45 seconds.

5 Using your hand, scoop up about a tablespoon of batter and stretch it slightly with your fingers. Tuck a piece of anchovy inside and drop the dough into the hot oil. Add more pieces of dough in the same way but do not overcrowd the pan.

6 Fry the fritters, in batches, for 4–6 minutes until they rise to the surface of the oil and turn crisp and golden, then lift them out with a slotted spoon and drain on kitchen paper. Serve at once – the hotter the better.

Marinated Anchovies

This is one of the simplest ways to prepare these tiny fish because it requires no cooking. Marinating is particularly associated with anchovies, which tend to lose their freshness very quickly. The Spanish term for marinated anchovies is boquerones, while anchoas is their word for the canned, salted variety.

Serves four

225g/8oz fresh anchovies, heads
    and tails removed, and split
    open along the belly
juice of 3 lemons
30ml/2 tbsp extra virgin olive oil
2 garlic cloves, finely chopped
15ml/1 tbsp chopped fresh
    parsley
flaked sea salt

1 Turn the anchovies on to their bellies, and press down with your thumb.

2 Using the tip of a small, sharp knife, carefully remove the backbones from the flattened fish, and arrange the anchovies skin side down in a single layer on a large plate.

3 Squeeze two-thirds of the lemon juice over the fish and sprinkle them with the salt. Cover and leave to stand for 1–24 hours, basting occasionally with the juices, until the flesh is white and no longer translucent.

4 Transfer the anchovies to a serving plate and drizzle with the olive oil and the remaining lemon juice. Scatter the fish with the chopped garlic and parsley, then cover with clear film (plastic wrap) and chill until ready to serve.

> **Cook's Tip**
> *Anchovies come from the Mediterranean Sea and from coastlines in southern Europe. These tiny, silver fish are delicious when fresh as in this recipe, but they are usually filleted, cured in salt then canned in oil, hence the saltiness in canned fish. This can be reduced by soaking them in cold water for 30 minutes, then draining and drying with kitchen towel.*

Anchovy Fritters Energy 416kcal/1753kJ; Protein 14.5g; Carbohydrate 64.9g, of which sugars 1.3g; Fat 12.7g, of which saturates 2.1g; Cholesterol 0mg; Calcium 141mg; Fibre 2.6g; Sodium 34.6mg.
Marinated Anchovies Energy 144kcal/597kJ; Protein 11.7g; Carbohydrate 0.1g, of which sugars 0.1g; Fat 10.7g, of which saturates 2.3g; Cholesterol 0mg; Calcium 55mg; Fibre 0.2g; Sodium 69mg.

Marinated Herrings

This is a classic Ashkenazi dish, sweet-and-sour and lightly spiced. It is delicious for Sunday brunch and is always welcomed at a Shabbat midday kiddush reception.

Serves 4–6

2–3 herrings, filleted
1 onion, sliced
juice of 1 1/2 lemons
30ml/2 tbsp white wine vinegar
25ml/1 1/2 tbsp sugar
10–15 black peppercorns
10–15 allspice berries
1.5ml/1/4 tsp mustard seeds
3 bay leaves, torn
salt

1 Soak the herrings in cold water for 5 minutes, then drain. Pour over enough water to cover them and soak for 2–3 hours, then drain. Again, pour over water to cover the herrings and leave to soak overnight in a cool place.

2 Hold the soaked herrings under cold running water and rinse very well, both inside and out.

3 Cut each fish into bitesize pieces, then place the pieces in a glass bowl or shallow dish.

4 Sprinkle the sliced onion over the fish, then add the lemon juice, vinegar, sugar, peppercorns, allspice, mustard seeds, bay leaves and salt. Add enough water to just cover. Cover the bowl with clear film (plastic wrap) and chill in the refrigerator for about 2 days to allow the flavours to blend thoroughly before serving.

Cook's Tip

Herring has been a staple food since 3,000 BCE. It is a good source of Omega 3 fatty acids and Vitamin D. This dish was originally made by Ashkenazi Jews but it is now popular all over the world. The marinated herrings can be served as a snack with dark rye bread, crisp bread, potatoes or salad, or as part of a buffet spread.

Minced Herring with Blinis

Herring is treated like caviar in this dish. Serve with freshly cooked blinis.

Serves 4

1 salted herring, cut into
 two fillets
about 10ml/2 tsp double
 (heavy) cream
2 hard-boiled eggs, chopped
1/2 onion, very finely chopped
15ml/1 tbsp fine fresh
 breadcrumbs
2.5ml/1/2 tsp mustard
15ml/1 tbsp chopped fresh parsley

about 5ml/1 tsp caster
 (superfine) sugar
ground white pepper

For the blinis

450ml/15fl oz/scant 2 cups milk
25g/1oz fresh yeast
60g/2 1/4oz/generous 1/2 cup
 buckwheat flour
about 90g/3 1/2oz/3/4 cup plain
 (all-purpose) flour
40g/1 1/2oz/3 tbsp butter
5ml/1 tsp salt
2 eggs, separated, plus 2 whites
butter for shallow frying

1 Soak the herring fillets in cold water for at least 2–3 hours or overnight. Remove the skin then chop the flesh very finely.

2 Add enough cream to the fish to form a paste, then add the hard-boiled eggs, onion, breadcrumbs, mustard and parsley. Add the sugar to taste and season with pepper.

3 To make the blinis, put 250ml/8fl oz/1 cup of the milk in a pan and heat until just warm. In a small bowl, blend the yeast with the milk, then add the buckwheat flour and 30g/1 1/4oz/generous 1/4 cup of the plain flour and mix together. Cover the bowl and leave the mixture to prove at room temperature for 1 hour.

4 Melt the butter in a pan, then leave to cool. Heat the remaining 200ml/7fl oz/scant 1 cup milk in a small pan until just warm. Whisk the milk into the yeast mixture. Stir in enough of the remaining plain flour to form a thick paste. Add the salt to the mixture, then beat in the egg yolks and melted butter. Whisk all the egg whites until stiff, then fold into the batter.

5 Heat the butter in a frying pan, add a tablespoonful of batter at a time and fry for 4 minutes, turning once, to make about 16 small, slightly risen blinis. Serve hot, with the minced herring.

Marinated Herrings Energy 94kcal/393kJ; Protein 7.7g; Carbohydrate 3.4g, of which sugars 3.2g; Fat 5.6g, of which saturates 1.4g; Cholesterol 21mg; Calcium 29mg; Fibre 0.1g; Sodium 52mg.
Minced Herrings Energy 443kcal/1851kJ; Protein 16.4g; Carbohydrate 40.7g, of which sugars 7.7g; Fat 25.2g, of which saturates 9.1g; Cholesterol 221mg; Calcium 212mg; Fibre 1.3g; Sodium 737mg.

Herring in Tomato Sauce with Egg and Dill

Salted herring is remarkably accepting of a variety of flavourings – sweet, spicy or a blend of the two. The fish is salted in autumn to preserve the catch, but the fillets can also be cured later in a bath of vinegar and sugar, with other flavourings. For this open sandwich, prepared herring in tomato sauce is topped with egg slices and garnished with red onion rings and dill in a classic combination dear to Danish hearts. This sandwich would make an attractive addition to a buffet spread or brunch.

Makes 4

4 fillets of pickled herring, cut into
   about 2.5cm/1in square
15ml/1 tbsp finely
   chopped onion
10ml/2 tsp red
   wine vinegar
45ml/3 tbsp tomato purée
2.5ml/½ tsp dry sherry
1.5ml/¼ tsp salt, or to taste
pinch of white pepper
25g/1oz/2 tbsp salted
   butter, softened
2 slices rye bread
2 hard-boiled eggs, sliced
12 small, thinly sliced
   red onion rings
4 small dill sprigs

1 To make the tomato herring, place the pickled herring pieces in a mixing bowl. Stir in the onion, red wine vinegar, tomato purée, sherry, salt and white pepper. Adjust seasonings to taste.

2 To make the sandwiches, butter the slices of bread to the edges and cut each slice in half. Arrange the herring pieces on the bread.

3 Garnish each sandwich by arranging three egg slices over the herring, then top with two or three onion rings and tuck a dill sprig into the onions.

Cook's Tips
You can use bought jars of pickled herring in tomato sauce.

Herrings with Carrot and Leek

Marinated herrings can be dressed in a number of different ways. Here, they are combined with the fresh taste of carrot and leek for a tasty appetizer. This Norwegian dish is often served at a cold table. The convention is that the herring dishes are eaten first, before any meat dishes. Every dish is eaten separately so that the flavours of each can be fully appreciated.

Serves 4 as an appetizer

2 salt herring fillets or 2 jars
   (150–200g/5–7oz) herring
   fillets in brine, drained (these
   do not need soaking)
200ml/7fl oz/¾ cup water
400ml/14fl oz/1⅔ cups
   wine vinegar
150g/5oz/¾ cup sugar
1 small carrot, finely sliced
½ small leek, white part only,
   finely sliced
2 shallots, quartered

1 Soak the herring fillets in cold water for 8–12 hours. Drain, rinse under cold water and place in a glass jar.

2 Put the water, vinegar and sugar in a large bowl and stir until the sugar has dissolved. Add the onion, bay leaf, allspice and peppercorns then pour over the herring fillets. Leave in a cold place for 6–12 hours before serving.

3 After soaking and marinating the herrings, cut the herring fillets into 2.5cm/1in thick pieces then arrange the pieces on a serving dish as if they were still whole.

4 Add a little of the marinade to the fillets and then the sliced carrot and leek. Place the quartered shallots around the edge of the dish and serve.

Cook's Tips
A typical accompaniment for marinated herrings would be buttered rye bread and a sliced cucumber salad dressed with a sour cream and fresh dill sauce. Serve with ice-cold snaps or chilled beer.

Herring with Egg Energy 177kcal/737kJ; Protein 8.9g; Carbohydrate 11.2g, of which sugars 5g; Fat 11g, of which saturates 4.1g; Cholesterol 119mg; Calcium 38mg; Fibre 1.1g; Sodium 363mg.
Herring with Carrot Energy 174kcal/731kJ; Protein 13.2g; Carbohydrate 10.9g, of which sugars 10.3g; Fat 8.5g, of which saturates 0.1g; Cholesterol 32mg; Calcium 24mg; Fibre 1.2g; Sodium 628mg.

Smoked Mackerel Pâté

The south-west of England and East Anglia in particular are known for smoking fish, especially freshly caught mackerel. This modern recipe provides an ideal way to use smoked mackerel – it's quick and easy, involves no cooking and is extremely versatile.

Serves 4–6

225g/8oz/1 cup crème fraîche
    or Greek (US strained
    plain) yogurt
finely grated rind of ½ lemon
few sprigs of parsley
225g/8oz smoked mackerel fillets
5–10ml/1–2 tsp
    horseradish sauce
1 tbsp lemon juice, or to taste
ground black pepper
crusty bread, hot toast or crisp
    plain crackers, to serve
lemon wedges, to serve

1 Put the crème fraîche or yogurt and lemon rind into a blender or food processor. Add a few sprigs of parsley.

2 Flake the mackerel, discarding the skin and removing any bones. Add the flaked fish to the blender. Blend on a medium speed until the mixture is almost smooth.

3 Add the horseradish sauce and lemon juice and blend briefly. Season with ground black pepper. Divide the pâté among individual serving dishes. Cover with clear film (plastic wrap) and refrigerate until required.

4 Garnish with parsley and serve with crusty bread, hot toast or crackers and lemon wedges for squeezing over.

Cook's Tips

Mackerel are inexpensive and nutritious; they are a source of vitamin A and B vitamins. Because they are a fairly rich oily fish, they are good served with any tangy or tart accompaniment to counteract the richness. Lemon or lime juice, tamarind paste or various fruits have all been used to prepare mackerel.

Sardines in Onion and Tomato Marinade

Both fish and poultry are frequently marinated in Portuguese cooking. The basic marinade consists of onion, garlic, bay leaves and good-quality wine vinegar, to which tomatoes or other vegetables may be added. The sardines that are fished off Portugal's cold Atlantic coast are particularly fine.

Serves 4–6

12 sardines, cleaned
plain (all-purpose) flour,
    for dusting
150ml/¼ pint/⅔ cup olive oil
2 onions, halved and thinly sliced
3 bay leaves
2 garlic cloves, chopped
150ml/¼ pint/⅔ cup white
    wine vinegar
2 ripe tomatoes, diced
sea salt
crusty bread, to serve

1 Dust the sardines with flour, shaking off any excess. Heat 75ml/5 tbsp of the olive oil in a heavy frying pan. Add the sardines, in batches, and cook over a medium heat, for about 1 minute each side. Remove with a slotted spatula and drain on kitchen paper.

2 In a clean pan, cook the onions, bay leaves and garlic with the rest of the olive oil over a low heat, stirring occasionally, for about 5 minutes, until softened. Add the vinegar and the tomatoes, and season with sea salt to taste.

3 Return the sardines to the pan. If they are not completely covered, add a little water or some more vinegar. Cook for a few minutes then transfer the mixture to a deep plate, allow to cool and leave to marinate in the refrigerator for 3 days. Serve with crusty bread.

Cook's Tips

Leave the sardine marinade for some days and don't be sparing with the vinegar, as it will be absorbed, and help to offset the slightly oily flavour of the sardines.

Mackerel Pâté Energy 344kcal/1421kJ; Protein 10.7g; Carbohydrate 0.5g, of which sugars 0.4g; Fat 33.3g, of which saturates 14.3g; Cholesterol 88mg; Calcium 57mg; Fibre 0.1g; Sodium 518mg.
Sardines Energy 335kcal/1392kJ; Protein 21.2g; Carbohydrate 4.3g, of which sugars 1.1g; Fat 26g, of which saturates 5.1g; Cholesterol 0mg; Calcium 92mg; Fibre 0.5g; Sodium 123mg.

Fried Whitebait with Sherry Salsa

Small freshly fried fish are offered in every tapas bar in Spain. Black-backed anchovies are the best, but need to be cooked within a day of catching. Tiny chanquetes are also good, but any small fish, such as whitebait, are suitable. Serve them with lemon wedges for squeezing over the fish.

Serves 4
225g/8oz whitebait
30ml/2 tbsp seasoned plain
  (all-purpose) flour
60ml/4 tbsp olive oil
60ml/4 tbsp sunflower oil

For the salsa
1 shallot, finely chopped
2 garlic cloves, finely chopped
4 ripe tomatoes, roughly chopped
1 small red chilli, seeded and
  finely chopped
30ml/2 tbsp olive oil
60ml/4 tbsp sweet oloroso sherry
30–45ml/2–3 tbsp chopped
  mixed fresh herbs, such as
  parsley or basil
25g/1oz/1½ cup stale white
  breadcrumbs
salt and ground black pepper

1 To make the salsa, place the shallot, garlic, tomatoes, chilli and olive oil in a pan. Cover and cook gently for 10 minutes.

2 Pour the sherry into the pan and season with salt and pepper to taste. Stir in the herbs and breadcrumbs, then cover and keep the salsa hot until the whitebait are ready.

3 Preheat the oven to 150°C/300°F/Gas 2. Wash the whitebait thoroughly, drain well and dry on kitchen paper, then dust in the seasoned flour.

4 Heat the oils in a heavy frying pan and cook the fish in batches until crisp and golden. Drain on kitchen paper and keep warm until all the fish are cooked. Serve with the salsa.

Cook's Tips
Whitebait are immature sprats or herrings. They are generally coated in a light batter and then cooked whole – the entire fish is eaten.

Fried Whitebait with Cayenne Pepper

For the perfect beach snack, try these crisp, spicy, bitesize fish with a squeeze of lime. They can be eaten out of hand or served with a simple tomato and onion salad dressed with lemon juice and a dash of olive oil.

Serves 4
50g/2oz/½ cup plain
  (all-purpose) flour
1.5ml/¼ tsp cayenne pepper
250g/9oz whitebait
vegetable oil, for deep-frying
salt and ground black pepper
lime wedges, to serve

1 Sift the flour and cayenne pepper into a deep bowl or large shallow dish. Season with plenty of salt and ground black pepper.

2 Thoroughly coat the whitebait in the seasoned flour, then shake off any excess flour and make sure the whitebait are separate. Do this in batches, placing the coated fish on a plate ready for frying.

3 Pour oil to a depth of 5cm/2in into a deep wide pan. Heat the oil until very hot, then add a batch of whitebait and fry for 2–3 minutes until golden.

4 Remove the batch from the pan using a slotted spoon then drain the fish well on kitchen paper. Repeat with the remaining whitebait.

5 Pile the fried whitebait on a plate, season with salt and serve immediately with the lime wedges.

Cook's Tips
Small fresh anchovies are also delicious cooked whole in this way. Or, make up a mixed seafood platter using whitebait, anchovies, squid and prawns (shrimp). Oily fish such as whitebait, herring and mackerel have health benefits; they are a rich source of omega 3 fatty acids which may help to reduce the risks of heart disease. Government guidelines suggest that eating one portion of oily fish weekly provides protection.

Whitebait with Salsa Energy 407kcal/1689kJ; Protein 26.8g; Carbohydrate 7.3g, of which sugars 0.2g; Fat 65.3g, of which saturates 0g; Cholesterol 0mg; Calcium 1183mg; Fibre 0.3g; Sodium 316mg.
Fried Whitebait Energy 722kcal/2989kJ; Protein 13g; Carbohydrate 13.1g, of which sugars 5.1g; Fat 32.8g, of which saturates 3.4g; Cholesterol 0mg; Calcium 526mg; Fibre 2g; Sodium 191mg.

Fried Squid with Salt and Pepper

Cooking squid couldn't be simpler. Salt and pepper are used to season, and that is all that is needed. The way the squid is cooked in this recipe is traditionally Chinese, and it is a Vietnamese favourite too. Ideal snack and finger food, the tender squid can be served on its own, with noodles or – as it is in the streets of Saigon – with baguette and chillies. Those who like chilli can replace the black pepper with chopped dried chilli or chilli powder. Butterflied prawns or shrimp, with the shells removed, are also delicious cooked in this way.

Serves 4

450g/1lb baby or medium squid
30ml/2 tbsp coarse salt
15ml/1 tbsp ground black pepper
50g/2oz/½ cup rice flour or
    cornflour (cornstarch)
vegetable or sesame oil, for frying
2 limes, halved

1 Prepare the squid by gently but firmly pulling the head away from the body. Sever the tentacles from the head and trim them, discarding the beak and the head. Remove and reserve the ink sac. Reach inside the body sac and pull out the 'quill' or backbone, then clean the squid inside and out, removing any skin. Rinse well in cold water.

2 Using a sharp knife, slice the squid into rings and pat them dry. Put them on a dish with the tentacles. Combine the salt and pepper with the rice flour or cornflour, pour it on to the squid rings and tentacles and toss well, making sure they are evenly coated.

3 Heat the oil in a wok or heavy pan for deep-frying. Cook the squid in batches, until the rings turn crisp and golden. Drain on kitchen paper and serve with lime to squeeze over.

Cook's Tips
To use the ink sac, put it in a bowl and pierce with a knife. Use the ink, diluted with water, to flavour and colour homemade pasta and risotto.

Pan-fried Baby Squid with Spices

Whether served as an appetizer in Africa or a meze in the Middle East, baby squid is highly prized. It needs very little cooking and tastes wonderful with this spicy sweet and sour sauce, which teams turmeric and ginger with honey and lemon juice.

Serves 4

8 baby squid, prepared,
    with tentacles
5ml/1 tsp ground turmeric
15ml/1 tbsp smen or olive oil
2 garlic cloves, finely chopped
15g/½oz fresh root ginger, peeled
    and finely chopped
5–10ml/1–2 tsp clear honey
juice of 1 lemon
10ml/2 tsp harissa
salt
small bunch of fresh coriander
    (cilantro), chopped, to garnish

1 Pat dry the squid bodies, inside and out, and dry the tentacles. Sprinkle the squid with the ground turmeric.

2 Heat the smen or olive oil in a large, heavy frying pan and stir in the garlic and ginger.

3 Just as the ginger and garlic begin to colour, add the squid and tentacles and fry quickly on both sides over a high heat. (Do not overcook the squid, it should be tender but not rubbery.)

4 Add the honey, lemon juice and harissa and stir to form a thick, spicy, caramelized sauce.

5 Season with salt, sprinkle with the chopped coriander and serve immediately.

Cook's Tips
Smen is a pungent, aged butter used in Moroccan cooking. It is also savoured with chunks of warm, fresh bread and is used to enhance other dishes including couscous and some tagines.

Fried Squid Energy 339Kcal/1405kJ; Protein 14g; Carbohydrate 5g, of which sugars 0g; Fat 29g, of which saturates 4g; Cholesterol 146mg; Calcium 70mg; Fibre 0g; Sodium 1.4g.
Baby Squid Energy 154Kcal/647kJ; Protein 19.8g; Carbohydrate 5.8g, of which sugars 4.3g; Fat 5.9g, of which saturates 1g; Cholesterol 281mg; Calcium 54mg; Fibre 1g; Sodium 144mg.

Fried Squid

There are few foods more appetizing than fried squid. In Greece, squid is generally rolled in flour and shallow-fried. There's an art to this, as the olive oil has to be at precisely the right temperature to keep the squid tender and moist. Fried squid can be served as a meze with salad or can accompany a soup or vegetable casserole.

Serves 4
900g/2lb medium squid
50g/2oz/½ cup plain
(all-purpose) flour
75ml/5 tbsp olive oil or sunflower
oil, for frying
large pinch of dried oregano
salt and ground black pepper
1 lemon, quartered, to serve

1 Prepare the squid, but do not slit the bodies open. Having removed the head, beak and quill, rinse the bodies thoroughly, inside and out, then drain well. Slice the bodies into 3–4cm/1¼–1½in wide rings.

2 Season the flour with salt and pepper and put it in a plastic bag. Add the squid, keeping the rings and tentacles separate, and toss until evenly coated. Shake off any excess flour.

3 Heat the oil in a large heavy or non-stick frying pan over a medium heat. When it is hot enough to sizzle, but is not smoking, add some squid rings. They should not touch each other.

4 Let the squid rings cook for 2–3 minutes or until pale golden, then use a fork to turn each piece over. Let each ring cook for 1–2 minutes more, until pale golden, then lift out with a slotted spoon and drain on a platter lined with kitchen paper.

5 Continue to cook the squid, but leave the floured tentacles to last, and take care, as they spit. The tentacles will need very little cooking as the oil will have become quite hot and they will become crisp almost immediately. Turn them after 1 minute and take them out as soon as they are crisp and golden all over.

6 Serve the squid sprinkled with some dried oregano. Garnish with the lemon wedges to squeeze over the squid.

Flash-fried Squid with Paprika Garlic

Squid are part of every tapas bar selection, and are usually deep-fried. Here is a modern recipe, which is unusual in that it uses fresh chillies. Serve the dish with a fino or manzanilla sherry as a tapas dish. Alternatively, serve the calamares on a bed of salad leaves, accompanied by bread, for a substantial first course to serve four.

Serves 6–8
500g/1¼lb very small squid,
cleaned
90ml/6 tbsp olive oil, plus extra
1 fresh red chilli, seeded and
finely chopped
10ml/2 tsp Spanish mild
smoked paprika
30ml/2 tbsp plain
(all-purpose) flour
2 garlic cloves, finely chopped
15ml/1 tbsp sherry vinegar
5ml/1 tsp grated lemon rind
30–45ml/2–3 tbsp finely chopped
fresh parsley
salt and ground black pepper

1 Using a sharp knife, cut the squid body sacs into rings and cut the tentacles into bitesize pieces.

2 Place the squid in a bowl and pour over 30ml/2 tbsp of the olive oil, half the chilli and the paprika. Season with a little salt and some pepper, cover with clear film (plastic wrap), place in the refrigerator and leave to marinate for about 2–4 hours.

3 Toss the squid in the flour and divide it into two batches. Heat the remaining oil in a wok or deep frying pan over a high heat until very hot.

4 Add the first batch of squid and quickly stir-fry for 1–2 minutes, or until the squid becomes opaque and the tentacles curl.

5 Add half the garlic. Stir, then turn out into a bowl. Repeat with the second batch, adding more oil if needed.

6 Sprinkle with the sherry vinegar, lemon rind, remaining chilli and parsley. Season and serve hot or cool.

Hot, Sweet and Sour Squid

The Indonesians and Malays love cooking prawns and squid in this way, and expertly crunch shells and suck tentacles to savour all the juicy chilli and tamarind flavouring. Sweetened with the ubiquitous kecap manis, the enticing aroma of these delicious squid will make your tastebuds tingle.

Serves 2–4
500g/1¼lb fresh baby squid
30ml/2 tbsp tamarind paste
30ml/2 tbsp chilli sauce
45ml/3 tbsp kecap manis
 (Indonesian sweet soy sauce)
juice of 1 kalamansi or
 ordinary lime
25g/1oz fresh root ginger, grated
2–4 green chillies, seeded and
 quartered lengthways
ground black pepper
fresh coriander (cilantro) leaves
 and lime wedges, to serve

1 Clean the squid and remove the head and ink sac. Pull out the backbone and rinse the body sac inside and out. Trim the head above the eyes, keeping the tentacles intact. Pat dry the body sac and tentacles and discard the rest.

2 In a small bowl, mix together the tamarind paste, chilli sauce, kecap manis and lime juice. Beat in the ginger and a little ground black pepper.

3 Spoon the mixture over the squid and, using your fingers, rub it all over the body sacs and tentacles. Cover and leave to marinate in the refrigerator for 1 hour.

4 Meanwhile, prepare the barbecue or heat a ridged griddle on the hob. Place the squid on the rack or griddle and cook for 3 minutes on each side, brushing them with the marinade as they cook. Serve immediately with the coriander leaves and lime wedges.

Variation
To make hot, sweet and sour prawns (shrimp), devein the prawns and remove the legs, then rinse, pat dry, and cut along the tail. Marinate and cook in the same way as the squid.

Dried Squid Satay

All sorts of dried fish and shellfish are a feature of south-east Asian cooking and at the local markets, dried squid can always be seen hanging from poles. In the Philippines, dried fish is usually deep-fried and served with garlic rice, and the dried squid is grilled in the street, luring passers-by with its sweet aroma. Simple and tasty, this dish is often made at the beach and served with iced fruit drinks or chilled serbesa (beer) to balance the saltiness. It is also good served with chunks of bread.

Serves 3–4
4 whole dried baby squid
30ml/2 tbsp light soy sauce
30ml/2 tbsp hoisin sauce
30ml/2 tbsp smooth
 peanut butter
juice of 1 kalamansi or
 ordinary lime
wooden or metal skewers
green mango or papaya salad,
 to serve

1 Cut each squid into four or five pieces. Put the soy sauce, hoisin sauce, peanut butter and lime juice in a bowl and mix well with a fork to form a thick, well blended marinade.

2 Toss the squid pieces in the peanut marinade, making sure they are completely coated, and leave to marinate at room temperature for about 30 minutes.

3 If using wooden skewers, soak them in water for about 30 minutes to prevent them from charring when you start cooking.

4 Meanwhile, prepare the barbecue or, if you are using the grill (broiler), preheat it on the maximum heat for 5 minutes before you start cooking.

5 Thread the pieces of squid on to the skewers. Place the satay on the barbecue or under the grill and cook for 2 minutes on each side, brushing occasionally with any remaining marinade.

6 Serve as an accompaniment to a drink or with chunks of bread and a green mango or papaya salad.

Sweet and Sour Squid Energy 110kcal/468kJ; Protein 20g; Carbohydrate 2.8g, of which sugars 1.1g; Fat 2.3g, of which saturates 0.5g; Cholesterol 281mg; Calcium 43mg; Fibre 0.6g; Sodium 943mg.
Squid Satay Energy 89kcal/374kJ; Protein 9.6g; Carbohydrate 2.2g, of which sugars 1.1g; Fat 4.7g, of which saturates 1.2g; Cholesterol 113mg; Calcium 11mg; Fibre 0.4g; Sodium 615mg.

Prawns with Baked Garlic and Roasted Tomatoes

Packed full of wonderful Mediterranean flavours, this simple, gutsy dish makes a marvellous first course for a dinner party.

Serves 4
4 small garlic bulbs
60–75ml/4–5 tbsp olive oil
500g/1¼lb baby plum tomatoes on the vine
16 raw large prawns (jumbo shrimp), in their shells
a few sprigs of fresh thyme
salt and ground black pepper
lemon wedges and warm crusty bread, to serve

1 Cut a small cross in the top of each bulb of garlic. Place the bulbs in a garlic baker, brush with half the olive oil and sprinkle with a little salt and ground black pepper.

2 Place the garlic baker in an unheated oven, set the temperature to 200°C/400°F/Gas 6 and bake the garlic for about 40 minutes. The garlic cloves should be soft and creamy – if not, bake for a further 10 minutes.

3 Place the tomatoes and prawns in a shallow earthenware baking dish. Drizzle over the remaining olive oil, sprinkle with thyme sprigs and season. Place the dish in the oven after the garlic has been cooking for 30 minutes; turn the prawns after 7 minutes.

4 Arrange the garlic, tomatoes and prawns on a warmed serving plate and serve with lemon wedges and plenty of crusty bread.

> **Cook's Tip**
> • If you can't find small garlic bulbs use one large one and bake it in the oven for about 50 minutes, or until the cloves are soft and creamy.
> • Spread a little of the baked garlic on the bread and drizzle with olive oil.

Butterflied Prawns in Chocolate Sauce

There is a long tradition in Spain, which originates in Mexico, of cooking savoury food – even shellfish – with chocolate. Known as langostinos en chocolate in Spanish, this is just the kind of culinary adventure that Basque chefs love.

Serves 4
8 large raw prawns (shrimp), in the shell
15ml/1 tbsp seasoned plain (all-purpose) flour
15ml/1 tbsp pale dry sherry
juice of 1 large orange
15g/½oz dark (bittersweet) chocolate, chopped
30ml/2 tbsp olive oil
2 garlic cloves, finely chopped
2.5cm/1in piece fresh root ginger, finely chopped
1 small dried chilli, seeded and chopped
salt and ground black pepper

1 Peel the prawns, leaving just the tail sections intact. Make a shallow cut down the back of each one and carefully pull out and discard the dark intestinal tract. Turn the prawns over so that the undersides are uppermost, and then carefully slit them open from tail to top, using a small sharp knife, cutting them almost, but not quite, through to the central back line.

2 Press the prawns down firmly to flatten them out. Coat with the seasoned flour and set aside.

3 Gently heat the sherry and orange juice in a small pan. When warm, remove from the heat and stir in the chopped chocolate until melted.

4 Heat the oil in a frying pan. Add the garlic, ginger and chilli and cook for 2 minutes until golden. Remove with a slotted spoon and reserve. Add the prawns, cut side down and cook for 2–3 minutes until golden brown with pink edges. Turn the prawns and cook for a further 2 minutes.

5 Return the garlic mixture to the pan and pour the chocolate sauce over. Cook for 1 minute, turning the prawns to coat them in the glossy sauce. Season to taste and serve hot.

Prawns with Garlic Energy 183Kcal/761kJ; Protein 11.7g; Carbohydrate 8g, of which sugars 4.3g; Fat 11.8g, of which saturates 1.8g; Cholesterol 98mg; Calcium 53mg; Fibre 2.3g; Sodium 107mg.
Prawns in Chocolate Energy 125kcal/520kJ; Protein 8.5g; Carbohydrate 6.5g, of which sugars 3.6g; Fat 6.9g, of which saturates 1.5g; Cholesterol 88mg; Calcium 44mg; Fibre 0.2g; Sodium 88mg.

King Prawns in Crispy Batter

A huge range of prawns is enjoyed in Spain, each with its appropriate cooking method. Langostinos are deep-water prawns, often with tiger stripes, and can be among the biggest. The best way to enjoy them is dipped in a simple batter and deep-fried.

Serves 4

120ml/4fl oz/½ cup water
1 large egg (US extra large)
115g/4oz/1 cup plain
  (all-purpose) flour
5ml/1 tsp cayenne pepper
12 raw king prawns (jumbo
  shrimp), in the shell
vegetable oil, for deep frying
flat leaf parsley, to garnish
lemon wedges, to serve (optional)

1 In a large bowl, whisk together the water and the egg. Whisk in the flour and cayenne pepper until smooth.

2 Peel the prawns, leaving just the tails intact. Make a shallow cut down the back of each prawn. Using the tip of the knife, pull out and discard the dark intestinal tract.

3 Heat the oil in a large pan or deep-fat fryer, until a cube of bread dropped into the oil browns in 1 minute.

4 Holding the prawns by their tails, dip them into the batter, one at a time, shaking off any excess. Carefully drop each prawn into the oil and fry for 2–3 minutes until crisp and golden. Drain on kitchen paper, garnish with parsley and serve with lemon wedges, if you like.

> **Cook's Tip**
> If you have any batter left over, use it to coat thin strips of vegetables such as sweet potato, beetroot (beet), carrot or (bell) pepper, or use small broccoli florets or whole baby spinach leaves. Deep-fry the vegetables until golden. Leaving the tails on the prawns makes them easier to pick up and eat, and also look very pretty once cooked.

Langoustines with Saffron and Tomato

The best langoustines come from the west coast of Scotland, where everything from a tiny shrimp to just smaller than a lobster is called a prawn. Langoustines, also known as Dublin Bay prawns or Norway lobsters, look like miniature lobsters, although they taste more like jumbo prawns or shrimp, and these can be substituted if you prefer.

Serves 4

5ml/1 tsp sea salt
20 live langoustines or Dublin Bay
  prawns (jumbo shrimp)
1 onion
15ml/1 tbsp olive oil
pinch of saffron threads
120ml/4fl oz/½ cup white wine
450g/1lb ripe fresh or canned
  tomatoes, roughly chopped
chopped fresh flat leaf parsley,
  to garnish
salt and ground black pepper

1 Bring a large pan of water to the boil, add the salt and plunge the shellfish into the pan. Let the water return to the boil then transfer the shellfish to a colander to cool.

2 When cooled, shell the langoustines or prawns and reserve four heads with two claws each. Keep the rest of the shells, heads and claws to make a flavourful stock for the sauce.

3 Chop the onions. Heat a large heavy pan and add 15ml/1 tbsp olive oil. Gently fry the chopped onion to soften. Stir in the saffron threads. Then add the shellfish debris, including the heads and the pincers. Stir to mix then reduce the heat.

4 Add the wine and then the tomatoes. Simmer to soften the tomatoes, about 5 minutes. Add water if it looks dry.

5 Strain through a sieve, pushing the debris to get as much moisture out as possible. The resulting sauce should be light in texture; if it is too thick, add some water. Check the seasoning.

6 Add the langoustines or prawns and warm for a few minutes. Serve in warmed soup plates garnished with the reserved langoustine or prawn heads and scattered with parsley.

King Prawns Energy 253kcal/1061kJ; Protein 13.1g; Carbohydrate 22.4g, of which sugars 0.4g; Fat 13.1g, of which saturates 1.8g; Cholesterol 145mg; Calcium 87mg; Fibre 0.9g; Sodium 113mg.
Langoustines Energy 107kcal/449kJ; Protein 9.8g; Carbohydrate 4.9g, of which sugars 4.5g; Fat 3.4g, of which saturates 0.6g; Cholesterol 98mg; Calcium 54mg; Fibre 1.3g; Sodium 598mg.

Hot Spicy Prawns with Coriander

Coriander has a long history. Native to the Mediterranean and the Middle East, it was known to the ancient Egyptians, and seeds have been found in the tombs of the pharaohs. Today, coriander is widely grown as a cash crop in North Africa, and it is often used to flavour tagines and similar dishes. The herb's affinity for cumin is well known, so it is not surprising to find the twin flavourings used in this spicy appetizer.

Serves 2–4

60ml/4 tbsp olive oil
2–3 garlic cloves, chopped
25g/1oz fresh root ginger, peeled and grated
1 fresh red or green chilli, seeded and chopped
5ml/1 tsp cumin seeds
5ml/1 tsp paprika
450g/1lb uncooked king prawns (jumbo shrimp), shelled
bunch of fresh coriander (cilantro), chopped
salt
1 lemon, cut into wedges, to serve

1 In a large, frying pan, heat the oil with the garlic. Stir in the ginger, chilli and cumin seeds. Cook briefly, until the ingredients give off a lovely aroma, then add the paprika and toss in the prawns.

2 Fry the prawns over a fairly high heat, turning them frequently, for 3–5 minutes, until just cooked. Season to taste with salt and add the coriander. Serve immediately, with lemon wedges for squeezing over the prawns.

Cook's Tips
• When buying garlic, choose plump garlic with tightly packed cloves and dry skin. Avoid any bulbs with soft, shrivelled cloves or green shoots.
• If you cannot find raw king prawns, use frozen instead. Thaw them out completely before you fry them with the garlic and spice mixture.

Ceviche

This is a fruity first course of marinated fresh fish. Take care in choosing the fish for this dish; it must be as fresh as possible and served on the day it is made, since it is 'cooked' by the action of the citrus juices, rather than by the usual method.

Serves 6

350g/12oz medium cooked prawns (shrimp)
350g/12oz scallops, removed from their shells, with corals
175g/6oz tomatoes
1 mango, about 175g/6oz
1 red onion, finely chopped
350g/12oz salmon fillet
1 fresh red chilli, seeded and chopped
12 limes
30ml/2 tbsp caster (superfine) sugar
2 pink grapefruit
3 oranges
salt and ground black pepper

1 Set aside two prawns for the garnish. Peel the remaining prawns and cut the scallops into 1.2cm/½in dice. Dice the tomatoes and place in a bowl. Peel the mango, dice the flesh and add it to the bowl with the red onion. Mix well.

2 Skin the salmon, then remove any pin bones with a pair of tweezers. Cut the fish into small pieces and mix with the tomato, mango and onion. Add the chilli and mix well.

3 Squeeze the juice from eight of the limes and add it to the tomato mixture, with the sugar and a little salt and pepper. Stir, cover and leave to marinate in a cool place for 3 hours.

4 Segment the grapefruit, oranges and remaining limes. Drain off as much excess lime juice as possible and mix the fruit segments into the marinated ingredients. Season to taste and serve, garnished with the reserved prawns.

Cook's Tips
To skin the salmon, place the fish in the freezer for 10 minutes first. Cut down to the skin at the narrow end of the fillet, hold that end firmly, turn the blade and slice the flesh off the skin.

Spicy Prawns Energy 382Kcal/1591kJ; Protein 40.8g; Carbohydrate 1.1g, of which sugars 0.9g; Fat 23.9g, of which saturates 3.4g; Cholesterol 439mg; Calcium 254mg; Fibre 1.9g; Sodium 440mg.
Ceviche Energy 147kcal/620kJ; Protein 21.9g; Carbohydrate 4.4g, of which sugars 2.2g; Fat 4.8g, of which saturates 1.1g; Cholesterol 175mg; Calcium 53mg; Fibre 1.2g; Sodium 186mg.

Deep-fried Sweet Potato and Prawn Patties

This dish, banh tom, is a Hanoi speciality. The street sellers in the city and the cafés along the banks of West Lake are well known for their varied and delicious banh tom. Traditionally, the patties are served with herb and lettuce leaves for wrapping and a sauce for dipping.

Serves 4

50g/2oz/½ cup plain
  (all-purpose) flour
50g/2oz/½ cup rice flour
scant 5ml/1 tsp baking powder
10ml/2 tsp sugar
2.5cm/1in fresh root ginger,
  peeled and grated
2 spring onions (scallions),
  finely sliced
175g/6oz small fresh prawns
  (shrimp), peeled and deveined
1 slim sweet potato, about
  225g/8oz, peeled and cut into
  fine matchsticks
vegetable oil, for deep-frying
salt and ground black pepper
chopped fresh coriander (cilantro),
  to garnish
nuoc cham or other dipping
  sauce, to serve

1 Sift the flours and baking powder into a bowl. Add the sugar and about 2.5ml/½ tsp each of salt and pepper. Gradually stir in 250ml/8fl oz/1 cup water, until thoroughly combined. Add the grated ginger and sliced spring onions and leave to stand for about 30 minutes.

2 Add the prawns and sweet potato to the batter and gently fold them in, making sure they are well coated. Heat enough oil for deep-frying in a wok or heavy pan. Place a heaped tablespoon of the mixture on to a metal spatula and pat it down a little. Lower it into the oil, pushing it off the spatula so that it floats in the oil. Fry the patty for 2–3 minutes, turning it over so that it is evenly browned. Drain on kitchen paper. Continue with the rest of the batter, frying the patties in small batches.

3 Arrange the patties on a dish, garnish with coriander, and serve immediately with nuoc cham or another dipping sauce of your choice.

Black-eyed Bean and Shrimp Fritters

This Brazilian snack, locally known as acarajé, is from Bahia. Women fry these patties to order. They are then cut open and filled with various sauces, all delectable but very messy to eat.

Makes 10

250g/9oz/1¼ cups black-eyed
  beans (peas)
40g/1½oz/¼ cup dried shrimp
1 onion, roughly chopped
palm oil and vegetable oil,
  for frying
salt
chilli oil, to serve

For the filling

30ml/2 tbsp palm oil
115g/4oz/⅔ cup dried shrimp
1 large onion, thinly sliced
2 fresh hot red chillies, seeded
  and finely chopped

1 Put the black-eyed beans in a bowl and cover with water. Soak overnight. Drain, then soak for a further 30 minutes in hot (but not boiling) water. Drain the beans and transfer to a board. Rub them between your hands to remove their skins. The patties will be very dry if the skins are not removed.

2 Transfer the beans to a bowl and cover with cold water. The loose skins will begin to rise to the surface. Remove them with a slotted spoon and throw them away. Stir the beans to encourage more skins to float to the surface, continuing until all the skins have been removed. Drain.

3 Blend the dried shrimp and onion in a food processor until smooth. Add the beans and blend until thick. Season with salt.

4 Mix equal quantities of palm oil and vegetable oil to a depth of 5cm/2in in a deep pan. Shape the acarajé mixture into 10 ovals. Heat the oil and fry batches of the fritters until golden. Lift out with a slotted spoon and drain on kitchen paper.

5 Make the filling. Heat the oil and sauté the shrimp for 2–3 minutes. Drain on kitchen paper. Add the onion, cook for 5 minutes, then add the chillies. Sauté for 1 minute. Cut each fritter open and fill with the onion mixture. Drizzle with chilli oil.

Patties Energy 276Kcal/1159kJ; Protein 11g; Carbohydrate 35g, of which sugars 6g; Fat 11g, of which saturates 1g; Cholesterol 85mg; Calcium 83mg; Fibre 81g; Sodium 0.2g.
Fritters Energy 225kcal/940kJ; Protein 15g; Carbohydrate 17g, of which sugars 3g; Fat 11g, of which saturates 2g; Cholesterol 78mg; Calcium 216mg; Fibre 1g; Sodium 677mg.

Coconut King Prawns

Popular throughout the Caribbean islands, these butterflied prawns look very pretty and they taste wonderful when partnered with a crisp coconut and chive coating.

Serves 4

12 raw king prawns
   (jumbo shrimp)
2 garlic cloves, crushed
15ml/1 tbsp lemon juice
50g/2oz/4 tbsp fine desiccated
   (dry unsweetened
   shredded) coconut
25g/1oz/²⁄₃ cup chopped
   fresh chives
150ml/¼ pint/²⁄₃ cup milk
2 eggs, beaten
salt and ground black pepper
oil, for deep-frying
lime or lemon wedges and fresh
   flat leaf parsley, to garnish

1 Peel and de-vein the prawns, leaving the tails intact, then deepen the incision made when de-veining the prawns, cutting from the back almost to the belly so that they can be opened out. Rinse the prawns under cold water and pat dry.

2 Mix the garlic and lemon juice with a little seasoning in a shallow dish, then add the prawns. Toss to coat, cover and marinate for about 1 hour.

3 Mix the coconut and chives in a separate shallow dish, and put the milk and eggs in two small bowls. Dip each prawn into the milk, then into the beaten egg and finally into the coconut and chive mixture.

4 Heat the oil in a large pan or deep-fryer and fry the prawns for about 1 minute, until golden. Lift out and drain on kitchen paper. Serve hot, garnished with lime or lemon wedges and parsley.

> **Cook's Tip**
> If raw king prawns (jumbo shrimp) are difficult to obtain, just substitute cooked prawns. However, the fresh raw prawns will absorb more flavour from the marinade, so they are the ideal choice.

Prawn Briouates

In Morocco, briouates are made with a special pastry called ouarka. Like filo, it is very thin and apt to dry out if not kept covered.

Makes about 24

175g/6oz filo pastry sheets
40g/1½oz/3 tbsp butter, melted
sunflower oil, for frying
1 spring onion (scallion) and fresh
   coriander (cilantro) leaves,
   to garnish
ground cinnamon and icing
   (confectioners') sugar, to serve

For the prawn (shrimp) filling
15ml/1 tbsp olive oil
15g/½oz/1 tbsp butter
2–3 spring onions (scallions),
   finely chopped
15g/½oz/2 tbsp plain
   (all-purpose) flour
300ml/½ pint/1¼ cups milk
2.5ml/½ tsp paprika
350g/12oz cooked peeled prawns
   (shrimp), chopped
salt and white pepper

1 First make the filling. Heat the olive oil and butter in a pan and gently fry the spring onions for 2–3 minutes until soft. Stir in the flour, and then gradually add the milk. Heat gently, stirring continuously, until the sauce is thickened and smooth. Simmer gently for 2–3 minutes, stirring.

2 Season the sauce with paprika, salt and pepper and stir in the prawns.

3 Take a sheet of filo pastry and cut it in half widthways, to make a rectangle about 18 x 14cm/7 x 5½in. Cover the remaining pastry with clear film (plastic wrap) to prevent it drying out.

4 Brush the pastry with melted butter and then place a heaped teaspoon of filling at one end. Roll up like a cigar, tucking in the sides as you go. Continue until you have used the pastry and filling.

5 Heat about 1cm/½in oil in a heavy pan and fry the briouates, in batches if necessary, for 2–3 minutes until golden, turning occasionally. Drain on kitchen paper, arrange on a serving plate and then serve garnished with a spring onion and coriander leaves, and sprinkled with cinnamon and icing sugar.

Coconut Prawns Energy 307kcal/1273kJ; Protein 22g; Carbohydrate 3g, of which sugars 3g; Fat 23g, of which saturates 10g; Cholesterol 297mg; Calcium 142mg; Fibre 3g; Sodium 234mg.
Briouates Energy 77Kcal/320kJ; Protein 4.3g; Carbohydrate 5.5g, of which sugars 0.7g; Fat 4.3g, of which saturates 1.6g; Cholesterol 17mg; Calcium 47mg; Fibre 0.2g; Sodium 251mg.

Crackling Rice Paper Fish Rolls

The rice in this dish is in the rice paper wrappers, which hold their shape during cooking, yet almost magically dissolve in your mouth when it comes to eating.

Makes 112

12 Vietnamese rice paper sheets
    (bahn trang), each about
    20 x 10cm/8 x 4in
45ml/3 tbsp plain flour mixed to
    a paste with 45ml/3 tbsp water
vegetable oil, for deep-frying
fresh herbs, to garnish

For the filling
24 asparagus spears, trimmed
225g/8oz raw prawns, peeled
    and deveined
25ml/1 1/2 tbsp olive oil
6 spring onions, finely chopped
1 garlic clove, crushed
2cm/3/4in piece of fresh root
    ginger, grated
30ml/2 tbsp chopped
    fresh coriander
5ml/1 tsp five-spice powder
5ml/1 tsp finely grated lime
    or lemon rind
salt and ground black pepper

1 Make the filling. Bring a saucepan of lightly salted water to the boil and cook the asparagus for 3–4 minutes until tender. Drain, refresh under cold water and drain again. Cut the prawns into 2cm/3/4in pieces.

2 Heat half of the oil in a small frying pan or wok and stir-fry the spring onions and garlic over a low heat for 2–3 minutes until soft. Using a slotted spoon, transfer the vegetables to a bowl and set aside.

3 Heat the remaining oil and stir-fry the prawns over a brisk heat for just a few seconds until they start to go pink. Add to the spring onion mixture with the ginger, coriander, five-spice powder, lime or lemon rind and a little pepper. Stir to mix.

4 To make each roll, brush a sheet of rice paper liberally with water and lay it on a clean surface. Place two asparagus spears and a spoonful of the prawn mixture just off centre. Fold in the sides and roll up to make a fat cigar. Seal the ends with a little of the flour paste.

5 Heat the oil in a wok or deep-fryer and fry the rolls in batches until golden. Drain well, garnish with herbs and serve.

Seaweed-wrapped Prawn Rolls

Japanese nori seaweed is used to enclose a fragrant filling of prawns, water chestnuts and fresh herbs and spices in these pretty steamed rolls. Ideal for entertaining, the rolls can be prepared in advance and stored in the refrigerator until ready to steam.

Serves 4

675g/1 1/2lb raw tiger prawns
    (shrimp), peeled and deveined
5ml/1 tsp finely chopped kaffir
    lime leaves
1 red chilli, seeded and chopped
5ml/1 tsp finely grated
    garlic clove
5ml/1 tsp finely grated fresh
    root ginger
5ml/1 tsp finely grated
    lime zest
60ml/4 tbsp very finely chopped
    fresh coriander (cilantro)
1 egg white, lightly beaten
30ml/2 tbsp chopped
    water chestnuts
4 sheets of nori
salt and ground black pepper
ketjap manis or soy sauce,
    to serve

1 Place the prawns in a food processor with the lime leaves, red chilli, garlic, ginger, lime zest and coriander.

2 Process until the mixture is smooth, add the egg white and water chestnuts, season and process until well combined. Transfer the mixture to a bowl, cover and chill in a refrigerator for 3–4 hours.

3 Lay the nori sheets on a clean, dry surface and spread the prawn mixture over each sheet, leaving a 2cm/3/4in border at one end. Roll up to form tight rolls, wrap in clear film (plastic wrap) and chill for 2–3 hours.

4 Unwrap the rolls and place on a board. Using a sharp knife, cut each roll into 2cm/3/4in lengths.

5 Place the slices in a bamboo steamer that has been lined with baking parchment, cover and place over a wok of simmering water (making sure the water does not touch the steamer). Steam the rolls for 6–8 minutes, or until they are cooked through. Serve warm or at room temperature with ketjap manis or soy sauce.

Prawn Rolls Energy 156kcal/661kJ; Protein 35g; Carbohydrate 1g, of which sugars 0g; Fat 1g, of which saturates 0g; Cholesterol 329mg; Calcium 202mg; Fibre 0g; Sodium 456mg.
Fish Rolls Energy 105kcal/438kJ; Protein 5g; Carbohydrate 8.8g, of which sugars 0.7g; Fat 5.6g, of which saturates 0.7g; Cholesterol 37mg; Calcium 36mg; Fibre 0.8g; Sodium 38mg.

Spicy Prawn and Scallop Satay

One of the tastiest satay dishes, this is succulent, spicy and extremely moreish. Serve as an appetizer with a fruity salad or pickled vegetables and lime.

Serves 4

250g/9oz shelled prawns (shrimp), deveined and chopped
250g/9oz shelled scallops, chopped
30ml/2 tbsp potato, tapioca or rice flour
5ml/1 tsp baking powder
12–16 wooden, metal, lemon grass or sugar cane skewers
1 lime, quartered, to serve

For the spice paste

2 shallots, chopped
2 garlic cloves, chopped
2–3 fresh red chillies, seeded and chopped
25g/1oz fresh galangal or fresh root ginger, chopped
15g/½oz fresh turmeric, chopped, or 2.5ml/½ tsp ground turmeric
2–3 lemon grass stalks, chopped
15ml/1 tbsp palm or groundnut (peanut) oil
5ml/1 tsp shrimp paste
15ml/1 tbsp tamarind paste
5ml/1 tsp palm sugar (jaggery)

1 To make the spice paste, pound the shallots, garlic, chillies, galangal, turmeric and lemon grass together.

2 Heat the oil in a wok, stir in the paste and fry until it becomes fragrant. Add the shrimp paste, tamarind and sugar and stir-fry, until the mixture darkens. Leave to cool.

3 In a bowl, pound the prawns and scallops together to form a paste, or blend them together in an electric blender or food processor.

4 Beat in the spice paste, followed by the flour and baking powder, until blended. Chill for about 1 hour.

5 If using wooden skewers, soak in water for about 30 minutes. Prepare the barbecue, or preheat the grill (broiler).

6 Take lumps of the shellfish paste and wrap it around the skewers. Barbecue or grill them for 3 minutes on each side, until golden brown. Serve with the lime wedges to squeeze over.

Grilled Prawns with Lemon Grass

The use of fresh, aromatic lemon grass for grilling, stir-frying or steaming shellfish is a classic feature of Indo-Chinese cooking. Next to every fish and shellfish stall in every market in Vietnam, there is bound to be someone doing just that – cooking up fragrant, citrus-scented snacks for you to eat as you wander around the market. The aromas will entice you to taste, but check what's cooking first, because the Vietnamese also like to cook frogs' legs and snails this way.

Serves 4

16 king prawns (jumbo shrimp), cleaned, with shells intact
120ml/4fl oz/½ cup nuoc mam
30ml/2 tbsp sugar
15ml/1 tbsp vegetable or sesame oil
3 lemon grass stalks, trimmed and finely chopped

1 Using a small sharp knife, carefully slice open each king prawn shell along the back and pull out the black vein, using the point of the knife. Try to keep the rest of the shell intact. Place the deveined prawns in a shallow dish and set aside.

2 Put the nuoc mam in a small bowl with the sugar, and beat together until the sugar has dissolved completely. Add the oil and lemon grass and mix well.

3 Pour the marinade over the prawns, using your fingers to rub it all over the prawns and inside the shells too. Cover the dish with clear film (plastic wrap) and chill for at least 4 hours.

4 Cook the prawns on a barbecue or under a conventional grill (broiler) for 2–3 minutes each side. Serve immediately with little bowls of water for rinsing sticky fingers.

> **Cook's Tip**
> *Big, juicy king prawns (jumbo shrimp) are best for this recipe, but you can use smaller ones if the very large king prawns are not available. Other shellfish, such as squid, are also good cooked in this way.*

Prawn and Scallop Energy 220kcal/922kJ; Protein 27g; Carbohydrate 11.5g, of which sugars 1g; Fat 7.3g, of which saturates 1g; Cholesterol 151mg; Calcium 99mg; Fibre 1.5g; Sodium 249mg.
Grilled Prawns Energy 174Kcal/726kJ; Protein 13g; Carbohydrate 11g, of which sugars 0g; Fat 9g, of which saturates 1g; Cholesterol 169mg; Calcium 30mg; Fibre 0.3g; Sodium 0.3g.

Chilli Crab Cakes

Served with a hot and spicy tomato dip, these Caribbean crab cakes are quite delicious. Use the freshest crab meat available and serve as a snack at any time.

Makes about 15
225g/8oz white crab meat
115g/4oz cooked potatoes, mashed
30ml/2 tbsp fresh herb seasoning
2.5ml/½ tsp prepared mild mustard
2.5ml/½ tsp ground black pepper
½ fresh hot chilli, seeded and chopped
2.5ml/½ tsp dried oregano, crushed

1 egg, beaten
15ml/1 tbsp shrimp paste (optional)
flour, for dusting
oil, for frying
lime wedges and fresh basil leaves, to garnish

For the tomato dip
15ml/1 tbsp butter or margarine
½ onion, finely chopped
2 canned plum tomatoes, drained and chopped
1 garlic clove, crushed
150ml/¼ pint/⅔ cup water
5–10ml/1–2 tsp malt vinegar
15ml/1 tbsp chopped fresh coriander (cilantro)
½ chilli, seeded and chopped

1 To make the crab cakes, combine the crab meat, mashed potato, herb seasoning, mustard, black pepper, chilli, oregano and egg in a large bowl. Add the shrimp paste, if using, and mix well. Cover and chill for 30 minutes.

2 Make the tomato dip. Melt the butter or margarine in a small pan. Add the onion, chopped tomato and garlic and sauté for about 5 minutes until the onion is soft.

3 Add the water, vinegar, coriander and chilli. Simmer for 10 minutes, then blend to a smooth purée in a food processor or blender. Pour into a bowl. Keep warm or chill, as required.

4 Using a spoon, shape the crab mixture into rounds and dust with flour. Heat a little oil in a large frying pan and fry the crab cakes, a few at a time, for 2–3 minutes on each side until golden brown. Remove with a fish slice, drain on kitchen paper and keep hot while cooking the remaining cakes. Serve with the tomato dip and garnish with lime wedges and basil leaves.

Hot Crab Soufflés

These delicious little soufflés must be served as soon as they are ready, so seat your guests at the table before taking them out of the oven.

Serves 6
50g/2oz/¼ cup butter
45ml/3 tbsp fine wholemeal (whole-wheat) breadcrumbs
4 spring onions (scallions), finely chopped

15ml/1 tbsp Malayan or mild Madras curry powder
25g/1oz/2 tbsp plain (all-purpose) flour
105ml/7 tbsp coconut milk or milk
150ml/¼ pint/⅔ cup whipping cream
4 egg yolks
225g/8oz white crab meat
mild green Tabasco sauce
6 egg whites
salt and ground black pepper

1 Use some of the butter to grease six ramekins or a 1.75 litre/3 pint/7½ cup soufflé dish. Sprinkle the breadcrumbs in the dishes or dish and roll them around to coat the base and sides completely, then tip out the excess breadcrumbs. Preheat the oven to 200°C/400°F/Gas 6.

2 Melt the remaining butter in a pan, add the spring onions and Malayan or mild Madras curry powder and cook over a low heat, stirring frequently, for about 1 minute, until softened. Stir in the flour and cook, stirring constantly, for 1 minute more.

3 Gradually, add the coconut milk or milk and the cream, stirring constantly. Cook over a low heat, still stirring, until smooth and thick. Remove the pan from the heat, stir in the egg yolks, then the crab. Season to taste with salt, black pepper and Tabasco sauce.

4 In a clean, grease-free bowl, whisk the egg whites with a pinch of salt until they are stiff. Using a metal spoon, stir one-third of the whites into the crab mixture to slacken, then fold in the remainder. Spoon into the dishes or dish.

5 Bake the soufflés until well risen, golden brown and just firm to the touch. Individual soufflés will take about 8 minutes, while a large soufflé will take 15–20 minutes. Serve immediately.

Crab Cakes Energy 285kcal/1187kJ; Protein 23.9g; Carbohydrate 10.3g, of which sugars 0.9g; Fat 16.7g, of which saturates 2.4g; Cholesterol 134mg; Calcium 178mg; Fibre 0.8g; Sodium 768mg.
Crab Soufflés Energy 270kcal/1122kJ; Protein 14g; Carbohydrate 11.6g, of which sugars 2.2g; Fat 18.9g, of which saturates 12.1g; Cholesterol 181mg; Calcium 123mg; Fibre 1g; Sodium 426mg.

Soft-shell Crabs with Chilli and Salt

If fresh soft-shell crabs are unavailable, you can buy frozen ones in Asian supermarkets. Allow two small crabs per serving, or one if they are large.

Serves 4
8 small soft-shell crabs, thawed if frozen
50g/2oz/½ cup plain (all-purpose) flour
60ml/4 tbsp groundnut (peanut) or vegetable oil

2 large fresh red chillies, or 1 green and 1 red chilli, seeded and thinly sliced
4 spring onions (scallions) or a small bunch of garlic chives, chopped
sea salt and ground black pepper

To serve
shredded lettuce, mooli (daikon) and carrot
light soy sauce, for dipping

1 Pat the crabs dry with kitchen paper. Season the flour with ground black pepper and coat the dried crabs lightly with the mixture.

2 Heat the oil in a shallow pan until very hot, then put in the crabs (you may need to do this in two batches). Fry for 2–3 minutes on each side, until the crabs are golden brown but still juicy in the middle. Drain the cooked crabs on kitchen paper and keep hot.

3 Add the sliced chillies and spring onions or garlic chives to the oil remaining in the pan and cook gently for about 2 minutes. Sprinkle over a generous pinch of salt, then spread the chilli and onion mixture on to the crabs.

4 Mix the shredded lettuce, mooli and carrot together. Arrange on plates, top each portion with two crabs and serve, with a bowl of light soy sauce for dipping.

> **Cook's Tip**
> Look for mooli (daikon) in Asian food stores. If you can't find any, use celeriac instead.

Stuffed Spider Crab

Spider crab has very sweet and succulent flesh. You can also prepare other kinds of crab in the same way.

Serves 2–3
1 bay leaf
6 black peppercorns
1 onion
4 fresh parsley sprigs

500ml/17fl oz/generous 2 cups white wine
1 live spider crab, about 1kg/2¼lb
1 egg yolk
175ml/6fl oz/¾ cup olive oil
15ml/1 tbsp pickles, drained and chopped
5ml/1 tsp Worcestershire sauce
few drops of Tabasco sauce
5ml/1 tsp brandy
1 hard-boiled egg, chopped
sea salt

1 Fill a large pan with water, measuring the quantity as you pour it in. Add the bay leaf, peppercorns, onion, parsley, white wine and 15ml/1 tbsp sea salt for every 1 litre/1¾ pints/4 cups water. Bring to the boil, add the crab, cover tightly and cook about 40 minutes. (Allow 20 minutes per 500g/1¼lb crab.)

2 Remove the crab from the pan and leave until cool enough to handle. Break off the claws and legs. Turn the crab upside down and break off the tail flap. Insert a sturdy knife between the body and the back shell and twist it. Using your thumbs, press the body away from the shell. Remove and discard the gills.

3 Scoop out the brown meat into a bowl. Cut the body in half and scoop out the white meat into another bowl. Crack the claws with the back of a heavy knife and pick out the white meat. Place the back shell on a board and press down on the piece of shell just behind the eyes. When it snaps, remove and discard it, including the stomach. Scoop the remaining brown meat into the first bowl. Scrub the back shell, dry and reserve.

4 Add the egg yolk to the brown meat then add the olive oil, a few drops at a time, whisking constantly. Once half of it has been added, add it steadily, whisking, until the mixture thickens. Fold in the white meat and pickles and add the Worcestershire sauce, Tabasco and brandy. Pile the mixture into the reserved shell and sprinkle with the hard-boiled egg. Serve the legs separately.

Soft-shell Crabs Energy 306kcal/1280kJ; Protein 37.6g; Carbohydrate 10g, of which sugars 0.5g; Fat 13g, of which saturates 1.5g; Cholesterol 144mg; Calcium 262mg; Fibre 0.5g; Sodium 1101mg.
Stuffed Crab Energy 507kcal/2093kJ; Protein 16.4g; Carbohydrate 0.3g, of which sugars 0.2g; Fat 48.6g, of which saturates 7.3g; Cholesterol 167mg; Calcium 40mg; Fibre 0g; Sodium 290mg.

Noodles with Crab and Mushrooms

This is a dish of contrasting flavours, textures and colours, and in Vietnam it is cooked with skill and dexterity. While one hand gently turns the noodles in the pan, the other takes chunks of fresh crab meat and drops them into the steaming wok to seal. Here the crab meat is cooked separately to make it easier for the uninitiated.

Serves 4

25g/1oz dried cloud ear (wood ear) mushrooms, soaked in warm water for 20 minutes
115g/4oz dried bean thread (cellophane) noodles, soaked in warm water for 20 minutes
30ml/2 tbsp vegetable or sesame oil
3 shallots, halved and thinly sliced
2 garlic cloves, crushed
2 green or red Thai chillies, seeded and sliced
1 carrot, peeled and cut into thin diagonal rounds
5ml/1 tsp sugar
45ml/3 tbsp oyster sauce
15ml/1 tbsp soy sauce
400ml/14fl oz/1⅔ cups water or chicken stock
225g/8oz fresh, raw crab meat, cut into bitesize chunks
ground black pepper
fresh coriander (cilantro) leaves, to garnish

1 Remove the centres from the soaked wood ear mushrooms and cut the mushrooms in half. Drain the soaked noodles and cut them into 30cm/12in pieces.

2 Heat a large, heavy pan and add 15ml/1 tbsp of the oil. Stir in the shallots, garlic and chillies, and cook until fragrant. Add the carrots and cook for 1 minute, then add the cloud ear mushrooms.

3 Stir in the sugar with the oyster and soy sauces, followed by the bean thread noodles. Add the water or stock, cover the pan and cook for 5 minutes, or until the noodles are soft.

4 Meanwhile, heat the remaining oil in a large, heavy pan. Add the crab meat and cook until it is nicely pink and tender. Season well with black pepper. Arrange the noodles and crab meat on a serving dish and garnish with coriander.

Saffron Mussels with White Wine

Mussels are easy to cook in a clay pot and they stay deliciously moist. The saffron adds a lovely pungent flavour as well as its distinctive yellow colour to the creamy sauce.

Serves 4

few threads of saffron
1kg/2¼lb mussels in their shells
25g/1oz/2 tbsp butter
2 shallots, finely chopped
2 garlic cloves, finely chopped
200ml/7fl oz/scant 1 cup dry white wine
60ml/4 tbsp double (heavy) cream or crème fraîche
30ml/2 tbsp chopped fresh parsley
salt and ground black pepper
French bread, to serve

1 Soak a large clay pot in cold water for about 20 minutes, then drain. Put the saffron in a small bowl, add 15ml/1 tbsp boiling water and leave to soak.

2 Scrub the mussels, pull off the beards and discard any open mussels that don't close when sharply tapped. Place all the closed mussels in the soaked clay pot.

3 Melt the butter in a frying pan, add the shallots and garlic and cook gently for 5 minutes, to soften. Stir in the wine and saffron water and bring to the boil. Pour the liquid over the mussels.

4 Cover the clay pot and place in an unheated oven. Set the oven to 220°C/425°F/Gas 7. Cook the mussels for about 15 minutes, then remove the pot from the oven and, firmly holding the lid on, shake the pot. Return the pot to the oven and cook for another 10 minutes, or until the mussels have opened.

5 Using a slotted spoon, transfer the mussels to four warmed serving bowls (discard any mussels that have not opened). Mix the cream or crème fraîche and parsley into the cooking liquid and season to taste.

6 Pour the cooking liquid over the mussels and serve immediately with French bread to soak up the sauce.

Noodles with Crab Energy 292Kcal/1224kJ; Protein 16g; Carbohydrate 30g, of which sugars 5g; Fat 13g, of which saturates 2g; Cholesterol 36mg; Calcium 29mg; Fibre 2.5g; Sodium 1g.
Mussels with Wine Energy 224Kcal/935kJ; Protein 13.5g; Carbohydrate 1.8g, of which sugars 1.4g; Fat 14.7g, of which saturates 8.5g; Cholesterol 64mg; Calcium 164mg; Fibre 0.2g; Sodium 201mg.

Mussels and Clams with Lemon Grass and Coconut Cream

Lemon grass has an incomparable flavour and aroma and is widely used in Thai cooking, especially with seafood. If you have difficulty obtaining fresh baby clams for this recipe, then use a few extra mussels instead.

Serves 6
1.8–2kg/4–4½lb mussels
450g/1lb baby clams

120ml/4fl oz/½ cup dry white wine
1 bunch spring onions (scallions), chopped
2 lemon grass stalks, chopped
6 kaffir lime leaves, chopped
10ml/2 tsp Thai green curry paste
200ml/7fl oz/scant 1 cup coconut cream
30ml/2 tbsp chopped fresh coriander (cilantro)
salt and ground black pepper
garlic chives, to garnish

1 Clean the mussels by pulling off the beards and scrubbing the shells. Discard any broken shells or any mussels that do not close when tapped sharply. Wash the clams.

2 Put the white wine in a large, heavy pan with the spring onions, chopped lemon grass stalks, chopped kaffir lime leaves and Thai green curry paste. Simmer until the wine has almost evaporated.

3 Add the mussels and clams to the pan, cover tightly and steam the shellfish over a high heat for 5–6 minutes, or until they open.

4 Using a slotted spoon, transfer the cooked mussels and clams to a heated serving bowl and keep hot. At this stage discard any shellfish that remain closed. Strain the cooking liquid into the clean pan and gently simmer until it is reduced to about 250ml/8fl oz/1 cup.

5 Stir in the coconut cream and fresh coriander, with plenty of salt and pepper to taste. Increase the heat and simmer gently until the sauce is piping hot. Pour the sauce over the mussels and clams and serve immediately, garnished with garlic chives.

Mussels with a Parsley Crust

The stormy atlantic coast of Spain produces the best mussels in the world. Known as mejillones in Spain, they grow to enormous size in a very short time. Here they are grilled with a deliciously fragrant topping of Parmesan cheese, garlic and parsley, which helps to prevent the mussels from becoming overcooked.

Serves 4
450g/1lb fresh mussels
45ml/3 tbsp water
15ml/1 tbsp melted butter
15ml/1 tbsp olive oil
45ml/3 tbsp freshly grated Parmesan cheese
30ml/2 tbsp chopped fresh parsley
2 garlic cloves, finely chopped
2.5ml/½ tsp coarsely ground black pepper
crusty bread, to serve

1 Scrub the mussels thoroughly, scraping off any barnacles with a round-bladed knife and pulling out the gritty beards. Sharply tap any open mussels and discard any that fail to close or whose shells are broken.

2 Place the mussels in a large pan and add the water. Cover the pan with a lid and steam for about 5 minutes, or until the mussel shells have opened.

3 Drain the mussels well and discard any that remain closed. Carefully snap off the top shell from each mussel, leaving the actual flesh still attached to the bottom shell. Balance the shells in a flameproof dish, packing them closely together to make sure that they stay level.

4 Preheat the grill (broiler) to high. Put the melted butter, olive oil, grated Parmesan cheese, parsley, garlic and black pepper in a small bowl and mix well to combine.

5 Place a small amount of the cheese and garlic mixture on top of each mussel and press down with the back of a spoon.

6 Grill (broil) the mussels for about 2 minutes, or until they are sizzling. Serve the mussels in their shells, with bread to mop up the delicious juices.

Mussels and Clams Energy 132Kcal/563kJ; Protein 19.6g; Carbohydrate 3.1g, of which sugars 3g; Fat 3.4g, of which saturates 0.6g; Cholesterol 44mg; Calcium 239mg; Fibre 0.3g; Sodium 288mg.
Mussels with Parsley Energy 110kcal/456kJ; Protein 5.4g; Carbohydrate 0.3g, of which sugars 0.3g; Fat 9.7g, of which saturates 4.7g; Cholesterol 21mg; Calcium 165mg; Fibre 0.6g; Sodium 156mg.

Garlic-stuffed Mussels

Mussels are a speciality of Wexford, on the south-east corner of Ireland, but they're also plentiful all around the coast, and safe to gather from the rocks anywhere down the west coast if the water is clean. Wild herbs, including garlic, have been used in Ireland for hundreds of years, so this way of cooking mussels is more Irish than it might sound.

Serves 4–6

2kg/4½lb fresh mussels
175g/6oz/¾ cup butter
4–6 garlic cloves
50g/2oz/1 cup fresh white
    breadcrumbs
15ml/1 tbsp chopped
    fresh parsley
juice of 1 lemon
brown bread, to serve

1 Wash the mussels in cold water. Pull off the beards, scrub the mussels well and scrape off any barnacles. Discard any mussels with broken shells, or those that do not close when sharply tapped on a hard surface.

2 Put the mussels into a shallow, heavy pan, without adding any liquid. Cover tightly and cook over a high heat for a few minutes, until all the mussels have opened. Discard any that fail to open.

3 Remove the top shell from each mussel and arrange the bottom shells with the mussels in a shallow flameproof dish.

4 Melt the butter in a small pan, add the crushed garlic, breadcrumbs, parsley and lemon juice. Mix well and sprinkle this mixture over the mussels.

5 Cook under a hot grill (broiler) until golden brown. Serve very hot, with freshly baked brown bread.

> **Cook's Tips**
> A glass of stout, such as Guinness, Beamish or Murphy's, goes down very well with these mussels.

Deep-fried Mussels in Beer Batter with Garlic-Flavoured Walnut Sauce

This recipe is a speciality from Istanbul and Izmir, where great vats of frying mussels are a familiar sight.

Serves 4–5
sunflower oil, for deep-frying
about 50 fresh mussels, cleaned,
    shelled and patted dry
    (see below)

For the batter
115g/4oz/1 cup plain
    (all-purpose) flour
5ml/1 tsp salt
2.5ml/½ tsp bicarbonate of soda
    (baking soda)

2 egg yolks
175–250ml/6–8fl oz/¾–1 cup
    beer or lager

For the sauce
75g/3oz/½ cup broken shelled
    walnuts
2 slices of day-old bread,
    sprinkled with water and left
    for a few minutes, then
    squeezed dry
2–3 garlic cloves, crushed
45–60ml/3–4 tbsp olive oil
juice of 1 lemon
dash of white wine vinegar
salt and ground black pepper

1 Make the batter. Sift the flour, salt and soda into a bowl. Make a well in the middle and add the egg yolks. Using a wooden spoon, beat in the beer and draw in the flour to make a smooth, thick batter. Set aside for 30 minutes.

2 Meanwhile, make the sauce. Pound the walnuts to a paste using a mortar and pestle, or whiz them in a blender. Add the bread and garlic, and pound to a paste. Drizzle in the olive oil, stirring all the time, and beat in the lemon juice and vinegar. The sauce should be smooth and thick – if it is too dry, stir in a little water. Season with salt and pepper and set aside.

3 Heat enough oil for deep-frying in a wok or other deep-sided pan. Dip each mussel into the batter and drop into the hot oil. Fry in batches for a minute or two until golden brown. Lift out with a slotted spoon and drain on kitchen paper.

4 Thread the mussels on wooden skewers and serve hot, accompanied by the garlic- flavoured dipping sauce.

Stuffed Mussels Energy 500Kcal/2082kJ; Protein 27.7g; Carbohydrate 10g, of which sugars 0.6g; Fat 39.2g, of which saturates 23.3g; Cholesterol 153mg; Calcium 319mg; Fibre 0.3g; Sodium 675mg.
Deep Fried Energy 439kcal/1827kJ; Protein 10.6g; Carbohydrate 24.6g, of which sugars 1.9g; Fat 33g, of which saturates 4g; Cholesterol 89mg; Calcium 115mg; Fibre 1.5g; Sodium 502mg.

Marinated Mussels

Large, ultra-fresh cultivated mussels, served raw on the half shell in a flavoursome vinaigrette, are a speciality of Brussels. They are particularly popular around the time of Brussel Kermis – Zuidfoor, an annual summer fair in the capital that lasts for one month, when locals and visitors are invited to sample mussels and escargots at several spots in the city, to celebrate the start of the new mussel season.

Serves 4–6

24 large live mussels, scrubbed
   and bearded
7.5ml/1½ tsp red wine vinegar or
   lemon juice
30ml/2 tbsp vegetable or olive oil
1 shallot, finely chopped
1 spring onion (scallion),
   finely chopped
1 medium ripe but firm tomato,
   finely chopped
salt and ground white pepper
30ml/2 tbsp freshly chopped
   parsley and 4–6 lemon wedges,
   to garnish
crusty bread, to serve

1 Discard any mussels that are not tightly closed, or which do not snap shut when sharply tapped. Holding a mussel firmly between the thumb and index finger of one hand, carefully lever it open from the side with a sharp, short-bladed knife. Insert the knife blade in the cavity and cut the muscle to which the mussel meat is attached. Work the knife blade around to free the mussel.

2 Place the mussel meat in a non-reactive bowl. Repeat the process with the remaining mussels. Wash and dry the mussel shells and reserve them.

3 In a separate bowl, whisk the vinegar or lemon juice with the oil. Season, then drizzle over the mussels. Fold in the shallot, spring onion and tomato. Cover and leave to marinate in the refrigerator for at least 1 hour.

4 To serve, arrange half the mussel shells on a large platter and place a marinated mussel on each, adding some tomato and onion from the marinade to each shell. Garnish the mussels with freshly chopped parsley and lemon wedges and serve with crusty bread.

Deep-fried Layered Shiitake and Scallops

In this dish, you can taste three kinds of softness: chewy shiitake, mashed naga-imo (a type of yam) with miso, and succulent scallop. The mixture creates a moment of heaven in your mouth.

Serves 4

4 scallops
8 large fresh shiitake mushrooms
225g/8oz naga-imo, unpeeled
20ml/4 tsp miso
50g/2oz/1 cup fresh breadcrumbs
cornflour (cornstarch), for dusting
vegetable oil, for deep-frying
2 eggs, beaten
salt
4 lemon wedges, to serve

1 Slice the scallops in two horizontally, then sprinkle with salt. Remove the stalks from the shiitake. Discard the stalks. Cut shallow slits on the top of the shiitake. Sprinkle with a little salt.

2 Heat a steamer and steam the naga-imo for 10–15 minutes, or until soft. Test with a skewer. Leave to cool. Wait until the naga-imo is cool enough to handle. Skin, then mash the flesh in a bowl with a masher, getting rid of any lumps. Add the miso and mix well. Take the breadcrumbs into your hands and break them down finely. Mix half into the mashed naga-imo, keeping the rest on a small plate.

3 Fill the underneath of the shiitake caps with a scoop of mashed naga-imo. Smooth down with the flat edge of a knife and dust the mash with cornflour. Add a little mash to a slice of scallop and place on top. Spread another 5ml/1 tsp mashed naga-imo on to the scallop and shape to completely cover. Make sure all the ingredients are clinging together. Repeat to make eight little mounds.

4 Heat the oil to 150°C/300°F. Place the beaten eggs in a shallow container. Dust the shiitake and scallop mounds with cornflour, then carefully dip into the egg. Coat well with the remaining breadcrumbs and deep-fry in the oil until golden. Drain well on kitchen paper. Serve hot with a wedge of lemon.

Marinated Mussels Energy 59kcal/246kJ; Protein 3.5g; Carbohydrate 1.8g, of which sugars 1.1g; Fat 4.3g, of which saturates 0.6g; Cholesterol 11mg; Calcium 14mg; Fibre 0.4g; Sodium 81mg.
Shiitake and Scallops Energy 221kcal/918kJ; Protein 11.2g; Carbohydrate 11.7g, of which sugars 1.5g; Fat 14.6g, of which saturates 2.3g; Cholesterol 107mg; Calcium 50mg; Fibre 1.1g; Sodium 183mg.

Steamed Scallops with Ginger, Spring Onion and Chives

Serve these juicy, fragrant scallops with their subtly spiced flavour as an indulgent main course for a special occasion. For the best results, use the freshest scallops you can find, and if you're worried about shucking them yourself, ask your fishmonger to do it for you.

Serves 4
24 king scallops in their
  shells, cleaned
15ml/1 tbsp very finely shredded
  fresh root ginger
5ml/1 tsp very finely
  chopped garlic
1 large red chilli, seeded and very
  finely chopped
15ml/1 tbsp light soy sauce
15ml/1 tbsp Chinese
  rice wine
a few drops of sesame oil
2–3 spring onions (scallions), very
  finely shredded
15ml/1 tbsp very finely chopped
  fresh chives
noodles or rice, to serve

1 Remove the scallops from their shells, then remove the membrane and hard white muscle from each one. Arrange the scallops on two plates. Rinse the shells, dry and set aside.

2 Fill two woks with 5cm/2in water and place a trivet in the base of each one. Bring to the boil.

3 Mix together the ginger, garlic, chilli, soy sauce, rice wine, sesame oil, spring onions and chives and spoon over the scallops.

4 Lower a plate of scallops into each of the woks. Turn the heat to low, cover and steam for 10–12 minutes, or until just cooked through. Divide the scallops among four, or eight, of the reserved shells and serve immediately with noodles or rice.

> **Cook's Tips**
> *An easy way to open scallops is to place them on a baking sheet in an oven preheated to 160°C/325°F/Gas 3 for a few moments, until they gape sufficiently to ease the shells apart.*

Spiced Clams

Spanish clams, especially in the North, are much larger than clams found elsewhere, and have more succulent bodies. This modern recipe uses Arab spicing to make a hot dip or sauce. Serve with plenty of fresh bread to mop up the delicious juices.

Serves 3–4
1 small onion, finely chopped
1 celery stick, sliced
2 garlic cloves, finely chopped
2.5cm/1in piece fresh root
  ginger, grated
30ml/2 tbsp olive oil
1.5ml/1/4 tsp chilli powder
5ml/1 tsp ground turmeric
30ml/2 tbsp chopped
  fresh parsley
500g/11/4lb small clams, in
  the shell
30ml/2 tbsp dry white wine
salt and ground black pepper
celery leaves, to garnish
fresh bread, to serve

1 Place the onion, celery, garlic and ginger in a large pan, add the olive oil, spices and chopped parsley and stir-fry for about 5 minutes. Add the clams to the pan and cook for 2 minutes.

2 Add the wine, then cover and cook gently for 2–3 minutes, shaking the pan occasionally. Season. Discard any clams that remain closed, then serve, garnished with the celery leaves.

> **Cook's Tips**
> • *There are many different varieties of clams fished off both coasts of Spain, and they are common fare in that country. There are many varieties; one of the best is the almeja fina (the carpet shell clam), which is perfect for this dish.*
> *They have grooved brown shells with a yellow lattice pattern. One of the largest clams is the concha fina, which measures 8cm/3in across.*
> • *Before cooking the clams, check that all the shells are closed. Any clams that do not open after cooking should be discarded.*
> • *Small clams can be opened in the microwave. Place them in a large bowl and cook on full power for 2 minutes. Remove opened mollusks and repeat until all are opened.*

Steamed Scallops Energy 157kcal/664kJ; Protein 29g; Carbohydrate 5g, of which sugars 1g; Fat 3g, of which saturates 1g; Cholesterol 56mg; Calcium 41mg; Fibre 0g; Sodium 432mg.
Spiced Clams Energy 126kcal/526kJ; Protein 12.5g; Carbohydrate 4.5g, of which sugars 2.2g; Fat 6g, of which saturates 0.9g; Cholesterol 50mg; Calcium 69mg; Fibre 0.6g; Sodium 906mg.

Classic Irish Oysters

The best native Irish oysters come from the Galway area on the west coast and, every September, festivals are held in Galway and Clarenbridge to celebrate the beginning of the new season. Dulse or dillisk, an edible seaweed, is an ideal garnish. Enjoy the oysters with freshly made brown soda bread and butter, and a glass of Guinness.

Serves 2–4
24 Galway oysters, in the shell
crushed ice and dulse or dillisk
*   (soaked if dried), to garnish*
soda bread and butter, and lemon
*   wedges, to serve*

1 Use a blunt-ended oyster knife or a strong knife with a short, blunt blade to shuck the oysters: insert the end of the knife between the shells near the hinge and work it until you cut through the muscle that holds the shells together. Catch the oyster liquid in a bowl.

2 When the oysters are all open, discard the flat shells. Divide the oysters, in the deep halves, among four serving plates lined with crushed ice and soaked dulse.

3 Strain the reserved liquid over the oysters. Serve with soda bread and butter and the lemon wedges.

Cook's Tips
• *Although they were once plentiful, Galway oysters are now a delicacy. They are eaten raw – buy them with their shells tightly clamped together, showing that they are still alive. The edible seaweed, dulse, or dillisk as it is also known, is an appropriate garnish for oysters.*
• *If you want oysters for a cooked dish, look for the widely cultivated, larger Pacific oysters, which are available all year round, unlike the native oyster which is found only when there's an 'r' in the month. Native oysters are named after their place of origin, such as the Irish Galway, the English Whitstable, Helford and Colchester. In America the best known of the eastern and Atlantic oysters is the Blue Point.*

Steamed Oysters with Zesty Tomato and Cucumber Salsa

A plate of lightly steamed fresh oysters makes a delicious appetizer for a special occasion. The fresh, zesty, aromatic salsa complements the delicate flavour and texture of the oysters perfectly and each irresistible mouthful feels like the ultimate indulgence.

Serves 4
12–16 oysters
30ml/2 tbsp sunflower oil

1 garlic clove, crushed
15ml/1 tbsp light soy sauce
sea salt, to serve

For the salsa
1 ripe plum tomato
1/2 small cucumber
1/4 small red onion
15ml/1 tbsp very finely chopped
*   coriander (cilantro)*
1 small red chilli, seeded and very
*   finely chopped*
juice of 1–2 limes
salt and ground black pepper

1 First prepare the salsa. Halve the tomato and remove the seeds, then finely dice the tomato, cucumber and red onion. Place in a bowl with the chopped coriander and red chilli. Add the lime juice and season to taste. Set aside (at room temperature) for 15–20 minutes.

2 Scrub the oyster shells under cold running water. Wrap one hand in a clean dish towel and hold the oyster with the cupped shell down and the narrow hinged end toward you. Using a special oyster knife or a strong knife with a short, blunt blade, push the point of the knife into the gap between the shells until the hinge breaks. Pull up the top shell. Sever the muscle that joins the oyster to the shell and lift off the top shell.

3 Arrange the oysters in their half shells in a bamboo steamer (using several tiers if necessary). Mix together the sunflower oil, garlic and soy sauce and spoon over the oysters.

4 Cover and place over a wok of simmering water (making sure it does not touch the water). Steam the oysters for 2–3 minutes, or until slightly firm on the outside. Arrange on a bed of sea salt, top each oyster with salsa and serve immediately.

Irish Oysters Energy 78Kcal/330kJ; Protein 13g; Carbohydrate 3.3g, of which sugars 0g; Fat 1.6g, of which saturates 0.3g; Cholesterol 68mg; Calcium 168mg; Fibre 0g; Sodium 612mg.
Steamed Oysters Energy 82kcal/339kJ; Protein 4.5g; Carbohydrate 2.4g, of which sugars 1.3g; Fat 6.1g, of which saturates 0.8g; Cholesterol 21mg; Calcium 60mg; Fibre 0.4g; Sodium 461mg.

Oysters Rockefeller

This is the perfect dish for those who prefer to eat their oysters lightly cooked. As a cheaper alternative, for those who are not as rich as Rockefeller, give mussels or clams the same treatment; they will also taste delicious.

Serves 6

450g/1lb/3 cups coarse sea salt, plus extra to serve
24 oysters, opened
115g/4oz/½ cup butter
2 shallots, finely chopped
500g/1¼lb spinach leaves, finely chopped
60ml/4 tbsp chopped fresh parsley
60ml/4 tbsp chopped celery leaves
90ml/6 tbsp fresh white or wholemeal (whole-wheat) breadcrumbs
10–20ml/2–4 tsp vodka
cayenne pepper
sea salt and ground black pepper
lemon or lime wedges, to serve

1 Preheat the oven to 220°C/425°F/Gas 7. Make a bed of coarse salt on two large baking sheets. Set the oysters in the half-shell in the bed of salt to keep them steady. Set aside.

2 Melt the butter in a large frying pan. Add the chopped shallots and cook them, stirring occasionally, over low heat for about 2–3 minutes until they are softened but not coloured. Stir in the spinach and let it wilt.

3 Add the parsley, celery leaves and breadcrumbs to the pan and fry gently for 5 minutes. Season with salt, ground black pepper and cayenne pepper.

4 Divide the stuffing among the oysters. Drizzle a few drops of vodka over each oyster. Bake in the preheated oven for about 5 minutes until the oysters are bubbling and golden brown. Serve on a heated platter on a shallow salt bed with lemon or lime wedges.

> **Cook's Tip**
> Frozen chopped spinach can be used. Thaw it in a colander over a bowl and press out as much liquid as possible.

Lemon, Chilli and Herb Steamed Razor Clams

Razor clams have beautiful striped gold and brown tubular shells and make a wonderful appetizer for a special meal. Here they are lightly steamed and tossed in a fragrant Italian-style dressing of chilli, lemon, garlic and parsley. It really is a marriage made in heaven. Serve with crusty bread for mopping up the juices. To serve as a main course, simply double the quantity.

Serves 4

12 razor clams
90–120ml/6–8 tbsp extra virgin olive oil
finely grated rind and juice of 1 small lemon
2 garlic cloves, very finely grated
1 red chilli, seeded and very finely chopped
60ml/4 tbsp chopped flat leaf parsley
salt and ground black pepper
mixed salad leaves and crusty bread, to serve

1 Wash the razor clams well in plenty of cold running water. Drain and arrange half the clams in a steamer, with the hinge-side downward.

2 Pour 5cm/2in water into a wok and bring to the boil. Carefully balance the steamer over the water and cover tightly. Steam for 3–4 minutes, or until the clams have fully opened. Carefully remove the clams from the wok and keep warm while you steam the remaining clams in the same way.

3 In a bowl, mix together the olive oil, grated lemon rind and juice, garlic, red chilli and chopped flat leaf parsley. Season well with salt and pepper. Spoon the mixture over the steamed clams and serve immediately with a crisp mixed-leaf salad and crusty bread.

> **Variation**
> You can use Venus clams or mussels in place of the razor shells if you prefer. You will need about 1kg/2¼lb. Clean the clams or mussels well before cooking.

Oysters Rockefeller Energy 210kcal/867kJ; Protein 6.4g; Carbohydrate 3.4g, of which sugars 2.1g; Fat 17g, of which saturates 10.1g; Cholesterol 60mg; Calcium 211mg; Fibre 2.3g; Sodium 406mg.
Razor Clams Energy 188kcal/775kJ; Protein 6.1g; Carbohydrate 2.9g, of which sugars 0.5g; Fat 16.9g, of which saturates 2.4g; Cholesterol 20mg; Calcium 47mg; Fibre 1.1g; Sodium 364mg.

Estonian Cod Salad with Horseradish and Dill

Fish is a frequent ingredient in salads from the Baltic region. Poaching, rather than frying fish, is most typical. When served with a light horseradish and dill sauce, this dish tastes marvellous.

Serves 4
675g/1½lb cod fillets
30ml/2 tbsp lemon juice
1 cucumber, thinly sliced
200g/7oz watercress or
    rocket (arugula)

For the dressing
10ml/2 tsp creamed horseradish
120ml/4fl oz/½ cup sour cream
15ml/1 tbsp mayonnaise
4 spring onions (scallions),
    finely chopped
small bunch of dill, finely chopped
salt and ground black pepper

1 Put the cod in a large frying pan and just cover with water. Bring to the boil and simmer for 4 minutes, or until cooked through. Test with a point of a knife; the flesh should flake easily and be milky white. Lift out of the pan, drain and put on a plate.

2 When the fish is cool enough to handle, remove and discard the skin. Gently break the fish into chunky flakes and drizzle with lemon juice.

3 To make the dressing, put the creamed horseradish in a bowl and stir in the sour cream, mayonnaise, onions and dill. Season with salt and pepper.

4 In a large bowl, gently combine the fish, cucumber, watercress or rocket and the dressing. Serve immediately while the fish is juicy and the salad leaves are crunchy.

> **Cook's Tip**
> *Most fairly firm fish can be used in place of the cod. Fish that are flavourful, such as herrings or smoked haddock are particular favourites.*

Cold Cod Salad

This salad, with its golden top, was created during the Soviet era when there was a shortage of food. If nothing else, cod, carrots and onions were always to be found in the supermarket 'Gastronom'. The salad is best if chilled overnight, so make it in advance.

Serves 6–8
600g/1lb 6oz cod fillets, skinned
5ml/1 tsp salt
4–5 black peppercorns
1 bay leaf
200ml/7fl oz/scant 1 cup
    rapeseed (canola) oil
3 large onions, diced
3 large carrots, grated
45ml/3 tbsp water
200g/7oz/scant 1 cup
    mayonnaise

1 Put the cod fillets in a pan and add water to just cover. Add the salt, peppercorns and bay leaf, bring gently to the boil then reduce the heat and simmer for 5–10 minutes. Drain and leave to cool.

2 Heat half of the oil in a large frying pan. Add the onions and fry, stirring, until golden brown. Remove from the pan and set aside to cool.

3 Heat the remaining oil in the frying pan, add the grated carrots and fry over medium heat, stirring, for 10 minutes. Pour in the water and continue cooking for 5–10 minutes, until the water has evaporated. Set aside.

4 Divide the cooled fish into small chunks, removing all bones, and spread on a large serving dish. Cover the fish with the onions and spread the carrots on top. Cover with mayonnaise. Chill for 2–3 hours or overnight before serving.

> **Variations**
> • *As an alternative, you can substitute the cod with perch, pike or other white fish.*
> • *Add other vegetables if you wish, such as spinach and broccoli and sprinkle with fresh chopped dill and parsley.*

Estonian Salad Energy 239kcal/997kJ; Protein 33.7g; Carbohydrate 2.1g, of which sugars 2.1g; Fat 10.6g, of which saturates 4.5g; Cholesterol 98mg; Calcium 137mg; Fibre 1.1g; Sodium 159mg.
Cold Cod Salad Energy 528kcal/2179kJ; Protein 15.3g; Carbohydrate 9.5g, of which sugars 7.5g; Fat 47.9g, of which saturates 6.6g; Cholesterol 63mg; Calcium 38mg; Fibre 2g; Sodium 225mg.

Whitefish, Celery and Onion Salad

Smoked whitefish is one of the glories of deli food and, made into a salad with mayonnaise and sour cream, it becomes indispensable as a brunch dish. Eat it with a stack of bagels, pumpernickel or rye bread. If you can't find smoked whitefish, use any other smoked firm white fish such as halibut or cod.

Serves 4–6

1 smoked whitefish, skinned and boned
2 celery sticks, chopped
½ red, white or yellow onion or 3–5 spring onions (scallions), chopped
45ml/3 tbsp mayonnaise
45ml/3 tbsp sour cream or Greek (US strained plain) yogurt
juice of ½–1 lemon
1 round lettuce
ground black pepper
5–10ml/1–2 tsp chopped fresh parsley, to garnish

1 Break the smoked whitefish into bitesize pieces. In a bowl, mix the celery, onion or spring onion, mayonnaise, and sour cream or yogurt, and add lemon juice to taste.

2 Fold the fish into the mixture and season with pepper. Arrange the lettuce leaves on serving plates, then spoon the salad on top. Serve chilled, sprinkled with chopped fresh parsley.

Cook's Tip

Whitefish is a member of the salmon family; it is silvery white and resembles trout. It is found in lakes and streams in North America and northern Europe, is available frozen and smoked, and the flavour and texture is pleasant. It is traditionally available smoked in Jewish delicatessens, where it is served with bagels, pumpernickel or rye bread, and cucumber salad. For centuries, it was dried and traded around the world. In the UK, whitefish may be a term used for other white fish such as cod, haddock, whiting or pollack, which are often smoked.

Soused Fish with Onions

This delicious dish, also known as 'escabeche', is at least five centuries old, and uses the preserving technique of boiling onions with vinegar. Here it is eaten as soon as it has cooled.

Serves 4

2 medium onions, thickly sliced lengthways
500ml/17fl oz/generous 2 cups water
175ml/6fl oz/¾ cup wine vinegar
500g/1¼lb firm-textured fish fillets, such as sea bass, bream, cod or haddock
115g/4oz plain (all-purpose) flour
200ml/7fl oz/scant 1 cup vegetable oil
4 garlic cloves, finely chopped
2 red chillies, seeded and sliced lengthways
30ml/2 tbsp red chilli sauce
2.5ml/½ tsp ground cumin
salt and ground black pepper

To accompany:

2 medium sweet potatoes
lettuce leaves
kalamata-type olives
115g/4oz feta cheese, crumbled
2 hard-boiled eggs, sliced

1 Put the onions in a pan with the water, 50ml/2fl oz/¼ cup of the vinegar and a pinch of salt. Bring to the boil, simmer for 2 minutes, then remove from the heat, drain and set aside.

2 Cut the fish into four portions. Season the flour with pepper and salt and toss the fish in it.

3 Heat 150ml/¼ pint/⅔ cup of the oil in a frying pan over medium heat and fry the fish for 6 minutes on each side, until cooked through. Remove and arrange them in a shallow dish.

4 Add the remaining oil to the frying pan over medium-high heat and fry the garlic until golden. Add the onions, the sliced chillies, chilli sauce and cumin, stir and add the rest of the vinegar. Season to taste. Remove from the heat and pour the contents of the pan over the fish. Leave to cool.

5 Cook the sweet potatoes in boiling water for 25 minutes, until they are tender. Drain, peel and slice. Serve each portion of fish with lettuce, some of the sauce and slices of sweet potato. Garnish with olives, feta and slices of hard-boiled eggs.

Whitefish Energy 112kcal/469kJ; Protein 10.1g; Carbohydrate 1g, of which sugars 1g; Fat 7.6g, of which saturates 1.9g; Cholesterol 28mg; Calcium 29mg; Fibre 0.3g; Sodium 421mg.
Soused Fish Energy 414kcal/1720kJ; Protein 41.9g; Carbohydrate 1.3g, of which sugars 1g; Fat 26.7g, of which saturates 3.2g; Cholesterol 104mg; Calcium 30mg; Fibre 0.2g; Sodium 137mg.

Cambodian Raw Fish Salad

Sweet-fleshed freshwater fish and shellfish are often eaten raw in Cambodia, plucked straight from the water, or tossed in a marinade. Wrapped in a lettuce leaf with extra leafy herbs, or served with noodles, this Cambodian salad, koy pa, is light and delicious.

Serves 4-6

450g/1lb white fish, such as sole or plaice
juice of 4 limes
30ml/2 tbsp tuk trey
4 spring onions (scallions), finely sliced
2 garlic cloves, finely sliced
1 fresh red chilli, seeded and finely sliced
1 small bunch fresh coriander (cilantro), stalks removed
lettuce leaves, to serve

1 Either fillet and skin the fish yourself, or ask your fishmonger to do it for you. Using a sharp knife, slice the fish into serving portions.

2 Place the sliced fish in a large glass bowl. Pour over the juice of 3 limes and toss well, making sure all the fish is coated Cover and chill in the refrigerator for 24 hours.

3 Drain the fish, discarding the liquid. Pat dry on kitchen towels.

4 Place in a clean bowl with the juice of the remaining lime, the tuk trey, spring onions, garlic, chilli and fresh coriander leaves.

5 Toss well together and serve with lettuce leaves.

Cook's Tip
Tuk trey is a Cambodian salad dressing made from fish sauce, vinegar, lime juice, sugar, salt, shallots and garlic. Tuk trey is very versatile; with the addition of chillies, it can also be adapted to make a dipping sauce, and the taste can be changed by varying the amount of fish sauce added to the dressing. Fish sauce, made from salted, fermented fish, is a strong liquid flavouring that is used in many south-east Asian cuisines.

Beansprouts with Salt Fish

This simple peasant dish has been elevated to gourmet status. The cardinal rule is to use the best salt fish available, ideally salted fillets of snapper or an expensive tropical fish called threadfin (ma yeow yu in Cantonese). If this is not obtainable, the closest substitute is salt cod.

Serves 4

100g/3¾oz salt fish fillet
60ml/4 tbsp vegetable oil
600g/1lb 6oz/2⅓ cups beansprouts
2 spring onions (scallions)
30ml/2 tbsp crushed garlic
15ml/1 tbsp light soy sauce

1 If you are using salt cod, soak it in water for at least 48 hours, changing the water frequently. Rinse the fish and pat dry on kitchen paper.

2 Cut the salt fish into small chunks. Heat the oil in a wok and fry the pieces of salt fish until they are fragrant and slightly brittle. With a slotted spoon, transfer them to a board. Let them cool slightly, then shred them roughly.

3 Wash the beansprouts, drain them thoroughly and remove any green husks. Cut the spring onions into 5cm/2in lengths.

4 Pour off all but 30ml/2 tbsp of the oil from the wok. Heat the remaining oil and fry the garlic until golden brown. Add the beansprouts and salt fish and stir rapidly for 2 minutes.

5 Add the spring onions and stir-fry for 1 minute. Drizzle over the soy sauce, stir for 1 minute more and serve immediately.

Cook's Tip
• Store beansprouts in the refrigerator and do not use them if they have turned dark or slimy. Rinse them thoroughly in cold running water before cooking them.
• Beansprouts are rich in vitamins A, and C as well as containing fibre and minerals.

Raw Fish Salad Energy 66Kcal/280kJ; Protein 14g; Carbohydrate 1.2g, of which sugars 1.1g; Fat 0.6g, of which saturates 0.1g; Cholesterol 35mg; Calcium 11mg; Fibre 0.2g; Sodium 402mg.
Salt Fish Energy 185kcal/772kJ; Protein 13.2g; Carbohydrate 6.5g, of which sugars 3.7g; Fat 12.1g, of which saturates 1.5g; Cholesterol 0mg; Calcium 68mg; Fibre 2.3g; Sodium 2157mg.

Smoked Trout Salad

Horseradish is as good a partner to smoked trout as it is to roast beef. In this recipe it is mixed with yogurt, mustard powder, oil and vinegar to make a deliciously piquant light salad dressing that complements the smoked trout perfectly.

Serves 4

1 oakleaf or other red lettuce
225g/8oz small tomatoes, cut into
   thin wedges
½ cucumber, peeled and
   thinly sliced
4 smoked trout fillets, each about
   200g/7oz, skinned and flaked

For the dressing
pinch of mustard powder
15–20ml/3–4 tsp white
   wine vinegar
30ml/2 tbsp light olive oil
100ml/3½fl oz/scant ½ cup
   natural (plain) yogurt
about 30ml/2 tbsp grated fresh or
   bottled horseradish
pinch of caster (superfine) sugar

1 Make the dressing. Mix the mustard powder and white wine vinegar in a bowl until smooth, then gradually whisk in the olive oil, yogurt, horseradish and sugar. Set aside for 30 minutes to allow all the flavours to develop.

2 Place the lettuce leaves in a large bowl. Stir the dressing again, then pour half of it over the leaves and toss them lightly using two wooden spoons.

3 Arrange the lettuce on four individual plates with the tomatoes, cucumber and trout. Spoon over the remaining dressing and serve immediately.

Cook's Tip
• Fresh grated horseradish varies in potency. It is pungently spicy, but if it is very strong, whisk only half the suggested amount into the dressing. If the only horseradish you can find is the creamed variety, you can still use it in the recipe, but mix it with the yogurt first.
• Dried horseradish is available but must be reconstituted before using.

Spiced Trout Salad

Most of the preparation for this delicious salad is done in advance so it is an ideal dish to come home to after a day on the beach or an afternoon walk. The trout is marinated in a mixture of coriander, ginger and chilli and served with cold baby roast potatoes.

Serves 4

2.5cm/1in piece fresh root ginger,
   peeled and finely grated
1 garlic clove, crushed
5ml/1 tsp hot chilli
   powder, optional
15ml/1 tbsp coriander seeds,
   lightly crushed
grated rind and juice of
   2 lemons
60ml/4 tbsp olive oil
450g/1lb trout fillet, skinned
900g/2lb new potatoes
5–10ml/1–2 tsp sea salt
ground black pepper
15ml/1 tbsp whole or
   chopped fresh chives,
   to garnish

1 Mix the ginger, garlic, chilli powder, if using, coriander seeds and lemon rind in a bowl. Whisk in the lemon juice with 15ml/1 tbsp of the olive oil to make a marinade.

2 Place the trout in a shallow, non-metallic dish and cover with the marinade. Turn the fish to make sure they are well coated, cover with clear film (plastic wrap) and chill for at least 2 hours or overnight.

3 Preheat the oven to 200°C/400°F/Gas 6. Place the potatoes in a roasting pan, toss them in 30ml/2 tbsp olive oil and season with salt and pepper. Roast for 45 minutes or until tender. Remove from the oven and set aside to cool.

4 Reduce the oven temperature to 190°C/375°F/Gas 5. Remove the trout from the marinade and place in a roasting pan. Bake for 20 minutes or until cooked through. Remove from the oven and leave to cool.

5 Cut the potatoes into chunks, flake the trout into bitesize pieces and toss the potatoes and fish together in a serving dish with the remaining olive oil. Sprinkle with the chives and serve.

Smoked Trout Energy 334kcal/1405kJ; Protein 50g; Carbohydrate 3g, of which sugars 3g; Fat 14g, of which saturates 3g; Cholesterol 168mg; Calcium 73mg; Fibre 2g; Sodium 123mg.
Spiced Trout Energy 437kcal/1834kJ; Protein 26g; Carbohydrate 37g, of which sugars 3g; Fat 22g, of which saturates 4g; Cholesterol 75mg; Calcium 41mg; Fibre 3g; Sodium 574mg.

Smoked Trout Pasta Salad

Choose hollow pasta shapes, such as shells or penne, which trap the creamy filling, creating tasty mouthfuls of trout, fennel and spring onion. The addition of dill is not only attractive, but also gives this salad a distinctive fresh flavour.

Serves 8
15g/¹/₂oz/1 tbsp butter
1 bulb fennel, finely chopped

6 spring onions (scallions),
   2 very finely chopped
   and 4 thinly sliced
225g/8oz smoked trout fillets,
   skinned and flaked
45ml/3 tbsp chopped fresh dill
120ml/4fl oz/¹/₂ cup
   mayonnaise
10ml/2 tsp lemon juice
30ml/2 tbsp whipping cream
450g/1lb small pasta shapes,
   such as shells
salt and ground black pepper
fresh dill sprigs, to garnish

1 Melt the butter in a small frying pan. Add the fennel and finely chopped spring onions and fry over a medium heat for 3–5 minutes. Transfer to a large bowl and leave to cool slightly.

2 Add the sliced spring onions, the flaked trout, dill, mayonnaise, lemon juice and cream to the bowl with the fennel. Season the mixture lightly with salt and pepper and mix gently until well blended together.

3 Bring a large pan of lightly salted water to the boil. Add the pasta. Cook according to the instructions on the packet until the pasta is al dente. Drain thoroughly in a colander and leave to cool.

4 Add the pasta to the vegetable and trout mixture and toss to coat evenly. Taste for seasoning. Serve the salad lightly chilled or at room temperature, garnished with the sprigs of dill.

Cook's Tip
This pasta salad works well with any type of fresh, cooked fish fillets, including salmon. Alternatively, you can use a 200g/7oz can of tuna in water in place of the trout.

Smoked Trout and Noodle Salad

It is important to use ripe juicy tomatoes for this fresh-tasting salad. For a special occasion you could replace the smoked trout with smoked salmon.

Serves 4
225g/8oz somen noodles
2 smoked trout, skinned
   and boned
2 hard-boiled eggs, chopped

30ml/2 tbsp snipped chives
lime halves, to serve (optional)

For the dressing
6 ripe plum tomatoes
2 shallots, finely chopped
30ml/2 tbsp tiny capers, rinsed
30ml/2 tbsp chopped
   fresh tarragon
finely grated rind and juice
   of ¹/₂ orange
60ml/4 tbsp extra virgin olive oil
salt and ground black pepper

1 To make the dressing, cut the tomatoes in half, remove the cores, and cut the flesh into chunks.

2 Place in a bowl with the shallots, capers, tarragon, orange rind, orange juice and olive oil. Season with salt and ground black pepper, and mix well. Leave the dressing to marinate at room temperature for 1–2 hours.

3 Cook the noodles in a large saucepan of boiling water until just tender. Drain and rinse under cold running water. Drain again well.

4 Toss the noodles with the tomato and onion dressing, then add salt and ground black pepper to taste. Arrange the noodles on a large serving platter or individual plates.

5 Flake the smoked trout over the noodles, then sprinkle the coarsely chopped eggs and snipped chives over the top. Serve the lime halves on the side, if you like.

Cook's Tip
Choose tomatoes that are firm, bright in colour and have a matt texture, avoiding any with blotched or cracked skins.

Trout Pasta Energy 369kcal/1548kJ; Protein 14.5g; Carbohydrate 42.7g, of which sugars 2.8g; Fat 16.8g, of which saturates 4g; Cholesterol 29mg; Calcium 31mg; Fibre 2.3g; Sodium 613mg.
Trout Noodle Energy 369kcal/1548kJ; Protein 14.5g; Carbohydrate 42.7g, of which sugars 2.8g; Fat 16.8g, of which saturates 4g; Cholesterol 29mg; Calcium 31mg; Fibre 2.3g; Sodium 613mg.

Trout and Ginger Salad

Fresh griddled trout and smoked trout are delicious on their own. Put them together, add a ginger dressing and you have a sensational first course that is easy to prepare.

Serves 4

15ml/1 tbsp olive oil
115g/4oz trout fillet, skinned
grated rind and juice of ½ lime
1 yellow (bell) pepper, finely chopped
1 red (bell) pepper, finely chopped
1 small bunch fresh coriander (cilantro), chopped
115g/4oz rocket (arugula)
115g/4oz smoked trout
ground black pepper

For the dressing

15ml/1 tbsp sesame oil
75ml/5 tbsp white wine vinegar
5ml/1 tsp soy sauce
2.5cm/1in piece fresh root ginger, peeled and grated

1 Heat a griddle pan, brush it with the oil, then fry the trout fillet for 5–8 minutes, until it is just cooked. Lift the fillet out of the pan and place it in a shallow bowl. Flake the trout into bitesize pieces, sprinkle the lime rind and juice over and set aside.

2 Make the dressing by mixing the sesame oil, vinegar, soy sauce and grated root ginger in a small jug (pitcher). Whisk thoroughly until the dressing is well combined.

3 Place the chopped yellow and red peppers, coriander and rocket in a large bowl and toss to combine. Transfer the salad to a serving dish.

4 Using kitchen scissors, cut the smoked trout into bitesize pieces. Arrange the smoked trout and griddled trout fillet on the salad. Sprinkle with black pepper. Whisk the ginger dressing again and drizzle it over the salad before serving.

> **Variation**
> *If you cannot find trout or smoked trout, use fresh salmon fillets and hot smoked salmon for a delicious change.*

Garlic Baked Trout with Avocado Salad

Packed full of flavour and with plenty of vitamins and minerals, this baked trout is a versatile main dish. Serve it with new potatoes, or cold with country bread.

Serves 4

6 plum tomatoes, halved
2 garlic cloves, thinly sliced
15g/½oz/½ cup fresh basil leaves
45ml/3 tbsp olive oil
4 trout fillets, each about 200g/7oz, skinned
2 avocados
juice of 1 lime
75g/3oz watercress
salt and ground black pepper
lime wedges, to garnish

1 Preheat the oven to 180°C/350°F/Gas 4. Place the tomatoes on a baking tray lined with baking parchment. Sprinkle the garlic and basil over the tomatoes and season well with black pepper. Drizzle 15ml/1 tbsp of the olive oil over and bake for 25 minutes. Remove from the oven.

2 Move the tomato halves closer together, if necessary, to make room for the trout. Place the fillets on the baking tray. Return the tray to the oven for a further 15 minutes. Test the fish with a fork to check it is cooked: if the flesh flakes easily it is ready. Remove the baking tray from the oven.

3 Meanwhile, cut the avocados in half, remove the stone (pit) and peel, then slice the flesh lengthways. In a small jug (pitcher), whisk the lime juice with the remaining olive oil. Season.

4 Divide the watercress among four individual serving plates. Top with the avocado slices. Drizzle the lime dressing over.

5 Using a fish slice, lift the cooked trout fillets carefully off the baking tray and place them on a board.

6 Arrange the cooked tomatoes over the watercress and pour over any cooking juices. Flake the trout into bitesize pieces and divide among the plates, arranging it attractively among the salad leaves. Garnish the plates with the lime wedges and serve.

Trout and Ginger Energy 178kcal/744kJ; Protein 13g; Carbohydrate 6g, of which sugars 5g; Fat 11g, of which saturates 2g; Cholesterol 40mg; Calcium 39mg; Fibre 2g; Sodium 125mg.
Garlic Trout Energy 178kcal/744kJ; Protein 13g; Carbohydrate 6g, of which sugars 5g; Fat 11g, of which saturates 2g; Cholesterol 40mg; Calcium 39mg; Fibre 2g; Sodium 125mg.

Marinated Salmon with Avocado

Use only the freshest of salmon for this delicious salad. The marinade of lemon and dashi-konbu 'cooks' the salmon.

Serves 4
250g/9oz very fresh salmon tail, skinned and filleted
juice of 1 lemon
10cm/4in dashi-konbu (seaweed), wiped with a damp cloth and cut into 4 strips
1 ripe avocado

4 shiso leaves, trimmed and cut in half lengthways
about 115g/4oz mixed leaves such as lamb's lettuce, frisée or rocket (arugula)
45ml/3 tbsp flaked (sliced) almonds, toasted until just slightly browned

For the miso mayonnaise
90ml/6 tbsp good-quality mayonnaise
15ml/1 tbsp shiro miso
ground black pepper

1 Cut the first salmon fillet in half crossways at the tail end where the fillet is not wider than 4cm/1½in. Next, cut the wider part in half lengthways. Cut the other fillet in the same way.

2 Pour the lemon juice and two of the dashi-konbu pieces into a wide shallow plastic container. Lay the salmon fillets in the base and sprinkle with the rest of the dashi-konbu. Marinate for 15 minutes, then turn once and leave for a further 15 minutes. The salmon should change to a pink 'cooked' colour. Remove from the marinade and wipe with kitchen paper.

3 Cut the salmon into 5mm/¼in thick slices against the grain. Halve the avocado and sprinkle with a little of the remaining marinade. Remove the avocado stone (pit), then slice to the same thickness as the salmon.

4 Mix the miso mayonnaise ingredients together. Spread 5ml/1 tsp on to the back of each of the shiso leaves, then mix the remainder with 15ml/1 tbsp of the marinade.

5 Arrange the salad on four plates. Top with the avocado, salmon, shiso leaves and almonds, and drizzle over the remaining miso mayonnaise.

Smoked Fish Salad

Oily fish – such as salmon, eels, sprats, perch, trout and herring – are well suited to being smoked. The fish used in this recipe are hot-smoked, a process that involves cooking and smoking the fish simultaneously over chips of burning wood (such as alder, apple or juniper) or, more recently, in an electric kiln. The smokiness and rich, oily flesh of the cooked fish is particularly suited to sharp dressings and pungent, relish-type sauces, such as this simple horseradish and mustard dressing.

Serves 4
500g/1¼lb smoked eel fillet
5ml/1 tsp Swedish mustard
5ml/1 tsp grated fresh horseradish
about 50ml/2fl oz/¼ cup double (heavy) cream
4 smoked sprat fillets
ground black pepper
lettuce and boiled new potatoes, to serve

For the dressing
100ml/3½fl oz/scant ½ cup double (heavy) cream
5ml/1 tsp mustard
5ml/1 tsp grated fresh horseradish
a little lemon juice

1 Remove the skin from the smoked eel by peeling it off with your fingers, much as you would skin a banana. Place the skinned, smoked eel on a board and cut about half of it into four neat fillets. Set aside.

2 Put the remaining smoked eel fillet in a food processor, add the mustard and horseradish and season with pepper. Blend until smooth, adding enough cream to form a firm paste.

3 Spoon a dollop of the smoked eel paste or pâté on to a bed of lettuce on four individual serving plates.

4 Carefully remove the skin from the smoked sprats using a small, sharp knife, then arrange the skinned fish around the pâté, together with the reserved smoked eel fillets.

5 To make the dressing, whisk together the cream, mustard, horseradish and a few drops of lemon juice, until stiff. Spoon on to the salad and serve with boiled new potatoes.

Salmon with Avocado Energy 422kcal/1745kJ; Protein 16g; Carbohydrate 2.1g, of which sugars 1.47g; Fat 38.9g, of which saturates 5.9g; Cholesterol 48mg; Calcium 53mg; Fibre 2g; Sodium 133mg.
Smoked Fish Energy 487kcal/2021kJ; Protein 30.8g; Carbohydrate 0.9g, of which sugars 0.7g; Fat 40.2g, of which saturates 17.3g; Cholesterol 285mg; Calcium 94mg; Fibre 0g; Sodium 257mg.

Asparagus and Smoked Fish Salad

A mixture of white and green asparagus with cherry tomatoes makes this a colourful salad.

Serves 4

600g/1lb 6oz white asparagus, peeled and cut diagonally into 1cm/½in pieces
300g/11oz green asparagus, peeled and sliced as above
20ml/4 tsp sunflower oil
1 onion, finely sliced
15ml/1 tbsp cider vinegar
15ml/1 tbsp apple juice
10 cherry tomatoes, halved
400g/14oz mixed smoked fish (salmon, trout, mackerel or eel)

salt, ground white pepper, sugar
finely chopped parsley, to garnish

For the green sauce

200ml/7fl oz/scant 1 cup yogurt
200ml/7fl oz/scant 1 cup sour cream
5ml/1 tsp medium-hot mustard
juice of ½ lemon
2 hard-boiled eggs, separated into yolk and white
10ml/2 tsp sunflower oil
150g/5oz fresh herbs (chervil, parsley, chives, watercress, sorrel, borage and salad burnet), very finely chopped
salt, ground white pepper, sugar

1 Cook the asparagus in separate pans for 4–5 minutes or until just tender. Drain and refresh under cold running water. Put the white asparagus in a bowl and set the green aside.

2 Heat the oil in a frying pan over medium heat and cook the onions for 2 minutes. Add the vinegar and apple juice and season with salt, pepper and sugar. Bring to the boil and remove from the heat. Pour the hot dressing over the white asparagus. Stir in the tomatoes and marinate for 1–2 hours.

3 To make the green sauce, mix the yogurt with the sour cream, mustard and lemon juice and season to taste with salt, pepper and sugar. Mash the egg yolk with a fork and blend with the oil, then stir into the yogurt and cream mixture. Finely dice the egg white and stir it into the dressing, with the herbs.

4 Drain the asparagus and tomatoes from the dressing and toss with the green asparagus and the chopped parsley. Arrange the salad on serving plates, surrounded by the sliced or flaked smoked fish. Serve the sauce on the side.

New Year Raw Fish Salad

To celebrate the lunar New Year, Chinese families in Malaysia and Singapore get together to eat special dishes, such as yu sheng, a raw fish salad, to ensure good luck and abundance.

Serves 4–6

175g/6oz fresh tuna or salmon, finely sliced
115g/4oz white fish fillet, finely sliced
25g/1oz fresh root ginger, peeled and finely chopped
2 garlic cloves, crushed
juice of 2 limes
225g/8oz daikon (white radish), cut into julienne strips
2 carrots, cut into julienne strips
1 small cucumber, peeled, seeded and cut into julienne strips

4 spring onions (scallions), trimmed and cut into julienne strips
1 pomelo, segmented and sliced
4 fresh lime leaves, finely sliced
50g/2oz preserved sweet melon, finely sliced
50g/2oz preserved sweet red ginger, finely sliced
ground black pepper
30ml/2 tbsp roasted peanuts, coarsely crushed, to garnish

For the dressing

30ml/2 tbsp sesame oil
15ml/1 tbsp light soy sauce
15ml/1 tbsp red vinegar
30ml/2 tbsp sour plum sauce
2 garlic cloves, crushed
10ml/2 tsp sugar

1 In a shallow, non-metallic, dish, toss the fish in the ginger, garlic and lime juice. Season with black pepper and set aside for at least 30 minutes.

2 Place the julienne strips of daikon, carrots, cucumber, spring onions, pomelo and lime leaves in a large bowl. Add the preserved melon and ginger.

3 In a small bowl, mix together the ingredients for the dressing. Adjust the sweet and sour balance to taste.

4 Just before serving, arrange the marinated fish on top of the vegetables in the bowl. Pour the dressing over the salad and sprinkle with the roasted peanuts. Place the bowl in the middle of the table and let everyone toss the salad with their chopsticks.

Asparagus and Fish Energy 644kcal/2664kJ; Protein 34.2g; Carbohydrate 13.4g, of which sugars 12.5g; Fat 50.9g, of which saturates 14.4g; Cholesterol 230mg; Calcium 319mg; Fibre 6.1g; Sodium 864mg.
Raw Fish Salad Energy 126Kcal/528kJ; Protein 13.2g; Carbohydrate 6.5g, of which sugars 6.4g; Fat 5.4g, of which saturates 1g; Cholesterol 22mg; Calcium 36mg; Fibre 1.3g; Sodium 222mg.

Tuna Salad Niçoise

Made with the freshest of ingredients, this classic Provençal salad makes a simple yet unbeatable summer dish. Serve with country-style bread and chilled white wine.

Serves 4

115g/4oz French beans, trimmed
   and cut in half
115g/4oz mixed salad leaves
½ small cucumber, thinly sliced
4 ripe tomatoes, quartered

50g/2oz can anchovies, drained
   and halved lengthways
4 eggs, hard-boiled
1 tuna steak, about 175g/6oz
olive oil, for brushing
½ bunch small radishes, trimmed
50g/2oz/½ cup small
   black olives
salt and ground black pepper

For the dressing
90ml/6 tbsp extra virgin olive oil
2 garlic cloves, crushed
15ml/1 tbsp white wine vinegar

1 To make the dressing, whisk together the oil, garlic and vinegar and season to taste with salt and pepper. Set aside.

2 Cook the French beans in a saucepan of boiling water for about 2 minutes until just tender, then drain.

3 Mix together the salad leaves, sliced cucumber, tomatoes and French beans in a large, shallow bowl. Halve the anchovies lengthways and shell and quarter the eggs.

4 Preheat the grill. Brush the tuna steak with olive oil and sprinkle with salt and black pepper. Grill for 3–4 minutes on each side until cooked through. Allow to cool, then flake with a fork.

5 Scatter the flaked tuna, anchovies, quartered eggs, radishes and olives over the salad. Pour over the dressing and toss together lightly to combine. Serve at once.

> **Cook's Tip**
> *Opinions vary on whether salad Niçoise should include potatoes but, if you like, include small cooked new potatoes.*

Red Rice Salad Niçoise

Red rice, with its sweet nuttiness, goes well in this classic salad.

Serves 6

675g/1½lb fresh tuna steaks
350g/12oz/1¾ cups Camargue
   red rice, cooked
fish or vegetable stock or water
450g/1lb French beans
450g/1lb broad beans, shelled
1 cos lettuce heart, torn
450g/1lb cherry tomatoes, halved
30ml/2 tbsp coarsely chopped
   fresh coriander
3 hard-boiled eggs, shelled
175g/6oz/1½ cups black olives
olive oil, for brushing

For the marinade
1 red onion, roughly chopped
2 garlic cloves
½ bunch fresh parsley
½ bunch fresh coriander
10ml/2 tsp paprika
45ml/3 tbsp olive oil
45ml/3 tbsp water
30ml/2 tbsp white wine vinegar
15ml/1 tbsp lime or lemon juice
salt and ground black pepper

For the dressing
30ml/2 tbsp lime or lemon juice
5ml/1 tsp Dijon mustard
½ garlic clove, crushed (optional)
60ml/4 tbsp olive oil
60ml/4 tbsp sunflower oil

1 Mix the ingredients for the marinade in a food processor for 30–40 seconds until finely chopped. Prick the tuna steaks all over with a fork, place them in a shallow dish and pour over the marinade, turning to coat each piece. Cover with clear film (plastic wrap) and leave in a cool place for 2–4 hours.

2 Mix the citrus juice, mustard and garlic (if using) in a bowl. Whisk in the oils, then season to taste. Stir 60ml/4 tbsp of the dressing into the rice, then transfer to a large serving dish.

3 Cook the French beans and broad beans. Drain. Remove the outer shell from the broad beans and add them to the rice. Add the lettuce to the salad with the tomatoes and coriander. Cut the eggs into sixths.

4 Preheat the grill. Arrange the tuna steaks on a grill pan. Brush each side with the marinade and olive oil. Grill for 3–4 minutes on each side, until the fish flakes easily. Allow the fish to cool a little, then break into pieces. Add to the salad with the olives and the remaining dressing. Decorate with the eggs and serve.

Salad Niçoise Energy 432kcal/1792kJ; Protein 23g; Carbohydrate 5g, of which sugars 5g; Fat 36g, of which saturates 6g; Cholesterol 252mg; Calcium 112mg; Fibre 3g; Sodium 890mg.
Red Rice Salad Energy 805kcal/3362kJ; Protein 42g; Carbohydrate 64g, of which sugars 7g; Fat 44g, of which saturates 7g; Cholesterol 147mg; Calcium 142mg; Fibre 7g; Sodium 1007mg.

Warm Niçoise Noodle Salad with Seared Tuna

The combination of seared fresh tuna and crisp, colourful Mediterranean vegetables with a herby dressing is very appealing.

Serves 4
2 fresh tuna steaks, each weighing
  about 225g/8oz
175g/6oz green beans, trimmed
3 eggs, hardboiled
350g/12oz dried egg noodles
225g/8oz cherry tomatoes, halved
50g/2oz/1/2 cup small black olives
a handful of fresh basil leaves, torn
salt and ground black pepper

For the marinade
30ml/2 tbsp lemon juice
75ml/5 tbsp olive oil
2 garlic cloves, crushed

For the warm dressing
90ml/6 tbsp extra virgin
  olive oil
30ml/2 tbsp wine vinegar or
  lemon juice
2 garlic cloves, crushed
2.5ml/1/2 tsp Dijon mustard
30ml/2 tbsp capers
45ml/3 tbsp chopped mixed
  herbs such as tarragon, chives,
  basil and chervil

1 To make the marinade, combine the lemon juice, olive oil and garlic in a glass dish. Season and mix well. Add the tuna and turn to coat in the marinade. Cover and leave to marinate in a cool place for 1 hour. Whisk all the ingredients for the dressing together in a small pan and leave to infuse.

2 Meanwhile, blanch the green beans for 4 minutes. Drain and refresh in cold water. Shell and quarter the eggs.

3 Put the noodles and beans into a bowl and pour boiling water over to cover. Leave for 5 minutes, then fork up the noodles. Heat the dressing and keep warm. Drain the noodles and beans, and toss with the dressing.

4 Heat a ridged griddle pan or heavy skillet until smoking. Drain the tuna steaks, pat dry and sear for 1–2 minutes on each side. Remove and immediately slice thinly. Add the tuna with the tomatoes and black olives to the noodles and beans, and toss well. Serve, scattered with the eggs and basil. Season well and eat while it is still warm.

Tuna Salad with Black-eyed Beans

Very simple and easy to prepare, this versatile salad is deliciously fresh tasting. It is popular with both adults and children and is a very useful store cupboard stand-by when unexpected guests arrive. It even works well for picnics.

Serves 6
1 apple
240g/8½oz canned tuna, drained
500g/1¼lb canned black-eyed
  beans (peas), drained
  and rinsed
1 small onion, chopped
30ml/2 tbsp chopped
  fresh parsley
75–105ml/5–7 tbsp olive oil
30–45ml/2–3 tbsp white wine
  vinegar

1 Peel, quarter and core the apple, then slice thinly. Put the apple, tuna, beans, onion and parsley in a salad bowl and mix gently.

2 Whisk together the olive oil and vinegar to taste in a bowl, then pour over the salad. Toss gently to coat.

Variations
• Instead of using canned tuna, use fresh. Preheat the grill (broiler). Brush a 225g/8oz tuna steak with olive oil and sprinkle with salt and ground black pepper. Grill) broil) for 3–4 minutes on each side until cooked through. Cool, then flake.
• A mixture of canned beans and sweetcorn, with the addition of yellow (bell) pepper, seeded and diced, red onion, sliced, and a few black or green olives, would make a very attractive salad.

Cook's Tip
If you want to make this salad a bit more substantial so that it can also be served as a main dish, just add 225g/8oz cooked pasta or cooked, diced potatoes and sprinkle with chopped hard-boiled egg to cover. Toss well to mix and serve with some crusty bread for a satisfying lunch.

Seared Tuna Energy 578kcal/2408kJ; Protein 46.4g; Carbohydrate 15g, of which sugars 10.6g; Fat 37.5g, of which saturates 7.1g; Cholesterol 235mg; Calcium 127mg; Fibre 4.7g; Sodium 585mg.
Tuna Salad Energy 139kcal/588kJ; Protein 15.4g; Carbohydrate 16.7g, of which sugars 4.6g; Fat 1.6g, of which saturates 0.3g; Cholesterol 20mg; Calcium 70mg; Fibre 5.6g; Sodium 454mg.

Bean Salad with Tuna

This makes a great first course or even a light main meal if served with a green salad, some garlic mayonnaise and plenty of warm, crusty bread.

Serves 4

250g/9oz/1⅓ cups dried haricot or cannellini beans, soaked overnight in cold water
1 bay leaf
200–250g/7–9oz fine French beans, trimmed
1 large red onion, very thinly sliced

45ml/3 tbsp chopped fresh flat leaf parsley
200–250g/7–9oz good-quality canned tuna in olive oil, drained
200g/7oz cherry tomatoes, halved
salt and ground black pepper
a few onion rings, to garnish

For the dressing

90ml/6 tbsp extra virgin olive oil
15ml/1 tbsp tarragon vinegar
5ml/1 tsp tarragon mustard
1 garlic clove, finely chopped
5ml/1 tsp grated lemon rind
a little lemon juice
pinch of caster sugar (optional)

1 Drain the beans and bring them to the boil in fresh water with the bay leaf added. Boil rapidly for 10 minutes, then reduce the heat and boil steadily for 1–1½ hours, until tender. Drain well. Discard the bay leaf.

2 Meanwhile, whisk all the dressing ingredients apart from the lemon juice and sugar in a jug or bowl until mixed. Season with salt, pepper, lemon juice and a pinch of caster sugar, if liked.

3 Blanch the French beans in plenty of boiling water for 3–4 minutes. Drain, refresh under cold water and drain thoroughly.

4 Place both types of beans in a bowl. Add half the dressing and toss to mix. Stir in the onion and half the chopped parsley, then season to taste with salt and pepper.

5 Flake the tuna into large chunks with a knife and toss it into the beans with the tomato halves.

6 Arrange the salad on four plates. Drizzle the remaining dressing over the salad and scatter the remaining parsley on top. Garnish with a few onion rings and serve immediately.

Swordfish with Citrus Dressing

Kajiki No Tataki Salad is a good example of how the Japanese try out new dishes from all over the world and soon start to arrange them in a Japanese way. Fresh fish is sliced thinly and seared or marinated, then served with salad leaves and vegetables.

Serves 4

75g/3oz daikon, peeled
50g/2oz carrot, peeled
1 Japanese or salad cucumber
10ml/2 tsp vegetable oil

300g/11oz skinned fresh swordfish steak, cut against the grain
2 cartons mustard and cress
15ml/1 tbsp toasted sesame seeds

For the dressing

105ml/7 tbsp shoyu
105ml/7 tbsp water and 5ml/ 1 tsp dashi-no-moto (stock granules)
30ml/2 tbsp toasted sesame oil
juice of ½ lime
rind of ½ lime, shredded into thin strips

1 Make the vegetable garnishes first. Use a very sharp knife, mandolin or vegetable slicer with a julienne blade to make very thin (about 4cm/1½in long) strands of daikon, carrot and cucumber. Soak the daikon and carrot in ice-cold water for 5 minutes, then drain well and keep in the refrigerator.

2 Mix together all the ingredients for the dressing and stir well, then chill.

3 Heat the oil in a small frying pan until smoking hot. Sear the fish for 30 seconds on all sides. Plunge it into cold water in a bowl to stop the cooking. Dry on kitchen paper and wipe off as much oil as possible.

4 Cut the swordfish steak in half lengthways then slice it into 5mm/¼in thick pieces in the other direction, against the grain.

5 Arrange the fish slices into a ring on individual plates. Mix the vegetable strands, mustard and cress and sesame seeds. Fluff up with your hands, then shape them into a sphere. Gently place it in the centre of the plate, on the swordfish. Pour the dressing around the plate's edge and serve immediately.

Bean Salad Energy 443kcal/1857kJ; Protein 29.1g; Carbohydrate 33.7g, of which sugars 6.4g; Fat 22.3g, of which saturates 3.3g; Cholesterol 25mg; Calcium 100mg; Fibre 11.9g; Sodium 162mg.
Swordfish Energy 223kcal/925kJ; Protein 15.4g; Carbohydrate 3.6g, of which sugars 3.3g; Fat 16.4g, of which saturates 2.5g; Cholesterol 31mg; Calcium 46mg; Fibre 0.9g; Sodium 1975mg.

Caesar Salad

This much-enjoyed salad was created by Caesar Cordoni in Tijuana in 1924. Be sure to use crunchy lettuce and add the soft eggs and garlic croûtons at the last minute.

Serves 6

175ml/6fl oz/³⁄₄ cup extra virgin
   olive oil
115g/4oz/2 cups French or Italian
   bread, cut in 2.5cm/1 in cubes

1 large garlic clove, crushed
1 cos lettuce
2 eggs, boiled for 1 minute
120ml/4fl oz/¹⁄₂ cup
   lemon juice
50g/2oz/²⁄₃ cup freshly grated
   (shredded) Parmesan cheese
6 anchovy fillets, drained and
   finely chopped (optional)
salt and ground
   black pepper

1 Heat 50ml/2fl oz/¹⁄₄ cup of the oil in a frying pan. Add the bread and garlic and fry, stirring and turning constantly, until the cubes are golden brown. Drain on kitchen paper and discard the garlic.

2 Tear large lettuce leaves into smaller pieces. Put all the lettuce in a bowl.

3 Add the remaining olive oil to the salad leaves and season with salt and pepper. Toss to coat well.

4 Break the soft-boiled eggs on top. Sprinkle with the lemon juice and toss to combine the ingredients.

5 Add the grated Parmesan cheese and anchovies, if using, then toss again. Scatter the croûtons on top of the salad and serve immediately.

> **Cook's Tip**
> If you would prefer a slightly tangier dressing, mix the olive oil with 30ml/2 tbsp white wine vinegar, 2.5ml/¹⁄₂ tsp ready-prepared mustard, 5ml/1 tsp sugar, and salt and ground black pepper. Whisk or shake well until the mixture is emulsified.

Egg and Bacon Caesar Salad

The key elements of this popular salad are sweet lettuce, crisp croutons and a mayonnaise-style dressing.

Serves 4–6

3 x 1cm/¹⁄₂in thick slices white
   bread, cubed
45ml/3 tbsp olive oil
1 large garlic clove, finely chopped
3–4 Little Gem (Bibb) lettuces or
   2 larger cos or romaine lettuces
12–18 quail's eggs

115g/4oz thinly sliced Parma,
   San Daniele or Serrano ham
40–50g/1¹⁄₂–2oz Parmesan
   cheese, grated (shredded)
salt and ground black pepper

For the dressing

1 large egg
1–2 garlic cloves, chopped
4 anchovy fillets in oil, drained
120ml/4fl oz/¹⁄₂ cup olive oil
10–15ml/2–3 tsp lemon juice
   or white wine vinegar

1 Preheat the oven to 190°C/375°F/Gas 5. Toss the bread cubes with the oil and garlic. Season to taste with salt and pepper. Turn out on to a baking tray and bake for 10–14 minutes, stirring once or twice, until golden brown all over.

2 Meanwhile, to make the dressing, boil the egg for 90 seconds, then plunge the egg into cold water. Shell and put in a food processor or blender. Add the garlic and anchovy fillets and process to mix. With the motor still running, gradually add the olive oil in a thin stream until creamy. Add the lemon juice or wine vinegar and season to taste with salt and pepper.

3 Separate the lettuce leaves and tear up if large. Place in a large salad bowl.

4 Put the quail's eggs in a pan, cover with cold water, then bring to the boil and boil for 2 minutes. Plunge the eggs into cold water, then part-shell them. Grill (broil) the ham for 2–3 minutes on each side, or until crisp.

5 Toss the dressing into the lettuce with 25g/1oz of the Parmesan. Add the croûtons. Cut the quail's eggs in half and add them to the salad. Crumble the ham into large pieces then scatter it over the salad with the remaining cheese. Serve immediately.

Caesar Salad Energy 198kcal/824kJ; Protein 5.6g; Carbohydrate 13.8g, of which sugars 1.7g; Fat 13.8g, of which saturates 2.1g; Cholesterol 50mg; Calcium 64mg; Fibre 0.9g; Sodium 400mg.
Egg Caesar Energy 447kcal/1855kJ; Protein 18g; Carbohydrate 11g, of which sugars 2g; Fat 37g, of which saturates 8g; Cholesterol 218mg; Calcium 165mg; Fibre 1g; Sodium 698mg.

Leek Salad with Anchovies, Eggs and Parsley

Chopped hard-boiled eggs and cooked leeks are a classic combination in French-style salads. This one makes a good first course, with some crusty bread, or a light main dish that can be finished with a tomato salad and/or a potato salad.

Serves 4
675g/1½lb thin or baby
   leeks, trimmed
2 large or 3 medium eggs
50g/2oz good-quality anchovy
   fillets in olive oil, drained
15g/½oz flat leaf parsley,
   chopped
a few black olives, stoned
   (pitted), optional
salt and ground black pepper

For the dressing
5ml/1 tsp Dijon mustard
15ml/1 tbsp tarragon vinegar
75ml/5 tbsp olive oil
30ml/2 tbsp double cream
1 small shallot, very
   finely chopped
pinch of caster sugar (optional)

1 Cook the leeks for 3–4 minutes. Drain, plunge into cold water, then drain again. Squeeze out excess water, then pat dry.

2 Place the eggs in a saucepan of cold water, bring to the boil and cook for 6–7 minutes. Drain, plunge into cold water, then shell and chop the eggs.

3 To make the dressing, whisk the mustard with the vinegar. Gradually whisk in the oil, followed by the cream. Stir in the shallot, then season to taste with salt, pepper and a pinch of caster sugar, if liked.

4 Leave the leeks whole or thickly slice them, then place in a serving dish. Pour most of the dressing over them and stir to mix. Leave for at least 1 hour, or until ready to serve, bringing them back to room temperature first, if necessary.

5 Arrange the anchovies on the leeks, then scatter with the eggs and parsley. Drizzle with the remaining dressing, season with black pepper and dot with a few olives, if using. Serve.

Chopped Herring Salad

Although the ingredients for this dish are simple, it is usually served at festive occasions. The herring fillets must be soaked overnight, so allow time to do this. You can buy ready-made forshmak in Russian delicatessens. It is delicious served with ice cold vodka.

Serves 6
250g/9oz salted or pickled
   herring fillets
2 eggs
45ml/3 tbsp rapeseed (canola) oil
1 onion, finely chopped
1 Granny Smith apple
40g/1 1/2oz/3 tbsp butter, at
   room temperature
1–2 spring onions (scallions),
   to garnish

1 If using salted herrings, soak the fillets in cold water overnight. The next day, rinse the herring fillets under running water and then drain.

2 Put the eggs in a pan, cover with cold water and bring to the boil. Reduce the heat and simmer for 10 minutes. Meanwhile, heat the oil in a frying pan, add the chopped onion and fry for about 5 minutes, until softened but not browned. Set aside.

3 When the eggs are hardboiled, drain them and leave under cold running water. When cool enough to handle, remove the shell and separate the yolks from the whites.

4 Peel, core and chop the apple and put in a food processor. Add the salted or pickled herring fillets, egg yolks and the butter and process to a paste. Transfer to a bowl and mix in the fried onion.

5 Finely chop the reserved egg whites and finely slice the spring onions. Put the salad on a serving plate and serve garnished with the chopped egg whites and spring onions.

Cook's Tips
Tasty salads such as this one are popular in Russia and would be served as zakuski or appetizers.

Leek Salad Energy 265kcal/1099kJ; Protein 9.4g; Carbohydrate 6.3g, of which sugars 4.8g; Fat 22.7g, of which saturates 5.6g; Cholesterol 113mg; Calcium 107mg; Fibre 4.1g; Sodium 533mg.
Herring Salad Energy 212kcal/875kJ; Protein 7.6g; Carbohydrate 3.2g, of which sugars 2.8g; Fat 18.9g, of which saturates 4.6g; Cholesterol 97mg; Calcium 32mg; Fibre 0.3g; Sodium 223mg.

Herring Salad with Beetroot and Sour Cream

This salad, served with black pumpernickel bread, is the traditional morning festive dish on Shabbat, which is a day of celebration. Serve the salad with cold boiled potatoes and allow your guests to cut the herring up and add to the salad however they like.

Serves 8

1 large tangy cooking apple
500g/1¼lb matjes herrings
(schmaltz herrings), drained and cut into slices
2 small pickled cucumbers, diced
10ml/2 tsp caster (superfine) sugar, or to taste
10ml/2 tsp cider vinegar or white wine vinegar
300ml/½ pint/1¼ cups sour cream
2 cooked beetroot (beets), diced
lettuce, to serve
sprigs of fresh dill and chopped onion or onion rings, to garnish

1 Peel, core and dice the apple. Put in a bowl, add the sliced herrings, diced cucumbers, sugar and cider or white wine vinegar and mix together. Add the sour cream and mix well to combine.

2 Add the beetroot to the herring mixture and chill in the refrigerator. Serve the salad on a bed of lettuce leaves, garnished with the sprigs of fresh dill and chopped onion or onion rings.

Cook's Tips

Beetroot (beets) makes a good partner for herring, and in countries such as Poland and Russia, beetroot is very popular; they are an essential part of many salads, and of course are often made into the delicious, satisfying soup known as borscht. They are also important before Christmas, when traditionally people fast and avoid dishes that contain fat and meat; instead they eat 'caviars' that have been prepared from vegetables such as beetroot and mushrooms.

Estonian Herring, Ham and Beetroot Salad

This is a very modern take on an old classic, Estonian rosolje. This dish is an essential on the smorgasbord table and it is a combination of herring, ham, potatoes and beetroot. It is a common item on menus in many restaurants, as it makes a perfect light snack.

Serves 4

2 fillets of pickled herring, drained and diced
1 large potato, boiled and diced
2 large cooked beetroot (beets), peeled and diced
1 small onion, grated
2 medium tart apples, cored and cut into thin wedges
2 gherkins, chopped
200g/7oz thick piece of ham, diced
2 thinly sliced hard-boiled eggs
salt and ground black pepper
30ml/2 tbsp finely chopped fresh dill, to garnish

For the dressing

100ml/3½fl oz/scant 1/2 cup sour cream
15ml/1 tbsp vinegar (any kind)
15ml/1 tbsp wholegrain mustard
1 medium beetroot (beet), finely grated
5ml/1 tsp creamed horseradish

1 To make the dressing, put the sour cream in a bowl and add the vinegar, mustard, grated beetroot and horseradish. Season to taste and combine well. Set aside.

2 Put the herring in a large bowl with the potato, beetroot, onion, apples, gherkins and ham. Season to taste with salt and ground black pepper and mix together gently.

3 Add the dressing to the mixed salad and gently toss together to combine. Top with the sliced hard-boiled eggs and garnish with dill, then serve.

Cook's Tips

Herring has an affinity to horseradish and mustard; to give this dish a little extra heat, add a small amount of freshly grated horseradish root.

Herring Salad Energy 315kcal/1323kJ; Protein 21.4g; Carbohydrate 19.5g, of which sugars 18.8g; Fat 17g, of which saturates 1.2g; Cholesterol 137mg; Calcium 58mg; Fibre 2.3g; Sodium 901mg.
Estonian Salad Energy 355kcal/1495kJ; Protein 25g; Carbohydrate 30.8g, of which sugars 22.2g; Fat 15.4g, of which saturates 4.5g; Cholesterol 160mg; Calcium 84mg; Fibre 4.2g; Sodium 1169mg.

Layered Herring Salad

This salad looks like a cake, and is internationally called Herring à la Russe.

Serves 8
250g/9oz salted herring fillets
3 carrots, total weight 250g/9oz
4 eggs
1 small red onion
200g/7oz/scant 1 cup
  mayonnaise
5–6 cooked beetroots (beets),
  total weight 300g/11oz
2 Granny Smith apples
45ml/3 tbsp chopped
  fresh dill

1 Soak the herring fillets in water overnight. The next day, rinse the herring under running water and then drain. Cut into small pieces and put in a bowl.

2 Put the whole carrots in a pan of cold water, bring to the boil then reduce the heat, cover and simmer for 10–15 minutes, until tender. Drain and put under cold running water. Set aside.

3 Meanwhile, put the eggs in a pan, cover with cold water and bring to the boil. Reduce the heat and simmer for 10 minutes. When the eggs are cooked, immediately drain and put under cold running water. Set aside.

4 Finely chop the onion and add to the herrings with 15ml/1 tbsp of the mayonnaise. Spread the herring mixture over a flat serving plate measuring about 25cm/10in in diameter.

5 Coarsely grate the carrots, beetroots and apples into small piles or bowls. Add a layer of grated beetroot over the herring mixture and spread 45–60ml/3–4 tbsp mayonnaise on top. Repeat with a layer of grated carrots and mayonnaise and then a layer of grated apple.

6 Finally spread a thin layer of mayonnaise over the top of the salad. Cover with clear film (plastic wrap) and chill in the refrigerator for at least 1 hour or overnight.

7 Just before serving shell the eggs and grate coarsely. Sprinkle the grated egg all over the salad so that it covers it completely and creates a final layer, then garnish with chopped dill.

Octopus Salad

Octopus is a popular appetizer and is often served at Christmas in Portugal. Served cold with plenty of parsley, the octopus flavour is less intense. This will serve eight people as a small snack or four for a large appetizer.

Serves 4–8
1 uncooked octopus, weighing
  2–3kg/4½–6½lb
105ml/7 tbsp olive oil
30–45ml/2–3 tbsp white
  wine vinegar
1 onion, finely chopped
1 bunch of parsley, chopped

For the stock
2 onions, quartered
1 leek, chopped
3 garlic cloves, crushed
10 black peppercorns
2 bay leaves
pinch of salt

1 Rinse the octopus in plenty of water and cut off the body. Turn the body inside out and pull out and discard the entrails. Remove the little strips from the sides of the body. Rinse thoroughly again and turn the right way out. Squeeze out the beak. Beat the tentacles lightly with a rolling pin or the flat side of a meat mallet.

2 Half fill a large pan with water and add all the ingredients for the stock. Bring to the boil, then lower the heat and simmer for 10 minutes.

3 Add the octopus and bring back to the boil. Lower the heat slightly so that the liquid continues to boil and cook for 1 hour. Check with a fork to see if the octopus is tender. If it is not, cook for a little longer but check frequently because it will toughen if overcooked. Strain the stock into a bowl and reserve. Discard the flavourings.

4 Whisk together the olive oil and vinegar in a bowl, then stir in the onion and parsley. Taste and add more vinegar if you like an acidic vinaigrette.

5 Cut the octopus tentacles into 2cm/¾in pieces and place in a dish. Pour the vinaigrette over them and leave to stand for several hours before serving.

Herring Salad Energy 130kcal/544kJ; Protein 12.1g; Carbohydrate 9.3g, of which sugars 8.7g; Fat 5.3g, of which saturates 0.8g; Cholesterol 95mg; Calcium 96mg; Fibre 2.2g; Sodium 1697mg.
Octopus Salad Energy 199kcal/834kJ; Protein 30g; Carbohydrate 0.5g, of which sugars 0.3g; Fat 8.6g, of which saturates 1.4g; Cholesterol 80mg; Calcium 60mg; Fibre 0.2g; Sodium 1mg.

Prawn, Melon and Chorizo Salad

This is a rich and colourful salad. It tastes best when made with fresh prawns.

Serves 4

450g/1lb/4 cups cooked white
   long grain rice
1 avocado
15ml/1 tbsp lemon juice
½ small melon, cut into wedges
15g/½oz/1 tbsp butter
½ garlic clove

115g/4oz raw prawns, peeled
   and deveined
25g/1oz chorizo sausage,
   finely sliced
flat leaf parsley, to garnish

For the dressing

75ml/5 tbsp natural yogurt
45ml/3 tbsp mayonnaise
15ml/1 tbsp olive oil
3 fresh tarragon sprigs
freshly ground black pepper

1 Put the cooked rice in a large salad bowl, breaking it up with your fingers if necessary.

2 Peel the avocado and cut it into chunks. Place in a mixing bowl and toss lightly with the lemon juice. Slice the melon off the rind, cut the flesh into chunks and add to the avocado.

3 Melt the butter in a small pan and fry the garlic for 30 seconds. Add the prawns and cook for about 3 minutes until evenly pink. Add the chorizo and stir-fry for 1 minute more, then tip the mixture into the bowl with the avocado and melon chunks. Mix lightly, then leave to cool.

4 Make the dressing by whizzing together all the ingredients in a food processor or blender. Stir half of the mixture into the rice and the remainder into the prawn and avocado mixture. Pile the salad on top of the rice. Chill for about 30 minutes before serving, garnished with flat leaf parsley sprigs.

> **Cook's Tips**
> The addition of chorizo, a Spanish sausage that contains paprika, adds a rich warming flavour to this dish. Because of the spice, any dish that chorizo is added to takes on a distinctive red colour.

Grilled Prawn Salad with Peanuts and Pomelo

This refreshing and fragrant salad is typical of the salads of central and southern Vietnam, where fruit, vegetables, meat, fish and shellfish are all tossed together in one dish.

serves 4

16–20 raw tiger prawns (shrimp),
   peeled and deveined
1 small cucumber, peeled and cut
   into matchsticks
1 pomelo, separated into
   segments and cut into
   bitesize pieces
1 carrot, peeled and cut into
   matchsticks
1 green Serrano chilli, seeded and
   finely sliced

30ml/2 tbsp roasted peanuts,
   roughly chopped
juice of half a lime
roughly 60ml/4 tbsp nuoc cham
vegetable oil, for griddling
1 small bunch of fresh basil, stalks
   removed, leaves torn
1 small bunch of coriander
   (cilantro), stalks removed, leaves
   chopped

For the marinade

30ml/2 tbsp nuoc mam
30ml/2 tbsp soy sauce
15ml/1 tbsp groundnut
   (peanut) oil
1 shallot, finely chopped
1 garlic clove, crushed
10ml/2 tsp raw cane sugar

1 In a wide bowl, combine all the marinade ingredients. Add the prawns, coating them all over, and set aside for 30 minutes.

2 Sprinkle the cucumber matchsticks with salt and leave for 15 minutes. Rinse and drain the cucumber and mix in a large bowl with the pomelo, carrot, chilli and peanuts. Add the lime juice and nuoc cham and toss well.

3 If using a barbecue, thread the prawns on to wooden skewers that have been soaked in water for 30 minutes.

4 Cook on a prepared barbecue for 2–3 minutes, turning them over from time to time. To griddle, wipe a hot griddle with a little oil, and cook the prawns on both sides until they turn opaque. Once cooked, toss the prawns into the salad with the herbs and serve.

Prawn Salad Energy 414kcal/1734kJ; Protein 10.8g; Carbohydrate 44.6g, of which sugars 8.8g; Fat 22.6g, of which saturates 5.8g; Cholesterol 75mg; Calcium 102mg; Fibre 1.5g; Sodium 236mg.
Grilled Prawn Salad Energy 219Kcal/912kJ; Protein 14g; Carbohydrate 14g, of which sugars 9g; Fat 12g, of which saturates 2g; Cholesterol 98mg; Calcium 121mg; Fibre 1.4g; Sodium 0.5g

Thai Prawn Salad with Garlic Dressing and Frizzled Shallots

In this salad, prawns and mango are tossed with a sweet-sour garlic dressing with a touch of chilli. The crisp frizzled shallots are a traditional addition.

Serves 4-6
675g/1½lb medium-size raw
    prawns, shelled with tails on
finely shredded rind of 1 lime
½ fresh red chilli, seeded and
    finely chopped
30ml/2 tbsp olive oil, plus extra
    for brushing
1 ripe but firm mango
2 carrots, cut into long thin shreds
10cm/4in piece cucumber, sliced
1 small red onion, thinly sliced
sprigs of fresh coriander (cilantro)
a few sprigs of fresh mint
45ml/3 tbsp roasted peanuts,
    roughly chopped
4 large shallots, thinly sliced and
    fried until crisp in 30ml/2 tbsp
    peanut oil
salt and ground black pepper

For the dressing
1 large garlic clove, chopped
10–15ml/2–3 tsp caster sugar
juice of 2 limes
15–30ml/1–2 tbsp Thai fish
    sauce (nam pla)
1 red chilli, seeded
5–10ml/1–2 tsp light rice vinegar

1 Place the prawns in a glass dish and add the lime rind and chilli. Season and spoon the oil over them. Marinate for 30 minutes.

2 For the dressing, place the garlic in a mortar with 10ml/2 tsp caster sugar and pound until smooth, then work in the juice of 1½ limes and 15ml/1 tbsp of the Thai fish sauce. Transfer the dressing to a bowl. Finely chop half the chilli. and add it to the bowl. Taste the dressing and add more seasoning to taste.

3 Peel and stone the mango, then cut it into very fine strips. Toss together the mango, carrots, cucumber and onion, and half the dressing. Arrange the salad on individual plates or in bowls.

4 Heat a frying pan until very hot. Brush with oil, then sear the prawns for 2–3 minutes on each side. Arrange the prawns on the salads. Sprinkle the remaining dressing over the salads with the coriander and mint. Shred the remaining chilli and sprinkle it over the salads with the peanuts and crisp-fried shallots. Serve.

Banana Blossom Salad with Prawns

Banana blossom is very popular – the purplish-pink sheaths are used for presentation, the petals as a garnish, and the creamy yellow heart is tossed in salads, where it is combined with leftover grilled chicken or pork, steamed or grilled prawns, or tofu.

Serves 4
2 banana blossom hearts
juice of 1 lemon

225g/8oz prawns (shrimp), cooked
    and shelled
30ml/2 tbsp roasted peanuts,
    finely chopped, fresh basil leaves
    and lime slices, to garnish

For the dressing
juice of 1 lime
30ml/2 tbsp white rice vinegar
60ml/4 tbsp nuoc mam or tuk trey
45ml/3 tbsp palm sugar
3 red Thai chillies, seeded and
    finely sliced
2 garlic cloves, peeled and
    finely chopped

1 Cut the banana blossom hearts into quarters lengthways and then slice them very finely crossways. To prevent them discolouring, tip the slices into a bowl of cold water mixed with the lemon juice and leave to soak for about 30 minutes.

2 To make the dressing, beat the lime juice, vinegar, and nuoc mam or tuk trey with the sugar in a small bowl, until it has dissolved. Stir in the chillies and garlic and set aside.

3 Drain the sliced banana blossom and put it in a bowl. Add the prawns and pour over the dressing. Toss well together and garnish with the roasted peanuts, basil leaves and lime slices.

> **Cook's Tip**
> Banana blossom doesn't actually taste of banana. Instead, it is mildly tannic, similar to an unripe persimmon – a taste and texture that complements chillies, lime and the local fish sauce. If you cannot find banana blossom hearts in Asian supermarkets, you can try this recipe with raw, or lightly steamed or roasted, fresh artichoke hearts.

Thai Prawn Salad Energy 292kcal/1222kJ; Protein 33.5g; Carbohydrate 13.4g, of which sugars 11.8g; Fat 11.9g, of which saturates 2g; Cholesterol 329mg; Calcium 160mg; Fibre 2.7g; Sodium 596mg.
Banana and Prawn Energy 103Kcal/438kJ; Protein 11g; Carbohydrate 15g, of which sugars 13g; Fat 0.5g, of which saturates 0.1g; Cholesterol 110mg; Calcium 54mg; Fibre 0.7g; Sodium 109mg.

Ghanaian Prawn and Plantain Salad

Usually served as a side dish, but substantial enough for lunch, this fresh-tasting salad is a colourful blend of fruits, vegetables, hard-boiled eggs and fish.

Serves 4

115g/4oz cooked, peeled prawns (shrimp)
1 garlic clove, crushed
7.5ml/1½ tsp vegetable oil
2 eggs
1 yellow plantain, halved

4 lettuce leaves
2 tomatoes
1 red (bell) pepper, seeded
1 avocado
juice of 1 lemon
1 carrot
200g/7oz can tuna or sardines, in brine, drained and flaked
1 fresh green chilli, finely chopped
30ml/2 tbsp chopped spring onions (scallions)
salt and ground black pepper

1 Put the prawns in a glass bowl, add the crushed garlic and a little seasoning. Heat the oil in a small pan, add the prawns and cook over a low heat for a few minutes. Transfer to a plate to cool.

2 Hard-boil the eggs, and then place them in cold water to cool. Shell the eggs and cut them into slices. Set aside.

3 Boil the plantain in a pan of water for 15 minutes, drain, cool, then peel and slice thickly. Set aside.

4 Shred the lettuce and arrange on a large serving plate. Slice the tomatoes and red pepper, and peel, stone (pit) and slice the avocado, sprinkling it with a little lemon juice. Arrange the vegetables on the plate over the lettuce. Cut the carrot into matchstick-size pieces and arrange over the other vegetables.

5 Add the plantain, eggs, prawns and tuna or sardines. Sprinkle with the remaining lemon juice, scatter the chilli and spring onions on top and season with salt and pepper to taste. Serve as a lunch-time salad or as a delicious side dish.

Seafood Salad with Fruity Dressing

White fish is briefly seared, then served with prawns and salad tossed in an oil-free apricot and apple dressing. The delicate fruit flavours complement the fish.

Serves 4

1 baby onion, sliced lengthways
lemon juice
400g/14oz very fresh sea bream or sea bass, filleted
30ml/2 tbsp sake

4 large king prawns (jumbo shrimp), heads and shells removed
about 400g/14oz mixed salad leaves

For the fruity dressing

2 ripe apricots, skinned and stoned (pitted)
¼ apple, peeled and cored
60ml/4 tbsp water and 5ml/1 tsp dashi-no-moto (stock granules)
10ml/2 tsp shoyu
salt and ground white pepper

1 Soak the onion slices in ice-cold water for 30 minutes. Drain well.

2 Bring a pan half-full of water to the boil. Add a dash of lemon juice and plunge the fish fillet into it. Remove after 30 seconds, and cool immediately under cold running water for 30 seconds to stop the cooking. Cut into 8mm/⅓in thick slices crossways.

3 Pour the sake into a small pan, bring to the boil, then add the prawns. Cook for 1 minute, or until their colour has completely changed to pink.

4 Cool immediately under cold running water for 30 seconds to again stop the cooking. Cut the prawns into 1cm/½in thick slices crossways.

5 Slice one apricot very thinly, then set aside. Purée the remaining dressing ingredients in a food processor. Add salt, if required, and pepper. Chill.

6 Lay a small amount of mixed leaves on four plates. Mix the fish, prawn, apricot and onion slices in a bowl. Add the remaining leaves with the dressing and toss well. Serve.

Ghanaian Prawn Energy 234Kcal/985kJ; Protein 22.1g; Carbohydrate 18g, of which sugars 8.5g; Fat 8.7g, of which saturates 2.1g; Cholesterol 177mg; Calcium 69mg; Fibre 3.3g; Sodium 265mg.
Seafood Salad Energy 135kcal/568kJ; Protein 22.3g; Carbohydrate 4.6g, of which sugars 4.3g; Fat 3.1g, of which saturates 0.5g; Cholesterol 100mg; Calcium 173mg; Fibre 1.5g; Sodium 359mg.

Seafood Salad

Ensalada de Mariscos is a very pretty arrangement of fresh mussels, prawns and squid rings served on a colourful bed of salad vegetables. In Spain, canned albacore tuna is also often included in this type of simple salad.

Serves six
115g/4oz prepared squid rings
12 fresh mussels, scrubbed and
    beards removed
1 large carrot
6 crisp lettuce leaves
10cm/4in piece cucumber,
    finely diced
115g/4oz cooked, peeled
    prawns (shrimp)
15ml/1 tbsp drained pickled
    capers

For the dressing
30ml/2 tbsp freshly squeezed
    lemon juice
45ml/3 tbsp virgin olive oil
15ml/1 tbsp chopped fresh
    parsley
salt and ground black pepper

1 Put the squid rings into a metal sieve or vegetable steamer. Place the sieve or steamer over a pan of simmering water, cover with a lid and steam the squid for 2–3 minutes until it just turns an opaque white. Cool under cold running water to prevent further cooking and drain the squid thoroughly on kitchen paper.

2 Discard any open mussels that do not close when sharply tapped. Cover the base of a large pan with water, add the mussels, then cover and steam for a few minutes until they open. Discard any mussels that remain closed.

3 Using a swivel-style vegetable peeler, cut the carrot into wafer-thin ribbons. Tear the lettuce into pieces and arrange on a serving plate. Scatter the carrot ribbons on top, then sprinkle over the diced cucumber.

4 Arrange the mussels, prawns and squid rings over the salad and scatter the capers over the top.

5 Make the dressing. Put all the ingredients in a small bowl and whisk well to combine. Drizzle over the salad. Serve at room temperature.

Potato, Mussel and Watercress Salad

The mussels found on the Galician coast are the best in the world. The Galicians are also very proud of their potatoes and their watercress. In ensalada de mejillones, patatas y berros a creamy, well-flavoured dressing enhances all the ingredients.

Serves 4
675g/1½lb salad potatoes
1kg/2¼lb mussels, scrubbed
    and beards removed
200ml/7fl oz/scant 1 cup dry
    white wine
15g/½oz fresh flat leaf
    parsley, chopped
1 bunch of watercress
    or rocket (arugula)
salt and ground black pepper
chopped fresh chives or
    spring onion (scallion) tops,
    to garnish

For the dressing
105ml/7 tbsp olive oil
15–30ml/1–2 tbsp white wine
    vinegar
5ml/1 tsp strong Dijon mustard
1 large shallot, very finely
    chopped
15ml/1 tbsp chopped fresh chives
45ml/3 tbsp double
    (heavy) cream
pinch of caster (superfine)
    sugar (optional)

1 Cook the potatoes in salted boiling water for 15–20 minutes, or until tender. Drain, cool, then peel. Slice the potatoes into a bowl and toss with 30ml/2 tbsp of the oil for the dressing.

2 Discard any open mussels. Bring the white wine to the boil in a large, heavy pan. Add the mussels, cover and boil vigorously, shaking the pan occasionally, for 3–4 minutes, until the mussels have opened. Discard any that do not open. Drain and shell the mussels, reserving the cooking liquid. Boil the reserved mussel cooking liquid until reduced to about 45ml/3 tbsp. Strain this through a fine sieve over the potatoes and toss to mix.

3 Make the dressing. Whisk together the remaining oil, 15ml/1 tbsp of the vinegar, the mustard, shallot and chives. Add the cream and whisk until thick. Season, adding more vinegar and/or a pinch of sugar to taste. Toss the mussels with the potatoes, then mix in the dressing and parsley. Arrange the watercress or rocket on a serving platter and top with the salad. Serve sprinkled with extra chives or a little spring onion.

Seafood Salad Energy 100kcal/415kJ; Protein 8.1g; Carbohydrate 2.6g, of which sugars 2g; Fat 6.4g, of which saturates 1g; Cholesterol 85mg; Calcium 50mg; Fibre 1.1g; Sodium 95mg.
Mussel Salad Energy 459kcal/1918kJ; Protein 17.2g; Carbohydrate 29.2g, of which sugars 3.8g; Fat 27.7g, of which saturates 7g; Cholesterol 45mg; Calcium 222mg; Fibre 2.5g; Sodium 231mg.

Shellfish Salad

This salad was created to take full advantage of the many types of delicious shellfish that can be caught off the west coast of Norway. It appears on all Norwegian cold tables for special occasions, with the shellfish chosen according to its availability and taste. When fresh shellfish is scarce or prohibitively expensive, frozen or canned are an alternative.

Serves 4

115g/4oz/1¾ cups
    mushrooms, sliced
juice ½ lemon
1 lobster, about 450g/1lb, cooked
    and with meat extracted
115g/4oz/1 cup cooked fresh or
    canned asparagus
1 crisp lettuce, shredded
16 cooked mussels
115g/4oz/½ cup cooked peeled
    prawns (shrimp)
2 tomatoes, skinned
    and quartered
chopped fresh dill, to garnish

For the dressing

30ml/2 tbsp white wine vinegar
90–120ml/6–8 tbsp olive oil
pinch of sugar
1 garlic clove, crushed (optional)
salt and ground black pepper

1 Chill all the salad ingredients in the refrigerator before use. To make the dressing, put the vinegar, oil, sugar and garlic, if using, in a bowl and whisk well together until the dressing is thick and emulsified. Season the dressing with salt and ground black pepper to taste.

2 Put the mushrooms in a serving bowl and sprinkle over the lemon juice.

3 Cut the lobster meat into bitesize pieces and add to the bowl. Cut the fresh or canned asparagus into 5cm/2in pieces and add to the bowl. Add the lettuce in a layer, then add layers of the mussels, prawns and tomatoes.

4 Pour the dressing over the salad ingredients and toss together. Garnish with the chopped fresh dill and serve immediately.

Crab Salad with Coriander

Crab, like other shellfish from the North Sea around Norway, is full of flavour. Norwegians love crab when it is simply dressed and accompanied with chopped hard-boiled eggs or served in a mixed salad, such as this one. The crab's richness blends with the cream, contrasting with the freshness of the apples and spring onions. Coriander gives an extra punch to the flavour.

Serves 4 as an appetizer, 2 as a light meal

1 head romaine lettuce
2 eating apples
juice 1 lemon
1 bunch spring onions
    (scallions), chopped
150ml/¼ pint/⅔ cup
    whipping cream
135ml/4½fl oz crème fraîche
30ml/2 tbsp chopped fresh
    coriander (cilantro), plus extra
    to garnish
brown and white meat of 2 crabs
salt

1 Shred the lettuce and arrange around the edge of a shallow serving bowl, reserving four small bowl-shaped leaves. Peel, quarter and core the apples then cut into small dice. Put in a bowl, add the lemon juice and toss together. Add the spring onions and mix together.

2 Whisk the cream in a large bowl until it stands in soft peaks, then fold in the crème fraîche. Add the apple mixture and chopped coriander.

3 Mix together the brown and white crab meat and season with salt to taste. Fold the meat into the cream mixture. Check the seasoning and spoon in to the centre of the reserved lettuce leaves. Serve, garnished with the chopped fresh coriander.

Cook's Tip

If you prefer the white meat of the crab, you could use about 225g/8oz of fresh or frozen white crab meat for this recipe and omit the brown meat. Or, buy fresh crab claws and remove the white meat using picks.

Shellfish Salad Energy 280kcal/1166kJ; Protein 23.2g; Carbohydrate 4.4g, of which sugars 3g; Fat 19g, of which saturates 2.9g; Cholesterol 127mg; Calcium 96mg; Fibre 1.8g; Sodium 357mg.
Crab Salad Energy 382kcal/1585kJ; Protein 20.6g; Carbohydrate 6.4g, of which sugars 6.2g; Fat 30.6g, of which saturates 19.3g; Cholesterol 151mg; Calcium 188mg; Fibre 1.4g; Sodium 571mg.

Creamy Lemon and Salmon Pappardelle

This is a fantastic all-in-one supper dish that tastes great and is made in just a few minutes – ideal for when you're really hungry but haven't much time. Serve it with a rocket salad dressed with extra virgin olive oil, balsamic vinegar and black pepper.

Serves 4
500g/1¼lb fresh pappardelle
    or tagliatelle
300ml/½ pint/1¼ cups single
    (light) cream
grated rind and juice of 2 lemons
225g/8oz smoked salmon pieces
2.5ml/½ tsp grated nutmeg
60ml/4 tbsp chopped
    fresh parsley
salt and ground black pepper
fresh Parmesan cheese shavings,
    to garnish
rocket (arugula) salad, to serve

1 Bring a large pan of lightly salted water to the boil and cook the pappardelle or tagliatelle for 3–5 minutes, or according to the instructions on the packet, until risen to the surface of the boiling water and just tender. Drain well.

2 Add the cream, lemon rind and juice to the pan and heat through gently until piping hot. Return the cooked pappardelle to the pan and stir thoroughly to coat the pasta with the creamy mixture.

3 Add the salmon pieces, grated nutmeg, chopped parsley and plenty of ground black pepper to the sauce in the pan and stir well to combine.

4 Divide the pasta among four warmed serving plates and top with the fresh Parmesan shavings. Serve immediately with the rocket salad.

Cook's Tips
To save time, use ready-shaved Parmesan cheese.

Spaghetti with Salmon and Prawns

This is a lovely, fresh-tasting pasta dish, perfect for an al-fresco meal in summer. Serve it as a main course lunch with warm Italian bread and a dry white wine.

Serves 4
300g/11oz salmon fillet
200ml/7fl oz/scant 1 cup dry
    white wine

a few fresh basil sprigs, plus extra
    basil leaves, to garnish
6 ripe Italian plum tomatoes,
    peeled and finely chopped
150ml/¼ pint/⅔ cup double
    (heavy) cream
350g/12oz/3 cups fresh or
    dried spaghetti
115g/4oz/⅔ cup peeled cooked
    prawns (shrimp), thawed and
    thoroughly dried if frozen
salt and ground black pepper

1 Put the salmon, skin side up, in a wide shallow pan. Add the wine, then the basil. Season the fish. Bring the wine to the boil, cover the pan and simmer gently for 5 minutes. Lift the fish out of the pan and set it aside to cool a little.

2 Add the tomatoes and cream to the liquid remaining in the pan and bring to the boil. Stir well, then reduce the heat and simmer, uncovered, for 10–15 minutes. Meanwhile, cook the pasta according to the instructions on the packet.

3 Flake the fish into chunks, discarding the skin and any bones. Add the fish to the sauce with the prawns. Season if needed.

4 Drain the pasta and put it in a warmed bowl. Pour the sauce over the pasta and toss to combine. Serve immediately, garnished with fresh basil leaves.

Cook's Tips
Check the salmon fillet carefully for small bones when you are flaking the flesh. Although the salmon is already filleted, you will always find a few stray 'pin' bones. Pick them out carefully using tweezers or your fingertips.

Salmon Pappardelle Energy 582kcal/2489kJ; Protein 28g; Carbohydrate 72g, of which sugars 4g; Fat 24g, of which saturates10g; Cholesterol 69mg; Calcium 167mg; Fibre 0g; Sodium 83mg.
Salmon Spaghetti Energy 701kcal/2941kJ; Protein 32.4g; Carbohydrate 70.4g, of which sugars 8.5g; Fat 30.6g, of which saturates 14.3g; Cholesterol 145mg; Calcium 94mg; Fibre 4.1g; Sodium 115mg.

Farfalle with Smoked Salmon and Dill

This quick, luxurious sauce for pasta has become very fashionable in Italy, but wherever you have it, it will taste delicious. Dill is the classic herb for cooking with fish, but if you don't like its aniseed flavour, substitute parsley or a little fresh tarragon.

Serves 4

6 spring onions (scallions), sliced
50g/2oz/¼ cup butter
90ml/6 tbsp dry white wine
  or vermouth
450ml/¾ pint/scant 2 cups double
  (heavy) cream
freshly grated nutmeg
225g/8oz smoked salmon
30ml/2 tbsp chopped fresh dill
freshly squeezed lemon juice
450g/1lb/4 cups farfalle
salt and ground black pepper
fresh dill sprigs, to garnish

1 Using a sharp cook's knife, slice the spring onions finely. Melt the butter in a large, heavy pan and fry the spring onions for about 1 minute, stirring occasionally, until softened.

2 Add the wine or vermouth and boil hard to reduce to about 30ml/2 tbsp. Stir in the cream and add salt, pepper and nutmeg to taste. Bring to the boil, then simmer for 2–3 minutes until slightly thickened.

3 Cut the smoked salmon slices into 2.5cm/1in squares and stir into the sauce, together with the dill. Add a little lemon juice to taste. Keep warm.

4 Cook the pasta in a large pan of boiling salted water, following the instructions on the packet. Drain well. Toss with the sauce. Spoon into serving bowls and serve immediately, garnished with sprigs of dill.

Cook's Tips
For a lighter touch, use half-fat crème fraîche instead of cream.

Penne with Cream and Smoked Salmon

No supper dish could be simpler, and it tastes delicious. Freshly cooked pasta is tossed with cream, smoked salmon and thyme. From start to finish it takes under 15 minutes to make.

Serves 4

350g/12oz/3 cups
  dried penne
115g/4oz thinly sliced
  smoked salmon
2–3 fresh thyme sprigs
25g/1oz/2 tbsp butter
150ml/¼ pint/⅔ cup double
  (heavy) cream
salt and ground black pepper

1 Bring a large pan of lightly salted water to the boil. Add the pasta and cook for about 12 minutes, or according to the instructions on the packet, until the penne are tender but still firm to the bite.

2 Meanwhile, using kitchen scissors or a small, sharp knife, cut the smoked salmon into thin strips, each about 5mm/¼in wide, and place on a plate. Strip the leaves from the thyme sprigs.

3 Melt the butter in a large pan. Stir in the cream with a quarter of the salmon and thyme leaves, then season with pepper. Heat gently for 3–4 minutes, stirring constantly. Do not allow the sauce to boil. Taste for seasoning.

4 Drain the pasta, return it to the pan, and toss it carefully in the cream and salmon sauce. Divide among four warmed bowls and top with the remaining salmon and thyme leaves. Serve immediately.

Cook's Tips
Substitute low fat cream cheese for half or all of the cream in the sauce, for a less rich mixture that still tastes smooth and delicious.

Salmon Farfalle Energy 1058kcal/4403kJ; Protein 29g; Carbohydrate 65g, of which sugars 4g; Fat 76g, of which saturates 45g; Cholesterol 201mg; Calcium 153mg; Fibre 4g; Sodium 1192mg.
Salmon Penne Energy 587kcal/2463kJ; Protein 17g; Carbohydrate 66g, of which sugars 4g; Fat 30g, of which saturates 16g; Cholesterol 79mg; Calcium 49 mg; Fibre 4g; Sodium 68mg.

Fusilli with Smoked Trout

In its creamy sauce, the smoked trout blends beautifully with the still crisp-tender vegetables in this classic pasta dish.

Serves 4–6

2 carrots, cut into matchsticks
1 leek, cut into matchsticks
2 celery sticks, cut into matchsticks
150ml/¼ pint/⅔ cup vegetable stock
225g/8oz smoked trout fillets, skinned and cut into strips
200g/7oz cream cheese
150ml/¼ pint/⅔ cup medium sweet white wine or fish stock
15ml/1 tbsp chopped fresh dill or fennel
225g/8oz/2 cups long curly fusilli or other dried pasta shapes
salt and ground black pepper
fresh dill sprigs, to garnish

1 Put the carrot, leek and celery matchsticks into a pan and add the stock. Bring to the boil and cook quickly for 4–5 minutes, until most of the stock has evaporated. Remove from the heat and add the smoked trout.

2 Put the cream cheese and wine or fish stock into a pan over a medium heat, and whisk until smooth. Add the dill or fennel and salt and pepper.

3 Cook the fusilli in a pan of salted boiling water according to the instructions on the packet. When the pasta is tender, but still firm to the bite, drain it thoroughly, and return it to the pan.

4 Add the sauce, toss lightly and transfer to a serving bowl. Top with the cooked vegetables and trout. Serve immediately, garnished with the dill sprigs.

> **Cook's Tips**
> *Two types of smoked trout are available: hot smoked and cold smoked. Hot smoked trout has a wonderful flavour and will enhance quiches and pâtés. Cold smoked trout has a more delicate flavour and is traditionally served with lemon, black pepper and bread. Both have a lower calorie count than salmon.*

Smoked Trout Cannelloni

Cannelloni usually has a meat and tomato filling, or one based on spinach and ricotta cheese. Smoked trout makes a delicious change in this version.

Serves 4–6

1 large onion, finely chopped
1 garlic clove, crushed
60ml/4 tbsp vegetable stock
2 x 400g/14oz cans chopped tomatoes
2.5ml/½ tsp dried mixed herbs
1 smoked trout, about 400g/14oz, or 225g/8oz fillets
75g/3oz/½ cup frozen peas, thawed
75g/3oz/1½ cups fresh breadcrumbs
16 no pre-cook cannelloni tubes
25ml/1½ tbsp freshly grated Parmesan cheese
salt and ground black pepper

For the white sauce
25g/1oz/2 tbsp butter
25g/1oz/¼ cup plain (all-purpose) flour
350ml/12fl oz/1½ cups skimmed milk
freshly grated nutmeg

1 Put the onion, garlic clove and stock in a large pan. Cover and simmer for 3 minutes. Remove the lid and cook until the stock has reduced entirely.

2 Stir in the tomatoes and dried herbs. Simmer uncovered for 10 minutes, or until the mixture is very thick.

3 Skin the trout and flake the flesh, discarding any bones. Put the fish in a bowl and add the tomato mixture, peas and breadcrumbs. Mix well, then season with salt and pepper.

4 Spoon the filling into the cannelloni tubes and arrange them in an ovenproof dish. Preheat the oven to 190°C/375°F/Gas 5.

5 Make the sauce. Put the butter, flour and milk into a pan and cook over medium heat, whisking constantly, until the sauce thickens. Simmer for 2–3 minutes, stirring all the time. Season to taste with salt, freshly ground black pepper and grated nutmeg.

6 Pour the sauce over the stuffed cannelloni and sprinkle with the grated Parmesan cheese. Bake for 30–45 minutes, or until the top is golden and bubbling. Serve immediately.

Smoked Trout Energy 410kcal/1735kJ; Protein 23.4g; Carbohydrate 62.3g, of which sugars 12g; Fat 9.3g, of which saturates 2.1g; Cholesterol 21mg; Calcium 186mg; Fibre 4.5g; Sodium 919mg.
Trout Cannelloni Energy 669Kcal/2811kJ; Protein 41.5g; Carbohydrate 74.5g, of which sugars 15.1g; Fat 24.9g, of which saturates 11.9g; Cholesterol 116mg; Calcium 353mg; Fibre 3.1g; Sodium 390mg.

Tuna Lasagne

Two popular Italian ingredients, tuna and pasta, combine to make a tasty lasagne that is sure to be a big hit with all the family.

Serves 6
12–16 fresh or dried
   lasagne sheets
15g/½oz butter
1 small onion, finely chopped
1 garlic clove, finely chopped
115g/4oz mushrooms,
   thinly sliced
60ml/4 tbsp dry white
   wine (optional)
white sauce (use 2 quantities, see
   page 98)
150ml/¼ pint/⅔ cup
   whipping cream
45ml/3 tbsp chopped
   fresh parsley
2 x 200g/7oz cans tuna, drained
2 canned pimientos, cut into strips
65g/2½oz/generous ½ cup
   frozen peas, thawed
115g/4oz mozzarella
   cheese, grated
30ml/2 tbsp freshly grated
   Parmesan cheese
salt and ground black pepper

1 For fresh lasagne, cook in a pan of salted boiling water until al dente. For dried lasagne, soak in a bowl of hot water for 3–5 minutes. Place the lasagne in a colander and rinse with cold water. Lay on a dish towel to drain.

2 Preheat the oven to 180°C/350°F/Gas 4. Melt the butter in a pan and cook the onion until soft.

3 Add the garlic and mushrooms to the pan and cook until soft, stirring occasionally. Pour in the wine, if using. Boil for 1 minute, then stir in the white sauce, cream and parsley. Season.

4 Spoon a thin layer of sauce over the base of a 30 x 23cm/12 x 9in baking dish. Cover with a layer of lasagne sheets.

5 Flake the tuna. Scatter half the tuna, pimiento strips, peas and grated mozzarella over the lasagne. Spoon one-third of the remaining sauce over the top and cover with another layer of lasagne.

6 Repeat the layers, ending with pasta and sauce. Sprinkle with the Parmesan. Bake for 30–40 minutes, or until lightly browned.

Seafood Lasagne

This dish can be as simple or as elegant as you like.

Serves 8
350g/12oz monkfish
350g/12oz salmon fillet
350g/12oz smoked haddock
1 litre/1¾ pints/4 cups milk
500ml/17fl oz/2¼ cups fish stock
2 bay leaves
1 small onion, halved
75g/3oz/6 tbsp butter, plus extra
   for greasing
45ml/3 tbsp plain (all-purpose) flour
150g/5oz/2 cups mushrooms,
   sliced
225–300g/8–11oz no pre-cook
   or fresh lasagne
60ml/4 tbsp freshly grated
   Parmesan cheese
salt, ground black pepper, grated
   nutmeg and paprika
rocket (arugula) leaves,
   to garnish

For the tomato sauce
30ml/2 tbsp olive oil
1 red onion, finely chopped
1 garlic clove, finely chopped
400g/14oz can chopped tomatoes
15ml/1 tbsp tomato purée (paste)
15ml/1 tbsp fresh basil leaves

1 Make the tomato sauce. Fry the onion and garlic over a low heat for 5 minutes. Stir in the tomatoes and tomato purée and simmer for 20–30 minutes, stirring occasionally. Season and add the basil. Put all the fish in a pan with the milk, stock, bay leaves or saffron and onion. Poach for 5 minutes. When cool, strain the liquid and reserve it. Remove skin and bones, then flake the fish.

2 Preheat the oven to 180°C/350°F/Gas 4. Melt the butter in a pan and stir in the flour. Cook for 2 minutes, stirring. Add the poaching liquid and bring to the boil, stirring. Add the mushrooms. Cook for 2 minutes. Season with salt, pepper and nutmeg.

3 Grease a shallow ovenproof dish. Spread a thin layer of the mushroom sauce over the dish. Stir the fish into the remaining mushroom sauce in the pan. Make a layer of lasagne, then a layer of fish and sauce. Add another layer of lasagne, then spread over all the tomato sauce. Continue to layer the lasagne and fish, finishing with a layer of fish and sauce.

4 Sprinkle over the cheese. Bake for 30–45 minutes, until golden. Remove from the oven and leave to stand for 10 minutes. Sprinkle with paprika. Garnish with rocket and serve.

Tuna Lasagna Energy 554Kcal/2315kJ; Protein 32.2g; Carbohydrate 28.9g, of which sugars 7.4g; Fat 34.7g, of which saturates 18.5g; Cholesterol 110mg; Calcium 371mg; Fibre 0.6g; Sodium 616mg.
Seafood Lasagne Energy 411kcal/1724kJ; Protein 32.2g; Carbohydrate 29.8g, of which sugars 3.6g; Fat 18.9g, of which saturates 7.8g; Cholesterol 71mg; Calcium 143mg; Fibre 1.9g; Sodium 525mg.

Fish with Fregola

This Sardinian speciality is a cross between a soup and a stew. Serve it with crusty Italian country bread to mop up the juices.

Serves 4–6
75ml/5 tbsp olive oil
4 garlic cloves, finely chopped
¹/₂ small fresh red chilli, seeded and finely chopped
1 handful flat leaf parsley, chopped

1 red snapper, about 450g/1lb, cleaned, with head and tail removed
1 grey mullet or porgy, about 500g/1 1/4lb, cleaned, with head and tail removed
350–450g/12oz–1lb cod fillet
400g/14oz can plum tomatoes
175g/6oz/1¹/₂ cups dried fregola
250ml/8fl oz/1 cup water
salt and ground black pepper

1 Heat 30ml/2 tbsp of the olive oil in a large flameproof casserole. Add the chopped garlic and chilli, with about half the chopped fresh parsley. Fry over a medium heat, stirring occasionally, for about 5 minutes.

2 Cut all of the fish into large chunks – including the skin and the bones in the case of the snapper and mullet – and add the pieces to the casserole. Sprinkle with a further 30ml/2 tbsp of the olive oil and fry for a few minutes more.

3 Add the tomatoes, then fill the empty can with water and add to the pan. Bring to the boil. Season to taste, lower the heat and cook for 10 minutes. Add the fregola and simmer for 5 minutes, then add the water and the remaining oil. Simmer for 15 minutes until the fregola is just tender.

4 If the sauce becomes too thick, add more water, then taste for seasoning. Serve hot, in warmed bowls, sprinkled with the remaining parsley.

> **Cook's Tips**
> • Fregola is a tiny pasta shape from Sardinia. If you can't find it, use a tiny soup pasta (pastina), such as corallini or semi de melone.

Pasta with Fresh Sardines

The ingredient that gives this dish its unique aniseed flavour is wild fennel.

Serves 4 to 6
1 sachet saffron powder
150g/5oz wild fennel (leaves and stalks), washed and trimmed
10ml/2 tsp fine salt
2 litres/3¹/₂ pints/8 cups cold water

1 large onion, chopped
90ml/6 tbsp olive oil
25g/1oz/¹/₃ cup pine nuts
30ml/2 tbsp sultanas (golden raisins), soaked in water
275g/10oz fresh or thawed frozen sardines, cleaned, boned and with heads removed
2 whole salted anchovies, boned and washed
400g/14oz fresh or dried bucatini
sea salt and ground black pepper

1 Soak the saffron in 45ml/3 tbsp cold water. Put the fennel in a large pan with the salt and the measured water. Bring to the boil, lower the heat and cover the pan. Simmer for 10 minutes. Drain the fennel and put it in a sieve (strainer) until cool enough to handle. Squeeze the fennel in your hands over a bowl, then chop it finely. Set the pan with the cooking water aside.

2 Put the onion in a pan and cover with water. Bring to the boil, then simmer for about 10 minutes or until the onion is soft. Add half the olive oil, the saffron with its soaking water, and the pine nuts to the cooked onion. Drain the sultanas and stir them into the pan. Simmer, stirring frequently, for 10 minutes.

3 Stir in the fennel and the sardines. Cover and cook gently for 4–5 minutes, until the sardines are cooked through.

4 Meanwhile, in a separate pan, cook the anchovies for 2–3 minutes in the remaining olive oil, then mash to a smooth purée. Stir in the anchovy purée to the sardines. Mix well and season to taste with salt and black pepper. Keep the mixture warm.

5 Return the pan used for cooking the fennel to the heat. Season. Bring to the boil, add the pasta and stir. Cook fresh pasta for about 4 minutes; dried pasta for 12–14 minutes. When the pasta is tender, drain it, transfer it to a warmed bowl and pour over the sauce. Toss thoroughly and serve.

Fish with Fregola Energy 300Kcal/1256kJ; Protein 29.6g; Carbohydrate 17.3g, of which sugars 2.3g; Fat 12.9g, of which saturates 1.7g; Cholesterol 44mg; Calcium 79mg; Fibre 1.1g; Sodium 126mg.
Sardines Energy 478kcal/2007kJ; Protein 20g; Carbohydrate 57.4g, of which sugars 9.1g; Fat 20.3g, of which saturates 3.1g; Cholesterol 0mg; Calcium 90mg; Fibre 3.4g; Sodium 226mg.

Vermicelli with Squid Ink

Using really fresh squid is key here, as this will ensure the sweetest and most fragrant finished dish.

Serves 4 to 6

whole fresh squid with ink sac
    (around 500g/1¼lb)
60ml/4 tbsp olive oil
2–3 whole garlic cloves, bruised
45ml/3 tbsp chopped
    fresh parsley
100ml/3½fl oz/scant ½ cup dry
    white wine
15ml/1 tbsp strattu or 45ml/3
    tbsp concentrated tomato
    purée (paste)
400g/14oz vermicelli
sea salt and ground black pepper

1 Rinse the squid. Holding one firmly, grasp the tentacles at the base and pull the head and entrails away from the body. Cut off the tentacles from the head and set them aside. Discard the head and the 'beak' but retain the ink sac, which looks like a black vein. Peel the membrane from the body, then pull out and discard the 'quill'. Cut the body of the squid into small cubes. Chop the tentacles finely. Repeat with the rest of the squid. Rinse and dry all the squid well.

2 Heat the olive oil over a medium heat in a large pan. Add the garlic cloves, fry until brown, then remove with a slotted spoon and discard. Add the squid to the garlic-flavoured oil. Stir in the parsley and plenty of pepper. Cover and simmer the mixture for 45 minutes.

3 Pour over the white wine and add the strattu or tomato purée. Stir well and continue to simmer, uncovered, for 20 minutes. Lower the heat, cover the pan again and cook for a further 30 minutes, adding a little hot water if needed.

4 About 15–17 minutes before serving, bring a large pan of salted water to the boil. Add the pasta, stir and cook for 10–12 minutes over a medium heat until just tender.

5 Meanwhile, add the ink sacs to the sauce and stir to mix.

6 Drain the pasta and return it to the pan. Pour the sauce over and mix. Cover and leave to stand for 5 minutes, then serve.

Tagliatelle with Cuttlefish and Shrimp

This is a very simple combination of tastes and textures, put together to create a sumptuous pasta dish. In some coastline areas of Italy, in the Abruzzi, empty, clean scallop shells are used to serve pasta dishes such as this one. It looks attractive, and the pasta stays wonderfully hot encased in the shells.

Serves 4

120ml/4fl oz/½ cup olive oil
1 garlic clove
a pinch of crushed chilli flakes
450g/1lb cuttlefish, cleaned and
    cut into small cubes
275g/10oz raw shrimp tails or
    prawns (shrimp), peeled and
    cut into small cubes
175ml/6fl oz/¾ cup
    dry white wine
3 ripe tomatoes, peeled, seeded
    and diced
350g/12oz fresh tagliatelle
sea salt
a handful of fresh flat leaf
    parsley, leaves chopped,
    to garnish

1 Put the olive oil, garlic clove and chilli flakes into a pan and fry gently until the garlic is golden brown.

2 Add the cuttlefish and shrimp tails or prawns, and stir together until the seafood is coated with the oil.

3 Add the white wine, bring to the boil and simmer gently for 1–2 minutes.

4 Add the diced tomatoes and stir well. Simmer for 5 minutes and season with salt.

5 Meanwhile, cook the tagliatelle in a large pan of salted boiling water, until the pasta is al dente.

6 Drain the pasta and return it to the pan. Add the sauce and mix together gently. Serve immediately, sprinkled with the fresh parsley.

Squid Energy 383kcal/1603kJ; Protein 18.9g; Carbohydrate 53.5g, of which sugars 0.3g; Fat 9.1g, of which saturates 1.4g; Cholesterol 188mg; Calcium 40mg; Fibre 0.3g; Sodium 100mg.
Cuttlefish Energy 630kcal/2654kJ; Protein 41.3g; Carbohydrate 67.4g, of which sugars 5.5g; Fat 20.5g, of which saturates 3g; Cholesterol 258mg; Calcium 152mg; Fibre 3.3g; Sodium 558mg.

Pasta with Mussels, Garlic and Tomatoes

This is one of the easiest ways to enjoy the delicious combination of pasta with shellfish. The recipe is a famous speciality of Campo Marino, a seaside resort on the Ionian coast in Puglia. Mussels are popular in the area, and the locals eat them raw with just a squeeze of lemon juice. In this recipe, they are flavoured simply with oil, garlic and parsley.

Serves 4

500g/1¼lb live mussels or cooked mussels in their shells
350g/12oz dried maccheroncini or spaghetti
60ml/4 tbsp olive oil
2 garlic cloves, finely chopped
45ml/3 tbsp chopped fresh parsley
400g/14oz chopped and seeded ripe tomatoes, drained
sea salt and ground black pepper

1 If using fresh mussels, discard any that are not tightly closed, or that do not snap shut when tapped sharply on the work surface. Scrub all the mussels carefully, remove the beards, and rinse them thoroughly.

2 Place the cleaned mussels in a wide frying pan. Cover the pan and place over medium-high heat for 5–6 minutes, shaking the pan frequently, until the mussels have opened. Any mussels that have not opened after this time should be discarded.

3 Remove all the mussels from the open shells, wipe off any traces of sand or sediment, and set them aside. Discard the shells.

4 Bring a large pan of lightly salted water to the boil and add the dried pasta. Stir, return to the boil and cook for 12–14 minutes or until just tender.

5 Meanwhile, heat the oil in a large frying pan and add the garlic and parsley. Fry for 5 minutes, then add the tomatoes. Season, stir, and cook over a high heat for about 8 minutes. Stir in the mussels.

Stir-fried Noodles with Soy Salmon

Teriyaki sauce forms the marinade for the salmon in this recipe and when added to the stir-fry, produces a lovely, shiny glaze on the fish. Served with soft-fried noodles, it makes a very tasty dish.

Serves 4

350g/12oz salmon fillet, skinned
30ml/2 tbsp shoyu (Japanese soy sauce)
30ml/2 tbsp sake
60ml/4 tbsp mirin or sweet sherry
5ml/1 tsp soft light brown sugar
10ml/2 tsp grated fresh root ginger
3 garlic cloves, 1 crushed, and 2 sliced into rounds
30ml/2 tbsp groundnut (peanut) oil
225g/8oz dried egg noodles, cooked and drained
50g/2oz/1 cup alfalfa sprouts
30ml/2 tbsp sesame seeds, lightly toasted

1 Using a sharp cook's knife, slice the salmon thinly. Spread out the slices in a large, shallow dish, keeping them in a single layer if possible.

2 In a bowl, mix together the soy sauce, sake, mirin or sherry, sugar, ginger and crushed garlic to make the teriyaki sauce. Pour the sauce over the salmon, cover and leave to marinate for about 30 minutes.

3 Preheat the grill (broiler). Drain the salmon, reserving the marinade. Place the salmon in a layer on a baking sheet. Cook under the grill for 2–3 minutes.

4 Meanwhile, heat a wok until hot, add the oil and swirl it around. Add the garlic rounds and cook until golden brown. Remove the garlic and discard.

5 Add the cooked noodles and reserved marinade to the wok and stir-fry for 3–4 minutes until the marinade has reduced to a syrupy glaze and coats the noodles. Toss in the alfalfa sprouts. Transfer immediately to warmed serving plates and top with the salmon. Sprinkle over the sesame seeds and serve.

Mussel Pasta Energy 452kcal/1910kJ; Protein 18.1g; Carbohydrate 68.3g, of which sugars 6.3g; Fat 13.8g, of which saturates 2g; Cholesterol 15mg; Calcium 128mg; Fibre 4.2g; Sodium 95mg.
Soy Salmon Energy 515kcal/2158kJ; Protein 27g; Carbohydrate 44g, of which sugars 4g; Fat 25g, of which saturates 5g; Cholesterol 61mg; Calcium 83mg; Fibre 3g; Sodium 680mg.

Buckwheat Noodles with Smoked Trout

The light, crisp texture of the pak choi balances the strong, earthy flavours of the mushrooms and buckwheat noodles and the smokiness of the trout.

Serves 4

350g/12oz buckwheat noodles
30ml/2 tbsp vegetable oil
115g/4oz/1½ cup fresh shiitake
   mushrooms, stems trimmed
   and quartered
2 garlic cloves, finely chopped
15ml/1 tbsp grated fresh
   root ginger
225g/8oz pak choi (bok choy)
1 spring onion (scallion), finely
   sliced diagonally
15ml/1 tbsp dark sesame oil
30ml/2 tbsp mirin or sweet sherry
30ml/2 tbsp soy sauce
2 smoked trout, skinned
   and boned
salt and ground black pepper
30ml/2 tbsp coriander (cilantro)
   leaves and 10ml/2 tsp sesame
   seeds, toasted, to garnish

1 Cook the buckwheat noodles in a pan of boiling water for 7–10 minutes, or following the instructions on the packet.

2 Meanwhile, heat the vegetable oil in a large frying pan. Add the shiitake mushrooms and sauté over a medium heat for 3 minutes. Add the garlic, ginger and pak choi, and continue to sauté for 2 minutes.

3 Drain the noodles and add them to the vegetables in the frying pan with the spring onion, sesame oil, mirin or sherry and soy sauce. Mix well and season with salt and pepper to taste.

4 Break the trout into bitesize pieces. Arrange the noodle mixture on individual serving plates. Place the smoked trout on top of the noodles. Garnish with coriander leaves and sesame seeds, and serve immediately.

> **Cook's Tip**
> Pak choi, also known as bok choy, has a crisp texture and tastes rather like a mixture of spinach and cabbage.

Malaysian Steamed Trout with Noodles

This simple dish, served on a bed of noodles, can be prepared quickly. It is suitable for any fish fillets.

Serves 4

8 pink trout fillets, about
   115g/4oz each, skinned
45ml/3 tbsp grated creamed
   coconut or desiccated (dry
   unsweetened shredded)
   coconut
grated rind and juice of 2 limes
45ml/3 tbsp chopped fresh
   coriander (cilantro)
15ml/1 tbsp groundnut
   (peanut) oil
2.5–5ml/½–1 tsp chilli oil
350g/12oz broad egg noodles
salt and ground black pepper
lime slices and coriander, to
   garnish

1 Cut four rectangles of baking parchment, each about twice the size of the trout fillets. Place a fillet on each piece and season lightly.

2 Mix together the coconut, lime rind and chopped coriander and spread one-quarter of the mixture over each trout fillet. Sandwich another trout fillet on top.

3 Mix the lime juice with the oils, adjusting the quantity of chilli oil to your own taste, and drizzle the mixture over the trout 'sandwiches'.

4 Prepare a steamer. Fold up the edges of the paper and pleat them over the trout to make parcels, ensuring they are sealed.

5 Place in the steamer insert and steam over the simmering water for about 10–15 minutes, depending on the thickness of the trout fillets.

6 Meanwhile, cook the noodles in a large pan of boiling water for 5–8 minutes, until just tender. Drain, toss with a little chilli oil, if you like, and divide among four warmed plates. Remove each trout 'sandwich' from its wrapper and place on top of the noodles. Garnish with the lime slices and coriander.

Smoked Trout Energy 562kcal/2363kJ; Protein 24g; Carbohydrate 69g, of which sugars 4g; Fat 22g, of which saturates 4g; Cholesterol 68mg; Calcium 74mg; Fibre 4g; Sodium 727mg.
Steamed Trout Energy 774kcal/3525kJ; Protein 56g; Carbohydrate 64g, of which sugars 3g; Fat 34g, of which saturates 12g; Cholesterol 180mg; Calcium 72mg; Fibre 4g; Sodium 265mg.

Steamed Fish Skewers on Herbed Rice Noodles

Fresh trout is perfect for summer entertaining. In this recipe, succulent fillets are marinated in a tangy citrus spice blend, then skewered and steamed before serving on a bed of herb noodles.

Serves 4
4 trout fillets, skinned
2.5ml/½ tsp turmeric
15ml/1 tbsp mild curry paste
juice of 2 lemons
15ml/1 tbsp sunflower oil
salt and ground black pepper

45ml/3 tbsp chilli-roasted peanuts, roughly chopped
chopped fresh mint, to garnish

For the noodles
300g/11oz rice noodles
15ml/1 tbsp sunflower oil
1 red chilli, seeded and finely sliced
4 spring onions (scallions), cut into slivers
60ml/4 tbsp roughly chopped fresh mint
60ml/4 tbsp roughly chopped fresh sweet basil

1 Trim each fillet and place in a large bowl. Mix together the turmeric, curry paste, lemon juice and oil and pour over the fish. Season with salt and black pepper and toss to mix well.

2 Place the rice noodles in a bowl and pour over enough boiling water to cover. Leave to soak for 3–4 minutes and then drain. Refresh in cold water, drain and set aside.

3 Thread two bamboo skewers through each trout fillet and arrange in two tiers of a baking bamboo steamer lined with baking parchment. Cover the steamer and place over a wok of simmering water (making sure the water doesn't touch the steamer). Steam the fish skewers for 5–6 minutes, or until the fish is just cooked through.

4 Meanwhile, in a clean wok heat the oil. Add the chilli, spring onions and noodles and stir-fry for about 2 minutes then stir in the herbs. Season and divide among four bowls or plates.

5 Top each bowl of noodles with a fish skewer and scatter over the chilli-roasted peanuts. Garnish with mint and serve immediately.

Crispy Egg Noodle Pancake with Prawns, Scallops and Squid

For this popular dish, the Vietnamese use thin Shanghai-style noodles, which are available in Chinese and Asian markets.

Serves 4
225g/8oz fresh egg noodles
45ml/3 tbsp vegetable oil, plus extra for brushing

For the seafood
15–30ml/1–2 tbsp vegetable oil
4cm/1½in fresh root ginger, peeled and cut into matchsticks

4 spring onions (scallions), trimmed and cut into pieces
1 carrot, peeled and cut into thin, diagonal slices
8 scallops (halved if large)
8 baby squid, cut in half lengthways
8 tiger prawns (shrimp), shelled and deveined
30ml/2 tbsp nuoc mam
45ml/3 tbsp soy sauce
5ml/1 tsp sugar
ground black pepper
fresh coriander (cilantro) leaves, to garnish
nuoc cham, to serve

1 Bring a large pan of water to the boil. Drop in the noodles, untangling them with a fork. Cook for about 5 minutes, or until tender. Drain and spread the noodles out into a wide, thick pancake on an oiled plate. Leave to dry out a little.

2 Heat 30ml/2 tbsp of the oil in a non-stick, heavy pan. Carefully slide the noodle pancake off the plate into the pan and cook over a medium heat until it is crisp and golden underneath. Add a little extra oil to the pan, flip the noodle pancake over and crisp the other side too.

3 Meanwhile, heat a wok or heavy pan and add the oil. Stir in the ginger and spring onions, and cook until they become fragrant. Add the carrot slices, tossing them in the wok, for 1–2 minutes. Add the scallops, squid and prawns, moving them around the wok, so that they sear while cooking. Stir in the nuoc mam, soy sauce and sugar and season with black pepper.

4 Transfer the pancake to a dish and place the seafood on top. Garnish with coriander and serve. To eat, drizzle with nuoc cham.

Fish Skewers Energy 544kcal/2277kJ; Protein 34g; Carbohydrate 63g, of which sugars 1g; Fat 17g, of which saturates 3g; Cholesterol 101mg; Calcium 64mg; Fibre 4g; Sodium 155mg.
Noodle Pancake Energy 807Kcal/3401kJ; Protein 83g; Carbohydrate 53g, of which sugars 48g; Fat 31g, of which saturates 5g; Cholesterol 97.5mg; Calcium 110mg; Fibre 2.3g; Sodium 1.6g.

Baked Trout with Rice, Tomatoes and Nuts

Trout is very popular in Spain, particularly in the North, where it is fished in many rivers. Here it is baked in foil with a rice stuffing in which sun-dried tomatoes have been used in place of chillies.

Serves 4

2 fresh trout, about 500g/1¼lb each
75g/3oz/¾ cup mixed unsalted almonds, pine nuts or hazelnuts
25ml/1½ tbsp olive oil, plus extra for drizzling
1 small onion, finely chopped
10ml/2 tsp grated fresh root ginger
175g/6oz/1½ cups cooked white long grain rice
4 tomatoes, peeled and very finely chopped
4 sun-dried tomatoes in oil, drained and chopped
30ml/2 tbsp chopped fresh tarragon
2 fresh tarragon sprigs
salt and ground black pepper
dressed green salad leaves, to serve

1 Preheat the oven to 190°C/375°F/Gas 5. If the trout is unfilleted, use a sharp knife to fillet it. Remove any tiny bones remaining in the cavity using a pair of tweezers.

2 Spread out the nuts in a shallow tin (pan) and bake for 3–4 minutes until golden brown, shaking the tin occasionally. Chop the nuts roughly.

3 Heat the olive oil in a small frying pan and fry the onion for 3–4 minutes until soft and translucent. Stir in the grated ginger, cook for a further 1 minute, then spoon into a mixing bowl. Stir the rice, tomatoes, sun-dried tomatoes, toasted nuts and tarragon into the onion mixture. Season the stuffing well.

4 Place the trout on individual large pieces of oiled foil and spoon the stuffing into the cavities. Add a sprig of tarragon and a drizzle of olive oil or oil from the sun-dried tomatoes.

5 Fold the foil over to enclose each trout, and put the parcels in a roasting pan. Bake for about 20 minutes or until the fish is just tender. Cut the fish into thick slices. Serve with the salad leaves.

Crayfish and Potato Stew with Fresh Cheese

The Peruvian variety of crayfish proliferate in the rivers of the south and there is no greater delicacy than fresh crayfish straight out of the water. The evaporated milk adds a touch of sweetness as well as a creamy texture.

Serves 6

675g/1½lb raw crayfish or king prawns (jumbo shrimp)
1kg/2¼lb floury potatoes
75ml/5 tbsp butter
1 small red onion, finely chopped
60ml/4 tbsp chilli sauce
5ml/1 tsp paprika
3 medium tomatoes, peeled, seeded and diced
5ml/1 tsp black mint (peppermint) leaves, finely sliced
500g/1¼lb queso fresco or mild feta cheese, cut into 2cm/¾in dice
120ml/4fl oz/½ cup evaporated milk
15ml/1 tbsp chopped parsley or mint leaves, to garnish
salt

1 Pour 350ml/12fl oz/1½ cups water into a large pan and bring to a boil. Drop the crayfish or prawns in, cover, and cook for about 10 minutes.

2 Strain and reserve the stock: there should be about 250ml/8fl oz/1 cup. Put aside six whole crayfish or prawns. Peel the rest, remove their heads, and devein.

3 Boil the potatoes in their skins in lightly salted water until tender, then peel them and cut into 1cm/½in slices.

4 Heat the butter in a large pan and cook the onion until softened. Stir in the chilli sauce, paprika, tomatoes and mint, and cook for 3 minutes. Add the crayfish or prawn tails, the reserved stock, cheese and sliced potatoes.

5 Bring to the boil and simmer for 5 minutes, or until the cheese has melted. Add the evaporated milk, season to taste with salt and simmer for 5 more minutes. Serve, garnished with parsley or mint leaves and the reserved whole crayfish or prawns.

Baked Trout Energy 458kcal/1920kJ; Protein 45.1g; Carbohydrate 19.4g, of which sugars 5g; Fat 22.8g, of which saturates 3.4g; Cholesterol 160mg; Calcium 146mg; Fibre 3.2g; Sodium 161mg.
Crayfish Stew Energy 541kcal/2262kJ; Protein 36.6g; Carbohydrate 34.1g, of which sugars 9.3g; Fat 29.5g, of which saturates 19g; Cholesterol 222mg; Calcium 411mg; Fibre 2.3g; Sodium 1639mg.

Rice Cakes with Smoked Salmon and Herbs

These elegant rice cakes are made using a risotto base. Or, you could use leftover long grain rice and add flavour with spring onions.

Serves 4
30ml/2 tbsp olive oil
1 medium onion, chopped
225g/8oz/generous 1 cup
  risotto rice
about 90ml/6 tbsp white wine
about 750ml/1¼ pints/3 cups
  fish or chicken stock
15g/1/2oz/2 tbsp dried porcini
  mushrooms, soaked for 10
  minutes in warm water to cover
15ml/1 tbsp chopped
  fresh parsley
15ml/1 tbsp snipped fresh chives
5ml/1 tsp chopped fresh dill
1 egg, lightly beaten
about 45ml/3 tbsp ground rice,
  plus extra for dusting
oil, for frying
60ml/4 tbsp soured cream
175g/6oz smoked salmon
salt and ground black pepper
dressed radicchio salad, to serve

1 Heat the olive oil in a pan and fry the onion for 3–4 minutes until soft. Add the rice and cook, stirring, until the grains are thoroughly coated in oil. Pour in the wine and stock, a little at a time, stirring constantly over a gentle heat until each quantity of liquid has been absorbed before adding more.

2 Drain the mushrooms and chop them into small pieces. When the rice is tender, and all the liquid has been absorbed, stir in the mushrooms, parsley, chives, dill and seasoning. Remove from the heat and set aside for a few minutes to cool.

3 Add the beaten egg, then stir in enough ground rice to bind the mixture – it should be soft but manageable. Dust your hands with ground rice and shape the mixture into four patties, about 13cm/5in in diameter and about 2cm/¾in thick.

4 Heat the oil in a pan and fry the rice cakes for 4–5 minutes until browned on both sides. Drain on kitchen paper and cool slightly. Place each rice cake on a plate and top with 15ml/1 tbsp soured cream. Twist two or three thin slices of smoked salmon on top, and serve with a dressed salad garnish.

Salt Cod Pancakes with Juicy Cabbage Rice

This dish is prepared all over Portugal; in some regions, the fish is cut into small pieces, in others, cooks use the whole fillet. The rice can be prepared with turnip tops, kidney beans and tomatoes.

Serves 4
400g/14oz salt cod, soaked
450ml/¾ pint/scant 2 cups milk
15ml/1 tbsp lemon juice
1 large (US extra large) egg
20ml/4 tsp olive oil
100g/3¾oz/scant 1 cup plain
  (all-purpose) flour
1 small onion, finely chopped
1 bunch of parsley, chopped
vegetable oil, for deep-frying

For the juicy cabbage rice
30ml/2 tbsp olive oil
1 onion, chopped
1 garlic clove, chopped
250g/9oz/1¼ cups risotto rice
1 small cabbage, shredded
salt

1 Remove the skin and bones from the fish and place the fillets in a dish. Mix together 300ml/½ pint/1¼ cups of the milk and lemon juice and pour over the fish. Marinate for 30 minutes.

2 Beat the egg with the olive oil in a bowl. Stir in the flour, onion, parsley and enough of the remaining milk to make a medium-thick paste.

3 Meanwhile, prepare the juicy cabbage rice. Heat the olive oil in a large pan. Add the onion and garlic and cook over a low heat, stirring occasionally, for 5 minutes, until softened.

4 Add the rice and cook, stirring frequently, for 1–2 minutes, until the grains are coated with oil. Pour in 750ml/1¼ pints/3 cups water and bring to the boil. Add the cabbage and season with salt. Cook for 15–20 minutes, until the rice is just tender.

5 Meanwhile, heat the oil for deep-frying to 180–190°C/350–375°F or until a cube of day-old bread browns in 40 seconds. Remove the fish fillets from the marinade and coat with the paste. Add to the oil and deep-fry for 5–7 minutes, until golden. Drain on kitchen paper, then serve with the rice.

Salmon Cakes Energy 475kcal/1978kJ; Protein 18.3g; Carbohydrate 55.9g, of which sugars 1.6g; Fat 17.8g, of which saturates 4.1g; Cholesterol 72mg; Calcium 56mg; Fibre 0.6g; Sodium 849mg.
Salt Cod Energy 687kcal/2874kJ; Protein 43.4g; Carbohydrate 77.6g, of which sugars 7.9g; Fat 22.9g, of which saturates 3.4g; Cholesterol 107mg; Calcium 164mg; Fibre 4.2g; Sodium 431mg.

Kedgeree with Smoked Haddock and Eggs

Of Indian origin, kedgeree came to Scotland via England and the landed gentry. It quickly became a popular dish using smoked fish for breakfast or high tea. This is a more manageable dish than the full Scottish breakfast if you are feeding several people, and it is often served in guesthouses and restaurants.

Serves 4–6

450g/1lb smoked haddock
300ml/½ pint/1¼ cups milk
175g/6oz/scant 1 cup long
  grain rice
pinch of grated nutmeg and
  cayenne pepper
50g/2oz/¼ cup butter
1 onion, peeled and chopped
2 hard-boiled eggs
salt and ground black pepper
chopped fresh parsley, to garnish
lemon wedges and toast, to serve

1 Poach the haddock in the milk, made up with just enough water to cover the fish, for about 8 minutes, or until just cooked. Skin the haddock, remove all the bones and flake the flesh with a fork. Set aside.

2 Bring 600ml/1 pint/2½ cups water to the boil in a large pan. Add the rice, cover closely with a lid and cook over a low heat for about 25 minutes, or until all the water has been absorbed by the rice. Season with salt and a grinding of black pepper, and the nutmeg and cayenne pepper.

3 Meanwhile, heat 15g/½oz/1 tbsp butter in a pan and fry the onion until soft and transparent. Set aside. Roughly chop one of the hard-boiled eggs, and slice the other into neat wedges. .

4 Stir the remaining butter into the rice and add the flaked haddock, onion and the chopped egg. Season to taste and heat the mixture through gently (this can be done on a serving dish in a low oven if more convenient).

5 To serve, pile up the kedgeree on a warmed dish, sprinkle generously with parsley and arrange the wedges of egg on top. Put the lemon wedges on the dish and serve hot with toast.

North African Fish with Pumpkin Rice

The slightly sweet pumpkin is a good partner for the mildly spicy fish.

Serves 4

450g/1lb sea bass
30ml/2 tbsp plain flour
5ml/1 tsp ground coriander
1.5–2.5ml/¼–½ tsp
  ground turmeric
1 wedge of pumpkin, about
  500g/1¼lb
30–45ml/2–3 tbsp olive oil
6 spring onions, sliced diagonally
1 garlic clove, finely chopped

275g/10oz/1½ cups basmati
  rice, soaked
550ml/18fl oz/2½ cups
  fish stock
salt and ground black pepper
lemon wedges and fresh coriander
  sprigs, to serve

For the spice mixture

45ml/3 tbsp finely chopped
  fresh coriander
10ml/2 tsp finely chopped fresh
  root ginger
½–1 fresh chilli, seeded and very
  finely chopped
45ml/3 tbsp lime or lemon juice

1 Remove and discard any skin or bones from the fish, and cut into chunks. Mix the flour, ground coriander, turmeric and salt and pepper in a plastic bag, add the fish and shake until the fish is evenly coated. Set aside. Make the spice mixture by mixing all the ingredients in a small bowl. Cut away the skin and scoop out the seeds from the pumpkin. Cut the flesh into 2cm/¾in chunks.

2 Heat 15ml/1 tbsp oil in a flameproof casserole and stir-fry the spring onions and garlic for a few minutes. Add the pumpkin and cook over a low heat, stirring frequently, for 4–5 minutes. Drain the rice, add it to the mixture and toss over a brisk heat for 2 minutes. Stir in the stock. Simmer, lower the heat, cover and cook for 12–15 minutes until the rice and the pumpkin are tender.

3 About 4 minutes before the rice is ready, heat the remaining oil in a frying pan and fry the spiced fish for about 3 minutes until the outside is lightly browned and crisp and the flesh is cooked but still moist. Stir the spice mixture into the rice and transfer to a serving dish. Lay the fish pieces on top. Serve immediately, garnished with coriander, and offer lemon to squeeze on the fish.

Kedgeree Energy 399kcal/1668kJ; Protein 28.9g; Carbohydrate 38g, of which sugars 2.2g; Fat 14.6g, of which saturates 7.6g; Cholesterol 181mg; Calcium 62mg; Fibre 0.5g; Sodium 974mg.
African Fish Energy 499kcal/2104kJ; Protein 29g; Carbohydrate 70g, of which sugars 3g; Fat 14g, of which saturates 2g; Cholesterol 90mg; Calcium 210mg; Fibre 2g; Sodium 379mg.

Creamy Fish Pilau

This dish is inspired by a fusion of cuisines – the method comes from India and uses that country's favourite rice, basmati, but the delicious wine and cream sauce is very much French in flavour.

Serves 4–6

450g/1lb fresh mussels, scrubbed
350ml/12fl oz/1½ cups
    white wine
fresh parsley sprig
about 675g/1½lb salmon
225g/8oz scallops
about 15ml/1 tbsp olive oil

40g/1½oz/3 tbsp butter
2 shallots, finely chopped
225g/8oz/3 cups button
    mushrooms, halved if large
275g/10oz/1½ cups basmati
    rice, soaked
300ml/½ pint/1¼ cups fish stock
150ml/¼ pint/⅔ cup
    double cream
15ml/1 tbsp chopped
    fresh parsley
225g/8oz large cooked prawns,
    peeled and deveined
salt and freshly ground
    black pepper
fresh flat leaf parsley sprigs,
    to garnish

1 Preheat the oven to 160°C/325°F/Gas 3. Place the mussels in a pan with 90ml/6 tbsp of the wine and parsley, cover and cook for 4–5 minutes until they have opened. Drain, reserving the cooking liquid. Remove the mussels from their shells, discarding any that have not opened. Cut the fish into bitesize pieces. Detach the corals from the scallops and cut the white scallop flesh into thick pieces.

2 Heat half the olive oil and butter and fry the shallots and mushrooms for 3–4 minutes. Transfer to a large bowl. Heat the remaining oil in the pan and fry the rice for 2 minutes, stirring until coated in oil. Spoon the rice into a deep casserole.

3 Pour the stock, remaining wine and reserved mussel liquid into the frying pan, and bring to the boil. Off the heat, stir in the cream and parsley. Pour over the rice then add the salmon and the scallop flesh, with the mushroom mixture. Mix. Cover the casserole and bake for 30–35 minutes, add the corals, cover and cook for 4 minutes more. Add the mussels and prawns, cover and cook for 3–4 minutes until the seafood is heated through and the rice is tender. Serve garnished with the parsley.

Mixed Fish Jambalaya

As with the Spanish paella, the ingredients used to make this classic Creole dish can be varied according to what is available. The name jambalaya is thought to have come from the French word for ham – jambon – and the Creole word for rice – à la ya.

Serves 4

30ml/2 tbsp oil
6 rashers (strips) rinded smoked
    streaky (fatty) bacon, chopped
1 onion, chopped
2 sticks celery, sliced
2 garlic cloves, crushed
5ml/1 tsp cayenne pepper
2 bay leaves

5ml/1 tsp dried oregano
2.5ml/½ tsp dried thyme
4 tomatoes, skinned, seeded and
    chopped
750ml/1¼ pints/3 cups boiling
    vegetable or fish stock
15ml/1 tbsp tomato
    purée (paste)
300g/10oz/1½ cups easy-cook
    (converted) rice
225g/8oz firm white fish, such
    as haddock, skinned, boned
    and cubed
115g/4oz cooked
    prawns (shrimp)
salt and ground black pepper
4 spring onions (scallions) and 4
    cooked prawns (shrimp) in their
    shells, to garnish

1 Heat the oil in a frying pan and cook the bacon over a medium-high heat for 2 minutes. Reduce the heat, add the onion and celery and cook for a further 5–10 minutes, or until soft and beginning to turn brown.

2 Transfer the mixture to a ceramic cooking pot and switch the slow cooker to high. Add the garlic, cayenne pepper, bay leaves, oregano, thyme, tomatoes, boiling stock and tomato purée. Stir well to mix, then cover with the lid and cook for about 1 hour.

3 Sprinkle the rice over the tomato mixture, followed by the cubes of fish. Season with salt and pepper and stir. Re-cover and cook for 45 minutes.

4 Add the prawns and stir, then cook until the fish and rice are tender and most of the liquid has been absorbed. Serve garnished with spring onions and prawns in their shells.

Fish Pilau Energy 428kcal/1787kJ; Protein 24.2g; Carbohydrate 39g, of which sugars 1.1g; Fat 15.2g, of which saturates 8.7g; Cholesterol 134mg; Calcium 130mg; Fibre 0.8g; Sodium 200mg.
Jambalaya Energy 243Kcal/1015kJ; Protein 23.2g; Carbohydrate 6.5g, of which sugars 5.4g; Fat 14g, of which saturates 3.4g; Cholesterol 126mg; Calcium 64mg; Fibre 1.6g; Sodium 1303mg.

Stuffed Squid

Characteristic to most of the Portuguese coast, the preparation of this recipe can vary. The squid meat can be replaced by tentacles. The stuffing can be prepared with other fish, such as hake, without the tomato in the stuffing.

Serves 4

1kg/2¼lb squid, preferably about 10cm/4in long
150ml/¼ pint/⅔ cup olive oil
4 onions, chopped
2 garlic cloves, chopped
100g/3¾oz cured ham, chopped
150g/5oz sausage or bacon, chopped
4 large ripe tomatoes, peeled and chopped
100g/3¾oz/generous ½ cup cooked rice
1 bay leaf
1 bunch of parsley, chopped
salt
cooked potatoes, to serve

1 Rinse the squid under cold running water, then pull the head away from the body – the entrails will come away with the head. Cut off the tentacles and squeeze out the beak. Chop the tentacles and discard the 'beak'. Pull out and discard the transparent 'quill' from the body sac and clean out any remaining membrane. Rinse the body sac and peel off the skin.

2 Heat 50ml/2fl oz/¼ cup of the olive oil in a pan. Add half the onions and half the garlic and cook over a low heat, stirring occasionally, for 5 minutes, until softened. Add the chopped tentacles, ham and sausage or bacon and cook for a few minutes more. Stir in about a quarter of the tomatoes and all the rice. Mix well and remove the pan from the heat

3 Spoon the filling into the body sacs of the squid, filling them just over half full. Secure the openings with wooden cocktail sticks (toothpicks).

4 Heat the remaining oil in a large pan. Add the remaining onions and garlic and cook over a low heat, stirring occasionally, for 5 minutes, until softened. Add the bay leaf and remaining tomatoes and about 150ml/¼ pint/⅔ cup water. Stir in the parsley and add the squid. Season with salt and simmer gently for about 20 minutes, until tender. Serve with cooked potatoes.

Braised Octopus with Rice

While it has a delicate flavour, octopus also has a reputation for being chewy. This texture largely depends on its origin and quality, but also on how it is cooked.

Serves 4

1 octopus, about 1.6kg/3½lb
150ml/¼ pint/⅔ cup olive oil
2 onions, chopped
300g/11oz/generous 1½ cups long grain rice
1 bay leaf

For the stock
2 onions, quartered
1 leek, chopped
3 garlic cloves, crushed
10 black peppercorns
2 bay leaves
pinch of salt

1 Rinse the octopus in water and cut off the body. Turn the body inside out and pull out and discard the entrails. Remove the little strips from the sides of the body. Rinse well again and turn the right way out. Squeeze out the 'beak'. Beat the tentacles with a rolling pin or the flat side of a meat mallet.

2 Half fill a large pan with water and add all the ingredients for the stock. Bring to the boil, then lower the heat and simmer for 10 minutes. Add the octopus and bring back to the boil. Lower the heat slightly so that the liquid continues to boil and cook for 1 hour. Check with a fork to see if the octopus is tender. If not, cook for a little longer but check frequently because it will toughen if overcooked.

3 Strain the stock into a bowl and reserve. Discard the flavourings. Chop the octopus body and cut the tentacles into short lengths, keeping the two parts separate. Preheat the oven to 160°C/325°F/Gas 3.

4 Heat 50ml/2fl oz/½ cup of the olive oil in a flameproof casserole. Add the onions and cook over a low heat for 10 minutes, until lightly browned. Add the rice, the octopus body, the bay leaf and 600ml/1 pint/2½ cups of the reserved stock. Transfer the casserole to the oven and braise for 30 minutes. Meanwhile, place the tentacles in an ovenproof dish, pour the remaining olive oil over them and heat through in the oven. Combine with the rice mixture before serving.

Stuffed Squid Energy 418kcal/1758kJ; Protein 37.7g; Carbohydrate 20.7g, of which sugars 7.4g; Fat 21.2g, of which saturates 5.9g; Cholesterol 456mg; Calcium 245mg; Fibre 2.6g; Sodium 508mg.
Braised Octopus Energy 871kcal/3646kJ; Protein 78.8g; Carbohydrate 69.7g, of which sugars 7g; Fat 30.9g, of which saturates 4.8g; Cholesterol 192mg; Calcium 178mg; Fibre 1.8g; Sodium 95mg.

Juicy Seafood Rice

All along the Portugese coast from north to south, any restaurant will serve this rice dish, made with the best produce the sea can supply. It is often served in the pan in which it is cooked, or in a terracotta pot placed in the centre of the table and shared by everyone. The rice used is carolino rice, with a short plump, white grain, which is similar to Italian risotto rice, but long grain rice is a good alternative.

Serves 4
50ml/2fl oz/¼ cup olive oil
1 onion, chopped
1 green (bell) pepper, seeded
and chopped
1 tomato, peeled and chopped
1 litre/1¾ pints/4 cups
shellfish stock
200g/7oz live clams, scrubbed
200g/7oz live cockles, scrubbed
200g/7oz live mussels, scrubbed
and beards removed
300g/11oz/generous 1½ cups
risotto rice
400g/14oz cooked peeled
prawns (shrimp)
30ml/2 tbsp chopped fresh
coriander (cilantro)

1 Heat the olive oil in a large pan. Add the onion and green pepper and cook over a low heat, stirring occasionally, for 5 minutes, until softened. Add the tomato and the stock and bring to the boil.

2 Open the clams, cockles and mussels. You can open clams and cockles by placing them in a large bowl in the microwave on high power for 2 minutes. Remove open mollusks and repeat the process until all of them have opened. Another way to open clams, cockles and mussels is by steaming them briefly in a little water and removing them from their shells as soon as they open. It is best to do this in small batches. Once opened, reserve the shellfish meat, keeping the shells to one side.

3 Add the rice to the pan, bring back to the boil and cook for about 12 minutes, until tender. The mixture should be moist; if necessary, add more stock. Add all the seafood and the coriander, heat through briefly and serve, decorated with the seafood shells, if using.

Seafood Rice

This rice dish mixes elements of classical Spanish cuisine with the abundant seafood of the South Pacific. This recipe is the Peruvian interpretation of the traditional Spanish paella, adapted to use Peruvian ingredients and flavourings.

Serves 4
150g/5oz clams
150g/5oz squid, cleaned
120ml/4fl oz/½ cup olive oil
1 large red onion, chopped
5 garlic cloves, finely chopped
15ml/1 tbsp paprika
250ml/8fl oz/1 cup white wine
250ml/8fl oz/1 cup fish stock
4 crab claws
200g/7oz whelks
200g/7oz New Zealand
greenshell mussels
200g/7oz scallops
250g/9oz/2 cups shelled peas
675g/11½lb/3 cups
cooked rice
1 red (bell) pepper, diced
1 chilli, seeded and finely sliced
salt and ground black pepper
handful fresh parsley, chopped,
to garnish

1 Clean the clams, discarding any that remain open when sharply tapped. Slice the bodies of the squid and leave the tentacles whole.

2 Heat the oil in a large frying pan over medium heat and fry the onion with the garlic for 10 minutes, until browned. Add the paprika and season with salt and pepper.

3 Pour in the wine and fish stock, raise the heat to high and cook the crab claws for about 8 minutes.

4 Add the whelks, squid bodies, squid tentacles and the clams and cook for a further 7 minutes. Then add the mussels, if fresh, and cook for another 5 minutes, then the scallops and peas and cook for another 3 minutes, reducing the heat to medium.

5 When all clam shells have opened, add the cooked rice and stir for a further 2 minutes until it is mixed in and heated through. Add the diced pepper and the sliced chilli. Sprinkle with chopped parsley before serving.

Juicy Seafood Energy 484kcal/2027kJ; Protein 32g; Carbohydrate 64.6g, of which sugars 4.2g; Fat 10.5g, of which saturates 1.5g; Cholesterol 213mg; Calcium 215mg; Fibre 1.7g; Sodium 292mg.
Seafood Rice Energy 714kcal/2997kJ; Protein 48.9g; Carbohydrate 65.3g, of which sugars 4.5g; Fat 26g, of which saturates 4.1g; Cholesterol 213mg; Calcium 177mg; Fibre 3.8g; Sodium 832mg.

Cuban Seafood Rice

This is the perfect dish for a large gathering. The more people you make it for, the more types of seafood you can add, and the tastier it will become.

Serves 8
450g/1lb raw prawns (shrimp)
1 litre/1¾ pints/4 cups fish stock
450g/1lb squid
16 clams, scrubbed
16 mussels, scrubbed
60ml/4 tbsp olive oil
1 onion, finely chopped
1 fresh red chilli, seeded and finely chopped
2 garlic cloves, crushed
350g/12oz/1⅔ cups long grain rice
45ml/3 tbsp chopped fresh coriander (cilantro)
Juice of 2 limes
salt and ground black pepper

1 Peel the prawns. Place the shells in a pan and add the fish stock. Bring to the boil, then simmer for 15 minutes. Strain into a bowl, discarding the shells. Clean the squid. Pull the tentacles from the body and remove the entrails and 'quill' and discard them. Pull away the membrane that covers the body. Cut between the tentacles and head, discarding the head. Leave the tentacles whole but discard the 'beak'. Cut the body into thin rounds. Pull away the 'beard' from the mussels and discard any open shells that fail to close when tapped. Place all the shellfish in a bowl, cover and put in the refrigerator.

2 Pour half the olive oil into a pan with a tight fitting lid. Place over a high heat. When the oil is very hot, add the squid and season well. Stir-fry for 2–3 minutes, until the squid curls and begins to brown. Remove the pieces from the pan and set aside. Add the prawns to the pan and cook for 2 minutes. The moment they turn pink, remove them from the heat.

3 Pour the remaining oil into the pan. Sauté the onion for 5 minutes. Add the chilli and garlic and cook for 2 minutes. Add the rice, and cook, stirring, for 1 minute. Add the prawn stock and bring to the boil. Cover and simmer, for 15–18 minutes. Add the clams and mussels and cover the pan. Cook for 3–4 minutes, until their shells open. Remove from the heat and discard any that have remained closed. Stir the cooked squid, prawns, coriander and lime juice into the rice. Season and serve.

Paella Valenciana

Valencia's paella has become a celebration dish in Spain.

Serves 6–8
90ml/6 tbsp white wine
450g/1lb fresh mussels, scrubbed
115g/4oz/scant 1 cup small shelled broad (fava) beans
150g/5oz green beans, cut into short lengths
90ml/6 tbsp olive oil
6 small skinless, boneless chicken breast portions, cut into large pieces
150g/5oz pork fillet, cubed
6–8 large raw prawn (shrimp) tails, deveined
2 onions, chopped
2–3 garlic cloves, finely chopped
1 red (bell) pepper, seeded and sliced
2 ripe tomatoes, peeled, seeded and chopped
60ml/4 tbsp chopped fresh parsley
900ml/1½ pints/3¾ cups chicken stock
pinch of saffron threads (0.25g), soaked in 30ml/2 tbsp water
350g/12oz/1¾ cups paella rice, washed and drained
225g/8oz frying chorizo, sliced
115g/4oz/1 cup peas
6–8 stuffed green olives, sliced
salt, paprika and black pepper

1 Heat the wine and add the mussels, discarding any that do not close when tapped. Cover and steam until opened. Reserve the liquid and mussels separately, discarding any that do not open. Briefly cook the broad beans and green beans then drain. Pop the broad beans out of their skins.

2 Heat 45ml/3 tbsp oil in a paella pan. Season the chicken with salt and paprika, and fry, skin downward until browned on all sides. Reserve. Season the pork with salt and paprika. Add 15ml/1 tbsp oil and fry the pork until browned. Reserve with the chicken. Fry the prawns in the same pan, reserve them separately.

3 Heat the remaining oil and fry the onions and garlic for 3–4 minutes. Add the red pepper, cook for 2–3 minutes, then stir in the tomatoes and parsley and cook until thick. Add the chicken stock, the reserved mussel liquid and the saffron liquid to the vegetables. Season and when bubbling, add all the rice. Stir, then add the chicken, pork, shellfish, beans, chorizo and peas. Cook for 10 minutes, moving the pan, until the rice is done, about 10 minutes more. Put the mussels and olives on top. Stand for 10 minutes, until all the liquid is absorbed. Serve from the pan.

Seafood Paella

This is a great dish to serve to guests on a special occasion.

Serves 4

60ml/4 tbsp olive oil
225g/8oz monkfish or cod fillets, skinned and cut into chunks
3 prepared baby squid, cleaned, body cut into rings and tentacles chopped
1 red mullet, filleted, skinned and cut into chunks (optional)
1 onion, chopped
3 garlic cloves, finely chopped
1 red pepper, seeded and sliced
4 tomatoes, peeled and chopped

225g/8oz/generous 1 cup risotto rice
450ml/³/₄ pint/scant 2 cups fish stock
150ml/¹/₄ pint/²/₃ cup white wine
4–5 saffron threads soaked in 30ml/2 tbsp hot water
115g/4oz cooked, peeled prawns, thawed if frozen
75g/3oz/³/₄ cup frozen peas
8 fresh mussels, scrubbed
salt and freshly ground black pepper
4 Mediterranean prawns, in the shell to garnish
lemon wedges, to serve

1 Heat half the oil in paella pan or a large frying pan and add the monkfish or cod fillets, the squid and the red mullet, if using. Stir-fry for 2 minutes, then transfer to a bowl and set aside.

2 Heat the remaining oil in the pan and add the onion, garlic and pepper. Fry for 6–7 minutes, stirring, until softened.

3 Stir in the chopped tomatoes and fry for 2 minutes, then add the rice. Stir to coat the grains with the oil, then cook for 2–3 minutes. Pour over the fish stock, wine and saffron water. Season and mix well.

4 Gently stir in the reserved cooked fish (with all the juices), then the peeled prawns and the peas. Push the mussels into the rice. Cover and cook over a gentle heat for about 30 minutes, or until the stock has been absorbed but the rice mixture is still relatively moist. Discard any mussels that remain closed.

5 Remove from the heat, and leave the paella to stand, covered, for 5 minutes. Arrange the whole prawns on top. Serve the paella with the lemon wedges.

Moroccan Paella

This is a spicy version of paella from Morocco.

Serves 6

2 skinless, boneless chicken breasts
150g/5oz prepared squid, sliced
275g/10oz cod or haddock fillets, skinned, cut into chunks
8–10 raw king prawns, peeled
8 scallops, trimmed and halved
350g/12oz fresh mussels
250g/9oz/1¹/₃ cups white long grain rice
30ml/2 tbsp sunflower oil

1 bunch spring onions (scallions, sliced
1 red pepper, seeded and sliced
400ml/14fl oz/1²/₃ cups chicken stock
250ml/8fl oz/1 cup passata
salt and ground black pepper

For the marinade

2 red chillies, seeded and chopped
fresh coriander (cilantro)
10–15ml/2–3 tsp ground cumin
15ml/1 tbsp paprika
2 garlic cloves
105ml/7 tbsp olive oil
juice of 1 lemon

1 Place the ingredients for the marinade in a food processor with salt and blend together. Cut the chicken into bitesize pieces and place in a bowl. Put the fish, prawns and scallops in another bowl. Divide the marinade between the fish and chicken. Cover with clear film (plastic wrap) and marinate for 2 hours. Scrub the mussels, discarding any that do not close when tapped, and chill. Put the rice in a bowl, cover with boiling water and set aside for 30 minutes. Drain the chicken and fish, reserving both marinades. Heat the oil in a paella pan and fry the chicken pieces until browned. Add the spring onions to the pan, fry for 1 minute, add the red pepper and fry for 3 minutes.

2 Transfer the chicken and then the vegetables to separate plates. Scrape all the marinade into the pan and cook for 1 minute. Drain the rice, add to the pan and cook for 1 minute. Add the stock, passata and reserved chicken, season and stir well. Cover and simmer for 10–15 minutes until the rice is almost tender. Add the reserved vegetables to the pan and place all the fish and mussels on top. Cover again with a lid or foil and cook for 10–12 minutes until the fish is cooked and the mussels have opened. Discard any mussels that remain closed. Serve immediately.

Seafood Paella Energy 585kcal/2445kJ; Protein 36.1g; Carbohydrate 60.9g, of which sugars 10.1g; Fat 20.4g, of which saturates 5.6g; Cholesterol 268mg; Calcium 132mg; Fibre 4.2g; Sodium 1055mg.
Moroccan Paella Energy 401kcal/1688kJ; Protein 46g; Carbohydrate 39.3g, of which sugars 4.4g; Fat 6.6g, of which saturates 1.1g; Cholesterol 200mg; Calcium 115mg; Fibre 1.4g; Sodium 343mg.

Prawn Pilau

Bengal is renowned for its fish and shellfish, and this pilau from Goa combines tasty prawns with a very simple preparation method. A flavoursome meal in itself, the dish also fits easily into a spread that includes meat, poultry and vegetable dishes as well.

Serves 4

275g/10oz/1⅓ cups basmati rice
4 tbsp sunflower oil or olive oil
5cm/2in piece of cinnamon
    stick, halved
6 green cardamom pods, bruised
4 cloves
2 bay leaves, crumpled
1 large onion, finely sliced
2 tsp ginger purée
1 green chilli, finely chopped, and
    seeded if preferred
2.5ml/½ tsp ground turmeric
1 tsp salt, or to taste
1 tbsp chopped fresh
    coriander (cilantro)
250g/9oz cooked and peeled
    prawns (shrimp)
sprigs of coriander leaves,
    to garnish

1 Wash the rice in several changes of cold water and soak for 20 minutes. Leave to drain.

2 In a heavy-based pan, heat the oil over a low heat and add the cinnamon, cardamom, cloves and bay leaves. Stir-fry the ingredients gently for 25–30 seconds and then add the onion. Increase the heat to medium, and fry until the onion is beginning to brown, around 7–8 minutes, stirring frequently to prevent the spices from burning.

3 Add the ginger purée and chilli and continue to fry until the onion is well browned.

4 Add the turmeric, salt, chopped coriander, prawns and rice. Stir gently to mix the ingredients. Stir-fry for 2–3 minutes, then and pour in 475ml/16fl oz/2 cups hot water. Bring this to the boil and let it cook, uncovered, for 2–3 minutes. Reduce the heat to low, cover the pan and cook for another 7–8 minutes.

5 Remove from the heat and let the dish stand for 5–6 minutes to absorb the flavour. Fluff up the pilau with a fork and transfer it to a serving dish. Garnish with sprigs of coriander.

Mussel and Rice Pilaff

This is a classic dish and a favourite one in Greece.

Serves 4 as a main course
6 as a first course

1.6kg/3½lb mussels, scrubbed
    and bearded
2 onions, thinly sliced
2 glasses white wine, about
    350ml/12fl oz/1½ cups
450ml/¾ pint/2 cups hot water
150ml/¼ pint/⅔ cup olive oil
5–6 spring onions
    (scallions), chopped
2 garlic cloves, chopped
large pinch of dried oregano
200g/7oz/1 cup long grain rice
45ml/3 tbsp finely chopped fresh
    flat leaf parsley
45–60ml/3–4 tbsp chopped
    fresh dill
salt and ground black pepper

1 Discard any mussels that do not close when tapped. Place the remainder in a large pan. Add about one-third of the onion slices, then pour in half the wine and 150ml/¼ pint/⅔ cup of the hot water. Cover and cook over a high heat for about 5 minutes, shaking the pan occasionally, until the mussels open.

2 Place a colander on top of a large bowl and transfer the open mussels to the colander, reserving their liquid. Discard any mussels that remain closed. Shell most of the mussels, discarding their shells, but keep a dozen mussels in their shells for garnish.

3 Line a sieve with fine muslin or kitchen paper and place it over a large bowl. Let the liquid remaining in the pan settle, then strain it through the lined sieve. Do the same with the liquid from the bowl, which drained from the cooked mussels.

4 Heat the olive oil, add the remaining onion slices and the spring onions and sauté over a medium heat until both start to turn golden. Add the garlic and the oregano, then the rice, and stir to coat the grains in the oil. Add the remaining wine, stirring until it has been absorbed, then stir in the remaining 300ml/ ½ pint/1¼ cups water, the reserved mussel liquid and the parsley. Season, cover and cook gently for 5 minutes, stirring occasionally.

5 Add the mussels, with those in their shells. Stir in half the dill. Add more hot water if needed. Cover and cook for 5–6 minutes, until the rice is cooked. Add the rest of the dill and serve.

Prawn Pilau Energy 440kcal/1835kJ; Protein 17.9g; Carbohydrate 64.1g, of which sugars 5.6g; Fat 12.4g, of which saturates 1.3g; Cholesterol 122mg; Calcium 94mg; Fibre 1.4g; Sodium 123mg.
Mussel Pilaff Energy 218kcal/924kJ; Protein 15g; Carbohydrate 36g, of which sugars 3g; Fat 2g, of which saturates 0g; Cholesterol 43mg; Calcium 66 mg; Fibre 2g; Sodium 261mg.

Monkfish Risotto

Monkfish is a versatile, firm-textured fish with a superb flavour, which is accentuated with lemon grass in this sophisticated risotto.

Serves 3–4
seasoned flour
about 450g/1lb monkfish,
    cut into cubes
30ml/2 tbsp olive oil
40g/1½oz/3 tbsp butter
2 shallots, finely chopped
1 lemon grass stalk,
    finely chopped
275g/10oz/1½ cups risotto rice,
    preferably Carnaroli
175ml/6fl oz/¾ cup dry
    white wine
1 litre/1¾ pints/4 cups
    simmering fish stock
30ml/2 tbsp chopped
    fresh parsley
salt and white pepper
dressed salad leaves, to serve

1 Spoon the seasoned flour over the monkfish cubes in a bowl. Toss the monkfish until coated.

2 Heat 15ml/1 tbsp of the oil with half the butter in a frying pan. Fry the monkfish cubes over a medium to high heat for 3–4 minutes until cooked, turning occasionally. Transfer to a plate and set aside.

3 Heat the remaining oil and butter in a saucepan and fry the shallots over a low heat for about 4 minutes until soft but not brown. Add the lemon grass and cook for 1–2 minutes more.

4 Tip in the rice. Cook for 2–3 minutes, stirring, until the rice is coated with oil and is slightly translucent. Gradually add the wine and the hot stock, stirring and waiting until each ladleful has been absorbed before adding the next.

5 When the rice is about three-quarters cooked, stir in the monkfish. Continue to cook the risotto, adding the remaining stock and stirring constantly until the grains of rice are tender, but still retain a bit of 'bite'. Season with salt and white pepper.

6 Remove the pan from the heat, stir in the parsley and cover with the lid. Leave the risotto to stand for a few minutes before serving with a garnish of dressed salad leaves.

Spicy Green Hoki

Any firm-fleshed fish can be used for this dish, which gains its rich colour from a mixture of fresh herbs. This recipe uses hoki, which is a fish in the hake family.

Serves 4
4 garlic cloves, roughly chopped
5cm/2in piece fresh root ginger,
    peeled and roughly chopped
2 fresh green chillies, seeded and
    roughly chopped
grated rind and juice of 1 lime
5ml/1 tsp coriander seeds
5ml/1 tsp five-spice powder
75ml/5 tbsp sesame oil
2 red onions, finely chopped
900g/2lb hoki fillets, skinned
400ml/14fl oz/1⅔ cups
    coconut milk
45ml/3 tbsp fish sauce
50g/2oz fresh coriander (cilantro)
50g/2oz fresh mint leaves
50g/2oz fresh basil leaves
6 spring onions (scallions),
    chopped
150ml/¼ pint/⅔ cup sunflower
    or groundnut (peanut) oil
sliced fresh green chilli and
    chopped fresh coriander
    (cilantro), to garnish

1 First make the spiced paste. Combine the garlic, fresh root ginger, green chillies and the lime juice in a food processor. Add the coriander seeds and five-spice powder, with half the sesame oil. Whiz to a fine paste, then set aside.

2 Heat a wok and stir-fry the red onions in the remaining sesame oil for 2 minutes. Add the fish and stir-fry for 1–2 minutes to seal on all sides.

3 Lift out the red onions and fish and put them on a plate. Add the spiced paste to the wok or pan and fry for 1 minute, stirring. Return the hoki fillets and red onions to the wok, pour in the coconut milk and bring to the boil.

4 Lower the heat, add the fish sauce and simmer for 5–7 minutes until the fish is cooked through.

5 Meanwhile, process the herbs, spring onions, lime rind and oil in a food processor to a coarse paste.

6 Stir into the fish curry. Garnish with chilli and coriander and serve with the cooked rice and lime wedges.

Monkfish Risotto Energy 431kcal/1802kJ; Protein 23.1g; Carbohydrate 56.4g, of which sugars 1.2g; Fat 9.1g, of which saturates 5.3g; Cholesterol 37mg; Calcium 37mg; Fibre 0.3g; Sodium 84mg.
Spicy Green Hoki Energy 608kcal/2527kJ; Protein 41g; Carbohydrate 13.3g, of which sugars 9.5g; Fat 43.8g, of which saturates 5.9g; Cholesterol 0mg; Calcium 168mg; Fibre 1.3g; Sodium 313mg.

Risotto with Stockfish

Stocco is dried stockfish: a medium-size cod that has been hung on wooden scaffolding to dry in the sun, then expertly salted and air dried. To transform this hard, unappetizing product into something edible, the fish must be cleaned and soaked in good quality tap water. The water that flows from the Apennine springs in the area of Mammola is said to be perfect for the task, and this, together with the skill of the local craftsmen, has given Calabrian stocco the reputation of being the finest in Italy.

Serves 4

25g/1oz/2 tbsp unsalted butter
1 onion, finely chopped
1.5 litres/2½ pints/6 cups fish stock (preferably made with trimmings from the dried fish)
500g/1¼lb stockfish (stocco) or dried salt cod, soaked, washed and flaked
175ml/6fl oz/¾ cup dry white wine
350g/12oz/1⅔ cups risotto rice
30ml/2 tbsp extra virgin olive oil
a handful of fresh flat leaf parsley, finely chopped

1 Melt the butter in a large heavy pan, add the onion and fry over a medium heat for 5 minutes or until golden brown. Meanwhile, set the stock simmering in a separate pan.

2 Stir the flaked stockfish into the onion, then add the wine and stir over the heat until the alcohol evaporates. Add the rice and toast the grains for 2–3 minutes, stirring constantly to prevent them from scorching.

3 When the rice is crackling hot, start adding the hot stock, one or two ladlefuls at a time. Stir constantly, and only add more liquid when the spoon leaves a clear wake behind it as it is drawn through the grains of rice. Do not ladle in more stock until the previous amount has been absorbed.

4 After about 20 minutes, when the rice grains are soft and plump, stir in the oil and the chopped fresh parsley. Remove the pan from the heat, cover it with a lid and set aside for about 4 minutes, then stir again gently and serve.

Stir-fried Prawns with Rice Noodles

One of the most appealing aspects of Asian food is its appearance. Ingredients are carefully chosen so that each dish, even a simple stir-fry such as this one, is balanced in terms of colour, texture and flavour.

Serves 4

130g/4½oz rice noodles
30ml/2 tbsp groundnut (peanut) oil
1 large garlic clove, crushed
150g/5oz large prawns (shrimp), peeled and deveined

15g/½oz dried shrimp
1 piece mooli (daikon), about 75g/3oz, grated
15ml/1 tbsp fish sauce
30ml/2 tbsp soy sauce
30ml/2 tbsp light muscovado (brown) sugar
30ml/2 tbsp lime juice
90g/3½oz/⅓ cup beansprouts
40g/1½oz/⅓ cup peanuts, chopped
15ml/1 tbsp sesame oil
chopped coriander (cilantro), 5ml/1 tsp dried chilli flakes and 2 shallots, finely chopped, to garnish

1 Soak the noodles in a bowl of boiling water for 5 minutes, or according to the packet instructions. Heat the oil in a wok or large frying pan. Add the garlic, and stir-fry over medium heat for 2–3 minutes, until golden brown.

2 Add the prawns, dried shrimp and grated mooli and stir-fry for a further 2 minutes. Stir in the fish sauce, soy sauce, sugar and lime juice.

3 Drain the noodles thoroughly, then snip them into smaller lengths with scissors. Add to the wok or pan with the beansprouts, peanuts and sesame oil. Toss to mix, then stir-fry for 2 minutes. Serve immediately, garnished with the coriander, chilli flakes and shallots.

Cook's Tip
Some cooks salt the mooli and leave it to drain, then rinse and dry it thoroughly before use.

Stockfish Energy 565kcal/2361kJ; Protein 30.3g; Carbohydrate 76g, of which sugars 4.5g; Fat 12.1g, of which saturates 4.3g; Cholesterol 72mg; Calcium 52mg; Fibre 1.1g; Sodium 126mg.
Stir-fried Prawns Energy 397kcal/1675kJ; Protein 21.3g; Carbohydrate 56.5g, of which sugars 3.2g; Fat 11.1g, of which saturates 2.4g; Cholesterol 89mg; Calcium 72mg; Fibre 3.3g; Sodium 567mg.

Salmon Risotto with Cucumber and Tarragon

This simple risotto is simpler than the usual risotto, since the stock is added all at once. If you prefer to make it the traditional way, ladle in the liquid gradually, adding the salmon about two-thirds of the way through cooking.

Serves 4

25g/1oz/2 tbsp butter
small bunch of spring onions
  (scallions), white parts, chopped
½ cucumber, peeled, seeded
  and chopped
350g/12oz/1¾ cups risotto rice
1.2 litres/2 pints/5 cups hot
  chicken or fish stock
150ml/¼ pint/⅔ cup dry
  white wine
450g/1lb salmon fillet, skinned
  and diced
45ml/3 tbsp chopped
  fresh tarragon
salt and freshly ground
  black pepper

1 Heat the butter in a large saucepan and add the spring onions and cucumber. Cook for 2–3 minutes without letting the spring onions colour.

2 Stir in the rice all at once, then pour in the chicken or fish stock and the wine. Bring to the boil, then lower the heat and simmer, uncovered, for 10 minutes, stirring occasionally to ensure the rice does not stick.

3 Stir in the diced salmon and season to taste with salt and freshly ground black pepper. Continue cooking for a further 5 minutes, stirring occasionally, then switch off the heat. Cover and leave to stand for 5 minutes.

4 Remove the lid, add the chopped tarragon and mix lightly. Spoon into a warmed bowl and serve.

> **Cook's Tips**
> *Carnaroli risotto rice would be excellent in this risotto, although if it is not available, Arborio can be used instead.*

Fried Chilli Fish with Spicy Rice

Cooking rice in fish stock gives it a splendid flavour.

Serves 6

45ml/3 tbsp olive oil
6 garlic cloves, smashed
1 dried chilli, seeded and chopped
250g/9oz ripe tomatoes, peeled,
  seeded and chopped
pinch of saffron threads
1.6kg/3½lb mixed fish fillets such
  as snapper, mullet, or bass
1 litre/1¾ pints/4 cups fish stock
30ml/2 tbsp dry white wine
1 tomato, finely diced
30ml/2 tbsp chopped fresh parsley
400g/14oz/2 cups paella rice
115g/4oz tiny unshelled shrimps
salt and ground black pepper

For the allioli

4 garlic cloves, finely chopped
2.5ml/½ tsp salt
5ml/1 tsp lemon juice
2 egg yolks
250ml/8fl oz/1 cup olive oil

1 To make the allioli, put the chopped garlic in a large mortar (or blender) with the salt and lemon juice and reduce to a purée. Add the egg yolks and mix thoroughly. Gradually work in the oil to make a thick, mayonnaise-like sauce.

2 Put 15ml/1 tbsp of the olive oil in a small pan and add the smashed garlic cloves and dried chilli. Fry for a few minutes then add the chopped tomato and saffron. Cook for a few minutes, then transfer to a processor and blend until smooth.

3 Heat the remaining 30ml/2 tbsp oil in a large pan or a wide flameproof casserole and fry the fish pieces until they begin to stiffen. Add the fish stock and the tomato sauce to the pan and cook gently for 3–4 minutes.

4 Transfer the fish to a serving dish. Season, sprinkle with the wine, diced tomato and parsley. Cover with foil and keep warm.

5 Add the rice to the stock, stir, season and bring to a simmer. Cook for 18–20 minutes. Before all the liquid is absorbed, stir in the shrimps. When the rice is tender, cover and turn off the heat. Stand until all the liquid is absorbed: about 5 minutes. Serve with the fish fillets and allioli.

Salmon Risotto Energy 506kcal/2122kJ; Protein 28.4g; Carbohydrate 51.3g, of which sugars 2.8g; Fat 20g, of which saturates 5.9g; Cholesterol 70mg; Calcium 91mg; Fibre 1.4g; Sodium 266mg.
Chilli Fish with Spicy Rice Energy 809kcal/3367kJ; Protein 56.9g; Carbohydrate 55.6g, of which sugars 1.9g; Fat 39g, of which saturates 5.8g; Cholesterol 198mg; Calcium 71mg; Fibre 0.7g; Sodium 412mg.

Shellfish Risotto with Mixed Mushrooms

This is a quick and easy risotto, where all the liquid is added at once. The method is well-suited to this shellfish dish, as it means all the ingredients cook together without requiring the cook's attention.

Serves 6
225g/8oz live mussels
225g/8oz live Venus or carpet shell clams
45ml/3 tbsp olive oil
1 onion, chopped
450g/1lb/2⅓ cups risotto rice
1.75 litres/3 pints/7½ cups simmering chicken or vegetable stock
150ml/¼ pint/⅔ cup white wine
225g/8oz/2–3 cups assorted wild and cultivated mushrooms, trimmed and sliced
115g/4oz raw peeled prawns, deveined
1 medium or 2 small squid, cleaned, trimmed and sliced
3 drops truffle oil (optional)
75ml/5 tbsp chopped mixed fresh parsley and chervil
celery salt and cayenne pepper

1 Scrub the mussels and clams clean and discard any that are open and do not close when sharply tapped. Set aside. Heat the oil in a large frying pan and fry the onion for 6–8 minutes until soft but not browned.

2 Add the rice, stirring to coat the grains in oil, then pour in the stock and wine and cook for 5 minutes. Add the mushrooms and cook for 5 minutes more, stirring occasionally.

3 Add the prawns, squid, mussels and clams and stir into the rice. Cover the pan and simmer over a low heat for 15 minutes until the prawns have turned pink and the mussels and clams have opened. Discard any of the mussels or clams that remain closed.

4 Switch off the heat. Add the truffle oil, if using, and stir in the herbs. Cover tightly and leave to stand for 5–10 minutes to allow all the flavours to blend. Season to taste with celery salt and a pinch of cayenne, pile into a warmed dish, and serve immediately.

Steamed Langoustine with Lemon Grass Risotto

Traditional Italian risotto is given a subtle Asian twist with the addition of fragrant lemon grass, Asian fish sauce and Chinese chives. The delicate citrus-flavoured rice is the perfect partner for simply steamed langoustines. If you cannot find fresh langoustines (also known as Dublin Bay prawns) you can use king prawns in their shells instead.

Serves 4
8 fresh langoustines
30ml/2 tbsp olive oil
15ml/1 tbsp butter
1 onion, finely chopped
1 carrot, finely diced
1 celery stick, finely diced
30ml/2 tbsp very finely chopped lemon grass
300g/11oz/1½ cups arborio rice
200ml/7fl oz/scant 1 cup dry white wine
1.5 litres/2½ pints/6¼ cups boiling vegetable stock
50ml/2fl oz/¼ cup fish sauce
30ml/2 tbsp finely chopped Chinese chives
salt and ground black pepper

1 Place the langoustines in a baking parchment-lined bamboo steamer, cover and place over a wok of simmering water. Steam for 6–8 minutes, remove from the heat and keep warm.

2 Heat the oil and butter in a wok and add the vegetables. Cook over a high heat for 2–3 minutes. Add the lemon grass and rice and stir-fry for 2 minutes.

3 Add the wine to the wok, reduce the heat and slowly stir until the wine is absorbed. Add about 250ml/8fl oz/1 cup of the stock and cook gently, stirring until absorbed. Continue adding the stock, about 120ml/4fl oz/½ cup at a time, stirring until fully absorbed before adding more. Cook until the rice is just tender.

4 Stir the fish sauce and the Chinese chives into the risotto, check the seasoning and serve on warmed plates. Top each serving with 2 langoustines.

Shellfish Risotto Energy 430kcal/1811kJ; Protein 12g; Carbohydrate 72g, of which sugars 4g; Fat 12g, of which saturates 3g; Cholesterol 66mg; Calcium 54mg; Fibre 3g; Sodium 1207mg.
Langoustine Energy 430kcal/1811kJ; Protein 12g; Carbohydrate 72g, of which sugars 4g; Fat 12g, of which saturates 3g; Cholesterol 66mg; Calcium 54mg; Fibre 3g; Sodium 1207mg.

Crab Risotto

This is a fresh-flavoured risotto which makes a wonderful main course or starter. You will need two crabs for this recipe, and it is a good dish to make when crabs are cheap and plentiful.

Serves 3–4
2 large cooked crabs
15ml/1 tbsp olive oil

25g/1oz/2 tbsp butter
2 shallots, finely chopped
275g/10oz/1½ cups risotto rice,
    preferably Carnaroli
75ml/5 tbsp Marsala or brandy
1 litre/1¾ pints/4 cups simmering
    fish stock
5ml/1 tsp chopped fresh tarragon
5ml/1 tsp chopped fresh parsley
60ml/4 tbsp double cream
salt and freshly ground
    black pepper

1 First remove the crab meat from each of the shells in turn. Hold the crab firmly in one hand and hit the back underside firmly with the heel of your hand. This should loosen the shell from the body. Using your thumbs, push against the body and pull away from the shell. From the inside of the shell, remove and discard the intestines. Discard the grey gills (dead man's fingers). Break off the claws and legs, then use a small hammer or crackers to break them open. Using a pick, remove the meat from the claws and legs. Place the meat on a plate.

2 Using a pick or a skewer, remove the white meat from the body cavities and place on the plate with the meat from the claws and legs, reserving some for garnish. Scoop out the brown meat from the shell and set aside with the white meat.

3 Heat the oil and butter in a pan and fry the shallots until soft but not browned. Add the rice. Cook for a few minutes, then add the Marsala or brandy, bring to the boil, and cook, stirring, until the liquid has evaporated. Add a ladleful of hot stock and cook, stirring, until all the stock has been absorbed. Continue in this way until about two-thirds of the stock has been added, then stir in all the crab meat and the herbs. Continue to cook the risotto, adding the remaining stock. When the rice is almost cooked but still has a slight 'bite', remove it from the heat, add the cream and season. Cover and leave to stand for 3 minutes to finish cooking. Serve garnished with the reserved white crab meat.

Truffle and Lobster Risotto

To capture the precious qualities of the fresh truffle, partner it with lobster and serve in a silky smooth risotto. Both truffle shavings and truffle oil are added toward the end of cooking to preserve the unique flavour of the truffle.

Serves 4
50g/2oz/4 tbsp unsalted butter
1 medium onion, chopped
350g/12oz/1¾ cups risotto rice,
    preferably Carnaroli

1 fresh thyme sprig
150ml/¼ pint/⅔ cup dry
    white wine
1.2 litres/2 pints/5 cups
    simmering chicken stock
1 freshly cooked lobster
45ml/3 tbsp chopped mixed fresh
    parsley and chervil
3–4 drops truffle oil
2 hard-boiled eggs
1 fresh black or white truffle
salt and freshly ground
    black pepper

1 Melt the butter, add the onion and fry until softened but not browned. Add the rice and stir well to coat with the butter. Cook until the rice is slightly translucent. Add the thyme, then the wine, and cook until it has been absorbed. Add the chicken stock a little at a time, stirring. Let each ladleful be absorbed before adding the next.

2 Twist off the lobster tail, cut the underside with scissors and remove the white tail meat. Carefully break open the claws with a small kitchen hammer and remove the flesh. Cut half the meat into large chunks, then roughly chop the remainder.

3 Stir in the chopped lobster meat, half the chopped herbs and the truffle oil. Remove the rice from the heat, cover and leave to stand for 5 minutes to allow the flavours to permeate throughout the risotto.

4 Divide among four warmed plates and place the lobster chunks on top in the centre of the risotto. Cut the hard-boiled eggs into wedges and arrange them around the lobster meat. Finally, shave a little fresh truffle over each portion and sprinkle with the remaining chopped fresh parsley and chervil. Serve the risotto immediately.

Crab Risotto Energy 496kcal/2060kJ; Protein 14.1g; Carbohydrate 56.4g, of which sugars 1.1g; Fat 18.7g, of which saturates 8.9g; Cholesterol 65mg; Calcium 25mg; Fibre 0.2g; Sodium 229mg.
Lobster Risotto Energy 520kcal/2172kJ; Protein 19.9g; Carbohydrate 71.3g, of which sugars 1.2g; Fat 14.3g, of which saturates 7.4g; Cholesterol 172mg; Calcium 68mg; Fibre 0.2g; Sodium 263mg.

Mussel Risotto

Fresh root ginger and coriander add a distinctive flavour to this dish, while the chillies give it a little heat.

Serves 3–4

900g/2lb fresh mussels, scrubbed
about 250ml/8fl oz/1 cup dry
   white wine
30ml/2 tbsp olive oil
1 onion, chopped
2 garlic cloves, crushed

1–2 fresh green chillies, seeded
   and finely sliced
2.5cm/1in piece of fresh root
   ginger, grated
275g/10oz/1½ cups risotto rice
900ml/1½ pints/3¾ cups
   simmering fish stock
30ml/2 tbsp chopped
   fresh coriander
30ml/2 tbsp double cream
salt and freshly ground
   black pepper

1 Discard any mussels that do not close when sharply tapped. Place in a large saucepan. Add 120ml/4fl oz/½ cup of the wine and bring to the boil. Cover the pan and cook the mussels for 4–5 minutes until they have opened, shaking the pan occasionally. Drain, reserving the liquid and discarding any mussels that have not opened. Remove most of the mussels from their shells, reserving a few in their shells for decoration. Strain the mussel liquid.

2 Heat the oil and fry the onion and garlic for 3–4 minutes until beginning to soften. Add the chillies. Cook over a low heat for 1–2 minutes, stirring often, then stir in the ginger and fry for 1 minute more. Add the rice and cook over a medium heat for 2 minutes, stirring, until the rice looks translucent.

3 Stir in the reserved cooking liquid from the mussels. When this has been absorbed, add the remaining wine and cook stirring, until absorbed. Add the fish stock, a little at a time, waiting until it has been absorbed before adding more. When the rice is three-quarters cooked, stir in the mussels. Add the coriander and season. Continue adding stock until it is creamy and the rice is tender but slightly firm in the centre.

4 Remove the risotto from the heat, stir in the cream, cover and stand for a few minutes. Serve immediately, decorated with the reserved mussels in their shells.

Sushi with Smoked Salmon

This sushi, known as oshi-zushi, dates back almost a thousand years. The earliest forms of sushi were made as a means of preserving fish. The cooked rice was used as a medium to produce lactic acid and was discarded after one year. Only the marinated fish was eaten.

Makes about 12

175g/6oz smoked salmon,
   thickly sliced

15ml/1 tbsp sake
15ml/1 tbsp water
30ml/2 tbsp shoyu
1 lemon, thinly sliced into
   6 x 3mm/⅛in rings

For the su-meshi
200g/7oz/1 cup Japanese short
   grain rice
40ml/8 tsp rice vinegar
20ml/4 tsp caster
   (superfine) sugar
5ml/1 tsp salt

1 To make the su-meshi, see Hand-rolled Sushi (p. 120, step 1).

2 Lay the smoked salmon on a chopping board and sprinkle with a mixture of the sake, water and shoyu. Leave to marinate for an hour, then wipe dry with kitchen paper.

3 Line a 25 x 7.5 x 5cm/10 x 3 x 2in plastic box with a sheet of clear film (plastic wrap), allowing the edges to hang over.

4 Spread half the smoked salmon to evenly cover the bottom of the plastic box. Add a quarter of the cooked rice and firmly press down with your hands dampened with rice vinegar until it is 1cm/½in thick. Add the remainder of the salmon, and press the remaining rice on top.

5 Cover the plastic box with the overhanging clear film. Place a weight, such as a heavy dinner plate, on top. Leave in a cool place overnight, or for at least 3 hours. If you keep it in the refrigerator, choose the least cool part.

6 Remove the compressed sushi from the container and unwrap. Cut into 2 cm/¾in slices and serve on a Japanese lacquered tray or a large plate. Quarter the lemon rings. Garnish with two slices of lemon on top of each piece and serve.

Mussel Risotto Energy 439kcal/1833kJ; Protein 17.2g; Carbohydrate 56.6g, of which sugars 1.4g; Fat 11.3g, of which saturates 3.5g; Cholesterol 37mg; Calcium 159mg; Fibre 0.2g; Sodium 146mg.
Sushi with Smoked Salmon Energy 68kcal/286kJ; Protein 4.7g; Carbohydrate 10.2g, of which sugars 0.2g; Fat 0.7g, of which saturates 0.1g; Cholesterol 5mg; Calcium 6mg; Fibre 0g; Sodium 452mg.

Hand-rolled Sushi

Roll your own filling in this fun way to enjoy sushi.

Serves 4–6
225g/8oz very fresh tuna steak
130g/4½oz smoked salmon
17cm/6½in cucumber cucumber
1 avocado, halved and stoned (pitted)
7.5ml/1½ tsp lemon juice
8 king prawns (jumbo shrimp), cooked and peeled
20 chives, trimmed and chopped into 6cm/2½in lengths
1 packet mustard and cress (fine curled cress), roots cut off

6–8 shiso leaves, cut in half lengthways

For the su-meshi
800g/1¾lb/2 cups Japanese short grain rice
75ml/5 tbsp rice vinegar
40ml/8 tsp caster (superfine) sugar
5ml/1 tsp salt

To serve
12 nori sheets, cut into four
mayonnaise
shoyu
45ml/3 tbsp wasabi paste
gari (thinly sliced ginger)

1 To make the su-meshi, rinse the rice in plenty of water. Drain in a sieve (strainer) for 1 hour. Put the rice into a deep pan with 250ml/ 8fl oz/1⅓ cups water to each 200g/7oz /1 cup rice. Cover and bring to the boil. Simmer for 12 minutes. Remove from the heat and leave for 10 minutes. Transfer the rice to a large bowl. Mix in the vinegar, sugar and salt, and fluff the rice. Place in a large serving bowl and cover with a damp dish towel.

2 Slice the tuna, with the grain, into 5mm/¼in slices, then into 1 x 6cm/½ x 2½in strips. Cut the salmon and cucumber into strips the same size as the tuna. Cut the avocado into 1cm/½in long strips and sprinkle on the lemon juice.

3 Arrange the fish, shellfish, avocado and vegetables on a plate. Place the nori sheets on a plate and put the mayonnaise, shoyu, wasabi and gari into separate bowls. Half-fill a glass with water and place four to six rice paddles inside.

4 To roll the sushi, take a sheet of nori and spread 45ml/3 tbsp rice on the sheet. Spread some wasabi on the rice, and place a few strips of the fillings on top. Roll it up as a cone and dip the end into the shoyu. Have some gari between rolls to refresh.

Hand-moulded Sushi

This is a wonderful way of appreciating fresh seafood.

Serves 4
400g/14oz/2 cups Japanese short grain rice, soaked for 20 minutes in water to cover
500ml/18fl oz/2½ cups water
55ml/3½ tbsp rice vinegar, plus extra for moulding
30ml/2 tbsp caster (superfine) sugar
10ml/2 tsp salt

4 raw king prawns (jumbo shrimp), head and shell removed, tails intact
4 scallops, white muscle only
425g/15oz assorted very fresh fish, such as salmon, tuna, sea bass and mackerel, skinned, cleaned and filleted
45ml/3 tbsp wasabi paste
pickled ginger, to garnish
shoyu (Japanese soy sauce), to serve

1 Drain the rice, then put it in a pan with the measured water. Bring to the boil, then reduce the heat, cover and simmer for 20 minutes, until all the water has been absorbed. Meanwhile, heat the vinegar, sugar and salt in a pan, stir well and cool. Fold into the hot rice, then remove the pan from the heat, cover and leave to stand for 20 minutes.

2 Insert a bamboo skewer or cocktail stick (toothpick) into each prawn lengthways. This stops the prawns curling up when cooked. Boil them in lightly salted water for 2 minutes, or until they turn pink. Drain and cool, then pull out the skewers. Cut open from the belly side but do not slice in two. With the point of a sharp knife, remove the black vein running down the back. Open each prawn out flat and place on a tray.

3 Slice the scallops horizontally in half, but not quite through. Gently open each scallop at this "hinge" to make a butterfly shape. Place on the tray, cut side down. Use a sharp knife to cut all the fish fillets into 7.5 x 4cm/3 x 1½in pieces, 5mm/¼in thick. Place all the raw fish and shellfish on the tray, cover with clear film (plastic wrap), then chill in the refrigerator for at least 1 hour, or up to 4 hours.

4 Spoon the vinegared rice into a bowl. Have ready a small bowl filled with water acidulated with rice vinegar for moulding. Take the tray of seafood from the refrigerator.

5 Wet your hand with the vinegared water and scoop about 25ml/1½ tbsp vinegared rice into your palm. Gently but firmly grip it to make a rectangular block. Do not squash the rice, but ensure that the grains stick together. The size of the blocks must be smaller than the toppings.

6 Put the rice block on a damp chopping board. Taking a piece of salmon topping in your palm, rub a little wasabi paste in the middle of it. Put the rice block on top of the salmon and gently press it. Form your palm into a cup and shape the topped rice to a smooth-surfaced mound. Place it on a serving tray. Work quickly, or the warmth of your hands may cause the salmon to lose its freshness.

7 Repeat this process until all of the rice and toppings are used. Serve immediately with a little shoyu dribbled on individual plates. To eat, pick up a sushi and dip the tip into the shoyu. Eat pickled ginger between different sushi to refresh the mouth.

Rolled Sushi Energy 191kcal/797kJ; Protein 8.2g; Carbohydrate 56.4g, of which sugars 7.7g; Fat 8.2g, of which saturates 1.4g; Cholesterol 19mg; Calcium 26mg; Fibre 0.9g; Sodium 442mg.
Moulded Sushi Energy 392kcal/16360kJ; Protein 29.3g; Carbohydrate 21.3g, of which sugars 0.2g; Fat 12.2g, of which saturates 2.1g; Cholesterol 77mg; Calcium 45mg; Fibre 0.1g; Sodium 86mg.

Jewel-box Sushi

In this sushi, a bowl is filled with su-meshi, and colourful toppings decorate it.

Serves 4

2 eggs, beaten
vegetable oil, for frying
50g/2oz mangetouts (snow
  peas), trimmed
1 nori sheet, cut into small shreds
15ml/1 tbsp shoyu
15ml/1 tbsp wasabi paste
salt
30–60ml/2–4 tbsp ikura, to garnish

For the su-meshi

200g/7oz/1 cup Japanese short
  grain rice
40ml/8 tsp rice vinegar
20ml/4 tsp caster (superfine) sugar
5ml/1 tsp salt

For the fish toppings

115g/4oz very fresh tuna steak,
  skin removed
90g/3½oz fresh squid, body only,
  cleaned and boned
4 king prawns (jumbo shrimp),
  cooked and peeled

For the shiitake

8 dried shiitake mushrooms, stalks
  discarded and soaked in
  350ml/12fl oz/1½ cups water
  for 4 hours
15ml/1 tbsp caster (superfine) sugar
60ml/4 tbsp mirin
45ml/3 tbsp shoyu

1 To make the su-meshi, see Hand-rolled Sushi (p. 120, step 1). Simmer the shiitake and the soaking water for 20 minutes. Add the sugar, mirin and shoyu. Drain and slice very thinly.

2 Beat the eggs in a bowl and add a pinch of salt. Heat a little oil in a frying pan and add enough egg to cover the pan thinly. Cook on both sides. Use the remaining egg to make several omelettes, roll into a tube and slice very thinly to make strands.

3 Slice the tuna across the grain into 7.5 × 4cm/3 × 1½in pieces, 5mm/¼in thick. Slice the squid crossways into 5mm/¼in strips. Par-boil the mangetouts for 2 minutes. Cut into 3mm/⅛in diagonal strips. Mix the nori with the shoyu and wasabi.

4 Place half the *su-meshi* in a bowl, cover with the nori mixture and the remaining *su-meshi*. Sprinkle over egg strands to cover the surface. Arrange the tuna slices in a fan shape with a fan of shiitake on top. Place the prawns and squid next to the tuna. Arrange the mangetouts and ikura decoratively on top.

Marinated Mackerel Sushi

Fresh mackerel fillets are marinated, then packed into a mould with sushi rice to make Saba-zushi. Start preparations 8 hours in advance to allow the fish to absorb the salt.

Makes about 12

500g/1¼lb mackerel, filleted
salt
rice vinegar
2cm/¾in fresh root ginger, peeled
  and finely grated, to garnish
shoyu, to serve

**For the su-meshi (vinegared
  rice)**

200g/7oz/1 cup Japanese short
  grain rice
40ml/8 tsp rice vinegar
20ml/4 tsp caster (superfine)
  sugar
5ml/1 tsp salt

1 Place the fillets skin-side down in a flat dish, cover with a thick layer of salt, and leave them for 3–5 hours.

2 To make the su-meshi, see Hand-rolled Sushi (p. 120, step 1).

3 Wipe the salt from the mackerel with kitchen paper. Remove all the remaining bones with tweezers. Lift the skin at the tail end of each fillet and peel towards the head end. Place the skinned fillets in a clean dish, and pour in enough rice vinegar to cover the fish completely. Leave for 20 minutes, then drain and wipe dry with kitchen paper.

4 Line a 25 × 7.5 × 4cm/10 × 3 × 1½in container with some clear film (plastic wrap), twice the size of the container. Lay the fillets in the container, skinned-side down, to cover the base. Cut the remaining mackerel to fill the gaps.

5 Put the su-meshi into the container, and press down firmly with dampened hands. Cover with the clear film (plastic wrap) and place a weight on top. Leave for at least 3 hours or overnight.

6 Remove the sushi from its container, then slice into 2cm/¾in pieces. After each slice, wipe the knife with kitchen paper dampened with rice vinegar. Arrange the sushi on a plate and add a little finely grated ginger. Serve with shoyu.

Jewel Box Energy 384kcal/1609kJ; Protein 23.1g; Carbohydrate 57.3g, of which sugars 7g; Fat 5g, of which saturates 1.3g; Cholesterol 203mg; Calcium 61mg; Fibre 0.4g; Sodium 1191mg.
Mackerel Sushi Energy 158kcal/659kJ; Protein 9g; Carbohydrate 15g, of which sugars 1.7g; Fat 6.8g, of which saturates 1.4g; Cholesterol 23mg; Calcium 9mg; Fibre 0g; Sodium 190mg.

Poached Cod with Parsnips

The Swedish fishing industry heavily relies on catching cod, which is second only to herring in terms of numbers fished. Cod and carrots are a traditional combination in Sweden, but this recipe rings the changes by also adding parsnips.

Serves 6
6 cod steaks, with skin on, about 150g/5oz each
30ml/2 tbsp sea salt
6 small carrots, sliced lengthways into quarters
3 parsnips, sliced lengthways into quarters
10g/¹/₂oz/1 tsp sugar
115g/4oz/¹/₂ cup butter
30ml/2 tbsp grated fresh horseradish
salt and ground white pepper
fresh parsley, chopped, to garnish

1 Cover the cod pieces in the salt and put aside in the refrigerator for 2–3 hours. (This salting process will help to firm the flesh and give it a mother-of-pearl shimmer.)

2 Put the carrots and parsnips in a pan. Add the sugar, a knob (pat) of the butter and salt and pepper and pour in enough water to cover the vegetables. Cut a piece of greaseproof (waxed) paper to fit the inside of the pan and place on top of the vegetables. (This allows the vegetables to cook in their own juice.) Simmer the vegetables, without a lid, for about 10 minutes until the water has evaporated.

3 Put the cod steaks on to an upside-down plate, sitting in the base of a pan, and pour a little water into the pan. Cover and steam the fish for about 8–10 minutes until just tender.

4 To make the horseradish sauce, melt the remaining butter then add the grated horseradish. Serve the cod garnished with parsley and accompanied by the sauce and the vegetables.

> **Cook's Tips**
> *This dish can also be made with pike or sea bass. If you use sea bass, it is advisable to cook it whole rather than in steaks.*

Cod Caramba

This colourful Mexican dish, with its contrasting crunchy topping and tender fish filling, can be made with any white fish such as coley or haddock.

Serves 6
450g/1lb cod fillets
225g/8oz smoked cod fillets
300ml/¹/₂ pint/1¹/₄ cups fish stock
50g/2oz/¹/₄ cup butter
1 onion, sliced
2 garlic cloves, crushed
1 green and 1 red (bell) pepper, seeded and diced
2 courgettes (zucchini), diced
115g/4oz/²/₃ cup drained canned or thawed frozen corn kernels
2 tomatoes, peeled and chopped
juice of 1 lime
Tabasco sauce
salt, ground black pepper and cayenne pepper

For the topping
75g/3oz tortilla chips
50g/2oz/¹/₂ cup grated Cheddar cheese
coriander (cilantro) sprigs, to garnish
lime wedges, to serve

1 Lay the fish in a shallow pan and pour over the fish stock. Bring to the boil, lower the heat, cover and poach for about 8 minutes, until the flesh flakes easily. Leave to cool slightly, then remove the skin and separate the flesh into large flakes. Keep hot.

2 Melt the butter in a pan, add the onion and garlic and cook gently over a low heat until translucent. Add the peppers, stir and cook for about 2 minutes. Stir in the courgettes and cook for 3 minutes more, until all the vegetables are tender.

3 Stir in the corn and tomatoes, then add lime juice and Tabasco to taste. Season with salt, black pepper and cayenne. Cook for 2 minutes to heat the corn and tomatoes, then stir in the fish and transfer to a dish that can safely be used under the grill (broiler).

4 Preheat the grill. Make the topping by crushing the tortilla chips, then mixing in the grated cheese. Add cayenne pepper to taste and sprinkle over the fish. Place the dish under the grill until the topping is crisp and brown. Garnish with coriander sprigs and lime wedges.

Poached Cod Energy 321kcal/1336kJ; Protein 28.8g; Carbohydrate 11.6g, of which sugars 7.9g; Fat 17.9g, of which saturates 10.3g; Cholesterol 111mg; Calcium 49mg; Fibre 3.2g; Sodium 265mg.
Cod Caramba Energy 293kcal/1223kJ; Protein 26.6g; Carbohydrate 15.8g, of which sugars 7.5g; Fat 13.9g, of which saturates 6.9g; Cholesterol 78mg; Calcium 123mg; Fibre 3.2g; Sodium 927mg.

Mackerel Escabeche

This traditional way of preserving fish in vinegar, was brought to Latin America by the Spanish and Portuguese. Oily fish, such as mackerel and sardines, lend themselves particularly well to this treatment. It takes at least a day, so allow plenty of time.

Serves 6

12 small mackerel fillets
juice of 2 limes
90ml/6 tbsp olive oil
2 red onions, thinly sliced
2 garlic cloves, thinly sliced
2 bay leaves
6 black peppercorns
120ml/4fl oz/½ cup red
   wine vinegar
50g/2oz/½ cup plain
   (all-purpose) flour
salt and ground black pepper

1 Place the mackerel fillets side by side in a large, shallow glass or china dish. Pour over the lime juice. Season with salt and pepper and cover. Marinate in the refrigerator for 20–30 minutes, but no longer.

2 Meanwhile, heat half the oil in a frying pan. Add the onions and cook over a low heat for 10 minutes, until softened but not coloured. Stir in the garlic and cook for 2 minutes. Add the bay leaves, peppercorns and vinegar to the pan and simmer over a very low heat for 5 minutes.

3 Pat the mackerel fillets dry and coat them in the flour. Heat the remaining oil in a large frying pan and fry the fish, in batches, for 2 minutes on each side.

4 Return the fish to the dish in which they were originally marinated. Pour the vinegar mixture over the fish. Leave to marinate for 24 hours before serving.

> **Cook's Tips**
> *If you are planning to keep the fish for more than one day, immerse it in the vinegar, then top with a thin layer of olive oil. Cover tightly. It will keep in the refrigerator for up to 1 month.*

Salt Cod with Red Peppers

Fiery and full of flavour, this winter dish comes from Basilicata, Italy, and was created for that time of year when there is a shortage of fresh vegetables and rough seas mean fish is in short supply. Salt fish needs to be soaked before cooking, so allow for this when planning when to serve the dish.

Serves 6

800g/1¾lb salt cod
75ml/5 tbsp extra virgin
   olive oil
275g/10oz bottled roasted red
   (bell) peppers, drained
3 garlic cloves, chopped
3 dried red chillies, chopped
a handful of fresh flat leaf
   parsley, chopped
sea salt (optional)

1 Soak the salt cod in enough cold water to cover for 24 hours, changing the water often. Drain well.

2 Trim the fish, removing any obvious bones, and put it in a pan. Pour over cold water to cover and heat to simmering. Cook for about 8 minutes until the fish is soft.

3 Drain well and remove the skin. Flake the cod, removing any remaining bones.

4 Heat the oil in a pan and add the roasted peppers, garlic, chillies and parsley. Fry over a medium heat for about 10 minutes, stirring frequently. Add a little water if necessary.

5 Add the flaked salt cod to the pan and mix well. Taste and add salt if necessary, although the fish may already be salty enough. Cook for 1–2 minutes to heat through. Serve on a heated platter.

> **Cook's Tips**
> *• Fresh fish can be used for this dish, but because it has a much more delicate taste than salt cod, the quantity of chilli should be reduced.*
> *• Reconstituted dried red (bell) peppers can be used instead of bottled roasted peppers.*

Escabeche Energy 518kcal/ 2147kJ; Protein 30g; Carbohydrate 11g, of which sugars 3g; Fat 39g, of which saturates 7g; Cholesterol 81mg; Calcium 42mg; Fibre 1g; Sodium 97mg.
Salt Cod Energy 207kcal/861kJ; Protein 25.1g; Carbohydrate 3.2g, of which sugars 3g; Fat 10.4g, of which saturates 1.5g; Cholesterol 61mg; Calcium 32mg; Fibre 1.2g; Sodium 85mg.

Haddock with Dill Sauce

Dill is Poland's favourite herb, and here it is used to lift the simple cream sauce that accompanies the moist fillets of poached haddock. Serve on its own, or with seasonal vegetables.

Serves 4

50g/2oz/¼ cup butter
4 haddock fillets, about
    185g/6½oz each
200ml/7fl oz/scant 1 cup milk
200ml/7fl oz/scant 1 cup
    fish stock
3–4 bay leaves
75ml/5 tbsp plain
    (all-purpose) flour
150ml/¼ pint/⅔ cup double
    (heavy) cream
1 egg yolk
30ml–45ml/2–3 tbsp chopped
    fresh dill
salt and ground black pepper,
    to taste
dill fronds and slices of lemon,
    to garnish (optional)

1 Melt 25g/1oz/2 tbsp butter in a frying pan, then add the haddock fillets, milk, fish stock, bay leaves, and salt and ground black pepper to taste.

2 Bring to a simmer, then poach the fish gently over a low heat for 10–15 minutes until tender.

3 Meanwhile, melt the remaining butter in a small pan, add the flour and cook, stirring, for 2 minutes.

4 Remove the pan from the heat and slowly add the double cream, whisking constantly to make a smooth sauce.

5 Stir in the egg yolk and chopped fresh dill, then return to the heat and simmer for 4 minutes, or until the sauce has thickened. Do not allow the sauce to boil. Season to taste with salt and ground black pepper.

6 Using a slotted spoon, remove the haddock fillets to a serving dish or four warmed serving plates and pour over the hot sauce.

7 Garnish the fish with dill fronds and slices of lemon, if you like, and serve immediately.

Haddock in Cider and Cream Sauce

Haddock, both smoked and unsmoked, is a popular fish in Ireland and it finds its way into dishes that are the backbone of the Irish repertoire, such as chowders. Cider, which is made in Ireland and often used in cooking, complements the haddock well. Small, new, boiled potatoes, matchstick carrots and peas or mangetouts are perfect accompaniments.

Serves 4

675g/1½lb haddock fillet
1 medium onion, thinly sliced
1 bay leaf
2 sprigs fresh parsley
10ml/2 tsp lemon juice
450ml/¾ pint/2 cups dry
    (hard) cider
25g/1oz/¼ cup cornflour
    (cornstarch)
30ml/2 tbsp single (light) cream
salt and ground black pepper

1 Cut the haddock fillet into four and place in a pan in a single layer. Add the onion, bay leaf, parsley, lemon juice and season. Pour in most of the cider, reserving 30ml/2 tbsp for the sauce. Cover and bring to the boil, then simmer for 10 minutes.

2 Strain 300ml/½ pint/1¼ cups of the fish liquor into a measuring jug (cup). In a pan, mix the cornflour with the reserved cider, then whisk in the fish liquor and bring to the boil, whisking for about 2 minutes, until smooth and thickened. Add more of the cooking liquor, if needed, to make a pouring sauce.

3 Remove the pan from the heat, stir in the single cream and season to taste with salt and freshly ground black pepper. To serve, remove any skin from the fish, arrange on hot plates with the onion over the vegetables and pour the sauce over.

Cook's Tips
A member of the cod family, silver-skinned haddock is sold whole, as steaks or as fillets. It is suitable for grilling (broiling), frying or smoking.

Haddock with Dill Energy 503kcal/2097kJ; Protein 36.6g; Carbohydrate 15.5g, of which sugars 1.2g; Fat 33.2g, of which saturates 19.6g; Cholesterol 191mg; Calcium 92mg; Fibre 1g; Sodium 207mg.
Haddock in Cider Energy 227Kcal/964kJ; Protein 32.8g; Carbohydrate 11.8g, of which sugars 5.2g; Fat 2.6g, of which saturates 1.1g; Cholesterol 65mg; Calcium 50mg; Fibre 0.5g; Sodium 128mg

Smoked Haddock with Spinach and Poached Egg

This is a really special breakfast treat. Use young spinach leaves in season and, of course, the freshest eggs. There is something about the combination of eggs, spinach and smoked fish that really perks you up in the morning.

Serves 4

4 undyed smoked haddock fillets
milk for poaching
75ml/2¹/₂fl oz/¹/₃ cup double
 (heavy) cream
25g/1oz/2 tbsp butter
250g/9oz fresh spinach, tough
 stalks removed
white wine vinegar
4 eggs
salt and ground black pepper

1 Over a low heat, poach the haddock fillets in just enough milk to come halfway up the fish, shaking the pan gently to keep the fish moist, for about 5 minutes. When cooked remove the fish and keep warm.

2 Increase the heat under the milk and allow to reduce by about half, stirring occasionally. Add the cream to the milk in the pan and heat until it bubbles up. Season to taste with salt and ground black pepper. The sauce should be thickened but should pour easily.

3 Heat a frying pan then add the butter. Add the spinach, stirring briskly for a few minutes. Season lightly then set aside, keeping it warm.

4 To poach the eggs, bring 4cm/1¹/₂in water to a simmer and add a few drops of vinegar. Gently crack two eggs into the water and cook for 3 minutes. Remove the first egg using a slotted spoon and rest in the spoon on some kitchen paper to remove any water. Repeat with the second egg, then cook the other two in the same way.

5 Place the spinach over the haddock fillets on four warmed serving plates and put a poached egg on top. Pour over the cream sauce and serve immediately.

Smoked Haddock with Vegetables

This light Lithuanian recipe is full of the fresh flavours of sautéed leeks, root vegetables and apples to complement the smoked haddock, which, as in almost all Baltic recipes, is poached. Smoked cod would be also be perfectly suitable instead of the haddock. Serve with rye bread to soak up the tasty juices.

Serves 4

5ml/1 tsp caraway seeds,
 lightly toasted
5ml/1 tsp butter
2 leeks, finely sliced
 lengthways
3–4 thin carrots, finely sliced
1 parsnip, finely sliced
 lengthways
2 apples, peeled and finely sliced
 in wedges
250ml/8fl oz/1 cup `
 vegetable stock
4 fillets smoked haddock,
 250g/9oz each, bones
 removed
salt and ground black pepper
30ml/2 tbsp finely chopped
 fresh parsley, to garnish

1 Put the caraway seeds in a dry pan over a medium-high heat and toast them for 1 minute, or until they release their aroma. Heat the butter in a deep pan over a medium-high heat and add the leeks, carrots, parsnip and apples.

2 Season to taste and add the caraway seeds. Turn the heat to medium and cook, stirring gently, for 3–5 minutes.

3 Add the stock and reduce the heat to low. Cook for 10–12 more minutes. Add the fish fillets to the stock, making sure that they are covered by the stock and vegetables. Cook for a further 5 minutes.

4 Remove the fish, using a slotted spoon, and arrange it in a deep serving plate. Spoon over some of the cooked vegetables and cooking liquid. Sprinkle with the chopped parsley and serve immediately.

> **Cook's Tips**
> *A light horseradish cream is a good accompaniment to this dish.*

Haddock with Spinach Energy 350kcal/1455kJ; Protein 27.5g; Carbohydrate 1.5g, of which sugars 1.4g; Fat 26.3g, of which saturates 14g; Cholesterol 277mg; Calcium 170mg; Fibre 1.3g; Sodium 969mg.
Haddock with Vegetables Energy 323kcal/1368kJ; Protein 51.1g; Carbohydrate 21.8g, of which sugars 17.2g; Fat 4.1g, of which saturates 1.2g; Cholesterol 93mg; Calcium 152mg; Fibre 8.3g; Sodium 1947mg.

White Fish Dumplings

Fish dumplings are served on a bed of summer vegetables with a creamy white wine sauce.

Serves 4

500g/1¼lb white fish fillets, plus their bones
2 eggs, separated
5ml/1 tsp salt
2.5ml/½ tsp ground white pepper
200ml/7fl oz/scant 1 cup double (heavy) cream
a pinch of cayenne pepper
25ml/1½ tbsp vegetable oil
1 onion, chopped
1 small celery stick, chopped
300ml/½ pint/1¼ cups white wine
50g/2oz/¼ cup unsalted (sweet) butter
30ml/2 tbsp plain (all-purpose) flour
15ml/1 tbsp chopped fresh dill
salt and ground black pepper
cooked early summer vegetables, such as peas, carrots, asparagus and spinach, to serve

1 Cut the fish into small dice, put in the bowl of a food processor and blend until finely chopped, slowly adding the egg whites, salt and pepper while blending. Put the fish paste in a bowl and place in the freezer for 20 minutes, until very cold but not frozen. Beat in 100ml/3½fl oz/scant ½ cup of the cream and cayenne pepper then set aside in the refrigerator.

2 Heat the oil in a pan, add the onion and celery and fry for about 5 minutes, until softened. Add the fish bones then cook for 10 minutes, until they start to smell cooked rather than raw. Pour in half of the wine and enough water to cover the bones. Bring to the boil, then reduce the heat and simmer for 20 minutes. Strain the stock through a sieve (strainer) into a clean pan. You should have about 400ml/14fl oz/1⅔ cups fish stock.

3 Simmer the stock. Use two tablespoons to shape the fish mixture into balls and drop these into the stock in two or three batches. Cook for 5 minutes, turning them gently. Transfer to an ovenproof dish and keep warm in a cool oven. Melt the butter in a pan, stir in the flour to make a roux, then stir in a ladleful of the fish stock. Slowly bring to the boil, stirring all the time, until the sauce thickens and has a smooth, velvety texture. Stir the remaining wine and cream into the sauce, return to the boil then remove from the heat. Whisk in the egg yolks and dill, pour the sauce over the dumplings and serve over the vegetables.

Fish Kebabs

To cook fish outside on skewers over coals or a wood fire and then serve with squeezed lemon and fresh tomato, is an ancient Russian tradition. Although incredibly simple to prepare, this dish is a popular choice in many Caucasian restaurants in Russia.

Serves 4

30ml/2 tbsp fresh lemon juice
60ml/4 tbsp smetana or crème fraîche
1kg/2¼lb firm white fish fillets, such as a halibut or monkfish
25g/1oz/2 tbsp butter
salt

For the garnish
4 spring onions (scallions)
1 lemon
4 tomatoes
30ml/2 tbsp finely chopped fresh parsley

1 Heat a barbecue or preheat the oven to 240°C/475°F/Gas 9.

2 To make the marinade, put the lemon juice and smetana or crème fraîche in a large bowl and mix together. Cut the fish into small chunks, season with salt, add to the marinade and stir to coat all over. Leave for 10–15 minutes for the fish to absorb the flavours.

3 Melt the butter in a small pan. Thread the fish chunks tightly together on to four metal skewers or wooden skewers that have been soaked in water. Pre-heat the grill (broiler) if using.

4 Cook the skewers on the barbecue, in the oven or under the grill for about 10 minutes, or until the fish is golden brown and firm. Baste the fish occasionally during cooking with the melted butter and the remaining marinade. Turn the skewers occasionally so that the fish cooks on all sides.

5 Meanwhile, prepare the garnish. Finely slice the spring onions and cut the lemon and tomatoes into wedges. To serve, put the skewers on a large serving dish and sprinkle over the spring onions and chopped fresh parsley. Arrange the lemon and tomatoes wedges around the fish skewers.

Fish Dumplings Energy 600kcal/2484kJ; Protein 27.7g; Carbohydrate 6.5g, of which sugars 2.4g; Fat 46.4g, of which saturates 24.8g; Cholesterol 248mg; Calcium 73mg; Fibre 0.5g; Sodium 205mg.
Fish Kebabs Energy 303kcal/1267kJ; Protein 46.1g; Carbohydrate 0.4g, of which sugars 0.4g; Fat 12.9g, of which saturates 7.6g; Cholesterol 145mg; Calcium 32mg; Fibre 0g; Sodium 191mg.

Grilled Fish in Vine Leaves

In this dish, the fish is first marinated in chermoula and then wrapped in vine leaves to seal in the flavours.

Serves 4
about 30 preserved vine leaves
4–5 large white fish fillets,
  skinned, such as haddock or ling

For the chermoula
small bunch of fresh coriander
  (cilantro), finely chopped
2–3 garlic cloves, chopped
5–10ml/1–2 tsp ground cumin
60ml/4 tbsp olive oil
juice of 1 lemon
salt

For the dipping sauce
50ml/2fl oz/¼ cup white wine
  vinegar or lemon juice
115g/4oz/½ cup caster
  (superfine) sugar
15–30ml/1–2 tbsp water
pinch of saffron threads
1 onion, finely chopped
2 garlic cloves, finely chopped
2–3 spring onions (scallions),
  finely sliced
25g/1oz fresh root ginger,
  peeled and grated
2 hot red or green chillies, seeded
  and finely sliced
small bunch fresh coriander
  (cilantro), finely chopped
small bunch of mint, chopped

1 To make the chermoula, blend the ingredients in a food processor, then set aside. Rinse the vine leaves then soak in cold water. Remove any bones from the fish, cut each fillet into eight. Coat the fish in the chermoula, cover and chill for 1 hour.

2 Meanwhile, prepare the dipping sauce. Heat the vinegar or lemon juice with the sugar and water until the sugar has dissolved. Bring to the boil and boil for about 1 minute, then cool. Add the remaining ingredients and mix well to combine. Spoon the sauce into small individual bowls and set aside.

3 Drain the vine leaves and pat dry. Lay a vine leaf flat on the work surface and place a piece of fish in the centre. Wrap up the fish and leaf into a small parcel. Repeat with the remaining fish and vine leaves. Thread the parcels on to kebab skewers and brush with any leftover marinade.

4 Heat the grill (broiler) on the hottest setting and cook the kebabs for 2–3 minutes on each side. Serve immediately, with the sauce for dipping.

Poached Fish in Spicy Tomato Sauce

A selection of white fish fillets are used in this Middle-Eastern dish – cod, haddock, hake or halibut are all good. Serve the fish with flat breads, such as pitta, and a spicy tomato relish. It is also good with couscous or rice and a green salad with a refreshing lemon and oil dressing.

Serves eight
600ml/1 pint/2½ cups fresh
  tomato sauce
2.5–5ml/½–1 tsp harissa
60ml/4 tbsp chopped fresh
  coriander (cilantro) leaves
1.5kg/3¼lb mixed white fish
  fillets, cut into chunks

1 Heat the tomato sauce with the harissa and coriander in a large pan. Add seasoning to taste and bring to the boil.

2 Remove the pan from the heat and add the fish to the hot sauce. Return to the heat and bring the sauce back to the boil.

3 Reduce the heat and simmer very gently for about 5 minutes, or until the fish is tender.

4 Test the fish with a fork: if the flesh flakes easily, then it is cooked.

5 Taste the sauce and adjust the seasoning, adding more harissa if necessary. Serve hot or warm.

Cook's Tips
Harissa, a hot chilli sauce spiced with cumin, garlic and coriander, is a standard ingredient in many North African dishes. The recipes for harissa vary depending on where it is prepared. It is commonly available in cans and jars. The sauce is fiery and should be used with care until you are familiar with the flavour. Start by adding a small amount and then add more after tasting the sauce. Harissa traditionally accompanies couscous, which is often served with meat or fish tagines, but it can be eaten with pasta or on pizza.

Grilled Fish Energy 432kcal/1818kJ; Protein 39g; Carbohydrate 35g, of which sugars 34g; Fat 17g, of which saturates 2g; Cholesterol 68mg; Calcium 214mg; Fibre 2g; Sodium 964mg.
Poached Fish Energy 194kcal/823kJ; Protein 37g; Carbohydrate 5g, of which sugars 4g; Fat 3g, of which saturates 0g; Cholesterol 68mg; Calcium 45mg; Fibre 1g; Sodium 450mg.

Fish Poached in Vinegar and Ginger

Paksiw in this dish's name (paksiw na isda) refers to a specific method of cooking with vinegar and sugar, rather like a sweet and sour dish, and is often used to give new zest to leftover pork and beef dishes. Although simple, it is a well-regarded method. Firm-fleshed fish turns out particularly well when prepared in this way.

Serves 4

30ml/2 tbsp garlic purée (paste)
30ml/2 tbsp grated ginger
5ml/1 tsp black peppercorns, crushed
300ml/½ pint/1¼ cups water
105ml/7 tbsp vinegar
2 whole fish (600g/1lb 6oz total weight) such as mullet, cod or snapper
15ml/1 tbsp patis (Filipino fish sauce)
15ml/1 tbsp vegetable oil
fresh coriander (cilantro) leaves

1 Blend the garlic purée, ginger, crushed peppercorns, water and vinegar in a non-metallic dish. Place in a flameproof dish.

2 Clean and gut the fish, trimming off any protruding fins and tail with scissors, and add to the dish. Bring to the boil, then simmer for 5 minutes, covered.

3 Turn the fish gently, and with a ladle add the patis and oil. Simmer for another 3 minutes.

4 Serve the fish hot, with the cooking liquid poured over it, garnished with coriander leaves and chilli strips.

> **Cook's Tip**
> *Although using a whole fish is the tradition, you could use fish fillets. This will remove the chore of dealing with bones, thus making the dish easier to serve and eat. You will need to be careful when turning the fish if you use fillets, as they will tend to break up, so you may need to reduce the cooking time slightly.*

Barbecued Salmon with Spices

In this Indian dish, the fish is cooked in a banana leaf parcel. The salmon really works well with the gutsy flavours of the spices.

Serves 6

50g/2oz fresh coconut, skinned and finely grated, or 65g/2½oz/scant 1 cup desiccated (dry unsweetened shredded) coconut, soaked in 30ml/2 tbsp water
1 large lemon, skin, pith and seeds removed, chopped
4 large garlic cloves, crushed
3 large fresh mild green chillies, seeded and chopped
50g/2oz fresh coriander (cilantro), roughly chopped
25g/1oz fresh mint leaves, roughly chopped
5ml/1 tsp ground cumin
5ml/1 tsp sugar
2.5ml/½ tsp fenugreek seeds, finely ground
5ml/1 tsp salt
2 large, whole banana leaves
6 salmon fillets, total weight about 1.2kg/2½lb, skinned

1 Place all the ingredients except the banana leaves and salmon in a food processor. Pulse to a fine paste. Scrape the mixture into a bowl, cover and chill for 30 minutes.

2 To make the parcels, cut each banana leaf widthways into three and cut off the hard outer edges of each piece. Put the pieces of leaf and the edge strips in a bowl of hot water. Soak for 10 minutes. Drain, rinse, and pour over boiling water to soften. Drain, then place the leaves, smooth-side up, on a board.

3 Smear the top and bottom of each with the coconut paste. Place one fillet on each banana leaf. Bring the trimmed edge of the leaf over the salmon, then fold in the sides. Bring up the remaining edge to cover the salmon and make a neat parcel. Tie each parcel securely with a leaf strip.

4 Lay each parcel on a sheet of foil, bring up the edges and scrunch together to seal. Position a lightly oiled grill rack over a moderately-hot barbecue. Place the salmon parcels on the grill rack and cook for about 10 minutes, turning over once.

5 Place on individual plates and leave to stand for 2–3 minutes. Remove the foil, then unwrap and eat the fish out of the parcel.

Fish in Vinegar Energy 157kcal/658kJ; Protein 28g; Carbohydrate 1.5g, of which sugars 0.4g; Fat 4.3g, of which saturates 0.9g; Cholesterol 78mg; Calcium 40mg; Fibre 0.3g; Sodium 411mg.
Salmon with Spices Energy 567kcal/2349kJ; Protein 34.9g; Carbohydrate 1g, of which sugars 0.8g; Fat 47.1g, of which saturates 7.5g; Cholesterol 113mg; Calcium 64mg; Fibre 0.6g; Sodium 1723mg.

Ginger Fishballs in Tomato and Preserved Lemon Sauce

These spicy balls of minced fish and ginger, cooked in a sauce of tomatoes and preserved lemon, are a speciality of the Jews of Morocco. Enjoy them accompanied by flat bread to scoop up the delicious sauce and lemon.

Serves 6

65g/2¹/₂oz bread (about 2 slices)
1kg/2¹/₄lb minced (ground) fish such as cod, haddock or whiting
2 onions, chopped
8 garlic cloves, chopped
2.5–5ml/¹/₂–1 tsp ground turmeric
2.5ml/¹/₂ tsp ground ginger
2.5ml/¹/₂ tsp ras al hanout or garam masala
1 bunch fresh coriander (cilantro), chopped, plus extra to garnish
1 egg
cayenne pepper, to taste
150ml/¹/₄ pint/²/₃ cup vegetable or olive oil or a combination of both
4 ripe tomatoes, diced
5ml/1 tsp paprika
1 preserved lemon, rinsed and cut into small strips
salt and ground black pepper
¹/₂ lemon, cut into wedges, to serve

1 Remove the crusts from the bread, put the bread in a bowl and pour over cold water. Soak for 10 minutes, then squeeze dry.

2 Add the fish to the bread with half the onions, half the garlic, half the turmeric, the ginger, half the ras al hanout, half the coriander, the egg and cayenne pepper and seasoning. Mix together and chill while you make the sauce.

3 To make the sauce, heat the oil in a pan, add the remaining onion and garlic and fry for about 5 minutes. Sprinkle in the remaining turmeric and ras al hanout and warm through.

4 Add the tomatoes, paprika and half the remaining coriander and cook over a medium heat until the tomatoes have formed a sauce consistency. Stir in the strips of preserved lemon.

5 With wet hands, roll pieces of the fish mixture into balls and flatten slightly. Add to the sauce. Cook for 15 minutes, turning twice. Garnish with coriander and serve with lemon wedges.

Moroccan Grilled Fish Brochettes

Serve these delicious skewers with potatoes, aubergine slices and strips of red peppers, which can be cooked on the barbecue alongside the fish brochettes. Accompany with a stack of warm, soft pitta breads or flour tortillas.

Serves 4–6

5 garlic cloves, chopped
2.5ml/¹/₂ tsp paprika
2.5ml/¹/₂ tsp ground cumin
2.5–5ml/¹/₂–1 tsp salt
2–3 pinches of cayenne pepper
60ml/4 tbsp olive oil
30ml/2 tbsp lemon juice
30ml/2 tbsp chopped fresh coriander (cilantro) or parsley
675g/1¹/₂lb firm-fleshed white fish, such as haddock, halibut, sea bass, snapper or turbot, cut into 2.5–5cm/1–2in cubes
3–4 green (bell) peppers, cut into 2.5–5cm/1–2in pieces
2 lemon wedges, to serve

1 Put the garlic, paprika, cumin, salt, cayenne pepper, oil, lemon juice and fresh coriander or parsley in a large bowl and mix together. Add the fish and toss to coat. Leave to marinate for at least 30 minutes, and preferably 2 hours, at room temperature, or chill overnight in the refrigerator.

2 About 40 minutes before you are going to cook the brochettes, light the barbecue. The barbecue is ready when the coals have turned white and grey.

3 Meanwhile, thread the fish cubes and pepper pieces alternately on to wooden or metal skewers.

4 Grill the brochettes on the barbecue for 2–3 minutes on each side, or until the fish is tender and lightly browned. Transfer to a warmed serving plate. Serve with lemon wedges for squeezing over the brochettes.

Cook's Tip
If you are using wooden skewers for the brochettes, soak them in cold water for 30 minutes before using to prevent them from burning.

Ginger Fishballs Energy 434kcal/1806kJ; Protein 34g; Carbohydrate 12g, of which sugars 5g; Fat 28g, of which saturates 4g; Cholesterol 115mg; Calcium 58mg; Fibre 2g; Sodium 179mg.
Fish Brochettes Energy 276kcal/1157kJ; Protein 33.3g; Carbohydrate 8g, of which sugars 7.6g; Fat 12.5g, of which saturates 1.9g; Cholesterol 61mg; Calcium 34mg; Fibre 2g; Sodium 118mg.

Steamed Fish with Sour Plums

Shantou restaurants take great pride in steamed fish dishes like this one. The addition of sour plums is a particularly inspired touch, especially when salmon, pomfret or sea bass is used, as the tartness of the plums really cuts the rich oils in the fish and perfectly balances the dish.

Serves 4

1 whole fish, about 500g/1¼lb,
   cleaned and scaled
4 canned sour plums
15ml/1 tbsp fish sauce
15ml/1 tbsp finely shredded fresh
   root ginger
2 spring onions (scallions),
   finely shredded
3–4 strips of streaky (fatty) bacon
chopped fresh coriander (cilantro),
   to serve

1 Rinse the fish inside and out. Dry with kitchen paper. Cut deep slashes on either side of the fish, where the flesh is thickest. Put the fish on a plate that will fit in your steamer. If the fish is too large, cut it in half.

2 Drain the sour plums and put them in a bowl. Mash to a rough purée, using a potato masher or a spoon. Spread the purée over the fish.

3 Dribble the fish sauce over the fish and scatter with the ginger and spring onions. Lay the strips of streaky bacon on top.

4 Put the plate in the steamer. Steam the fish over rapidly boiling water for about 15 minutes or until it is cooked through. Transfer everything to a warm platter, garnish with the coriander and serve immediately.

> **Cook's Tips**
> • Pomfret is a tropical fish and is commonly used in south-east Asian cuisine. It has firm but tender, white flesh and is a perfect partner to Asian flavourings such as ginger or lemon grass.
> • Sea bass is a favourite in Chinese cooking, since it also tastes excellent with Asian flavours.

Poached Turbot with Saffron Sauce

The saffron sauce complements the firm white flesh of the turbot well. Turbot is a treat by any standards and this is a rich elegant dish, most suitable for entertaining. Offer rice, or new boiled potatoes, and mangetouts or peas with the turbot.

Serves 4

pinch of saffron threads

50ml/2fl oz/¼ cup single
   (light) cream
1 shallot, finely chopped
175g/6oz/¾ cup cold
   unsalted (sweet) butter, cut into
   small cubes
175ml/6fl oz/¾ cup dry sherry
475ml/16fl oz/2 cups fish stock
4 medium turbot fillets, about
   150–175g/5–6oz
   each, skinned
flat leaf parsley leaves,
   to garnish

1 Put the saffron threads into the single cream and allow them to infuse (steep) for 10 minutes. Cook the chopped shallot very gently in a large heavy-based frying pan with 15g/½oz/1 tbsp of the butter until it is soft.

2 Put the cooked shallot, with the dry sherry and fish stock, into a fish kettle or other large, heavy pan. Lay the turbot fillets in the pan, without overlapping them, and bring gently to the boil. Reduce the heat immediately and simmer gently for about 5 minutes, depending on the thickness of the turbot fillets.

3 When cooked, remove the fillets from the poaching liquid with a slotted fish slice or metal spatula and lay them on a heated dish. Cover and keep warm.

4 To make the sauce: bring the poaching liquor to the boil and boil fast to reduce it to 60ml/4 tbsp.

5 Add the cream and saffron and bring back to the boil. Remove from the heat, add the butter, whisking constantly until a smooth sauce has formed.

6 Pour the sauce on to warmed serving plates, lay the turbot on top and sprinkle with parsley leaves to serve.

Steamed Fish Energy 188kcal/791kJ; Protein 20.4g; Carbohydrate 9.3g, of which sugars 9.2g; Fat 8g, of which saturates 2.4g; Cholesterol 45mg; Calcium 51mg; Fibre 1.7g; Sodium 658mg.
Poached Turbot Energy 544Kcal/2256kJ; Protein 27.4g; Carbohydrate 1.4g, of which sugars 1.4g; Fat 42.4g, of which saturates 25.4g; Cholesterol 100mg; Calcium 97mg; Fibre 0.1g; Sodium 376mg.

Turbot with Egg and Prawns

Turbot, known as the king of flat fish because of its firm, white flesh and delicate flavour, is found mostly in the North Sea on the west coast of Sweden. This fish is also caught in the south-west of the Baltic Sea, where freshwater fish are found in salt water. In Sweden, turbot is often irreverently called 'dass lock', meaning toilet seat, which is a reference to its expansive flat shape. If unavailable, halibut, sole or flounder are all good alternatives.

Serves 6–8

1kg/2¼lb whole turbot, gutted
1 leek, finely chopped
1 bunch fresh parsley, chopped
1 lemon, sliced
salt and ground black pepper

For the sauce
250g/9oz/1 cup plus
   2 tbsp butter
1 egg
175g/6oz shell-on cooked
   prawns (shrimp)
15ml/1 tbsp grated fresh
   horseradish

1 Preheat the oven to 180°C/350°F/Gas 4. Lay the gutted turbot on a large sheet of foil.

2 Mix together the chopped leek and chopped parsley and season with salt and pepper.

3 Use the leek and parsley mixture to stuff the body cavity of the turbot and then add the lemon slices. Wrap the turbot in the foil and bake the fish in the preheated oven for about 45 minutes.

4 To make the sauce, hard boil the egg and leave to cool. Then mash the hard-boiled egg in a bowl.

5 Melt the butter and set aside. Remove the shells from the prawns and add them to the mashed hard-boiled egg with the butter and grated horseradish.

6 Serve the turbot on a large serving dish, accompanied by the sauce.

Halibut Steaks with Lemon Butter

Poles often simply grill or fry fresh fish, and this elegant dish is a good example. This simple treatment of spreading the steaks with parsley, lemon and butter before cooking ensures the flesh is moist and enables the flavours to permeate the fish without overpowering its delicate flavour.

Serves 4

4 halibut steaks, about
   185g/6½oz each
150g/5oz/10 tbsp
   butter, softened
30ml/2 tbsp chopped
   fresh parsley
30ml/2 tbsp lemon juice
salt and ground black pepper,
   to taste
lemon wedges, to serve
parsley sprigs, to garnish
   (optional)

1 Preheat the grill (broiler) to medium. Season the fish with salt and pepper on both sides.

2 Mix together the butter, parsley and lemon juice, then spread over both sides of each fish steak.

3 Line a grill pan with foil, then put the steaks on the foil. Place under the grill and cook for 7–8 minutes on each side, until tender.

4 Transfer the halibut steaks to warmed plates. Serve immediately, with lemon wedges for squeezing over, and garnished with parsley sprigs if using.

Variation
White fish such as plaice fillets can also be used in this recipe.

Cook's Tips
Halibut is a member of the flat fish family and is one of the largest edible fishes. It has firm, white flesh and a pleasing, mild flavour. It is a versatile fish that lends itself to almost any kind of preparation.

Turbot Energy 350kcal/1448kJ; Protein 20.8g; Carbohydrate 0.8g, of which sugars 0.7g; Fat 29.2g, of which saturates 17.1g; Cholesterol 113mg; Calcium 71mg; Fibre 0.5g; Sodium 337mg.
Halibut Energy 464kcal/1928kJ; Protein 38.2g; Carbohydrate 0.6g, of which sugars 0.5g; Fat 34.3g, of which saturates 20.1g; Cholesterol 141mg; Calcium 83mg; Fibre 0.6g; Sodium 337mg.

Marinated Steamed Sea Bass

This recipe comes from Tumbes, the region in Peru that is closest to the Equator with a tropical climate and wonderful seafood. Using an ancient technique, the fish is steamed with a little vinegar or chicha, which is a drink made from fermented corn.

Serves 2

1 sea bass, weighing about 500g/1¼lb, scaled and cleaned

2.5ml/½ tsp ground black pepper
2.5ml/½ tsp ground cumin
45ml/3 tbsp red wine vinegar
75ml/5 tbsp vegetable oil
1 large red onion, chopped
1 small tomato, chopped
1 small piece of red (bell) pepper, diced
1 chilli, seeded and finely chopped
15ml/1 tbsp grated garlic
10ml/2 tsp paprika
salt
boiled cassava and rice, if using, to serve

1 Season the sea bass with pepper, cumin and salt. Pour the vinegar over it and leave to marinate for 15 minutes.

2 Heat the oil in a large frying pan and fry the onion for 5 minutes over medium heat. When it starts to brown, add the chopped tomato, diced pepper, chopped chilli, garlic and paprika and cook for a further 5 minutes.

3 Lay the fish in the pan and pour in its seasonings and vinegar. Cover the pan and leave the fish to steam for 15 minutes at medium heat.

4 Using a fork, carefully check that the fish is cooked: if the flesh flakes easily, remove from the heat. Serve the fish accompanied by the tomato mixture, boiled cassava and white rice, if using.

Cook's Tips
Cassava is a tropical vegetable with starchy roots, that is rather like a yam. After peeling, the creamy white flesh is cooked and eaten instead of potatoes. It is often made into cassava flour, which is used for baking cakes and breads.

Sea Bass Steamed in Coconut Milk

This is a delicious recipe for any whole white fish, such as sea bass or cod, or for large chunks of trout or salmon. The recipe also works well in the oven – place the fish, tucked in foil, on a baking tray and bake. Serve this dish with plain or sticky rice or a Vietnamese salad.

Serves 4

200ml/7fl oz coconut milk
10ml/2 tsp raw cane or muscovado (molasses) sugar

about 15ml/1 tbsp sesame or vegetable oil
2 garlic cloves, finely chopped
1 red Thai chilli, seeded and finely chopped
4cm/1½in fresh root ginger, peeled and grated
750g/1lb 10oz sea bass, gutted and skinned on one side
1 star anise, ground
1 bunch of fresh basil, stalks removed
30ml/2 tbsp cashew nuts
sea salt and ground black pepper

1 Heat the coconut milk with the sugar in a small pan, stirring until the sugar dissolves, then remove from the heat. Heat the oil and fry the garlic, chilli and ginger until they begin to brown. Add the mixture to the coconut milk and mix well to combine.

2 Place the fish, skin side down, on a wide piece of foil and tuck up the sides to form a boat-shaped container. Cut diagonal slashes into the flesh on the top and rub with the ground star anise. Season and spoon the coconut milk over the top.

3 Scatter half the basil leaves on top of the fish and pull the sides of the foil over the top, so that it is almost enclosed. Place the foil packet in a steamer. Cover the steamer, bring the water to the boil, reduce the heat and simmer for 20–25 minutes.

4 Meanwhile, roast the cashew nuts in the small frying pan, adding a little extra oil if necessary. Drain the nuts on kitchen paper, then grind them to crumbs. Lift the cooked fish out of the foil and transfer it to a serving dish.

5 Spoon the cooking juices over, sprinkle with the cashew nut crumbs and garnish with the remaining basil leaves. Serve immediately.

Steamed Sea Bass Energy 592kcal/2471kJ; Protein 50.6g; Carbohydrate 27.8g, of which sugars 21.2g; Fat 31.8g, of which saturates 4g; Cholesterol 120mg; Calcium 77mg; Fibre 5.7g; Sodium 750mg.
Sea Bass in Coconut Milk Energy 235Kcal/983kJ; Protein 26g; Carbohydrate 8g, of which sugars 6g; Fat 11g, of which saturates 2g; Cholesterol 100mg; Calcium 217mg; Fibre 0.3g; Sodium 0.3g

Skate with Bitter Salad Leaves

This dish is popular in Galicia, which is famous for both its skate and its watercress. Skate has a delicious sweet flavour, enhanced here by orange. It contrasts well with any bitter leaves – buy a bag of mixed salad leaves for contrasting textures and flavours.

Serves 4
800g/1¾lb skate wings
15ml/1 tbsp white wine vinegar
4 black peppercorns
1 fresh thyme sprig
175g/6oz bitter salad leaves, such as frisée, rocket (arugula), radicchio, escarole, lamb's lettuce (mâche) and watercress
1 orange
2 tomatoes, peeled, seeded and diced

For the dressing
15ml/1 tbsp white wine vinegar
45ml/3 tbsp extra virgin olive oil
1 bunch spring onions (scallions), whites finely chopped
salt, paprika and black pepper
crusty bread, to serve

1 Put the skate wings into a large shallow pan, cover with cold water and add the vinegar, peppercorns and thyme. Bring to the boil, then poach gently for 8–10 minutes, until the flesh comes away easily from the bones.

2 Make the dressing. Whisk together the vinegar, oil and spring onions and season with salt, paprika and pepper.

3 Put the salad leaves in a large bowl, pour over the dressing and toss well. Remove the rind from the orange using a zester, then peel it, removing all the pith. Slice into thin rounds.

4 Flake the fish, discarding the bones, and add to the salad. Add a pinch of zest, the orange slices and tomatoes, toss gently and serve with bread.

> **Cook's Tips**
> *The edible parts of skate are the winglike pectoral fins or 'wings'. The flesh is white and firm and similar to scallops. It can be baked, poached or fried.*

Ray with Black Butter

The butter in this classic dish is not really black but a deep nutty brown, and its flavour complements the sweetish flesh perfectly. Ray has soft ribs instead of bones, but the skin is very hard to remove from the raw fish, so make sure the fishmonger does this for you. Offer boiled new potatoes and a side salad to accompany the ray. Have everything ready before starting to cook the fish, as it must be served immediately while the butter is still sizzling.

Serves 4
675g/1½lb ray wings, skinned
half a small onion, sliced
bay leaf
a few parsley stalks
1 slice of lemon
75g/3oz/6 tbsp butter
50g/2oz capers
2.5ml/½ tsp white wine vinegar
chopped fresh parsley, to garnish (optional)

1 Cut the ray wings into four serving pieces. Put 600ml/1 pint/2½ cups water into a wide pan with the onion, bay leaf, parsley stalks and lemon.

2 Bring to boiling point, then add the ray pieces and, when the water comes to the boil, reduce the heat to a gentle simmer. The cooking time will depend on the thickness of the ray, so cook very gently for about 15–20 minutes, or until the flesh lifts easily away from the cartilage.

3 Remove the fish as soon as it is tender, and transfer it to four warmed serving plates. Meanwhile, melt the butter in a small pan over medium heat and cook until it turns a deep golden brown. Add the capers and white wine vinegar, and pour over the cooked ray. Sprinkle the chopped parsley over the fish quickly, and serve straight away while it is sizzling hot.

> **Cook's Tips**
> *Capers are the flower buds of a bush that grows in the Mediterranean region. The buds are picked then preserved in salt and vinegar, and their unique flavour develops.*

Skate Energy 230kcal/965kJ; Protein 31.6g; Carbohydrate 4.8g, of which sugars 4.8g; Fat 9.5g, of which saturates 1.3g; Cholesterol 0mg; Calcium 118mg; Fibre 1.5g; Sodium 247mg.
Ray Energy 253Kcal/1055kJ; Protein 25.8g; Carbohydrate 1.3g, of which sugars 1g; Fat 16.1g, of which saturates 9.8g; Cholesterol 40mg; Calcium 75mg; Fibre 0.2g; Sodium 317mg.

Sole with Vodka Sauce and Caviar

Caviar was once served only with silver spoons to protect the taste. Today, caviar is served on white buttered toast or blinis, or as a luxurious garnish to a delicious fish.

Serves 4
500–600g/1lb 4oz–1lb 6oz sole, flounder or plaice fillets
200ml/7fl oz/scant 1 cup fish stock
60ml/4 tbsp caviar
salt
4 lemon wedges and fresh dill, to garnish

hot boiled potatoes, to serve

For the vodka sauce
25–40g/1–1½oz/2–3 tbsp butter
5–6 shallots, finely diced
5ml/1 tsp plain white (all-purpose) flour
200ml/7fl oz/scant 1 cup double (heavy) cream
200ml/7fl oz/scant 1 cup fish stock
100ml/3½fl oz/scant ½ cup dry white wine
30ml/2 tbsp vodka
salt and ground black pepper

1 Season the fish fillets with salt. Roll up and secure each fillet with a cocktail stick (toothpick).

2 Heat the stock in a small pan. Place the fish rolls in the pan, cover and simmer for 5–8 minutes, until the fish is tender. Remove from the pan and keep warm.

3 Meanwhile, make the sauce. Melt the butter in a pan, add the shallots and fry gently for 3–5 minutes, until softened but not browned. Add the flour and stir until well mixed.

4 Gradually add the cream and stock until smooth. Slowly bring to the boil, stirring, until the sauce bubbles. Reduce the heat and simmer for 3–5 minutes, until the sauce thickens. Remove the shallots with a slotted spoon. Add the wine and vodka and bring to the boil. Season with salt and pepper to taste.

5 Pour the sauce over the base of four warmed plates. Place the fish rolls on top and add a spoonful of caviar to each. Garnish with lemon and dill and serve with hot boiled potatoes.

Quenelles of Sole

Traditionally, these light fish 'dumplings' are made with pike, but they are even better made with sole or other white fish.

Serves 6
450g/1lb sole fillets, skinned and cut into large pieces and boned
4 egg whites
600ml/1 pint/2½ cups double (heavy) cream

freshly grated nutmeg
salt and ground black pepper
chopped fresh parsley, to garnish

For the sauce
1 small shallot, finely chopped
60ml/4 tbsp dry vermouth
120ml/4fl oz/½ cup fish stock
150ml/¼ pint/⅔ cup double (heavy) cream
50g/2oz/¼ cup butter, diced

1 Put the sole pieces in a food processor. Season. Switch the machine on and, with the motor running, add the egg whites one at a time through the feeder tube to make a smooth purée. Press the purée through a metal sieve placed over a bowl. Stand the bowl of purée in a larger bowl and surround it with plenty of crushed ice or ice cubes.

2 Whip the cream until very thick, but not stiff. Gradually fold it into the fish mixture. Season, then stir in nutmeg to taste. Cover the bowl and refrigerate for several hours.

3 To make the sauce, combine the shallot, vermouth and fish stock in a small pan. Bring to the boil and cook until reduced by half. Add the cream and boil until it has a thick consistency. Strain and return to the pan. Whisk in the butter, one piece at a time, until creamy. Season. Keep hot, but do not allow to boil.

4 Bring a wide shallow pan of lightly salted water to the boil, then reduce the heat to very low. Using two tablespoons dipped in hot water, shape the fish mousse into ovals. As each quenelle is shaped, slip it into the simmering water.

5 Poach the quenelles in batches for 8–10 minutes, until firm to the touch but still slightly creamy inside. Lift out using a slotted spoon, drain on kitchen paper and keep hot. Serve on warm plates; pour the sauce around, garnish with parsley and serve.

Sole with Vodka Energy 470kcal/1952kJ; Protein 27.9g; Carbohydrate 3.2g, of which sugars 1.9g; Fat 35g, of which saturates 20.4g; Cholesterol 188mg; Calcium 103mg; Fibre 0.3g; Sodium 548mg.
Quenelles 771kcal/3180kJ; Protein 17.7g; Carbohydrate 3.3g, of which sugars 3g; Fat 75.4g, of which saturates 46.1g; Cholesterol 227mg; Calcium 89mg; Fibre 0.1g; Sodium 195mg.

Monkfish Kebabs

Monkfish is a prized firm-fleshed fish that is ideal for dishes like kebabs, as it will not fall apart when cooked.

Serves 4
900g/2lb fresh monkfish
tail, skinned
3 (bell) peppers, preferably
red, green and yellow
juice of 1 lemon
60ml/4 tbsp olive oil
bay leaves, halved (optional)
salt and ground black pepper
rolls or pitta bread and
lemon juice (optional), to serve

For the spicy barbecue sauce
15ml/1 tbsp olive oil
1 onion, finely chopped
1 garlic clove, finely chopped
300ml/½ pint/1¼ cups water
30ml/2 tbsp wine vinegar
30ml/2 tbsp soft brown sugar
10ml/2 tsp mild mustard
grated rind and juice
of ½ lemon
pinch of dried thyme
30ml/2 tbsp Worcestershire sauce
60–75ml/4–5 tbsp
tomato ketchup
30ml/2 tbsp tomato purée
(paste) (optional)

1 Trim the monkfish and cut it into bitesize cubes. Cut each pepper into quarters, and then seed and halve each quarter.

2 Combine the lemon juice and oil in a bowl and add seasoning. Turn the fish and pepper pieces in the mixture and leave to marinate for 20 minutes (this will add flavour and offset the natural dryness of the fish). Soak four wooden skewers in cold water for 30 minutes. This prevents them from burning during cooking.

3 To make the spicy barbecue sauce, heat the oil in a pan and fry the onion and garlic until soft but not browned. Add all the remaining ingredients, bring to the boil and simmer for 15 minutes to make a fairly chunky sauce.

4 Preheat a very hot grill (broiler) or barbecue, and oil the grill rack. Thread pieces of fish and pepper alternately, with the occasional half bay leaf, if you like. Cook for about 10 minutes, turning and basting frequently.

5 Serve in rolls or pitta bread, with the sauce, or simply with a squeeze of fresh lemon juice, if you like.

Roast Monkfish with Garlic

Monkfish tied up and cooked in this way is known in French as a 'gigot', because it resembles a leg of lamb. The combination of monkfish and garlic is superb. For a contrast in colour, serve it with vibrant green beans.

Serves 4–6
1kg/2¼lb monkfish
tail, skinned
14 fat garlic cloves
5ml/1 tsp fresh thyme leaves
30ml/2 tbsp olive oil
juice of 1 lemon
2 bay leaves
salt and ground black pepper

1 Preheat the oven to 220°C/425°F/Gas 7. Remove any membrane from the monkfish tail and cut out the central bone. Peel two garlic cloves and cut them into thin slivers. Sprinkle a quarter of these and half the thyme leaves over the cut side of the fish, then close it up and use kitchen string to tie it into a neat shape. Pat dry with kitchen paper.

2 Make incisions on either side of the fish and push in the remaining garlic slivers. Heat half the olive oil in a frying pan that can safely be used in the oven. When the oil is hot, put in the monkfish and brown it all over for about 5 minutes, until evenly coloured. Season with salt and pepper, sprinkle with lemon juice and sprinkle over the remaining thyme.

3 Tuck the bay leaves under the monkfish, arrange the remaining (unpeeled) garlic cloves around it and drizzle the remaining oil over the fish and the garlic. Transfer the pan to the oven for 20–25 minutes, until the fish is cooked through.

4 Place on a warmed serving dish with the garlic and some green beans. To serve, remove the string and cut the monkfish into 2cm/¾in thick slices.

Cook's Tips
• The garlic heads can be used whole.
• When serving the monkfish, invite each guest to pop out the soft garlic pulp with a fork and spread it over the monkfish.

Monkfish Kebabs Energy 377Kcal/1586kJ; Protein 37.4g; Carbohydrate 24.1g, of which sugars 23.1g; Fat 15.3g, of which saturates 2.4g; Cholesterol 32mg; Calcium 54mg; Fibre 2.8g; Sodium 382mg.
Roast Monkfish Energy 259kcal/1091kJ; Protein 45.7g; Carbohydrate 4.1g, of which sugars 0.4g; Fat 6.7g, of which saturates 1.1g; Cholesterol 40mg; Calcium 27mg; Fibre 1g; Sodium 51mg.

Grilled Red Mullet with Bay Leaves

Red mullet are called salmonetes – little salmon – in Spain because of their delicate, pale pink colour. They are simple to cook on a barbecue, with bay leaves for flavour and a dribble of tangy dressing instead of a marinade.

Serves 4
4 red mullet, about 225–275g/
  8–10oz each, cleaned
  and descaled
olive oil, for brushing
fresh herb sprigs, such as fennel,
  dill, parsley, or thyme
2–3 dozen fresh or dried bay
  leaves

For the dressing
90ml/6 tbsp olive oil
6 garlic cloves, finely chopped
1/2 dried chilli, seeded and
  chopped
juice of 1/2 lemon
15ml/1 tbsp parsley

1 Prepare the barbecue or preheat the grill (broiler) with the shelf 15cm/6in from the heat source.

2 Brush each fish with oil and stuff the cavities with the herb sprigs. Brush the grill pan with oil and lay bay leaves across the cooking rack. Place the fish on top and cook for 15–20 minutes until cooked through, turning once.

3 To make the dressing, heat the olive oil in a small pan and fry the chopped garlic with the dried chilli. Add the lemon juice and strain the dressing into a small jug (pitcher). Add the chopped parsley and stir to combine.

4 Serve the mullet on warmed plates, drizzled with dressing.

> **Cook's Tip**
> • Nicknamed the woodcock of the sea, red mullet are one of the fish that are classically cooked uncleaned to give them extra flavour. In this recipe however, the fish are cleaned and herbs are used to add extra flavour to the fish.

Red Mullet with Chermoula and Preserved Lemons

The coriander and chilli chermoula marinade gives this dish its distinct flavour. Served with saffron couscous and a crisp, herb-filled salad, this is delicious as a main course.

Serves 4
30–45ml/2–3 tbsp olive oil, plus
  extra for brushing
1 onion, chopped
1 carrot, chopped
1/2 preserved lemon, finely chopped
4 plum tomatoes, peeled and
  chopped
600ml/1 pint/2 1/2 cups fish stock
  3–4 new potatoes, peeled
  and cubed
4 small red mullet or snapper,
  gutted and filleted
handful of black olives, pitted
  and halved
small bunch of fresh coriander
  (cilantro), chopped
small bunch of mint, chopped
salt and ground black pepper

For the chermoula
small bunch of fresh coriander
  (cilantro), finely chopped
2–3 garlic cloves, chopped
5–10ml/1–2 tsp ground cumin
pinch of saffron threads
60ml/4 tbsp olive oil
juice of 1 lemon
1 red chilli, seeded and chopped
5ml/1 tsp salt

1 To make the chermoula, process the ingredients together in a food processor, then set aside.

2 Heat the olive oil in a pan. Add the onion and carrot and cook until softened but not browned. Stir in half the preserved lemon, along with 30ml/2 tbsp of the chermoula, the tomatoes and the stock. Bring to the boil, reduce the heat, cover and simmer for 30 minutes. Add the potatoes and simmer for a further 10 minutes, until they are tender.

3 Preheat the grill (broiler) and brush a grill pan with oil. Brush the fish fillets with oil and a little of the chermoula. Season, then place the fillets, skin-side up, on the sheet or pan and cook under the grill for 5–6 minutes. Meanwhile, stir the olives, the remaining chermoula and preserved lemon into the sauce and check the seasoning. Serve the fish fillets in wide bowls, spoon the sauce over and sprinkle liberally with coriander and mint.

Grilled Red Mullet Energy 451kcal/1876kJ; Protein 38g; Carbohydrate 1g, of which sugars 0g; Fat 33g, of which saturates 4g; Cholesterol 0mg; Calcium 135mg; Fibre 0g; Sodium 183mg.
Mullet with Chermoula Energy 501kcal/2086kJ; Protein 40g; Carbohydrate 9g, of which sugars 7g; Fat 35g, of which saturates 4g; Cholesterol 0mg; Calcium 200mg; Fibre 3g; Sodium 1325mg.y

Fragrant Red Snapper in Banana Leaves

Banana leaves make a good wrapping for steamed fish.

Serves 4

4 small red snapper, grouper, tilapia or red bream, gutted and cleaned
4 large squares of banana leaf (about 30cm/12in square)
50ml/2fl oz/¼ cup coconut cream
90ml/6 tbsp chopped coriander (cilantro)
90ml/6 tbsp chopped mint
juice of 3 limes
3 spring onions (scallions), finely sliced
4 kaffir lime leaves, shredded
2 red chillies, seeded and sliced
4 lemon grass stalks, split lengthways
salt and ground black pepper
steamed rice and steamed Asian greens, to serve

1 Using a sharp knife, score the fish diagonally on each side. Bring a wok of water to the boil and dip each square of banana leaf into it for 15–20 seconds. Rinse under cold water and dry with kitchen paper.

2 Place the coconut cream, chopped herbs, lime juice, spring onions, lime leaves and chillies in a bowl and stir well to mix. Season with salt and pepper.

3 Lay each banana leaf out flat on a work surface and place a fish and a split lemon grass stalk in the centre of each one. Spread the herb mixture over each fish.

4 Wrap the banana leaf around each one to form four neat parcels. Secure each parcel tightly with a bamboo skewer or a cocktail stick (toothpick).

5 Place the parcels in a single layer in one or two tiers of a large bamboo steamer and place over a wok of simmering water. Cover tightly and steam for 15–20 minutes, or until the fish is cooked through.

6 Remove the fish from the steamer and serve immediately, still in their banana-leaf wrappings, with steamed rice and Asian greens.

Paper-wrapped and Steamed Red Snapper

Originally, this elegant dish featured a red snapper wrapped in layered Japanese hand-made paper soaked in sake and tied with ribbons.

Serves 4

4 small red snapper fillets, no greater than 18 x 6cm/ 7 x 2½in, or whole snapper, 20cm/8in long, gutted but head, tail and fins intact
8 asparagus spears, hard ends discarded
4 spring onions (scallions)
60ml/4 tbsp sake
grated rind of ½ lime
½ lime, thinly sliced
5ml/1 tsp shoyu (optional)
salt

1 Sprinkle the fish fillets with salt and chill for 20 minutes. Preheat the oven to 180°C/350°F/ Gas 4. To make the parcels, lay greaseproof (waxed) paper measuring 38 x 30cm/15 x 12in on a work surface. Use two pieces for each. Fold up one-third of the paper and turn back 1cm/½in from one end to make a flap.

2 Fold 1cm/½in in from the other end to make another flap. Fold the top edge down to fold over the first flap. Interlock the two flaps to form a long rectangle. At each end, fold the top corners down diagonally, then fold the bottom corners up to meet the opposite folded edge to make a triangle. Press flat with your palm. Repeat the process to make four parcels.

3 Cut 2.5cm/1in from the tip of the asparagus, and slice in half lengthways. Slice the asparagus stems and spring onions diagonally into thin ovals. Parboil the tips for 1 minute, drain. Set aside.

4 Open the parcels. Place the asparagus and the spring onions inside. Sprinkle with salt and place the fish on top. Add more salt and some sake, then the lime rind. Refold the parcels.

5 Pour hot water into a roasting pan fitted with a wire rack to 1cm/½in below the rack. Place the parcels on the rack. Cook in the centre of the oven for 20 minutes. The fish should be changed to white. Insert a thin slice of lime and two asparagus tips into each parcel. Serve with shoyu, if you like.

Snapper in Banana Leaves Energy 185kcal/781kJ; Protein 39.4g; Carbohydrate 0.9g, of which sugars 0.8g; Fat 2.7g, of which saturates 0.6g; Cholesterol 74mg; Calcium 87mg; Fibre 0.1g; Sodium 168mg.
Steamed Snapper Energy 110kcal/465kJ; Protein 20.6g; Carbohydrate 1g, of which sugars 0.9g; Fat 1.5g, of which saturates 0.3g; Cholesterol 37mg; Calcium 51mg; Fibre 0.6g; Sodium 79mg.

Salmon with Light Hollandaise and Asparagus

This summery dish is light and colourful. Asparagus makes the ideal accompaniment for salmon when it is in season.

Serves 4
bunch of 20 asparagus
  spears, trimmed
4 salmon portions, such as steaks,
  about 200g/7oz each

15ml/1 tbsp olive oil
juice of ½ lemon
25g/1oz/2 tbsp butter
salt and ground black pepper

For the hollandaise sauce
45ml/3 tbsp white wine vinegar
6 peppercorns
1 bay leaf
3 egg yolks
175g/6oz/¾ cup butter, softened

1 Peel the lower stems of the asparagus. Stand in a deep pan; cook in salted boiling water for about 1 minute, or until just becoming tender, then remove from the pan and cool quickly under cold running water to prevent further cooking. Drain.

2 To make the hollandaise sauce: in a small pan, boil the vinegar and 15ml/1 tbsp water with the peppercorns and bay leaf until reduced to 15ml/1 tbsp. Leave to cool. Cream the egg yolks with 15g/½oz/1 tbsp butter and a pinch of salt. Strain the vinegar into the eggs and set the bowl over a pan of boiling water. Remove from the heat. Whisk in the remaining butter, no more than 10g/¼oz/1½ tsp at a time, until the sauce is shiny and looks like thick cream. Season with salt and pepper.

3 Heat a ridged griddle pan or grill (broiler) until very hot. Brush the salmon with olive oil, sprinkle with the lemon juice and season with salt and black pepper.

4 Cook the fish on the griddle or under a grill for 3–5 minutes on each side, depending on the thickness of the fish. The fish should be seared on the outside, moist and succulent within.

5 Melt the butter in a separate large pan and gently reheat the asparagus in it for 1–2 minutes before serving with the fish and hollandaise sauce.

Salmon Steaks with Warm Potato Salad

Salmon is a favourite fish in Denmark for special occasions, festivals and significant anniversaries. Warm potato salad is another Danish favourite, and its buttery, tangy dressing complements the salmon.

Serves 6
3 bunches fresh dill
6 salmon steaks, each about
  2.5cm/1in thick (1.3kg/3lb
  total weight)
475ml/16fl oz/2 cups water
250ml/8fl oz/1 cup dry
  white wine

15ml/1 tbsp white vinegar
5ml/1 tsp salt
5 whole allspice berries
2 bay leaves
6 small dill sprigs, to garnish
6 lemon slices, to garnish

For the warm potato salad
1.2kg/2½lb potatoes, peeled
175g/6oz chopped onion
175ml/6fl oz/¾ cup water
45ml/3 tbsp cider vinegar
10ml/2 tsp caster
  (superfine) sugar
5ml/1 tsp mustard powder
salt and ground white pepper
25g/1oz/2 tbsp butter
45ml/3 tbsp chopped parsley

1 Place the dill in the bottom of a 23 × 33cm/9 × 13in rectangular baking dish. Arrange the salmon over the dill. Mix the water, wine, vinegar and salt and add the allspice and bay leaves. Pour over the salmon. Bring the liquid to a simmer, lower the heat, cover and cook for 10–15 minutes.

2 Boil the potatoes whole in lightly salted water for 20–25 minutes, until tender. To make the dressing, place the onion in a pan with the water. Bring to the boil over a medium-high heat, and cook for 5 minutes, until the onion is transparent. Stir in the vinegar, sugar and mustard and season to taste, adding more water if necessary. Stir in the butter until melted. Keep warm.

3 Drain the potatoes. While still warm, cut them into slices and layer in a bowl. Pour over the dressing, add the parsley and toss gently. When the fish flakes easily with a fork, skim off any scum and lift out the fish and drain. Remove the skin and put on plates. Garnish with dill and lemon and serve with the potato salad.

Salmon Hollandaise Energy 834Kcal/3449kJ; Protein 46.5g; Carbohydrate 2.8g, of which sugars 2.7g; Fat 7.7g, of which saturates 31.6g; Cholesterol 358mg; Calcium 102mg; Fibre 2.1g; Sodium 401mg.
Salmon Steaks Energy 578kcal/2420kJ; Protein 47.6g; Carbohydrate 36.3g, of which sugars 6g; Fat 27.9g, of which saturates 6.5g; Cholesterol 117mg; Calcium 67mg; Fibre 2.4g; Sodium 146mg.

Salmon and Scallop Lemon Grass Brochettes

Using lemon grass as skewers isn't a culinary gimmick. The subtle flavour that emanates from the lemon grass gives the ingredients – in this case, salmon and scallops – a fragrance that seems perfectly in keeping with the delicacy of this superb dinner dish.

Serves 4
8 lemon grass stalks
225g/8oz salmon fillet, skinned
8 queen scallops, with their corals if possible
8 baby onions, peeled and blanched
½ yellow (bell) pepper, cut into eight squares
100g/4oz/½ cup butter
juice of ½ lemon
30ml/2 tbsp dry vermouth
5ml/1 tsp chopped fresh tarragon
salt, ground white pepper and paprika

1 Preheat the grill (broiler) to medium-high. Cut off the top 7.5–10cm/3–4in of each lemon grass stalk. Reserve the bulb ends for another dish.

2 Cut the salmon fillet into twelve 2cm/¾in cubes. Thread the salmon, scallops, corals if available, onions and pepper squares on to the lemon grass sticks and arrange the brochettes side by side in a grill (broiler) pan.

3 Melt half the butter in a small pan, add the lemon juice and a pinch of paprika and then brush all over the brochettes. Grill (broil) the skewers for about 2–3 minutes on each side, turning and basting the brochettes every minute, until the fish and scallops are just cooked, but are still very juicy. Transfer to a platter and keep hot.

4 Pour the dry vermouth and the leftover cooking juices from the brochettes into a pan and boil fiercely to reduce by half. Add the remaining butter and melt, stirring all the time. Stir in the tarragon and add salt and white pepper to taste. Pour the tarragon butter sauce over the brochettes and serve.

Poached Salmon Steaks with Sandefjord Butter

For sheer simplicity, this dish takes a lot of beating. Sandefjord butter is named after a town near the mouth of the Oslofjord. A shipping centre since the 14th century, it is now a seaside resort. The 'butter' is actually a classic butter sauce and is the traditional Norwegian accompaniment to many fish dishes.

45ml/3 tbsp salt
5ml/1 tsp whole peppercorns
1 lemon slice
1 onion slice

For the Sandefjord butter
100ml/3½ fl oz/scant ½ cup double (heavy) cream
225g/8oz/1 cup chilled unsalted butter, cut into small cubes
30–45ml/2–3 tbsp chopped fresh parsley or chives

To serve
boiled potatoes
cucumber salad

Serves 4
4 salmon steaks, each about 175g/6oz
1 litre/1¾ pints/4 cups water

1 Put the fish steaks, in a single layer, in a pan and add the water to cover the steaks. If there is not enough water, add a little more. Add the salt, peppercorns, lemon and onion slice. Bring to the boil then lower the heat to below simmering point. (The water should just throw up the occasional bubble.) Poach the fish for 6–8 minutes, until the flesh easily loosens from the backbone.

2 To make the Sandefjord butter, pour the cream into a pan and slowly bring to the boil. Lower the heat and add the butter, in small pieces, whisking all the time until well incorporated before adding another piece. Do not allow the sauce to boil or it will separate. If you wish, the sauce can be kept warm by putting it in a bowl standing over a pan of gently simmering water.

3 Just before serving, add the parsley or chives to the sauce. Serve the fish with boiled potatoes and a cucumber salad, accompanied with the Sandefjord butter.

Salmon and Scallops Energy 336kcal/1391kJ; Protein 17g; Carbohydrate 7g, of which sugars 5g; Fat 27g, of which saturates 14g; Cholesterol 90mg; Calcium 40mg; Fibre 1g; Sodium 212mg.
Poached Salmon Energy 771kcal/3184kJ; Protein 26.3g; Carbohydrate 1.1g, of which sugars 1g; Fat 73.6g, of which saturates 40g; Cholesterol 217mg; Calcium 71mg; Fibre 0.6g; Sodium 406mg.

Salted Salmon in Dill Sauce

Salted salmon is a refreshing alternative to the more well known gravlax recipe. However, salted salmon is plumper, smoother and fresher.

Serves 6–8

200g/7oz/2 cups sea salt
50g/2oz/½ cup caster (superfine) sugar
1kg/2¼lb salmon, scaled, filleted and boned
1 litre/1¾ pints/4 cups water
675–900g/1½–2lb new potatoes

For the béchamel and dill sauce
25g/1oz/2 tbsp butter
45ml/3 tbsp plain (all-purpose) flour
750ml/1¼ pints/3 cups milk
120ml/4fl oz/½ cup double (heavy) cream
a little freshly grated nutmeg (optional)
25g/1oz/¼ cup chopped fresh dill
salt and ground black pepper

1 Mix together 100g/4oz/1 cup of the salt and the sugar. Cover the salmon fillets with the mixture and put in a plastic bag. Seal the bag and put the fish on a plate in the refrigerator overnight.

2 The next day, make a brine by mixing the remaining salt and the water in a bowl. Place the salmon in the brine and leave in the refrigerator for another night.

3 Remove the salmon from the brine and cut into 5mm/¼in slices. If large, cut the potatoes in half then cook in boiling water for about 20 minutes until tender.

4 Meanwhile, make the béchamel sauce. Melt the butter in a pan, add the flour and cook over a low heat for 1 minute, stirring. Remove from the heat and slowly add the milk, stirring all the time, to form a smooth sauce.

5 Return to the heat and cook, stirring, for 2–3 minutes until the sauce boils and thickens. Stir in the cream, nutmeg if using, season to taste and heat gently.

6 Drain the potatoes and add to the sauce with the dill. Serve the salted salmon with the potatoes in béchamel and dill.

Salmon Kebabs with Coconut

Inspired by flavours from the West Indies, this recipe combines the traditional flavours of coconut and lime to provide a counterpoint to the subtle taste of salmon and scallops.

Serves 6
450g/1lb salmon fillet, skinned
1 small fresh coconut

2 limes
12 scallops
45ml/3 tbsp freshly squeezed lime juice
30ml/2 tbsp soy sauce
30ml/2 tbsp clear honey
15ml/1 tbsp soft light brown sugar
ground black pepper

1 Using a sharp knife, cut the salmon into bitesize chunks and place these in a shallow bowl.

2 Halve the coconut and pour the liquor into a jug (pitcher). Using a small, sharp knife, carefully remove the coconut flesh from the inside of the shell and cut it into chunks, making them about the same size as the salmon.

3 Cut each lime into six thick slices. Thread the coconut meat, salmon, scallops and pieces of lime alternately on to six skewers.

4 Add the lime juice, soy sauce, honey and sugar to the coconut liquor to make the marinade. Mix well and stir in some pepper. You will probably not need to add any salt, owing to the addition of soy sauce to the marinade.

5 Place the prepared kebabs in a single layer in a shallow non-metallic dish. Pour the marinade over. Cover and chill for at least 3 hours.

6 Shake off excess marinade from the kebabs and place them on the grill pan.

7 Grill (broil) for 4 minutes on each side, turning once and basting occasionally with the marinade, until the salmon is lightly browned.

Salted Salmon Energy 407kcal/1699kJ; Protein 26.4g; Carbohydrate 22.6g, of which sugars 5.9g; Fat 24g, of which saturates 9.7g; Cholesterol 85mg; Calcium 155mg; Fibre 1g; Sodium 118mg.
Salmon Kebabs Energy 322kcal/1339kJ; Protein 22g; Carbohydrate 9g, of which sugars 8g; Fat 22g, of which saturates 13g; Cholesterol 48mg; Calcium 30mg; Fibre 5g; Sodium 439mg.

Salmon with Tropical Fruit Salsa

Fresh salmon, cooked on the barbecue, is good enough to serve on its own, but tastes even better with this colourful and tasty combination of mango, papaya and chilli.

Serves 4
4 salmon steaks or fillets, each about 175g/6oz

finely grated rind and juice of 1 lime

For the tropical fruit salsa
1 small, ripe mango
1 small, ripe papaya
1 fresh red chilli
45ml/3 tbsp chopped fresh coriander (cilantro)
salt and ground black pepper

1 Lay the pieces of salmon side by side in a wide dish and sprinkle over half the lime rind and juice. Season well.

2 To make the tropical fruit salsa, take a thick slice off either side of the mango stone (pit), and then remove the stone. Finely chop the mango flesh and put it in a bowl.

3 Discard the skin. Halve the papaya, scoop out and discard the seeds and remove the skin. Chop the flesh and add it to the mango.

4 Cut the chilli in half lengthways. For a milder flavour, remove the seeds, or leave the seeds in to make the salsa hot and spicy. Finely chop the chilli and add to the fruit. Add the fresh coriander to the bowl and mix gently with a large spoon. Stir in the remaining lime rind and juice. Season to taste.

5 Cook the salmon on an oiled barbecue grill over medium-hot coals for 5–8 minutes, turning once, until the fish is cooked throught and lightly browned. Serve the salmon with the tropical fruit salsa.

> **Cook's Tips**
> If fresh red chillies are not available, use about 2.5ml/½ tsp of chilli paste from a jar, or add a dash of chilli sauce.

Tangy Grilled Salmon with Pineapple

Fresh pineapple really brings out the flavour of salmon. Here, it is combined with lime juice to make a light and refreshing dish.

Serves 4
grated rind and juice of 2 limes
15ml/1 tbsp olive oil, plus extra for greasing
1cm/½in piece fresh root ginger, peeled and grated

1 garlic clove, crushed
30ml/2 tbsp clear honey
15ml/1 tbsp soy sauce
4 salmon fillets, each about 200g/7oz
1 small pineapple
30ml/2 tbsp sesame seeds
ground black pepper
fresh chives, to garnish
wild rice, to serve

1 Make the marinade. Put the lime rind in a bowl and stir in the lime juice, olive oil, ginger, garlic, honey and soy sauce. Taste and add a little ground black pepper. Place the salmon fillets in a single layer in a shallow, non-metallic dish. Pour the marinade over the salmon. Cover and chill for at least 1 hour, turning the salmon halfway through.

2 Cut the skin off the pineapple, removing as many of the small black 'eyes' as possible. Cut the pineapple into four thick slices. Use an apple corer to remove the tough central core from each slice and cut away any remaining eyes with a small knife.

3 Preheat the grill (broiler) to high. Sprinkle the sesame seeds over a piece of foil and place under the grill for a minute or two until they turn golden brown. Set aside.

4 Grease the grill pan and cover with a layer of foil. Using a slotted spoon, remove the salmon fillets from the marinade and place them in a single layer on the foil. Add the pineapple rings, placing one on top of each piece of salmon.

5 Grill (broil) the fish and pineapple for 10 minutes. Brush occasionally with the marinade and turn over once, until the fish is cooked through and the pineapple rings are golden brown. Place each fillet on a bed of wild rice. Top with the pineapple. Sprinkle with sesame seeds and garnish with chives.

Salmon with Salsa Energy 350kcal/1463kJ; Protein 36g; Carbohydrate 9g, of which sugars 8g; Fat 19g, of which saturates 3g; Cholesterol 88mg; Calcium 52mg; Fibre 2g; Sodium 82mg.
Salmon with Pineapple Energy 423kcal/1771kJ; Protein 41g; Carbohydrate 16g, of which sugars 15g; Fat 22g, of which saturates 4g; Cholesterol 100mg; Calcium 61mg; Fibre 1g; Sodium 360mg.

Salmon with Spicy Pesto

This is a great way to bone salmon steaks to give a solid piece of fish. The pesto uses sunflower kernels and chilli as its flavouring rather than the classic basil and pine nuts.

Serves 4
4 salmon steaks, each about
 225g/8oz
30ml/2 tbsp sunflower oil

finely grated rind and
 juice of I lime
salt and ground black pepper

For the pesto
6 fresh mild red chillies, seeded
 and roughly chopped
2 garlic cloves
30ml/2 tbsp pumpkin or
 sunflower seeds
finely grated rind and
 juice of I lime
75ml/5 tbsp olive oil

I Place a salmon steak flat on a board. Insert a very sharp knife close to the top of the bone. Staying close to the bone all the time, cut to the end of the steak to release one side of the steak. Repeat with the other side.

2 Place one piece of salmon skin side down and hold it firmly with one hand. Insert a small sharp knife under the skin and, working away from you, cut the flesh off in a single piece. Repeat with the remaining salmon steaks. Wrap each piece of fish into a circle, with the thinner end wrapped around the fatter end. Tie with string (twine). Place in a shallow bowl.

3 Rub the oil into the boneless fish rounds. Add the lime juice and rind to the bowl. Cover and marinate in the refrigerator for 2 hours.

4 Make the pesto. Put the chillies, garlic, pumpkin or sunflower seeds, lime rind and juice and seasoning into a food processor. Process until well mixed. With the machine running, gradually add the olive oil through the feeder tube. The pesto will thicken and emulsify. Scrape it into a bowl. Preheat the grill (broiler).

5 Drain the salmon and place the rounds in a grill pan. Grill (broil) for 5 minutes on each side or until opaque. Serve with the spicy pesto.

Salmon Teriyaki

This is a well-known Japanese dish, which uses a sweet and shiny sauce for marinating as well as for glazing the ingredients.

Serves 4
4 small salmon fillets with skin on,
 each weighing about 150g/5oz
50g/2oz/1 cup
 beansprouts, washed
50g/2oz mangetouts (snow peas)

20g/3⁄4oz carrot,
 cut into thin strips
salt

For the teriyaki sauce
45ml/3 tbsp shoyu
 (Japanese soy sauce)
45ml/3 tbsp sake
45ml/3 tbsp mirin or sweet sherry
15ml/I tbsp plus I0ml/2 tsp
 caster (superfine) sugar

I Make the teriyaki sauce. Mix the shoyu, sake, mirin and 15ml/I tbsp caster sugar in a pan. Heat, stirring, to dissolve the sugar. Cool for I hour. Place the salmon fillets, skin side down, in a shallow glass dish. Pour over the teriyaki sauce. Marinate for 30 minutes.

2 Meanwhile, bring a pan of lightly salted water to the boil. Add the beansprouts, then after I minute, the mangetouts. Leave for I minute then add the thin carrot strips. Remove the pan from the heat after I minute, then drain the vegetables and keep warm.

3 Preheat the grill (broiler) to medium. Take the salmon fillet out of the sauce, shake to remove excess sauce and pat dry with kitchen paper. Reserve the sauce. Lightly oil a grilling (broiling) tray. Grill (broil) the salmon for about 6 minutes, turning once, until golden.

4 Meanwhile, pour the remaining teriyaki sauce into a small pan, add the remaining sugar and heat until dissolved. Brush the salmon with the sauce.

5 Continue to grill the salmon until the surface of the fish bubbles. Turn over and repeat on the other side. Heap the vegetables on to serving plates. Place the salmon on top and spoon over the rest of the sauce.

Salmon with Pesto Energy 694kcal/2871kJ; Protein 47g; Carbohydrate 2g, of which sugars 1g; Fat 55g, of which saturates 8g; Cholesterol 113mg; Calcium 59mg; Fibre 0g; Sodium 103mg.
Salmon Teriyaki Energy 239kcal/995kJ; Protein 24.8g; Carbohydrate 2.1g, of which sugars 1.7g; Fat 13.3g, of which saturates 2.3g; Cholesterol 58mg; Calcium 93mg; Fibre 0.3g; Sodium 323mg.

Umbrian Stuffed Grilled Trout

This is a very simple
Umbrian recipe for trout.
The region, being landlocked,
relies on either freshwater
fish from the rivers and
lakes, or on preserved fish
such as baccalà (salted cod)
or canned fish. In Umbria,
the trout caught in the river
Nera are highly prized and
much sought after. This
recipe serves two people,
so to feed more people
you'll need a large barbecue.

Serves 2

2 medium sized trout, cleaned
    and gutted
120ml/8 tbsp soft breadcrumbs
juice of 1 lemon
150ml/10 tbsp extra virgin
    olive oil, plus extra for brushing
30ml/2 tbsp chopped fresh flat
    leaf parsley
sea salt and ground black pepper

1 Light the barbecue and wait until you have a heap of hot,
even red embers. Position the grill rack. Rinse the trout under
cold running water inside and out. Pat dry with kitchen paper.

2 In a small bowl, mix the breadcrumbs with the lemon juice,
half the olive oil and the parsley and season to taste with salt
and pepper.

3 Stuff the inside of each trout with this mixture. Score each
trout lightly on each side through the skin, and rub the
remaining oil all over the fish.

4 Lay the fish on a grill rack and cook for about 10 minutes
on each side, until the trout is cooked through, brushing
with more oil during the cooking process. Serve while still hot,
and remove the fillets from the fish.

Cook's Tips

*Trout is very versatile; it can be baked, steamed, grilled and
poached and stuffed before cooking. It is also very good
served cold with various sauces, mayonnaise and creamy
salad dressings.*

Hot and Fragrant Trout

This wickedly hot marinade
could be used with any
firm-fleshed fish or meat.
It also makes a wonderful
spicy dip for grilled or
barbecued meat.

Serves 4

2 large fresh green chillies,
    seeded and roughly chopped
5 shallots, peeled

5 garlic cloves, peeled
30ml/2 tbsp fresh lime juice
30ml/2 tbsp Thai fish sauce
15ml/1 tbsp palm sugar or light
    muscovado (molasses) sugar
4 kaffir lime leaves, rolled into
    cigarette shapes and
    finely sliced
2 trout, about 350g/12oz
    each, cleaned

1 Wrap the green chillies, shallots and garlic cloves in a foil
package. Place under a hot grill (broiler) for 10 minutes, until
the vegetables have softened.

2 As soon as the foil package is cool enough to handle, unwrap
it and tip the contents into a mortar or food processor. Blend
to a paste. Add the lime juice, fish sauce, sugar and lime leaves
and mix well.

3 With a teaspoon, stuff this paste inside the fish. Smear a little
on the skin too. Grill (broil) the fish for about 5 minutes on
each side, until just cooked through. Carefully lift the fish on to
a platter. Serve with rice.

Cook's Tips

*• Thai fish sauce (nam pla) is made from anchovies, which are
salted, then fermented in wooden barrels. The sauce, which is
ubiquitous in Thai cooking, accentuates the flavour of food.
• Kaffir lime leaves release a distinctive lemony flavour when
roughly chopped or torn. They are obtainable in Asian food
stores. They will keep for several days, or can be frozen.
• Slightly sweet coconut rice is the perfect accompaniment to
this spicy trout. To make it, simply substitute coconut milk for
half of the water in your usual rice recipe. Ready-to-use
coconut milk is available in cartons and cans.*

Stuffed Trout Energy 661kcal/2761kJ; Protein 40.9g; Carbohydrate 34.9g, of which sugars 1.2g; Fat 40.7g, of which saturates 6.2g; Cholesterol 147mg; Calcium 114mg; Fibre 1g; Sodium 475mg.
Fragrant Trout Energy 267kcal/1125kJ; Protein 36g; Carbohydrate 11g, of which sugars 8g; Fat 9g, of which saturates 2g; Cholesterol 117mg; Calcium 54mg; Fibre 1g; Sodium 394mg.

Trout with Curried Orange Butter

Trout are perfect for midweek meals, especially served with this delicious tangy butter.

Serves 4
25g/1oz/2 tbsp butter, softened
5ml/1 tsp curry powder
5ml/1 tsp grated orange rind
4 small trout, gutted,
  heads removed
vegetable or sunflower oil,
  for brushing
salt and ground black pepper
orange wedges, to garnish
boiled new potatoes, to serve

1 Mix the softened butter, curry powder and orange rind together in a bowl with salt and plenty of ground black pepper. Wrap in foil and freeze for 10 minutes.

2 Brush the fish all over with oil and sprinkle well with seasoning. Make three diagonal slashes through the skin and flesh on each side of the fish. Cut the flavoured butter into small pieces and carefully insert into the slashes in the fish.

3 Place the fish on the grill (broiling) pan and cook under a preheated high grill (broiler) or hot barbecue for 3–4 minutes on each side, depending on the size of the fish. Garnish with wedges of orange before serving with boiled new potatoes.

Cook's Tip
The curry powder for this recipe can be made at home from a blend of dry spices. The following mix could also be used as the basis for any curry dish. It is a fairly mild recipe but you could increase the quantity of dried chilli for a hotter taste. Place 50g/2oz/½ cup whole coriander seeds, 60ml/4 tbsp whole cumin seeds, 30ml/2 tbsp each of whole fennel seeds and fenugreek seeds, 4 dried red chillies and 5 curry leaves together in a large frying pan. Dry roast for 8–10 minutes, shaking the pan until the spices darken and release a rich aroma. Allow the roasted spices to cool, then grind to a fine powder in a spice mill. Place in a large glass bowl and add 15ml/1 tbsp chilli powder, 15ml/1 tbsp ground turmeric and 2.5ml/½ tsp salt and mix well. Store in an airtight container.

Chinese-style Steamed Trout

Steamed trout may sound plain, but this treatment of the fish, marinated in a black bean, ginger and garlic mixture is superb.

Serves 6
2 trout, each about 675–800g/
  1½–1¾lb
25ml/1½ tbsp salted black beans
2.5ml/½ tsp granulated sugar
30ml/2 tbsp finely shredded
  fresh root ginger
4 garlic cloves, thinly sliced
30ml/2 tbsp Chinese rice wine
  or dry sherry
30ml/2 tbsp light soy sauce
4–6 spring onions (scallions),
  finely shredded
45ml/3 tbsp groundnut
  (peanut) oil
10ml/2 tsp sesame oil

1 Wash the fish inside and out under cold running water, then pat dry on kitchen paper. Using a sharp knife, slash 3–4 deep crosses on either side of each fish.

2 Place half the black beans and the sugar in a small bowl and mash together with the back of a fork. When the beans are thoroughly mashed, stir in the remaining whole beans.

3 Place a little ginger and garlic inside the cavity of each fish, then lay them on a plate or dish that will fit inside a large steamer. Rub the bean mixture into the fish, working it into the slashes, then sprinkle the remaining ginger and garlic over the top. Cover with clear film (plastic wrap) and place the fish in the refrigerator for at least 30 minutes.

4 Remove the fish from the refrigerator and place the steamer over a pan of boiling water. Sprinkle the rice wine or sherry and half the soy sauce over the fish and place the plate of fish inside the steamer. Steam for 15–20 minutes, or until the fish is cooked and the flesh flakes easily when tested with a fork.

5 Using a fish slice (metal spatula), lift the fish on to a serving dish. Sprinkle the fish with the remaining soy sauce, then sprinkle with the shredded spring onions. In a small pan, heat the groundnut oil until very hot, then trickle it over the spring onions and fish. Sprinkle the sesame oil over the fish and serve.

Trout with Curried Butter Energy 354kcal/1481kJ; Protein 44g; Carbohydrate 0g, of which sugars 0g; Fat 20g, of which saturates 6g; Cholesterol 164mg; Calcium 45mg; Fibre 0g; Sodium 141mg.
Steamed Trout Energy 427kcal/1788kJ; Protein 53g; Carbohydrate 2g, of which sugars 1g; Fat 23g, of which saturates 4g; Cholesterol 179mg; Calcium 57mg; Fibre 1g; Sodium 226mg.

Thai Marinated Sea Trout

Sea trout has a superb texture and a flavour like that of wild salmon. It is best served with strong but complementary flavours, such as chillies and lime, that cut the richness of its flesh.

Serves 6

6 sea trout cutlets, each about
    115g/4oz, or wild or
    farmed salmon
2 garlic cloves, chopped
1 fresh long red chilli, seeded
    and chopped
45ml/3 tbsp chopped `
    Thai basil
15ml/1 tbsp palm sugar or
    granulated sugar
3 limes
400ml/14fl oz/1²⁄₃ cups
    coconut milk
15ml/1 tbsp Thai fish sauce

1 Place the sea trout cutlets side by side in a large shallow dish. Using a pestle, pound the garlic and chilli in a large mortar to break both up roughly. Add 30ml/2 tbsp of the Thai basil with the sugar and continue to pound to a rough paste.

2 Grate the rind from 1 lime and squeeze it. Mix the rind and juice into the chilli paste, with the coconut milk. Pour the mixture over the cutlets. Cover and chill for about 1 hour. Cut the remaining limes into wedges.

3 Take the fish out of the refrigerator so that it can return to room temperature. Remove the cutlets from the marinade and place them in an oiled hinged wire fish basket or directly on the lightly oiled grill. Cook the fish for 4 minutes on each side, trying not to move them. They may stick to the grill rack if not seared first.

4 Strain the remaining marinade into a pan, reserving the contents of the sieve. Bring the marinade to the boil, then simmer gently for 5 minutes, stirring. Stir in the contents of the sieve and continue to simmer for 1 minute more. Add the Thai fish sauce and the remaining Thai basil.

5 Lift each fish cutlet on to a plate, pour over the sauce and serve with the lime wedges.

Braised Carp in Ginger Sauce

Braising fish in water and aromatics is a cooking method that is typical of both the Fujian school of cooking and the neighbouring province of Guangzhou, China. The recipe is very easy to make – the fish is simply braised in a tasty stock – but the combination of flavours works very well.

Serves 4

1 large carp, about 1kg/2¼lb,
    cleaned and scaled
400ml/14fl oz/1²⁄₃ cups water
15ml/1 tbsp grated fresh
    root ginger
45ml/3 tbsp dark soy sauce
30ml/2 tbsp sesame oil
5ml/1 tsp sugar
pinch of salt and ground
    black pepper
4 cloves
15ml/1 tbsp cornflour
    (cornstarch) mixed with
    30ml/2 tbsp water
spring onions, to garnish
    (optional)

1 Rinse the carp inside and out. Pat dry with kitchen paper. Make deep cuts diagonally across both sides of the fish. If the fish is too large for your wok, cut it into two pieces.

2 Pour the water into the wok and add the grated ginger, soy sauce, sesame oil, sugar, salt, pepper and cloves. Bring to the boil. Carefully lower the fish into the liquid. Reduce the heat and braise the fish for 15 minutes or until it is cooked through. Lift the fish out and put it on a serving dish. Keep hot.

3 Stir the cornflour mixture into the liquid remaining in the wok. Bring to the boil and cook, stirring constantly, for 2 minutes or until the sauce thickens. Spoon the sauce over the fish, garnish with spring onions, if using, and serve immediately.

Cook's Tip

Carp is usually sold whole, so ask your fishmonger to clean and scale the fish for you. Carp do not have many bones and their flesh is sweet and firm, therefore it is best cooked whole to keep the fish moist.

Thai Trout Energy 174kcal/735kJ; Protein 23g; Carbohydrate 7g, of which sugars 6g; Fat 6g, of which saturates 1g; Cholesterol 77mg; Calcium 48mg; Fibre 0g; Sodium 230mg.
Braised Carp Energy 211kcal/883kJ; Protein 22.2g; Carbohydrate 5.4g, of which sugars 1.9g; Fat 11.4g, of which saturates 1.9g; Cholesterol 84mg; Calcium 62mg; Fibre 0g; Sodium 590mg.

Carp in Wine Sauce

This Old Polish carp dish from Krakow forms part of the Christmas Eve meal.

Serves 4–6
400g/14oz carp, cut into
   thick portions
750ml/1¼ pints/3 cups water
350ml/12fl oz/1½ cups
   red wine
30ml/2 tbsp lemon juice
1 small celeriac, sliced
2 onions, sliced
6–8 black peppercorns
2.5ml/½ tsp ground ginger

grated rind of 1 lemon
salt and ground black pepper,
   to taste

For the sauce
15ml/1 tbsp butter
15ml/1 tbsp plain
   (all-purpose) flour
45ml/3 tbsp lemon juice
15ml/1 tbsp redcurrant jelly
15ml/1 tbsp clear honey
120ml/4fl oz/½ cup red wine
30ml/2 tbsp currants
30ml/2 tbsp chopped
   blanched almonds

1 Rinse the fish pieces, then sprinkle with salt and leave in a cool place for 20 minutes.

2 Meanwhile, make the stock. Put the water, wine, lemon juice, celeriac, onions, peppercorns, ginger, seasoning and lemon rind in a large pan. Bring to the boil and simmer, uncovered, for 15 minutes. Leave to cool.

3 Place the fish in a shallow pan and pour over the stock and vegetables. Simmer, uncovered, over a low heat for about 15 minutes, or until the fish flakes easily. Remove the fish to a serving plate using a slotted spoon, and keep warm.

4 Skim out the vegetables and press through a fine sieve to form a purée. Add the purée to the stock in the pan. You should have 500ml/17fl oz/2¼ cups stock. Add more water to make up the volume if necessary.

5 To make the sauce, melt the butter in a pan over a medium heat, then add the flour and cook, stirring, for 2 minutes. Stir in the stock. Add the lemon juice, redcurrant jelly, honey and red wine, and cook for 7 minutes. Stir in the currants and almonds, then bring to the boil. Pour the sauce over the carp and serve.

Pike with Hard-boiled Eggs

This dish of poached pike with hard-boiled eggs and parsley is a traditional part of the Christmas Eve meal in Poland, although it is eaten at other times of the year too.

Serves 4
2 carrots, roughly chopped
2 parsnips, roughly chopped

¼ celery stick, roughly chopped
1 leek, roughly chopped
1 large onion, roughly chopped
4–5 black peppercorns
2–3 bay leaves
1.8kg/4lb pike, cleaned, scaled
   and cut into 4 steaks
25g/1oz/2 tbsp butter
3 hard-boiled eggs, chopped
15ml/1 tbsp chopped fresh
   parsley

1 Put the carrots in a large pan and add the parsnips, celery, leek, onion, peppercorns, bay leaves and fish.

2 Pour over enough cold water to cover. Bring to the boil and simmer, uncovered, for 15–20 minutes, or until the fish flakes easily.

3 Meanwhile, melt the butter in a small pan, then add the chopped hard-boiled eggs and parsley, and heat through.

4 Remove the fish from the pan with a slotted spoon and transfer to a warm serving plate.

5 Liberally sprinkle the fish with the lemon juice, then pour over the hot hard-boiled egg and parsley mixture and serve immediately.

Cook's Tip
• The addition of egg makes this a nourishing and sustaining dish, perfect for cold weather. If you are unable to buy pike, use river trout instead.
• Pike has a good flavour and texture and can be cooked in almost any way; it lends itself to steaming, poaching, baking, stuffing or frying.
• Pike is traditionally used for gefilte fish and quenelles.

Carp in Wine Sauce Energy 213kcal/891kJ; Protein 13.2g; Carbohydrate 9.5g, of which sugars 7.5g; Fat 8g, of which saturates 2.1g; Cholesterol 50mg; Calcium 58mg; Fibre 0.6g; Sodium 52mg.
Pike with Egg Energy 327kcal/1368kJ; Protein 39.8g; Carbohydrate 0.2g, of which sugars 0.1g; Fat 18.8g, of which saturates 6.2g; Cholesterol 290mg; Calcium 124mg; Fibre 0.2g; Sodium 178mg.

Grilled Swordfish Skewers

Souvlakia are chunks of fish or meat that are threaded on long metal skewers, often with pieces of pepper and onions. The word is derived from souvla, the long metal spit that is inserted into a whole lamb or goat to spit-roast it over an open fire.

Serves 4

2 red onions, quartered
2 red or green (bell) peppers,
  quartered and seeded
20–24 thick cubes of swordfish,
  prepared weight
  675–800g/1½–1¾lb
75ml/5 tbsp extra virgin olive oil
1 garlic clove, crushed
large pinch of dried oregano
salt and ground black pepper

1 Separate the onion quarters in to pieces, each composed of two or three layers. Slice each pepper quarter in half widthways.

2 Make the souvlakia by threading five or six pieces of swordfish on to each of four long metal skewers, alternating with pieces of the pepper and onion. Lay the souvlakia across a grill pan or roasting tray and set aside while you make the basting sauce.

3 Whisk the olive oil, garlic and oregano in a bowl. Add salt and pepper and whisk again. Brush the souvlakia generously on all sides with the basting sauce.

4 Preheat the grill (broiler) to the highest setting. Slide the grill pan or roasting tray underneath the grill. Cook for 8–10 minutes, turning the skewers several times, until the fish is cooked and the peppers and onions have begun to scorch around the edges. When you turn the skewers, brush them with the basting sauce. Serve the souvlakia immediately, with a cucumber, onion and olive salad.

Cook's Tips
The fishmonger will prepare the cubes of swordfish for you, but if you prefer to do this yourself you will need 800g/1¾lb swordfish. The cubes should be about 5cm/2in square.

Sardine Frittata with Herbs

It may seem odd to cook sardines in an omelette, but they are surprisingly delicious this way. Frozen sardines are fine for this dish. Serve the frittata with crisp sautéed potatoes and thinly sliced cucumber crescents.

Serves 4

4 fat sardines, cleaned, filleted
  and with heads removed,
  thawed if frozen
juice of 1 lemon
45ml/3 tbsp olive oil
6 large (US extra large) eggs
30ml/2 tbsp chopped
  fresh parsley
30ml/2 tbsp chopped
  fresh chives
1 garlic clove, chopped
salt, ground black pepper
  and paprika

1 Open out the sardines and sprinkle the fish with lemon juice, a little salt and paprika. Heat 15ml/1 tbsp olive oil in a frying pan and fry the sardines for about 1–2 minutes on each side to seal them. Drain on kitchen paper, trim off the tails and set aside until required.

2 Separate the eggs. In a bowl, whisk the yolks lightly with the parsley, chives and a little salt and pepper. Beat the whites in a separate bowl with a pinch of salt until fairly stiff. Preheat the grill (broiler) to medium-high.

3 Heat the remaining olive oil in a large frying pan, add the garlic and cook over low heat until just golden. Gently mix together the egg yolks and whites and ladle half the mixture into the pan.

4 Cook gently until just beginning to set on the base, then arrange the sardines on the frittata and sprinkle them lightly with paprika.

5 Pour over the remaining egg mixture and cook until the frittata has browned underneath and is beginning to set on top.

6 Put the pan under the grill and cook until the top of the frittata is golden. Cut into wedges and serve immediately.

Swordfish Energy 427kcal/1778kJ; Protein 36g; Carbohydrate 11g, of which sugars 9g; Fat 27g, of which saturates 4g; Cholesterol 77mg; Calcium 37mg; Fibre 3g; Sodium 249mg.
Sardine Frittata Energy 342kcal/1422kJ; Protein 28.9g; Carbohydrate 0.2g, of which sugars 0.2g; Fat 25.3g, of which saturates 6g; Cholesterol 285mg; Calcium 137mg; Fibre 0.4g; Sodium 220mg.

Mackerel with Wild Fennel

Le Marche is a coastal region and fish plays an important part of the daily diet in the towns and villages that dot the shoreline. Fishermen and their families will generally eat their smaller catch, often salted to preserve it for longer, and will sell the larger and more profitable fish. Although mackerel isn't considered to be a much sought-after fish, it tastes superb when cooked with care and with some thoughtfully chosen ingredients, such as fennel.

Serves 4

1.2kg/2½lb fresh
   mackerel, cleaned
45ml/3 tbsp olive oil
6 small onions or
   shallots, chopped
4 carrots, chopped
1 large celery stick, chopped
a small handful of wild fennel
   fronds, chopped
a small bunch of fresh flat leaf
   parsley, leaves chopped
1 garlic clove, chopped
5cm/2in piece of unwaxed orange
   peel, chopped
juice of ½ orange
15ml/1 tbsp tomato purée
   (paste) diluted with 15ml/
   1 tbsp hot water or stock
sea salt and ground
   black pepper

1 Boil the mackerel in lightly salted water until cooked through. Gently remove the cooked fish from the pan and fillet them carefully. Discard the bones, head and skin.

2 Put the oil in a large pan and gently fry the onions or shallots, carrots, celery, fennel, parsley, garlic and orange peel for 10 minutes. Season with salt and ground black pepper.

3 Add the orange juice. Stir and reduce the heat to low. Simmer, stirring frequently, for 15 minutes.

4 Stir in the diluted tomato purée. Cook for 15 minutes more, until the sauce has thickened.

5 Arrange the fish on a serving platter and pour over the sauce. Serve immediately, or chill to serve cold.

Mackerel with Rhubarb Sauce

Mackerel are available in Ireland for most of the year, but they are really at their best in early summer, just when rhubarb is growing strongly – a happy coincidence, as the tartness of rhubarb offsets the richness of the oily fish to perfection.

Serves 4

4 whole mackerel, cleaned
25g/1oz/2 tbsp butter
1 onion, finely chopped
90ml/6 tbsp fresh white
   breadcrumbs

15ml/1 tbsp chopped fresh parsley
finely grated rind of 1 lemon
freshly grated nutmeg
1 egg, lightly beaten
melted butter or olive
   oil, for brushing
sea salt and ground black pepper

For the sauce

225g/8oz rhubarb
   (trimmed weight), cut into
   1cm/½in lengths
25–50g/1–2oz/2–4 tbsp caster
   (superfine) sugar
25g/1oz/2 tbsp butter
15ml/1 tbsp chopped fresh
   tarragon (optional)

1 Ask the fishmonger to bone the mackerel, or do it yourself: open out the body of the cleaned fish, turn flesh side down on a board and run your thumb firmly down the backbone – when you turn the fish over, the bones should lift all at once. complete section.

2 Melt the butter in a pan and cook the onion gently for 5–10 minutes, until softened but not browned. Add the breadcrumbs, parsley, lemon rind, salt, pepper and grated nutmeg. Mix well, and then add the beaten egg to bind.

3 Divide the mixture among the four fish, wrap the fish over and secure with cocktail sticks (toothpicks). Brush with melted butter or olive oil. Preheat the grill (broiler) and cook under a medium heat for about 8 minutes on each side.

4 Meanwhile, make the sauce: put the rhubarb into a pan with 75ml/2½fl oz/⅓ cup water, 25g/1oz/2 tbsp of the sugar and the butter. Cook until the rhubarb is tender. Taste for sweetness and add extra sugar if necessary. The sauce needs to be quite sharp. Serve the mackerel with the sauce garnished with the tarragon.

Mackerel with Fennel Energy 743kcal/3084kJ; Protein 57.7g; Carbohydrate 1.8g, of which sugars 1.4g; Fat 56g, of which saturates 11.1g; Cholesterol 159mg; Calcium 42mg; Fibre 0.4g; Sodium 189mg.
Mackerel with Rhubarb Energy 728Kcal/3034kJ; Protein 48.2g; Carbohydrate 27.5g, of which sugars 9.8g; Fat 48g, of which saturates 14.3g; Cholesterol 193mg; Calcium 129mg; Fibre 1.8g; Sodium 398mg.

Mackerel with Gooseberry Relish

Off Scotland's west coast it is still possible to fish for mackerel yourself and quite often at the weekends part-time fishermen can be found selling fresh mackerel at the harbours. Mackerel is very good for you, and the tart gooseberries give you a serving of fruit too.

Serves 4

4 whole mackerel
60ml/4 tbsp olive oil

For the sauce

250g/9oz gooseberries
25g/1oz/2 tbsp soft light
    brown sugar
5ml/1 tsp wholegrain mustard
salt and ground black pepper

1 For the sauce, wash and trim the gooseberries and then roughly chop them, so there are some pieces larger than others.

2 Cook the gooseberries in a little water with the sugar in a small pan. A thick and chunky purée will form. Add the mustard and season to taste with salt and ground black pepper.

3 Preheat the grill (broiler) to high and line the grill pan with foil. Using a sharp knife, slash the fish two or three times down each side then season and brush with the olive oil. Place the fish in the grill pan and grill (broil) for about 4 minutes on each side until cooked or a few minutes longer if they are large. The slashes will open up to speed cooking and the skin should be lightly browned. To check that they are cooked properly, use a small sharp knife to pierce the skin and look for uncooked flesh.

4 Serve the mackerel with dollops of the gooseberry relish over them. Pass the remaining sauce around at the table.

Cook's Tip
• Turn the grill (broiler) on well in advance as the fish need a fierce heat to cook quickly. If you like the fish but hate the smell, try barbecuing outside.
• The foil lining in the grill pan is to catch the smelly drips. Simply roll it up and throw it away afterwards, leaving a nice clean grill pan.

Grilled Squid Stuffed with Feta

A favourite dish in Greece is grilled squid stuffed with feta cheese. A large, fresh leafy salad or a vegetable dish, such as fresh green beans with tomato sauce or slow-cooked okra casserole with tomatoes, could be served with the squid.

Serves 4

4 medium squid, total weight
    about 900g/2lb
4–8 finger-length slices of
    feta cheese
90ml/6 tbsp olive oil
2 garlic cloves, crushed
3–4 fresh marjoram sprigs, leaves
    removed and chopped
salt and ground black pepper
lemon wedges, to serve

1 Prepare the squid, following the instructions on page 150, but keep the bodies intact. Rinse them thoroughly, inside and out, and drain well. Lay the squid bodies and tentacles in a shallow dish that will hold them in a single layer. Tuck the pieces of cheese between the squid.

2 To make the marinade, pour the oil into a jug (pitcher) or bowl and whisk in the garlic and marjoram. Season to taste with salt and pepper.

3 Pour the marinade over the squid and the cheese, then cover and leave in a cool place to marinate for 2–3 hours, turning once.

4 Insert one or two pieces of cheese and a few bits of marjoram from the marinade in each squid and place them in a lightly oiled grill (broiler) pan or tray. Thread the tentacles on skewers.

5 Preheat the grill to a fairly low setting or prepare a barbecue. Grill the stuffed squid gently for about 6 minutes, then turn them over carefully. Grill them for 1–2 minutes more, then add the skewered tentacles. Grill them for 2 minutes on each side, until they start to scorch.

6 Serve the stuffed squid with the tentacles. Add a few lemon wedges, for squeezing over the seafood.

Squid Stuffed with Breadcrumbs and Serrano Ham

This traditional Filipino dish of baby squid, stuffed with a tasty mixture of breadcrumbs and Spanish ham and then cooked in wine, once again reflects the nation's colonial past. A dish for celebrations and festivals feasts, these stuffed squid are delicious served with rice or noodles and a fresh and simple seaweed salad.

Serves 4
16 fresh baby squid
15ml/1 tbsp palm or groundnut (peanut) oil
2–3 shallots, finely chopped
2–3 garlic cloves, finely chopped
115g/4oz Serrano ham, finely chopped
5–10ml/1–2 tsp paprika
1 small bunch flat leaf parsley, finely chopped, reserving a few leaves to garnish
6–8 slices white bread, crusts removed, made into breadcrumbs
300ml/½ pint/1¼ cups dry white wine
300ml/½ pint/1¼ cups chicken stock
2–3 bay leaves
salt and ground black pepper
cooked rice, to serve

1 To prepare the squid, pull off the head and reach into the body sac to pull out all the innards and the 'quill'. Rinse the sac inside and out and peel off the skin. Cut off the tentacles above the eyes, chop and reserve, discarding the 'beak'. Pat the sacs dry.

2 Heat the oil in a heavy pan, stir in the shallots and garlic and fry until beginning to colour. Add the squid tentacles and Serrano ham and fry for 2–3 minutes. Stir in the paprika and parsley and toss in the breadcrumbs to absorb the juices and flavours. Season with salt and pepper. If the mixture is dry, splash in 15–30ml/1–2 tbsp of the wine. Leave to cool.

3 Fill the squid sacs with the stuffing and thread a cocktail stick (toothpick) through the ends. Bring the wine and stock to the boil. Add the bay leaves, reduce the heat and add the squid. Cover and simmer for 5–10 minutes until tender. Pile rice on to four plates, place the squid on top and add some of the cooking juices. Garnish with the reserved parsley leaves and serve.

Steamed Shellfish with Tamarind Dip

There are abundant ways to eat the seafood harvest of South-east Asia, and in Indonesia and the Philippines this is one of the most popular dishes.

Serves 4–6
2 whole lobsters, each weighing about 450g/1lb
3–4 medium crabs
24 mussels
24 scallops or clams
24 tiger prawns (jumbo shrimp)
6 spring onions (scallions), sliced
150ml/¼ pint/⅔ cup suka (Filipino coconut vinegar) or rice vinegar
6 garlic cloves, crushed
about 50g/2oz fresh root ginger, finely sliced
6–8 black peppercorns
lime wedges, to garnish

To serve
tamarind sauce and limes
cooked rice
green papaya salad

1 Scrub the lobsters, crabs, mussels and scallops or clams under cold running water, removing any beards, barnacles, and discarding any clams, mussels or scallops that remain open when sharply tapped.

2 Fill the bottom of two large steamers with at least 5cm/2in water, then divide the spring onions, suka, garlic, ginger and peppercorns between them. Cover the steamers and bring to the boil. Place the lobster and crab in the basket of one steamer and the small shellfish in the other. (Steam the shellfish in batches and top up the water if it gets low.)

3 Cover the pans and steam the lobsters and crabs for 10 minutes and the smaller shellfish for 5 minutes, until they turn opaque and the mussel and clam or scallop shells open.

4 Discard any mussels, clams and scallops that have not opened.

5 Transfer the cooked shellfish to a warmed serving dish, garnish with lime wedges and serve with tamarind sauce and limes, accompanied by rice and a green papaya salad.

Stuffed Squid Energy 344kcal/1449kJ; Protein 28.9g; Carbohydrate 25.5g, of which sugars 4.2g; Fat 9.6g, of which saturates 1.5g; Cholesterol 298mg; Calcium 104mg; Fibre 1.8g; Sodium 701mg.
Steamed Shellfish Energy 312kcal/1315kJ; Protein 61g; Carbohydrate 3.4g, of which sugars 0.5g; Fat 6.1g, of which saturates 1g; Cholesterol 309mg; Calcium 193mg; Fibre 0.6g; Sodium 769mg.

Lobster and Crab Steamed in Beer, with Ginger and Basil

In spite of its appearance, this is one of the easiest recipes in this book. Depending on the size and availability of the lobsters and crabs, you can make it for as many people as you like, because the quantities are simple to adjust.

serves 4

4 uncooked lobsters, about
    450g/1lb each
4–8 uncooked crabs, about
    225g/8oz each
about 600ml/1 pint/2½
    cups beer
4 spring onions (scallions),
    trimmed and chopped into
    long pieces
4cm/1½in fresh root ginger,
    peeled and finely sliced
2 green or red Thai chillies,
    seeded and finely sliced
3 lemon grass stalks, finely sliced
1 bunch of fresh dill,
    fronds chopped
1 bunch each of fresh basil and
    coriander (cilantro), stalks
    removed, leaves chopped
about 30ml/2 tbsp nuoc mam,
    plus extra for serving
juice of 1 lemon
salt and ground black pepper

1 Clean the lobsters and crabs well and rub them with salt and pepper. Place half of them in a large steamer and pour the beer into the base. Scatter half the spring onions, ginger, chillies, lemon grass and herbs over the lobsters and crabs, and steam for about 10 minutes, or until the lobsters turn red. Lift them on to a serving dish. Cook the remaining half in the same way.

2 Add the lemon grass, herbs and nuoc mam to the simmering beer, stir in the lemon juice, then pour into a dipping bowl. Serve the shellfish hot, dipping the lobster and crab meat into the broth and adding extra splashes of nuoc mam, if you like.

Cook's Tip
Whether you cook the lobsters and crabs at the same time depends on the number of people you are cooking for and the size of your steamer. However, they don't take long to cook so it is easy to steam them in batches.

Steamed Mussels with Celery

One of the best ways of preparing Belgium's national dish is to simply steam the mussels in their own juices with celery and onions. This allows the delectable flavour of the mussels to shine through. In Belgium, the mussels are traditionally served in individual casseroles; the lids can be inverted to hold the empty shells.

Serves 4

4kg/9lb live mussels
40g/1½oz/3 tbsp butter, softened
2 onions, roughly chopped
3–4 celery sticks, roughly chopped
salt and ground white pepper
chopped fresh parsley, to garnish

To serve
fries or crusty bread
pickles or mayonnaise

1 Scrub the mussels until the shells are shiny black and smooth. Remove the beards, if present. If any of the shells are cracked or broken, discard them, along with any mussels that are open and that do not snap shut if tapped.

2 Melt the butter in a large heavy pan over medium heat. Add the onions and sauté for 5 minutes until softened and glazed. Add the celery and sauté for 5 minutes more. Add the mussels and season with salt and pepper. Cover the pan and place over high heat for 3–4 minutes or until the mussels open, shaking the pan occasionally to distribute the steam.

3 Discard any mussels that have failed to open. Taste the liquid in the pan and adjust the seasoning if necessary, then spoon the mussels and the liquid into bowls or pots. Sprinkle with parsley and serve with fries or crusty bread. Offer pickles, mayonnaise or mustard vinaigrette on the side.

Cook's Tip
• Additional flavourings include leek or carrot slices, chopped garlic, thyme and/or bay leaves.
• A splash of white wine, added before cooking, improves the dish, as well as a little hot mustard.

Lobster and Crab Energy 264Kcal/1112kJ; Protein 48g; Carbohydrate 4g, of which sugars 1g; Fat 7g, of which saturates 1g; Cholesterol 210mg; Calcium 185mg; Fibre 0.5g; Sodium 1.3g.
Steamed Mussels Energy 393kcal/1658kJ; Protein 46.5g; Carbohydrate 17.3g, of which sugars 6g; Fat 15.5g, of which saturates 6.2g; Cholesterol 181mg; Calcium 183mg; Fibre 1.9g; Sodium 1048mg.

Fish and Chips

Here is one of England's national dishes. Use white fish of your choice – cod, haddock, hake, huss, plaice, skate or whiting – and cook in batches so that each piece of fish and all the chips are perfectly crisp. Salt and vinegar are the traditional accompaniments.

Serves 4

115g/4oz/1 cup self-raising (self-rising) flour
150ml/¼ pint/⅔ cup water
675g/1½lb potatoes
oil, for deep frying
675g/1½lb skinned cod fillet, cut into four pieces
salt and pepper
lemon wedges, to serve

1 Stir the flour and salt together in a bowl, then make a well in the centre. Gradually whisk in the water to make a smooth batter. Leave for 30 minutes.

2 Using a sharp knife, cut the potatoes into strips about 1cm/½in wide and 5cm/2in long. Put the potatoes in a colander and rinse them with cold water, then drain and dry well.

3 Heat the oil in a deep-fat fryer or large heavy pan to 150°C/300°F. Using a wire basket, lower the potatoes in batches into the hot oil and cook for 5–6 minutes, shaking the basket occasionally until the chips are soft but not browned. Remove the chips from the oil and drain them thoroughly on kitchen paper.

4 Increase the heat of the oil in the fryer to 190°C/375°F. Season the pieces of fish with salt and pepper. Stir the batter, then dip the fish into it, one piece at a time, allowing the excess to drain off.

5 Working in two batches if necessary, lower the fish into the hot oil and fry for 6–8 minutes, until crisp and brown. Drain the fish on kitchen paper and keep warm.

6 Make sure the oil is hot again then add a batch of chips, cooking for 2–3 minutes, until brown and crisp. Keep hot while cooking the other batches. Sprinkle with salt and serve with the fish, accompanied by lemon wedges.

British Fried Fish Patties

These patties are the fried version of gefilte fish and are probably the original way that they were made when brought to England by Portuguese Jews in the sixteenth century.

Makes 12–14

450g/1lb haddock fillet, skinned
450g/1lb cod fillet, skinned
2 eggs
50–65g/2–2½oz matzo meal, plus extra for coating
10ml/2 tsp salt
5ml/1 tsp sugar
15ml/1 tbsp vegetable oil
15ml/1 tbsp chopped fresh parsley
2 onions, chopped
vegetable oil, for frying
ground black pepper
chrain or other spicy condiment, to serve

1 Mince (grind) or finely chop the fish in a food processor or by hand. Add the eggs, matzo meal, salt, sugar, oil, parsley, onions and a little pepper. Combine to form a batter.

2 The batter should be firm enough to shape into a soft patty. If it is too thin, add a little more matzo meal and if too thick, add 15–30ml/1–2 tbsp water. Cover and chill for at least 1 hour.

3 Form the mixture into round patties measuring about 6cm/2½in in diameter and 2cm/¾in thick.

4 Put some matzo meal on a plate and use to coat each patty. Place the coated patties on another plate.

5 Heat the oil in a pan until it is hot enough to brown a cube of bread in 30 seconds. Add the patties, taking care not to overcrowd the pan, and fry for 7–8 minutes, turning occasionally, until they are golden brown on both sides. Place on kitchen paper to drain. Serve hot or cold with one or more spicy condiments.

> **Cook's Tip**
> To make a Sephardi version, add a little chopped garlic to the fish mixture and fry the patties in olive oil.

Fish and Chips Energy 521kcal/2188kJ; Protein 36.3g; Carbohydrate 48.9g, of which sugars 2.6g; Fat 21.3g, of which saturates 2.7g; Cholesterol 78mg; Calcium 126mg; Fibre 2.6g; Sodium 223mg.
Fish Patties Energy 123kcal/513kJ; Protein 13.4g; Carbohydrate 3.8g, of which sugars 0.9g; Fat 6.1g, of which saturates 0.8g; Cholesterol 54mg; Calcium 15mg; Fibre 0.2g; Sodium 332mg.

Baltic Fish Croquettes

The people of the Baltic States love croquettes. This recipe would use whichever fish is in season, ideally a mixture of smoked and unsmoked. A cold potato salad and gherkins are traditional and tasty accompaniments.

Serves 4

900g/2lb white fish fillet
   (smoked or preferably a
   combination of smoked
   and unsmoked), bones and
   skin removed
60ml/4 tbsp white breadcrumbs,
   plus 75ml/5 tbsp for coating
100ml/3½fl oz/scant ½ cup milk
75–90ml/5–6 tbsp vegetable oil
1 large onion, thinly sliced
2 eggs, beaten
100ml/3½fl oz/scant ½ cup
   sour cream
15ml/1 tbsp finely chopped
   fresh marjoram
15ml/1 tbsp creamed
   horseradish
2 eggs for rolling croquettes
75ml/5 tbsp flour for
   rolling croquettes
salt and ground black pepper

1 Chop the fish as finely as you can – you can pulse it in a food processor, but make sure that you don't purée it. Transfer the fish into a large bowl.

2 Put the breadcrumbs and milk into a small bowl to soak, squeeze the breadcrumbs dry, and discard the excess milk. Add the breadcrumbs to the fish.

3 Heat 15ml/1 tbsp oil in a frying pan over a medium heat and add the onion. Cook for 3–4 minutes, or until soft but not browned. Add to the fish mixture.

4 Add the eggs to the bowl, with the sour cream, marjoram and horseradish. Season and mix together. Shape the mixture into croquettes as shown. Dip in the egg and the flour, coat in the breadcrumbs and chill for 30 minutes.

5 Heat 30–45ml/2–3 tbsp of the remaining oil in a large non-stick frying pan over a medium heat, and add the fish croquettes in batches, cooking evenly on all sides for 10–12 minutes, or until golden brown and crispy. Serve hot.

Trout a la Navarra

This trout dish is named after the Spanish region of Navarre and features tender fish wrapped in slices of dry-cured ham.

Serves 4

4 brown or rainbow trout, about
   250g/9oz each, cleaned
50g/2oz/¼ cup melted butter,
   plus extra for greasing
16 thin slices Serrano ham, about
   200g/7oz
salt and ground black pepper
buttered potatoes, to
   serve (optional)

1 Extend the belly cavity of each trout, cutting up one side of the backbone. Slip a knife behind the rib bones to loosen them (sometimes just flexing the fish will make the bones pop up). Chop these off from both sides with scissors, and season the fish well inside.

2 Preheat the grill (broiler) to high, with a shelf in the top position. Line a baking tray with kitchen foil and grease it with a little butter.

3 Working with the fish on the foil, fold a piece of ham into each belly. Use smaller or broken bits of ham for this, and reserve the eight best slices.

4 Brush each trout with a little butter, seasoning the outside lightly with salt and ground black pepper. Wrap two slices of ham around each one, crossways, tucking the ends into the belly of the fish.

5 Grill (broil) the trout for about 4 minutes, then carefully turn them over with a metal spatula, rolling them across on the belly, so the ham wrapping does not come loose, and grill for a further 4 minutes until cooked through – the flesh will flake easily when tested with the tip of a knife.

6 Serve the trout very hot, with any spare butter spooned over the top and around the sides. Diners should open the trout on their plates, and eat them from the inside, pushing the flesh off the skin.

Baltic Fish Energy 402kcal/1684kJ; Protein 28.1g; Carbohydrate 33.2g, of which sugars 3.3g; Fat 18.3g, of which saturates 3g; Cholesterol 148mg; Calcium 79mg; Fibre 1.8g; Sodium 622mg.
Trout a la Navarra Energy 369kcal/1546kJ; Protein 48g; Carbohydrate 0.6g, of which sugars 0.6g; Fat 19.4g, of which saturates 8.8g; Cholesterol 216mg; Calcium 66mg; Fibre 0g; Sodium 821mg.

Haddock with Fennel Butter

Fresh fish tastes fabulous cooked in a simple herb butter. Here the aniseed flavour of fennel complements the haddock beautifully to make a simple dish ideal for a dinner party. If you can buy only small haddock fillets, fold them in half before baking, or use cod as an alternative. Serve tiny new potatoes and a herb salad with the fish to make a light, summery main course.

Serves four
675g/1½ lb haddock fillet,
   skinned and cut into
   4 portions
50g/2oz/¼ cup butter
1 lemon
45ml/3 tbsp coarsely
   chopped fennel

1 Preheat the oven to 220°C/425°F/Gas 7. Season the fish on both sides with salt and pepper. Melt a quarter of the butter in a frying pan, preferably non-stick, and cook the fish over a medium heat briefly on both sides.

2 Transfer the fish to a shallow ovenproof dish. Cut four wafer-thin slices from the lemon and squeeze the juice from the remainder over the fish. Place the lemon slices on top and then bake for 15–20 minutes, or until the fish is cooked.

3 Meanwhile, melt the remaining butter in the frying pan and add the fennel and a little seasoning.

4 Transfer the cooked fish to plates and pour the cooking juices into the herb butter. Heat gently for a few seconds, then pour the herb butter over the fish. Serve immediately.

Cook's Tip
Fennel is a rounded, white bulb with stalks rather like celery, although its bright green, feathery fronds look more like dill. Its delicate aniseed flavour partners well with fish, but it can be eaten as a vegetable on its own or served with cheese sauce, risotto, or in soups. Its crisp texture also makes it ideal to eat raw in salads.

Smoked Haddock Omelette

This creamy, smoked haddock soufflé omelette is also known as Omelette Arnold Bennett, after the famous author who frequently dined in the Savoy Hotel in London. It is now served all over the world, using good Scottish smoked haddock and cheese.

Serves 2
175g/6oz smoked haddock fillet,
   poached and drained
50g/2oz/½ cup butter, diced
175ml/6fl oz/¾ cup whipping or
   double (heavy) cream
4 eggs, separated
40g/1½oz/⅓ cup mature (sharp)
   Cheddar cheese, grated
ground black pepper
watercress, to garnish

1 Remove the skin and any bones from the haddock fillet by carefully pressing down the length of each fillet with your fingertips. Discard them. Using a fork and following the grain of the flesh, flake the flesh into large chunks.

2 Melt half the butter with 60ml/4 tbsp of the cream in a fairly small non-stick pan. Wait until the mixture is hot but not boiling, and then add the chunks of flaked fish. Stir together gently, making sure that you do not break up the flakes of fish.

3 Bring slowly to the boil, stirring continuously. Once it is boiling, cover the pan with a lid, remove from the heat and set aside to cool for at least 20 minutes.

4 Preheat the grill (broiler) to high. Mix the egg yolks with 15ml/1 tbsp of the cream. Season with ground black pepper, then stir into the fish. In a separate bowl, mix the cheese and the remaining cream. Stiffly whisk the egg whites, then fold into the fish mixture.

5 Heat the remaining butter in an omelette pan until it is slightly bubbling. Add the fish mixture and cook until it is browned underneath.

6 Pour the cheese mixture over the omelette evenly and grill (broil) until it is bubbling. Serve with fresh bread and garnish with watercress.

Haddock with Fennel Energy 231kcal/970kJ; Protein 32.3g; Carbohydrate 0.3g, of which sugars 0.3g; Fat 11.3g, of which saturates 6.7g; Cholesterol 87mg; Calcium 29mg; Fibre 0.3g; Sodium 190mg.
Haddock Omelette Energy 821kcal/3396kJ; Protein 36.1g; Carbohydrate 2.6g, of which sugars 2.6g; Fat 74g, of which saturates 42.6g; Cholesterol 577mg; Calcium 280mg; Fibre 0g; Sodium 1123mg.

Halibut Fillets with Parsley Sauce

Norsemen considered halibut 'the fish of the gods' and a holy fish, and linked it to Baldur, the wise and kind 'white god'. In Denmark, this traditional dish is often served with steamed cauliflower and buttered new potatoes, but buttered shredded green cabbage or braised leeks would also work well.

Serves 4

900g/2lb halibut fillet
2 eggs, beaten
10ml/2 tsp water
75g/3oz/1½ cup fine
   breadcrumbs
10ml/2 tsp salt
2.5ml/½ tsp white pepper
50g/2oz/4 tbsp butter
4 lemon wedges, to garnish

For the parsley sauce
50g/2oz/4 tbsp butter
60ml/4 tbsp plain
   (all-purpose) flour
350ml/12fl oz/1½
   cups milk
45ml/3tbsp chopped fresh parsley
salt

1 Cut the halibut into four pieces. Whisk the eggs and water together in a shallow dish. Place the breadcrumbs in a second shallow dish. Dip the fish into the egg mixture, then into the breadcrumbs, to coat both sides evenly. Sprinkle with salt and pepper. Allow the fish to rest at least 10 minutes before starting to cook it.

2 To make the parsley sauce, melt the butter in a pan over a medium heat, and whisk in the flour. Reduce the heat and cook the roux for 3–5 minutes until pale beige. Slowly add the milk into the roux; cook, whisking constantly, for about 5 minutes, until the sauce comes to the boil and becomes smooth and thick. Season, add the parsley and simmer for 2 minutes. Cover and keep warm.

3 Melt the butter in a large pan over a medium-high heat. Place the halibut fillets in the pan, and cook for about 4 minutes on each side, turning once, until the coating is golden brown and the fish flakes easily with a fork.

4 Serve the halibut fillets with the sauce spooned over accompanied by freshly cooked vegetables.

Halibut with Leek and Ginger

When buying halibut steaks, it is best to avoid the tail end, because there is more bone than flesh, and the steaks will tend to dry out quickly. However, the flesh of halibut is delicious: it is white and firm and has a good flavour.

Serves 4

2 leeks
50g/2oz piece fresh
   root ginger
4 halibut steaks, approximately
   175g/6oz each
   (see Cook's Tip)
15ml/1 tbsp olive oil
75g/3oz/6 tbsp butter

1 Trim the leeks, discarding the coarse outer leaves, the very dark green tops and the root end. Cut them into 5cm/2in lengths then slice into thin matchsticks. Wash thoroughly.

2 Peel the fresh ginger then slice it very thinly and cut the slices into thin sticks.

3 Dry the halibut steaks on kitchen paper. Heat a large pan with the olive oil and add 50g/2oz/¼ cup of the butter. As it begins to bubble place the fish steaks carefully in the pan, skin side down. Allow the halibut to colour – this will take 3–4 minutes. Then turn the steaks over, reduce the heat and cook for about a further 10 minutes.

4 Remove the fish from the pan, set aside and keep warm. Add the leek and ginger to the pan, stir to mix then allow the leek to soften (they may colour slightly but this is fine). Once softened, season with a little salt and ground black pepper. Cut the remaining butter into small pieces then, off the heat, gradually stir into the pan. Serve the halibut steaks on warmed plates with the leek and ginger mixture over the fish. Accompany with mashed potato.

Cook's Tips
• Ask your fishmonger to skin flattish halibut steaks that are not too thick so you can cook them in a pan rather than in the oven.

Halibut with **Parsley** Energy 594kcal/2493kJ; Protein 58.2g; Carbohydrate 30.4g, of which sugars 5g; Fat 27.6g, of which saturates 14.1g; Cholesterol 227mg; Calcium 234mg; Fibre 0.9g; Sodium 487mg.
Halibut with **Leek** Energy 364kcal/1520kJ; Protein 39.1g; Carbohydrate 2.7g, of which sugars 2.1g; Fat 21.9g, of which saturates 10.8g; Cholesterol 101mg; Calcium 75mg; Fibre 1.9g; Sodium 221mg.

Pollock with Onions

Pollock is a member of the cod family. It is a favourite, less expensive alternative to cod and it is often served along the Norwegian coast. The flesh is much firmer than cod and has a slightly pearly hue. It is full of flavour and forms a delicious partnership with the fried onions that feature in this dish.

Serves 4

50g/2oz/½ cup plain (all-
   purpose) flour
675g/1½lb pollock fillet,
   skinned and cut into
   4 serving portions
50g/2oz/4 tbsp butter
15ml/1 tbsp vegetable oil
2 large onions, sliced
5ml/1 tsp sugar
200ml/7fl oz/scant
   1 cup water
salt and ground black pepper

To serve
boiled potatoes
a green vegetable, such
   as cabbage

1 Preheat the oven to 180°C/350°F/Gas 4. Put the flour on a large plate and season with salt and pepper. Dip the fish portions in the flour to coat on both sides.

2 Put a knob of the butter and the oil in a large frying pan and heat until the butter has melted. Add the floured fish and fry quickly on both sides until browned. Place in an ovenproof dish.

3 Melt the remaining butter in the same pan, add the onions, season with salt and pepper and fry gently for about 10 minutes until softened and golden brown.

4 Add the sugar, increase the heat and allow the onion to caramelize slightly.

5 Spread the onions over the fish. Add the water to the frying pan, stirring to lift any sediment on the bottom of the pan, bring to the boil then pour over the fish and onions.

6 Bake in the oven for about 20 minutes, until the fish is tender. Serve the pollack with boiled potatoes and a green vegetable, such as cabbage.

Stuffed White Fish Wrapped in Bacon

Caught mainly off the east coast of Ireland, and available all year round, plentiful but rather bland fish such as whiting and lemon sole, plaice and flounder, are good for this recipe. Serve with boiled new potatoes and a fresh, green vegetable.

Serves 4

4 good-size or 8 small fish fillets,
   such as whiting, trimmed
4 streaky (fatty) bacon
   rashers (strips)

For the stuffing
50g/2oz/¼ cup butter
1 onion, finely chopped
50g/2oz/1 cup fine fresh brown
   breadcrumbs
5ml/1 tsp finely chopped
   fresh parsley
a good pinch of mixed
   dried herbs
sea salt and ground
   black pepper

To serve
new potatoes
green beans or broccoli

1 Preheat the oven to 190°C/375°F/Gas 5. Trim the fish fillets. If they are fairly big, cut them in half lengthways; leave small ones whole.

2 Trim off and discard the rind and any gristle from the streaky bacon rashers.

3 To make the stuffing, melt the butter in a small pan, add the onion and cook gently until softened but not browned. Add the breadcrumbs, parsley and herbs. Season to taste.

4 Divide the stuffing between the fillets, roll them up and wrap a bacon rasher around each one.

5 Secure the rolls with wooden cocktail sticks (toothpicks) and place them in a single layer in the base of a shallow buttered baking dish.

6 Cover with foil and bake in the preheated oven for about 15 minutes, removing the cover for the last 5 minutes. Serve the stuffed fish with potatoes and green beans or broccoli.

Pollack Energy 298kcal/1247kJ; Protein 32.9g; Carbohydrate 16g, of which sugars 5g; Fat 11.8g, of which saturates 6.7g; Cholesterol 104mg; Calcium 52mg; Fibre 1.3g; Sodium 180mg.
Stuffed Fish Energy 344Kcal/1436kJ; Protein 38.1g; Carbohydrate 12.5g, of which sugars 2.4g; Fat 15.9g, of which saturates 8.2g; Cholesterol 120mg; Calcium 44mg; Fibre 0.8g; Sodium 662mg.

Fried Fish with Shellfish Sauce

The historic port of Callao has been full of culinary treasures since the 16th century, when it was the region's centre of trade. This dish is typical of Callao's famous seafood recipes.

Serves 6

12 mussels
12 cockles
12 clams
6 small squid
12 king prawns (jumbo shrimp)
12 scallops
6 white fish fillets, such as sea
  bass, haddock or sole
50g/2oz plain (all-purpose) flour
250ml/8fl oz/1 cup vegetable oil
1 large red onion, diced
15ml/1 tbsp chilli sauce
5ml/1 tsp paprika
2.5ml/½ tsp ground cumin
1 glass white wine
salt and ground black pepper
lime wedges and boiled potatoes
  or rice, to serve

1 Scrub and clean the mussels, discarding any that are open and fail to close when tapped sharply, and put them in a pan with a little water. Bring to the boil over a high heat, cover, and cook until opened. Drain, discarding any that fail to open after about 5 minutes. Using a teaspoon, detach the flesh from the shells. Discard the shells.

2 Steam and shell the cockles and clams in the same way. Clean and slice the squid, peel and devein the prawns and slice the scallops. Season the fish fillets with salt and pepper and dust with flour. Heat the oil in a frying pan, reserving 30–45ml/2–3 tbsp, and fry the fillets over a high heat, turning once, until golden and cooked through. Transfer them to a serving dish and keep warm.

3 Heat the remaining oil in a large pan over medium heat and fry the onion for about 10 minutes, until golden brown. Stir in the chilli sauce, paprika and cumin and season well.

4 Add all the prepared shellfish to the pan and cook, stirring, for 2 minutes, then add the wine, cover the pan and simmer for about 5 minutes. Pour the seafood sauce over the fried fish and serve immediately, with lime wedges to squeeze over the fish, and accompanied by rice or boiled potatoes.

Fish with Mushroom and Dill Sauce

Dill and flat leaf parsley are the herbs most often used in Russian cuisine, and both go superbly with most fish dishes. In this recipe the fish is accompanied by a creamy mushroom sauce with a rich taste of fresh dill.

Serves 4

4 perch fillets, total weight
  500–600g/1lb 4oz–1lb 6oz,
  skinned
5ml/1 tsp salt
plain white (all-purpose) flour
35–50g/1½–2oz/3–4 tbsp butter
hot boiled new potatoes, to serve

For the dill sauce

2 onions
20 fresh mushrooms
45ml/3 tbsp rapeseed
  (canola) oil
15ml/1 tbsp plain white
  (all-purpose) flour
200ml/7fl oz/scant 1 cup
  fish stock
250ml/8fl oz/1 cup double
  (heavy) cream
100ml/3½fl oz/scant ½ cup
  crème fraîche
100ml/3½fl oz/scant ½ cup dry
  white wine
1 large bunch fresh dill, chopped
1–2 dashes soy sauce
salt and white pepper

1 To make the sauce, chop the onions and slice the mushrooms. In a large frying pan, heat the oil, add the onions and fry, over a medium high heat, for 3–5 minutes until softened but not browned. Add the sliced mushrooms and fry for a further 5–10 minutes.

2 Meanwhile, season the fish fillets with the salt and coat with the flour. Heat the butter in a large non-stick frying pan over a medium heat. Add the fish and fry for 3 minutes on each side or until golden brown and crisp.

3 Sprinkle the flour into the onions and mushrooms and stir until mixed. Gradually stir in the stock until smooth. Bring to the boil, stirring all the time, until the sauce boils and thickens. Stir the cream and crème fraîche into the sauce. Reduce the heat and simmer for 3 minutes.

4 Meanwhile, add the wine to the sauce and season with the soy sauce, and salt and pepper. Stir in the dill. Spoon the sauce over the fish in the pan, reheat and serve with new potatoes.

Fried Fish Energy 343kcal/1429kJ; Protein 31.1g; Carbohydrate 9.1g, of which sugars 0.9g; Fat 18.4g, of which saturates 2g; Cholesterol 133mg; Calcium 86mg; Fibre 0.4g; Sodium 668mg.
Fish with Dill Sauce Energy 706kcal/2924kJ; Protein 31.2g; Carbohydrate 15.6g of which sugars 7.5g; Fat 56.3g, of which saturates 30.7g; Cholesterol 191mg; Calcium 98mg; Fibre 1.8g; Sodium 137mg.

Fish Fillets in Creamy Mustard Sauce

This dish is from northern Germany. You can use any kind of fish that is good for pan-frying, or a mix of different kinds. The mustard sauce is made with grainy mustard to add texture to the dish. Fried potatoes with bacon and onions are a perfect accompaniment.

Serves 4

300ml/½ pint/1¼ cups fish stock
100ml/3½oz/scant ½ cup single (light) cream

10ml/2 tsp grainy mustard
1kg/2¼lb boiled potatoes, thinly sliced
150g/5oz bacon, diced into cubes
1 onion, finely chopped
small bunch chives, chopped
800g/1¾lb fish fillets (cod, salmon, trout, pike or perch)
juice of 1 lemon
oil, for frying
salt and ground white pepper
fresh dill, to garnish

1 Heat the fish stock and season it, if necessary, with salt and pepper. Add the cream and mustard and simmer for 5 minutes to make the sauce.

2 Heat some oil in a frying pan over high heat and fry the potato slices and the bacon until browned and crisp. Add the onion and fry for another 5 minutes. Season with salt and pepper and stir in the chives.

3 Meanwhile, season the fish with lemon juice, salt and pepper. Heat some oil in another pan and fry the fillets, turning once, until golden on both sides. Arrange the potatoes on a serving plate with the fish round them and pour the sauce around. Garnish with fresh dill.

> **Cook's Tip**
> *Any other firm-fleshed white fish, such as cod or haddock, can be used instead of the perch, and you can substitute frozen or wild mushrooms, such as porcini, for the sauce.*

Corn Purée with Fried Fish

Peruvian corn was developed in the age of the Incas, or maybe even earlier. There are two basic kinds: one from the coast, which has a large white kernel with a bland flavour, and one from the mountains, which is sweeter and crisper. This recipe can be made with the kind of fresh corn on the cob that is available everywhere.

Serves 4

4 fresh corn cobs
500ml/17fl oz/generous 2 cups water

25g/1oz fresh coriander (cilantro)
150ml/5fl oz/⅔ cup vegetable oil
1 medium red onion, finely chopped
2 chicken or vegetable stock (bouillon) cubes
1.5ml/¼ tsp ground cumin
10ml/2 tsp chilli sauce
4 fish fillets, such as mahi mahi or halibut
40g/1½oz plain (all-purpose) flour
salt and ground black pepper
lime halves, to serve

1 Slice the kernels off the corn cobs and blend them with half the water in a blender or food processor. Transfer to a bowl and set aside.

2 Put the coriander in the blender with half the remaining water, and blend to a purée.

3 Heat 30ml/2 tbsp of the oil in a deep pan and fry the onion until golden. Add the stock cubes, cumin, chilli sauce and the remaining water. Stir until the stock cubes have dissolved.

4 Add the blended corn kernels and simmer for 5–10 minutes, stirring constantly to avoid the mixture sticking. Stir in the coriander purée and cook for 1 minute, then remove from the heat. Pour into a serving dish and keep warm.

5 Season the fish fillets with salt and pepper and dust them with flour. Fry them in the remaining oil, turning once, until golden on both sides and cooked through. Serve immediately with the corn purée and half a lime.

Fish in Mustard Sauce Energy 570kcal/2387kJ; Protein 47.9g; Carbohydrate 42.5g, of which sugars 5.1g; Fat 24.1g, of which saturates 6.9g; Cholesterol 126mg; Calcium 62mg; Fibre 2.7g; Sodium 738mg.
Corn Purée with Fish Energy 508kcal/2122kJ; Protein 31.7g; Carbohydrate 35.3g, of which sugars 10.6g; Fat 27.5g, of which saturates 3g; Cholesterol 69mg; Calcium 57mg; Fibre 2.4g; Sodium 393mg.

Fish in Tangy Tomato Sauce

Meals in Assam always end with a dish made with tomatoes and lime juice along with a flavoursome sprinkling of whole spices. Quick and easy to make, this dish makes a refreshing, healthy and delicious choice for a dinner. Any firm white fish can be used.

Serves 4

675g/1½lb fillets of tilapia, monk fish or other firm white fish
1 tsp ground turmeric
1 tsp salt or to taste
3 tbsp mustard oil
½ tsp black mustard seeds
½ tsp nigella seeds
10–12 fenugreek seeds
2 green chillies, sliced lengthways, and seeded if you prefer
2 small potatoes, about 200g/7oz, finely chopped
250ml/8fl oz/1 cup warm water
400g/14oz chopped canned tomatoes with their juice
1 tbsp lime juice
1 tbsp chopped fresh coriander (cilantro) leaves
plain boiled rice, to serve

1 Cut the fish into 5cm/2in pieces and lay them on a large plate. Sprinkle half of the turmeric and half the salt over them and rub both gently into the fish.

2 Heat the oil over a medium to high heat until it starts to smoke but not burn (the oil must be very hot), then fry the fish fillets in batches until the edges turn brown. Drain the fish pieces on absorbent kitchen paper.

3 Take the pan off the heat and add the mustard seeds, nigella seeds and fenugreek seeds, followed by the chillies. Return the pan to the heat and add the potatoes. Fry these together until the potatoes are golden brown.

4 Add the remaining turmeric and salt, and pour in 250ml/ 8fl oz/1 cup warm water. Bring the pan to the boil, reduce the heat to low and cook for a further 5–6 minutes.

5 Add the tomatoes and cook for another 5 minutes. Next, add the fried fish and cook for 5 minutes. Stir in the lime juice and coriander and remove from the heat. Serve with a large spoonful of plain boiled rice.

Fried Fish with Onion and Tomato Sauce

A century ago Chorrillos was a fishing village to the south of Lima, but its beaches made it a very popular resort. Today it is a district of the city, but the fishing boats are still there, bringing their catch to the kiosks that serve fried fish.

Serves 6

6 white fish fillets, such as cod, haddock or sea bass
50g/2oz plain (all-purpose) flour
250ml/8fl oz/1 cup vegetable oil
3 medium red onions, sliced into rings
3 garlic cloves, finely chopped
4 medium tomatoes, peeled, seeded and diced
2 fresh chillies, seeded and thinly cut lengthways
15ml/1 tbsp chilli sauce
2.5ml/½ tsp dried oregano
juice of 1 lime
salt and ground black pepper
parsley leaves, to garnish
rice or boiled potatoes, to serve

1 Season the fish with salt and pepper and dust with flour. Heat the oil in a frying pan, reserving 30ml/2 tbsp, and fry the fillets, turning once, until golden and cooked through. Transfer them to a plate and keep warm.

2 Heat the reserved oil over medium heat and fry the onions until they are browned. Add the garlic, tomatoes, chilli strips and chilli sauce and the dried oregano. Cook for 5 minutes.

3 Spoon the onion and tomato mixture into a serving dish and lay the fish on top, or transfer the sauce to a bowl and serve on the side.

4 Sprinkle the fish with lime juice and garnish with parsley. Serve with rice or boiled potatoes.

Variations
For a different flavour, use any fresh herbs you have to hand, such as coriander (cilantro, dill or chives).

Fried Fish Energy 412kcal/1712kJ; Protein 29.6g; Carbohydrate 14.6g, of which sugars 6.3g; Fat 26.5g, of which saturates 2.8g; Cholesterol 69mg; Calcium 50mg; Fibre 1.9g; Sodium 97mg.
Fish in Tomato Sauce Energy 345kcal/1445kJ; Protein 23g; Carbohydrate 28.3g, of which sugars 5.6g; Fat 16.3g, of which saturates 4.2g; Cholesterol 144mg; Calcium 105mg; Fibre 2g; Sodium 338mg.

Fish Baked with Cardamom, Cinnamon and Cloves

This fish recipe is cooked by sealing food into a heavy pan with a tight-fitting lid so that steam and flavour cannot escape.

Serves 4

675g/1½lb tilapia or monkfish
  fillets, or any other firm,
  white fish
1½ tbsp lemon juice
1 tsp salt
2.5cm/1in piece of cinnamon
  stick, broken up
seeds of 6 green cardamom pods
1 tsp cumin seeds
2 tsp coriander seeds
1 tbsp white poppy seeds
1 tbsp sesame seeds
4 tbsp sunflower oil or olive oil
1 large onion, finely chopped
2 tsp garlic purée
2 tsp ginger purée
½–1 tsp chilli powder
½ tsp ground turmeric
115g/4oz/½ cup thick set natural
  (plain) yogurt, whisked
2 medium tomatoes, sliced
2–3 tbsp chopped coriander
  (cilantro) leaves

1 Cut the fish fillets into 5cm/2in pieces and sprinkle with the lemon juice and half the salt. Rub in gently and set aside for 20 minutes to absorb the flavours. Preheat the oven to 160°C/325°F/Gas Mark 3. Grind the cinnamon, cardamom seeds, cumin, coriander, poppy and sesame seeds in a coffee grinder until finely ground. Set aside.

2 In a small pan, heat the oil over a medium heat and add the onion. Fry until it is soft and translucent, but not brown. Add the garlic and ginger, continue to fry for 2 minutes, then add the ground ingredients, chilli powder and turmeric. Cook, stirring constantly, for 1 minute, then add the remaining salt and the yogurt. Mix thoroughly and remove from the heat.

3 In a roasting pan (15cm × 30cm/6in × 12in), spread half the spice mixture, half the tomatoes and half the chopped coriander. Arrange the fish on top in a single layer. Carefully spread the remaining spice mix, chopped coriander and tomatoes over the fish. Cover the pan with a piece of foil, sealing the edges completely. Bake in the centre of the oven for 35–40 minutes. Transfer to a dish and strain the juices over.

Mini Saffron Fish Cakes with Sweet Cucumber and Cinnamon Salad

This scented cucumber salad makes a superbly refreshing accompaniment for the fish cakes. Both the fish cakes and salad include the sweet and spicy flavours that are so popular in Moroccan food.

Serves 4

450g/1lb white fish fillets, such as
  sea bass, ling or haddock,
  skinned and cut into chunks
10ml/2 tsp harissa
rind of ½ preserved lemon,
  finely chopped
small bunch of fresh coriander
  (cilantro), finely chopped
1 egg
5ml/1 tsp honey
pinch of saffron threads, soaked
  in 5ml/1 tsp water
sunflower oil, for frying
salt and ground black pepper

For the salad
2 cucumbers, peeled
  and grated
juice of 1 orange
juice of ½ lemon
15–30ml/1–2 tbsp orange
  flower water
15–20ml/3–4 tsp sugar
2.5ml/½ tsp ground cinnamon

1 Make the salad in advance to allow time to chill. Place the cucumber in a strainer over a bowl and sprinkle with some salt. Leave to drain for about 10 minutes. Using your hands, squeeze out the excess liquid and place the cucumber in a bowl.

2 In a small jug (pitcher), combine the orange and lemon juice, orange flower water and sugar and pour over the cucumber. Toss well, sprinkle with cinnamon and chill for at least 1 hour.

3 To make the fish cakes, put the fish in a food processor. Add the harissa, preserved lemon, coriander, egg, honey, saffron with its soaking water, and seasoning, and whizz until smooth. Divide into 16 portions. Use wet hands to prevent the mixture sticking. Roll each portion into a ball and flatten in the palm of your hand.

4 Heat the oil and fry the fish cakes in batches, until golden brown on each side. Drain on kitchen paper and keep hot until all the fish cakes are cooked. Serve with the cucumber salad.

Fish with Cardamom Energy 353kcal/1473kJ; Protein 36.2g; Carbohydrate 17.8g, of which sugars 10.6g; Fat 15.9g, of which saturates 2.3g; Cholesterol 0.2mg; Calcium 320mg; Fibre 2.2g; Sodium 126mg.
Mini Fish Cakes Energy 284kcal/1181kJ; Protein 25g; Carbohydrate 10g, of which sugars 10g; Fat 16g, of which saturates 2g; Cholesterol 148mg; Calcium 200mg; Fibre 1g; Sodium 107mg.

Calabrian Fish, Cheese and Chilli Patties

These are the Calabrian version of fishcakes – hot and spicy with plenty of garlic and some grated goat's cheese for extra pungency. The fish that is traditionally used is stocco, or stockfish, a member of the cod family. It is dried, and then salted, as opposed to baccalà which is salted without being dried. Stockfish from Mammola in Calabria is recommended for this recipe, but another type could be used, if it can withstand the other flavours in the dish.

Serves 4 to 6

1kg/2¼lb stockfish, preferably
    Stocco di Mammola, soaked
    in water until soft
115g/4oz/2 cups soft white
    breadcrumbs
75g/3oz hard goat's
    cheese, grated
45ml/3 tbsp chopped fresh flat
    leaf parsley
1 dried red chilli, chopped
3 garlic cloves, finely chopped
2 eggs, beaten
60ml/4 tbsp olive oil
400g/14oz can chopped
    tomatoes
sea salt

1 Drain the soaked stockfish, clean and trim it, then flake and chop it finely, removing any bones. Put the fish in a large bowl.

2 Add the breadcrumbs, cheese, parsley, chilli and half the garlic. Stir in enough beaten egg to bind the mixture, and it is firm enough to shape the patties. Shaping the patties is easier if the mixture is lightly chilled, so if there is time, put it into the refrigerator for 30 minutes.

3 Divide the mixture into 8–12 portions and shape into patties. Set aside. Heat the olive oil in a large frying pan and add the remaining garlic. Fry over gentle heat for about 3 minutes. As soon as the garlic begins to brown, stir in the canned tomatoes. Simmer the sauce for about 10 minutes.

4 Season with salt to taste, then add the stockfish patties and spoon the sauce over to coat. Cover the pan and simmer for 10–15 minutes until cooked, then serve immediately.

Cinnamon Fishcakes with Currants, Pine Nuts and Herbs

Whether served as a hot meze or as a main course with a salad, these fresh, tasty fishcakes are delicious flavoured with cinnamon and the ubiquitous triad of herbs – parsley, mint and dill. They are delicious for lunch or supper with a salad. Sage and basil could also be used, and sunflower seeds are interchangeable with the pine nuts.

serves 4

450g/1lb skinless fresh white
    fish fillets, such as haddock
    or sea bass
2 slices of day-old bread,
    sprinkled with water, left for a
    few minutes, then squeezed dry
1 red onion, finely chopped
30ml/2 tbsp currants, soaked in
    warm water for 5–10 minutes
    and drained
30ml/2 tbsp pine nuts
1 bunch each of fresh flat leaf
    parsley, mint and dill, chopped
1 egg
5–10ml/1–2 tsp tomato purée
    (paste) or ketchup
15ml/1 tbsp ground cinnamon
45–60ml/3–4 tbsp plain
    (all-purpose) flour
45–60ml/3–4 tbsp sunflower oil
salt and ground black pepper

To serve

1 small bunch of fresh flat
    leaf parsley
1–2 lemons or limes, cut
    into wedges

1 In a bowl, break up the fish with a fork. Add the bread, onion, currants and pine nuts, toss in the herbs and mix well.

2 In another small bowl, beat the egg with the tomato purée and 10ml/2 tsp of the cinnamon. Pour the mixture over the fish and season with salt and pepper, then mix with your hands and mould into small balls.

3 Mix the flour on a plate with the remaining cinnamon. Press each ball into a flat cake and coat in the flour.

4 Heat the oil in a wide, shallow pan and fry the fishcakes in batches for 8–10 minutes, until golden brown. Lift out and drain on kitchen paper. Serve hot on a bed of parsley, with lemon or lime wedges for squeezing.

Fish Patties Energy 346kcal/1450kJ; Protein 38.2g; Carbohydrate 17.3g, of which sugars 2.9g; Fat 14.2g, of which saturates 4g; Cholesterol 152mg; Calcium 87mg; Fibre 1.5g; Sodium 353mg.
Cinnamon Fish Cakes Energy 317kcal/1324kJ; Protein 26.1g; Carbohydrate 17.8g, of which sugars 2.5g; Fat 16.2g, of which saturates 1.9g; Cholesterol 99mg; Calcium 79mg; Fibre 1.6g; Sodium 169mg.

Piran Baked Fish

The old seaport of Piran lies at the tip of the peninsula on the Slovene coastline. This beautiful historic town welcomes many visitors every year, who are treated to the delightful taste of this unusual baked fish and vegetable dish, served in many local restaurants.

Serves 4

675g/1½lb white fish fillets, such as pike, carp or perch

40g/1½oz/¼ cup raisins
30ml/2 tbsp lemon juice
30ml/2 tbsp cold water
45ml/3 tbsp olive oil
2 onions, peeled and sliced
2 leeks, thinly sliced
2 garlic cloves, crushed
1 carrot, peeled and diced
115g/4oz green beans, cut into 2.5cm/1in lengths
60ml/4 tbsp chopped fresh dill
salt and ground black pepper

1 Preheat the oven to 180°C/350°F/ Gas 4. Grease an ovenproof dish and arrange the fish fillets in a single layer along the bottom.

2 Put the raisins in a small bowl with the lemon juice and the water. Leave to soak for a few minutes while cooking the vegetables.

3 Heat the olive oil in a frying pan and gently cook the onions and leeks for 5 minutes, until they begin to soften. Stir in the garlic, carrot and green beans and cook for an additional 3–4 minutes.

4 Add the raisins and soaking liquid. Gently heat until they are piping hot. Season with salt and a few twists of ground black pepper to taste.

5 Spoon the vegetable mixture over the fish and then tightly cover with a piece of foil. Bake for 20–25 minutes, or until the fish and vegetables are tender and cooked.

6 Sprinkle the top of the fish with the chopped dill before serving this dish with a generous helping of polenta or some steamed tender new potatoes.

Hake with Spinach and Egg and Lemon Sauce

Fish cooked with various greens has its roots in monastic life. Religious observance required that fish be eaten on certain days, and monastery cooks added interest to what might otherwise have been a bland meal by including wild greens. In the modern kitchen, they have been substituted with vegetables such as spinach, celery, leeks, turnip tops and fennel.

Serves 4

500g/1¼lb fresh spinach, trimmed
4 x 200g/7oz fresh hake steaks or 4 pieces of cod fillet
30ml/2 tbsp plain (all-purpose) flour
75ml/5 tbsp extra virgin olive oil
175ml/6floz/¾ cup white wine
3–4 strips of pared lemon rind
salt and ground black pepper

For the egg and lemon sauce
2.5ml/½ tsp cornflour (cornstarch)
2 large (US extra large) eggs
juice of ½ lemon

1 Place the spinach in a large pan with the water that clings to the leaves after washing. Cover the pan tightly and cook over a medium heat for 5–7 minutes. Turn the leaves occasionally using a wooden spoon. Drain and set the spinach aside.

2 Dust the fish lightly with the flour and shake off any excess. Heat the olive oil in a large frying pan, add the pieces of fish and sauté gently, for 2–3 minutes on each side, until golden. Pour the wine over the fish, add the lemon rind and some seasoning and carefully shake the pan from side to side to blend the flavourings. Lower the heat and simmer gently for a few minutes until the wine has reduced a little.

3 Add the spinach. Simmer for 3–4 minutes more, then remove from the heat and stand for a few minutes before adding the sauce. To make the egg and lemon sauce, mix the cornflour with a little water. Beat the eggs in a separate bowl, add the cornflour and lemon juice and mix well together until smooth. Pour the sauce over the fish and spinach, heat over a very gentle heat and shake to mix. If it seems dry, add a little warm water. Allow to cook gently for 2–3 minutes and serve.

Piran Baked Fish Energy 373kcal/1564kJ; Protein 33.5g; Carbohydrate 22.5g, of which sugars 19.3g; Fat 17.3g, of which saturates 2.9g; Cholesterol 113mg; Calcium 149mg; Fibre 5.3g; Sodium 97mg.
Hake with Spinach Energy 490kcal/2041kJ; Protein 45g; Carbohydrate 9g, of which sugars 2g; Fat 28g, of which saturates 4g; Cholesterol 173mg; Calcium 275mg; Fibre 5g; Sodium 424mg.

Hake with Turnip Tops and Onions

This recipe comes from Povoa de Varzim, a fishing harbour north of Porto. Hake is highly prized in the north and served in many different ways. A member of the cod family, it has a deliciously soft texture and an excellent flavour, but should be handled carefully as it is quite fragile.

Serves 4

105ml/7 tbsp olive oil

2 small onions, chopped
2 garlic cloves, chopped
5ml/1 tsp sweet paprika
1 bay leaf
15ml/1 tbsp white vine vinegar
150ml/¼ pint/⅔ cup fish stock
    or water
4 hake steaks, about
    225g/8oz each
200g/7oz turnip tops (the green
    part of the turnip)
8 potatoes, boiled without peeling
4 hard-boiled eggs, halved
salt

1 Preheat the oven to 180°C/350°F/Gas 4. Heat 30ml/2 tbsp of the olive oil in a flameproof casserole. Add the onions, garlic, paprika and bay leaf and cook over a low heat, stirring occasionally, for 5 minutes, until the onions have softened.

2 Add the vinegar and the stock or water, then place the hake in the casserole and season with salt. Cover and cook in the oven for 15 minutes.

3 Meanwhile, steam the turnip tops or cook in a little boiling water for 3–5 minutes, then drain if necessary. Press them through a sieve (strainer) into a bowl, mix with 15ml/1 tbsp of the remaining olive oil and keep warm.

4 Peel the potatoes and cut into quarters. Heat the remaining olive oil in a sauté pan or frying pan, add the potatoes and cook over a medium-low heat, turning occasionally, for 7–8 minutes until light golden brown.

5 Using a slotted spatula, transfer the fish to a large serving plate. Add the potatoes, turnip tops and eggs and spoon over the onion sauce. Serve immediately.

Hake and Clams with Salsa Verde

Merluza en salsa verde is a favourite Basque way of cooking hake, which is one of the most popular and plentiful fish in Spain. As they bake, the clams open up and add their delicious sea juices to the green wine and parsley sauce.

Serves 4

4 hake steaks, about
    2cm/¾in thick
50g/2oz/½ cup plain (all-purpose)
    flour, for dusting,
    plus 30ml/2 tbsp

60ml/4 tbsp olive oil
15ml/1 tbsp lemon juice
1 small onion, finely chopped
4 garlic cloves, finely chopped
150ml/¼ pint/⅔ cup
    fish stock
150ml/¼ pint/⅔ cup
    white wine
90ml/6 tbsp chopped
    fresh parsley
75g/3oz/¾ cup frozen
    petits pois
16 fresh clams, cleaned
salt and ground black pepper

1 Preheat the oven to 180°C/350°F/Gas 4. Season the fish, then dust with flour. Heat half the oil in a large pan, add the fish and fry for 1 minute on each side. Transfer to an ovenproof dish and sprinkle with the lemon juice.

2 Heat the remaining oil in a clean pan and fry the onion and garlic, stirring, until soft. Stir in the 30ml/2 tbsp flour and cook for about 1 minute. Slowly add the stock and wine to the pan, stirring until thickened. Add 75ml/5 tbsp of the parsley and the petits pois to the sauce and season with plenty of salt and ground black pepper.

3 Pour the sauce over the fish, and bake for 15–20 minutes, adding the clams 3–4 minutes before the end of the cooking time. Discard any clams that do not open once cooked, then sprinkle the fish with the remaining parsley and serve.

Cook's Tips
This dish often includes fresh young asparagus tips as well as peas. Simply replace half the peas with asparagus tips.

Hake with Turnip Tops Energy 614kcal/2571kJ; Protein 51g; Carbohydrate 36.2g, of which sugars 5.7g; Fat 30.7g, of which saturates 5.2g; Cholesterol 242mg; Calcium 102mg; Fibre 3.4g; Sodium 326mg.
Hake and Clams Energy 347kcal/1449kJ; Protein 34.2g; Carbohydrate 13.2g, of which sugars 1.4g; Fat 15.2g, of which saturates 2.2g; Cholesterol 51mg; Calcium 109mg; Fibre 2.4g; Sodium 460mg.

Pan-fried Red Mullet with Basil and Citrus

Red mullet is popular all over the Mediterranean. This Italian recipe combines it with oranges and lemons, which grow in abundance in the south of the country.

Serves 4

4 red mullet, weighing about
   225g/8oz each, filleted
90ml/6 tbsp olive oil

10 peppercorns, crushed
2 oranges, one peeled and sliced,
   and one squeezed
1 lemon
flour, for dusting
15g/½oz/1 tbsp butter
2 canned anchovies, drained
   and chopped
60ml/4 tbsp shredded fresh basil
salt and ground black pepper

1 Place the fish fillets in a shallow glass or china dish in a single layer. Pour over the olive oil and sprinkle with the crushed peppercorns. Arrange the orange slices on top of the fish. Cover the dish, and leave to marinate in the refrigerator for at least 4 hours.

2 Halve the lemon. Remove the skin and pith from one half using a small sharp knife, and slice thinly. Squeeze the juice from the other half.

3 Lift the fish out of the marinade and pat dry on kitchen paper. Reserve the marinade and orange slices. Season the fish with salt and pepper and dust lightly with flour.

4 Heat 45ml/3 tbsp of the marinade in a frying pan. Add the fish and fry for 2 minutes on each side. Remove from the pan and keep warm. Discard the residue that is left in the pan.

5 Melt the butter in the pan with any of the remaining original marinade. Add the anchovies and cook, stirring, until completely softened and mashed.

6 Stir in the orange and lemon juice, then check the seasoning and simmer until slightly reduced. Stir in the basil. Pour the sauce over the fish. Serve with the orange and lemon slices.

Red Mullet in the Style of Livorno

The ancient port city of Livorno – Leghorn in English – is renowned for two famous fish specialities. One of these is the dense fish stew or soup called cacciucco, the other is this recipe for cooking sweet red mullet. The smaller the mullet, the better the flavour, but they are quite bony, so some people prefer to use large fillets rather than the whole fish – although the purists will claim that the flavour is nowhere near as delicious.

Serves 6

12 small red mullet, scaled,
   cleaned and gutted
30–45ml/2–3 tbsp plain
   (all-purpose) flour
75ml/5 tbsp olive oil
250ml/8fl oz/1 cup dry
   white wine
½ onion, finely chopped
1 garlic clove, chopped
1 bay leaf
a handful of fresh flat leaf parsley
   leaves, chopped
400g/14oz can tomatoes,
   strained and chopped
sea salt and ground
   black pepper

1 Dry the fish carefully inside and out with kitchen paper and coat them lightly with flour.

2 Heat the oil in a frying pan and fry the mullet for about 4 minutes.

3 Turn the fish over carefully, without breaking them, then add the dry white wine, chopped onion, chopped garlic, bay leaf, flat leaf parsley leaves and season with a little salt and ground black pepper.

4 Shake the pan, then spoon the flavouring ingredients over the fish.

5 Allow the alcohol from the wine to evaporate for 1–2 minutes, then add the canned tomatoes.

6 Cover with a lid and simmer gently for a further 5 minutes. Serve immediately.

Pan-fried Mullet Energy 328kcal/1364kJ; Protein 24.5g; Carbohydrate 0.4g, of which sugars 0.3g; Fat 25.5g, of which saturates 2.9g; Cholesterol 0mg; Calcium 123mg; Fibre 1g; Sodium 411mg.
Mullet Livorno Energy 279kcal/1165kJ; Protein 24.9g; Carbohydrate 5.7g, of which sugars 2.9g; Fat 14.7g, of which saturates 1.4g; Cholesterol 0mg; Calcium 106mg; Fibre 0.9g; Sodium 133mg.

Marinated Fried Fish with Ginger and Chilli

Fish and shellfish are a strong feature of the cuisine in the coastal region of southern India. Kerala, in the southernmost part of the country, produces some of the finest fish and shellfish dishes. These are flavoured with local spices, grown in the fabulous spice plantations that are the pride and joy of the state.

Serves 4–6

1 small onion, coarsely chopped
4 garlic cloves, crushed
5cm/2in piece fresh root ginger, chopped
5ml/1 tsp ground turmeric
10ml/2 tsp chilli powder
4 red mullet or snapper
vegetable oil, for shallow-frying
5ml/1 tsp cumin seeds
3 fresh green chillies, finely sliced
salt
lemon or lime wedges, to serve

1 In a food processor, grind the first five ingredients with salt to a smooth paste.

2 Make several slashes on both sides of the fish and rub them with the paste. Leave to rest for 1 hour. Excess fluid will be released as the salt dissolves, so lightly pat the fish dry with kitchen paper, without removing the paste.

3 Heat the vegetable oil and fry the cumin seeds and sliced chillies for 1 minute.

4 Add the fish, in batches if necessary, and fry on one side. When the first side is sealed, turn them over very gently to ensure they do not break. Fry until golden brown on both sides and fully cooked. Drain and serve hot, with lemon or lime wedges.

> **Variation**
> To enhance the flavour, add 15ml/1 tbsp chopped fresh coriander (cilantro) leaves to the spice paste in step 1.

Marinated Red Mullet

This popular Latin American recipe is based on a Spanish way of cooking fish en escabeche by first frying it, then marinating it. If you are unable to find fresh mullet, snapper, sea bream or tilapia are all good alternatives.

Serves 6

7.5ml/1½ tsp mild Spanish paprika, preferably Spanish smoked pimentón
45ml/3 tbsp plain (all-purpose) flour
120ml/4fl oz/½ cup olive oil
6 red mullet, each weighing about 300g/11oz, filleted
2 aubergines (eggplants), sliced or cut into long wedges
2 red or yellow (bell) peppers, seeded and thickly sliced
1 large red onion, thinly sliced
2 garlic cloves, sliced
15ml/1 tbsp sherry vinegar
juice of 1 lemon
brown sugar, to taste
15ml/1 tbsp chopped fresh oregano
18–24 black olives
45ml/3 tbsp chopped fresh flat leaf parsley
salt and ground black pepper

1 Mix 5ml/1 tsp of the paprika with the flour and season well with salt and black pepper. Heat half the oil in a large frying pan. Dip the fish into the flour, coating both sides, and fry for 4–5 minutes, until browned. Place the fish in a glass or china dish suitable for marinating it.

2 Add 30ml/2 tbsp of the remaining oil to the pan and fry the aubergine wedges until softened and browned. Drain well on a piece of kitchen paper, then add the aubergine to the fish.

3 Add another 30ml/2 tbsp oil to the pan and cook the peppers and onion gently for 6–8 minutes, until softened. Add the garlic and remaining paprika, then cook for a further 2 minutes. Stir in the sherry vinegar and lemon juice with 30ml/ 2 tbsp water and simmer. Season with a pinch of sugar.

4 Stir in the oregano and olives, then spoon over the fish. Set aside to cool, then cover and marinate in the fridge for several hours or overnight. About 30 minutes before serving, bring the fish and vegetables back to room temperature. Stir in the parsley just before serving.

Fried Fish Energy 222kcal/929kJ; Protein 27g; Carbohydrate 2g, of which sugars 1g; Fat 12g, of which saturates 2g; Cholesterol 45mg; Calcium 48mg; Fibre 0g; Sodium 97mg.
Marinated Mullet Energy 335kcal/1406kJ; Protein 31.9g; Carbohydrate 18.4g, of which sugars 11.5g; Fat 15.5g, of which saturates 1.4g; Cholesterol 0mg; Calcium 166mg; Fibre 4.6g; Sodium 347mg.

Crusted Garlic and Wild Thyme Monkfish

Monkfish is a lovely juicy fish; it is hard to believe that until recently it was thrown back into the sea or sold breaded as 'scampi' because its firm texture was not fashionable. Now it is considered a prime fish that needs simple cooking. Garlic is excellent with it as are aromatic herbs such as wild thyme and fennel.

Serves 4
4 monkfish tails (see Cook's Tip)
garlic and herb butter (blend
   115g/4oz/½ cup softened
   butter or margarine, 2 cloves
   finely chopped garlic and
   15ml/1 tbsp. finely
   chopped parsley)
115g/4oz/generous 1 cup dried
   breadcrumbs (see Cook's Tip)
salt and ground black pepper

1 Preheat the oven to 220°C/425°F/Gas 7. Make two or three diagonal slashes down each side of the fish, working from the bone to the edge.

2 Season the fish with salt and freshly ground black pepper. Using your fingertips, rub the garlic butter liberally all over, ensuring that you have pushed a good quantity into each of the diagonal slashes.

3 Sprinkle the breadcrumbs over the fish, place on a baking tray and bake for 10–15 minutes. The cooked tails should be golden brown, with white slashes where the cuts have opened up to reveal the succulent flesh inside.

Cook's Tips
• Buy monkfish tails weighing about 250g/9oz each. Ask your fishmonger to trim off all the skin and purple membrane surrounding the fillets but to leave the fish on the bone.
• The best breadcrumbs are made with day-old bread. Break the bread up with your fingers and then roughly in a food processor to make coarse breadcrumbs. Dry out overnight. The next day process the dried bread again to obtain fine dry crumbs.

Roasted Sea Bream

This is a classic way of cooking a whole fish. The sauce is juicy and combines superbly with the taste of the bream. You can use other fish instead of sea bream, but red bream is essential to make the most of this delicious dish. It is traditional to cook the fish whole, but you can also roast individual portions using the same method.

Serves 4
1 red bream or porgy, weighing
   1.6–2kg/3½–4½lb, scaled
   and cleaned
105ml/7 tbsp olive oil
2 onions, sliced
2 garlic cloves, chopped
2 bay leaves
2 ripe tomatoes, peeled and diced
50ml/2fl oz/¼ cup white wine
sea salt
chopped fresh parsley, to garnish
potatoes and vegetables, to serve

1 Preheat the oven to 180°C/350°F/Gas 4. Using a sharp knife, slash the fish twice on each side. Place it in a large, shallow ovenproof dish or roasting pan, drizzle with 60ml/4 tbsp of the olive oil and sprinkle with sea salt. Place in the preheated oven and roast for about 10 minutes, until the fish is half cooked.

2 Meanwhile, heat the remaining oil in a frying pan. Add the sliced onions, garlic and bay leaves and cook over a low heat, stirring occasionally, for 5 minutes, until the onions are soft and translucent but not browned. Add the diced tomatoes and the white wine. Bring to the boil then simmer gently to warm the sauce through.

3 When the fish has been in the oven for about 10 minutes, spoon the onion mixture over it, return to the oven and roast for a further 10 minutes. Transfer to a serving dish, sprinkle with the parsley and serve immediately with cooked potatoes and vegetables.

Cook's Tips
Sea bream is a white fish with firm flesh and a delicious succulent flavour. Unless the fish is very large and can be cut into fillets, it is best to cook bream whole.

Sea Bream Energy 403kcal/1679kJ; Protein 32.5g; Carbohydrate 11.5g, of which sugars 8.6g; Fat 24.7g, of which saturates 2.8g; Cholesterol 67mg; Calcium 106mg; Fibre 2.3g; Sodium 201mg.
Monkfish Energy 272kcal/1130kJ; Protein 11.4g; Carbohydrate 9.9g, of which sugars 0.5g; Fat 21.1g, of which saturates 13.1g; Cholesterol 62mg; Calcium 26mg; Fibre 0.3g; Sodium 258mg.

Monkfish with Pimiento and Cream Sauce

This recipe comes from Rioja country, where a special horned red pepper grows and is used to make a spicy sauce. Here, red peppers are used with a little chilli while cream makes a mellow pink sauce. To drink, choose a Marques de Cáceres white Rioja.

Serves 4

2 large red (bell) peppers
1kg/2¼lb monkfish tail
  or 900g/2lb halibut
plain (all-purpose) flour,
  for dusting
30ml/2 tbsp olive oil
25g/1oz/2 tbsp butter
120ml/4fl oz/½ cup white Rioja
  or dry vermouth
½ dried chilli, seeded
  and chopped
8 raw prawns (shrimp), in
  the shell
150ml/¼ pint/⅔ cup double
  (heavy) cream
salt and ground black pepper
fresh flat leaf parsley,
  to garnish

1 Preheat the grill (broiler) to high and cook the peppers for 8–12 minutes, turning occasionally, until they are soft, and the skins blackened. Leave, covered, until cool enough to handle. Skin and discard the stalks and seeds. Put the flesh into a blender, strain in the juices and purée.

2 Cut the monkfish or halibut into eight steaks (freeze the bones for stock). Season well and dust with flour.

3 Heat the oil and butter in a large frying pan and fry the fish for 3 minutes on each side. Remove to a warm dish.

4 Add the wine or vermouth and chilli to the pan and stir to deglaze the pan. Add the prawns and cook them briefly, then lift out and reserve.

5 Boil the sauce to reduce by half, then strain into a small jug (pitcher). Add the cream to the pan and boil briefly to reduce. Return the sauce to the pan, stir in the puréed peppers and check the seasonings. Pour the sauce over the fish and serve garnished with the cooked prawns and parsley.

Pugliese Baked Bream

The fish for this dish is cooked on a base of sliced potatoes that has been flavoured with garlic, fresh parsley and grated Pecorino. The cheese needs to be really pungent and peppery, so choose one that is mature and full of flavour. Serve this dish with a green salad and some slow-roasted tomatoes for a really fantastic meal.

Serves 4

1 large gilthead bream, cleaned
  and scaled, about 1kg/2¼lb
500g/1¼lb potatoes
150ml/¼ pint/⅔ cup
  extra virgin olive oil,
  plus extra for basting
a handful of fresh flat leaf
  parsley, chopped
4 garlic cloves, finely chopped
75g/3oz Pecorino cheese, grated
sea salt and ground
  black pepper

1 Preheat the oven to 200°C/400°F/Gas 6. Rinse the fish thoroughly and pat it dry.

2 Peel the potatoes, slice them about 1cm/½in thick and place them in a bowl of cold water. Leave to soak until required.

3 Use half of the oil to coat the fish generously, both inside and out. Season with salt and pepper and tuck half the parsley and garlic into the cavity.

4 Drain the potatoes and rub the slices dry in a clean cloth.

5 Put the potatoes into a baking dish that is large enough to hold the fish. Add the rest of the oil with the remaining parsley and garlic. Mix well. Spread the potatoes evenly in the dish, season them with salt and pepper, then sprinkle with the cheese.

6 Lay the fish on top of the potatoes. Bake for about 40 minutes or until the potatoes are tender and the fish is cooked through, basting occasionally with a little olive oil.

7 Serve the fish and potatoes immediately, straight from the baking dish.

Baked Bream Energy 456kcal/1894kJ; Protein 31.8g; Carbohydrate 0.4g, of which sugars 0.3g; Fat 36.5g, of which saturates 7.4g; Cholesterol 19mg; Calcium 340mg; Fibre 0.6g; Sodium 334mg.
Monkfish with Pimiento Energy 500kcal/2087kJ; Protein 49.7g; Carbohydrate 7.2g, of which sugars 6.9g; Fat 27.1g, of which saturates 13.7g; Cholesterol 140mg; Calcium 70mg; Fibre 1.4g; Sodium 113mg.

Monkfish with Rocket Pesto

Colourful Mediterranean vegetables complement richly flavoured monkfish.

Serves 4
900g/2lb monkfish tail
50g/2oz rocket (arugula)
30ml/2 tbsp pine nuts
1 garlic clove, chopped
25g/1oz/⅓ cup freshly grated
 Parmesan cheese
90ml/6 tbsp olive oil
45ml/3 tbsp lemon juice
2 red (bell) peppers, halved
2 yellow (bell) peppers, halved
1 red onion, cut into wedges
2 courgettes (zucchini), sliced
4 fresh rosemary sprigs
salt and ground black pepper

1 Preheat the oven to 220°C/425°F/Gas 7. Remove skin or membrane from the monkfish. Using a sharp knife cut along one side of the central bone, close to the bone and remove the fish fillet. Repeat on the other side. Set aside.

2 Place the rocket, pine nuts, garlic, Parmesan cheese, 45ml/ 3 tbsp of the olive oil and 15ml/1 tbsp of the lemon juice in a food processor or blender and process to a smooth paste.

3 Lay one fish fillet out flat, cut-side up and spread with the pesto. Place the remaining fillet on top, cut-side down. Tie the fish with string at regular intervals to seal together. Sprinkle with plenty of salt and pepper to season and set aside. Cut each pepper half into three lengthways. Remove the core and seeds.

4 Place the pepper in an ovenproof casserole with the onion wedges and slices of courgette. In a small bowl, mix 15ml/1 tbsp of the olive oil and the remaining lemon juice. Sprinkle over the vegetables. Mix and season with salt and pepper.

5 Tuck the rosemary sprigs among the vegetables. Cover the casserole, place in the oven and cook the vegetables for 20 minutes. Place the monkfish parcel in the centre of the vegetables and brush it with 15ml/1 tbsp of the olive oil. Sprinkle the remaining oil over the vegetables. Cover again, return to the oven until the monkfish is cooked through and turns opaque. To serve, cut the fish into thick slices, removing the string, if you prefer, and serve with the cooked vegetables.

Pan-fried Sole with Lemon and Capers

Flat fish of different varieties abound in the Mediterranean Sea and are usually fried simply, and served with lemon wedges to squeeze over the top. Intensely flavoured capers, which grow extensively in the Balearic Islands, make a pleasant tangy addition to this classic dish.

Serves 2
30–45ml/2–3 tbsp plain
 (all-purpose) flour
4 sole, plaice or flounder fillets,
 or 2 whole small flat fish
45ml/3 tbsp olive oil
25g/1oz/2 tbsp butter
60ml/4 tbsp lemon juice
30ml/2 tbsp pickled
 capers, drained
salt and ground black pepper
fresh flat leaf parsley, to garnish
lemon wedges, to serve

1 Sift the flour on to a plate and season well with salt and ground black pepper. Dip the fish fillets into the flour, to coat evenly on both sides.

2 Heat the oil and butter in a large shallow pan until foaming. Add the fish fillets and fry over a medium heat for 2–3 minutes on each side.

3 Lift out the fillets carefully with a metal spatula and place them on a warmed serving platter. Season with salt and ground black pepper.

4 Add the lemon juice and capers to the pan, heat through and pour over the fish. Garnish with parsley and serve at once with lemon wedges.

Cook's Tip
This is a flavourful, and very quick, way to serve the fillets of any white fish, particularly flat fish such as sole or plaice. The delicate flavour of the fish is enhanced by the tangy lemon juice and capers.

Monkfish with Pesto Energy 477Kcal/1991kJ; Protein 47g; Carbohydrate 14.7g, of which sugars 13.7g; Fat 25.8g, of which saturates 4.5g; Cholesterol 42mg; Calcium 160mg; Fibre 4.3g; Sodium 139mg.
Pan-fried Sole Energy 533kcal/2223kJ; Protein 37g; Carbohydrate 16g, of which sugars 1g; Fat 36g, of which saturates 10g; Cholesterol 147mg; Calcium 70mg; Fibre 1g; Sodium 268mg.

Grilled Sole with Chive Butter

The very best way of transforming simple grilled fish into a luxury dish is by topping it with a flavoured butter, as in this recipe.

Serves 4
115g/4oz/½ cup unsalted (sweet) butter, softened, plus extra, melted
5ml/1 tsp diced lemon grass
pinch of finely grated lime rind
1 kaffir lime leaf, very finely shredded (optional)
45ml/3 tbsp chopped chives or chopped chive flowers, plus extra chives or chive flowers to garnish
2.5–5ml/½–1 tsp Thai fish sauce
4 sole, skinned
salt and ground black pepper
lemon or lime wedges, to serve

1 Put the butter in a bowl and cream it with a wooden spoon. Add the lemon grass, lime rind, lime leaf, if using, and chives or chive flowers. Mix well, making sure all the ingredients are thoroughly combined, then season to taste with Thai fish sauce, salt and pepper.

2 Chill the butter mixture to firm it a little, then form it into a roll and wrap in foil or clear film (plastic wrap). Chill until firm. Preheat the grill (broiler).

3 Brush the fish with melted butter. Place it on the grill (broiling) rack and season. Grill (broil) for about 5 minutes on one side.

4 Carefully turn the pieces of fish over and grill the other side for 4–5 minutes, until the fish is firm and just cooked. Test the flesh with a fork, it should flake easily.

5 Meanwhile, cut the chilled butter into thin slices. Put the fish on individual plates and top with the butter. Garnish with chives and serve with lemon or lime wedges.

Cook's Tips
• Finer white fish fillets, such as plaice, can be cooked in this way, but reduce the cooking time slightly.
• The flavoured butter can be made ahead and frozen.

Plaice fillets with Sorrel and Lemon Butter

Sorrel is a wild herb that is now grown commercially. It is very good in salads and, roughly chopped, partners this slightly sweet-fleshed fish very well. Plaice – such a pretty fish with its orange spots and fern-like frills – is a delicate fish that works well with this sauce. Cook it simply like this to get the full natural flavours of the ingredients.

Serves 4
200g/7oz/scant 1 cup butter
500g/1¼lb plaice fillets, skinned and patted dry
30ml/2 tbsp chopped fresh sorrel
90ml/6 tbsp dry white wine
a little lemon juice

1 Heat half the butter in a large frying pan and, just as it is melted, place the fillets skin side down. Cook briefly, just to firm up, reduce the heat and turn the fish over. The fish will be cooked in less than 5 minutes. Try not to let the butter brown or allow the fish to colour.

2 Remove the fish fillets from the pan and keep warm between two plates. Cut the remaining butter into chunks. Add the chopped sorrel to the pan and stir. Add the wine then, as it bubbles, add the butter, swirling it in piece by piece and not allowing the sauce to boil. Stir in a little lemon juice.

3 Serve the fish with the sorrel and lemon butter spooned over, with some crunchy green beans and perhaps some new potatoes, if you like.

Cook's Tip
Sorrel is a herb that has a sour, slightly acidic flavour that becomes stronger as it matures. It should have bright green crisp leaves, and should not be used if the leaves are wilted or yellow. If you cannot find sorrel, you could try this recipe with tarragon or thyme instead.

Grilled Sole Energy 349kcal/1447kJ; Protein 27.4g; Carbohydrate 0.5g, of which sugars 0.5g; Fat 26.3g, of which saturates 15g; Cholesterol 136mg; Calcium 49mg; Fibre 0g; Sodium 591mg.
Plaice Energy 494kcal/2047kJ; Protein 25.7g; Carbohydrate 0.5g, of which sugars 0.5g; Fat 43.3g, of which saturates 26.4g; Cholesterol 170mg; Calcium 98mg; Fibre 0.3g; Sodium 501mg.

Chilli-spiced Fried Plaice

In this beautiful Japanese dish the flesh of the fish and also the skeleton is deep-fried to such crispness that you can eat it all.

Serves 4
4 small plaice or flounder, about 500–675g/1¼–1½lb total weight, gutted
60ml/4 tbsp cornflour (cornstarch)

vegetable oil, for deep-frying
salt

For the condiment
130g/4½oz mooli (daikon), peeled
4 dried chillies, seeded
1 bunch of chives, finely chopped, plus whole chives to garnish

For the sauce
20ml/4 tsp rice vinegar
20ml/4 tsp shoyu

1 Use a very sharp knife to make deep cuts around the gills and across the tail of the fish. Cut through the skin from the head down to the tail along the centre. Slide the tip of the knife under the flesh near the head and gently cut the fillet from the bone. Fold the fillet with your hand as you cut, as if peeling it from the bone. Keep the knife horizontal.

2 Repeat for the other half, then turn the fish over and do the same to get four fillets from each fish. Place in a dish and sprinkle with a little salt on both sides. Keep the bony skeletons.

3 For the condiment, pierce the mooli with a skewer in four places to make holes, then insert the chillies. Leave for 15 minutes, then grate finely. Squeeze out the moisture with your hand. Press a quarter of the grated mooli and chilli into an egg cup, then turn out on to a plate. Make three more mounds.

4 Cut the fish fillets into four slices crossways and coat in cornflour. Heat the oil in a wok or pan to 175°C/345°F. Deep-fry the fillets, two to three at a time, until light golden brown. Raise the temperature to 180°C/350°F. Dust the skeletons with cornflour and cook until crisp. Drain and sprinkle with salt.

5 For the sauce, mix the rice vinegar and shoyu in a bowl. Arrange the fish on the plates with the mooli moulds and chives. To eat, mix the condiment and fish with the sauce.

Pan-fried Sea Bream with Lime and Tomato Salsa

The most popular way of cooking a fresh piece of fish is to pan fry it or grill it. In this recipe a simple salsa is flashed in the pan at the end of cooking, to make a light sauce.

Serves 4
4 sea bream fillets
juice of 2 limes

30ml/2 tbsp chopped coriander (cilantro)
1 fresh red chilli, seeded and finely chopped
2 spring onions (scallions), sliced
45ml/3 tbsp olive oil, plus extra to serve
2 large tomatoes, diced
salt
cooked white rice, to serve

1 Place the fish fillets in a shallow china or glass dish large enough to hold them all in a single layer.

2 Mix the lime juice, coriander, chilli and spring onions in a jug (pitcher). Stir in half the oil, then pour this marinade over the fish.

3 Cover and marinate for around 15–20 minutes. Do not be tempted to marinate the fish for longer than this or the acid in the marinade will start to 'cook' it.

4 Heat the remaining oil in a large heavy frying pan over a high heat. Lift each piece of fish from the marinade and pat dry with kitchen paper.

5 Season the fish with salt and place in the hot pan, skin side down. Cook for 2 minutes, then turn and cook for a further 2 minutes, until the flesh is opaque all the way through.

6 Add the marinade and the chopped tomatoes to the pan. Bring the sauce to the boil and cook for about 1 minute, until the tomatoes are lightly cooked but still retain their shape.

7 Drizzle a little olive oil over the fish and serve on individual warm plates, with white rice and the tomato salsa.

Chilli-spiced Plaice Energy 219kcal/911kJ; Protein 13.8g; Carbohydrate 13.3g, of which sugars 1.7g; Fat 12.6g, of which saturates 1.6g; Cholesterol 34mg; Calcium 60mg; Fibre 1g; Sodium 808mg.
Sea Bream Energy 166kcal/698kJ; Protein 27.3g; Carbohydrate 2g, of which sugars 2g; Fat 5.5g, of which saturates 0.2g; Cholesterol 57mg; Calcium 84mg; Fibre 1g; Sodium 173mg.

Sea Bass with Parsley and Lime Butter

The delicate but firm, sweet flesh of sea bass goes beautifully with citrus flavours. Serve with roast fennel and sautéed diced potatoes or, for a summer lunch, with new potatoes and salad.

Serves 6
50g/2oz/¼ cup butter
6 sea bass fillets, about
   150g/5oz each
grated rind and juice of
   1 large lime
30ml/2 tbsp chopped fresh parsley
salt and ground black pepper

1 Heat the butter in a large frying pan and add three of the sea bass fillets, skin side down. Cook for 3–4 minutes, or until the skin has turned crisp and golden. Turn the fish over and cook for a further 2–3 minutes, or until cooked through. If the flesh flakes easily when tested with a knife, it is cooked.

2 Carefully remove the fillets from the pan with a metal spatula. Place each on a serving plate and keep them warm. Cook the remaining fish in the same way and transfer to serving plates.

3 Add the lime rind and juice to the pan with the chopped parsley, and season with salt and black pepper. Allow to bubble for 1–2 minutes, then pour a little over each fish portion and serve immediately.

Variation
Instead of serving this with sautéed diced potatoes, offer fat home-made oven chips (French fries) with fresh herbs and a little lime to echo the flavouring used in the butter for the fish. Slice 4 large waxy potatoes thickly and spread them in a single layer in a roasting pan. Sprinkle with 30ml/2 tbsp chopped fresh herbs and the finely grated rind of 1 lime. Drizzle with 30ml/2 tbsp olive oil and dot with the same quantity of butter. Cover with foil and bake at 200°C/400°F/Gas 6 for 1–1¼ hours, removing the foil after 30 minutes and stirring the chips at least twice.

Sea Bass Baked in Salt

This is a restaurant speciality, especially popular along the Bosphorus in Istanbul and the waterfront restaurants in Izmir. A good-sized fish, completely masked in sea salt, is baked until the salt is as hard as rock. It is then transported to the eager diners by proud waiters, who crack open the salt casing with a heavy mallet and remove the top layer of skin to reveal the bleached white flesh of the cooked fish beneath. This ancient method of cooking intensifies the freshness of the fish, conjuring up the taste of the sea, but it does require a lot of salt. For supreme enjoyment, little else is needed – sauces would disguise the freshness. Serve with lemon, freshly ground black pepper and a rocket salad.

Serves 2–4
1.2kg/2½lb very fresh sea bass
   (see below), gutted, with head
   and tail left on
about 1kg/2¼lb coarse sea salt
ground black pepper and lemon
   wedges, to serve

1 Preheat the oven to 190°C/375°F/ Gas 5. Rinse the fish inside and out. Find an ovenproof dish to fit the fish and cover the bottom with a thick layer of salt, pressing it down with the heel of your hand. Place the fish on top and shovel spoonfuls of salt over it until it is covered, then press gently to compact it.

2 Put the dish in the oven and bake for 1 hour, until the salt has formed a hard crust. Place the dish on the table and crack open the salt crust with a heavy object, such as a meat cleaver or a pestle. Carefully peel off the top layer of salt, removing the skin of the fish with it. Serve chunks of the delicate white flesh immediately, with black pepper and a squeeze of lemon.

Cook's Tips
In Turkey, bluefish is popular for this dish, but if you are unable to get it sea bass is an acceptable alternative. You could equally well use any other firm-fleshed white fish, such as turbot or sole.

Sea Bass with Parsley Energy 213kcal/890kJ; Protein 29g; Carbohydrate 0g, of which sugars 0g; Fat 11g, of which saturates 5g; Cholesterol 138mg; Calcium 199mg; Fibre 0.1g; Sodium 200mg.
Sea Bass in Salt Energy 175kcal/737kJ; Protein 33.8g; Carbohydrate 0g, of which sugars 0g; Fat 4.4g, of which saturates 0.7g; Cholesterol 140mg; Calcium 228mg; Fibre 0g; Sodium 1103mg.

Fillets of Brill in Red Wine Sauce

Forget the old maxim that red wine and fish do not go well together. The robust sauce adds colour and richness to this excellent dish, which is more than elegant enough for a dinner party. Halibut and John Dory are also good cooked this way.

Serves 4

4 fillets of brill, about
175–200g/6–7oz
each, skinned
150g/5oz/10 tbsp chilled butter,
diced, plus extra for greasing
115g/4oz shallots, thinly sliced
200ml/7fl oz/scant 1 cup red wine
200ml/7fl oz/scant 1 cup
fish stock
salt and ground white pepper
fresh flat leaf parsley leaves or
chervil, to garnish

1 Preheat the oven to 180°C/350°F/Gas 4. Season the fish fillets on both sides with salt and ground black pepper. Generously butter a shallow flameproof dish, which is large enough to take all the brill fillets in a single layer. Spread the shallots in an even layer in the dish and lay the fish fillets on top. Season well with salt and ground pepper.

2 Pour in the red wine and fish stock, cover the dish with a lid or foil and then bring the liquid to just below boiling point. Transfer the dish to the oven and bake for 6–8 minutes, or until the brill is just cooked.

3 Using a fish slice (metal spatula), lift the fish and shallots on to a serving dish, cover with foil and keep hot.

4 Transfer the dish to the stove and bring the cooking liquid to the boil over a high heat. Cook it until it has reduced by half. Lower the heat and whisk in the chilled butter, one piece at a time, to make a smooth, shiny sauce. Season with salt and ground white pepper, set the sauce aside and keep hot.

5 Divide the shallots among four warmed plates and lay the brill fillets on top. Pour the sauce over and around the fish and garnish with the fresh flat leaf parsley or chervil.

Milkfish Stuffed with Pork and Peas

Although milkfish is widely used throughout south-east Asia, it is regarded as the national fish of the Philippines, where it is known as bangus.

Serves 3–4

1–2 fresh milkfish, sea bass or
mackerel, gutted and cleaned,
total weight 1.2–1.3kg/2¹⁄₂–3lb
15ml/1 tbsp palm or groundnut
(peanut) oil
2–3 shallots, finely chopped
2 garlic cloves, finely chopped

115g/4oz minced (ground) pork
30ml/2 tbsp light soy sauce
400g/14oz can petits pois (baby
peas), drained and rinsed
15ml/1 tbsp groundnut (peanut)
oil, for frying
15g/¹⁄₂oz/1 tbsp butter
salt and ground black pepper

To serve

45–60ml/3–4 tbsp suka (Filipino
coconut vinegar)
2 red chillies, seeded and
finely chopped

1 Preheat the oven to 180°C/350°F/Gas 4. Put the fish on a flat surface and gently bash the body (not the head) with a rolling pin to soften the flesh. Gently massage the skin away from the flesh, being careful not to tear the skin.

2 Using a sharp knife, make an incision on the underside of the fish, just below the gills, and squeeze the flesh from the tail end through this opening, keeping the head and backbone intact. Remove all the small bones from the flesh.

3 Heat the oil in a heavy frying pan, stir in the shallots and garlic and fry until they turn golden brown. Add the pork and fry for 2–3 minutes, then stir in the fish flesh. Add the soy sauce and peas, and season. Stuff the fish and pork mixture into the fish. Secure the opening with a cocktail stick (toothpick). Fry the fish on both sides in the oil and the butter until browned.

4 Wrap the fish in a sheet of aluminium foil and place it on a baking tray. Bake in the oven for 35 minutes. Mix the suka and chillies to make a dressing for the fish. Remove the fish from the oven and slice it thickly. Serve with the spiced suka. to spoon over the fish.

Brill Energy 515Kcal/2142kJ; Protein 35.6g; Carbohydrate 2.6g, of which sugars 1.9g; Fat 36.7g, of which saturates 19.5g; Cholesterol 156mg; Calcium 98mg; Fibre 0.4g; Sodium 452mg.
Milkfish Energy 397kcal/1665kJ; Protein 53.3g; Carbohydrate 12.7g, of which sugars 3.4g; Fat 15.4g, of which saturates 4.6g; Cholesterol 102mg; Calcium 116mg; Fibre 4.9g; Sodium 413mg.

Sweet and Sour Snapper

Originating in the northern region of Shandong, China, this dish comprises a whole deep-fried fish served with a medley of vegetables.

Serves 4

4 dried Chinese black mushrooms
1 whole snapper or similar fish, about 800g/1¾lb, cleaned and scaled
15ml/1 tbsp salt
45ml/3 tbsp cornflour (cornstarch)
oil for deep- and shallow-frying
15ml/1 tbsp thinly sliced root ginger
15ml/1 tbsp crushed garlic
1 spring onion, cut into 2.5cm/1in lengths, plus extra, to garnish
30ml/2 tbsp thinly sliced bamboo shoots
½ red (bell) pepper, thinly sliced

For the sauce

60ml/4 tbsp Kao Liang wine vinegar
15ml/1 tbsp sugar
15ml/1 tbsp light soy sauce
10ml/2 tsp cornflour (cornstarch) mixed with 45ml/3 tbsp water
200ml/7fl oz/scant 1 cup water or stock

1 Soak the mushrooms in boiling water for 20–30 minutes, until soft. Rinse the fish inside and out, then pat dry with kitchen paper. Make deep cuts diagonally across both sides of the fish. Rub with the salt, rinse and pat dry. Dust the fish with cornflour.

2 Heat the oil in a wok that is large enough to hold the fish comfortably. Carefully lower the fish into the oil and fry over medium heat for 7–8 minutes, until the skin is crisp and golden brown and the fish is cooked through. Remove it from the wok and drain on kitchen paper. Place the fish on a serving platter with a decent lip to hold the sauce, and keep hot.

3 Drain the mushrooms and slice them thinly, discarding the stems. In a clean wok, heat 30ml/2 tbsp oil and stir-fry the ginger and garlic for 1 minute. Add the spring onions, bamboo shoots and pepper, with the sliced mushrooms. Stir-fry for 2 minutes more.

4 Mix all the sauce ingredients in a bowl. Add to the wok, bring to the boil and simmer for 1 minute, until the sauce thickens. Pour over the fish and garnish with more spring onions. Serve.

Fish Moolie

This is a very popular South-east Asian fish curry in a coconut sauce, which is truly delicious. Choose a firm-textured fish so that the pieces stay intact during the brief cooking process. Monkfish, halibut or cod work well in this dish.

Serves 4

500g/1¼lb monkfish or other firm-textured fish fillets, skinned and cut into 2.5cm/1in cubes
2.5ml/½ tsp salt
50g/2oz/⅔ cup desiccated (dry unsweetened shredded) coconut
6 shallots, chopped
6 blanched almonds
2–3 garlic cloves, roughly chopped
2.5cm/1in piece fresh root ginger, peeled and sliced
2 lemon grass stalks, trimmed
10ml/2 tsp ground turmeric
45ml/3 tbsp vegetable oil
2 × 400ml/14fl oz cans coconut milk
1–3 fresh red chillies, seeded and sliced into rings
salt and ground black pepper
fresh chives, to garnish
plain boiled or steamed basmati rice, to serve

1 Put the fish cubes in a shallow dish and sprinkle with the salt. Dry fry the coconut in a wok, turning all the time until it is crisp and golden, then transfer into a food processor and process to an oily paste. Scrape into a bowl and reserve.

2 Add the shallots, almonds, garlic and ginger to the food processor. Chop the bulbous part of each lemon grass stalk and add to the processor with the turmeric. Process the mixture to a paste. Bruise the remaining lemon grass stalks.

3 Heat the oil in a wok. Cook the shallot and spice mixture for about 2–3 minutes. Stir in the coconut milk and bring to the boil, stirring. Add the fish, most of the chilli and the lemon grass stalks. Cook for 3–4 minutes.

4 Stir in the coconut paste and cook for a further 2–3 minutes only. Adjust the seasoning.

5 Remove the lemon grass. Transfer the moolie to a hot serving dish and sprinkle with the remaining slices of chilli. Garnish with chopped and whole chives and serve with rice.

Snapper Energy 332kcal/1389kJ; Protein 25.4g; Carbohydrate 14.2g, of which sugars 1.1g; Fat 19.8g, of which saturates 2.6g; Cholesterol 46mg; Calcium 61mg; Fibre 0.2g; Sodium 884mg.
Fish Moolie Energy 319kcal/1335kJ; Protein 22.4g; Carbohydrate 16.7g, of which sugars 14.9g; Fat 18.6g, of which saturates 8.3g; Cholesterol 18mg; Calcium 96mg; Fibre 3g; Sodium 249mg.

Carp with Tamarind and Galangal

This dish is popular in Cambodia and Vietnam. For a simpler version, toss the cooked fish in the herbs and serve with noodles or rice and a salad.

Serves 4
500g/1¼lb carp fillets, cut
    into 3 or 4 pieces
30ml/2 tbsp sesame oil
10ml/2 tsp ground turmeric
1 small bunch each fresh
    coriander (cilantro) and basil,
    stalks removed

20 lettuce leaves or rice
    paper wrappers
nuoc cham (Vietnamese fish
    sauce) or other dipping sauce,
    to serve

For the marinade
30ml/2 tbsp tamarind paste
15ml/1 tbsp soy sauce
juice of 1 lime
1 green or red Thai chilli, chopped
2.5cm/1in galangal root, peeled
    and grated
a few sprigs of fresh coriander
    (cilantro) leaves, finely chopped

1 Mix together all the marinade ingredients in a bowl. Toss the fish pieces in the marinade, cover with clear film (plastic wrap) and chill in the refrigerator for at least 6 hours, or overnight.

2 Lift the pieces of fish out of the marinade and lay them on a plate. Heat a wok or heavy pan, add the oil and stir in the turmeric. Working quickly, so that the turmeric doesn't burn, stir-fry the fish pieces, for 2–3 minutes. Add any remaining marinade to the pan and cook for a further 2–3 minutes.

3 To serve, divide the fish among four plates, sprinkle with the coriander and basil, and add some lettuce leaves or rice paper wrappers and a small bowl of dipping sauce to each serving.

4 To eat, tear off a bitesize piece of fish, place it on a wrapper with a few herb leaves, fold it up into a roll, then dip it into the sauce.

> **Cook's Tip**
> *Any freshwater fish can be used for this recipe but, because it is stirred in a wok, you will need one with firm, thick flesh.*

Carp with Horseradish Sauce

Carp is a traditional fish on Polish menus, and has been bred since the 13th century. There are several varieties, the best being the mirror or king carp.

Serves 4
750ml/1¼ pints/3 cups
    cold water
120ml/4fl oz/½ cup vinegar
1 medium carp, about
    400g/14oz, cut into 4 fillets

115g/4oz/1 cup plain
    (all-purpose) flour
115g/4oz/½ cup butter
250ml/8fl oz/1 cup dry
    white wine
30ml/2 tbsp grated
    fresh horseradish
2 egg yolks, beaten
30ml/2 tbsp chopped
    fresh chives
salt and ground black pepper,
    to taste

1 Mix the water and vinegar in a bowl, then soak the carp in the liquid for 1 hour.

2 Pat dry on kitchen paper, then coat the fish in flour.

3 Melt the butter over a high heat, add the fish and fry for 3–4 minutes on each side, until golden brown.

4 Add the wine and season, then cover and simmer for 10–15 minutes.

5 Transfer the fish to a serving dish and keep warm.

6 Add the horseradish and egg yolks to the juices in the pan and simmer for 5 minutes, or until thickened.

7 Pour the sauce over the warm fish and garnish with chopped chives. Serve immediately.

> **Cook's Tips**
> *Some fish, such as carp, which are caught in lakes, ponds and rivers can have a muddy taste, so require soaking in water and vinegar before use.*

Sour Carp with Tamarind Energy 298kcal/1246kJ; Protein 24g; Carbohydrate 19g, of which sugars 5g; Fat 14g, of which saturates 2g; Cholesterol 121mg; Calcium 120mg; Fibre 0g; Sodium 300mg.
Carp with Horseradish Energy 500kcal/2083kJ; Protein 22.3g; Carbohydrate 23.2g, of which sugars 1.3g; Fat 31.6g, of which saturates 16.7g; Cholesterol 229mg; Calcium 135mg; Fibre 1.5g; Sodium 229mg.

Baked Pike in Sour Cream

This freshwater fish has lean creamy-white flesh and needs to be kept moist during cooking. Here it is gently baked in a creamy sauce. Serve with sautéed potatoes.

Serves 4–6
1.5kg/3lb whole pike
1 bay leaf
15ml/1 tbsp olive oil

50g/2oz/1/4 cup butter
1 onion, chopped
1 garlic clove, chopped
115g/4oz/11/2 cups wild
   mushrooms, thickly sliced
15ml/1 tbsp plain
   (all-purpose) flour
175ml/6fl oz/3/4 cup
   sour cream
15ml/1 tbsp chopped
   fresh parsley
salt and ground black pepper

1 Preheat the oven to 190°C/375°F/ Gas 5. Clean, skin and fillet the pike, putting the bones and skin into a pan. Pour over just enough cold water to cover (use a little white wine instead of some of the water, if you wish) and add the bay leaf. Slowly bring to the boil, reduce the heat and gently simmer, uncovered, for 20 minutes.

2 Heat the oil and half the butter in a frying pan and cook the onion for 7–8 minutes, until soft. Add the garlic and mushrooms and cook for 2 more minutes. Strain the fish stock and reserve 300ml/1/2 pint/11/4 cups. Add the stock to the onion and mushroom mixture and simmer for 5 minutes.

3 Use the remaining butter to thickly grease an ovenproof dish. Arrange the fillets snugly in the dish and season with salt and pepper. Blend the flour with the sour cream and pour into the onion and mushroom mixture. Bring to the boil, stirring, and carefully pour over the fish. Cover the dish with foil and bake for 30 minutes, until the fish is tender. Serve, sprinkled with parsley.

Cook's Tips
Pike is a very bony fish and even the fillets should be checked for tiny pin bones.

Oven-roasted Carp

This freshwater fish has a firm flesh and is delicious when it is cooked on a base of sliced local new potatoes and caramelized white onions. The fish is covered with smoked streaky bacon before being baked in the oven, which helps to seal in the flavour and baste the fish as it cooks. The dish is delectable served with a helping of steamed cabbage.

Serves 4
25g/1oz/2 tbsp butter,
   preferably unsalted
500g/11/4lb new potatoes
15ml/1 tbsp olive oil
1 large onion, thinly sliced
1 garlic clove, crushed
10ml/2 tsp cider vinegar
about 900g/2lb whole carp,
   cleaned 115g/4oz rindless
   smoked streaky (fatty) bacon
   rashers (strips)
salt and ground black pepper

1 Preheat the oven to 180°C/350°F/Gas 4. Use half of the butter to grease an ovenproof dish (the dish needs to be large enough to fit the fish fillets side by side).

2 Bring a large pan of lightly salted water to the boil. Scrub the new potatoes and cut into 2cm/3/4in thick slices. Add to the water, bring back to the boil and simmer for 10 minutes, until they are almost tender.

3 Remove from the pan with a slotted spoon and place in the bottom of the prepared dish. Spoon over 60ml/4 tbsp of the cooking liquid.

4 While the potatoes are cooking, heat the remaining butter and oil in a frying pan and gently cook the onions for 10 minutes over a medium heat until they are beginning to brown.

5 Add the garlic and cook for a further 2 minutes until golden. Stir in the cider vinegar. Spoon the onions over the potatoes. Place the carp fillets on top of the onions, then season. Arrange the bacon rashers on top. Cover with foil and bake in the oven for 20 minutes. Remove the foil and bake for a further 15–20 minutes or until the bacon is browned and the fish is tender and flakes easily with a fork. Serve immediately with green cabbage.

Oven Roasted Carp Energy 438kcal/1836kJ; Protein 41.6g; Carbohydrate 20.1g, of which sugars 1.6g; Fat 21.8g, of which saturates 7.8g; Cholesterol 177mg; Calcium 64mg; Fibre 1.3g; Sodium 554mg.
Baked Pike Energy 310kcal/1299kJ; Protein 40.2g; Carbohydrate 3.1g, of which sugars 1.2g; Fat 15.3g, of which saturates 5.7g; Cholesterol 178mg; Calcium 92mg; Fibre 0.3g; Sodium 158mg.

Catfish with a Spicy Coconut Sauce

In this popular Indonesian dish, catfish is simply fried and served with a fragrant and spicy sauce.

Serves 4
200ml/7fl oz/¾ cup coconut milk
30ml/2 tbsp coconut cream
30ml/2 tbsp rice flour, tapioca
    flour or cornflour (cornstarch)
5ml/1 tsp ground coriander
8 fresh catfish fillets
30ml/2 tbsp coconut or corn oil
salt and ground black pepper
fresh coriander (cilantro) leaves,
    to garnish
boiled rice and 1 lime, quartered,
    to serve

For the spice paste
2 shallots, chopped
2 garlic cloves, chopped
2 fresh red chillies, seeded
    and chopped
25g/1oz fresh galangal, chopped
15g/½ oz fresh turmeric,
    chopped, or 2.5ml/½ tsp
    ground turmeric
2–3 lemon grass stalks, chopped
15ml/1 tbsp palm or groundnut
    (peanut) oil
5ml/1 tsp terasi (Indonesian
    shrimp paste)
15ml/1 tbsp tamarind paste
5ml/1 tsp palm sugar (jaggery)

1 For the spice paste, use a mortar and pestle or food processor to pound the shallots, garlic, chillies, galangal, turmeric and lemon grass to a paste.

2 Heat the oil in a wok or heavy pan, stir in the paste and fry until it becomes fragrant and begins to colour. Add the terasi, tamarind paste and sugar and continue to stir until the paste darkens. Stir the coconut milk and cream into the spice paste and boil for about 10 minutes, until the milk and cream separate, leaving behind an oily paste. Season to taste.

3 Meanwhile, on a large plate, mix the flour with the coriander and season with salt and pepper. Toss the catfish fillets in the flour so that they are lightly coated all over.

4 Heat the oil in a heavy frying pan and fry the fillets for about 2 minutes on each side, until golden. Using a fish slice, transfer the fish to warmed dishes with helpings of rice in them. Spoon the coconut sauce over the fish and add lime wedges for squeezing.

Salmon Baked with Potatoes and Thyme

This is very simple and absolutely delicious. Pepper-crusted salmon fillets are baked on a bed of potatoes and onions braised in thyme-flavoured vegetable or fish stock.

Serves 4
675g/1½lb waxy potatoes,
    thinly sliced
1 onion, thinly sliced
10ml/2 tsp fresh thyme leaves

450ml/¾ pint/scant 2 cups
    vegetable or fish stock
40g/1½oz/3 tbsp butter,
    finely diced
4 salmon fillets, each about
    150g/5oz, skinned
30ml/2 tbsp olive oil
15ml/1 tbsp black peppercorns,
    roughly crushed
salt and ground black pepper
fresh thyme sprigs, to garnish
mangetouts (snow peas) or sugar
    snap peas, to serve

1 Preheat the oven to 190°C/375°F/Gas 5. Layer the potato and onion slices in a shallow baking dish, such as a lasagne dish, seasoning each layer and sprinkling with thyme. Pour over the stock, dot with butter, cover with foil and place in the oven.

2 Bake the potatoes for 40 minutes then remove the foil and bake for a further 20 minutes, or until they are almost cooked.

3 Meanwhile, brush the salmon fillets with olive oil and coat with crushed black peppercorns, pressing them in, if necessary, with the back of a spoon.

4 Place the salmon on top of the potatoes, cover with foil and bake for 15 minutes, or until the salmon is opaque, removing the foil for the last 5 minutes. Garnish with fresh thyme sprigs and serve with mangetouts or sugar snap peas.

Cook's Tip
Take care not to overcook the salmon. Although it is an oily fish, it does dry out very easily. In this recipe, cooking the fish with stock helps to keep the fish moist.

Catfish Energy 338kcal/1412kJ; Protein 38.1g; Carbohydrate 11.9g, of which sugars 4.9g; Fat 15.3g, of which saturates 5.7g; Cholesterol 92mg; Calcium 56mg; Fibre 0.9g; Sodium 190mg.
Salmon Energy 549kcal/2290kJ; Protein 34g; Carbohydrate 31g, of which sugars 4g; Fat 33g, of which saturates 9g; Cholesterol 96mg; Calcium 60mg; Fibre 3g; Sodium 442mg.

Salmon with Leeks and Peppers

Cooking salmon in paper parcels is a healthy option. The fish and vegetables cook in their own juices, so they retain their nutrients.

Serves 6

25ml/1½ tbsp groundnut (peanut) oil
2 yellow (bell) peppers, seeded and thinly sliced
4cm/1½in fresh root ginger, peeled and finely shredded
1 large fennel bulb, thinly sliced, fronds chopped and reserved
1 fresh green chilli, seeded and finely shredded
2 large leeks, cut into 10cm/4in lengths and shredded lengthways
30ml/2 tbsp chopped fresh chives
10ml/2 tsp light soy sauce
6 portions salmon fillet, each weighing about 150–175g/ 5–6oz, skinned
10ml/2 tsp toasted sesame oil
salt and ground black pepper

1 Heat the oil in a large frying pan. Add the yellow peppers, ginger and fennel bulb and cook, stirring occasionally, for 5–6 minutes, until they are softened, but not browned.

2 Add the chilli and leeks to the pan and cook, stirring occasionally, for about 3 minutes. Stir in half the chives and the soy sauce and season to taste. Set aside to cool slightly.

3 Preheat the oven to 190°C/375°F/Gas 5. Cut six 35cm/14in rounds of baking parchment or foil and set aside.

4 When the vegetable mixture is cool, divide it equally among the paper or foil rounds and top each with a piece of fish.

5 Drizzle each portion of fish with a little sesame oil and sprinkle with the remaining chives and the chopped fennel fronds. Season with a little more salt and ground black pepper.

6 Fold the baking parchment or foil over to enclose the fish, rolling and twisting the edges together to seal the parcels.

7 Place the parcels on a baking sheet and bake for 15–20 minutes, or until the parcels have puffed up. Transfer the parcels to six warmed plates and serve immediately.

Foil-baked Salmon

Baking the whole salmon in a foil package ensures that the flesh remains wonderfully moist. It can be served hot, with new potatoes and cucumber salad, or cold with a salad, for a summer lunch.

Serves 6

1 salmon, about 1kg/2¼lb, cleaned and trimmed
1 small bunch fresh dill, roughly chopped
4 garlic cloves, finely chopped
115g/4oz/½ cup unsalted (sweet) butter
50ml/2fl oz/¼ cup dry white wine
juice of ½ lemon
10–12 black peppercorns
4–5 fresh bay leaves
salt and ground black pepper, to taste
slices of lemon, to garnish
boiled new potatoes and cucumber salad, to serve

1 Preheat the oven to 200°C/400°F/Gas 6. Place the salmon in the centre of a large piece of foil.

2 In a small bowl, mix together the chopped fresh dill, garlic and butter, to form a smooth paste. Add the wine and lemon juice, and mix to combine.

3 Spread the mixture inside the cavity of the fish, and all over the outside. Put the peppercorns and bay leaves inside the cavity, then season the skin with salt and pepper, to taste.

4 Bring the edges of the foil up and seal together to make a loose parcel.

5 Put the fish in the preheated oven and cook for about 30–40 minutes, or until the fish is tender and cooked.

6 Remove from the oven and divide the fish into 6 portions. If you like, remove the skin before serving. Insert the prongs of a fork between the flesh and the skin at one end and roll the skin around the prongs. Transfer the fish to warmed plates.

7 Pour over any juices caught in the foil, and serve immediately with boiled new potatoes and cucumber salad.

Salmon with Leeks Energy 379kcal/1575kJ; Protein 35g; Carbohydrate 4g, of which sugars 4g; Fat 24g, of which saturates 4g; Cholesterol 83mg; Calcium 52mg; Fibre 2g; Sodium 198mg.
Baked Salmon Energy 242kcal/1005kJ; Protein 20.3g; Carbohydrate 0.1g, of which sugars 0.1g; Fat 17.9g, of which saturates 6.2g; Cholesterol 68mg; Calcium 23mg; Fibre 0g; Sodium 96mg.

Filo-wrapped Salmon

Select a chunky variety of tomato sauce for this simple but delicious recipe. When working with filo pastry, keep it covered with clear film (plastic wrap) or a damp dish towel, since once it's exposed to air it dries out quickly and becomes brittle and difficult to handle.

Serves 3–4

about 130g/4½oz filo pastry
  (6–8 large sheets)
about 30ml/2 tbsp olive oil,
  for brushing
450g/1lb salmon fillets
550ml/18fl oz/2½ cups fresh
  tomato sauce

1 Preheat the oven to 200°C/400°F/Gas 6. Take a sheet of filo pastry, brush all over with a little olive oil and cover with a second sheet of pastry. Place a piece of fish on top of the pastry, towards the bottom edge, then top with one or two spoonfuls of the tomato sauce, spreading it in an even layer.

2 Roll the fish in the pastry, taking care to enclose the filling completely. Brush with a little olive oil. Place on a baking sheet and repeat with the remaining fish and pastry, placing each parcel on the baking sheet but keeping them apart. You should have about half the sauce remaining, to serve with the fish.

3 Bake for 10–15 minutes, or until golden. Meanwhile, reheat the remaining sauce. Serve the filo-wrapped salmon immediately with the remaining tomato sauce.

Cook's Tip
To save time, use a bottled tomato sauce in this dish. There is a vast selection these days and a quick trawl through the pasta sauces at the supermarket will offer a wide choice. A simple tomato and basil sauce, or one including mushrooms, would work well. Alternatively, try puttanesca sauce, which includes black olives, chilli, garlic and anchovies. It has a robust flavour but if you use it sparingly it will not overwhelm the flavour of the salmon.

Fish Cakes

Baked in the oven, fish cakes are a steadfast favourite throughout Denmark. Serve the fish cakes with remoulade, buttered potatoes and pickled cucumber salad to make a complete supper.

Serves 4

450g/1lb cod or plaice fillet
225g/8oz salmon fillet
175g/6oz smoked salmon
30ml/2 tbsp finely chopped onion
40g/1½oz/3 tbsp melted butter
3 eggs
25g/1oz/¼ cup plain
  (all-purpose) flour
salt and white pepper
pickled cucumber salad, to serve

1 Place the cod and salmon fillets in a shallow dish, and sprinkle with 15ml/1 tbsp salt to draw some of the moisture out. Leave the fish to rest for 10 minutes, then pat dry with kitchen paper.

2 Place the cod and salmon, with the smoked salmon, in a food processor. Add the onion, butter, eggs and flour and pulse until smooth; season with salt and pepper and spoon into a bowl.

3 Preheat the oven to 190°C/375°F/Gas 5. Lightly grease a 23 x 33cm/9 x 13in baking tray. With damp hands, form the fish mixture into 16 slightly flattened, round patties, and place them on the prepared tray.

4 Bake the fish cakes in the preheated oven for 30–35 minutes, until they are cooked through and lightly browned. Serve immediately with pickled cucumber salad.

Cook's Tip
• *Serve the fish cakes with mustard sauce instead of remoulade. Instead of baking they can be fried or grilled (broiled).*
• *Make smaller fishcakes to serve as an appetizer with a salad garnish, or with vegetables for a main course for children.*
• *Before processing the fish, check for any small bones and pick them out with tweezers.*

Filo-wrapped Salmon Energy 460kcal/1924kJ; Protein 28.1g; Carbohydrate 31.3g, of which sugars 5.9g; Fat 25.8g, of which saturates 5.5g; Cholesterol 70mg; Calcium 85mg; Fibre 2.7g; Sodium 519mg.
Fish Cakes Energy 407kcal/1700kJ; Protein 48.5g; Carbohydrate 5.5g, of which sugars 0.6g; Fat 21.4g, of which saturates 7.9g; Cholesterol 259mg; Calcium 64mg; Fibre 0.3g; Sodium 1029mg.

Salmon with Green Peppercorns

Salmon benefits from being served with a piquant accompaniment. Lemon and lime are the obvious choices, but capers and green peppercorns also serve to counter the rich taste of the fish.

Serves 4
15g/½oz/1 tbsp butter
2–3 shallots, finely chopped
15ml/1 tbsp brandy (optional)
60ml/4 tbsp white wine
90ml/6 tbsp fish or chicken stock
120ml/4fl oz/½ cup
   whipping cream
30–45ml/2–3 tbsp green
   peppercorns in brine, rinsed
15–30ml/1–2 tbsp vegetable oil
4 pieces salmon fillet, each
   about 175g/6oz
salt and ground black pepper
fresh parsley, to garnish

1 Melt the butter in a heavy pan over a medium heat. Add the shallots and cook over low to medium heat for 1–2 minutes, until just softened but not coloured.

2 Add the brandy, if using, then pour in the white wine and stock. Bring to the boil. Boil vigorously to reduce by three-quarters, stirring occasionally.

3 Reduce the heat, then add the cream and half the peppercorns, crushing them slightly against the sides of the pan with the back of a spoon. Cook very gently for 4–5 minutes, until the sauce has thickened slightly.

4 Strain the sauce into a clean pan and stir in the remaining peppercorns. Keep the sauce warm over a very low heat, stirring occasionally, while you cook the salmon fillets.

5 Heat the oil in a large, heavy frying pan over a medium-high heat. Lightly season the salmon. When the oil is very hot, add the salmon. Sear the fillets on both sides, then lower the heat and cook for 4–6 minutes, until the flesh is opaque throughout.

6 Arrange the fish on warmed plates and pour over the sauce. Garnish with parsley and serve.

Salmon Fishcakes

The secret of a good fishcake is to make it with freshly prepared fish and potatoes, homemade breadcrumbs and plenty of interesting seasoning.

Serves 4
450g/1lb cooked salmon fillet
450g/1lb freshly cooked
   potatoes, mashed
25g/1oz/2 tbsp butter, melted
10ml/2 tsp wholegrain mustard
15ml/1 tbsp each chopped
   fresh dill and chopped fresh
   flat leaf parsley
grated rind and juice of ½ lemon
15g/½oz/1 tbsp plain
   (all-purpose) flour
1 egg, lightly beaten
150g/5oz/generous 1 cup
   dried breadcrumbs
60ml/4 tbsp sunflower oil
salt and ground white pepper
rocket (arugula) leaves and fresh
   chives, to garnish
lemon wedges, to serve

1 Flake the cooked salmon, watching carefully for and discarding any skin and bones. Place the flaked salmon in a bowl with the mashed potato, melted butter and wholegrain mustard. Mix well then stir in the dill and parsley, lemon rind and juice. Season.

2 Divide the mixture into eight portions and shape each into a ball, then flatten into a thick disc. Dip the fish cakes first in flour, then in egg and finally in breadcrumbs, making sure they are evenly coated.

3 Heat the oil in a frying pan until very hot. Fry the fishcakes in batches until golden brown and crisp all over. As each batch is ready, drain on kitchen paper and keep hot.

4 Warm some plates and then place two fishcakes on to each warmed plate, one slightly on top of the other. Garnish with rocket leaves and chives, and serve with lemon wedges.

Cook's Tips
Almost any fresh white or hot-smoked fish is suitable; smoked cod and haddock are particularly good. A mixture of smoked and unsmoked fish also works well.

Salmon with Peppercorns Energy 526kcal/2180kJ; Protein 36.3g; Carbohydrate 2.9g, of which sugars 2.3g; Fat 40g, of which saturates 13.5g; Cholesterol 127mg; Calcium 63mg; Fibre 0.4g; Sodium 110mg.
Salmon Fishcakes Energy 586kcal/2453kJ; Protein 29.8g; Carbohydrate 49.9g, of which sugars 3.2g; Fat 31g, of which saturates 7.2g; Cholesterol 117mg; Calcium 79mg; Fibre 1.3g; Sodium 266mg.

Baked Salmon with Green Sauce

When buying a whole salmon, there are several points to consider – the skin should be bright and shiny, the eyes should be bright and the tail should look fresh and moist. Baking the salmon in foil produces a moist result, rather like poaching, but with the ease of baking. Garnish the fish with thin slices of cucumber and dill to conceal any flesh that may look ragged after skinning, and serve with lemon wedges.

Serves 6–8
2–3kg/4½–6¾lb salmon, cleaned with head and tail left on
3–5 spring onions (scallions), thinly sliced
1 lemon, thinly sliced
600ml/1 pint/2½ cups watercress sauce or herb mayonnaise

1 Preheat the oven to 180°C/350°F/Gas 4. Rinse the salmon and lay it on a large piece of foil. Stuff the fish with the sliced spring onions and layer the lemon slices inside and around the fish, then sprinkle with plenty of salt and ground black pepper.

2 Loosely fold the foil around the fish and fold the edges over to seal. Bake for about 1 hour.

3 Remove the fish from the oven and leave to stand, still wrapped in the foil, for about 15 minutes, then unwrap the parcel and leave the fish to cool.

4 When the fish is cool, carefully lift it on to a large plate, retaining the lemon slices. Cover the fish tightly with clear film (plastic wrap) and chill for several hours.

5 Before serving, discard the lemon slices from around the fish. Using a blunt knife to lift up the edge of the skin, carefully peel the skin away from the flesh, avoiding tearing the flesh, and pull out any fins at the same time.

6 Chill the watercress sauce or herb mayonnaise before serving. Transfer the fish to a serving platter and serve the sauce separately.

Salmon with Stilton

A rich blue Stilton and herb butter makes a flavoursome sauce for salmon steaks baked in wine. Serve this totally mouthwatering mélange with new potatoes, stir-fried red and yellow peppers and mangetouts.

Serves 4
115g/4oz Stilton cheese
25g/1oz/2 tbsp butter, softened
15ml/1 tbsp chopped fresh chives, plus extra, to garnish
15ml/1 tbsp chopped fresh thyme leaves
1 garlic clove, crushed
30ml/2 tbsp olive oil
4 salmon steaks
60ml/4 tbsp dry white wine
salt and ground black pepper
new potatoes and stir-fried red and yellow (bell) peppers and mangetouts (snow peas), to serve

1 Crumble the Stilton and place it in a food processor with the softened butter. Process until smooth. Scrape the Stilton butter into a small bowl.

2 Stir in the 15ml/1 tbsp chives, with the thyme and garlic. Season to taste. Stilton is salty, so you will probably only need to add pepper. Preheat the oven to 180°C/350°F/Gas 4.

3 Place the butter on a piece of foil and shape into an oblong. Wrap this in the foil and seal tightly. Chill the butter by placing it in the refrigerator until it is firm.

4 Brush a sheet of foil, large enough to enclose all the steaks, with olive oil. Support the foil on a baking sheet. Place the steaks on the foil, drizzle the wine over, season and seal the foil tightly. Bake for 20–30 minutes or until cooked through.

5 Unwrap the chilled butter and cut it into four equal portions. Remove the salmon from the oven, carefully open the package and use a fish slice (metal spatula) to transfer each steak to a warmed serving plate.

6 Top each salmon steak with a portion of butter and garnish with the extra chives. Serve immediately with new potatoes and stir-fried red and yellow peppers and mangetouts.

Baked Salmon Energy 783kcal/3242kJ; Protein 38.7g; Carbohydrate 1g, of which sugars 0.9g; Fat 69.3g, of which saturates 21.3g; Cholesterol 173mg; Calcium 102mg; Fibre 0.5g; Sodium 418mg.
Salmon with Stilton Energy 604kcal/2508kJ; Protein 47g; Carbohydrate 1g, of which sugars 0g; Fat 45g, of which saturates 15g; Cholesterol 141mg; Calcium 148mg; Fibre 0g; Sodium 355mg.

Salmon with Whisky and Cream

This dish combines two of the finest flavours of Scotland – salmon and whisky. It takes very little time to make, so cook it at the last moment. Serve quite plainly.

Serves 4

4 thin pieces of salmon fillet, about 175g/6oz each

5ml/1 tsp chopped fresh thyme leaves
50g/2oz/¼ cup butter
75ml/5 tbsp whisky
150ml/¼ pint/⅔ cup double (heavy) cream
juice of ½ lemon (optional)
salt and ground black pepper
fresh dill sprigs, to garnish

1 Season the salmon with salt, pepper and thyme. Melt half the butter in a frying pan large enough to hold two pieces of salmon side by side.

2 When the butter is foaming, fry the first two pieces of salmon for 2–3 minutes on each side, until they are golden on the outside and just cooked through.

3 Pour in 30ml/2 tbsp of the whisky and ignite it. When the flames have died down, carefully transfer the salmon to a plate and keep it hot. Heat the remaining butter and cook the second two pieces of salmon in the same way. Keep them hot.

4 Pour the cream into the pan and bring to the boil, stirring constantly and scraping up the cooking juices from the base of the pan. Allow to bubble until reduced and slightly thickened. Season and add the last of the whisky and a squeeze of lemon.

5 Place the salmon pieces on individual warmed plates, pour the sauce over and garnish with dill. New potatoes and crisp green beans are good with this dish.

Variation
The combination of seafood and whisky also works well with prawns, just substitute the salmon for prawns.

Salmon with Lemon & Tofu Sauce

The elegant simplicity of this dish makes it an ideal choice for a dinner party. Moreover, it is very quick and easy to prepare while looking and tasting wonderful.

Serves 2

2 salmon steaks or fillets, each weighing about 130–150g/4½–5oz
5cm/2in piece fresh root ginger, cut into thin sticks
2 garlic cloves, finely chopped

1 small red chilli, seeded and finely chopped
bunch of fresh dill, parsley or coriander (cilantro), tough stems removed
sea salt and ground black pepper
15ml/1 tbsp sesame seeds, toasted, to garnish

For the sauce
175g/6oz silken tofu
grated rind and juice of 1 lemon
50ml/3½ tbsp water

1 Line a bamboo steaming basket or metal steaming tray with baking parchment, then arrange the salmon steaks or fillets on top.

2 Pile the ginger, garlic and chilli, and half of the dill, parsley or coriander on top of the fish and season with salt and pepper, then cover and steam for 5–10 minutes, or until the fish is opaque and just cooked through.

3 Meanwhile, make the sauce by blending all the ingredients and the remaining herbs in a blender or food processor until smooth. Transfer to a small pan and gently warm through, stirring frequently.

4 Serve the fish with the sauce spooned over the top and garnished with the toasted sesame seeds.

Cook's Tip
Steaming is a wonderful way of cooking fish, ensuring that the maximum flavour is retained. If you like, the water beneath the steamer can be scented by the addition of some lemon grass or a strip of pared lemon rind.

Salmon with Lemon Energy 387kcal/1612kJ; Protein 39.5g; Carbohydrate 1.4g, of which sugars 0.9g; Fat 24.9g, of which saturates 3.9g; Cholesterol 75mg; Calcium 578mg; Fibre 1.9g; Sodium 81mg
Salmon with Whisky Energy 637kcal/2637kJ; Protein 36g; Carbohydrate 1g, of which sugars 1g; Fat 50g, of which saturates 22g; Cholesterol 166mg; Calcium 61mg; Fibre 0g; Sodium 163mg.

Rainbow Trout in Lemon and Mustard Marinade

In this recipe, whole trout are marinated in a mixture of mustard oil, chilli, lemon juice and rind. They are then baked and served with a spicy hot seasoning poured over the top. This dish is sumptuous served with vegetable side dishes such as potato in mustard oil.

Serves 4

4 rainbow trout, about 250g/9oz each, scaled and gutted

For the marinade

4 tbsp mustard oil
1 tsp salt or to taste
1 tsp fennel seeds
1/2 tsp crushed dried chilli
grated rind and juice of 1 lemon
1/2 tsp ground turmeric

For the sauce

2 tbsp mustard oil
1/2 tsp mustard seeds
1 medium onion, finely chopped
1/2 tsp crushed dried chilli
3 tbsp chopped fresh coriander
(cilantro) leaves

1 Lay the fish on a flat surface and make three diagonal slits on each side. Put them in a shallow dish. Mix the marinade ingredients together and pour over the fish. Gently rub in the marinade, working it well into the slits. Set aside for 1 hour.

2 Preheat the oven to 180°C/350°F/Gas Mark 4. Line a roasting pan with foil and brush it generously with oil. Lay the fish in the pan and cook in the centre of the oven for 20 minutes.

3 For the sauce, heat the oil over a medium heat. When it is smoking, remove the pan from the heat and add the mustard seeds, then the onion. Fry the onion until translucent.

4 Add the crushed chilli and cook for 1 minute. Pour in 120ml/4fl oz/1/2 cup warm water and cook it for 2–3 minutes. Transfer the fish to a serving dish.

5 Add the fish juices to the onion sauce, then stir in the chopped coriander and cook for 1 minute. Spoon the sauce over the fish and serve with plain basmati rice.

Hot Smoked Salmon

This is a fantastic way of smoking salmon on a barbecue in no time at all. The mojo makes a mildly spicy companion.

Serves 6

6 salmon fillets, each about 175g/6oz, with skin
15ml/1 tbsp sunflower oil
salt and ground black pepper
2 handfuls hickory wood chips, soaked in cold water for as much time as you have available, preferably for about 30 minutes

For the mojo

1 ripe mango, diced
4 drained canned pineapple slices, diced
1 small red onion, finely chopped
1 fresh long mild red chilli, seeded and finely chopped
15ml/1 tbsp good-quality sweet chilli sauce
grated rind and juice of 1 lime
leaves from 1 small lemon basil plant or 45ml/3 tbsp fresh coriander (cilantro) leaves, shredded or chopped

1 First, make the mojo by putting the mango and diced pineapple in a bowl. Add the chopped onion, and seeded and chopped chilli, and stir well to mix. Add the chilli sauce, lime rind and juice, and the herb leaves. Stir to mix well. Cover tightly with clear film (plastic wrap) and leave in a cool place until needed.

2 Rinse the salmon fillets and pat dry, then brush each with a little oil. Place the fillets skin side down on a lightly oiled grill (broiler) rack over medium-hot coals. Cover the barbecue with a lid or tented heavy-duty foil and cook the fish for 3–5 minutes.

3 Drain the hickory chips into a colander and sprinkle about a third of them as evenly as possible over the coals. Carefully drop them through the slats in the grill racks, taking care not to scatter the ash as you do so.

4 Replace the barbecue cover and continue cooking for a further 8 minutes, adding a small handful of hickory chips twice more during this time. Serve the salmon hot or cold, with the mango and pineapple mojo.

Hot Smoked Salmon Energy 364kcal/1519kJ; Protein 35.9g; Carbohydrate 7.8g, of which sugars 7.4g; Fat 21.2g, of which saturates 3.6g; Cholesterol 88mg; Calcium 58mg; Fibre 1.3g; Sodium 82mg.
Trout Energy 368.8kcal/1542kJ; Protein 40.7g; Carbohydrate 9.1g, of which sugars 5.9g; Fat 19.2g, of which saturates 3g; Cholesterol 160mg; Calcium 114.5mg; Fibre 2g; Sodium 153mg.

Baked Trout with a Gremolata Crust

A gremolata crust is a delicious combination of breadcrumbs with finely chopped parsley, lemon rind and garlic. It is traditionally sprinkled over the classic veal dish, osso bucco, but is equally good with fish.

Serves 4
1 small aubergine
  (eggplant), cubed
1 red (bell) pepper,
  finely diced
1 yellow (bell) pepper,
  finely diced
1 small red onion,
  finely chopped
30ml/2 tbsp olive oil
350g/12oz trout fillets
juice of 1 lime
salt and ground
  black pepper
chunks of bread, to serve

For the gremolata crust
grated rind of 1 lemon
grated rind of 1 lime
25g/1oz/1/2 cup fresh
  breadcrumbs
30ml/2 tbsp chopped fresh flat
  leaf parsley
1 garlic clove, finely chopped

1 Preheat the oven to 200°C/400°F/Gas 6. Place the aubergine, peppers and onion in a roasting pan. Add the oil and stir to coat all the vegetables. Sprinkle with plenty of salt and ground black pepper. Cook for 40 minutes or until the edges of the vegetables have begun to char.

2 Make the gremolata by mixing the lemon and lime rind with the breadcrumbs, chopped parsley and chopped garlic. Add plenty of salt and ground black pepper.

3 Place the trout fillets on top of the vegetables in the roasting pan and cover the surface of the fish with the breadcrumb mixture. Return to the oven for a further 15 minutes or until the fish is fully cooked and the gremolata topping is golden and crunchy.

4 Divide the fish and vegetables among four individual warmed serving plates and sprinkle the lime juice over to taste. Serve with chunks of bread to soak up all the juices.

Trout Burgers

These home-made fish burgers really are a treat. They provide the ideal way of persuading children who claim they don't like fish to try it. Cook chilled burgers on the barbecue, if you prefer, on a lightly oiled grill rack.

Makes 8
350g/12oz trout fillet, skinned
150ml/1/4 pint/2/3 cup milk
150ml/1/4 pint/2/3 cup
  hot fish stock
4 spring onions (scallions),
  thinly sliced
350g/12oz cooked
  potatoes, peeled
5ml/1 tsp tartare sauce
1 egg, beaten
50g/2oz/1 cup fresh white
  breadcrumbs
60ml/4 tbsp semolina
salt and ground white pepper
vegetable oil, for shallow frying

To serve
120ml/4fl oz/1/2 cup
  mayonnaise
45ml/3 tbsp drained canned
  whole kernel corn
1 red (bell) pepper, seeded
  and finely diced
8 burger buns
4 ripe tomatoes, sliced
salad leaves

1 Place the trout in a frying pan with the milk, stock and spring onions. Simmer for 5 minutes or until the fish is cooked. Lift it out of the pan and set it aside. Strain the stock through a sieve into a bowl, reserving the spring onions.

2 Mash the potatoes roughly and stir in the tartare sauce, egg and breadcrumbs. Flake the trout and add the reserved spring onions. Fold into the potato mixture and season.

3 Divide the potato mixture into eight and shape into burgers, using your hands. Coat thoroughly in the semolina and pat them into shape. Arrange on a plate and place in the refrigerator for 1 hour, so that they firm up.

4 In a bowl, mix the mayonnaise for serving with the corn kernels and diced red pepper. To serve, split open the buns and spread a little of the mayonnaise over each half. Fill with a few salad leaves, a couple of tomato slices and a fish burger. Serve immediately.

Baked Trout Energy 237kcal/992kJ; Protein 20g; Carbohydrate 12g, of which sugars 7g; Fat 13g, of which saturates 2g; Cholesterol 59mg; Calcium 43mg; Fibre 3g; Sodium 92mg.
Trout Burgers Energy 461kcal/1936kJ; Protein 18g; Carbohydrate 47g, of which sugars 6g; Fat 23g, of which saturates 4g; Cholesterol 72mg; Calcium 120mg; Fibre 4g; Sodium 484mg.

Hot Trout with Red Vegetables

This Mediterranean-style sandwich is so easy to prepare and makes a tasty weekend lunch. Choose your favourite bread, but make sure it is really fresh.

Serves 4
2 red (bell) peppers
8 cherry tomatoes
60ml/4 tbsp extra virgin olive oil
30ml/2 tbsp lemon juice
4 thin trout fillets, each about 115g/4oz, skinned
2 small ciabatta loaves
15ml/1 tbsp red pesto
30ml/2 tbsp mayonnaise
115g/4oz rocket (arugula)
salt and ground black pepper

1 Preheat the oven to 180°C/350°F/Gas 4. Place the peppers and tomatoes in a roasting pan and drizzle half the olive oil over. Bake for 25–30 minutes or until the pepper skins are blackened. Set aside to cool.

2 In a small bowl or jug (pitcher), whisk the remaining oil with the lemon juice and a little salt and freshly ground black pepper. Place the trout in a shallow, non-metallic dish and pour over the oil and lemon juice. Turn the fish to coat.

3 Peel the skin off the cooked peppers and discard the core and seeds. Cut the pepper flesh into strips. Slice each ciabatta loaf in half vertically, then carefully cut each half in half horizontally.

4 Mix the pesto and mayonnaise together and spread over the bread. Divide the rocket among four halves of the bread and top with the trout fillet, pepper strips and roasted tomatoes. Place the remaining bread on top and serve.

Cook's Tip
• You can use any bread you like but make sure you slice the bread thickly.
• Small loaves of olive-oil bread, such as ciabatta and focaccia, are ideal for these sandwiches. Try the sun-dried tomato and black olive versions, too.

Pan-fried Citrus Trout with Basil

The clean taste of oranges and lemons and the aromatic scent of basil combine beautifully in this recipe to create a light and tangy sauce for trout fillets.

Serves 4
4 trout fillets, each about 200g/7oz
2 lemons
3 oranges
105ml/7 tbsp olive oil
45ml/3 tbsp plain (all-purpose) flour
25g/1oz/2 tbsp butter
5ml/1 tsp soft light brown sugar
15g/½ oz/½ cup fresh basil leaves
salt and ground black pepper

1 Arrange the trout fillets in the base of a non-metallic shallow dish. Grate the rind from one lemon and two oranges, then squeeze these fruits and pour the combined juices into a jug (pitcher). Slice the remaining fruits and reserve to use as a garnish.

2 Add 75ml/5 tbsp of the oil to the citrus juices. Beat with a fork and pour over the fish. Cover and leave to marinate in the refrigerator for at least 2 hours.

3 Preheat the oven to 150°C/300°F/Gas 2. Using a fish slice or metal spatula, carefully remove the trout from the marinade. Season the fish and coat each in flour. Heat the remaining oil in a frying pan and add the fish. Fry for 2–3 minutes on each side until cooked, then transfer to a plate and keep hot in the oven.

4 Add the butter and the marinade to the pan and heat gently, stirring until the butter has melted. Season with salt and pepper, then stir in the sugar. Continue cooking gently for 4–5 minutes until the sauce has thickened slightly. Finely shred half the basil leaves and add them to the pan. Pour the sauce over the fish and garnish with the remaining basil and the orange and lemon slices.

Cook's Tip
Basil leaves bruise easily, so they should always be shredded by hand or used whole rather than cut with a knife.

Hot Trout Energy 487kcal/2033kJ; Protein 29g; Carbohydrate 26g, of which sugars 26g; Fat 30g, of which saturates 5g; Cholesterol 84mg; Calcium 106mg; Fibre 2g; Sodium 313mg.
Pan-fried Trout Energy 266kcal/1119kJ; Protein 40.5g; Carbohydrate 7.9g, of which sugars 7.7g; Fat 8.3g, of which saturates 0.2g; Cholesterol 0mg; Calcium 140mg; Fibre 1.7g; Sodium 177mg.

Trout with Tamarind and Chilli Sauce

Sometimes trout can taste rather bland, but this spicy sauce really gives it a zing. If you like your food very spicy, add an extra chilli.

Serves 4

4 trout, cleaned
6 spring onions (scallions), sliced
60ml/4 tbsp soy sauce
15ml/1 tbsp vegetable oil
30ml/2 tbsp chopped fresh
 coriander (cilantro) and strips
 of fresh red chilli, to garnish

For the sauce

50g/2oz tamarind pulp
105ml/7 tbsp boiling water
2 shallots, coarsely chopped
1 fresh red chilli, seeded
 and chopped
1cm/½in piece fresh root ginger,
 peeled and chopped
5ml/1 tsp soft light brown sugar
45ml/3 tbsp Thai fish sauce

1 Slash the trout diagonally four or five times on each side. Place them in a shallow dish that is large enough to hold them all in a single layer.

2 Fill the cavity of each trout with spring onions and douse each fish with soy sauce. Carefully turn the fish over to coat both sides with the sauce. Sprinkle any remaining spring onions over the top.

3 To make the sauce, put the tamarind pulp in a small bowl and pour over the boiling water. Mash well with a fork until softened and combined.

4 Transfer the tamarind mixture to a food processor or blender, and add the shallots, fresh chilli, ginger, sugar and fish sauce. Process to a coarse pulp. Scrape into a bowl.

5 Heat the oil in a large frying pan or wok and cook the trout, one at a time if necessary, for about 5 minutes on each side, until the skin is crisp and browned and the flesh cooked.

6 Transfer the trout to warmed serving plates and spoon over some of the sauce. Sprinkle with the coriander and chilli and serve with the remaining sauce.

Cheese-topped Trout

Succulent strips of filleted trout are topped with a mixture of Parmesan, pine nuts, herbs and breadcrumbs before being drizzled with lemon butter and grilled.

Serves 4

50g/2oz/1 cup fresh white
 breadcrumbs
50g/2oz Parmesan cheese, grated
25g/1oz/⅓ cup pine
 nuts, chopped

15ml/1 tbsp chopped fresh parsley
15ml/1 tbsp chopped fresh
 coriander (cilantro)
30ml/2 tbsp olive oil
4 thick trout fillets, about
 225g/8oz each
40g/1½oz/3 tbsp butter
juice of 1 lemon
salt and ground black pepper
lemon slices, to garnish
steamed baby asparagus and
 carrots, to serve

1 In a mixing bowl, combine the breadcrumbs, Parmesan cheese, pine nuts, parsley and coriander. Add the oil.

2 Cut each trout fillet into two strips. Firmly press the breadcrumb mixture on to the top of each strip of trout.

3 Preheat the grill (broiler) to high. Grease the grill (broiling) pan with 15g/½oz of the butter. Melt the remaining butter in a small pan and stir in the lemon juice.

4 Place the breadcrumb-topped fillets on the greased grill pan and pour the lemon butter over.

5 Grill (broil) the trout for 10 minutes or until the fillets are just cooked. Place two trout strips on each plate, garnish with lemon slices and serve with steamed asparagus and carrots.

> **Variations**
> • If you don't have any fresh coriander (cilantro), increase the amount of fresh parsley.
> • Dried peaches or apricots could be chopped finely and added to the stuffing, with perhaps a little finely grated lemon rind to enhance the fruity flavour.

Trout with Tamarind Energy 82kcal/346kJ; Protein 12g; Carbohydrate 2g, of which sugars 1.6g; Fat 3g, of which saturates 0.6g; Cholesterol 48mg; Calcium 24mg; Fibre 0.3g; Sodium 245mg.
Cheese-topped Trout Energy 524kcal/2185kJ; Protein 51.3g; Carbohydrate 10.3g, of which sugars 0.9g; Fat 31.1g, of which saturates 8.9g; Cholesterol 34mg; Calcium 214mg; Fibre 1g; Sodium 422mg.

Stuffed Trout with Tarragon Sauce

Tarragon and trout make a marvellous team. Here trout are filled with a herby stuffing before being baked in wine and served with a creamy tarragon sauce.

Serves 4

90ml/6 tbsp fresh white
  breadcrumbs
30ml/2 tbsp chopped
  fresh tarragon
1 egg, beaten

4 whole trout, each about
  200g/7oz, cleaned and boned
1 small onion, sliced
150ml/¼ pint/⅔ cup dry
  white wine
8 fresh tarragon sprigs
25g/1oz/2 tbsp butter
15ml/1 tbsp plain
  (all-purpose) flour
150ml/¼ pint/⅔ cup single
  (light) cream
salt and ground black pepper
a steamed green vegetable and
  lime wedges, to serve

1 Preheat the oven to 190°C/375°F/Gas 5. Mix the breadcrumbs with half the tarragon in a bowl. Season, then bind the mixture with the beaten egg. Spread a layer of tarragon stuffing inside the cavity of each trout, pressing the mixture down firmly. Season the trout well.

2 Place the trout in a single layer in a shallow baking dish. Add the onion slices and wine to the dish and top each fish with a sprig of tarragon. Cover the dish with foil. Bake for 20–25 minutes. Remove the trout from the dish, reserving the cooking liquid. Remove the heads, tails and skin, then place the fish in a hot ovenproof dish. Cover with foil and keep warm in the oven.

3 Strain the cooking liquid into a measuring jug (cup) and make up with water to 150ml/¼ pint/⅔ cup of liquid. Melt the butter in a pan, stir in the flour and cook, stirring constantly, for 1–2 minutes. Gradually add the cooking liquid, stirring constantly. Add the cream in the same way and bring to the boil. Continue to stir as the mixture thickens to a smooth sauce. Season and add the remaining tarragon.

4 Blanch the remaining tarragon sprigs in boiling water. Drain. Place the trout on plates, pour over the sauce and garnish with the tarragon sprigs. Serve with a steamed green vegetable.

Trout with Almonds

Fresh trout is best cooked simply, to bring out its sweet flavour, and this classic method of preparation remains one of the best.

Serves 4

4 whole trout, head and tail
  intact, cleaned
8 lemon slices
a handful of finely chopped flat
  leaf parsley

30ml/2 tbsp vegetable oil
100ml/3½fl oz/scant ½ cup dry
  white wine
115g/4oz/½ cup unsalted
  (sweet) butter
75g/3oz/1 cup flaked (sliced)
  almonds, lightly toasted
30ml/2 tbsp finely chopped fresh
  flat leaf parsley
juice of 1 small lemon
salt and ground black pepper
lemon wedges, to garnish

1 Rinse the trout under running water. Pat dry with kitchen paper. With scissors, cut away the fins. Turn each fish on its back and ease open the cavity. Season inside and out and place two lemon slices and a quarter of the parsley in each cavity. Close with cocktail sticks (toothpicks).

2 Heat two 30cm/12in non-stick pans or oval fish pans over medium-high heat and add 15ml/1 tbsp oil to each. Place two trout, skin side down, in each pan and sauté for 4 minutes, then turn over and cook for 3 minutes on the other side. As soon as the flesh becomes opaque and flakes when tested with the tip of a sharp knife, transfer to individual serving plates, using a large spatula or fish slice. Cover with foil.

3 Using one pan over medium high heat, pour in the wine and heat for 3 minutes, scraping the pan to incorporate the sediment.

4 Add the butter and a pinch of salt to the mixture. When it begins to brown, add half the almonds. Shake the pan over the heat for 5 minutes, without letting the butter burn. When the almonds are golden, add the parsley and lemon juice.

5 Spoon the foaming butter and almonds over the warm fish and serve with extra lemon wedges and the remaining toasted almonds sprinkled over the top.

Stuffed Trout Energy 462kcal/933kJ; Protein 44g; Carbohydrate 11g, of which sugars 2g; Fat 25g, of which saturates 11g; Cholesterol 226mg; Calcium 108mg; Fibre 1g; Sodium 221mg.
Trout with Almonds Energy 475kcal/1978kJ; Protein 39.2g; Carbohydrate 7.6g, of which sugars 0.8g; Fat 32.2g, of which saturates 12.4g; Cholesterol 187mg; Calcium 101mg; Fibre 1.2g; Sodium 249mg.

Blue Trout

The blue sheen on the trout in this recipe is a German speciality and is easily achieved by first scalding the fish and then fanning to cool it. Traditionally, the fish would be left to cool by the kitchen window in a breeze or draught.

Serves 4

4 trout, about 175g/6oz each

5ml/1 tsp salt
600ml/1 pint/2½ cups white wine vinegar
1 onion, sliced
2 bay leaves
6 whole black peppercorns
bay leaves and lemon slices, to garnish
115g/4oz/½ cup melted butter, creamed horseradish sauce and green beans, to serve

1 Preheat the oven to 180°C/350°F/Gas 4. Rub both sides of the trout with salt and place in a non-aluminium roasting tin or fish kettle.

2 Bring the vinegar to the boil and slowly pour over the trout. Fan the fish as it cools or leave to stand in a draught for 5 minutes.

3 Bring the vinegar back to the boil, then add the sliced onion, bay leaves and peppercorns.

4 Cover the tin with foil and cook in the oven for 30 minutes, or until the fish is cooked through.

5 Transfer the fish to warmed serving dishes, garnish with bay leaves and lemon slices, and serve with melted butter, creamed horseradish sauce and green beans.

Cook's Tips
• Sprinkling boiling vinegar over the fish turns the slime on its skin a steely blue colour, hence the name "au bleu".
• The cooked fish can be served either hot or cold.
• If necessary, the fish should be scaled before being served. Using a fish scaler will make this task straightforward.

FRIED AND BAKED

Bacon-wrapped Trout with Oatmeal

This stuffing is based on a Scottish speciality, called skirlie, which is a mixture of oatmeal and onion.

Serves 4
10 dry-cured streaky bacon rashers (fatty bacon slices)
40g/1½oz/3 tbsp butter
1 onion, finely chopped
115g/4oz/1 cup oatmeal
30ml/2 tbsp chopped fresh parsley
30ml/2 tbsp chopped fresh chives
4 trout, each about 350g/12oz, cleaned and boned

juice of ½ lemon
salt and ground black pepper
watercress, cherry tomatoes and lemon wedges, to serve

For the herb mayonnaise
6 watercress sprigs
15ml/1 tbsp chopped fresh chives
30ml/2 tbsp roughly chopped fresh parsley
90ml/6 tbsp lemon mayonnaise
30ml/2 tbsp crème fraîche
2.5–5ml/½–1 tsp tarragon mustard

1 Preheat the oven to 190°C/375°F/Gas 5. Chop two of the bacon rashers. Melt 25g/1oz/2 tbsp of the butter in a large frying pan and cook the chopped bacon briefly. Add the finely chopped onion and fry gently for 5–8 minutes, until softened. Add the oatmeal and cook until it darkens and absorbs the fat, but do not allow it to overbrown. Stir in the parsley and chives, with salt and pepper to taste. Cool.

2 Wash and dry the trout, then stuff with the oatmeal mixture. Wrap each fish in two bacon rashers and place in an ovenproof dish. Dot with the remaining butter and sprinkle with the lemon juice. Bake for 20–25 minutes, until the bacon browns and crisps a little.

3 Meanwhile, make the mayonnaise. Place the watercress, chives and parsley in a sieve and pour boiling water over them. Drain, rinse under cold water, and drain well on kitchen paper.

4 Purée the herbs in a mortar with a pestle. Stir the puréed herbs into the lemon mayonnaise with crème fraîche. Add tarragon mustard to taste and mix. When cooked, transfer the trout to serving plates. Serve with watercress, cherry tomatoes and lemon wedges, accompanied by the herb mayonnaise.

Blue Trout Energy 479kcal/1990kJ; Protein 36g; Carbohydrate 4g, of which sugars 3g; Fat 33g, of which saturates 17g; Cholesterol 179mg; Calcium 51mg; Fibre 1g; Sodium 753mg.
Trout with Oatmeal Energy 997kcal/4164kJ; Protein 85g; Carbohydrate 25g, of which sugars 3g; Fat 63g, of which saturates 19g; Cholesterol 326mg; Calcium 118 mg; Fibre 3g; Sodium 1190mg.

Tuna Steaks with Red Onion Salsa

Red onions are ideal for this salsa, not only for their mild and sweet flavour, but also because they look so appetizing. Salad, rice or bread and a bowl of thick yogurt flavoured with chopped fresh herbs are good accompaniments.

Serves 4

4 tuna loin steaks, about
    175–200g/6–7oz each
5ml/1 tsp cumin seeds, toasted
    and crushed
pinch of dried red chilli flakes
grated rind and juice of 1 lime
30–60ml/2–4 tbsp extra virgin
    olive oil
salt and ground black pepper

lime wedges and fresh coriander
    sprigs, to garnish

For the salsa

1 small red onion, finely chopped
200g/7oz red or yellow cherry
    tomatoes, roughly chopped
1 avocado, peeled, stoned (pitted)
    and chopped
2 kiwi fruit, peeled and chopped
1 fresh red chilli, seeded and
    finely chopped
15g/½oz fresh coriander,
    chopped
6 fresh mint sprigs, leaves
    only, chopped
5–10ml/1–2 tsp Thai fish sauce
about 5ml/1 tsp muscovado
    (molasses) sugar

1 Wash the tuna steaks and pat dry. Sprinkle with half the cumin, the dried chilli, salt, pepper and half the lime rind. Rub in 30ml/2 tbsp of the oil and set aside in a glass or china dish for about 30 minutes.

2 Meanwhile, make the salsa. Mix the onion, tomatoes, avocado, kiwi fruit, chilli, coriander and mint. Add the remaining cumin, the rest of the lime rind and half the lime juice. Add the fish sauce and sugar to taste. Leave for 15–20 minutes, then add more Thai fish sauce, lime juice and olive oil if required.

3 Heat a ridged, cast iron grill (griddle) pan. Cook the tuna, allowing about 2 minutes on each side for rare tuna or a little longer for a medium result.

4 Serve the tuna steaks garnished with lime wedges and coriander sprigs. Serve the salsa separately or spoon on to the plates with the tuna.

Calabrian Tuna Steaks

The flavours in this recipe work very well together, making the most of the taste of fresh tuna and creating a satisfying dish, with just enough chilli to add a hint of fire.

Serves 4

4 even-sized fresh tuna steaks,
    total weight about 800g/1¾lb
60ml/4 tbsp olive oil
30ml/2 tbsp plain
    (all-purpose) flour

60ml/4 tbsp dry white wine
50g/2oz pancetta, chopped
1 large garlic clove, chopped
1 onion, chopped
30ml/2 tbsp chopped
    fresh parsley
4 anchovy fillets in oil, drained
    and boned
400g/14oz can chopped
    tomatoes, drained
½ dried red chilli, chopped
sea salt and ground black pepper

1 Rinse the tuna steaks in cold water, drain and pat dry. Season the steaks thoroughly on both sides with salt and pepper.

2 Heat half the olive oil in a frying pan large enough to hold the tuna steaks in a single layer. Coat the steaks lightly in flour, add them to the pan and fry them over a medium heat for 3 minutes on each side. Sprinkle with the wine and allow the alcohol to boil off for 1 minute. Using a spatula, lift out the fish and drain on kitchen paper. Place on a plate and spoon over the pan juices.

3 Heat the remaining oil in the pan. Add the pancetta, garlic, onion and half the parsley. Fry gently for 5 minutes, stirring.

4 Add the anchovy fillets and mash them into the hot mixture with a fork. After 1 minute, stir in the tomatoes. Add the chilli and simmer over very low heat for 15 minutes.

5 Slide the tuna steaks back into the pan and spoon some of the tomato mixture over them. Heat through thoroughly for about 8 minutes, turning them over gently once.

6 Serve the tuna topped with the sauce and sprinkled with the remaining parsley.

Tuna Steaks Energy 389kcal/1628kJ; Protein 43.2g; Carbohydrate 7.9g, of which sugars 6.8g; Fat 20.7g, of which saturates 4.4g; Cholesterol 49mg; Calcium 55mg; Fibre 2.5g; Sodium 180mg.
Calabrian Tuna Energy 472kcal/1976kJ; Protein 51.7g; Carbohydrate 10.2g, of which sugars 4.2g; Fat 24.2g, of which saturates 5.1g; Cholesterol 64mg; Calcium 64mg; Fibre 1.5g; Sodium 380mg.

Seared Tuna with Ginger and Chilli

Tuna steaks are wonderful seared and served slightly rare with a punchy sauce or salad. In this recipe the salad is served just warm as a bed for the tender tuna. Add a dab of harissa as a condiment to create a dish that will transport you to the warmth of the North African coastline. If you can't get tuna, try using salmon steaks instead.

Serves 4
30ml/2 tbsp olive oil
5ml/1 tsp harissa
5ml/1 tsp clear honey
4 x 200g/7oz tuna steaks
salt and ground black pepper
lemon wedges, to serve

For the salad
30ml/2 tbsp olive oil
a little butter
25g/1oz fresh root ginger, peeled
 and finely sliced
2 garlic cloves, finely sliced
2 green chillies, seeded and
 finely sliced
6 spring onions (scallions), cut into
 bitesize pieces
2 large handfuls of watercress
juice of ½ lemon

1 Mix the olive oil, harissa, honey and salt, and rub it over the tuna steaks.

2 Heat a frying pan, grease it with a little oil and sear the tuna steaks for about 2 minutes on each side. They should still be pink on the inside.

3 Keep the tuna warm while you quickly prepare the salad: heat the olive oil and butter in a heavy pan.

4 Add the ginger, garlic, chillies and spring onions, cook until the mixture begins to colour, then add the watercress. When the watercress begins to wilt, toss in the lemon juice and season well with salt and plenty of ground black pepper.

5 Tip the warm salad on to a serving dish or individual plates. Slice the tuna steaks and arrange on top of the salad.

6 Serve the tuna steaks immediately with lemon wedges for squeezing over.

Fish Kebabs

Any firm-fleshed fish, such as tuna, trout, salmon, monkfish or sea bass, can be used for kebabs, but the classic made with meaty chunks of swordfish is a firm favourite in restaurants. Usually served as a main course with a rocket and herb salad, it is a light and tasty dish.

serves 4
500g/1¼lb boneless swordfish
 loin or steaks, cut into
 bitesize chunks
1 lemon, halved lengthways
 and sliced
1 large tomato, halved, seeded
 and cut into bitesize pieces
2 hot green peppers (see below)
 or 1 green (bell) pepper,
 seeded and cut into
 bitesize pieces
a handful of bay leaves
lemon wedges, to serve

For the marinade
1 onion, grated
1–2 garlic cloves, crushed
juice of ½ lemon
30–45ml/2–3 tbsp olive oil
5–10ml/1–2 tsp tomato
 purée (paste)
salt and ground black pepper

1 Mix the marinade ingredients in a shallow bowl. Toss in the chunks of swordfish and set aside for about 30 minutes.

2 Thread the fish on to skewers, alternating with the lemon, tomato and peppers and the occasional bay leaf. If there is any marinade left, brush it over the kebabs.

3 Put a cast-iron griddle pan over a medium heat until very hot. Place the skewers on the pan and cook for 2–3 minutes on each side until the kebab ingredients are quite charred.

4 Serve the kebabs hot with lemon wedges for squeezing.

> **Cook's Tips**
> In Turkish hot green peppers are called 'çarliston biber'. They are light green, and shaped like Turkish slippers. Most are sweet, and mainly used raw in meze and salads, but some have a hint of heat and are good for cooked dishes like kebabs.

Seared Tuna Energy 428kcal/1788kJ; Protein 48g; Carbohydrate 2g, of which sugars 2g; Fat 25g, of which saturates 5g; Cholesterol 56mg; Calcium 58mg; Fibre 0g; Sodium 101mg.
Fish Kebabs Energy 225kcal/940kJ; Protein 23.9g; Carbohydrate 7.8g, of which sugars 7.2g; Fat 11.1g, of which saturates 2g; Cholesterol 51mg; Calcium 18mg; Fibre 1.9g; Sodium 177mg.

Calabrian Baked Swordfish

The perfect accompaniment for this delicious swordfish dish is a platter of grilled vegetables such as peppers, courgettes, carrots, red onion slices and aubergines.

Serves 4
4 thick swordfish steaks, about 175g/6oz each
225g/8oz/4 cups soft white breadcrumbs
150g/5oz Pecorino cheese, grated
45ml/3 tbsp finely chopped fresh flat leaf parsley
90ml/6 tbsp extra virgin olive oil
juice of 1 lemon
sea salt and ground black pepper

1 Rinse and dry the swordfish steaks. Preheat the oven to 180°C/350°F/Gas 4.

2 Put the breadcrumbs in a bowl and add the grated cheese and parsley. Season with salt and pepper to taste and mix well.

3 Use a little of the olive oil to grease a baking dish which is just large enough to hold the steaks snugly in one layer. Brush the steaks with oil on both sides.

4 Spread half the breadcrumb mixture over the base of the dish, and lay the swordfish steaks on top. Season the fish with salt and pepper.

5 Cover with the rest of the breadcrumb mixture, then drizzle with the remaining oil. Bake for 10 minutes, then take the dish out of the oven, pour the lemon juice evenly over the crumb topping and return to the oven for 10 minutes more. Serve.

Variations
• *Use tuna steaks instead of swordfish, adjusting the cooking times if necessary, depending upon the thickness of the fish.*
• *Flavour the breadcrumb topping by adding some chopped olives and rinsed and chopped capers.*

Griddled Swordfish with Roasted Tomatoes and Cinnamon

The sun-ripened tomatoes of Morocco are naturally full of flavour and sweetness, and when roasted with sugar and spices they simply melt in the mouth. As an accompaniment to chargrilled fish, they are sensational. These delectable tomatoes can also be stored in sealed containers in the refrigerator, ideal for impromptu barbecues. In this recipe, they add a delicious fruitiness that complements the meaty texture of the swordfish.

Serves 4
1kg/2¼lb large vine or plum tomatoes, peeled, halved and seeded
5–10ml/1–2 tsp ground cinnamon
pinch of saffron threads
15ml/1 tbsp orange flower water
60ml/4 tbsp olive oil
45–60ml/3–4 tbsp sugar
4 x 225g/8oz swordfish steaks
rind of ½ preserved lemon, finely chopped
small bunch of fresh coriander (cilantro), finely chopped
handful of blanched almonds
knob (pat) of butter
salt and ground black pepper

1 Preheat the oven to 110°C/225°F/Gas ¼. Place the tomatoes on a baking sheet. Sprinkle with the cinnamon, saffron and orange flower water. Trickle half the oil over, being sure to moisten every tomato half, and sprinkle with sugar.

2 Place the tray in the bottom of the oven and cook the tomatoes for about 3 hours, then turn the oven off and leave them to cool.

3 Brush the remaining olive oil over the swordfish steaks and season with salt and pepper. Lightly oil a pre-heated cast-iron griddle and cook the steaks for 3–4 minutes on each side. Sprinkle the chopped preserved lemon and coriander over the steaks towards the end of the cooking time.

4 In a separate pan, fry the almonds in the butter until golden and sprinkle them over the tomatoes. Then serve the steaks immediately with the tomatoes.

Swordfish Steaks with Mango and Avocado Salsa

Meaty swordfish steaks, marinated in a tangy mix of lime juice, coriander and chilli, are served here with a vibrant fruity salsa.

Serves 4

4 swordfish steaks, about
   150g/5oz each
lime wedges and shredded spring
   onions (scallions), to garnish

For the marinade
rind and juice of 2 limes
2 garlic cloves, crushed

1 red chilli, seeded and chopped
30ml/2 tbsp olive oil
30ml/2 tbsp chopped fresh
   coriander (cilantro)
salt and ground black pepper

For the salsa
1 mango
4 spring onions (scallions), sliced
1 red chilli, seeded and chopped
30ml/2 tbsp chopped fresh dill or
   coriander (cilantro)
30ml/2 tbsp lime juice
30ml/2 tbsp olive oil
1 ripe avocado

1 Place the swordfish steaks in a shallow non-metallic dish. Mix together the marinade ingredients and pour over the swordfish. Cover and leave to marinate in the refrigerator for 2 hours.

2 Soak a fish clay pot in cold water for 20 minutes, then drain. To prepare the salsa, peel the mango and slice the flesh off the stone (pit). Cut the flesh into rough dice. Add the spring onions, chilli, dill or coriander, lime juice and olive oil. Toss the ingredients together, cover and set aside to allow the flavours to blend.

3 Place the swordfish steaks in the clay pot and pour over the marinade. Cover and place in an unheated oven. Set the oven to 220°C/425°F/Gas 7 and bake for 15–20 minutes, or until the fish is cooked. The time will vary depending on the thickness of the steaks.

4 To complete the salsa, cut the avocado in half, remove the stone (pit), then dice the flesh. Stir it into the prepared salsa ingredients and mix. Serve the swordfish steaks with a mound of salsa, garnished with lime wedges and shredded spring onions.

Deep-fried and Marinated Small Fish

The influence of early Europeans, or Nanban, who first brought deep-frying to Japan a few hundred years ago, is still evident in this dish, known as Kozakana Nanban-zuke.

Serves 4
450g/1lb sprats (US small
   whitebait)
plain (all-purpose) flour, for
   dusting

1 small carrot
⅓ cucumber
2 spring onions (scallions)
4cm/1½in piece fresh root
   ginger, peeled
1 dried red chilli
75ml/5 tbsp rice vinegar
60ml/4 tbsp shoyu
15ml/1 tbsp mirin
30ml/2 tbsp sake
vegetable oil, for deep-frying

1 Wipe the sprats dry with kitchen paper, then put them in a small plastic bag with a handful of flour. Seal and shake vigorously to coat the fish.

2 Cut the carrot and cucumber into thin strips by hand or using a mandolin or food processor. Cut the spring onions into three, then slice into thin, lengthways strips. Slice the ginger into thin, lengthways strips and rinse in cold water. Drain. Seed and chop the chilli into thin rings.

3 In a mixing bowl, mix the rice vinegar, shoyu, mirin and sake together to make a marinade. Add the chilli and all the sliced vegetables. Stir well using a pair of chopsticks.

4 Pour plenty of oil into a deep pan and heat to 180°C/350°F. Deep-fry the fish five or six at a time until golden brown. Drain on layered kitchen paper, then plunge the hot fish into the marinade. Leave to marinate for at least an hour, stirring occasionally.

5 Serve the fish cold in a shallow bowl and put the marinated vegetables on top. This dish will keep for about a week in the refrigerator.

Swordfish Energy 311Kcal/1297kJ; Protein 29g; Carbohydrate 5.5g, of which sugars 5.3g; Fat 19.4g, of which saturates 3.3g; Cholesterol 69mg; Calcium 30mg; Fibre 1.3g; Sodium 212mg.
Small Fish Energy 307Kcal/1273kJ; Protein 17.4g; Carbohydrate 4.2g, of which sugars 4g; Fat 23.7g, of which saturates 3.6g; Cholesterol 83mg; Calcium 91mg; Fibre 0.2g; Sodium 961mg.

Roast Mackerel with Spicy Chermoula Paste

Chermoula is a marinade used in African cooking. There are many variations on the flavourings used, but it is usually based on a blend of coriander, lemon and garlic, and often includes saffron and paprika. It is popular with fish, but can also be used with poultry and meat.

Serves 4

4 whole mackerel, cleaned and gutted
30–45ml/2–3 tbsp chermoula paste
75ml/5 tbsp olive oil
2 red onions, sliced
salt and ground black pepper

1 Preheat the oven to 190°C/375°F/Gas 5. Place each fish on a large sheet of baking parchment. Using a sharp knife, slash into the flesh of each fish several times.

2 In a small bowl, mix the chermoula with the olive oil, and spread the paste over the skin of the mackerel, rubbing the mixture into the cuts.

3 Sprinkle the red onions over the mackerel, and season with salt and pepper. Scrunch the ends of the baking parchment together to seal. Place the four parcels on a baking tray.

4 Bake for 20 minutes, until the mackerel is cooked through. Serve the fish on warmed plates, still in their paper parcels, to be unwrapped at the table.

Cook's Tips

• Buy only very fresh mackerel: they should be firm with a bright eye and smell of the sea.
• Chermoula paste is now readily available in most large supermarkets. It can be mixed with oil and other ingredients and used as a marinade, or simply brushed on to fish and meat before cooking.

Mackerel in Lemon Samfaina

Samfaina is a sauce from the east coast of Spain and the Costa Brava. It shares the same ingredients as ratatouille and is rather like a chunky vegetable stew. This version is particularly lemony, to offset the richness of the mackerel.

Serves 4

2 large mackerel, filleted, or 4 fillets
plain (all-purpose) flour, for dusting

30ml/2 tbsp olive oil
lemon wedges, if serving cold

For the samfaina sauce

1 large aubergine (eggplant)
60ml/4 tbsp olive oil
1 large onion, chopped
2 garlic cloves, finely chopped
1 large courgette (zucchini), sliced
1 red and 1 green (bell) pepper, seeded and cut into squares
800g/1¾lb ripe tomatoes, roughly chopped
1 bay leaf
salt and ground black pepper

1 Make the sauce. Peel the aubergine, then cut the flesh into cubes, sprinkle with salt and leave in a colander for 30 minutes.

2 Heat half the oil in a flameproof casserole large enough to fit the fish. Fry the onion over a medium heat until it colours. Add the garlic, then the courgettes and peppers and stir-fry.

3 Add the tomatoes and bay leaf, partially cover and simmer over the lowest heat, letting the tomatoes just soften without losing their shape.

4 Rinse off the salt from the aubergine. Using three layers of kitchen paper, squeeze the cubes dry. Heat the remaining oil in a frying pan until smoking. Put in one handful of aubergine cubes, then the next, stirring with a wooden spoon and cooking over a high heat until the cubes are brown on all sides. Stir into the tomato sauce.

5 Cut each fillet into three, and dust the filleted side with flour. Heat the oil in a frying pan over a high heat and put the fish in, floured side down. Fry for 3 minutes until golden. Turn and cook for another 1 minute, then slip the fish into the sauce and simmer, covered, for 5 minutes. Adjust the seasonings then serve.

Roast Mackerel Energy 353kcal/1470kJ; Protein 19.9g; Carbohydrate 16.7g, of which sugars 9.1g; Fat 23.4g, of which saturates 5.9g; Cholesterol 63mg; Calcium 54mg; Fibre 0.7g; Sodium 90mg.
Mackerel with Lemon Energy 621kcal/2591kJ; Protein 34.3g; Carbohydrate 32.4g, of which sugars 29.4g; Fat 40.6g, of which saturates 7.6g; Cholesterol 66mg; Calcium 134mg; Fibre 19.4g; Sodium 111mg.

Grilled Mackerel with Gooseberry Relish

With a variety of health benefits, mackerel is a nutritious fish, and the tart gooseberries give you a serving of fruit, too.

Serves 4

4 whole mackerel

60ml/4 tbsp olive oil

For the sauce

250g/9oz gooseberries

25g/1oz/2 tbsp soft light brown sugar

5ml/1 tsp wholegrain mustard

salt and ground black pepper

1 For the sauce, wash and trim the gooseberries, and then chop them roughly, so that some pieces are larger than others.

2 Cook the gooseberries in a little water with the sugar in a small pan. A thick and chunky purée will form. Add the mustard and season to taste with salt and ground black pepper.

3 Preheat the grill (broiler) to high and line the grill (broiling) pan with foil. Using a sharp knife, slash the fish two or three times down each side, then season and brush with the olive oil.

4 Place the fish in the grill pan and cook for about 4 minutes on each side until cooked. You may need to cook them for a few minutes longer if they are particularly large. The slashes will open up to speed cooking and the skin should be lightly browned. To check that they are cooked properly, use a small sharp knife to pierce the skin and check for uncooked flesh.

5 Place the mackerel on warmed plates and spread generous dollops of the gooseberry relish over them. Pass the remaining sauce around at the table.

> **Cook's Tip**
> Turn the grill (broiler) on well in advance as the fish need a fierce heat to cook quickly. If you like fish but hate the smell of them cooking, try barbecuing them outside.

Baked Stuffed Sardines

Beccafico, literally translated from the Italian as 'pecker of figs', are little birds that like to hang by their feet from ripe figs and peck away at the sweet flesh. You might see a resemblance between them and the stuffed sardines, with their rounded bellies and beak-like tails. This particular recipe comes from the eastern side of Sicily.

Serves 4

800g/1¾lb fresh sardines or thawed frozen sardines

50g/2oz/⅓ cup sultanas (golden raisins), soaked in warm water for 15 minutes

120ml/4fl oz/½ cup olive oil

60ml/4 tbsp fresh white breadcrumbs

50g/2oz/⅔ cup pine nuts

30ml/2 tbsp chopped fresh parsley

sea salt and ground black pepper

6 salted anchovies, rinsed, dried and boned

3–4 dried bay leaves

1 Preheat the oven to 180°C/350°F/Gas 4. If using fresh sardines, slit them along the belly and remove the innards under running water. Place each sardine flat on its back, tail pointing toward you. Twist off the head by pulling it toward you so that it comes away with the spine and other bones, leaving the tail intact.

2 Drain the sultanas and pat them dry with kitchen paper. Put half the oil into a pan and add 15ml/1 tbsp of the breadcrumbs. Heat, stirring gently, so that the crumbs absorb the oil. Remove the breadcrumbs from the heat and stir in the sultanas, pine nuts and parsley. Season with pepper, then chop the anchovies finely and stir them into the mixture. Add salt if needed.

3 Using half the remaining oil, grease a baking dish that will hold all the fish in a single layer. Depending upon the size of the sardines, you can either put the stuffing in the body cavity or wrap the flattened fish around the filling and roll them up. Secure with a cocktail stick (toothpick). Arrange the stuffed sardines in the dish with their tails pointing upward and the bay leaves tucked in between the fish. Drizzle with the remaining oil and scatter over the remaining breadcrumbs. Bake for 30 minutes and serve immediately or allow to cool.

Mackerel Energy 576kcal/2390kJ; Protein 38.1g; Carbohydrate 8.4g, of which sugars 8.4g; Fat 43.5g, of which saturates 8.2g; Cholesterol 108mg; Calcium 43mg; Fibre 1.5g; Sodium 128mg.
Sardines Energy 596kcal/2481kJ; Protein 36.1g; Carbohydrate 21.1g, of which sugars 9.8g; Fat 41.3g, of which saturates 6.8g; Cholesterol 0mg; Calcium 215mg; Fibre 1.3g; Sodium 467mg.

Stuffed Sardines

This delicious Tuscan recipe for fresh sardines or plump, overgrown anchovies could not be simpler and relies very much on the fish being freshly caught. Like many recipes from this region, the ingredients are quite generous and call for about ten fish per person, although you may prefer to reduce the quantities slightly. Once the fish have been filleted, any that have been damaged in the process are added to the bread filling. To remove the scales without them flying all over the kitchen, local cooks use a piece of newspaper soaked in water, to rub vigorously over the fish.

Serves 4
2–3 stale crusty white bread rolls, crusts removed
about 120ml/4fl oz/½ cup milk
40 fresh sardines or large anchovies, scaled and filleted
3 eggs, beaten
45ml/3 tbsp freshly grated Parmesan cheese
2 garlic cloves, chopped
a handful of fresh flat leaf parsley, leaves chopped
1 dried red chilli
about 90ml/6 tbsp plain (all-purpose) flour
about 2 litres/3½ pints/9 cups sunflower oil, for deep-frying
sea salt

1 Soak the bread in the milk to cover, then squeeze dry. Use any damaged fish fillets for the filling. Put all the perfectly shaped fillets to one side.

2 Mix the bread with the damaged fish, half the beaten eggs, the grated Parmesan cheese, garlic, parsley, chilli and a pinch of salt. Blend it all together to make a firm paste with your hands or a fork.

3 Sandwich two fillets together with a generous spoonful of the filling in the middle, then gently coat in the remaining beaten egg and then the flour. Repeat for the remaining fillets.

4 Heat the oil in large pan until sizzling, then fry the fish, in batches, until crisp and golden brown; about 2 minutes. Drain on kitchen paper and serve.

Baked Sardines with Thyme and Purple Basil

With the hillsides covered in herbs, aromatic fish dishes like this one are a common feature of the Aegean and Mediterranean coasts. Purple basil, which has a mild aniseed taste, is used frequently, although green holy basil and lemon basil work just as well. Served with chunks of fresh, crusty bread to mop up the sauce, and a green salad, this is all you need for a tasty, satisfying meal. Whole mackerel and anchovies can also be prepared and cooked this way.

Serves 4
8 large sardines, scaled, gutted and thoroughly washed
6–8 fresh thyme sprigs
juice of ½ lemon
2 x 400g/14oz cans chopped tomatoes, drained of juice
60–75ml/4–5 tbsp olive oil
4 garlic cloves, smashed flat
5ml/1 tsp sugar
1 bunch of fresh purple basil
salt and ground black pepper
lemon wedges, to serve

1 Preheat the oven to 180°C/350°F/ Gas 4.

2 Place the sardines side by side in an ovenproof dish, place a sprig of thyme between each one and squeeze the lemon juice over them.

3 In a bowl, mix the tomatoes, olive oil, garlic and sugar. Season and stir in most of the basil leaves, then tip the mixture over the sardines. Bake, uncovered, for 25 minutes.

4 Sprinkle the remaining basil leaves over the top and serve hot, with lemon wedges.

Cook's Tip
To accentuate the aniseed flavour of the sauce, add a pinch of ground fennel or a few fennel seeds, then serve the sardines with some fresh bread for a tasty light lunch or snack. If you prefer you can buy fillets of sardine.

Stuffed Sardines Energy 621kcal/2594kJ; Protein 35.8g; Carbohydrate 37.2g, of which sugars 2.6g; Fat 37.7g, of which saturates 9.3g; Cholesterol 155mg; Calcium 343mg; Fibre 1.3g; Sodium 505mg.
Baked Sardines Energy 219kcal/915kJ; Protein 11.7g; Carbohydrate 7.3g, of which sugars 7.3g; Fat 16.2g, of which saturates 3.1g; Cholesterol 0mg; Calcium 57mg; Fibre 2g; Sodium 78mg.

Baltic Herring Fillets with Caper Butter Sauce

This recipe is a modern take on a traditional recipe using Baltic herrings. In earlier years, no Finn would waste vodka in cooking, mostly because it was too expensive and hard to come by. The flavour of the ubiquitous dill adds that authentic Finnish flavour to this otherwise simple dish.

Serves 4

a little butter, for greasing
50g/2oz/1 cup fine fresh
    breadcrumbs
600g/1lb 6oz Baltic herring fillets
salt

For the caper butter

100g/3¾oz/scant ½ cup butter,
    softened
15ml/1 tbsp vodka
30ml/2 tbsp chopped fresh dill
15ml/1 tbsp capers
1 large pinch cayenne pepper

1 Preheat the oven to 200°C/400°F/Gas 6. Grease a shallow, ovenproof dish with butter and sprinkle 15ml/1 tbsp of the breadcrumbs over the base.

2 To make the caper butter, put the softened butter in a bowl and beat until it is light and fluffy, then whisk in the vodka, dill, capers and cayenne pepper.

3 Season the fish with salt then fold each fillet in half, so that the skin sides are on the outside. Lightly press the folded fish together with your fingers. Arrange the fillets in the prepared dish.

4 Spread the caper butter over the fish, then sprinkle over the remaining breadcrumbs. Bake the fish in the oven for 25 minutes or until the top is crisp and golden brown.

> **Cook's Tips**
> For a truly authentic flavour, use Finnish vodka, but other varieties will be good in the sauce, too.

Fried Mustard Herrings with Mangetouts

Because of the Swedish mustard and dill that are used in the gravlax sauce this dish has a classic Swedish character. The herrings have to be fresh as they lose their delicious flavour if they are kept for too long. The mangetouts can be replaced with sugar snap peas.

Serves 6

6 fresh herrings, filleted
50g/2oz/1 cup fresh breadcrumbs
150g/5oz/1¼ cups plain (all-
    purpose) flour
50g/2oz/¼ cup butter

15ml/1 tbsp vegetable oil
450g/1lb mangetouts
    (snow peas)
salt and ground black pepper
mashed potatoes, to serve

**For the mustard and
    dill sauce**

100g/4oz Swedish mustard
100g/4oz/½ cup sugar
15ml/1 tbsp cider vinegar
5ml/1 tsp salt
ground black pepper
300ml/½ pint/1¼ cups
    vegetable oil
100g/4oz chopped fresh
    dill fronds

1 To make the sauce, put the mustard, sugar, vinegar, salt and pepper to season into a bowl, mix together then very slowly drizzle the oil into the mixture, whisking it all the time until you have a thick, shiny sauce. Add the chopped dill.

2 If necessary, remove any fins or scales from the herring fillets then rinse under cold running water and dry on kitchen paper. Cut the fillets in half lengthways then add to the bowl of sauce. Place in the refrigerator overnight to marinate.

3 Put the breadcrumbs and flour on a large plate and season with salt and ground black pepper. Coat the fish fillets, on both sides, in the mixture. Heat the butter and oil in a large frying pan, add the herring fillets and fry on both sides until golden brown.

4 Meanwhile, put the mangetouts in a steamer and cook for 5 minutes. Serve the herrings with the mangetouts and mashed potatoes.

Baltic Herring Energy 545kcal/2261kJ; Protein 28.6g; Carbohydrate 10.1g, of which sugars 0.7g; Fat 42.8g, of which saturates 19.3g; Cholesterol 134mg; Calcium 126mg; Fibre 0.7g; Sodium 444mg.
Mustard Herring Energy 730kcal/3032kJ; Protein 25.1g; Carbohydrate 30.7g, of which sugars 4.5g; Fat 57.2g, of which saturates 11.9g; Cholesterol 68mg; Calcium 152mg; Fibre 2.7g; Sodium 728mg.

Fried Salt Herring with Red Onion Compote

By the 12th century, salt herring was a staple food in Scandinavia.

Serves 4
8 salted herring fillets (about
   675g/1½lb total weight)
15g/3oz/1½ cup fine
   breadcrumbs
40g/1½oz/3 tbsp butter
2.5ml/½ tsp white pepper

For the red onion compote
675g/1½lb red onions, diced
75ml/2½fl oz/⅓ cup
   cider vinegar
350ml/12fl oz/1½ cups red wine
250ml/8fl oz/1 cup water
50ml/2fl oz/¼ cup honey
15ml/1 tbsp soft light
   brown sugar
10ml/2 tsp butter
salt and ground black pepper

1 Rinse the herring well in cold water. Place in a bowl of cold water, cover and leave to soak overnight in the refrigerator. Taste the herring for saltiness. If it is too salty, rinse the fillets again. Or, drain, pat dry with kitchen paper and place on a plate.

2 To make the red onion compote, place the chopped onion in a pan and add the vinegar and red wine. Bring to the boil and cook, uncovered, over a medium heat for about 30 minutes, stirring occasionally, until the liquid has evaporated.

3 Stir in the water, honey, brown sugar and butter, and season with salt and pepper. Cook for a further 15 minutes, stirring occasionally, until reduced and thick. Cover and keep warm until needed.

4 Place the breadcrumbs in a dish and dip the herring fillets into the crumbs to coat both sides. Sprinkle with pepper. Melt the butter in a frying pan over a medium-high heat.

5 Fry the herring fillets, in batches, turning once, for 4 minutes on each side, until the coating is golden and the fish is cooked and flakes easily with a fork. Remove the fish from the pan, drain on kitchen paper, and keep warm until all the fillets are cooked. Spoon the compote over the fish then serve immediately.

Jansson's Temptation

This anchovy pie is another warming dish for the winter months. The dish is named after a well-known Swedish opera singer whose name was Jansson, who served it to his guests after a performance at the opera house in Stockholm. In Sweden, a meal such as this, called 'vickning', is served late in the evening at the end of a good party, and is always accompanied by snaps. It is also excellent served as part of a smörgåsbord selection.

Serves 6
6 large potatoes
1 Spanish (Bermuda) onion,
   thinly sliced
120ml/4fl oz/½ cup milk
250ml/8fl oz/1 cup double
   (heavy) cream
100g/3½oz can
   Swedish anchovies
salt and ground
black pepper

1 Preheat the oven to 180°C/350°F/Gas 4.

2 Peel and grate the potatoes. Put in a sieve (strainer) and wash under cold running water to remove any excess starch.

3 Drain well and put in a bowl. Add the sliced onion and mix together then put in a shallow, ovenproof dish.

4 Mix together the milk and cream. Put both the liquid and the fish from the can of anchovies into the milk mixture and stir together. Pour the mixture over the potatoes and season with salt and pepper

5 Bake in the oven for 50 minutes until golden and bubbling.

Cook's Tip
• *This dish is delicious served on its own or with a salad and is also perfect when eaten with cold sliced ham.*
• *If you cannot get Swedish anchovies, use ordinary salted anchovies and soak them in milk for a couple of hours to remove the saltiness.*

Salt Herring Energy 672kcal/2805kJ; Protein 35.9g; Carbohydrate 43.5g, of which sugars 23.7g; Fat 34.1g, of which saturates 12.3g; Cholesterol 114mg; Calcium 186mg; Fibre 2.8g; Sodium 460mg.
Anchovies Energy 419kcal/1738kJ; Protein 19.3g; Carbohydrate 6.4g, of which sugars 3.9g; Fat 35.4g, of which saturates 5.6g; Cholesterol 24mg; Calcium 145mg; Fibre 2.4g; Sodium 1526mg.

Marinated Eels

In the many ditches, rivers and slow-moving streams of the Tuscan plains, eels are caught and turned into delicious, simple dishes for the table. This is a very old recipe from the Pisa area, and is served cold as part of an antipasto. After 48 hours or so in the marinade, the strong, slightly muddy flavour of the eel is much reduced and the vinegar acts as a good foil to the natural oiliness of the fish.

Serves 4
900g/2lb very fresh eels
coarse sea salt, for cleaning
150ml/¼ pint/⅔ cup extra virgin
    olive oil
3 garlic cloves
1 dried red chilli
3 fresh sage leaves
1 rosemary sprig
300ml/½ pint/1¼ cups white
    wine vinegar
sea salt

1 Clean the outside of the eels carefully to remove all trace of slime, using coarse sea salt or gritty wood ash. Split and gut them carefully, then wash and dry them all over. Cut them into finger-length chunks.

2 Heat the oil in a frying pan and fry the eel chunks until golden brown all over. Remove them with a slotted spoon and drain on kitchen paper. Place in a bowl to cool.

3 Using the same oil, fry the garlic, chilli, sage and rosemary together for 3 minutes.

4 Add the white wine vinegar to the frying pan and then boil to reduce by about one-third. Season with salt.

5 Pour this marinade over the eels and cover the bowl. Leave to marinate for about 48 hours before serving.

> **Cook's Tip**
> Eel is an oily fish that is rich in vitamins A and D. It can be grilled, stewed and baked.

Fried Eel with Potatoes in Cream Sauce

A legacy of Denmark's rural past, fried eel is a choice delicacy. Served with boiled or creamed potatoes and accompanied by icy aquavit and beer, this seasonal dish is a summer speciality.

Serves 4
1kg/2¼lb eel, skinned and
    cleaned
1 egg
5ml/1 tsp water
25g/1oz/½ cup fine
    breadcrumbs, toasted
10ml/2 tsp salt
2.5ml/½ tsp white pepper
40g/1½oz/3 tbsp butter
2 lemons, sliced into wedges,
    to garnish

For the potatoes
800g/1¾lb potatoes, peeled
5ml/1 tsp salt
40g/1½oz/3 tbsp butter
20g/¾oz/3 tbsp plain (all-
    purpose) flour
475ml/16fl oz/2 cups single
    (light) cream
salt and white pepper, to taste
45ml/3 tbsp chopped fresh
    parsley, to garnish

1 Cut the eel into 10cm/4in lengths. Whisk together the egg and water in a shallow dish. Place the breadcrumbs in a second shallow dish. Dip the eel first into the egg mixture, then into the breadcrumbs to coat both sides evenly. Sprinkle with salt and pepper. Leave the fish to rest for at least 10 minutes.

2 Melt the butter in a large pan over a medium-high heat. Add the eel pieces and cook, turning once, for about 10 minutes on each side, depending on thickness, until the coating is golden brown and the eel is tender. Remove from the pan and drain on kitchen paper. Keep warm.

3 Meanwhile, boil the potatoes in salted water for about 20 minutes. Drain, slice and keep warm. Melt the butter in a pan and stir in the flour. Cook, stirring, for 5 minutes until the roux is pale beige. Slowly stir in the cream and cook for about 5 minutes, stirring constantly, until the sauce has thickened. Season to taste. Stir the potato slices into the cream sauce. Serve with the fried eel, sprinkled with parsley and garnished with lemon wedges.

Marinated Eels Energy 603kcal/2499kJ; Protein 37.4g; Carbohydrate 0g, of which sugars 0g; Fat 50.4g, of which saturates 10g; Cholesterol 338mg; Calcium 43mg; Fibre 0g; Sodium 200mg.
Fried Eels Energy 978kcal/4074kJ; Protein 50.2g; Carbohydrate 43.7g, of which sugars 5.6g; Fat 68.2g, of which saturates 32.3g; Cholesterol 483mg; Calcium 184mg; Fibre 2.3g; Sodium 448mg.

Smoked Eel on Röstis with Dill and Horseradish

This light dish comes from one of the best restaurants in Riga. Strips of smoked eel top crisp rösti and salad leaves, finished with a dollop of a creamy horseradish and dill dressing. Try the same recipe with smoked haddock or smoked salmon.

Serves 4

2 large baking potatoes, peeled
20g/¾oz clarified
  or regular butter
115g/4oz salad leaves
200g/7oz smoked eel, cut into
  8 thin strips

**For the dill and creamed
  horseradish**
200g/7oz crème fraîche
5ml/1 tsp creamed horseradish
15ml/1 tbsp finely chopped
  fresh dill
salt and ground black pepper

1 To make the dill and creamed horseradish, put the crème fraîche in a large bowl with the creamed horseradish and dill. Combine and season with salt and pepper.

2 Grate the potatoes fairly coarsely and put into a colander to drain. Sprinkle them with a little salt to help draw out the excess moisture. Wrap the potato in a piece of muslin (cheesecloth) and squeeze to remove the remaining moisture.

3 Heat the butter in a frying pan over a medium-low heat. Take a large spoonful of the grated potatoes and shape into a round about 7.5cm/3in in diameter.

4 Make three more röstis in the same way. Put into the pan (you may need to cook in batches) and cook for about 5 minutes on each side, or until golden brown. Remove from the pan and keep warm while you cook the remainder.

5 Put a rösti on each serving plate, then top with a handful of the salad leaves. Arrange two strips of the smoked eel on top and garnish with some of the dill and creamed horseradish. Serve immediately.

Eels in Green Herb Sauce

In this classic dish the Belgian herbs chervil and sorrel, as well as spinach and parsley, are used. These are added towards the end of the cooking time so their full flavour comes through.

Serves 4–6

1.6kg/3½lb fresh small river eels,
  skinned, gutted and cut into
  5cm/2in lengths (ask your
  fishmonger to do this)
2 egg yolks
juice of 1 large lemon
120ml/4fl oz/½ cup water
25g/1oz/2 tbsp butter, plus extra
  for thickening sauce if needed
2–3 shallots, finely chopped
1 sprig of thyme
1 bay leaf
300ml/½ pint/1¼ cups
  white wine
200ml/7fl oz/scant 1 cup
  fish stock
50g/2oz/1 cup fresh chervil,
  roughly chopped
50g/2oz/1 cup fresh parsley,
  roughly chopped
200g/7oz spinach, leaves torn
  and tough stems removed
15ml/1 tbsp each of chopped
  fresh sorrel, mint, sage, savory
  and tarragon
salt and ground black pepper

For the garnish
30ml/2 tbsp freshly chopped
  parsley
4 lemon wedges

1 Rinse the portions of eel and pat them dry with kitchen paper. Mix together the egg yolks, lemon juice and water. Set the mixture aside. Melt the butter in a frying pan and sauté the shallots for 2–3 minutes over low heat until almost softened.

2 Meanwhile, strip the leaves from the thyme and put them into a mortar with the bay leaf. Crush with a pestle. Rub the mixture into the pieces of eel, then add to the pan. Season.

3 Fry the eel on both sides for 8 minutes until golden, then add the wine and enough fish stock to cover. Cover and simmer for 15 minutes, remove from the pan and put the eel on a plate. Remove from the heat. Add the chervil, parsley and spinach, with the remaining herbs. Blend in a food processor to chop the herbs further. Blend in the egg yolk mixture and add a little butter to thicken. Return to the pan if necessary. Replace the pieces of eel in the sauce and warm through. Stir until the sauce thickens. Serve, garnished with lemon wedges and parsley.

Smoked Eels Energy 403kcal/1677kJ; Protein 11.8g; Carbohydrate 22.1g, of which sugars 3.4g; Fat 30.4g, of which saturates 17.9g; Cholesterol 143mg; Calcium 55mg; Fibre 1.6g; Sodium 119mg.
Eels in Herb Sauce Energy 290kcal/1213kJ; Protein 32.7g; Carbohydrate 1.9g, of which sugars 1.6g; Fat 13.4g, of which saturates 2.8g; Cholesterol 76mg; Calcium 218mg; Fibre 1.2g; Sodium 183mg.

Stir-fried Squid and Mangetout

Like many people who live near the sea, the Cantonese have a passion for all shellfish. Squid and octopus are especially popular, both at home and as premium restaurant dishes. They demand skilful cooking as they rapidly become rubbery and unpalatable if overdone.

Serves 4

175g/6oz squid tubes, cleaned
15ml/1 tbsp vegetable oil
30ml/2 tbsp garlic, crushed
175g/6oz mangetouts
 (snow peas), trimmed
30ml/2 tbsp oyster sauce
2.5ml/½ tsp ground
 black pepper
30ml/2 tbsp sesame oil
10ml/2 tsp cornflour (cornstarch)
105ml/7 tbsp water

1 Using a sharp knife or kitchen scissors, slice through the side of each squid tube and open them out so that they lie flat.

2 Cross-hatch the surface of each piece of squid by making deep cuts at 1cm/½in intervals, first in one direction and then in the other. Cut each piece of squid in half lengthways.

3 Heat the vegetable oil in a wok and fry the crushed garlic for 30 seconds. Toss in the mangetouts and the pieces of squid and fry over high heat for 2 minutes.

4 Add the oyster sauce, ground black pepper and sesame oil and stir for 1 minute.

5 Mix the cornflour with the water in a small bowl. Add the mixture to the wok and stir until the sauce thickens and bubbles. Spoon into a serving bowl and serve immediately.

> **Cook's Tip**
> • If you rub squid with bicarbonate of soda (baking soda) the flesh becomes more tender and succulent. You do not need much – a scant teaspoon will be plenty.
> • Extract the ink from the ink sacs of the squid and reserve to colour pasta or to flavour squid dishes.

Cuttlefish with Swiss Chard

Cuttlefish are usually sold pre-prepared, or the fishmonger will do this for you; if not, see the instructions in the cook's tip below. This recipe is typical of the type of cooking that is found in the Mediterranean regions of Slovenia, where the dish is served with polenta.

Serves 6

45ml/3 tbsp olive oil
1 onion, sliced
2 garlic cloves, chopped
675g/1½lb prepared
 cuttlefish, sliced
1.5kg/3¼lb Swiss chard or
 large spinach leaves, washed
 and shredded
bunch of fresh parsley, trimmed
 and chopped
30–45ml/2–3 tbsp water or light
 vegetable stock

1 Heat the olive oil in a pan. Add the onion and garlic and cook for about 15 minutes, until the onion is soft.

2 Add the cuttlefish and fry for a few minutes, stirring and turning the slices, until firm and lightly cooked.

3 Sprinkle with chopped parsley and pour in the water or stock, just enough to cover the bottom of the pan and braise the cuttlefish without covering it. Gently simmer for 5 minutes, stirring occasionally.

4 Add the rinsed Swiss chard and season. Simmer and cook for 10 minutes, stirring until the chard is reduced and the cuttlefish is tender. The cooking juices will evaporate to leave the mixture moist but not wet. Serve.

> **Cook's Tip**
> To clean the cuttlefish, cut off the tentacles in front of the eyes and remove the mouth. Remove the head, cut open the body from top to bottom and remove the cuttlebone and innards. Scrape the inside clean and rinse well. Remove the skin from the outside of the body and from the tentacles if they are large.

Stir-fried Squid Energy 141kcal/589kJ; Protein 8.5g; Carbohydrate 6.8g, of which sugars 3.6g; Fat 9.1g, of which saturates 1.3g; Cholesterol 98mg; Calcium 27mg; Fibre 1.1g; Sodium 173mg.
Cuttlefish Energy 196kcal/813kJ; Protein 25.2g; Carbohydrate 4.8g, of which sugars 4.3g; Fat 8.3g, of which saturates 1.3g; Cholesterol 124mg; Calcium 494mg; Fibre 5.4g; Sodium 767mg.

Light and Fragrant Tiger Prawns with Cucumber and Dill

This simple, elegant dish has a fresh, light flavour and is equally good served as a simple supper or for a dinner party. The delicate flavour of fresh prawns goes really well with mild cucumber and fragrant dill, but if you prefer a more robust dish, toss in a handful of chives as well.

Serves 4

500g/1¼lb raw tiger prawns
    (jumbo shrimp), peeled
    with tail on
500g/1¼lb cucumber
30ml/2 tbsp butter
15ml/1 tbsp olive oil
15ml/1 tbsp finely chopped garlic
45ml/3 tbsp chopped fresh dill
juice of 1 lemon
salt and ground black pepper
steamed rice or noodles,
    to serve

1 Using a small, sharp knife, carefully make a shallow slit along the back of each prawn and use the point of the knife to remove the black vein. Set the prawns aside.

2 Peel the cucumber and slice in half lengthways. Using a small teaspoon, gently scoop out all the seeds and discard. Cut the cucumber into 4 x 1cm/1½ x ½in sticks.

3 Heat a wok over a high heat, then add the butter and oil. When the butter has melted, add the cucumber and garlic and stir-fry over a high heat for 2–3 minutes. Add the prepared prawns to the wok and continue to stir-fry over a high heat for 3–4 minutes, or until the prawns turn pink and are just cooked through, then remove from the heat.

4 Add the fresh dill and lemon juice to the wok and toss to combine. Season well with salt and ground black pepper and serve immediately with steamed rice or noodles.

Cook's Tip
The best rice to use is jasmine, also known as Thai fragrant rice.

Prawn and Bread Mash with Pan-fried Tiger Prawns

Bread soups are associated with fish and shellfish, especially salt cod and prawns.

Serves 4

500g/1¼lb raw prawns (shrimp),
    in their shells
4 tiger prawns (jumbo shrimp),
    about 140g/4¾oz each, in
    their shells
150ml/¼ pint/⅔ cup olive oil
5ml/1 tsp sweet paprika
500g/1¼lb dry white bread,
    crusts removed and cubed
3 garlic cloves, finely chopped
piri piri sauce, to taste

45ml/3 tbsp chopped fresh
    coriander (cilantro)
2 egg yolks

For the shellfish stock
150ml/¼ pint/¾ cup olive oil
2 onions, quartered
1 leek, cut in small pieces
3 carrots, cubed
3 garlic cloves, chopped
1 bunch of parsley
3 bay leaves
6 grains of black pepper
250ml/8fl oz/1 cup white wine
500ml/17fl oz/generous 2 cups
    fresh tomato juice
2kg/4½lb shrimp heads and shells

1 Cook the prawns in boiling water for 2–3 minutes. Drain, refresh in cold water and drain. Pull off the heads and peel the prawns, reserving the heads and shells. Set aside. Peel the tiger prawns, keeping the heads on, reserving the shells. Set aside.

2 For the shellfish stock heat the oil and fry the shrimp heads and shells for about 10 minutes, stirring. Mash the mixture. Add the vegetables, blend and add the rest of the ingredients. Cover with 3–5 litres/5–7 pints of water and cook for 2 hours. Pass the stock through a sieve (strainer).

3 In a pan, fry the tiger prawns in 45ml/3 tbsp of olive oil, sprinkle with the paprika and fry for 2 minutes on each side. Add some stock and return to the heat for 2–3 minutes.

4 Put the bread, shellfish stock, garlic and remaining olive oil in a pan and cook, stirring for 5 minutes, until the mixture is smooth but not dry. Add the reserved prawns, piri piri to taste, and the coriander. Add the egg yolks. Serve with the prawns and the sauce.

Tiger Prawns 192kcal/798kJ; Protein 23.2g; Carbohydrate 2.5g, of which sugars 1.9g; Fat 9.8g, of which saturates 4.4g; Cholesterol 260mg; Calcium 123mg; Fibre 0.9g; Sodium 287mg.
Prawn and Bread Energy 640kcal/2688kJ; Protein 27.5g; Carbohydrate 62.7g, of which sugars 3.6g; Fat 32.8g, of which saturates 4.9g; Cholesterol 319mg; Calcium 253mg; Fibre 2.5g; Sodium 2232mg.

Scallops with Black Pudding and Potato, Celery and Apple Mash

This recipe is a modern twist on a classic Estonian recipe using sweet and delicate scallops, topped with black pudding and nestled on a sweet–savoury mash. Estonians love black pudding and the flavour combinations used here contrast well. The dish is light, yet packed with unexpected flavours.

Serves 4
400g/14oz good-quality, soft
   black pudding (blood
   sausage), chopped
extra virgin olive oil, for greasing
12 large scallops
salt and ground black pepper
chopped fresh chervil, to garnish
juice of 1 lemon, to serve

For the mash
4–5 celery sticks, chopped into
   small pieces
400g/14oz potatoes, peeled
   and diced
1 large cooking apple, peeled
   and diced
a pinch of freshly grated nutmeg
knob (pat) of butter (optional)

1 To make the mash, put the celery, potato and apple in a pan and cover with water. Bring to the boil and cook until soft. Drain and mash, or pass through a potato ricer. Season, and add a touch of nutmeg and some butter. You need a firm mash so that it will stay in shape when serving. Keep warm.

2 Preheat the oven to 160°C/325°F/Gas 3. Put the black pudding in a roasting pan and roast for 10–12 minutes. Remove and keep warm.

3 Add a smear of oil to a heavy non-stick frying pan or griddle and heat over high heat. Cook the scallops for about 2 minutes on each side, or until golden brown.

4 To serve, make three small heaps of mash, about 45ml/3 tbsp each, on each serving plate, about 5cm/2in apart. Put a scallop on top of each heap, then top with a small pile of the cooked black pudding. Sprinkle with fresh chervil and squeeze a little lemon juice over the top. Season and serve.

Herb and Chilli-seared Scallops on Wilted Pak Choi

Tender, succulent scallops are simply divine marinated in fresh chilli, fragrant mint and aromatic basil, then quickly seared in a piping hot wok. If you can't find king scallops for this recipe, use twice the quantity of smaller queen scallops.

Serves 4
20–24 king scallops, cleaned
120ml/4fl oz/½ cup olive oil
finely grated zest and juice
   of 1 lemon
30ml/2 tbsp finely chopped mixed
   mint and basil
1 red chilli, seeded and finely
   chopped
salt and ground black pepper
500g/1¼lb pak choi (bok choy)

1 Place the scallops in a shallow, non-metallic bowl in a single layer. In a clean bowl, mix together half the oil, the lemon zest and juice, chopped herbs and chilli and spoon over the scallops. Season well with salt and black pepper, cover and set aside.

2 Using a sharp knife, cut each pak choi lengthways into four pieces.

3 Heat a wok over a high heat. When hot, drain the scallops (reserving the marinade) and add to the wok. Cook for about 1 minute on each side, or until cooked to your liking.

4 Pour the marinade over the scallops and remove the wok from the heat. Transfer the scallops and juices to a platter and keep warm.

5 Wipe out the wok with a piece of kitchen paper and place the wok over a high heat. Add the remaining oil and add the pak choi. Stir-fry over a high heat for 2–3 minutes, until the leaves are wilted.

6 Divide the greens among four warmed serving plates, then top with the reserved scallops and their juices and serve immediately.

Scallops with Black Pudding Energy 457kcal/1916kJ; Protein 26.8g; Carbohydrate 38.5g, of which sugars 5.2g; Fat 22.8g, of which saturates 8.9g; Cholesterol 97mg; Calcium 161mg; Fibre 2.2g; Sodium 1087mg.
Chilli Scallops Energy 410kcal/1714kJ; Protein 44.5g; Carbohydrate 8.3g, of which sugars 2.1g; Fat 22.3g, of which saturates 3.5g; Cholesterol 82mg; Calcium 286mg; Fibre 3.2g; Sodium 494mg.

Seafood Pie with Rösti Topping

This oven-baked dish is a mixture of white fish and shellfish with a creamy sauce and finished with a grated potato topping.

Serves 4
750g/1lb 10oz potatoes, unpeeled and scrubbed
50g/2oz/¼ cup butter, melted
350g/12oz cod or haddock fillets, skinned and cut into bitesize pieces
115g/4oz cooked, peeled prawns (shrimp)
115g/4oz cooked, shelled mussels
8–12 shelled queen scallops
50g/2oz/¼ cup butter
1 onion, finely chopped
50g/2oz/½ cup plain (all-purpose) flour
200ml/7fl oz/scant 1 cup dry white wine
300ml/½ pint/1¼ cups fish or vegetable stock
105ml/7 tbsp double (heavy) cream
30ml/2 tbsp chopped fresh dill, plus extra sprigs to garnish
15ml/1 tbsp chopped fresh parsley
60ml/4 tbsp freshly grated Parmesan cheese

1 Place the potatoes in a large pan. Cover with cold water and bring to the boil. Cook for 10–15 minutes until just tender.

2 Drain the potatoes and set aside until cool enough to handle. Peel and coarsely grate the cooled potatoes into a bowl. Stir in the melted butter and season well with salt and pepper.

3 Preheat the oven to 220°C/425°F/Gas 7. Divide the pieces of cod or haddock and the prawns, mussels and scallops among four individual 18cm/7in rectangular earthenware dishes.

4 Melt the butter in a large pan, add the onion and cook for 6–8 minutes or until softened and light golden. Sprinkle in the flour and stir thoroughly until well blended.

5 Remove the pan from the heat and pour in the wine and stock, stirring until smooth. Bring to the boil, then stir in the cream, herbs and season to taste. Pour the sauce over the fish.

6 Sprinkle the potato evenly over the fish and sauce in the dishes and top with the Parmesan. Bake for 25 minutes until the topping is crisp and the fish is cooked. Serve hot, garnished with dill.

Cod, Basil, Tomato and Potato Pie

Natural and smoked fish make a great combination, especially with the hint of tomato and basil. Served with a green salad, it makes an ideal dish for lunch or a family supper.

Serves 8
1kg/2¼lb smoked cod
1kg/2¼lb white cod
900ml/1½ pint/3¾ cups milk
1.2litres/2 pints/5 cups water
2 basil sprigs
1 lemon thyme sprig
150g/5oz/10 tbsp butter
1 onion, chopped
75g/3oz/⅔ cup plain flour
30ml/2 tbsp chopped fresh basil
4 firm plum tomatoes, peeled and chopped
12 medium main crop floury potatoes
salt and ground black pepper
crushed black pepper corns, to garnish
lettuce leaves, to serve

1 Place both kinds of fish in a roasting tin with 600ml/1 pint/2½ cups of the milk, the water and the herb sprigs. Bring to a simmer and cook gently for about 3–4 minutes. Leave the fish to cool in the liquid for about 20 minutes. Drain the fish, reserving the cooking liquid for use in the sauce. Flake the fish, removing any skin and bone.

2 Melt 75g/3oz/6 tbsp of the butter in a large pan, add the onion and cook for about 5 minutes until softened and tender but not browned. Sprinkle over the flour and half the chopped basil. Gradually add the reserved fish cooking liquid, adding a little more milk if necessary to make a fairly thin sauce, stirring constantly to make a smooth consistency. Bring to the boil, season with salt and pepper, and add the remaining basil.

3 Remove the pan from the heat, add the fish and tomatoes and stir gently to combine. Pour into an ovenproof dish.

4 Preheat the oven to 180°C/350°F/Gas 4. Cook the potatoes in boiling water until tender. Drain then add the remaining butter and milk, and mash. Season to taste and spoon over the fish mixture, using a fork to create a pattern. You can freeze the pie at this stage. Bake for 30 minutes until the top is golden. Sprinkle with the pepper corns and serve hot with lettuce.

Seafood Pie Energy 770kcal/3215kJ; Protein 47.3g; Carbohydrate 44.5g, of which sugars 4.5g; Fat 42.4g, of which saturates 25.5g; Cholesterol 236mg; Calcium 298mg; Fibre 2.7g; Sodium 626mg.
Cod and Potato Pie Energy 474kcal/1989kJ; Protein 49.6g; Carbohydrate 30.7g, of which sugars 4.6g; Fat 17.8g, of which saturates 10.2g; Cholesterol 155mg; Calcium 62mg; Fibre 2.5g; Sodium 1672mg.

Cod Fillet Baked with Sliced Potatoes

Cod fillet bakes perfectly, its mild flavour enhanced by the herbs and its juices adding flavour to the sliced potatoes underneath.

Serves 4

2 large potatoes, sliced
600ml/1 pint/2½ cups water or fish stock
900g/2lb cod fillet, skinned and cut into 4 pieces
1 small bunch dill
1 small leek, shredded
50g/2oz/¼ cup butter
olive oil, to drizzle
salt and ground black pepper

For the sauce

150ml/¼ pint/⅔ cup single (light) cream
shredded leek, to garnish
chopped dill, to garnish

1 Preheat the oven to 200°C/400°F/Gas 6. Cook the potatoes in the water or fish stock for 7–10 minutes or until tender. Drain and reserve the stock.

2 Season the cod pieces. Divide the potatoes into four portions. Arrange each one in an overlapping fan shape on a greased non-stick roasting pan.

3 Season the potatoes and cut some of the dill over each fan, reserving a little for the sauce. Sprinkle over the leeks, reserving some for the sauce, and add a knob of the butter.

4 Arrange the fish over the sliced potatoes. Sprinkle the remaining leeks and sliced potatoes on top of the fish and drizzle the olive oil over the top. Bake, uncovered, for 15–20 minutes.

5 Meanwhile, to make the sauce, rapidly boil the reserved stock in a pan for 10 minutes or until reduced by two-thirds.

6 Stir in the cream and the remaining dill. Boil for 5 minutes to thicken slightly.

7 Remove the fish from the oven and garnish with the shredded leek and chopped dill. Place the individual portions on plates and serve with the sauce.

Cod Tallinn-style

This is a simple and easy recipe to use with cod or any other fish that is available. Strips of fish are dipped in flour and quickly fried, then baked with a sour cream, dill, mustard and cheese topping. Simple, quick and full of flavour, it just needs a salad and new potatoes to serve.

Serves 4

20g/¾oz/1½ tbsp butter
45ml/3 tbsp plain (all-purpose) flour
800g/1¾lb chunky fillet of cod, cut into thick strips
juice of ½ lemon
75ml/2½fl oz/⅓ cup thick sour cream
30ml/2 tbsp dill, finely chopped
5ml/1 tsp mild wholegrain mustard
50g/2oz/½ cup grated mild Emmenthal cheese
salt and ground black pepper

1 Preheat the oven to 200°C/400°F/Gas 6. Melt the butter in a large frying pan over a medium heat.

2 Put the flour on a plate and roll the fish strips in it to coat them evenly. Drop the fish into the melted butter.

3 Season to taste and cook for 2–3 minutes, or until lightly golden, turning halfway through. Add the lemon juice.

4 Remove the fish using a slotted spoon, and arrange, skin side down, on an ovenproof dish, alongside each other.

5 Put the sour cream, dill and mustard in a small bowl and mix together. Spread the mixture on top of the fish strips and then sprinkle with the grated cheese. Bake for about 6–8 minutes, or until the top is golden brown and the cheese has melted. Serve hot.

> **Cook's Tips**
> Avoid using Atlantic cod. Choose Pacific (bottom longline) cod for best sustainability.

Cod Fillet Energy 428kcal/1788kJ; Protein 44.7g; Carbohydrate 19.1g, of which sugars 4g; Fat 19.5g, of which saturates 11.6g; Cholesterol 153mg; Calcium 74mg; Fibre 2.1g; Sodium 259mg.
Cod Tallinn Energy 331kcal/1384kJ; Protein 41.8g; Carbohydrate 9.9g, of which sugars 1.2g; Fat 13.7g, of which saturates 8g; Cholesterol 127mg; Calcium 165mg; Fibre 0.9g; Sodium 296mg.

Baked Salt Cod with Potatoes, Tomatoes and Olives

Salt cod has been a winter staple in Greece for generations. It is particularly popular in the spring, and the following dish is often on the menu at city restaurants on Fridays during Lent. The dried, creamy-coloured sides of cod can often be seen in the market in Athens and on the stalls in many street markets

Serves 4
675g/1½lb salt cod

800g/1¾lb potatoes, peeled and cut into small wedges
1 large onion, finely chopped
2–3 garlic cloves, chopped
leaves from 1 fresh rosemary sprig
30ml/2 tbsp chopped fresh flat leaf parsley
120ml/4fl oz/½ cup extra virgin olive oil
400g/14oz can chopped tomatoes
15ml/1 tbsp tomato purée (paste)
300ml/½ pint/1¼ cups hot water
5ml/1 tsp dried oregano
12 black olives
ground black pepper

1 Soak the cod in cold water overnight, changing the water as often as possible in the course of the evening and during the following day. The cod does not have to be skinned for this dish, but you should remove any obvious fins or bones.

2 Preheat the oven to 180°C/350°F/Gas 4. Mix the potatoes, onion, garlic, rosemary and parsley in a large roasting pan. Grind in plenty of pepper. Add the olive oil and toss to coat.

3 Drain the cod and cut it into serving pieces. Arrange the pieces of cod between the vegetables and spread with the tomatoes. Stir the tomato purée into the hot water until dissolved, then pour the mixture over the contents of the tin. Sprinkle the oregano on top. Bake for 1 hour, basting the fish and potatoes occasionally with the pan juices.

4 Remove the roasting pan from the oven, sprinkle the olives on top, then cook it for 30 minutes more, adding more hot water if the mixture seems to be drying out. Garnish with fresh herbs. Serve hot or cold.

Salt Cod with Potato Mash Gratin

This recipe is reminiscent of the well-known French salt cod purée, brandade. Many similar dishes are produced in other Mediterranean countries, using salt or dried cod, which is also known as stockfish. Serve with an assortment of lettuces, seasoned with parsley vinaigrette. A smaller portion of this recipe is ideal as an appetizer.

Serves 8
1kg/2¼lb potatoes, unpeeled
800g/1¾lb salt cod, soaked
105ml/7 tbsp olive oil
200ml/7fl oz/scant 1 cup single (light) cream
2 garlic cloves, chopped
1 small bunch of parsley, chopped
pinch of freshly grated nutmeg
salt

1 Cook the potatoes in a large pan of lightly salted boiling water for 20–30 minutes, until tender. Drain well, then peel and mash with a fork. Meanwhile, preheat the oven to 200°C/400°F/Gas 6.

2 Bring another large pan of water to the boil. Add the fish and bring back to the boil, then immediately remove the pan from the heat. Leave to stand for 5 minutes.

3 Remove the fish from the pan with a slotted spatula and leave to cool slightly. Remove and discard the skin and bones. Mix the fish with the potatoes, then blend in the olive oil and cream and the garlic. Stir in the parsley and nutmeg and season with salt, if necessary.

4 Spoon the mixture into an ovenproof dish and bake for about 20 minutes. Serve hot.

> **Cook's Tips**
> Salt cod can often be bought from Italian and Spanish groceries, as well as from Greek food stores. It is often sold in small squares, ready for soaking and draining. If you buy it in the piece, cut it into 7cm/2¾in squares after soaking.

Baked Salt Cod Energy 692kcal/2886kJ; Protein 55g; Carbohydrate 43g, of which sugars 8g; Fat 33g, of which saturates 4g; Cholesterol 0mg; Calcium 431mg; Fibre 5g; Sodium 267mg.
Salt Cod Gratin Energy 366kcal/1535kJ; Protein 35.9g; Carbohydrate 21.4g, of which sugars 2.4g; Fat 15.8g, of which saturates 4.7g; Cholesterol 73mg; Calcium 65mg; Fibre 1.7g; Sodium 423mg.

Thyme and Juniper-baked Haddock

Baking fish in sour cream with typical flavourings from the region is a method of cooking often employed in the Baltic. This recipe uses haddock, but it can be adapted to almost any fish. Delicious served hot or cold, and prepared with either a whole fillet of fish or cut into serving pieces, the dish tastes great with potatoes and steamed vegetables.

Serves 4

4 thick haddock fillets, about
   200g/7oz each, skin on,
   bones removed
15ml/1 tbsp finely chopped fresh
   thyme leaves
2.5ml/½ tsp juniper
   berries, crushed
1.5ml/¼ tsp sugar
400ml/14fl oz/1⅔ cups thick
   sour cream
30ml/2 tbsp finely chopped
   fresh dill
salt and ground black pepper

1 Preheat the oven to 180°C/350°F/Gas 4. Arrange the haddock fillets in an ovenproof dish that is just large enough to hold them in a single layer. Season with salt and pepper.

2 In a bowl, mix together the thyme, juniper berries and sugar, then rub this mixture into the fillets.

3 Stir the sour cream and pour over the fish. Sprinkle with the dill and bake for 20–30 minutes, depending on the thickness of the fillets. The fish is cooked when it flakes easily when separated with the point of a knife. Serve.

> **Cook's Tips**
> • Avoid using trawl haddock, a fishing method that has resulted in overfishing. A more sustainable option is hook-and-line haddock. Good sustainable alternative fish choices are Pacific cod and Pacific halibut.
> • Juniper berries grow in both Europe and North America. They are naturally very bitter and are only ever eaten when they are cooked in meat dishes, fish recipes, sauces and stuffings. The berries are always crushed before use, to release their unique flavour.

Pale Smoked Haddock Flan

The classic combination of potatoes and smoked fish is reworked in pastry.

Serves 4

For the pastry
225g/8oz/2 cups plain
   (all-purpose) flour
pinch of salt
115g/4oz/1½ cup cold butter,
   cut into chunks
cold water, to mix

For the filling
2 pale smoked haddock fillets
   (approximately 200g/7oz)
600ml/1 pint/2½ cups full-fat
   (whole) milk
3–4 black peppercorns
sprig of fresh thyme
150ml/¼ pint/⅔ cup double
   (heavy) cream
2 eggs
200g/7oz potatoes, diced
ground black pepper

1 Preheat the oven to 200°C/400°F/Gas 6. Use a food processor to make the pastry. Put the flour, salt and butter into the food processor bowl and process until the mixture resembles fine breadcrumbs.

2 Pour in a little cold water (about 40ml/8 tsp) and continue to process until the mixture forms a ball. If this takes longer than 30 seconds add a dash or two more water.

3 Wrap the pastry ball in clear film (plastic wrap) and leave to rest in a cool place for about 30 minutes. Roll out the dough and use to line a 20cm/8in flan tin (quiche pan). Prick the base of the pastry all over with a fork then bake blind in the preheated oven for 20 minutes.

4 Put the haddock in a pan with the milk, peppercorns and thyme. Poach for 10 minutes. Remove the fish from the pan and flake into small chunks. Allow the poaching liquor to cool.

5 Whisk the cream and eggs together thoroughly, then whisk in the cooled poaching liquid.

6 Layer the flan case with the fish and potato, season with pepper. Pour the cream mixture over the top. Put the flan in the oven and bake for 40 minutes, until lightly browned on top and set. Serve.

Haddock Flan Energy 734kcal/3064kJ; Protein 23.8g; Carbohydrate 58.4g, of which sugars 8.2g; Fat 46.8g, of which saturates 27.9g; Cholesterol 225mg; Calcium 280mg; Fibre 2.3g; Sodium 636mg.
Juniper Haddock Energy 370kcal/1547kJ; Protein 41g; Carbohydrate 4g, of which sugars 4g; Fat 21g, of which saturates 13g; Cholesterol 132mg; Calcium 136 mg; Fibre 0g; Sodium 176mg.

Seafood Gougère

This is an easy-to-prepare
yet impressive supper dish.

Serves 4

130g/4½oz/1 cup plus 2 tbsp
    plain (all-purpose) flour
1.5ml/¼ tsp salt
130g/4½oz/9 tbsp butter
200ml/7fl oz/scant 1 cup water
3 eggs, beaten
150g/5oz Gruyère cheese, grated

250g/9oz smoked haddock fillet
1 bay leaf
250ml/8fl oz/1 cup milk
1 small red onion, chopped
150g/5oz/2–2½ cups white
    (button) mushrooms, sliced
5ml/1 tsp mild curry paste
fresh lemon juice
30ml/2 tbsp chopped fresh parsley
salt and ground black pepper

1 Lightly grease an ovenproof dish. Sift 100g/3¾ oz/scant 1 cup
of the flour on to a sheet of baking parchment and add the salt.
Place 75g/3oz/6 tbsp of the butter in a pan. Add the water and
heat gently. When the butter has melted, bring the water to the
boil, tip in the flour mixture and beat well. When the mixture
comes away from the sides of the pan and forms a soft,
smooth paste, remove the pan from the heat and cool for 5
minutes. Slowly work the beaten eggs into the dough, beating
well, until the mixture has the consistency of creamy mashed
potato. Stir in two-thirds of the grated cheese.

2 Spoon the choux pastry around the edge of the prepared
dish, so it comes well up the sides. Set aside. Preheat the oven
to 180°C/350°F/ Gas 4. Put the haddock in a baking dish with
the bay leaf. Add the milk, cover and bake for 15 minutes. Lift
out the fish, set aside. Discard the bay leaf but retain the milk.

3 Melt the remaining butter in a frying pan. Add the onion and
mushrooms and sauté for 5 minutes. Mix in the curry paste, if
using, then the remaining flour. Stir in the hot milk. Heat, stirring,
until the sauce is smooth. Simmer for 2–3 minutes, then add
the lemon juice, parsley, and season to taste. Increase the oven
temperature to 200°C/400°F/Gas 6. Skin the haddock and flake
the flesh and spoon it into the centre of the uncooked choux
pastry, with the mushroom mixture. Sprinkle over the rest of
the cheese. Bake for 35–40 minutes until the filling is cooked
and the gougère has risen and is golden brown. Serve at once.

Smoked Fish Soufflé

The fluffy savoury soufflé
comes from French cuisine,
but was made in grand
English kitchens by 19th-
century chefs such as
Antonin Carême, who
cooked for the Prince
Regent. Serve it puffed up
and straight out of the oven,
before it has time to settle
and fall.

Serves 4

225g/8oz skinless smoked
    haddock
300ml/½ pint/1¼ cups milk
2 bay leaves (optional)
40g/1½oz/3 tbsp butter, plus
    extra for greasing
40g/1½oz/5 tbsp plain
    (all-purpose) flour
55g/2oz mature Cheddar cheese
5ml/1 tsp English (hot) mustard
4 egg yolks
5 egg whites
ground black pepper

1 Put the fish into a pan just large enough to hold it in a single
layer, and add the milk and bay leaves (if using). Heat slowly
until the milk is very hot, with small bubbles rising to the
surface, but not boiling. Cover and simmer very gently for 5–8
minutes until the fish is just cooked.

2 Lift out the fish with a slotted spoon, reserving the cooking
liquid, and remove any bones. Discard the bay leaves and break
the fish into flakes. Preheat the oven to 190°C/375°F/Gas 5 and
butter a 20cm/8in soufflé dish.

3 Melt the butter in a pan, stir in the flour and cook gently for
1 minute, stirring. Remove from the heat and gradually stir in
the reserved cooking liquid. Cook, stirring constantly until the
sauce thickens and comes to the boil.

4 Remove from the heat. Stir in the cheese, mustard, pepper
and fish. Beat in the egg yolks, one at a time. Whisk the egg
whites until stiff. Stir a little egg white into the sauce then use a
large metal spoon to fold in the rest.

5 Pour the mixture into the prepared dish and cook in the hot
oven for about 40 minutes until risen and just firm to the
touch. Serve immediately.

Seafood Gougère Energy 698kcal/2909kJ; Protein 33g; Carbohydrate 36g, of which sugars 4g; Fat 48g, of which saturates 28g; Cholesterol 308mg; Calcium 541mg; Fibre 3g; Sodium 1099mg.
Fish Soufflé Energy 325kcal/1356kJ; Protein 24.4g; Carbohydrate 11.4g, of which sugars 3.8g; Fat 20.3g, of which saturates 10.7g; Cholesterol 272mg; Calcium 247mg; Fibre 0.3g; Sodium 706mg.

Fillets of Sea Bream in Filo Pastry

Any firm fish fillets can be used for this dish – bass, grouper, red mullet and snapper are particularly good. Each little parcel is a meal in itself and can be prepared several hours in advance, which makes this an ideal recipe for entertaining.

Serves 4

8 small waxy salad potatoes, preferably red-skinned
200g/7oz spinach, stalks removed
30ml/2 tbsp olive oil
16 filo pastry sheets, thawed if frozen
4 sea bream or porgy fillets, about 175g/6oz each, scaled but not skinned
50g/2oz/¼ cup butter, melted
120ml/4fl oz/½ cup fish stock
250ml/8fl oz/1 cup whipping cream
salt and ground black pepper
finely diced red (bell) pepper, to garnish

1 Preheat the oven to 200°C/400°F/Gas 6. Cook the potatoes in a pan of salted boiling water for 15–20 minutes, until just tender. Drain and leave to cool. Set about half the spinach leaves aside. Shred the remaining leaves by piling up six at a time, rolling them up like a cigar and slicing them with a sharp knife.

2 Thinly slice the potatoes. Brush a baking sheet with a little of the oil. Lay a sheet of filo pastry on the sheet, brush it with oil, then lay a second sheet crossways over the first. Repeat with two more sheets. Arrange a quarter of the sliced potatoes in the centre, season and add a quarter of the shredded spinach. Lay a fish fillet on top, skin-side up. Season.

3 Loosely fold the filo pastry up and over to make a neat parcel. Make three more parcels; place on the baking sheet. Brush with half the butter. Bake for about 20 minutes, until the filo is puffed up and golden brown.

4 Meanwhile, make the spinach sauce. Heat the remaining butter in a pan, add the reserved spinach and cook gently for 3 minutes, stirring, until it wilts. Stir in the stock and cream. Heat almost to boiling point, stirring so that the spinach breaks down. Season to taste and keep hot until the fish parcels are ready. Serve garnished with red pepper. Hand the sauce separately.

Monkfish in Beer on a Bed of Leeks

For a long time, superstitious fishermen believed that monkfish brought bad luck and any that were caught were thrown back into the sea. Fortunately, the sweet taste and dense flesh has since earned it a place on the national menu, and the fish has gained greater appreciation by Belgian fish lovers owing to its rather sweet taste and dense flesh.

Serves 4

4 medium fillets of monkfish
50g/2oz/¼ cup unsalted (sweet) butter
2 leeks, white parts only, finely chopped
25ml/1½ tbsp plain (all-purpose) flour
5ml/1 tsp mustard (optional)
300ml/½ pint/1¼ cups Belgian Abbey beer or dry white wine
1–2 tbsp capers, rinsed and dried
salt and ground black pepper
15ml/1 tbsp chopped fresh chives, chervil or parsley, to garnish
cooked potatoes or rye bread, and lemon wedges, to serve

1 Preheat the oven to 180°C/350°F/Gas 4. Rinse the fish fillets and pat them dry. Season both sides with salt and pepper, and set aside.

2 Melt the butter in a frying pan over medium heat. Add the leeks and sauté for 3 minutes. Add the flour and stir for about 2 minutes until it has been absorbed. Stir in the mustard, if using, and continue to stir while gradually adding the beer or wine to the pan.

3 When the sauce thickens, after about 5 minutes, season it, then scrape it into a baking dish. Level the surface. Arrange the fish fillets on the sauce, and sprinkle over the capers. Cover the dish with foil and bake for about 30 minutes, or until the fish flakes when tested with the tip of a sharp knife.

4 Garnish with the herbs and serve with the potatoes or rye bread, offering the lemon wedges separately for squeezing.

Sea Bream Energy 651kcal/2710kJ; Protein 35.8g; Carbohydrate 23.2g, of which sugars 3.3g; Fat 46.8g, of which saturates 23.2g; Cholesterol 159mg; Calcium 222mg; Fibre 2g; Sodium 359mg.
Monkfish Energy 268kcal/1125kJ; Protein 33.3g; Carbohydrate 2.6g, of which sugars 2g; Fat 11.6g, of which saturates 6.8g; Cholesterol 55mg; Calcium 65mg; Fibre 2.3g; Sodium 123mg.

Stuffed Lemon Sole Fillets with Gratin Sauce

These mushroom-stuffed fillets of white fish are a modern take on an old Latvian recipe. A light Parmesan and tarragon sauce makes a succulent topping for the stuffed fish.

Serves 4

4 large lemon sole fillets (or any other white fish fillet), about 200g/7oz each, skinned and bones removed
10g/¼oz/½ tbsp butter
300g/11oz wild mushrooms, finely chopped
5ml/1 tsp finely chopped fresh tarragon
60ml/4 tbsp white wine
60ml/4 tbsp double (heavy) cream
salt and ground black pepper
For the sauce
7.5ml/1½ tsp butter
1 shallot, finely chopped
15ml/1 tbsp cornflour (cornstarch)
200ml/7fl oz/scant 1 cup fish stock
115g/4oz/1¼ cups freshly grated Parmesan cheese
15ml/1 tbsp finely chopped fresh tarragon

1 Lay the fish fillets on your work surface, skin side down. Season with salt and pepper. Melt the butter and add the mushrooms. Stir for 4–5 minutes, then add the tarragon.

2 Add the wine and cream, and cook 5–6 more minutes, or until the liquid has evaporated. Remove from the heat and allow to cool.

3 Preheat the oven to 180°C/350°F/Gas 4. Divide the mushroom mixture among the fish fillets, spreading it along the fillets. Roll up the fillets, making sure that the mushroom filling remains inside. Secure with cocktail sticks (toothpicks) and arrange in an ovenproof dish just large enough to hold the fish.

4 To make the sauce, melt the butter and add the shallot. Sauté for 1–2 minutes. Stir in the cornflour, then gradually add the stock, and combine well to make a smooth sauce. Cook over a low heat for 5 minutes, then add the Parmesan and tarragon. Pour the sauce over the fillets and bake for 20–25 minutes, or until golden brown. Remove from the oven and serve.

Seafood Pie

A well-made fish pie is absolutely delicious, and is particularly good made with a mixture of fresh and smoked fish. Cooked shellfish, such as mussels, can be included too.

Serves 4–5

450g/1lb haddock or cod fillet
225g/8oz smoked haddock or cod
150ml/¼ pint/⅔ cup milk
150ml/¼ pint/⅔ cup water
1 slice of lemon
1 small bay leaf
a few fresh parsley stalks

For the sauce

25g/1oz/2 tbsp butter
25g/1oz/¼ cup plain (all-purpose) flour
5ml/1 tbsp lemon juice, or to taste
45ml/3 tbsp chopped fresh parsley
ground black pepper

For the topping

450g/1lb potatoes, boiled and mashed
25g/1oz/2 tbsp butter

1 Preheat the oven to 190°C/375°F/Gas 5. Rinse the fish, cut it into bitesize pieces and put into a pan with the milk, water, lemon, bay leaf and parsley stalks. Bring slowly to the boil, then simmer gently for 15 minutes until tender. Strain and reserve 300ml/½ pint/1¼ cups of the cooking liquor. Leave the fish to cool, then flake the flesh and discard the skin and bones. Set aside.

2 To make the sauce, melt the butter in a heavy pan, add the flour and cook for 1–2 minutes over low heat stirring constantly. Gradually add the reserved cooking liquor, stirring well to make a smooth sauce.

3 Simmer the sauce gently for 1–2 minutes, then remove from the heat and stir in the flaked fish, chopped parsley and lemon juice. Season to taste with pepper. Turn into a buttered 1.75 litre/3 pint/7½ cup pie dish or shallow casserole, cover with the potato for the topping and dot with the butter.

4 Cook in the oven for about 20 minutes, or until thoroughly heated through. The top should be golden brown and crunchy. Divide the pie among 4–5 warmed plates and serve with a lightly cooked green vegetable, such as fresh broccoli spears.

Lemon Sole Energy 420kcal/1757kJ; Protein 46g; Carbohydrate 5.1g, of which sugars 1.3g; Fat 23.9g, of which saturates 13.2g; Cholesterol 178mg; Calcium 393mg; Fibre 0.2g; Sodium 545mg.
Seafood Pie Energy 336Kcal/1413kJ; Protein 35.1g; Carbohydrate 24.3g, of which sugars 0.9g; Fat 11.6g, of which saturates 6.7g; Cholesterol 87mg; Calcium 45mg; Fibre 1.7g; Sodium 587mg.

Fish Pie with Saffron Mash

This is the ultimate fish pie. Breaking through the golden potato crust reveals prawns and chunks of cod swathed in a creamy parsley sauce.

Serves 6

750ml/1¼ pints/3 cups milk
1 onion, chopped
1 bay leaf
2–3 peppercorns
450g/1lb each of fresh cod fillet
   and smoked haddock fillet
350g/12oz cooked tiger prawns
   (jumbo shrimp), shelled, with tails
75g/3oz/6 tbsp butter
75g/3oz/¾ cup plain
   (all-purpose) flour
60ml/4 tbsp chopped fresh parsley
1.3kg/3lb floury potatoes, peeled
large pinch saffron threads, soaked
   in 45ml/3 tbsp hot water
75g/3oz/6 tbsp butter
250ml/8fl oz/1 cup milk
45ml/3 tbsp chopped fresh dill
salt and ground black pepper

1 Put the milk, chopped onion, bay leaf and peppercorns into a pan. Bring to the boil, simmer for about 10 minutes, and set aside. Lay the cod and haddock fillets, skin side up, in a pan. Strain over the milk, place over a gentle heat and simmer for 5–7 minutes until the fish is opaque. Lift it out of the milk and transfer to a plate. Reserve the milk.

2 When the fish is cool enough to handle, pull off the skin and flake the flesh into large pieces, removing any bones as you go. Transfer to a large bowl and add the shelled prawns.

3 Melt the butter in a small pan. Stir in the flour and cook for a minute or so, then gradually stir in the flavoured milk from the pan until you achieve a smooth consistency. Whisk well and simmer gently for 15 minutes until thick and a little reduced, then taste and season with salt and pepper. Stir in the parsley. Pour the sauce over the fish. Carefully mix together, transfer the mixture to a pie dish and leave to cool.

4 Preheat the oven to 180°C/350°F/Gas 4. Boil the potatoes in salted water until tender, drain and mash until smooth. Using an electric whisk, beat in the saffron and its soaking water, then the butter, milk and dill to make light, fluffy mashed potato. When the fish mixture has cooled and set, pile the mash on top. Bake for 30–40 minutes, or until the potato is golden and crisp.

Classic Fish Pie

Originally a fish pie was based on the 'catch of the day'. Now we can choose either the fish we like best, or the variety that offers best value for money.

Serves 4

butter, for greasing
450g/1lb mixed fish, such as
   cod or salmon fillets and
   peeled prawns (shrimp)
finely grated rind of 1 lemon
450g/1lb floury potatoes
25g/1oz/2 tbsp butter
salt and ground black pepper
1 egg, beaten

For the sauce
15g/½oz/1 tbsp butter
15ml/1 tbsp plain
   (all-purpose) flour
150ml/¼ pint/⅔ cup milk
45ml/3 tbsp chopped fresh parsley

1 Preheat the oven to 220°C/425°F/Gas 7. Grease an ovenproof dish and set aside. Cut the fish into bitesize pieces. Season the fish, sprinkle over the lemon rind and place in the base of the prepared dish. Set aside while you make the topping.

2 Cook the potatoes in a pan of boiling salted water for about 10–15 minutes until tender.

3 Meanwhile, make the sauce. Melt the butter in a pan, add the flour and cook, stirring, for a few minutes. Remove from the heat and gradually whisk in the milk. Return to the heat and bring to the boil, then reduce the heat to a simmer, whisking constantly, until the sauce has thickened and achieved a smooth consistency. Add the parsley and season to taste. Pour over the fish mixture.

4 Drain the potatoes well and then mash with the butter. Pipe or spoon the potatoes on top of the fish mixture. Brush the beaten egg over the potatoes. Bake for 45 minutes until the top is golden brown. Serve hot.

> **Cook's Tip**
> If using frozen fish defrost it thoroughly first, as a lot of water from the fish will ruin your pie.

Fish Pie with Saffron Energy 458kcal/1921kJ; Protein 29.4g; Carbohydrate 32.8g, of which sugars 5.8g; Fat 25g, of which saturates 3.7g; Cholesterol 74mg; Calcium 216mg; Fibre 1g; Sodium 867mg.
Classic Fish Pie Energy 301kcal/1262lkJ; Protein 26.5g; Carbohydrate 24.1g, of which sugars 2.6g; Fat 11.6g, of which saturates 6.2g; Cholesterol 132mg; Calcium 76mg; Fibre 1.6g; Sodium 173mg.

Fish Pie

This traditional fish pie, using a combination of white fish and smoked haddock, has a distinct Welsh flavour. This version uses a puff pastry topping, which, if you wish, can easily be replaced with mashed potato.

Serves 4
225g/8oz skinless white fish, such as hake, haddock or cod
225g/8oz skinless smoked haddock or cod
425ml/¾ pint/scant 2 cups milk
25g/1oz/2 tbsp butter
25g/1oz/½ cup plain (all-purpose) flour
good pinch of freshly grated nutmeg
1 leek, thinly sliced
200g/7oz shelled cooked cockles (small clam)
30ml/2 tbsp laverbread (optional)
30ml/2 tbsp finely chopped fresh parsley
1 sheet ready-rolled puff pastry
salt and ground black pepper

1 Preheat the oven to 200°C/400°F/Gas 6. Put the white and smoked fish in a pan with the milk. Heat until the milk barely comes to the boil, then cover and poach gently for about 8 minutes or until the fish is just cooked. Lift the fish out, reserving the liquid. Break into flakes, discarding any bones.

2 Melt the butter, stir in the flour and cook for 1–2 minutes. Remove and stir in the reserved cooking liquid. Stir over medium heat until the sauce thickens.

3 Stir in the fish flakes and their juices. Add nutmeg and season to taste. Add the leek, cockles, laverbread, if using, and parsley to the sauce and spoon into a 1.2 litre/2 pint ovenproof dish.

4 Brush the edges of the dish with water. Unroll the pastry and lay it over the top of the dish, trimming it to fit.

5 Use the pastry off-cuts to make decorative fish or leaves for the top, brushing each one with a little water to help them stick.

6 Put into the hot oven and cook for about 30 minutes, or until the pastry is puffed and golden brown.

Fish Pie with Sweet Potato Topping

This unusual fish pie is crowned with a subtly sweet topping of mashed potato and sweet potato.

30–45ml/2–3 tbsp plain (all-purpose) flour
15ml/1 tbsp chopped fresh parsley
salt and ground black pepper

Serves 4
175g/6oz/1 cup basmati rice
450ml/¾ pint/scant 2 cups well-flavoured stock
175g/6oz/1½ cups podded broad (fava) beans
675g/1½lb cod fillets, skinned
450ml/¾ pint/scant 2 cups milk

For the topping
450g/1lb sweet potatoes, peeled and cut in large chunks
450g/1lb floury white potatoes, peeled and cut in large chunks
milk and butter, for mashing
10ml/2 tsp freshly chopped parsley
5ml/1 tsp freshly chopped dill
15ml/1 tbsp single (light) cream (optional)

For the sauce
40g/1½oz/3 tbsp butter

1 Preheat the oven to 190°C/375°F/Gas 5. Put the rice in a pan with the stock. Bring to the boil, then cover and simmer for 10 minutes until tender. Cook the beans in lightly salted water until tender. Drain thoroughly. When cool, remove their skins.

2 For the topping, cook the sweet and white potatoes separately in boiling salted water until tender. Drain, then mash with milk and butter and spoon into separate bowls. Beat the parsley and dill into the sweet potatoes, with the cream, if using.

3 Place the fish in a pan and pour in milk to cover. Dot with 15g/½oz/1 tbsp of the butter and season. Simmer for 5 minutes until tender. Remove from the pan. Make up the cooking liquid to 450ml/¾ pint/scant 2 cups with the remaining milk.

4 Make a white sauce. Melt the butter in a pan, stir in the flour and cook for 1 minute. Gradually add the milk mixture, stirring, until a white sauce forms. Stir in the parsley, taste and season.

5 Spread the rice on the bottom of a gratin dish. Add the beans and fish and pour over the sauce. Top with the potatoes in a pattern. Dot with butter and bake for 15 minutes until browned.

Fish Pie Energy 573kcal/2401kJ; Protein 36.8g; Carbohydrate 41g, of which sugars 7.3g; Fat 31.2g, of which saturates 4.7g; Cholesterol 92mg; Calcium 270mg; Fibre 1.2g; Sodium 1084mg.
Fish Pie with Sweet Potato Energy 604kcal/2545kJ; Protein 41.6g; Carbohydrate 88g, of which sugars 8.6g; Fat 10.7g, of which saturates 5.7g; Cholesterol 99mg; Calcium 94mg; Fibre 6.9g; Sodium 223mg.

Smoked Salmon Quiche

The ingredients in this light quiche perfectly complement the melt-in-the-mouth pastry made with potatoes.

Serves 6
For the pastry
115g/4oz floury maincrop
   potatoes, diced
225g/8oz/2 cups plain
   (all-purpose) flour, sifted
115g/4oz/½ cup butter, diced
½ egg, beaten
10ml/2 tsp chilled water

For the filling
275g/10oz smoked salmon
6 eggs, beaten
150ml/¼ pint/⅔ cup full-cream
   (whole) milk
300ml/½ pint/1¼ cups double
   (heavy) cream
30–45ml/2–3 tbsp chopped
   fresh dill
30ml/2 tbsp capers, chopped
salt and ground black pepper
salad leaves and chopped fresh
   dill, to serve

1 For the potato pastry, boil the potatoes in a pan of salted water for 15 minutes or until tender. Drain well and return to the pan. Mash the potatoes until smooth and set aside to cool completely.

2 Place the flour in a bowl and rub in the butter to form fine crumbs. Beat in the potatoes and egg. Bring the mixture together; if it is too heavy, add a little chilled water until it is pliable and able to be rolled out.

3 Roll the pastry out on a floured surface and use to line a deep 23cm/9in round, loose-based, fluted flan tin (pan). Chill for 1 hour.

4 Preheat the oven to 200°C/400°F/Gas 6. Place a baking sheet in the oven to preheat it. Chop the salmon into bitesize pieces and set aside.

5 For the filling, beat the eggs, milk and cream together, then stir in the dill and capers and season with pepper. Add the salmon and stir to mix.

6 Prick the base of the pastry case (pie shell) well and pour the mixture into it. Bake on a baking sheet for 35–45 minutes until cooked through. Serve warm with salad leaves and dill.

Thai-style Seafood Pasties

Thai-style food is popular along the West Coast of America, where rice is one of the most important crops.

Makes 18
500g/1¼lb puff pastry, thawed
   if frozen
1 egg, beaten with
   30ml/2 tbsp water
fresh coriander leaves and lime
   twists, to garnish

For the filling
275g/10oz skinned white fish
   fillets, such as cod or haddock
plain flour, seasoned
8–10 large raw prawns
15ml/1 tbsp sunflower oil
about 75g/3oz/6 tbsp butter
6 spring onions, finely sliced
1 garlic clove, crushed
225g/8oz/2 cups cooked Thai
   fragrant rice
4cm/1½in piece of fresh root
   ginger, grated
10ml/2 tsp chopped fresh coriander
5ml/1 tsp finely grated lime rind

1 Preheat the oven to 190°C/375°F/Gas 5. Make the filling. Cut the fish into 2cm/¾in cubes and dust with the flour. Peel and devein the prawns and cut each one into four pieces.

2 Heat half of the oil and 15g/½oz/1 tbsp of the butter in a frying pan. Add the spring onions and fry for 2 minutes. Add the garlic and fry for about 5 minutes more, until the onions are very soft. Transfer to a large bowl.

3 Heat the remaining oil and a further 25g/1oz/2 tbsp of the butter in a clean pan. Fry the fish pieces briefly. When they begin to turn opaque, transfer them to the bowl with the spring onions. Cook the prawns in the pan. When they begin to change colour, lift them out and add them to the bowl.

4 Add the rice, with the ginger, coriander and lime rind. Mix. Dust the work surface with flour. Roll out the pastry and cut into 10cm/4in rounds. Place spoonfuls of filling on the pastry rounds. Dot with butter. Dampen the edges of the pastry with the egg wash, fold one side of the pastry over the filling and press the edges together firmly. Place them on a greased baking sheet. Decorate with pastry trimmings, if you like. Brush with egg wash and bake for 12–15 minutes. Garnish with lime twists.

Salmon Quiche Energy 338kcal/1413kJ; Protein 24.3g; Carbohydrate 17.9g, of which sugars 10.2g; Fat 19.4g, of which saturates 7g; Cholesterol 199mg; Calcium 167mg; Fibre 0.7g; Sodium 665mg.
Seafood Pasties Energy 171kcal/715kJ; Protein 8.6g; Carbohydrate 18.7g, of which sugars 0.9g; Fat 7g, of which saturates 2.3g; Cholesterol 48mg; Calcium 34mg; Fibre 0.4g; Sodium 99mg.

Lemony Salmon Loaf with Cucumber

This easy all-in-one loaf would make a tasty lunch.

Serves 4–6
150ml/¼ pint/⅔ cup milk
2 eggs, beaten
115g/4oz/2 cups fresh white
  breadcrumbs
butter, for greasing
75g/3oz celery
400g/14oz can salmon, drained

grated rind and juice of 1 lemon
salt and ground black pepper

For the sauce
1 cucumber, peeled, seeded
  and chopped
25g/1oz/2 tbsp butter
15ml/1 tbsp plain
  (all-purpose) flour
rind and juice of ½ lemon
1 egg yolk

1 Mix the milk, eggs and breadcrumbs in a large bowl and leave to stand for 10 minutes. Preheat the oven to 180°C/350°F/ Gas 4. Grease a 450g/1lb loaf tin (pan) with butter. Chop the celery finely and set it aside.

2 Place the drained salmon in a bowl and flake with a fork. Add to the breadcrumb mixture with the celery, lemon rind and juice. Season to taste. Stir the mixture until blended. Pour into the prepared loaf tin and bake for 1 hour or until a skewer inserted into the centre of the loaf comes out clean. Leave the loaf in the tin to cool slightly.

3 Make the sauce. Place the cucumber pieces in a small pan, cover with cold water and simmer until just tender. Remove the cucumber and set it aside. Pour the cooking liquid into a measuring jug (cup). Add enough water to make up the liquid to 300ml/½ pint/1¼ cups.

4 Melt the butter, stir in the flour and cook, stirring constantly, for 1 minute, then add the reserved liquid, stirring until it boils and thickens. Add the lemon rind and juice, then the cucumber. Beat the egg yolk in a bowl and stir in a little of the hot sauce. Pour into the pan and heat gently, until the sauce thickens more. Season to taste. Loosen the loaf from the sides of the tin and invert it on a serving dish. Slice and serve with the sauce.

Salmon Bake

Subtly flavoured with dill and onion, this warming bake combines two of the most common ingredients in Finland: salmon and potatoes.

Serves 4
25g/1oz/2 tbsp unsalted (sweet)
  butter, softened
8 potatoes, thinly sliced
300g/11oz pressed salmon with
  dill, sliced (see below)
1 onion, finely chopped
30ml/2 tbsp chopped fresh dill

3 eggs, beaten
400ml/14fl oz/1⅔ cups milk
5ml/1 tsp salt
2.5ml/½ tsp ground
  white pepper

**For the pressed salmon with
  dill (Graavilohi)**
90ml/6 tbsp coarse sea salt
90ml/6 tbsp sugar
90ml/6 tbsp chopped fresh dill
30ml/2 tbsp brandy
5ml/1 tsp ground black pepper
1 small or ½ large fresh
  salmon, filleted

1 To make the pressed salmon and dill, put the salt, sugar, dill, brandy and pepper in a bowl and mix together. Rub the mixture over both sides of the salmon fillets. Place the flesh sides of the fillets together, so that the skin sides are on the outside, to form a whole fish, then wrap in foil.

2 Place the wrapped fish in a deep dish or roasting pan and place a heavy weight or weights, such as cans, on the top. Put in the refrigerator and leave for 12 hours. Turn the fish over, replace the weights and leave for a further 12 hours. Scrape off the marinade and pat the fish dry with kitchen paper.

3 To prepare the salmon bake, preheat the oven to 200°C/400°F/Gas 6. Grease a deep, ovenproof dish with a little of the butter.

4 Arrange half the potato slices in a layer over the base of the dish, then add a layer of salmon and a layer of onion. Sprinkle over the dill and end with a layer of the remaining potato slices.

5 Mix the eggs, milk, salt and pepper together and pour over the dish. Dot the remaining butter on top. Bake in the oven for 1 hour, until the potatoes are tender. Serve immediately.

Salmon Loaf Energy 219kcal/918kJ; Protein 17g; Carbohydrate 14g, of which sugars 3g; Fat 11g, of which saturates 5g; Cholesterol 65mg; Calcium 129mg; Fibre 1g; Sodium 404mg.
Salmon Bake Energy 338kcal/1413kJ; Protein 24.3g; Carbohydrate 17.9g, of which sugars 10.2g; Fat 19.4g, of which saturates 7g; Cholesterol 199mg; Calcium 167mg; Fibre 0.7g; Sodium 665mg.

Salmon, Potato and Mushroom Bake

This layered bake is a variation of a popular dish in Latvia. The hint of caraway goes well with the rich salmon and mushrooms.

Serves 4–6

135ml/4½fl oz/scant ⅔ cup vegetable oil
4 baking potatoes, peeled and thinly sliced
10g/¼oz/½ tbsp butter
300g/11oz/generous 4 cups mushrooms, thinly sliced
1 large onion, finely sliced in rings
1.5ml/½ tsp caraway seeds
500g/1¼lb thin salmon fillets, bones and skin removed
2 large eggs, beaten
300ml/½ pint/1¼ cups single (light) cream
200g/7oz/3½ cups fresh rye breadcrumbs
salt and ground black pepper

1 Preheat the oven to 180°C/350°F/Gas 4. Heat 75–90ml/5–6 tbsp oil in a large non-stick frying pan over a medium heat. Add the potatoes a few at a time, and cook for 5–8 minutes, or until they are almost tender and lightly browned. (You may need to cook them for a little longer, depending on how thinly you have sliced them.) Remove with a slotted spoon and set aside.

2 Add the butter to the pan and add the mushrooms. Sauté for about 4 minutes, or until soft. Season to taste and remove the mushrooms from the pan.

3 Add the remaining oil to the pan and cook the onion rings for 4–5 minutes, or until lightly browned and soft. Line individual serving dishes, or a 20cm/8in square ovenproof dish, with most of the pre-cooked potatoes in a solid layer, overlapping the slices slightly.

4 Spoon over the mushrooms, and then top with the onion rings. Grind the caraway seeds using a mortar and pestle, and sprinkle over the top.

5 Top with the salmon fillets and finish with a layer of the remaining potatoes. Combine the eggs and cream in a bowl and pour over the bake. Sprinkle with the breadcrumbs. Bake individual dishes for 20–25 minutes, and the larger dish for 35–40 minutes, or until golden brown. Serve hot.

Egg and Salmon Puff Parcels

These elegant parcels hide a mouthwatering mixture of flavours, and make a delicious appetizer or lunch dish. Serve with curry-flavoured mayonnaise or hollandaise sauce.

Serves 6

75g/3oz/scant ½ cup long grain rice
300ml/½ pint/4 cups good-quality fish stock
350g/12oz tail pieces of salmon
juice of ½ lemon
15ml/1 tbsp chopped fresh dill
15ml/1 tbsp chopped fresh parsley
10ml/2 tsp mild curry powder
6 small eggs, soft-boiled and cooled
425g/15oz flaky or puff pastry
1 egg, beaten
salt and ground black pepper

1 Place the rice in a large pan and cook according to the instructions on the packet, using fish stock instead of water, then drain, tip into a bowl and set aside to cool. Preheat the oven to 220°C/425°F/Gas 7.

2 Place the salmon in a large pan and cover with cold water. Gently heat until the water is not quite simmering and cook the fish for 8–10 minutes until it flakes easily when tested.

3 Lift the salmon out of the pan and remove the bones and skin. Flake the fish into the rice, add the lemon juice, herbs, curry powder and seasoning, and mix well. Peel the eggs.

4 Roll out the pastry and cut into six 15cm/6in squares. Brush the edges with the beaten egg. Place a spoonful of the rice mixture in the middle of each square, push an egg into the centre and top with a little more of the rice mixture.

5 Pull over the pastry corners to the middle to form a neat parcel. Press the joins together with your fingers firmly to seal.

6 Brush the parcels with beaten egg, place on a baking sheet and bake for 20 minutes, then reduce the oven temperature to 190°C/375°F/Gas 5. Cook for 10 minutes, more or until golden and crisp underneath. Cool the pastries slightly before serving.

Salmon Bake Energy 689kcal/2877kJ; Protein 27.2g; Carbohydrate 57.6g, of which sugars 7.1g; Fat 40.4g, of which saturates 11.2g; Cholesterol 149mg; Calcium 144mg; Fibre 3.4g; Sodium 422mg.
Salmon Puff Parcels Energy 494kcal/2063kJ; Protein 23.4g; Carbohydrate 36.9g, of which sugars 1.1g; Fat 29.7g, of which saturates 2.7g; Cholesterol 219mg; Calcium 112mg; Fibre 0.8g; Sodium 326mg.

Salmon in Puff Pastry

This is an elegant party dish, made with rice, eggs and salmon, enclosed in pastry.

Serves six

450g/1lb puff pastry, thawed
  if frozen
1 egg, beaten
3 hard-boiled eggs
90ml/6 tbsp single cream
200g/7oz/1¾ cups long grain
  cooked rice
30ml/2 tbsp finely chopped
  fresh parsley
10ml/2 tsp chopped fresh tarragon
675g/1½lb fresh salmon fillets
40g/1½oz/3 tbsp butter
juice of ½ lemon
salt and ground
  black pepper

1 Preheat the oven to 190°C/375°F/Gas 5. Roll out two-thirds of the pastry into an oval, measuring about 35cm/14in in length. Cut into a curved fish shape and place on a greased baking sheet. Use the trimmings to make narrow strips. Brush one side of each strip with beaten egg and secure in place around the rim of the pastry to make a raised edge. Prick the base all over with a fork, then bake for 8–10 minutes until the sides are well risen and the pastry is lightly golden. Leave to cool.

2 In a bowl, mash the hard-boiled eggs with the cream, then add the cooked rice. Add the parsley and tarragon and season well. Spoon this mixture on to the prepared pastry. Cut the salmon into 2cm/¾in chunks. Melt the butter until it sizzles, then add the salmon. Turn the pieces over in the butter so that they begin to colour but do not cook through. Remove from the heat and arrange the salmon on the rice. Stir the lemon juice into the butter in the pan, then spoon over the salmon pieces.

3 Roll out the remaining pastry and cut out a semi-circle piece to cover the head and a tail shape to cover the tail. Brush both pieces of pastry with beaten egg and place on the fish, pressing down firmly to secure. Score a criss-cross pattern on the tail.

4 Cut the remaining pastry into small circles and, starting from the tail end, arrange them in overlapping lines for scales. Add an extra one for an eye. Brush the shape with beaten egg. Bake for 10 minutes, then reduce the temperature to 160°C/325°F/Gas 3 and cook for 15–20 minutes until golden. Serve.

Salmon Coulibiac

Serves 8
For the filling
50g/2oz/¼ cup butter
350g/12oz/5 cups chestnut
  mushrooms, sliced
105ml/7 tbsp white wine
juice of ½ lemon
675g/1½lb salmon fillet, skinned
115g/4oz/scant ½ cup
  long grain rice
30ml/2 tbsp chopped
  fresh dill
1 large onion, chopped
4 hard-boiled eggs, shelled, sliced
butter, for greasing
flour, for dusting
450g/1lb puff pastry
1 egg, beaten
salt and ground black pepper
lemon and dill sprigs, to garnish

1 First make the filling. Melt most of the butter in a large frying pan. Add the mushrooms and cook for 3 minutes. Pour in 60ml/4 tbsp of the wine and boil for 2 minutes, then simmer for 5 minutes. Stir in most of the remaining wine and the lemon juice. Place the salmon on top of the cooked mushrooms, cover with foil and steam for 8–10 minutes, until just cooked. Remove the salmon from the pan and set aside. With a slotted spoon, transfer the mushrooms to a bowl. Pour the cooking liquid into a large pan. Add the rice and cook for 10–15 minutes, until tender, adding water if needed.

2 Remove from the heat and stir in the dill and seasoning. Melt the remaining butter and fry the onion until golden. Set aside. Grease a large baking sheet. Using baking parchment, cut out a fish-shaped template that will fit easily on the baking sheet. Roll out just less than half the pastry and use the template to cut a fish shape. Place on the baking sheet. Leaving the edges clear, spread out half the mushrooms and top with half the rice, half the onion and half the eggs. Add the salmon, cutting it to fit, then repeat the layers in reverse.

3 Roll out the remaining pastry and cut a larger fish shape. Brush the base pastry rim with egg, fit the pastry top and seal the edges. Chill for 1 hour. Preheat the oven to 220°C/425°F/Gas 7. Cut four slits in the pastry, brush with egg and bake for 10 minutes. Reduce the oven temperature to 190°C/375°F/Gas 5 and bake for 30 minutes until golden. Garnish with lemon wedges and dill sprigs and serve.

Salmon in Pastry Energy 668kcal/2782kJ; Protein 31g; Carbohydrate 36.6g, of which sugars 0.7g; Fat 45.3g, of which saturates 14g; Cholesterol 209mg; Calcium 98mg; Fibre 1.1g; Sodium 389mg.
Salmon Coulibiac Energy 519kcal/2166kJ; Protein 26g; Carbohydrate 34g, of which sugars 1g; Fat 32g, of which saturates 6g; Cholesterol 174mg; Calcium 76mg; Fibre 3g; Sodium 297mg.

Gratin of Cod with Mustard

While the cod crisis continues in Scottish waters, those in north-west Europe are advised not to eat Atlantic cod. However, you can now buy good-quality farmed cod and elsewhere in the world cod or its local equivalents are still available. If you need an alternative then a thick, flaky-textured, moist white-fleshed fish is what is required.

Serves 4

4 cod steaks, approximately
   175g/6oz each
200g/7oz/1¾ cups grated
   Cheddar cheese, such as
   Isle of Mull
15ml/1 tbsp wholegrain mustard
75ml/5 tbsp double
   (heavy) cream
salt and ground black pepper

1 Preheat the oven to 200°C/400°F/Gas 6. Check the fish for bones and remove any pin bones with tweezers.

2 Butter the base and sides of an ovenproof dish then place the fish fillets skin side down in the dish and season.

3 In a small bowl, mix the grated cheese and mustard together with enough cream to form a spreadable but thick paste. Make sure that the cheese and mustard are thoroughly blended to ensure an even taste. Season lightly with salt and ground black pepper.

4 Spread the cheese mixture thickly and evenly over each fish fillet, using up all of the mixture.

5 Bake in the preheated oven for about 20 minutes, until the top of the gratin is browned and bubbling and the fish underneath is flaky and tender. Serve immediately on warmed plates.

Variation
If you don't have wholegrain mustard, use any ready-made mustard that you have to hand.

Filo Fish Pies

These light filo-wrapped fish pies can be made with any firm white fish fillets, such as orange roughy, cod, halibut or hoki. Serve with salad leaves and mayonnaise.

Serves 6
400g/14oz spinach, trimmed
1 egg, lightly beaten
2 garlic cloves, crushed
450g/1lb orange roughy or other
   white fish fillet
juice of 1 lemon
50g/2oz/¼ cup butter, melted
8–12 filo pastry sheets, thawed
   if frozen, quartered
15ml/1 tbsp finely chopped chives
200ml/7fl oz/scant 1 cup half-fat
   crème fraîche
15ml/1 tbsp chopped fresh dill
salt and ground black pepper

1 Preheat the oven to 190°C/375°F/Gas 5. Wash the spinach, then cook it in a lidded heavy pan with just the water that clings to the leaves. As soon as the leaves are tender, drain, squeeze as dry as possible and chop. Put the spinach in a bowl, add the egg and garlic, season with salt and pepper and set aside. Dice the fish and place it in a bowl. Stir in the lemon juice. Season with salt and pepper and toss lightly.

2 Brush the inside of six 13cm/5in tartlet tins (muffin pans) with a little of the melted butter. Fit a piece of filo pastry into the tins, draping it so that it hangs over the sides. Brush with butter, then add another sheet at right-angles to the first. Brush with butter. Continue to line the tins in this way.

3 Spread the spinach evenly over the pastry. Add the diced fish and season well. Stir the chives into the crème fraîche and spread the mixture over the top of the fish. Sprinkle with dill.

4 Draw the overhanging pieces of pastry together and scrunch lightly to make a lid. Brush with butter. Bake for about 15–20 minutes, until golden brown. Serve immediately.

Variation
To make one large pie, use a 20cm/8in tin (pan) and bake in the oven for 45 minutes.

Gratin of Cod Energy 445kcal/1852kJ; Protein 46g; Carbohydrate 9.1g, of which sugars 2.2g; Fat 14g, of which saturates 8.2g; Cholesterol 84mg; Calcium 170mg; Fibre 1.7g; Sodium 213mg.
Filo Fish Pies Energy 233kcal/972kJ; Protein 18.4g; Carbohydrate 33.2g, of which sugars 3.7g; Fat 8.6g, of which saturates 1.4g; Cholesterol 41mg; Calcium 77mg; Fibre 2.1g; Sodium 276mg.

Filo-wrapped Fish

This delicious dish comes from Jerusalem, where, typically, fish are wrapped in filo pastry and served with a zesty tomato sauce.

Serves 3–4

450g/1lb salmon or cod steaks
1 lemon
30ml/2 tbsp olive oil, plus extra for brushing
1 onion, chopped
2 celery sticks, chopped
1 green (bell) pepper, diced
5 garlic cloves, chopped
400g/14oz fresh or canned tomatoes, chopped
120ml/4fl oz/½ cup passata (bottled strained tomatoes)
30ml/2 tbsp chopped fresh flat leaf parsley
2–3 pinches of ground allspice or ground cloves
cayenne pepper, to taste
pinch of sugar
about 130g/4½oz filo pastry (6–8 large sheets)
salt and ground black pepper

1 Sprinkle the salmon or cod steaks with salt and black pepper and a squeeze of lemon juice. Set aside and prepare the sauce.

2 Heat the olive oil in a pan, add the chopped onion, celery and pepper and fry for about 5 minutes, until the vegetables are softened. Add the garlic and cook for a further 1 minute, then add the tomatoes and passata and cook until the tomatoes are the consistency of a sauce. Stir the parsley into the sauce, then season with allspice or cloves, cayenne pepper, sugar and salt and pepper.

3 Preheat the oven to 200°C/400°F/Gas 6. Take a sheet of filo pastry, brush with a little olive oil and cover with a second sheet. Place a piece of fish on top of the pastry, toward the bottom edge, then top with 1–2 spoonfuls of the sauce, spreading it evenly.

4 Roll the fish in the pastry, taking care to enclose the filling completely. Arrange on a baking sheet and repeat with the remaining fish and pastry. You should have about half the sauce remaining, to serve with the fish.

5 Bake for 10–15 minutes, or until golden. Reheat the remaining sauce if necessary. Serve with the remaining sauce.

Salmon and Prawn Tart

This tart is unusual because it is made with raw salmon, which means that the fish stays moist. Cooking it this way gives a lovely succulent result. This versatile dish may be served hot with vegetables or cool with mixed salad leaves and tomato wedges.

Serves 6

350g/12oz shortcrust pastry, thawed if frozen
225g/8oz salmon fillet, skinned
225g/8oz/2 cups cooked peeled prawns (shrimp)
2 eggs, plus 2 egg yolks
150ml/¼ pint/⅔ cup whipping cream
200ml/7fl oz/scant 1 cup milk
15ml/1 tbsp chopped fresh dill
salt, ground black pepper and paprika
lime slices, tomato wedges and fresh dill sprigs, to garnish

1 Roll out the pastry on a floured work surface and use it to line a 20cm/8in quiche dish or tin (pan). Prick the base all over and mark the edges with the tines of the fork. It need not be too neat. Chill for about 30 minutes.

2 Meanwhile, preheat the oven to 180°C/350°F/Gas 4. Bake the pastry case (pie shell) for about 30 minutes, until golden brown. Reduce the oven temperature to 160°C/325°F/Gas 3.

3 Cut the salmon into 2cm/¾in cubes. Arrange the salmon and prawns evenly in the pastry case. Dust with paprika.

4 In a bowl, beat together the eggs and yolks, cream, milk and dill and season to taste. Pour over the salmon and prawns. Bake for about 30 minutes, until the filling is just set. Serve hot or at room temperature, garnished with lime slices, tomato wedges and dill.

Cook's Tip

For a more economical version of this flan, omit the prawns (shrimp) and use some extra salmon instead, or use a mixture of salmon and white fish.

Filo Fish Energy 496kcal/2063kJ; Protein 20.6g; Carbohydrate 26.7g, of which sugars 1.3g; Fat 34.8g, of which saturates 8.1g; Cholesterol 249mg; Calcium 111mg; Fibre 1.5g; Sodium 217mg.
Salmon and Prawn Energy 517kcal/2151kJ; Protein 22g; Carbohydrate 29g, of which sugars 3g; Fat 35g, of which saturates 14g; Cholesterol 242mg; Calcium 159mg; Fibre 1g; Sodium 372mg.

Sour Fish and Vegetable Bake

This layered eel and vegetable bake is slowly baked in the oven, resulting in marvellously tender fish that is full in flavour.

Serves 4

675g/1½lb eel, skinned and boned
900ml/1½ pints/3¾ cups fish
  or vegetable stock
1.2 litres/2 pints/5 cups water
450g/1lb/4 cups shredded
  white cabbage
50g/2oz/¼ cup butter
1 large onion, chopped
2 pickled cucumbers, sliced
12 green olives
15ml/1 tbsp capers, drained
75g/3oz/1½ cups fresh white
  breadcrumbs
salt and ground black pepper
parsley, to garnish

1 Cut the eel into large pieces. Bring the fish or vegetable stock to a gentle simmer in a large, heavy pan, then add the eel and cook for about 4 minutes.

2 Remove the fish pieces from the pan with a slotted spoon. Reserve 150ml/¼ pint/⅔ cup of the stock and set aside, leaving the remaining stock in the pan.

3 Pour the measured water into the pan of stock. Bring to the boil, then add the shredded cabbage. Simmer for 2 minutes, then strain well.

4 Melt half of the butter in the pan. Cook the onion for about 5 minutes, stirring occasionally, until beginning to turn soft. Stir in the strained cabbage and reserved stock, then bring to the boil. Cover the pan with a tight-fitting lid and cook over low heat for about 1 hour, until tender. Season with salt and plenty of ground black pepper.

5 Preheat the oven to 200°C/400°F/Gas 6. Spoon half the cabbage into a baking dish. Top with the eel and the cucumbers. Spoon over the remaining cabbage and any remaining stock.

6 Sprinkle the olives, capers and the breadcrumbs over the top. Melt the remaining butter and drizzle over the top. Bake for 25–30 minutes, or until the breadcrumbs are lightly browned. Garnish with parsley sprigs.

Trout with Cucumber and Horseradish

Horseradish is one of the principal aromatics in Finnish cooking, and it is especially good with salmon or trout. Used with care, it gives zest to a dish rather than overpowers it. If you are able to use fresh horseradish and grate it yourself, so much the better.

Serves 4

1 cucumber, thinly sliced
75g/3oz/6 tbsp butter, softened,
  plus extra for greasing
5ml/1 tsp Dijon mustard
20g/¾oz grated horseradish
a few drops of lemon juice
600g/1lb 6oz trout fillet, cut into
  twelve 50g/2oz thin slices
45ml/3 tbsp water or white wine
salt and ground black pepper

1 Sprinkle the cucumber slices with 2.5ml/½ tsp salt and mix together. Sandwich the slices between two plates, place a small weight on top and leave in the refrigerator for 30 minutes. Squeeze out any juices from the cucumber.

2 Preheat the oven to 200°C/400°F/Gas 6. Grease an ovenproof dish with butter and sprinkle over the base. Beat the softened butter until it is light and fluffy, then add the mustard, horseradish, lemon juice and pepper, and beat until well mixed.

3 Arrange the trout slices in the prepared dish in four servings, each consisting of three overlapping slices. Spread these with the horseradish butter. Arrange the cucumber slices across the top of each serving, to look like fish scales.

4 Add water or white wine to the dish, cover with foil, and bake for 6–7 minutes. Transfer each serving to a plate and serve hot.

Cook's Tip

It is very easy to overcook trout, which makes it dry. You need to remember that residual heat on the outside of the fish will continue to cook the centre for as long as it remains warm, so it should be served as soon as it is ready.

Fish Bake Energy 508kcal/2117kJ; Protein 33.1g; Carbohydrate 25.2g, of which sugars 9.9g; Fat 31.2g, of which saturates 11.8g; Cholesterol 282mg; Calcium 146mg; Fibre 4.2g; Sodium 623mg.
Trout Energy 314kcal/1306kJ; Protein 29.7g; Carbohydrate 1g, of which sugars 0.9g; Fat 21.3g, of which saturates 9.8g; Cholesterol 40mg; Calcium 27mg; Fibre 0.3g; Sodium 236mg.

Trout and Asparagus Pie

Crisp filo pastry filled with layers of trout, ricotta cheese, asparagus and mushrooms makes a dramatic-looking dish that is extremely easy to make.

Serves 6–8

115g/4oz asparagus
75g/3oz/6 tbsp butter
1 small onion, chopped
115g/4oz/1½ cups button
  (white) mushrooms, sliced
30ml/2 tbsp chopped fresh flat
  leaf parsley
250g/9oz/generous 1 cup
  ricotta cheese
115g/4oz/½ cup
  mascarpone cheese
450g/1lb trout fillet, skinned
8 filo pastry sheets,
  each measuring
  45 x 25cm/18 x 10in
salt and ground black pepper
butter, for greasing
flat leaf parsley, to garnish

1 Preheat the oven to 200°C/400°F/Gas 6. Grease a 23cm/9in springform cake tin (pan). Blanch the asparagus for 3 minutes. Drain, refresh under cold water and drain again.

2 Heat 25g/1oz/2 tbsp of the butter in a frying pan and add the onion. Cook for 3–5 minutes or until softened. Add the mushrooms and cook for 2 minutes more. Stir in the parsley and season well with salt and black pepper. In a bowl combine the ricotta and mascarpone cheeses. Stir in the onion mixture. Melt the remaining butter in a small pan.

3 Line the cake tin with the filo pastry sheets, brushing each layer with melted butter and leaving the edges hanging over the sides of the tin. While you are working with one filo pastry sheet, keep the rest covered with a damp, clean dishtowel so that they do not dry out. Place half the ricotta mixture in the base of the filo-lined tin. Remove any pin bones from the trout fillets, then arrange them in a layer over the ricotta. Season well.

4 Top with the asparagus and the remaining ricotta mixture. Bring the overhanging edges of the pastry over the top, and brush the layers with the remaining butter. Bake the pie for 25 minutes. Cover with foil and cook for a further 15 minutes. To serve, remove from the tin and place it on a warmed serving plate. Serve in slices, garnished with parsley.

Tuna and Mascarpone Bake

A one-dish meal ideal for informal entertaining that marries the smoky flavour of seared tuna with a sweet and herby Italian sauce. The dish has a grated potato base as well as a topping made of diced potato chunks.

Serves 4

4 tuna steaks, about 175g/6oz each
400g/14oz can chopped
  tomatoes, drained
2 garlic cloves, crushed
30ml/2 tbsp chopped
  fresh basil
250g/9oz/generous 1 cup
  mascarpone cheese
3 large potatoes
25g/1oz/2 tbsp
  butter, diced
salt and ground black pepper

1 Preheat the oven to 200°C/400°F/Gas 6. Heat a griddle (grill) pan on the stove and sear the fish steaks for 2 minutes on each side, seasoning with a little black pepper. Set aside while you prepare the sauce.

2 Mix the chopped tomatoes, garlic, basil and cheese together in a bowl and season to taste with salt and plenty of ground black pepper.

3 Peel the potatoes, then grate half of them and dice the other half. Blanch them in separate pans of lightly salted water for about 3 minutes. Drain thoroughly and set aside to cool slightly. When the grated potato is cool enough to handle, squeeze out any excess moisture.

4 Lightly grease a 1.75 litre/3 pint/7½ cup ovenproof dish. Spoon a little sauce and some grated potato into it. Lay the tuna over the grated potato with more sauce and the remaining grated potato. Sprinkle the diced butter and the diced potatoes over the top. Bake for 30 minutes until cooked through and brown on top. Serve immediately.

> **Variation**
> This dish can easily be made into a side dish, simply leave out the tuna and prepare the other ingredients as before.

Trout Pie Energy 310kcal/1293kJ; Protein 17g; Carbohydrate 13g, of which sugars 3g; Fat 21g, of which saturates 12g; Cholesterol 87mg; Calcium 109mg; Fibre 1g; Sodium 236mg.
Baked Tuna Energy 205kcal/853kJ; Protein 19.5g; Carbohydrate 0.1g, of which sugars 0.1g; Fat 14.1g, of which saturates 6.5g; Cholesterol 27mg; Calcium 11mg; Fibre 0g; Sodium 132mg.

Trout with Filo and Almond Crust

Beautiful presentation is a real plus when it comes to serving fish, and this trout is as pretty as a picture with its filo wrapping dusted with almonds. Almonds are used in the delicious stuffing, too, making this a tasty and satisfying main course.

Serves 4

4 whole trout, each about
    175g/6oz, cleaned
40g/1½oz/3 tbsp butter
1 small onion, finely chopped
115g/4oz/1 cup
    ground almonds
30ml/2 tbsp chopped
    fresh parsley
finely grated rind of 1 lemon
12 sheets filo pastry
salt and ground black pepper
lemon slices and parsley sprigs,
    to garnish

1 Preheat the oven to 200°C/400°F/Gas 6. Season the trout generously with salt and black pepper.

2 Melt 25g/1oz/2 tbsp of the butter in a large pan and cook the onion for 1–2 minutes until soft and translucent. Do not allow the onion to brown.

3 Stir 75g/3oz/¾ cup of the ground almonds into the onions in the pan, then add the chopped parsley and the lemon rind. Mix.

4 Gently stuff the cavity of each trout with one-quarter of the mixture. Press the mixture down firmly to mould it to the shape of the cavity.

5 Melt the remaining butter. Cut three sheets of filo pastry into strips and brush with the melted butter. Wrap the strips around one fish, with the buttered side inside. Leave the head and the tail free. Place on a baking sheet. Wrap the remaining trout.

6 Brush the top of the pastry casing with melted butter and sprinkle the remaining ground almonds over the fish.

7 Bake for 20–25 minutes until the pastry is golden brown. Place on warmed individual serving dishes, garnish with the lemon slices and parsley sprigs and serve.

Tuna and Egg Galette

Ready-rolled puff pastry is used in this easy-to-make colourful pie. If you prefer to make your own pastry, you will need 500g/1¼lb.

Serves 4

2 sheets of ready-rolled puff pastry
1 egg, beaten
60ml/4 tbsp olive oil
175g/6oz tuna steak
2 onions, sliced
1 red (bell) pepper, chopped
2 garlic cloves, crushed
45ml/3 tbsp capers, drained
5ml/1 tsp grated lemon rind
30ml/2 tbsp lemon juice
5 eggs
salt and ground black pepper
30ml/2 tbsp chopped flat leaf
    parsley, to garnish

1 Preheat the oven to 190°C/375°F/Gas 5. Lay one sheet of puff pastry on a lightly floured baking sheet and cut to a 28 x 18cm/11 x 7in rectangle. Glaze the whole sheet with beaten egg.

2 Cut the second sheet of puff pastry to the same dimensions. Cut out the centre and reserve for another recipe, leaving a 2.5cm/1in border. Carefully lift the pastry border on to the first sheet. Brush the border with beaten egg and prick the base with a fork. Bake the pastry case in the hot oven for about 15 minutes until golden and well risen.

3 Heat 30ml/2 tbsp of the oil in a frying pan and fry the tuna steak for about 3 minutes on each side until golden but still pale pink in the middle. Transfer to a plate and flake into small pieces.

4 Add the remaining oil to the pan and fry the onions, red pepper and garlic for 6–8 minutes until softened, stirring occasionally. Remove the pan from the heat and stir in the tuna, capers and lemon rind and juice. Season well.

5 Spoon the filling into the pastry case and level the surface with the back of a spoon. Break the eggs into the filling, cover the tart with lightly oiled foil, and return to the oven for about 10 minutes, or until the eggs have just cooked through. Garnish with chopped parsley and serve at once.

Trout with Filo Energy 649kcal/2716kJ; Protein 46g; Carbohydrate 37g, of which sugars 4g; Fat 35g, of which saturates 8g; Cholesterol 139mg; Calcium 11mg; Fibre 4g; Sodium 293mg.
Tuna Galette Energy 544kcal/2263kJ; Protein 21.7g; Carbohydrate 27.7g, of which sugars 4.6g; Fat 39.5g, of which saturates 10.1g; Cholesterol 260mg; Calcium 102mg; Fibre 1.9g; Sodium 320mg.

Creamy Anchovy and Potato Bake

This classic Scandinavian dish of potatoes, onions and anchovies cooked with cream makes a hearty winter lunch or simple supper, served with a refreshing salad. In Norway and Sweden, it is often served as a hot appetizer.

Serves 4

1kg/2¼ lb maincrop potatoes
2 onions
25g/1oz/2 tbsp butter
2 x 50g/2oz cans anchovy fillets
150ml/¼ pint/⅔ cup single (light) cream
150ml/¼ pint/⅔ cup double (heavy) cream
15ml/1 tbsp chopped fresh parsley
ground black pepper
fresh crusty bread, to serve

1 Peel the potatoes and cut into slices slightly thicker than 1cm/½in. Cut the slices into strips slightly more than 1cm/½in wide. Peel the onions and cut into very thin rings.

2 Use half of the butter to grease the base and sides of a ceramic cooking pot, and layer half the potatoes and onions in the base of the dish.

3 Drain the anchovies, reserving 15ml/1 tbsp of the oil. Cut the anchovies into thin strips and lay these over the potatoes and onions, then layer the remaining potatoes and onions on top.

4 Combine the single cream and anchovy oil in a small jug (pitcher) and season with a little ground black pepper. Pour the mixture evenly over the potatoes and dot with butter.

5 Cover and cook on high for 3½ hours, or until the potatoes and onions are tender. Brown under a hot grill (broiler), if you like, then drizzle over the double cream and sprinkle with parsley and pepper. Serve with fresh crusty bread.

> **Cook's Tip**
> This recipe can also be served as an appetizer for six, or as a side dish to accompany a main meal.

Octopus and Pasta Bake

This slow-cooked combination of octopus and pasta in a spicy tomato sauce is quite an everyday affair in Greece.

Serves 4

2 octopuses, total weight about 675–800g/1½–1¾lb, cleaned
150ml/¼ pint/⅔ cup extra virgin olive oil
2 large onions, sliced
3 garlic cloves, chopped
1 fresh red or green chilli, seeded and thinly sliced
1–2 bay leaves
5ml/1 tsp dried oregano
1 piece of cinnamon stick
2–3 grains allspice (optional)
1 glass red wine, 175ml/6fl oz/¾ cup
30ml/2 tbsp tomato purée (paste) diluted in 300ml/ ½ pint/1¼ cups warm water
300ml/½ pint/1¼ cups boiling water
225g/8oz/2 cups penne or small dried macaroni-type pasta
ground black pepper

1 Rinse the octopuses, removing all sand from the suckers. Cut the octopuses into large cubes and place them in a heavy pan over a low heat. Cook gently; they will produce some liquid, the colour of the flesh will change and they will eventually become bright scarlet. Keep turning the pieces of octopus with a wooden spatula until all the liquid has evaporated.

2 Add the olive oil to the pan and sauté the octopus pieces for 4–5 minutes. Add the onions to the pan and cook for a further 4 minutes, stirring constantly until they start to turn golden. Stir in the garlic, chilli, bay leaf, oregano, cinnamon stick and allspice, if using. As soon as the garlic becomes aromatic, pour in the wine and let it bubble and evaporate for a couple of minutes.

3 Pour in the diluted tomato purée, add pepper, cover and cook gently for 1½ hours or until the octopus is perfectly soft. Stir occasionally and add a little hot water if needed.

4 Preheat the oven to 160°C/325°F/Gas 3. Bring the octopus mixture to the boil, add the boiling water and stir in the dried pasta. Tip the mixture into a roasting dish. Bake for 30–35 minutes, stirring occasionally. Add a little hot water if it starts to look dry. Serve hot.

Anchovy Bake Energy 378Kcal/1580kJ; Protein 11.3g; Carbohydrate 37.9g, of which sugars 6.4g; Fat 21.2g, of which saturates 11.4g; Cholesterol 54mg; Calcium 1460mg; Fibre 11.5g; Sodium 133mg.
Octopus Bake Energy 874kcal/3662kJ; Protein 71g; Carbohydrate 53g, of which sugars 10g; Fat 43g, of which saturates 6g; Cholesterol 168 mg; Calcium 162mg; Fibre 5g; Sodium 27mg.

Smoked Mussel and Potato Bake

This slow-baked dish uses smoked mussels, which have a creamy texture and rich flavour, delicious with sour cream and chives. You can easily substitute smoked oysters for the mussels.

Serves 4

2 large maincrop potatoes,
  cut in half
butter, for greasing
2 shallots, finely diced
2 x 85g/3¼oz cans
  smoked mussels
1 bunch chives, chopped
300ml/½ pint/1¼ cups
  sour cream
175g/6oz/1½ cups mature
  Cheddar cheese, grated
salt and ground black pepper
mixed vegetables, to serve

1 Preheat the oven to 180°C/350°F/Gas 4. Cook the potatoes in a large pan of lightly salted boiling water for 15 minutes until they are just tender. Drain and leave to cool slightly. When cool enough to handle, cut the potatoes into even 3mm/⅛in slices.

2 Grease the base and sides of a 1.2 litre/2 pint/5 cup casserole dish. Lay a few potato slices over the base of the dish. Sprinkle a few shallots over and season well.

3 Drain the oil from the mussels into a bowl. Slice the mussels and add them again to the reserved oil. Stir in the chives and sour cream with half of the cheese. Spoon a little of the sauce over the layer of potatoes.

4 Continue to layer the potatoes, shallots and the sauce in the dish. Finish with a layer of potatoes and sprinkle over the remainder of the cheese.

5 Bake for 30–45 minutes. Remove from the oven and serve while hot with a selection of mixed vegetables.

Cook's Tip
For a dinner party, instead of serving the bake in a large dish, once it has cooked, stamp out rounds using a 5cm/2in cutter and serve on a bed of salad leaves.

Prawns with Tomatoes and Feta

This luxurious and unusual dish is traditionally cooked in a yiouvetsi – a round baking dish without a lid. It is made from glazed, dark red earthenware. Serve it as a first course for six, with plenty of crusty bread for mopping up the sauce, or with rice as a main course for four people.

Serves 4

75ml/5 tbsp extra virgin olive oil
1 onion, chopped
½ red (bell) pepper, seeded
  and cubed
675g/1½lb ripe tomatoes, peeled
  and roughly chopped
generous pinch of sugar
2.5ml/½ tsp dried oregano
450g/1lb peeled (but with the tail
  shells intact) raw tiger or king
  prawns (jumbo shrimp), thawed
  if frozen
30ml/2 tbsp finely chopped fresh
  flat leaf parsley
75g/3oz feta cheese, cubed
salt and ground black pepper

1 Heat the oil in a frying pan, add the onion and sauté gently for a few minutes until translucent. Add the cubed red pepper and cook, stirring occasionally, for 2–3 minutes more.

2 Stir in the chopped tomatoes, sugar and oregano, then season with salt and pepper to taste.

3 Cook gently over a low heat for about 15 minutes, stirring occasionally, until the sauce reduces slightly and thickens.

4 Preheat the oven to 180°C/350°F/Gas 4. Stir the prawns and parsley into the tomato sauce, tip it into a baking dish and spread evenly. Sprinkle the cheese cubes on top, then bake for 30 minutes. Serve hot with a fresh green salad.

Cook's Tip
Feta is a Greek cheese that is traditionally made from ewes' milk, but now is often made from cow's milk. It is preserved in brine and has a slightly salty taste and crumbly texture.

Mussel Bake Energy 348kcal/1457kJ; Protein 16.7g; Carbohydrate 25.8g, of which sugars 3.4g; Fat 20.6g, of which saturates 3g; Cholesterol 30mg; Calcium 178mg; Fibre 1.8g; Sodium 288mg.
Prawns with Feta Energy 328kcal/1362kJ; Protein 19g; Carbohydrate 10g, of which sugars 9g; Fat 24g, of which saturates 6g; Cholesterol 172mg; Calcium 159mg; Fibre 3g; Sodium 442mg.

Baked Crab with Garlic and Ginger

The Vietnamese have made this French-inspired dish their own with a combination of bean thread noodles and cloud ear mushrooms. It is time-consuming to cook the crabs yourself, so you can use freshly cooked crab meat from your fishmonger or supermarket. Buy it in the shell, or ask the fishmonger for some shells, as you will also need four small, empty shells in which to cook the crab. Alternatively, you can bake this in individual dishes.

Serves 4

25g/1oz dried bean thread
    (cellophane) noodles
6 dried cloud ear (wood ear)
    mushrooms
450g/1lb fresh crab meat
15ml/1 tbsp vegetable oil
10ml/2 tsp nuoc mam
2 shallots, finely chopped
2 garlic cloves, finely chopped
2.5cm/1in fresh root ginger,
    peeled and grated
1 small bunch coriander (cilantro),
    stalks removed, leaves chopped
1 egg, beaten
25g/1oz/2 tbsp butter
salt and ground black pepper
fresh dill fronds, to garnish
nuoc cham, to serve

1 Preheat the oven to 180°C/350°F/Gas 4. Soak the bean thread noodles and cloud ear mushrooms separately in bowls of lukewarm water for 15 minutes, then squeeze them dry and chop finely.

2 In a bowl, mix together the chopped noodles and mushrooms with the crab meat. Add the oil, nuoc mam, shallots, garlic, ginger and coriander. Season, then stir in the beaten egg.

3 Spoon the mixture into four small crab shells or use individual ovenproof dishes, packing it in tightly, and dot the top of each one with a little butter.

4 Place the shells on a baking tray and cook for about 20 minutes, or until the tops are nicely browned.

5 Garnish with dill and serve immediately with a little nuoc cham to drizzle over the top.

Crab Bake

Plentiful all around the Irish coast, crabs are popular on bar menus, especially fresh crab open sandwiches. Cork dry gin, which is made in Midleton, County Cork, brings an extra dimension to this delicious dish. Serve hot with rice, or fresh crusty bread, and a side salad.

Serves 4 as a first course

225g/8oz cooked white
    crab meat
juice of ½ lemon
15ml/1 tbsp chopped fresh herbs,
    such as parsley, chives
    and fennel

20ml/4 tsp Cork dry gin
5ml/1 tsp smooth Dijon mustard
5ml/1 tsp wholegrain
    Dijon mustard
60ml/4 tbsp grated hard
    cheese, such as Dubliner
ground black pepper

For the béchamel sauce

1 small onion
3 cloves
300ml/½ pint/1¼ cups milk
½ bay leaf
25g/1oz/2 tbsp butter
25g/1oz/¼ cup plain
    (all-purpose) flour

1 First make an infusion for the béchamel sauce: stud the onion with the cloves, and then put it into a small pan with the milk and bay leaf. Bring slowly to the boil, then allow to infuse (steep) for 15 minutes, and strain.

2 Preheat the oven to 180°C/350°F/Gas 4 and butter four gratin dishes. Toss the crab meat in the lemon juice. Divide it among the dishes and add a pinch of herbs to each. Sprinkle each dish with 5ml/1 tsp gin and pepper.

3 Melt the butter for the sauce in a pan, stir in the flour and cook over a low heat for 1–2 minutes. Gradually add the infused milk, stirring constantly to make a smooth sauce. Simmer over a low heat for 1–2 minutes.

4 Blend the béchamel sauce with the two mustards and use to cover the crab. Sprinkle the cheese on top, and bake for 20–25 minutes, or until the surface is hot and bubbling. Serve immediately.

Baked Crab Energy 289Kcal/1206kJ; Protein 26g; Carbohydrate 8g, of which sugars 2g; Fat 17g, of which saturates 5g; Cholesterol 145mg; Calcium 39mg; Fibre 24g; Sodium 800mg.
Crab Bake Energy 224Kcal/936kJ; Protein 17.4g; Carbohydrate 9.6g, of which sugars 4.5g; Fat 11.9g, of which saturates 7.4g; Cholesterol 73mg; Calcium 282mg; Fibre 0.4g; Sodium 489mg.

Cockle Pie

This Pembrokeshire dish, Pastai gocos, is sprinkled with grated cheese and browned under the grill, though it could equally well be topped with shortcrust or puff pastry and cooked in a hot oven. Serve the former with crusty bread and the latter with a crisp salad. Make it in one large dish or in individual ones.

Serves 4 as a starter, 2 as a main dish

425ml/¾ pint/scant 2 cups milk
25g/1oz/2 tbsp butter, cut into small pieces
25g/1oz/¼ cup plain (all-purpose) flour
150–200g/5½–7oz shelled cooked cockles (small clams)
100g/3½oz/1 cup mature cheese, such as Llanboidy or Llangloffan, grated
about 60ml/4 tbsp fresh breadcrumbs
salt and ground black pepper

1 To make the sauce, put the milk, butter, flour and seasoning into a pan. Over medium heat and stirring constantly with a whisk, bring to the boil and bubble gently for 2–3 minutes until thick, smooth and glossy.

2 Stir in two-thirds of the cheese. Add the cockles and bring just to the boil.

3 Spoon the mixture into one large dish or four individual flameproof dishes. Then toss together the remaining cheese and the breadcrumbs.

4 Sprinkle the cheese and breadcrumb mixture over the cockle sauce. Put under a hot grill (broiler) until bubbling and golden. Serve immediately.

Cook's Tip

• *Add some chopped fresh herbs (chives or parsley are good), laverbread, softened sliced leeks or some crisp-fried bacon pieces to the white sauce.*
• *This dish is equally delicious made with mixed seafood.*

Clam Stovies

Clams are now harvested in the lochs, especially in Loch Fyne where some of the best Scottish clams are grown on ropes. Limpets or cockles can also be used if you can buy them fresh or collect them yourself along the seashore.

Serves 4

2.5 litres/4 pints/10 cups clams
potatoes (see step 3)
oil, for greasing
chopped fresh flat leaf parsley, to garnish
50g/2oz/¼ cup butter
salt and ground black pepper

1 Wash the clams and soak them overnight in fresh cold water. This will clean them out and get rid of any sand and other detritus.

2 Preheat the oven to 190°C/375°F/Gas 5. Put the clams into a large pan, cover with water and bring to the boil. Add a little salt then simmer until the shells open. Reserve the cooking liquor. Shell the clams, reserving a few whole.

3 Weigh the shelled clams. You will need three times their weight in unpeeled potatoes.

4 Peel and slice the potatoes thinly. Lightly oil the base and sides of a flameproof, ovenproof dish. Arrange a layer of potatoes in the base of the dish, add a layer of the clams and season with a little salt and ground black pepper.

5 Repeat until the ingredients are all used, finishing with a layer of potatoes on top. Finally, season lightly.

6 Pour in some of the reserved cooking liquor to come about halfway up the dish. Dot the top with the butter then cover with foil.

7 Bring to the boil on the stove over a medium-high heat, then bake in the preheated oven for 2 hours until the top is golden brown.

8 Serve hot, garnished with chopped fresh flat leaf parsley.

Clam Stovies Energy 320kcal/1348kJ; Protein 17.3g; Carbohydrate 36.7g, of which sugars 3.3g; Fat 12.6g, of which saturates 7g; Cholesterol 57mg; Calcium 188mg; Fibre 2.9g; Sodium 262mg.
Cockle Pie Energy 294kcal/1231kJ; Protein 16.8g; Carbohydrate 21.6g, of which sugars 5.6g; Fat 15.7g, of which saturates 9.9g; Cholesterol 64mg; Calcium 376mg; Fibre 0.5g; Sodium 562mg.

Cod and Bean Stew with Saffron and Paprika

In this dish, everything is cooked in one pot – the chunks of fresh, flaky cod, made yellow with saffron, with their flavour offset by the smoked, spiced beans.

Serves 6–8
1 large red (bell) pepper
45ml/3 tbsp olive oil
4 rashers (strips) streaky (fatty) bacon, roughly chopped
4 garlic cloves, finely chopped
1 onion, sliced
10ml/2 tsp paprika
5ml/1 tsp hot pimentón (smoked Spanish paprika)

large pinch of saffron threads
400g/14oz jar Spanish butter (lima) beans or canned haricot (navy) beans, drained and rinsed
about 600ml/1 pint/2½ cups fish stock, or water and
  60ml/4 tbsp Thai fish sauce
6 plum tomatoes, quartered
350g/12oz fresh skinned cod fillet, cut into large chunks
45ml/3 tbsp chopped fresh coriander (cilantro), plus a few sprigs to garnish
salt and ground black pepper
crusty bread, to serve

1 Preheat the grill (broiler) and line the pan with foil. Halve the red pepper and scoop out the seeds. Place, cut-side down, in the grill pan and grill (broil) under a hot heat for about 10–15 minutes, until the skin is charred. Put the pepper in a plastic bag, seal and leave for 10 minutes. Remove from the bag, peel off the skin and discard. Chop the pepper into large pieces.

2 Heat the olive oil in a pan, then fry the bacon and garlic for 2 minutes, then add the onion. Cover the pan and cook for 5 minutes. Stir in the paprika and pimentón, the saffron and its soaking water, and salt and pepper. Stir the beans into the pan and add enough stock to cover. Simmer, uncovered, for about 15 minutes, stirring occasionally. Stir in the pepper and tomato. Add the cubes of cod and stir in the sauce.

3 Cover and simmer for 5 minutes until cooked. Stir in the chopped coriander. Serve the stew in warmed soup plates or bowls, garnished with the coriander sprigs. Eat with lots of crusty bread.

Cod with Caramelized Onions

After long slow cooking, onions become caramelized and turn a deep golden colour with a fabulously rich, sweet flavour, which is enhanced by the addition of balsamic vinegar.

Serves 4
40g/1½oz/3 tbsp butter
10ml/2 tsp olive oil
1.2kg/2½lb yellow onions, peeled and finely sliced

5ml/1 tsp caster (superfine) sugar
30ml/2 tbsp balsamic vinegar
30ml/2 tbsp vegetable stock, white wine or water
4 x 150g/5oz thick cod fillets

For the caper butter
115g/4oz/½ cup butter, softened
30ml/2 tbsp capers, drained and chopped
30ml/2 tbsp chopped fresh coriander (cilantro)
salt and ground black pepper

1 Put the butter and oil in a ceramic cooking pot and heat on high for about 15 minutes, until melted. Add the sliced onions and stir to coat well in the butter and oil. Cover the pot with the lid, then place a folded dish towel over the top to retain the heat. Cook for 2 hours, stirring halfway through cooking time.

2 Sprinkle the sugar over the onions and mix. Replace the lid and folded dish towel and cook on high for 4 hours, stirring two or three times, to ensure the onions colour evenly. At the end of the cooking time, they should be a dark golden colour.

3 Add the vinegar to the onions and stir in the stock, wine or water. Cover again and cook for 1 hour; the onions should now be tender. Season and stir well. Arrange the cod fillets over the onions and cook for a final 1 hour, or until the fish flakes easily.

4 Make the caper butter. Cream the butter in a bowl until soft, then beat in the capers, coriander, salt and pepper. Roll up the butter in foil, clear film (plastic wrap) or greaseproof (waxed) paper to form a short log shape. Twist the ends to secure them. Chill in the refrigerator or freezer until firm.

5 To serve, spoon the onions and fish on to warmed serving plates. Slice off discs of the butter and top each piece of fish with two slices. Serve, with the butter melting over the hot fish.

Cod and Bean Stew Energy 186kcal/778kJ; Protein 14g; Carbohydrate 12g, of which sugars 5g; Fat 9g, of which saturates 2g; Cholesterol 29mg; Calcium 43mg; Fibre 4g; Sodium 355mg.
Cod with Onions Energy 534Kcal/2213kJ; Protein 31.3g; Carbohydrate 25g, of which sugars 18.1g; Fat 35g, of which saturates 20.6g; Cholesterol 152mg; Calcium 96mg; Fibre 4.2g; Sodium 334mg.

Mixed Seafood in Spiced Coconut Broth

The assortment of seafoods in this piquant blend of chillies and spices makes the dish a feast for the tastebuds. It is delicious served with basmati rice.

Serves 4

500g/1¼lb mixture of white fish fillets and assorted seafood, such as prawns (shrimp), mussels, scallops, crab claws, and squid
2 tbsp sunflower oil or plain olive oil
10–12 curry leaves
1 medium onion, finely chopped
200ml/7fl oz/¾ cup canned coconut milk
2 tsp lemon juice
salt to taste

For the purée:
4 dried red chillies
2.5cm/1in piece of fresh root ginger, chopped
3–4 garlic cloves, roughly chopped
2 tsp coriander seeds
1 tsp cumin seeds
½ tsp ground turmeric
6 black peppercorns
1 tbsp malt vinegar
sprigs of fresh coriander (cilantro), to garnish

1 Shell, trim and clean the seafood as required. Grind the chillies, ginger, spices and other purée ingredients in a food processor or blender, or use a mortar and pestle.

2 Heat the oil in a medium-sized shallow pan and add the curry leaves, followed by the chopped onion.

3 Stir-fry over a medium heat until the onion is translucent, then add the puréed ingredients and sauté gently for 2 minutes.

4 Add the seafood, but not the white fish. Mix gently and cook for 2 minutes. Pour in the coconut milk, bring it to the boil, then add the white fish, lower the heat and simmer for 5–7 minutes until the white fish is cooked.

5 Add the lemon juice and salt and mix gently. Serve, garnished with sprigs of fresh coriander, accompanied by plain boiled basmati rice.

Hungarian Paprika-spiced Fish Goulash

This wholesome meal is a cross between a stew and a soup. It is traditionally served with half a hot cherry pepper, which is placed in the centre of the plate. The goulash is then ladled over it.

Serves 6

2kg/4½lb mixed fish
4 large onions, sliced
2 garlic cloves, crushed
½ small celeriac, diced
handful of parsley stalks or cleaned parsley roots
30ml/2 tbsp paprika
1 green (bell) pepper, sliced
5–10ml/1–2 tsp tomato purée (paste)
salt
90ml/6 tbsp sour cream and 3 cherry peppers (optional), to serve

1 Skin and fillet the fish and cut the flesh into chunks. Put all the fish heads, skin and bones into a large pan, together with the onions, garlic, celeriac, parsley stalks, paprika and salt. Cover with water and bring to the boil. Reduce the heat and simmer for 1¼–1½ hours. Strain the stock.

2 Place the fish and green pepper in a large frying pan and pour over the stock. Blend the tomato purée with a little stock and pour it into the pan.

3 Heat gently but do not stir, or the fish will break up. Cook for just 10–12 minutes but do not boil. Season to taste.

4 Ladle into warmed deep plates or bowls and top with a generous spoonful of sour cream and a halved cherry pepper, if liked.

> **Cook's Tip**
> *Use any firm-textured fish to make goulash, such as cod, haddock or halibut. In Hungary freshwater fish such as carp, pike or eel may be used, and it is sometimes said that the more varieties of fish go into a soup the better it will be.*

Mixed Seafood Energy 218kcal/913kJ; Protein 25.3g; Carbohydrate 13g, of which sugars 8.1g; Fat 7.7g, of which saturates 1g; Cholesterol 58mg; Calcium 64mg; Fibre 1.4g; Sodium 136mg.
Paprika Fish Goulash Energy 420kcal/1761kJ; Protein 64.1g; Carbohydrate 15.2g, of which sugars 12g; Fat 5.8g, of which saturates 2.2g; Cholesterol 162mg; Calcium 104mg; Fibre 3g; Sodium 259mg.

Haddock in Cheese Sauce

A relative of cod, haddock is one of the nation's preferred white fish, though unfortunately North Sea supplies have declined considerably in recent years. Other white fish can be used in place of haddock in this flavourful dish – try hake, coley or whiting.

Serves 4
1kg/2¼lb haddock fillets
300ml/½ pint/1¼ cups milk
1 small onion, thinly sliced
2 bay leaves
a few black peppercorns
25g/1oz/2 tbsp butter
25g/1oz/2 tbsp flour
5ml/1 tsp English (hot) mustard
115g/4oz mature hard cheese
    such as Cheddar, grated
salt and ground black pepper

1 Put the fish in a pan large enough to hold it in a single layer. Add the milk, onion, bay leaves and peppercorns and heat slowly until small bubbles are rising to the surface.

2 Cover and simmer very gently for 5–8 minutes, until the fish is just cooked. Lift out with a slotted spoon, straining and reserving the cooking liquid. Flake the fish, removing any bones.

3 To make the sauce, melt the butter in a saucepan, stir in the flour and cook gently, stirring all the time, for about 1 minute (do not allow it to brown). Remove from the heat and gradually stir in the strained milk. Return the pan to the heat and cook, stirring, until the mixture thickens and comes to the boil. Stir in the mustard and three-quarters of the cheese and season to taste.

4 Stir the fish into the sauce and spoon the mixture into flameproof dishes. Sprinkle with the remaining cheese. Put under a hot grill (broiler) until golden. Serve with crusty bread.

> **Cook's Tip**
> The fish can be left whole if you prefer, spoon the sauce over them before grilling. This dish can be made with smoked haddock, use fillets that have been mildly smoked.

Haddock and Beer Casserole

The earthy flavour of wild mushrooms perfectly complements the delicate taste of the haddock steaks and creamy sauce in this satisfying dish. Cooking it in beer ensures that the flesh is moist and makes a distinctive and delicious addition to the sauce.

Serves 4
150g/5oz/2 cups
    wild mushrooms
50g/2oz/¼ cup butter
2 large onions, roughly chopped
2 celery sticks, sliced
2 carrots, sliced
4 haddock steaks, about
    85g/6½oz each
300ml/½ pint/1¼ cups
    light lager
4 bay leaves
25g/1oz/¼ cup plain
    (all-purpose) flour
200ml/7fl oz/scant 1 cup double
    (heavy) cream
salt and ground black pepper,
    to taste
dill sprigs, to garnish

1 Preheat the oven to 190°C/375°F/Gas 5. Brush the wild mushrooms to remove any grit and only wash the caps briefly if necessary. Dry with kitchen paper and chop them.

2 Melt 25g/1oz/2 tbsp butter in a flameproof casserole, then add the onions, mushrooms, celery and carrots. Fry for about 8 minutes, or until golden brown.

3 Place the haddock steaks on top of the vegetables, then pour over the lager. Add the bay leaves and season well with salt and pepper. Put the casserole in the preheated oven and cook for 20–25 minutes, or until the fish flakes easily when tested.

4 Remove the fish and vegetables from the casserole with a slotted spoon and transfer to a serving dish. Cover and keep warm while you make the sauce.

5 Melt the remaining butter in a medium pan, then stir in the flour and cook, stirring, for 2 minutes. Pour in the liquid from the casserole, mix well and simmer for 2–3 minutes.

6 Add the cream to the sauce and heat, without boiling. Serve the fish and vegetables with the sauce, garnished with dill sprigs.

Haddock and Cheese Energy 430kcal/1809kJ; Protein 58.2g; Carbohydrate 9.6g, of which sugars 4.5g; Fat 17.4g, of which saturates 10.6g; Cholesterol 136mg; Calcium 351mg; Fibre 0.4g; Sodium 446mg.
Haddock and Beer Energy 564kcal/2346kJ; Protein 37g; Carbohydrate 17.9g, of which sugars 10.5g; Fat 38.8g, of which saturates 23.5g; Cholesterol 158mg; Calcium 106mg; Fibre 3.4g; Sodium 231mg.

Haddock with Spicy Puy Lentils

Dark brown Puy lentils have a delicate taste and texture and hold their shape during cooking, which makes them good for cooking in a ceramic slow cooker. Red chilli pepper and ground cumin add a hint of heat and spice without overpowering the flavour of the fish.

Serves 4

175g/6oz/³/₄ cup Puy lentils
600ml/1 pint/2½ cups near-
   boiling vegetable stock
30ml/2 tbsp olive oil
1 onion, finely chopped
2 celery sticks, finely chopped
1 red chilli, halved, seeded
   and finely chopped
2.5ml/½ tsp ground cumin
four thick 150g/5oz pieces of
   haddock fillet or steak
10ml/2 tsp lemon juice
25g/1oz/2 tbsp butter, softened
5ml/1 tsp finely grated
   lemon rind
salt and ground black pepper
lemon wedges, to garnish

1 Put the lentils in a sieve (strainer) and rinse under cold running water. Drain well, then transfer to a ceramic cooking pot. Pour over the hot vegetable stock, cover with the lid and switch the slow cooker on to high.

2 Heat the oil in a frying pan, add the onion and cook gently for 8 minutes. Stir in the celery, chilli and cumin, and cook for a further 2 minutes, or until soft but not coloured. Add the mixture to the lentils, stir, re-cover and cook for about 2½ hours.

3 Meanwhile, rinse the haddock pieces and pat dry on kitchen paper. Sprinkle them with the lemon juice. In a clean bowl, beat together the butter, lemon rind, salt and a generous amount of ground black pepper.

4 Put the haddock on top of the lentils in the cooking pot, then dot the lemon butter over the top of the fish. Cover and cook for 45 minutes–1 hour, or until the fish flakes easily when tested with a sharp knife or a fork, the lentils are tender and most of the stock has been absorbed. If you like, remove the skin from the haddock, then serve immediately, garnished with the lemon wedges.

Spiced Halibut and Tomato Curry

The chunky cubes of white fish contrast beautifully with the rich red spicy tomato sauce and taste just as good as they look. Halibut is used here, but you can use any type of firm white fish for this recipe.

Serves 4

60ml/4 tbsp lemon juice
60ml/4 tbsp rice wine vinegar
30ml/2 tbsp cumin seeds
5ml/1 tsp turmeric
5ml/1 tsp chilli powder
5ml/1 tsp salt
750g/1lb 11oz thick halibut
   fillets, skinned and cubed
60ml/4 tbsp sunflower oil
1 onion, finely chopped
3 garlic cloves, finely grated
30ml/2 tbsp finely grated
   fresh root ginger
10ml/2 tsp black mustard seeds
2 x 400g/14oz cans
   chopped tomatoes
5ml/1 tsp sugar
chopped coriander (cilantro)
   and sliced green chilli,
   to garnish
natural (plain) yogurt,
   to drizzle (optional)
basmati rice, pickles and
   poppadums, to serve

1 Mix together the lemon juice, vinegar, cumin, turmeric, chilli powder and salt in a shallow glass bowl. Add the cubed fish and turn to coat evenly. Cover and put in the refrigerator to marinate for 25–30 minutes.

2 Meanwhile, heat a wok over a high heat and add the oil. When hot, add the onion, garlic, ginger and mustard seeds. Reduce the heat to low and cook very gently for about 10 minutes, stirring occasionally.

3 Add the tomatoes and sugar to the wok, bring to a boil, reduce the heat, cover and cook gently for 15–20 minutes, stirring occasionally. Add the fish and its marinade to the wok, stir gently to mix, then cover and simmer gently for 15–20 minutes, or until the fish is cooked through and flakes easily with a fork.

4 Serve the curry ladled into shallow bowls with basmati rice, pickles and poppadums. Garnish with fresh coriander and green chillies, and drizzle over some natural yogurt if liked.

Haddock with Lentils Energy 381kcal/603kJ; Protein 40g; Carbohydrate 25g, of which sugars 3g; Fat 15g, of which saturates 5g; Cholesterol 67mg; Calcium 73mg; Fibre 1g; Sodium 155mg.
Spiced Halibut Energy 366Kcal/1538kJ; Protein 38.9g; Carbohydrate 25.2g, of which sugars 3.2g; Fat 12.8g, of which saturates 4.3g; Cholesterol 82mg; Calcium 64mg; Fibre 4.7g; Sodium 353mg.

Halibut with Peppers and Coconut Milk

This aromatic dish comes from the state of Bahia, on the east coast of Brazil. Cooked and served in an earthenware dish, it is usually accompanied by white rice and cassava flour to soak up the sauce.

Serves 6

6 halibut, cod, haddock or
   monkfish fillets, each 115g/4oz
juice of 2 limes
8 fresh coriander (cilantro) sprigs
2 fresh red chillies, seeded
   and chopped
3 tomatoes, sliced into thin rounds

1 red (bell) pepper, seeded and
   sliced into thin rounds
1 green (bell) pepper, seeded and
   sliced into thin rounds
1 small onion, sliced into
   thin rounds
200ml/7fl oz/scant 1 cup
   coconut milk
60ml/4 tbsp palm oil
salt
cooked white rice, to serve

**For the flavoured
   cassava flour**
30ml/2 tbsp palm oil
1 medium onion, thinly sliced
250g/9oz/2¼ cups cassava flour

1 Place the fish fillets in a large, shallow dish and cover with water. Pour in the lime juice and set aside for 30 minutes. Drain the fish thoroughly and pat dry with kitchen paper. Arrange the fish in a single layer in a heavy pan which has a tight-fitting lid.

2 Sprinkle the coriander and chillies over the fish, then top with a layer each of tomatoes, peppers and onion. Pour the coconut milk over, cover and stand for 15 minutes before cooking.

3 Season with salt, then place the pan over a high heat and bring to the boil, then simmer for 5 minutes. Remove the lid, pour in the palm oil, cover again and simmer for 10 minutes.

4 Meanwhile make the flavoured cassava flour. Heat the oil in a frying pan over a low heat. Stir in the onion slices and cook for 8–10 minutes until soft and golden. Stir in the cassava flour and cook, stirring constantly, for 1–2 minutes until lightly toasted and evenly coloured by the oil. Season with salt. Serve the halibut with the rice and flavoured cassava flour.

Jamaican Fish Curry

Although the rice is simply boiled for this recipe, it is an integral part of this dish and quickly takes on the flavour of the deliciously spicy sauce.

Serves 4

2 halibut steaks, total weight
   about 500–675g/1¼–1½lb
30ml/2 tbsp groundnut oil
2 cardamom pods
1 cinnamon stick
6 allspice berries
4 cloves
1 large onion, chopped
3 garlic cloves, crushed

10–15ml/2–3 tsp grated fresh
   root ginger
10ml/2 tsp ground cumin
5ml/1 tsp ground coriander
2.5ml/½ tsp cayenne pepper
   or to taste
4 tomatoes, peeled, seeded
   and chopped
1 sweet potato, about 225g/8oz,
   cut into 2cm/¾in cubes
475ml/16fl oz/2 cups fish stock
   or water
115g/4oz creamed coconut
1 bay leaf
225g/8oz/generous 1 cup white
   long grain rice
salt

1 Rub the halibut steaks well with salt and set aside. Heat the oil in a flameproof casserole and stir-fry the cardamom pods, cinnamon stick, allspice berries and cloves for about 3 minutes to release the aroma.

2 Add the onion, garlic and ginger. Continue cooking for 4–5 minutes over a gentle heat until the onion is fairly soft, stirring frequently, then add the cumin, coriander and cayenne pepper and cook briefly, stirring all the time.

3 Stir in the tomatoes, sweet potato, fish stock or water, creamed coconut and bay leaf. Season well with salt. Bring to the boil, then lower the heat, cover and simmer for 15–18 minutes until the sweet potato is tender.

4 Cook the rice according to your preferred method. Add the fish steaks to the pan of sauce and spoon the sauce over to cover them completely. Put a lid on the pan and simmer for about 10 minutes until the fish is just tender and flakes easily. Spoon the rice into a serving dish, spoon over the curry sauce and arrange the halibut steaks on top. Serve immediately.

Halibut with Peppers Energy 392kcal/1648kJ; Protein 29g; Carbohydrate 50g, of which sugars 18g; Fat 8g, of which saturates 3g; Cholesterol 40mg; Calcium 80mg; Fibre 2g; Sodium 123mg.
Fish Curry Energy 639kcal/2669kJ; Protein 34.2g; Carbohydrate 62g, of which sugars 8.3g; Fat 28.4g, of which saturates 18.7g; Cholesterol 44mg; Calcium 74mg; Fibre 2.4g; Sodium 115mg.

Tagine of Monkfish

Chermoula, a lemony garlic and coriander paste, gives fish an unmistakable Moroccan flavour.

Serves 4

900g/2lb monkfish tail, cut into chunks
15–20 small new potatoes, scrubbed, scraped or peeled
45–60ml/3–4 tbsp olive oil
4–5 garlic cloves, thinly sliced
15–20 cherry tomatoes
2 green (bell) peppers, grilled (broiled) until black, skinned, seeded and cut into strips
large handful of kalamata or fleshy black olives
oil, to drizzle
about 100ml/3½fl oz/scant ½ cup water
salt and ground black pepper

For the chermoula

2 garlic cloves
5ml/1 tsp coarse salt
10ml/2 tsp ground cumin
5ml/1 tsp paprika
juice of 1 lemon
small bunch of fresh coriander (cilantro), roughly chopped
15ml/1 tbsp olive oil

1 Use a mortar and pestle to make the chermoula: pound the garlic with the salt to a smooth paste. Add the cumin, paprika, lemon juice and chopped coriander, and gradually mix in the oil.

2 Reserve a little chermoula for cooking, then rub the rest of the paste over the monkfish. Cover and leave to marinate in a cool place for 1 hour. Par-boil the potatoes for about 10 minutes. Drain, then cut them in half lengthways.

3 Heat the olive oil in a heavy pan and stir in the garlic. When the garlic begins to colour, add the tomatoes and cook until just softened. Add the peppers to the tomatoes and garlic, together with the remaining chermoula, and season to taste. Spread the potatoes over the base of a tagine, or shallow pan. Spoon three-quarters of the tomato and pepper mixture over and place the marinated fish chunks on top, with their marinade.

4 Spoon the rest of the tomato and pepper mixture over the fish and add the olives. Drizzle olive oil over the dish and add the water. Heat until simmering, cover the tagine or pan and cook for 15 minutes, until the fish is cooked. Serve with warm crusty bread to mop up the delicious juices.

Lemon Sole and Parma Ham Roulades

In this elegant dish, Parma ham and delicately textured lemon sole are rolled around a subtle herb and lemon stuffing. Serve this dish for a special dinner party with new potatoes tossed in butter, and lightly steamed asparagus.

Serves 4

10ml/2 tsp unsalted (sweet) butter, at room temperature
120ml/4fl oz/½ cup dry white wine
4 large lemon sole fillets, about 150g/5oz each
8 thin slices of Parma ham, about 130g/4½oz in total
50g/2oz/½ cup chopped toasted walnuts
75g/3oz/1½ cups fresh white breadcrumbs
30ml/2 tbsp finely chopped fresh parsley
2 eggs, lightly beaten
5ml/1 tsp finely grated lemon rind
ground black pepper
new potatoes and steamed green vegetables, to serve

1 Smear the inside of a ceramic cooking pot with the butter. Pour in the wine and switch the slow cooker to high. Skin the fish fillets and check that all the bones have been removed, then pat dry with kitchen paper.

2 Remove most of the fat from the Parma ham. Lay two overlapping slices on a board and place a sole fillet on top, skinned side up.

3 Mix the walnuts, breadcrumbs, parsley, eggs, lemon rind and pepper together and spread a quarter of the mixture over the fish fillet, then press down gently. Starting at the thicker end of the fillet, carefully roll up the fish and ham to enclose the filling.

4 Repeat with the remaining Parma ham, fish and filling, then secure each roll with a cocktail stick (toothpick).

5 Place the fish seam-side down in the ceramic cooking pot. Cover, then turn the temperature down to low. Cook for 1½–2 hours, or until the fish flakes easily. Remove the cocktail sticks and serve straight away with freshly cooked vegetables.

Monkfish Energy 406Kcal/1710kJ; Protein 39.6g; Carbohydrate 25.2g, of which sugars 6.5g; Fat 17.1g, of which saturates 2.7g; Cholesterol 32mg; Calcium 98mg; Fibre 5.4g; Sodium 915mg.
Lemon Sole Energy 363Kcal/1521kJ; Protein 38g; Carbohydrate 9.6g, of which sugars 1.5g; Fat 17.3g, of which saturates 3.6g; Cholesterol 201mg; Calcium 134mg; Fibre 0.8g; Sodium 714mg.

Burbot Stew

Burbot is a large freshwater fish that looks similar to a monkfish, and which has soft but well-flavoured flesh. This hearty chowder can be served on its own as a tasty appetizer or with bread for a sustaining main meal.

Serves 4

1kg/2¼lb burbot or monkfish, with their bones, if filleted
20g/¾oz/1½ tbsp unsalted (sweet) butter
1 onion, chopped
1 small celery stick, chopped
1 small leek, chopped
1 bay leaf
10 whole allspice
5 white peppercorns
1.5 litres/2½ pints/ 6¼ cups water
1 carrot, finely diced
500g/1¼lb potatoes, cubed
5ml/1 tsp plain white (all-purpose) flour
200ml/7fl oz/scant 1 cup double (heavy) cream
salt and ground white pepper
dill sprigs, to garnish

1 Fillet the fish or, if the fishmonger fillets it for you, ask him to reserve the bones and head. Cut the fish into large chunks.

2 Heat the butter in a pan, add the onion, celery, leek, fish bones, fish head and any fish trimmings. Fry for about 5 minutes until the vegetables are beginning to soften.

3 Add the bay leaf, allspice, peppercorns, 15ml/1 tbsp salt and 1 litre/1¾ pints/4 cups of the water. Bring to the boil, then lower the heat and simmer very gently for 30 minutes.

4 Strain the stock through a sieve (strainer) into a clean pan. (You should be left with about 1 litre/1¾ pints/4 cups of liquid or add extra water to make up the correct amount.)

5 Add the carrot and potato to the stock and bring to the boil. Lower the heat and simmer until the potato is nearly cooked. Add the fish to the pan and return to simmering point, then sprinkle over the flour and continue to simmer for a further 5 minutes, or until the fish is just cooked.

6 Stir in the cream, then taste and season according to taste. Pour into serving dishes and serve garnished with a sprig of dill.

Skate with Tomato and Olive Sauce

The classic way of serving skate is with a browned butter sauce, but here it is given a Mediterranean twist with tomatoes, olives, orange and a dash of Pernod. If time allows, soak the skate in salted water for a few hours before cooking, to firm up the flesh.

Serves 4

15ml/1 tbsp olive oil
1 small onion, finely chopped
2 fresh thyme sprigs
grated rind of ½ orange
15ml/1 tbsp Pernod
400g/14oz can chopped tomatoes
50g/2oz/1 cup stuffed green olives
1.5ml/¼ tsp caster (superfine) sugar
4 small skate wings
plain (all-purpose) flour, for coating
salt and ground black pepper
15ml/1 tbsp basil leaves, to garnish
lime wedges, to serve

1 Heat the oil in a pan, add the onion and fry gently for about 10 minutes. Stir in the thyme and orange rind and cook for 1 minute. Add the Pernod, tomatoes, olives, sugar and a little salt and ground black pepper, and heat until just below boiling point.

2 Tip the mixture into a ceramic pot and switch on to high. Cover with the lid and cook for 1½ hours.

3 Meanwhile, rinse the skate wings under cold water and pat dry on kitchen paper. Sprinkle the flour on a large, flat dish and season well with salt and ground black pepper.

4 Coat each skate wing in the flour, shaking off any excess, then place on top of the tomato sauce.

5 Re-cover the ceramic cooking pot and reduce the temperature to low. Cook for 1½–2 hours, or until the skate is cooked and flakes easily.

6 Place the fish on to warmed serving plates and spoon over the sauce. Sprinkle over the basil leaves and serve with a wedge of lime for squeezing over.

Burbot Stew Energy 582kcal/2431kJ; Protein 47.6g; Carbohydrate 25.8g, of which sugars 6.4g; Fat 32.6g, of which saturates 19.7g; Cholesterol 119mg; Calcium 77mg; Fibre 2.8g; Sodium 117mg.
Skate with Tomato Energy 144Kcal/606kJ; Protein 15.5g; Carbohydrate 8.1g, of which sugars 3.7g; Fat 4.8g, of which saturates 0.7g; Cholesterol 35mg; Calcium 37mg; Fibre 1.4g; Sodium 366mg.

Grouper Stewed with Grapes

Fish stews are found in all Mediterranean cuisines and in other coastal regions of southern Europe. This one, originating from the Atlantic islands of the Azores, has an original touch as it uses green grapes, which add an elegant acidity to the flavour.

Serves 4
50ml/2fl oz/¼ cup olive oil
1 small onion, chopped
1 garlic clove, chopped
1 green (bell) pepper, seeded and chopped
1 bay leaf
1 ripe tomato, peeled and diced
5ml/1 tsp saffron threads
20 green grapes
200ml/7fl oz/scant 1 cup fish stock
4 grouper fillets with skin, each weighing about 175g/6oz
1 small bunch of mint, chopped

1 Preheat the oven to 180°C/350°F/Gas 4. Heat the oil in a flameproof casserole. Add the onion, garlic, green pepper and bay leaf and cook over a low heat, stirring occasionally, for 5 minutes, until the onion has softened.

2 Add the tomato and saffron and cook for a few minutes more, then add the grapes and stock and bring to the boil.

3 Place the fish in the casserole, skin side up, cover and cook in the oven for about 20 minutes, until the fish is cooked through and tender. Sprinkle with the mint and serve immediately.

Cook's Tips
Groupers are found in warm waters such as those of the Indian Ocean, the Mediterranean, the Caribbean and south-east Asia. They are sought after in fish markets for their remarkable flavour. The skin of grouper has a pronounced taste so you may wish to remove it before cooking. Although groupers may grow very large, their flavour is still excellent and the flesh is white and firm. They lend themselves to almost any form of cooking and can be baked, poached, grilled, fried and steamed. They can stand up to spicy sauces and accompaniments.

Red Mullet with Fennel

These pretty pink fish have a firm flesh and sweet flavour, which is enhanced by serving it with fennel.

Serves 4
10ml/2 tsp fennel seeds
5ml/1 tsp chopped fresh thyme
30ml/2 tbsp chopped fresh parsley
1 clove garlic, crushed
10ml/2 tsp olive oil
4 red mullet, weighing about 225g/8oz each
lemon wedges, to serve

For the fennel
8 ripe tomatoes
2 fennel bulbs
30ml/2 tbsp olive oil
120ml/4fl oz/½ cup boiling fish or vegetable stock
10ml/2 tsp balsamic vinegar
salt and ground black pepper

1 Crush the fennel seeds using a mortar and pestle, then work in the thyme and parsley, garlic and olive oil. Clean and scale the fish and trim off the fins. Use a sharp knife to make deep slashes on each side of the fish.

2 Push the herb paste into the cuts in the fish and spread any excess inside the body cavities. Place the fish on a plate, cover with clear film (plastic wrap) and leave to marinate. On a warm day, place the fish in the refrigerator and bring to room temperature 20 minutes before cooking.

3 Meanwhile, prepare the bed of fennel. Put the tomatoes in a heatproof bowl, cover with boiling water and stand for 1 minute. Drain and cool under cold running water and peel off the skins. Quarter the tomatoes, seed and cut into small dice.

4 Trim the feathery fronds from the fennel, then cut the bulbs into 1cm/½ in slices from the top to the root end. Heat the oil in a frying pan and cook the fennel slices over a medium heat for about 10 minutes, or until just starting to colour.

5 Transfer the fennel to a ceramic cooking pot. Add the tomatoes, stock, balsamic vinegar, salt and pepper, cover with the lid and cook on high for 2 hours. Stir the fennel sauce, then place the fish on top in a single layer. Cover and cook for 1 hour, or until the fish is cooked through. Serve with lemon wedges.

Grouper Energy 248kcal/1037kJ; Protein 33.2g; Carbohydrate 6.7g, of which sugars 6.1g; Fat 9.9g, of which saturates 1.4g; Cholesterol 81mg; Calcium 51mg; Fibre 1.9g; Sodium 114mg.
Red Mullet Energy 194Kcal/816kJ; Protein 26.5g; Carbohydrate 4.2g, of which sugars 4.1g; Fat 8.1g, of which saturates 1.2g; Cholesterol 63mg; Calcium 95mg; Fibre 3.0g; Sodium 239mg.

Fisherman's Casserole

This simple recipe can be adapted to whichever fish are available on the day.

Serves 4

500g/1¼lb mixed fish fillets, such as haddock, bass, red mullet, salmon
500g/1¼lb mixed shellfish, such as squid strips, mussels, cockles and prawns (shrimp)
15ml/1 tbsp oil
25g/1oz/2 tbsp butter
1 medium onion, finely chopped
1 carrot, finely chopped
3 celery sticks, finely chopped
30ml/2 tbsp plain (all-purpose) flour
600ml/1 pint/2½ cups fish stock
300ml/½pt/1¼ cups dry (hard) cider
350g/12oz small new potatoes, halved
150ml/¼ pint/⅔ cup double (heavy) cream
handful of chopped mixed herbs such as parsley, chives and dill
salt and ground black pepper

1 Wash the fish fillets and dry on kitchen paper. With a sharp knife, remove the skin, feel carefully for any bones and extract them. Cut the fish into large, even chunks.

2 Prepare the shellfish, shelling the prawns if necessary. Scrub the mussels and cockles, discarding any with broken shells or that do not close when given a sharp tap. Pull off the beards and discard.

3 Heat the oil and butter in a saucepan, add the onion, carrot and celery and cook, stirring occasionally, until beginning to soften. Add the flour, and cook for 1 minute.

4 Remove the pan from the heat and gradually stir in the fish stock and cider. Return the pan to the heat and cook, stirring continuously, until the mixture comes to the boil and thickens.

5 Add the potatoes. Bring the sauce back to the boil, cover and simmer for 10–15 minutes until the potatoes are nearly tender. Add all the fish and shellfish and stir in gently.

6 Stir in the cream. Gently simmer, then cover the pan and cook for 5–10 minutes or until the fish is cooked through and all the shells have opened. Season and add the herbs, then serve.

Aromatic Fish Stew

Lemon grass and ginger give this simple, delicate stew of fish, prawns, new potatoes and broccoli an appetizing aromatic flavour.

Serves 4

25g/1oz/2 tbsp butter
1 large onion, chopped
20ml/4 tsp plain (all-purpose) flour
400ml/14fl oz/1⅔ cups light fish stock
150ml/¼ pint/⅔ cup white wine
2.5cm/1in piece fresh root ginger, peeled and finely chopped
2 lemon grass stalks, trimmed and finely chopped
450g/1lb new potatoes, scrubbed and halved if necessary
450g/1lb white fish fillets
275g/10oz small broccoli florets
150ml/¼ pint/⅔ cup double (heavy) cream
175g/6oz large, cooked, peeled prawns (shrimp)
60ml/4 tbsp chopped fresh garlic chives
salt and ground black pepper
crusty bread, to serve

1 Melt the butter in a large pan. Add the onions and cook for 3–4 minutes. Stir in the flour and cook for 1 minute.

2 Stir in the fish stock, white wine, ginger, lemon grass and new potatoes. Season with salt and pepper and bring to the boil. Cover and cook for 15 minutes, or until the potatoes are almost tender.

3 Remove the skin from the fish fillets and cut the fillets into large chunks. Add the chunks of fish to the pan with the broccoli and cream. Stir gently.

4 Simmer gently for 4 minutes, taking care not to break up the fish, then add the prawns and heat through in the sauce. Adjust the seasoning and sprinkle in the chives. Serve in heated bowls with plenty of crusty bread.

Cook's Tip
Don't overcook the prawns, or they will toughen. Just add them at the last minute and heat through.

Fish Casserole Energy 583kcal/2439kJ; Protein 49.3g; Carbohydrate 25.3g, of which sugars 6.1g; Fat 30.2g, of which saturates 16.5g; Cholesterol 354mg; Calcium 199mg; Fibre 2.5g; Sodium 404mg.
Fish Stew Energy 515kcal/2148kJ; Protein 34.9g; Carbohydrate 27.6g, of which sugars 5.9g; Fat 27.4g, of which saturates 16.2g; Cholesterol 202mg; Calcium 131mg; Fibre 3.7g; Sodium 218mg.

Fragrant Spanish Fish Stew

This splendid fish feast is a favourite throughout Spain.

Serves 6
60ml/4 tbsp olive oil
8 small squid, cleaned
plain (all-purpose) flour,
    for dusting
500g/1¼lb skinless, boneless
    white fish such as monkfish
    and cod, cut in large chunks
30ml/2 tbsp Ricard or Pernod
450ml/¾ pint/2 cups fish stock
250ml/8fl oz/1 cup white wine
450g/1lb mussels, cleaned
16 raw king prawns (jumbo
    shrimp), with heads, deveined

115g/4oz prawns (shrimp)
salt and ground black pepper
45ml/3 tbsp chopped fresh
    parsley, to garnish

For the broth
30ml/2 tbsp oil
1 large onion, finely chopped
2 garlic cloves, finely chopped
500g/1¼lb ripe tomatoes, peeled,
    seeded and chopped
2 bay leaves
1 dried chilli, seeded and chopped
5ml/1 tsp paprika
pinch of saffron threads
salt and ground black pepper

1 To make the broth, heat the oil in a flameproof casserole and soften the onion and garlic. Add the tomatoes, bay leaves, chilli, paprika and saffron and cook gently to make a sauce.

2 Meanwhile, heat the oil in a large pan. Put in the squid tentacles, face down, and cook for 45 seconds, to make 'flowers'. Reserve on a plate. Flour and fry the fish pieces for 2 minutes on each side. Cut the squid bodies into rings and fry. Pour the Ricard or Pernod into a ladle, flame it and pour over the fish remaining in the pan. Remove the fish and reserve.

3 Add the fish stock and the wine to the sauce and bring to a simmer. Add the mussels, cover for 2 minutes, then remove to a plate, discard any closed mussels, and remove the upper shells. Add the raw prawns to the casserole for 3–4 minutes, then lift out and reserve.

4 About 20 minutes before serving, add the white fish to the casserole, followed by the squid rings and then the shellfish, keeping the liquid simmering gently. Season to taste. Sprinkle over the mussels and squid flowers and garnish with parsley.

Italian Fish Stew

This stew is a veritable feast of fish and shellfish in a delicious tomato broth – ideal for a family lunch.

Serves 4
30ml/2 tbsp olive oil
1 onion, thinly sliced
a few saffron threads
5ml/1 tsp dried thyme
large pinch of cayenne pepper
2 garlic cloves, finely chopped
2 x 400g/14oz cans tomatoes,
    drained and chopped
175ml/6fl oz/¾ cup white wine

2 litres/3½ pints/8 cups
    hot fish stock
350g/12oz white, skinless fish
    fillets, such as haddock or cod,
    cut into pieces
450g/1lb monkfish,
    cut into pieces
450g/1lb mussels, scrubbed
225g/8oz small squid, cleaned
    and cut into rings
30ml/2 tbsp chopped fresh basil
    or parsley
salt and ground black pepper
thickly sliced bread, to serve

1 Heat the olive oil in a large, heavy pan. Add the onion, saffron threads, thyme, cayenne pepper and salt, to taste. Stir well and cook over a low heat for 10 minutes, until the onion is soft. Add the garlic and cook for 1 minute more.

2 Stir in the chopped tomatoes, dry white wine and hot fish stock. Bring to the boil and boil for 1 minute, then reduce the heat and simmer gently for 15 minutes.

3 Add the fish pieces to the tomato mixture in the pan and stir gently. Simmer the stew for a further 3 minutes.

4 Add the mussels and squid rings and simmer for about 2 minutes, until the mussels open. Discard any that remain closed. Stir in the basil or parsley and season to taste. Ladle into warmed soup bowls and serve with bread.

Cook's Tip
Cayenne pepper has quite a hot, spicy flavour and was originally made from a type of chilli from the Cayenne region of French Guiana. It should be used sparingly.

Spanish Fish Stew Energy 463kcal/1940kJ; Protein 30g; Carbohydrate 32.3g, of which sugars 13.8g; Fat 21.7g, of which saturates 6.5g; Cholesterol 61mg; Calcium 80mg; Fibre 4.2g; Sodium 738mg.
Italian Fish Stew Energy 337Kcal/1423kJ; Protein 49.8g; Carbohydrate 8.3g, of which sugars 7.3g; Fat 8.8g, of which saturates 1.5g; Cholesterol 196mg; Calcium 112mg; Fibre 2.2g; Sodium 226mg.

Sour Fish, Star Fruit and Chilli Stew

Somewhere between a stew and a soup, this refreshing dish is just one of many variations on the theme of sour fish stew found throughout South-east Asia. The star fruit are added towards the end of cooking so that they retain a bite.

Serves 4 to 6
30ml/2 tbsp coconut or palm oil
900ml/1½ pints/3¾ cups water
2 lemon grass stalks, bruised
25g/1oz fresh root ginger, finely sliced
about 675g/1½lb freshwater or saltwater fish, such as trout or sea bream, cut into thin steaks

2 firm star fruit (carambola), sliced
juice of 1–2 limes

For the spice paste
4 shallots, chopped
4 red chillies, seeded and chopped
2 garlic cloves, chopped
25g/1oz galangal, chopped
25g/1oz fresh turmeric, chopped
3–4 candlenuts, chopped

To serve
1 bunch fresh basil leaves
1 lime, cut into wedges
steamed rice

1 Using a mortar and pestle or food processor, grind all the spice paste ingredients together to form a coarse paste.

2 Heat the oil in a wok or wide, heavy pan, stir in the spice paste and fry until fragrant. Pour in the water and add the lemon grass and ginger. Bring to the boil, stirring all the time, then reduce the heat and simmer for 10 minutes.

3 Slip the fish steaks into the pan, making sure there is enough cooking liquid to cover the fish and adding more water if necessary. Simmer gently for 3–4 minutes, then add the star fruit and lime juice. Simmer for a further 2–3 minutes, until the fish is cooked.

4 Divide the fish and star fruit between four to six warmed serving bowls and add a little of the cooking liquid. Garnish with basil leaves and a wedge of lime to squeeze over it. Serve the stew with bowls of steamed rice, which is moistened by spoonfuls of the remaining cooking liquid.

Fish Goulash

A remnant of Austro-Hungarian rule, goulash remains a favourite and is often made with fish rather than meat. It is flavoured with paprika and served with sour cream.

Serves 4
1.2kg/2½lb mixed fish
2 bay leaves
30ml/2 tbsp olive oil
1 large onion, chopped
2 celery sticks, chopped
1 green (bell) pepper, seeded and chopped

2 garlic cloves, chopped
75g/3oz lean smoked back bacon rashers (strips), rinded and diced
15ml/1 tbsp plain (all-purpose) flour
15ml/1 tbsp paprika, plus extra for sprinkling
5ml/1 tsp chopped fresh thyme
200g/7oz can chopped tomatoes
75g/3oz fine green beans, cut into bitesize lengths
30ml/2 tbsp chopped fresh parsley
salt and ground black pepper
sour cream, to serve

1 Skin and fillet the fish and cut the flesh into large chunks. Put all the fish bones into a large pan together with the bay leaves. Barely cover with cold water and bring to the boil. Gently simmer for 30 minutes, skimming the surface occasionally. Strain the stock.

2 Heat the oil in a large pan, add the onion and gently cook for 5 minutes, until the onion is softened and translucent. Stir in the celery, green pepper, garlic and bacon, and cook for a further 3–4 minutes. Stir in the flour and paprika and cook for 1 more minute. Gradually add 600ml/1 pint/ 2½ cups of the fish stock.

3 Add the thyme and chopped tomatoes and then season with salt and pepper. Cover and simmer for 5 minutes or until the vegetables are almost tender.

4 Add the green beans, fish chunks and parsley and cook for about 10 minutes or until the fish and all the vegetables are cooked. Ladle into warmed deep plates or bowls and serve with a generous spoonful of sour cream and a sprinkle of paprika.

Sour Fish Stew Energy 240kcal/1001kJ; Protein 25.9g; Carbohydrate 7.3g, of which sugars 4.7g; Fat 12.1g, of which saturates 1.2g; Cholesterol 0mg; Calcium 27mg; Fibre 1.7g; Sodium 67mg.
Fish Goulash Energy 382kcal/1603kJ; Protein 60.2g; Carbohydrate 9.4g, of which sugars 4.9g; Fat 11.7g, of which saturates 2.4g; Cholesterol 148mg; Calcium 60mg; Fibre 1.9g; Sodium 486mg.

Moroccan Fish Tagine

This spicy, aromatic dish proves just how exciting an ingredient fish can be.

Serves 8

1.3kg/3lb firm fish fillets, skinned and cut into 5cm/2in chunks
60ml/4 tbsp olive oil
1 large aubergine (eggplant), cut into 1cm/½in cubes
2 courgettes (zucchini), cut into 1cm/½in cubes
4 onions, chopped
400g/14oz can chopped tomatoes
400ml/14fl oz/1⅔ cups passata (bottled strained tomatoes)
200ml/7fl oz/scant 1 cup fish stock
1 preserved lemon, chopped
90g/3½oz/scant 1 cup olives
60ml/4 tbsp chopped fresh coriander (cilantro), plus extra coriander leaves to garnish
salt and ground black pepper

For the harissa

3 large fresh red chillies, seeded and chopped
3 garlic cloves, peeled
15ml/1 tbsp ground coriander
30ml/2 tbsp ground cumin
5ml/1 tsp ground cinnamon
grated rind of 1 lemon
30ml/2 tbsp sunflower oil

1 Make the harissa. Whizz the ingredients in a food processor to a smooth paste. Put the fish in a wide bowl and add 30ml/2 tbsp of the harissa. Toss to coat, cover and chill for at least 1 hour.

2 Heat half the olive oil in a heavy pan. Add the aubergine cubes and fry for about 10 minutes, or until they are golden. Add the courgettes and fry for a further 2 minutes. Remove the vegetables from the pan and set aside.

3 Add the remaining olive oil to the pan, add the onions and cook over a low heat for 10 minutes until golden. Stir in the remaining harissa and cook for 5 minutes, stirring occasionally.

4 Add the vegetables and combine with the onions, then stir in the chopped tomatoes, the passata and fish stock. Bring to the boil, then lower the heat and simmer for about 20 minutes.

5 Stir the fish chunks and preserved lemon into the pan. Add the olives and stir gently. Cover and simmer over a low heat for 15–20 minutes. Season to taste. Stir in the chopped coriander. Serve with couscous, if you like, and garnish with coriander leaves.

Fish with Spinach and Lime

Fresh herbs and hot spices are combined to make the charmoula marinade that is used to flavour this delicious Moroccan-style dish.

Serves 4

675g/1½lb white fish, such as haddock, cod or sea bass
sunflower oil, for frying
500g/1¼lb potatoes, sliced
1 onion, chopped
1–2 garlic cloves, crushed
5 tomatoes, peeled and chopped
375g/13oz fresh spinach, chopped
lime wedges, to garnish

For the charmoula

6 spring onions (scallions), chopped
10ml/2 tsp fresh thyme
60ml/4 tbsp chopped parsley
30ml/2 tbsp chopped fresh coriander (cilantro)
10ml/2 tsp paprika
generous pinch of cayenne pepper
60ml/4 tbsp olive oil
grated rind of 1 lime and 60ml/4 tbsp lime juice
salt

1 Cut the white fish into large even-size pieces, discarding any skin and bones. Place the fish in a large shallow dish.

2 Blend the ingredients for the charmoula. Season with salt. Pour over the fish, stir to mix and leave in a cool place, covered with clear film (plastic wrap), to marinate for 2–4 hours.

3 Heat about 5mm/¼in oil in a heavy pan, add the potato slices and cook, turning occasionally, until they are cooked through and golden brown. Drain the potatoes on kitchen paper. Pour off all but 15ml/1 tbsp of the oil from the pan and add the onion, garlic and tomatoes. Cook over a gentle heat for 5–6 minutes, stirring occasionally, until the onion is soft. Place the potatoes on top then add the spinach.

4 Place the marinated fish pieces on the spinach in the pan and pour over all of the marinade. Cover the pan and cook for 15–18 minutes. After 8 minutes of the cooking time, stir the contents of the pan, so that the fish at the top are distributed throughout the dish. Cover the pan and continue cooking, but check occasionally – the dish is cooked once the fish is just tender and opaque and the spinach has wilted. Serve the dish hot, with wedges of lime and warm crusty bread, if you like.

Fish Tagine Energy 263Kcal/1099kJ; Protein 32.3g; Carbohydrate 8.3g, of which sugars 7g; Fat 11.3g, of which saturates 1.7g; Cholesterol 75mg; Calcium 57mg; Fibre 3.2g; Sodium 360mg.
Fish with Spinach Energy 433Kcal/1810kJ; Protein 37.3g; Carbohydrate 28.9g, of which sugars 9.4g; Fat 19.3g, of which saturates 2.8g; Cholesterol 78mg; Calcium 206mg; Fibre 5.2g; Sodium 260mg.

Goan Fish Casserole

The cooking of Goa is a mixture of Portuguese and Indian; the addition of tamarind gives a tangy note to the spicy coconut sauce.

Serves 4

7.5ml/1½ tsp ground turmeric
5ml/1 tsp salt
450g/1lb monkfish fillet, cut into eight pieces
15ml/1 tbsp lemon juice
5ml/1 tsp cumin seeds
5ml/1 tsp coriander seeds
5ml/1 tsp black peppercorns
1 garlic clove, chopped
5cm/2in piece fresh root ginger, finely chopped
25g/1oz tamarind paste
150ml/¼ pint/⅔ cup hot water
30ml/2 tbsp vegetable oil
2 onions, halved and sliced lengthways
400ml/14fl oz/1⅔ cups coconut milk
4 mild green chillies, seeded and cut into thin strips
16 large raw prawns (shrimp), peeled
30ml/2 tbsp chopped fresh coriander (cilantro) leaves, to garnish

1 Mix the turmeric and salt in a small bowl. Place the monkfish in a dish and sprinkle over the lemon juice, then rub the turmeric mixture over the fish fillets to coat them completely. Cover and chill until ready to cook. Put the cumin seeds, coriander seeds and black peppercorns in a blender or small food processor and blend to a powder. Add the garlic and ginger and process for a few seconds more.

2 Preheat the oven to 200°C/400°F/Gas 6. Mix the tamarind paste with the hot water and set aside. Heat the oil in a frying pan, add the onions and cook for 5–6 minutes, until softened and golden. Transfer the onions to an ovenproof dish.

3 Add the fish to the pan, and fry over a high heat, turning to seal all sides. Remove the fish from the pan and place on top of the onions. Add the spice mixture and cook for 1–2 minutes. Add the tamarind liquid, coconut milk and chillies and bring to the boil. Pour the sauce into the ovenproof dish to coat the fish.

4 Cover the dish and cook in the oven for 10 minutes. Add the prawns, cover again and return it to the oven for 5 minutes. Check the seasoning, sprinkle with coriander leaves and serve.

Green Fish Curry

Fresh-tasting, spicy curries made with coconut milk are a classic of Thai cuisine.

Serves 4

1 onion, chopped
1 large fresh green chilli, halved, seeded and chopped, plus extra slices to garnish
1 garlic clove, crushed
50g/2oz/½ cup cashew nuts
2.5ml/½ tsp fennel seeds
30ml/2 tbsp desiccated (dry unsweetened shredded) coconut
150ml/¼ pint/⅔ cup water
30ml/2 tbsp vegetable oil
1.5ml/¼ tsp cumin seeds
1.5ml/¼ tsp ground coriander
1.5ml/¼ tsp ground cumin
150ml/¼ pint/⅔ cup double (heavy) cream
4 white fish fillets, such as cod or haddock, skinned
1.5ml/¼ tsp ground turmeric
30ml/2 tbsp lime juice
salt
45ml/3 tbsp chopped fresh coriander (cilantro), plus extra to garnish
boiled rice, to serve

1 Place the onion, chilli, garlic, cashew nuts, fennel seeds and coconut in a food processor with 45ml/3 tbsp of the water and blend to a smooth paste, then stir in the water.

2 Heat the oil in a frying pan and fry the cumin seeds for 1 minute. Add the coconut paste and fry for 5 minutes, then stir in the ground coriander, cumin and remaining water. Bring to the boil, then let the mixture bubble for 1 minute. Transfer the mixture to a ceramic cooking pot. Stir in the cream, cover with the lid and switch the slow cooker to high. Cook for 1½ hours.

3 Towards the end of cooking time, prepare and marinate the fish. Cut the fillets into 5cm/2in chunks and put them in a glass bowl. Combine the turmeric, lime juice and a pinch of salt in a separate bowl and pour it over the fish. Use your hands to rub it into the fish. Cover with clear film (plastic wrap) and leave to marinate for 15 minutes.

4 Stir the fish into the sauce, re-cover and cook for 30 minutes to 1 hour, or until the fish flakes easily. Stir in the coriander. Spoon the curry into a warmed bowls. Garnish with chopped coriander and sliced green chilli, and serve with rice.

Fish Casserole Energy 220Kcal/926kJ; Protein 28g; Carbohydrate 12.8g, of which sugars 10.5g; Fat 6.8g, of which saturates 1g; Cholesterol 113mg; Calcium 103mg; Fibre 1.4g; Sodium 720mg.
Fish Curry Energy 511Kcal/2118kJ; Protein 36.1g; Carbohydrate 6.4g, of which sugars 3.9g; Fat 37.9g, of which saturates 18.8g; Cholesterol 132mg; Calcium 50mg; Fibre 2g; Sodium 153mg.

Fish in Aromatic Sauce

This well-loved dish from West Bengal is flavoured with mustard oil and a combination of five whole spices that produces a memorable aromatic taste.

Serves 4–5

675g/1½lb fillets of tilapia or
    other firmwhite fish, cut into
    5cm/2in pieces
5ml/1 tsp ground turmeric
5ml/1 tsp salt or to taste
4 tbsp mustard oil
1.5ml/¼ tsp black mustard seeds
1.5ml/¼ tsp cumin seeds
1.5ml/¼ tsp fennel seeds

1.5ml/¼ tsp nigella seeds
5–6 fenugreek seeds
2 bay leaves
2 dried red chillies, left whole
2 fresh green chillies, chopped
2.5ml/½ tsp ground cumin
5ml/1 tsp ground coriander
75g/3oz chopped canned
    tomatoes, with their juice
115g/4oz potatoes, cut into
    1cm/½in cubes
115g/4oz aubergine (eggplant),
    cut into 1cm/½in pieces
50g/2oz/½ cup frozen peas
30ml/2 tbsp chopped fresh
    coriander (cilantro)
plain boiled rice, to serve

1 Lay the fish on a large plate and rub in half the turmeric and half the salt. Set aside. Heat 30ml/2 tbsp of the mustard oil over a medium heat, and when it is almost smoking, switch off the heat source and add the mustard seeds, followed by the cumin, fennel, nigella and fenugreek seeds.

2 Add the bay leaves, and the red and green chillies. Return the pan to the heat and add the cumin, coriander and remaining turmeric. Stir over a medium heat for 30 seconds then add the tomatoes. Cook for 4–5 minutes.

3 Add in all the potato cubes and the aubergine pieces, along with about 350ml/12fl oz/1½ cups warm water and the remaining salt. Bring the pan to the boil, then reduce the heat to low, cover and cook for 15 minutes, stirring occasionally.

4 Meanwhile, heat the remaining oil in a frying pan until almost smoking. Fry the fish in batches until well browned and drain on absorbent paper. Add the fried fish to the curry along with the peas. Cook for 4–5 minutes, then stir in the chopped coriander and remove from the heat. Serve with plain boiled rice.

Malay Fish Curry

The fish curries of Malaysia differ slightly from region to region, but most of them include Indian spices and coconut milk. The Malay food stalls often feature a fish, chicken or beef curry, which is usually served with bread or rice, pickles and extra chillies.

Serves 4

30ml/2 tbsp vegetable oil
7.5ml/1½ tsp tamarind paste
8 thick fish cutlets, about
    90g/3½oz, such as grouper,
    red snapper, trout
    or mackerel
800ml/1½ pints coconut milk
salt

fresh coriander (cilantro) leaves,
    roughly chopped, to garnish
rice or crusty bread,
    to serve

For the curry paste
4 shallots, chopped
4 garlic cloves, chopped
50g/2oz fresh root ginger, peeled
    and chopped
25g/1oz fresh turmeric, chopped
4–6 dried red chillies, softened
    in warm water, seeded
    and chopped
15ml/1 tbsp coriander
    seeds, roasted
15ml/1 tbsp cumin seeds, roasted
10ml/2 tsp fish curry powder
5ml/1 tsp fennel seeds
2.5ml/½ tsp black peppercorns

1 First make the curry paste. Using a mortar and pestle or food processor, grind the shallots, garlic, ginger, turmeric and chillies to a paste and transfer to a bowl.

2 Again, using the mortar and pestle or food processor, grind the roasted coriander and cumin seeds, fish curry powder, fennel seeds and peppercorns to a powder and add to the paste in the bowl. Bind with 15ml/1 tbsp water and thoroughly mix together.

3 Heat the oil in a wok or heavy pan. Stir in the curry paste and fry until fragrant. Add the tamarind paste and mix well. Add the fish cutlets and cook for 1 minute on each side. Pour in the coconut milk, mix well and bring to the boil. Reduce the heat and simmer for 10–15 minutes until the fish is cooked. Season to taste with salt. Scatter the coriander over the top and serve with plain or yellow rice, or with chunks of crusty bread to mop up the sauce.

Fish in Aromatic Sauce Energy 242kcal/1011kJ; Protein 27.1g; Carbohydrate 7.4g, of which sugars 1.4g; Fat 11.9g, of which saturates 1.5g; Cholesterol 0mg; Calcium 184mg; Fibre 1.2g; Sodium 83mg.
Fish Curry Energy 304kcal/1281kJ; Protein 38g; Carbohydrate 16g, of which sugars 13g; Fat 12g, of which saturates 2g; Cholesterol 67mg; Calcium 193mg; Fibre 0g; Sodium 373mg.

Dry Fish Stew with Coriander

A seco is a 'dry' style of stew that can be made with fish or meat. The recipe, from northern Peru, uses coriander and other locally grown ingredients. The cooking of the north includes many versions of seco made with chicken, kid and lamb.

Serves 6
6 white fish fillets, such as cod or
  swordfish
1 large red onion, sliced lengthways
1 red (bell) pepper, thinly sliced
3 garlic cloves
2.5cm/1in piece fresh root ginger
100g/3¾oz chopped fresh
  coriander (cilantro)
1.5ml/¼ tsp ground cumin
45ml/3 tbsp chilli sauce
120ml/4fl oz/½ cup
  vegetable oil
120ml/4fl oz/½ cup white beer
250g/9oz/2 cups shelled peas
juice of 1 lime
salt and ground black pepper
boiled rice, to serve

1 Arrange the fish fillets in a wide saucepan and cover with the slices of onion and red pepper.

2 Put the garlic cloves, fresh root ginger, coriander, cumin, chilli sauce and oil into a blender or food processor and blend to a purée.

3 Spoon the mixture over the fish and leave to marinate in the saucepan for about 15 minutes.

4 Put the pan on a high heat until the fish is starting to sizzle, pour in the beer and add the peas and bring to the boil. Reduce the heat, cover the pan and simmer for 15 minutes.

5 When the fish is cooked, squeeze the lime juice over the top, and serve with rice.

Cook's Tips
Because swordfish is inclined to be rather dry, any recipe that marinates the fish in a mixture of spices and oil is ideal. Although it is a white fish, swordfish has a firm, meaty texture.

Fish Stew with Lemon Grass

Lemon grass and ginger give this delicate stew of fish, prawns, new potatoes and broccoli an appetizing aromatic flavour.

Serves 4
25g/1oz/2 tbsp butter
175g/6oz onions, chopped
20ml/4 tsp plain
  (all-purpose) flour
400ml/14fl oz/1⅔ cups
  light fish stock
150ml/¼ pint/⅔ cup
  white wine
2.5cm/1in piece fresh root ginger,
  peeled and finely chopped
2 lemon grass stalks, trimmed
  and finely chopped
450g/1lb new potatoes,
  scrubbed and halved
  if necessary
450g/1lb white fish fillets
175g/6oz large, cooked, peeled
  prawns (shrimp)
275g/10oz small broccoli florets
150ml/¼ pint/⅔ cup double
  (heavy) cream
60ml/4 tbsp chopped fresh
  garlic chives
salt and ground black pepper
crusty bread, to serve

1 Melt the butter in a large pan. Add the onions and cook for 3–4 minutes. Stir in the flour and cook for 1 minute.

2 Stir in the stock, wine, ginger, lemon grass and potatoes. Season and bring to the boil. Cover and cook for 15 minutes, or until the potatoes are almost tender.

3 Remove the skin from the fish fillets and cut the fillets into large chunks. Add the chunks of fish to the pan with the prawns, broccoli and cream. Stir gently.

4 Simmer gently for 5 minutes, taking care not to break up the fish. Adjust the seasoning and sprinkle in the chives. Serve with plenty of crusty bread.

Cook's Tips
If you cannot find lemon grass, you could use the grated zest of a lemon instead. The main flavouring of the two ingredients is very similar.

Fish with Crab Meat and Aubergine

Combining crab with salmon and aubergine creates a sophisticated dish.

Serves 4
450–675g/1–1½lb salmon fillet, skinned and cut into 4 pieces
2 garlic cloves, crushed
juice of ½ lemon
15ml/1 tbsp vegetable oil
15g/½oz/1 tbsp butter
1 onion, cut into rings
175g/6oz fresh or canned crab meat
salt and ground black pepper

For the aubergine (eggplant) sauce
25g/1oz/2 tbsp butter or margarine
30ml/2 tbsp chopped spring onion (scallion)
2 tomatoes, skinned and chopped
½ red (bell) pepper, seeded and finely chopped
1 large aubergine (eggplant), peeled and chopped
450ml/¾ pint/scant 2 cups fish or vegetable stock
salt and ground black pepper

1 Place the salmon fillet in a shallow, non-metallic dish, season with the garlic and a little salt and pepper. Sprinkle with the lemon juice, cover with clear film (plastic wrap) and set aside to marinate in a cool place for 1 hour.

2 Meanwhile, make the aubergine sauce. Melt the butter or margarine in a pan and fry the spring onion and tomatoes for 5 minutes. Add the red pepper and aubergine, mix, then add 300ml/½ pint/1¼ cups of the stock. Simmer for 20 minutes, until the aubergines are mushy and the liquid has been absorbed and then mash the mixture together well with a fork.

3 To cook the salmon, heat the oil and butter in a large frying pan. When the butter has melted, scatter the onion rings over the bottom of the pan and lay the salmon pieces on top. Cover each piece of salmon with crab meat and then spoon the aubergine mixture on top.

4 Pour the remaining stock around the salmon, cover with a lid and cook over a low to moderate heat, until the salmon is cooked through and flakes easily when tested with a knife. The sauce should be thick and fairly dry. Arrange the fish on serving plates, spoon the sauce over and serve at once.

Salmon and Black-eyed Bean Stew

The addition of fresh salmon to this stew helps to make it an extremely nourishing dish, as well as a delicious winter warmer.

Serves 2
150g/5oz salmon fillet, skinned and any bones removed
400g/14oz canned black-eyed beans (peas) in brine
50g/2oz fresh shiitake mushrooms, stalks removed
1 small carrot, peeled
½ mooli (daikon), peeled
5g/⅛oz dashi-konbu (dried kelp seaweed), about 10cm/4in square
60ml/4 tbsp water
15ml/1 tbsp shoyu (Japanese soy sauce)
7.5ml/1½ tsp mirin or dry sherry
sea salt
2.5cm/1in fresh root ginger, peeled and thinly sliced into thin threads, to garnish

1 Slice the salmon into 1cm/½in-thick strips. Place in a colander, sprinkle with sea salt and leave for 1 hour. Wash away the salt and cut the salmon strips into 1cm/½in cubes. Parboil for 30 seconds, then drain. Gently rinse under cold water to prevent the cubes from cooking further.

2 Soak the ginger in cold water for about 30 minutes, then drain well.

3 Drain the can of black-eyed beans into a medium pan. Reserve the liquid from the can.

4 Chop all the fresh vegetables into 1cm/½in cubes. Wipe the dashi-konbu with kitchen paper, then snip with scissors. Cut everything as close to the same size as possible.

5 Put the parboiled salmon, dashi-konbu and vegetables into the pan containing the liquid from the can of beans. Pour the beans on top and add the 60ml/4 tbsp water and 1.5ml/¼ tsp salt. Bring to the boil. Reduce the heat to low and cook for 6 minutes or until the carrot is cooked.

6 Add the shoyu and cook for a further 4 minutes. Add the mirin or sherry and remove the pan from the heat. Mix well. Leave to rest for 1 hour. Serve warm or cold, with the ginger threads.

Fish with Crab Energy 372Kcal/1548kJ; Protein 32.4g; Carbohydrate 6.5g, of which sugars 5.8g; Fat 24.3g, of which saturates 7.9g; Cholesterol 109mg; Calcium 98mg; Fibre 3.1g; Sodium 360mg.
Salmon Stew Energy 342kcal/1440kJ; Protein 30g; Carbohydrate 37g, of which sugars 6g; Fat 10g, of which saturates 2g; Cholesterol 38mg; Calcium 78mg; Fibre 1g; Sodium 614mg.

Northern Thai Fish Curry

Thin, soupy, strongly flavoured curries are typical of the northern region of Thailand. Fragrant lemon grass, zesty galangal and salty Thai fish sauce come together to give this fish dish its characteristic Thai flavour. Serve with lots of sticky rice to soak up the flavourful juices.

Serves 4
450g/1lb salmon fillet
475ml/16fl oz/2 cups near-boiling
    vegetable stock
4 shallots, very finely chopped
1 garlic clove, crushed
2.5cm/1in piece fresh galangal or
    ginger, finely chopped
1 lemon grass stalk,
    finely chopped
2.5ml/½ tsp dried chilli flakes
15ml/1 tbsp Thai fish sauce
5ml/1 tsp palm sugar or light
    muscovado (brown) sugar

1 Wrap the salmon fillet in clear film (plastic wrap) and place in the freezer for 30–40 minutes to firm up slightly. Unwrap the fish, and carefully remove and discard the skin. Using a sharp knife, cut the fish into 2.5cm/1in cubes and remove any stray bones with your fingers or a pair of tweezers.

2 Place the cubed fish in a bowl, cover with clear film (plastic wrap) and leave to stand at room temperature.

3 Meanwhile, pour the hot vegetable stock into a ceramic cooking pot and switch the slow cooker to high. Add the shallots, garlic, galangal or ginger, lemon grass, chilli flakes, fish sauce and sugar and mix. Cover and cook for 2 hours.

4 Add the salmon to the stock and cook for 15 minutes. Turn off the slow cooker and leave to stand for a further 10–15 minutes, or until the fish is cooked through. Serve immediately.

> **Cook's Tip**
> *Allow the fish to return to room temperature before adding to the stock, so that the temperature of the liquid doesn't fall below simmering point.*

Coconut Salmon

Salmon is quite a robust fish, and responds well to being cooked with this fragrant blend of spices, garlic and chilli.

Serves 4
15ml/1 tbsp oil
1 onion, finely chopped
2 fresh green chillies, seeded
    and chopped
2 garlic cloves, crushed
2.5cm/1in piece fresh root
    ginger, grated

175ml/6fl oz/¾ cup
    coconut milk
10ml/2 tsp ground cumin
5ml/1 tsp ground coriander
4 salmon steaks,
    each about 175g/6oz
10ml/2 tsp chilli powder
2.5ml/½ tsp ground turmeric
15ml/1 tbsp white wine vinegar
1.5ml/¼ tsp salt
fresh coriander (cilantro) sprigs,
    to garnish
rice tossed with spring onions
    (scallions), to serve

1 Heat the oil in a pan, add the onion, chillies, garlic and ginger and fry for 5–6 minutes, until fairly soft. Place in a food processor with 120ml/4fl oz/½ cup of the coconut milk and blend until smooth.

2 Tip the paste into a ceramic cooking pot. Stir in 5ml/1 tsp of the cumin, the ground coriander and the rest of the coconut milk. Cover and cook on high for 1½ hours.

3 About 20 minutes before the end of cooking time, arrange the salmon steaks in a single layer in a shallow glass dish. Combine the remaining 5ml/1 tsp cumin, the chilli powder, turmeric, vinegar and salt in a bowl to make a paste. Rub the mixture over the salmon steaks and leave to marinate at room temperature while the sauce finishes cooking.

4 Add the salmon steaks to the sauce, arranging them in a single layer and spoon some of the coconut sauce over the top to keep the fish moist while it cooks. Cover with the lid, reduce the temperature to low and cook for 45 minutes–1 hour, or until the salmon is opaque and tender.

5 Transfer the fish to a serving dish, spoon over the sauce and garnish with fresh coriander. Serve with the rice.

Fish Curry Energy 216Kcal/902kJ; Protein 23.2g; Carbohydrate 2.7g, of which sugars 2.2g; Fat 12.6g, of which saturates 2.1g; Cholesterol 56mg; Calcium 30mg; Fibre 0.2g; Sodium 522mg.
Coconut Salmon Energy 363Kcal/1512kJ; Protein 35.9g; Carbohydrate 5.1g, of which sugars 4.2g; Fat 22.2g, of which saturates 3.8g; Cholesterol 88mg; Calcium 59mg; Fibre 0.5g; Sodium 275mg.

Trout in Wine Sauce with Plantain

In the West Indies, where this recipe originated, the fish used would probably be dolphinfish or snapper, but this is also a wonderful treatment for trout.

Serves 4

4 trout fillets
15ml/1 tbsp crushed garlic
7.5ml/1½ tsp coarse-grain black pepper
7.5ml/1½ tsp paprika
7.5ml/1½ tsp celery salt
7.5ml/1½ tsp curry powder
5ml/1 tsp caster (superfine) sugar
25g/1oz/2 tbsp butter
150ml/¼ pint/⅔ cup white wine
150ml/¼ pint/⅔ cup fish stock
10ml/2 tsp clear honey
15–30ml/1–2 tbsp chopped fresh parsley
1 yellow plantain
oil, for frying

1 Put the trout fillets in a dish. Mix the garlic, pepper, paprika, celery salt, curry powder and sugar in a bowl. Sprinkle over the trout and marinate for 1 hour.

2 Melt the butter in a large frying pan and sauté the marinated trout fillets, in batches if necessary, for about 5 minutes or until cooked through, turning once. Transfer to a warm plate and keep hot. Add the wine, fish stock and honey to the pan. Bring to the boil and simmer to reduce slightly. Return the fillets to the pan and spoon over the sauce. Sprinkle with parsley and simmer gently for a few minutes.

3 Peel the plantain and cut it into rounds. Heat a little oil in a frying pan and fry the plantain until soft and golden brown, turning once.

4 Transfer the fish to warmed serving plates, stir the sauce and pour it over. Garnish with the fried plantain.

> **Cook's Tip**
> This recipe can also be prepared on a barbecue. Cook the fish and wine sauce in a frying pan but wrap the unpeeled plantain in foil and bake it on the barbecue for about 10 minutes, or until tender, before cutting it into rounds.

Basque-style Tuna

In Spain, this traditional fisherman's stew is known as marmitako. It used to be cooked at sea on the fishing boats, and takes its name from the cooking pot, known in France as a marmite. In this version, a slow cooker is used to catch all the rich flavourings, which go perfectly with the robust taste of tuna.

Serves 4

30ml/2 tbsp olive oil
1 onion, finely chopped
1 clove garlic, finely chopped
75ml/2½fl oz/⅓ cup white wine, preferably Spanish
150ml/¼ pint/⅔ cup boiling fish or vegetable stock
200g/7oz can chopped tomatoes
5ml/1 tsp paprika
2.5ml/½ tsp dried crushed chillies
450g/1lb waxy new potatoes, cut into 1cm/½in chunks
1 red and 1 yellow (bell) pepper, seeded and chopped
1 small sprig of fresh rosemary
1 bay leaf
450g/1lb fresh tuna, cut into 2.5cm/1in chunks
salt and ground black pepper
crusty bread, to serve

1 Heat the oil in a large frying pan, add the onion and fry gently for 10 minutes until soft and translucent. Stir in the garlic, followed by the wine, stock, tomatoes, paprika and chillies.

2 Bring the mixture to just below boiling point, then carefully pour the mixture into a ceramic cooking pot.

3 Add the chunks of potato, red and yellow pepper, rosemary and bay leaf to the pot and stir to combine. Cover the slow cooker with the lid and cook on high for 2–2½ hours, or until the potatoes are just tender, then season the sauce to taste with salt and a little ground black pepper.

4 Stir the chunks of tuna into the sauce. Cover and cook for 15–20 minutes, or until the fish is firm and opaque.

5 Remove the rosemary and bay leaf, then ladle the stew into warmed dishes, grind over a little more black pepper and serve with crusty bread.

Trout in Wine Sauce Energy 478kcal/2005kJ; Protein 36g; Carbohydrate 30g, of which sugars 8g; Fat 8g, of which saturates 25g; Cholesterol 131mg; Calcium 52mg; Fibre 2g; Sodium 679mg
Basque Tuna Energy 297Kcal/1256kJ; Protein 30.1g; Carbohydrate 27.5g, of which sugars 9.6g; Fat 6.g, of which saturates 1.2g; Cholesterol 57mg; Calcium 39mg; Fibre 3.2g; Sodium 397mg.

John Dory with Light Curry Sauce

The spicy taste of this dish should be very subtle, so use a mild curry powder. Serve the fish with pilau rice and mango chutney.

Serves 4
4 John Dory fillets, about
    175g/6oz each, skinned
15ml/1 tbsp sunflower oil
25g/1oz/2 tbsp butter
salt and ground black pepper
15ml/1 tbsp fresh coriander
    (cilantro) leaves and 1 small
    mango, diced, to garnish
pilau rice and mango chutney,
    to serve

For the curry sauce
30ml/2 tbsp sunflower oil
1 carrot, chopped
1 onion, chopped
1 celery stick, chopped
white of 1 leek, chopped
2 garlic cloves, crushed
50g/2oz creamed coconut
    (coconut cream), crumbled
2 tomatoes, peeled, seeded
    and diced
2.5cm/1in piece fresh root
    ginger, grated
15ml/1 tbsp tomato purée (paste)
5–10ml/1–2 tsp mild curry powder
500ml/17fl oz/generous 2 cups
    chicken or fish stock

1 Make the sauce. Heat the oil in a pan; add the vegetables and garlic. Cook gently until soft but not brown.

2 Add the coconut, tomatoes and ginger. Cook for 1–2 minutes, then stir in the tomato purée and curry powder to taste. Add the stock, stir and season.

3 Bring to the boil, then lower the heat, cover the pan and cook over the lowest heat for about 50 minutes. Stir once or twice to prevent burning. Leave to cool, then pour into a food processor or blender and process until smooth. Return to a clean pan and reheat gently, adding a little water if too thick.

4 Season the fish fillets with salt and pepper. Heat the oil in a large frying pan, add the butter and heat until sizzling. Put in the fish and cook for about 2–3 minutes on each side, until pale golden and cooked through. Drain on kitchen paper.

5 Serve on a bed of rice. Arrange the fillets on individual warmed plates and pour the sauce around. Garnish with finely diced mango and coriander leaves, and serve with chutney.

Swordfish in Barbecue Sauce

Slow cooking is an ideal way to cook any firm fish steaks. The warmly spiced smoky sauce goes particularly well with meaty fish, such as swordfish, shark and tuna. Choose smaller, thicker fish steaks rather than large, thinner ones, so that they will fit in a slow cooker.

Serves 4
15ml/1 tbsp sunflower oil
1 small onion, very finely chopped
1 garlic clove, crushed
2.5ml/½ tsp chilli powder
15ml/1 tbsp Worcestershire sauce
15ml/1 tbsp soft light
    brown sugar
15ml/1 tbsp balsamic vinegar
15ml/1 tbsp American mustard
150ml/¼ pint/⅔ cup
    tomato juice
4 swordfish steaks, about
    115g/4oz each
salt and ground black pepper
fresh flat leaf parsley sprigs,
    chopped parsley and lemon
    wedges, to garnish
boiled or steamed rice, to serve

1 Heat the oil in a frying pan, add the onion and cook gently for 10 minutes, until soft. Stir in the garlic and chilli powder and cook for a few seconds, then add the Worcestershire sauce, sugar, vinegar, mustard and tomato juice. Heat gently, stirring, until nearly boiling.

2 Pour half the sauce into a ceramic cooking pot. Rinse the swordfish steaks, pat dry on kitchen paper and arrange in a single layer on top of the sauce. Top with the remaining sauce.

3 Cover the slow cooker with a lid and switch on to high. Cook for 2–3 hours, or until the fish is tender and cooked.

4 Using a fish slice, carefully transfer the fish to warmed serving plates and spoon the barbecue sauce over the top. Garnish with sprigs of flat-leaf parsley, lemon wedges and a little chopped fresh parsley, and serve immediately with rice.

Cook's Tip
For a really smoky barbecue flavour use a crushed dried chipotle chilli instead of the chilli powder.

John Dory Energy 333kcal/1391kJ; Protein 34.9g; Carbohydrate 12.5g, of which sugars 11.5g; Fat 16.3g, of which saturates 4.9g; Cholesterol 13mg; Calcium 102mg; Fibre 2.6g; Sodium 291mg.
Swordfish Energy 158Kcal/670kJ; Protein 27.3g; Carbohydrate 4.9g, of which sugars 4.5g; Fat 3.5g, of which saturates 0.6g; Cholesterol 59mg; Calcium 21mg; Fibre 0.2g; Sodium 414mg.

Catfish Cooked in a Clay Pot

Wonderfully easy and tasty, this southern-style dish, called ca kho to, is a classic in most Vietnamese homes. In the south, clay pots are regularly used for cooking and they enhance both the look and taste of this traditional dish. However, you can use any heavy pot or pan. It is delicious served with chunks of baguette to mop up the caramelized, smoky sauce at the bottom of the pot, but you could easily serve it with steamed rice or vegetables.

Serves 4

30ml/2 tbsp sugar
15ml/1 tbsp sesame or
    vegetable oil
2 garlic cloves, crushed
45ml/3 tbsp nuoc mam
350g/12oz catfish fillets, cut
    diagonally into 2 or 3 pieces
4 spring onions (scallions), cut into
    bitesize pieces
ground black pepper
chopped fresh coriander (cilantro),
    to garnish

1 Tip the sugar into a clay pot or heavy pan, and add 15ml/1 tbsp water to wet it. Heat the sugar until it begins to brown, then add the oil and garlic.

2 Stir the nuoc mam into the caramel mixture and add 120ml/4fl oz/½ cup boiling water, then toss in the catfish pieces, making sure they are well coated with the sauce.

3 Cover the pot, reduce the heat and simmer for about 5 minutes.

4 Remove the lid, season with black pepper and gently stir in the spring onions. Simmer for a further 3–4 minutes to thicken the sauce, garnish with fresh coriander, and serve immediately straight from the pot.

Cook's Tip
Adding a salty fish sauce (nuoc mam), anchovies or olives to catfish counteracts its rather bland flavour.

Eel Stew

One excellent way to cook eel is in escabeche, when it is poached or fried and then marinated, but eel stew is another popular option. Different regions of Portugal cook this stew with a variety of other fish. One common method is to combine several types of fish, such as sardines, skate or conger eel.

Serves 4

1kg/2½lb eel fillets, cut into
    4cm/1½in slices
500g/1¼lb potatoes, cut into
    5mm/¼in slices
2 onions, very thinly sliced
2 bay leaves, torn into pieces
2 garlic cloves, chopped
50ml/2fl oz/¼ cup white wine
105ml/7 tbsp olive oil
1 bunch of parsley, chopped
5–7.5ml/1–1½ tsp
    ground ginger
salt
bread, to serve

1 If you haven't asked your fishmonger to prepare the eels, prepare them yourself by cutting off the heads and sprinkling the skin with salt so you can easily remove it. Rinse the eel fillets well in cold running water then cut them up into small slices .

2 Make a layer of sliced potatoes in a large pan, then make a layer of onions, followed by a layer of fish. Season with pieces of bay leaf, some garlic, a little wine and olive oil and a sprinkling of parsley, ginger and salt. Continue making layers in this way until all the ingredients have been used up.

3 Sprinkle in 100ml/3½fl oz/scant ½ cup water, cover and cook on a low heat for about 30 minutes, until the fish is cooked through and the vegetables are tender. Serve with bread.

Cook's Tips
• *You can add some green and red (bell) pepper between the layers.*
• *The eels can also be cooked in 4cm/1½in boned pieces, in which case make the potato slices thicker since the eel will take longer to cook.*

Catfish Energy 160kcal/671kJ; Protein 16g; Carbohydrate 10g, of which sugars 8g; Fat 6g, of which saturates 1g; Cholesterol 40mg; Calcium 26mg; Fibre 0g; Sodium 552mg.
Eel Stew Energy 738kcal/3074kJ; Protein 45.5g; Carbohydrate 30.4g, of which sugars 9g; Fat 48.3g, of which saturates 10.1g; Cholesterol 375mg; Calcium 113mg; Fibre 3.6g; Sodium 245mg.

Eel Braised in Caramel Sauce with Butternut Squash

Although this dish is found in different parts of Vietnam, it is traditionally a northern dish and it is there, in the highlands, that it is best sampled. The eels are caught in the Red, Black and Song Ma rivers, which contribute to the local name of this dish, 'three rivers eel'. If you can't find eel, use mackerel. The fat rendered from these fish melts into the caramel sauce, making it deliciously velvety. When it is cooked in this way, the eel is usually served with noodles or rice.

Serves 4

45ml/3 tbsp raw cane sugar
30ml/2 tbsp soy sauce
45ml/3 tbsp nuoc mam
2 garlic cloves, crushed
2 dried chillies
2–3 star anise
4–5 peppercorns
350g/12oz eel on the bone, cut
    into 2.5cm/1in-thick chunks
200g/7oz butternut squash, cut
    into bitesize chunks
4 spring onions (scallions), cut into
    bitesize pieces
30ml/2 tbsp sesame oil
5cm/2in fresh root ginger, peeled
    and cut into matchsticks
salt
chopped fresh coriander (cilantro),
    to garnish

1 Put the sugar in a heavy pan or wok with 30ml/2 tbsp water, and gently heat it until it turns golden. Remove the pan from the heat and stir in the soy sauce and nuoc mam with 120ml/4fl oz/½ cup water. Add the garlic, chillies, star anise and peppercorns and return to the heat.

2 Add the eel chunks, squash and spring onions, making sure the fish is well coated in the sauce, and season with salt. Reduce the heat, cover the pan and simmer for about 20 minutes to let the eel braise gently in the sauce and steam.

3 Meanwhile, heat a small wok, tip in the oil and stir-fry the ginger until crisp and golden. Remove and drain on kitchen paper. When the eel is nicely tender, arrange it on a serving dish, scatter the crispy ginger over it, and garnish with a little fresh coriander.

Spicy Prawn Casserole

This popular prawn dish is often served as hot meze in the fish restaurants of Izmir and Istanbul, but it is also good served as a main meal. The Mediterranean version, found in the coastal regions of south-west Turkey, is flavoured with a dose of garlic, red pepper and coriander seeds. Cooked in one big earthenware pot, güveç, or in small individual ones as here, it is delicious served with a green salad and some chunky bread.

Serves 4

30–45ml/2–3 tbsp olive oil
1 onion, cut in half lengthways
    and finely sliced along
    the grain
1 green (bell) pepper, seeded and
    finely sliced
2–3 garlic cloves, chopped
5–10ml/1–2 tsp coriander seeds
5–10ml/1–2 tsp Turkish red
    pepper,
or 1 fresh red chilli, seeded and
    chopped
5–10ml/1–2 tsp sugar
splash of white wine vinegar
2 x 400g/14oz cans chopped
    tomatoes
1 small bunch of fresh flat leaf
parsley, chopped
500g/1 1/4lb fresh raw prawns
    (shrimp), shelled, thoroughly
    cleaned and drained
about 120g/4oz kasar peyniri,
    Parmesan or a strong dry
    Cheddar, grated
salt and ground black pepper

1 Heat the oil in a heavy pan, stir in the onion, green pepper, garlic, coriander seeds and red pepper or chilli and cook until they begin to colour.

2 Stir in the sugar, vinegar, tomatoes and parsley, then cook gently for about 25 minutes, until you have a chunky sauce.

3 While the sauce is cooking, preheat the oven to 200°C/400°F/Gas 6. Season the sauce with salt and pepper and toss in the prawns, making sure they are mixed in well.

4 Spoon the mixture into individual earthenware pots and sprinkle the top with the grated cheese.

5 Bake for 25 minutes, or until the cheese is nicely browned on top.

Eel in Caramel Sauce Energy 204Kcal/857kJ; Protein 11g; Carbohydrate 20g, of which sugars 14g; Fat 10g, of which saturates 1g; Cholesterol 0mg; Calcium 76mg; Fibre 1g; Sodium 1.1g.
Spicy Prawn Casserole Energy 338kcal/1413kJ; Protein 35.9g; Carbohydrate 11.2g, of which sugars 10.8g; Fat 16.9g, of which saturates 7.3g; Cholesterol 274mg; Calcium 481mg; Fibre 2.9g; Sodium 585mg.

Octopus Stew

In Galicia, octopus stews are popular, and a common tapas dish is a simple stew with paprika, served on little wooden plates. Here the octopus is stewed with tomatoes and potatoes, to make a main course.

Serves 4–6

1kg/2¼lb octopus, cleaned
45ml/3 tbsp olive oil
1 large red onion, chopped
3 garlic cloves, finely chopped
30ml/2 tbsp brandy
300ml/½ pint/1¼ cups dry white wine
800g/1¾lb ripe plum tomatoes, peeled and chopped or 2 x 400g/14oz cans chopped tomatoes
1 dried red chilli, seeded and chopped
1.5ml/¼ tsp paprika
450g/1lb small new potatoes
15ml/1 tbsp chopped fresh rosemary
15ml/1 tbsp fresh thyme leaves
1.2 litres/2 pints/5 cups fish stock
30ml/2 tbsp chopped fresh flat leaf parsley leaves
salt and ground black pepper
rosemary sprigs, to garnish
salad leaves and French bread, to serve

1 Cut the octopus into large pieces, put in a pan and pour over enough cold water to cover. Season with salt, bring to the boil, then lower the heat and simmer for 30 minutes to tenderize it. Drain and cut into bitesize pieces.

2 Heat the oil in a large shallow pan. Fry the onion until lightly coloured, then add the garlic and fry for 1 minute. Add the octopus and fry for 2–3 minutes, stirring, until coloured.

3 Pour the brandy over the octopus and ignite it. When the flames have died down, add the wine, bring to the boil and bubble gently for about 5 minutes. Stir in the chopped tomatoes, with the chilli and paprika, then add the potatoes, rosemary and thyme. Simmer gently for 5 minutes.

4 Pour in the fish stock and season. Cover and simmer for 20–30 minutes, stirring occasionally, until the octopus and potatoes are tender and the sauce has thickened slightly. To serve, check the seasoning and stir in the parsley. Garnish with rosemary and accompany with salad and bread.

Chilean Squid Casserole

This hearty stew is ideal on a cold evening. The potatoes disintegrate to thicken and enrich the sauce, making a warming, comforting main course.

Serves 6

800g/1¾lb squid
45ml/3 tbsp olive oil
5 garlic cloves, crushed
4 fresh jalapeño chillies, seeded and finely chopped
2 celery sticks, diced
500g/1¼lb small new potatoes or baby salad potatoes, scrubbed, scraped or peeled and quartered
400ml/14fl oz/1⅔ cups dry white wine
400ml/14fl oz/1⅔ cups fish stock
4 tomatoes, diced
30ml/2 tbsp chopped fresh flat leaf parsley
salt
white rice or arepas (corn breads), to serve

1 Clean the squid under cold water. Pull the tentacles away from the body. The squid's entrails will come out easily. Remove the 'quill' from inside the body cavity and discard it. Wash the body thoroughly.

2 Pull away the membrane that covers the body. Cut between the tentacles and head, discarding the head and entrails. Leave the tentacles whole but discard the hard 'beak' in the middle. Cut the body into thin rounds.

3 Heat the oil, add the garlic, chillies and celery and cook for 5 minutes. Stir in the potatoes, then add the wine and stock. Bring to the boil, then simmer, covered, for 25 minutes.

4 Remove from the heat and stir in the squid, tomatoes and parsley. Cover the pan and leave to stand until the squid is cooked. Serve immediately.

> **Cook's Tip**
> Adding the tomatoes and parsley at the end gives a freshness to the sauce. If you prefer an even heartier dish, add these ingredients to the pan with the potatoes.

Octopus Stew Energy 325kcal/1369kJ; Protein 32.7g; Carbohydrate 20.5g, of which sugars 8.2g; Fat 8.4g, of which saturates 1.5g; Cholesterol 80mg; Calcium 86mg; Fibre 2.8g; Sodium 24mg.
Chilean Squid Energy 254kcal/1071kJ; Protein 23g; Carbohydrate 18g, of which sugars 4g; Fat 10g, of which saturates 2g; Cholesterol 300mg; Calcium 30mg; Fibre 2g; Sodium 310mg.

Mediterranean Squid with Olives and Red Wine

Although many Muslims do not drink alcohol, there are some surprisingly good wines in Turkey, and along the Mediterranean and Aegean coasts some restaurants incorporate wine in dishes. This could be due to their proximity to Greece or, perhaps, to the influence of Western tourists. Whatever the reason, this is one of the most memorable squid dishes from around the Mediterranean coast. Chunks of crusty bread and a leafy rocket salad make good accompaniments.

Serves 4

30–45ml/2–3 tbsp olive oil
2 red onions, cut in half lengthways
 and sliced along the grain
3–4 garlic cloves, chopped
about 750g/1lb 10oz fresh squid,
 cleaned and cut into
 thick rings
45–60ml/3–4 tbsp black
 olives, pitted
5–10ml/1–2 tsp ground cinnamon
5–10ml/1–2 tsp sugar
about 300ml/1/2 pint/1 1/4 cups
 red wine
2 bay leaves
1 small bunch each of fresh
 flat leaf parsley and dill,
 finely chopped
salt and ground black pepper
lemon wedges, to serve

1 Heat the oil in a heavy pan and cook the onions and garlic until golden. Add the squid rings and toss them in the pan for 2–3 minutes, until they begin to colour. Toss in the olives, cinnamon and sugar, pour in the wine and add the bay leaves.

2 Boil, then lower the heat and cover the pan. Cook for 35–40 minutes, until most of the liquid has reduced and the squid is tender. Season and add the herbs. Serve with lemon wedges.

Cook's Tip
Rinse the squid and peel off the skin, then sever the head and trim the tentacles with a sharp knife. With your finger, pull out the 'quill' and remove the ink sac and any mushy bits. Rinse the empty pouch inside and out and pat dry.

Cuttlefish with Potatoes

Cuttlefish is sweeter and more tender than squid, provided you buy small or medium-size specimens. If the only ones available are very large, cook them for a little longer than stated in the recipe. This wonderful dish is often eaten during Lent.

**Serves 4 as a main course
6 as a first course**
1kg/2 1/4lb fresh cuttlefish

150ml/1/4 pint/2/3 cup extra
 virgin olive oil
1 large onion, about 225g/8oz,
 chopped
1 glass white wine, about
 175ml/6fl oz/3/4 cup
300ml/1/2 pint/1 1/4 cups
 hot water
500g/1 1/4lb potatoes, peeled
 and cubed
4–5 spring onions
 (scallions), chopped
juice of 1 lemon
60ml/4 tbsp chopped fresh dill
salt and ground black pepper

1 Prepare the cuttlefish as for squid, following the instructions on page 245. Rinse and drain the pieces well, then slice them in 2cm/3/4in wide ribbons.

2 Heat the oil in a heavy pan, add the onion and sauté for about 5 minutes until light golden. Add the cuttlefish and sauté until all the water they exude has evaporated and the flesh starts to change colour. This will take 10–15 minutes.

3 Pour in the wine and, when it has evaporated, add the water. Cover and cook for 10 minutes, then add the potatoes, spring onions, lemon juice, and salt and pepper. There should be enough water to almost cover the ingredients; top up if necessary. Cover and cook gently for 40 minutes or until the cuttlefish is tender, stirring occasionally. Add the dill and cook for 5 minutes. Serve hot.

Cook's Tip
Cuttlefish has a tender yet firm texture and a mild, sweet flavour. When cooked, the flesh turns milky white. It can be used in any recipe that calls for squid.

Squid with Olives Energy 304kcal/1275kJ; Protein 30.3g; Carbohydrate 11.4g, of which sugars 6.8g; Fat 10.1g, of which saturates 1.7g; Cholesterol 422mg; Calcium 62mg; Fibre 1.7g; Sodium 468mg.
Cuttlefish Energy 423kcal/1761kJ; Protein 29g; Carbohydrate 18g, of which sugars 3g; Fat 26g, of which saturates 4g; Cholesterol 183mg; Calcium 123mg; Fibre 2g; Sodium 625mg.

King Prawns in Almond Sauce

A delectable seafood curry from Mauritius, where the prawns are large and succulent and christophene – or cho-cho as it's locally known – is a popular vegetable.

Serves 4

450g/1lb raw king prawns (jumbo shrimp)
600ml/1 pint/2½ cups water
3 thin slices fresh root ginger, peeled
10ml/2 tsp curry powder
2 garlic cloves, crushed
15g/½oz/1 tbsp butter or margarine
60ml/4 tbsp ground almonds
1 fresh green chilli, seeded and finely chopped
45ml/3 tbsp single (light) cream
salt and ground black pepper

For the vegetables

15ml/1 tbsp mustard oil
15ml/1 tbsp vegetable oil
1 onion, sliced
½ red (bell) pepper, seeded and thinly sliced
½ green (bell) pepper, seeded and thinly sliced
1 christophene, peeled, stoned (pitted) and cut into strips

1 Shell the prawns and place the shells in a pan with the water and ginger. Simmer, uncovered, for 15 minutes until reduced by half. Strain into a jug (pitcher), discard the shells and ginger.

2 De-vein the prawns, place in a bowl and season with the curry powder, garlic and salt and pepper and set aside.

3 Heat the mustard and vegetable oils in a large frying pan, add the vegetables and stir-fry for 5 minutes. Season, spoon into a dish and keep warm.

4 Wipe out the frying pan, then melt the butter or margarine in the pan and sauté the prawns for about 5 minutes, until pink. Spoon over the bed of vegetables, cover and keep warm.

5 Add the ground almonds and chilli to the pan, stir-fry for a few seconds and then add the reserved stock and bring to the boil. Reduce the heat, stir in the cream and cook for a few minutes, without boiling. Pour the sauce over the vegetables and prawns before serving.

Prawn and New Potato Stew

New potatoes with plenty of flavour, such as Jersey Royals, Maris Piper or Nicola varieties, are essential when making this effortless stew. Use a good quality jar of tomato and chilli sauce; there are now plenty available in many stores and supermarkets. For a really easy supper dish, serve the stew with warm, crusty bread to mop up the delicious sauce, and a mixed green salad.

Serves 4

675g/1½lb small new potatoes, scrubbed
15g/½oz/½ cup fresh coriander (cilantro)
350g/12oz jar tomato and chilli sauce
300g/11oz cooked peeled prawns (shrimp), thawed and drained if frozen

1 Cook the potatoes in lightly salted, boiling water for about 15 minutes, until tender. Drain and return to the pan.

2 Finely chop half the coriander and add to the pan with the tomato and chilli sauce and 90ml/6 tbsp water.

3 Bring to the boil, reduce the heat, cover and simmer gently for 5 minutes.

4 Stir in the prawns and heat briefly until they are warmed through. Do not overheat the prawns or they will quickly shrivel, becoming tough and tasteless.

5 Spoon into shallow bowls and serve sprinkled with the remaining coriander leaves, torn into pieces.

> **Cook's Tip**
> Vary the ingredients according to your store cupboard and your personal taste. If you want a milder dish, simply replace the tomato and chilli sauce with plain tomato sauce or passata. Add a chopped spring onion (scallion) for extra flavour.

King Prawns Energy 301Kcal/1251kJ; Protein 24.3g; Carbohydrate 6.1g, of which sugars 5.1g; Fat 20.1g, of which saturates 4.8g; Cholesterol 234mg; Calcium 154mg; Fibre 2.4g; Sodium 244mg.
Prawn Stew Energy 216kcal/919kJ; Protein 18g; Carbohydrate 33g, of which sugars 7g; Fat 2g, of which saturates 0g; Cholesterol 146mg; Calcium 90mg; Fibre 2g; Sodium 520mg.

King Prawns in a Coconut and Nut Cream

Coconut milk is used to make a luxurious sauce thickened with cashews, peanuts and breadcrumbs.

Serves 6

130g/4½oz/2¼ cups fresh white
   breadcrumbs
105ml/7 tbsp coconut milk
30 raw king prawns (jumbo
   shrimp), about 900g/2lb
400ml/14fl oz/1⅔ cups
   fish stock
2 large tomatoes, chopped

1 onion, quartered
2 fresh red chillies, seeded and
   roughly chopped
130g/4½oz dried shrimps
45ml/3 tbsp palm oil
2 garlic cloves, crushed
25g/1oz fresh root ginger, grated
75g/3oz/¾ cup roasted peanuts
50g/2oz/½ cup cashew nuts
60ml/4 tbsp coconut cream
juice of 1 lime
salt and ground black pepper
chopped fresh coriander (cilantro)
   and hot chilli oil, to serve

1 Place the breadcrumbs in a bowl and stir in the coconut milk. Leave to soak for at least 30 minutes. Purée, in a blender or food processor, then scrape into a bowl and set aside.

2 Peel the fresh prawns and set them aside in a cool place. Place the shells in a pan and add the fish stock and tomatoes. Bring to the boil, then simmer for 30 minutes. Strain into a bowl, pressing the prawn shells against the sides of the sieve with a wooden spoon to extract as much flavour as possible. Reserve the prawn stock but discard the shells.

3 Put the onion, chillies and shrimps in a blender or food processor and blend to a purée. Scrape into a pan and add the oil. Cook gently for 5 minutes. Add the garlic and ginger and cook for 2 minutes. Grind all the nuts in a food processor to a fine powder. Add to the pan and cook for 1 minute more. Stir in the breadcrumb purée and prawn stock and bring to the boil. Reduce the heat and continue to cook, stirring constantly, for 6–8 minutes, until thick and smooth. Add the coconut cream, lime juice and prawns. Stir over the heat for 3 minutes until the prawns are cooked. Season. Serve, add chopped coriander and a couple of drops of chilli oil to each portion.

Aromatic Prawn Laksa

This is a hearty dish, and is perfect when you are tired. Tiger prawns, vegetables and noodles are tangled together in a savoury coconut broth – flavours and textures that both soothe and stimulate the appetite.

Serves 4

6 dried red chillies
1 onion, chopped
1 small piece fresh root ginger,
   peeled and grated
5ml/1 tsp ground turmeric
45ml/3 tbsp Thai fish sauce
finely grated rind of 1 lime

8 macadamia nuts
5ml/1 tsp ground coriander
60ml/4 tbsp vegetable oil
475ml/16fl oz/2 cups fish stock
750ml/1¼ pints/3 cups coconut
   milk from a can or carton
225g/8oz dried flat rice noodles
60ml/4 tbsp thick coconut milk,
   made by dissolving grated
   creamed coconut in boiling
   water, or 120ml/4fl oz/½ cup
   coconut cream
400g/14oz raw headless tiger
   prawns (shrimp), shelled
   and deveined, with tails left
225g/8oz/4 cups fresh
   beansprouts
coriander (cilantro) sprigs, to serve

1 Soak the chillies in warm water for 30 minutes. Drain them, cut them in half and remove the seeds. Put the chillies, onion, ginger, turmeric, fish sauce, lime rind, macadamia nuts, ground coriander and half of the vegetable oil into a food processor or blender and process to form a smooth paste.

2 Heat the remaining oil in a pan, add the paste and fry for 5 minutes, stirring all the time to prevent sticking. Add the fish stock and simmer for a further 5 minutes.

3 Pour in the canned coconut milk, stirring constantly to prevent curdling. Bring to the boil and simmer, uncovered, for about 5 minutes. Meanwhile, cook the noodles in a separate pan of boiling water according to the packet instructions, drain and toss in a little oil. Set aside.

4 Stir the thick coconut milk and prawns into the soup. Simmer for a further 2–3 minutes. To serve, add noodles to serving bowls. Add the beansprouts and prawns, pour over the soup, add coriander and serve.

King Prawn Energy 368kcal/1538kJ; Protein 23g; Carbohydrate 19g, of which sugars 6g; Fat 23g, of which saturates 9g; Cholesterol 139mg; Calcium 321mg; Fibre 3g; Sodium 1296mg.
Prawn Laksa Energy 544kcal/2276kJ; Protein 29g; Carbohydrate 63g, of which sugars 13g; Fat 19g, of which saturates 3g; Cholesterol 244mg; Calcium 192mg; Fibre 4g; Sodium 1143mg.

Crayfish and Potato Stew with Fresh Cheese

The Peruvian variety of crayfish proliferate in the rivers of the south and there is no greater delicacy than fresh crayfish straight out of the water. The evaporated milk adds a touch of sweetness as well as a creamy texture.

Serves 6
675g/1½lb raw crayfish or king
 prawns (jumbo shrimp)
1kg/2¼lb floury potatoes
75ml/5 tbsp butter
1 small red onion, finely chopped
60ml/4 tbsp chilli sauce
5ml/1 tsp paprika
3 medium tomatoes, peeled,
 seeded and diced
5ml/1 tsp black mint
 (peppermint) leaves,
 finely sliced
500g/1¼lb queso fresco
 or mild feta cheese,
 cut into 2cm/¾in dice
120ml/4fl oz/½ cup
 evaporated milk
15ml/1 tbsp chopped parsley
 or mint leaves, to garnish
salt

1 Pour 350ml/12fl oz/1½ cups water into a large pan and bring to a boil. Drop the crayfish or prawns in, cover, and cook for 10 minutes.

2 Strain and reserve the stock: there should be about 250ml/8fl oz/1 cup. Put aside six whole crayfish or prawns. Peel the rest, remove their heads, and devein.

3 Boil the potatoes in their skins in lightly salted water until tender, then peel them and cut into 1cm/½in slices.

4 Heat the butter in a large pan and cook the onion until softened. Stir in the chilli sauce, paprika, tomatoes and mint, and cook for 3 minutes. Add the crayfish or prawn tails, the reserved stock, cheese and sliced potatoes.

5 Bring to the boil and simmer for 5 minutes. Add the evaporated milk, season to taste with salt and simmer for 5 more minutes. Serve, garnished with chopped parsley or mint leaves and the reserved whole crayfish or prawns.

Soft-shell Crab, Prawn and Corn Gumbo

A well-flavoured chicken and shellfish stock gives this dish the authentic taste of a traditional Louisiana gumbo.

Serves 6
30ml/2 tbsp vegetable oil
1 onion, chopped
1 garlic clove, chopped
115g/4oz rindless streaky
 bacon, chopped
40g/1½oz/⅓ cup plain flour
1 celery stick, chopped
1 red pepper, seeded
 and chopped
1 red chilli, seeded and chopped
450g/1lb plum tomatoes, chopped
2 large cobs of corn
4 soft-shell crabs, washed well
30ml/2 tbsp chopped
 fresh parsley
small bunch of spring onions,
 roughly chopped
salt and ground black pepper

For the stock
350g/12oz whole
 uncooked prawns
2 large chicken wings
1 carrot, thickly sliced
3 celery sticks, sliced
1 onion, sliced
handful of parsley stalks
2 bay leaves
1.5 litres/2½ pints/6¼
 cups water

1 To make the stock, peel the prawns and put the shells into a pan. Set the prawns aside. Add the remaining ingredients to the pan. Bring to the boil and skim. Cover and cook for 1 hour.

2 To make the gumbo, heat the oil in a large pan, add the onion and garlic and cook for 3–4 minutes. Add the bacon and cook for 3 minutes. Stir in the flour and cook for 3–4 minutes. When the mixture is turning golden, strain in the stock, stirring continuously. Add the celery, pepper, chilli and tomatoes, bring to the boil and simmer for 5 minutes. Cut the corn cobs into 2.5cm/1in slices, and add to the gumbo.

3 To prepare the crabs, remove the eyes and mouth, then cut across the face and hook out the stomach, a jelly-like sac. Turn the crab over and pull off the tail flap. Lift up both sides of the shell and pull out the gills or dead man's fingers. Quarter the crabs, then add to the gumbo with the prawns. Simmer for 15 minutes. Season, then stir in the parsley and spring onions. Serve.

Crayfish Stew Energy 541kcal/2262kJ; Protein 36.6g; Carbohydrate 34.1g, of which sugars 9.3g; Fat 29.5g, of which saturates 19g; Cholesterol 222mg; Calcium 411mg; Fibre 2.3g; Sodium 1639mg.
Crab Gumbo Energy 342kcal/1430kJ; Protein 30g; Carbohydrate 22g, of which sugars 9g; Fat 16g, of which saturates 3g; Cholesterol 147mg; Calcium 88mg; Fibre 4g; Sodium 638mg.

Louisiana Seafood Gumbo

Gumbo is a soup, but it is served over rice as a main course.

Serves 6
450g/1lb fresh mussels, cleaned
450g/1lb raw prawns, in the shell
1 cooked crab, about 1kg/2¼lb
small bunch of parsley, leaves
    chopped and stalks reserved
150ml/¼ pint/⅔ cup
    vegetable oil
115g/4oz/1 cup plain flour

1 green pepper, seeded
    and chopped
1 large onion, chopped
2 celery sticks, sliced
3 garlic cloves, finely chopped
75g/3oz smoked spiced sausage,
    skinned and sliced
275g/10oz/1½ cups white long
    grain rice
6 spring onions, shredded
cayenne pepper, to taste
Tabasco sauce, to taste
salt

1 Bring 250ml/8fl oz/1 cup water to the boil in a pan. Add the mussels, cover and cook over a high heat, shaking the pan frequently, for 3 minutes. Lift out opened mussels with tongs into a sieve set over a bowl. Discard any that fail to open. Shell the mussels and discard the shells. Return the liquid from the bowl to the pan and make up to 2 litres/3½ pints/8 cups with water.

2 Peel the prawns and set aside, reserving a few for the garnish. Put the shells and heads into the saucepan. Remove all the meat from the crab, separating the brown and white meat. Add all the pieces of shell to the saucepan with 5ml/2 tsp salt. Bring the shellfish stock to the boil and skim off the froth. Add the parsley stalks and simmer for 15 minutes. Cool the stock, strain it into a measuring jug and make up to 2 litres/3½ pints/8 cups with water.

3 Heat the oil and add the flour. Stir constantly until the roux is golden. Add the pepper, onion, celery and garlic. Cook for 3 minutes until the onion is soft. Add the sausage and reheat the stock. Stir the brown crab meat into the roux, then gradually ladle in the hot stock, stirring, until it is smooth. Simmer the gumbo for 30 minutes. Cook the rice until the grains are tender. Add the prawns, mussels, white crab meat and spring onions to the gumbo. Return to the boil, season with salt, cayenne and Tabasco sauce. Add the parsley leaves. Serve the soup over the hot rice.

Spicy Shellfish Couscous

This couscous is flavoured with harissa, a spicy chilli paste, then baked.

Serves 4–6
500g/1¼lb/3 cups couscous
5ml/1 tsp salt
600ml/1 pint/2½ cups warm water
45ml/3 tbsp sunflower oil
5–10ml/1–2 tsp harissa
25g/1oz/2 tbsp butter, diced

For the shellfish broth
500g/1¼lb mussels in their shells,
    scrubbed, beards removed
500g/1¼lb uncooked prawns
    (shrimp) in their shells

juice of 1 lemon
50g/2oz/¼ cup butter
2 shallots, finely chopped
5ml/1 tsp coriander seeds,
    roasted and ground
5ml/1 tsp cumin seeds, roasted
    and ground
2.5ml/½ tsp ground turmeric
2.5ml/½ tsp cayenne pepper
5–10ml/1–2 tsp plain
    (all-purpose) flour
600ml/1 pint/2½ cups fish stock
120ml/4fl oz/½ cup double
    (heavy) cream
salt and ground black pepper
small bunch of fresh coriander
    (cilantro), finely chopped

1 Preheat the oven to 180°C/350°F/Gas 4. Place the couscous in a bowl. Add salt to the warm water, then pour over the couscous, stirring. Set aside for 10 minutes. Stir the oil into the harissa to make a paste, then rub it into the couscous to break up any lumps. Transfer to an ovenproof dish, dot with butter, cover with foil and cook in the oven for about 20 minutes.

2 Put the mussels and prawns in a pan, add the lemon juice and 50ml/2fl oz/¼ cup water, cover and cook for 3–4 minutes, shaking the pan, until the mussels have opened. Drain the shellfish, reserving the liquor, and discard any closed mussels.

3 Heat the butter in a large pan. Cook the shallots for 5 minutes. Add the spices and fry for 1 minute. Off the heat, stir in the flour, the fish stock and shellfish cooking liquor. Bring to the boil, stirring. Add the cream and simmer for 10 minutes. Season. Shell two-thirds of the mussels and prawns, then add the shellfish and most of the fresh coriander to the pan. Heat through, then sprinkle with the remaining coriander. Fluff up the couscous with a fork or your fingers, working in the melted butter. Serve, ladling the broth over the couscous.

Shellfish Tagine

The distinctive mixture of spices and chillies used in tagines – charmoula – is a classic Moroccan marinade for many fish, meat and vegetable dishes.

Serves 4
60ml/4 tbsp olive oil
4 garlic cloves, sliced
1–2 green chillies, seeded
   and chopped
a large handful of flat leaf parsley,
   roughly chopped
5ml/1 tsp coriander seeds
2.5ml/½ tsp ground allspice
6 cardamom pods, split open
2.5ml/½ tsp ground turmeric
15ml/1 tbsp lemon juice
350g/12oz scorpion fish, red
   mullet or red snapper fillets, cut
   into large chunks
225g/8oz squid, cleaned
   and cut into rings
1 onion, chopped
4 tomatoes, seeded and chopped
300ml/½ pint/1¼ cups warm
   fish or vegetable stock
225g/8oz large, raw
   prawns (shrimp)
15ml/1 tbsp chopped fresh
   coriander (cilantro)
salt and ground black pepper
lemon wedges, to garnish
couscous or rice and crusty bread,
   to serve

1 Place the olive oil, garlic, chillies, parsley, coriander seeds, allspice and cardamom pods in a mortar and pound to a smooth paste using a pestle. Stir in the ground turmeric, salt, pepper and lemon juice.

2 Place the fish in a large glass bowl with the squid, add the spice paste and mix together. Cover and leave to marinate in the refrigerator for about 2 hours, or longer, if time allows.

3 Place the onion, tomatoes and fish or vegetable stock in a tagine, place in an unheated oven and set the oven to 200°C/400°F/Gas 6. Cook the vegetables for 20 minutes.

4 Remove the fish from the marinade, then drain. Set aside the squid and any excess marinade, then place the fish in the tagine with the vegetables. Cover and cook in the oven for 5 minutes. Add the prawns, squid rings and remaining marinade to the tagine and mix. Cover the tagine and return it to the oven for 5–10 minutes, or until all the fish, prawns and squid are cooked. Season and add the chopped coriander. Serve with lemon wedges.

Spicy Seafood Stew

Most Peruvian stews containing chilli and potatoes have their origins in the south of the country. However, that does not mean they are exclusively prepared in that region. This traditional dish is found in every seafood restaurant throughout the country. It is most often accompanied by boiled rice.

Serves 6
500g/1¼lb floury potatoes,
75ml/5 tbsp vegetable oil
1 medium red onion,
   finely chopped
3 garlic cloves, finely chopped
30ml/2 tbsp chilli sauce
250ml/8fl oz/1 cup dry white
   wine or light beer
1kg/2¼lb mixed seafood, such
   as mussels, whelks, scallops,
   squid, king prawns (jumbo
   shrimp), cleaned
30ml/2 tbsp potato flour (starch)
   or cornflour (cornstarch)
salt and ground black pepper

1 Boil the potatoes in their skins in salted water for 20 minutes, until tender. Drain and peel. Cut into slices and keep warm in a serving dish.

2 While the potatoes are cooking, heat the oil in a large pan and fry the onion and garlic for 10 minutes until the onion is golden. Add the chilli sauce, pour in the wine or beer and simmer for about 15 minutes.

3 Add the seafood mixture to the pan and season with salt and pepper. Simmer for a further 5 minutes.

4 Slake the potato flour or cornflour in 45ml/3 tbsp cold water and add to the stew. Simmer, stirring constantly. As soon as it thickens, remove from the heat and pour the sauce over the potato slices. Serve immediately.

> **Cook's Tip**
> Whelks are a saltwater shellfish rather like a snail. Their meat is salty, chewy and juicy, but can become rubbery if overcooked.

Shellfish Tagine Energy 301Kcal/1261kJ; Protein 37.2g; Carbohydrate 7.1g, of which sugars 5.5g; Fat 14g, of which saturates 2.2g; Cholesterol 269mg; Calcium 128mg; Fibre 2.2g; Sodium 251mg.
Seafood Stew Energy 335kcal/1405kJ; Protein 32g; Carbohydrate 22.7g, of which sugars 5.4g; Fat 10.6g, of which saturates 1.2g; Cholesterol 325mg; Calcium 161mg; Fibre 1.7g; Sodium 385mg.

Yellow Prawn Curry

This south-east Asian speciality lives up to its name with an intense turmeric yellow colour that matches the strong flavours.

Serves 4

30ml/2 tbsp coconut or palm oil
2 shallots, finely chopped
2 garlic cloves, finely chopped
2 red chillies, seeded and
   finely chopped
25g/1oz fresh turmeric, finely
   chopped, or 10ml/2 tsp
   ground turmeric
25g/1oz fresh root ginger,
   finely chopped

2 lemon grass stalks, finely sliced
10ml/2 tsp coriander seeds
10ml/2 tsp shrimp paste
1 red (bell) pepper, seeded and
   finely sliced
4 kaffir lime leaves
about 500g/1¼lb fresh prawns
   (shrimp), shelled and deveined
400g/14oz can coconut milk
salt and ground black pepper
1 green chilli, seeded and sliced,
   to garnish

To serve
cooked rice
4 fried shallots or fresh chillies,
   seeded and sliced lengthways

1 Heat the oil in a wok or heavy frying pan. Stir in the shallots, garlic, chillies, turmeric, ginger, lemon grass and coriander seeds and fry until the fragrant aromas are released.

2 Stir in the shrimp paste and cook for 2–3 minutes. Add the red pepper and lime leaves and stir-fry for a further 1 minute.

3 Add the prawns to the pan. Pour in the coconut milk, stirring to combine, and bring to the boil. Cook for 5–6 minutes until the prawns are cooked. Season with salt and pepper to taste.

4 Spoon the prawns on to a warmed serving dish and sprinkle with the sliced green chilli to garnish. Serve with rice and fried shallots or the fresh chillies on the side.

Variation

Big, juicy prawns are delectable in this dish, but you can easily substitute them with scallops, squid or mussels, or a combination of all three, depending on what is available.

Goan Prawn Curry

Goan dishes use generous amounts of chilli, mellowed by coconut milk and palm vinegar. In this delicious coconut-enriched prawn curry, cider vinegar makes an equally good alternative to palm vinegar.

Serves 4

500g/1¼lb peeled king or tiger
   prawns (jumbo shrimp)
2.5ml/½ tsp salt, plus extra to taste
30ml/2 tbsp palm or cider vinegar
60ml/4 tbsp sunflower or olive oil

1 large onion, finely chopped
10ml/2 tsp crushed fresh root ginger
10ml/2 tsp crushed garlic
2.5ml/½ tsp ground cumin
5ml/1 tsp ground coriander
2.5ml/½ tsp ground turmeric
2.5ml/½ tsp chilli powder
2.5ml/½ tsp ground black pepper
75g/3oz/1 cup creamed coconut,
   chopped, or 250ml/8floz/1 cup
   coconut cream
4 green chillies
30ml/2 tbsp chopped fresh
   coriander (cilantro) leaves
plain boiled rice, to serve

1 Put the prawns in a non-metallic bowl and add the measured salt and vinegar. Mix and set aside for 10–15 minutes.

2 Heat the sunflower or olive oil in a medium pan and add the onion. Fry over medium heat until the onion is translucent.

3 Add the ginger and garlic and continue to fry for about 2 minutes over a low heat, until lightly browned.

4 Mix the cumin, coriander, turmeric, chilli powder and pepper in a bowl and add 30ml/2 tbsp water to make a pouring consistency. Add to the onion and cook, stirring, for 4–5 minutes until the mixture is dry and the oil separates from the spice mix.

5 Next, pour in 200ml/7fl oz/¾ cup warm water, the creamed coconut and salt to taste. Stir until the coconut has dissolved.

6 Add the prawns along with all the juices in the bowl, bring the pan to the boil, reduce the heat and cook for another 5–7 minutes. When the prawns curl up, they are cooked.

7 Add the whole chillies and simmer for 2–3 minutes. Stir in the chopped coriander. Serve with plain boiled rice.

Yellow Curry Energy 230kcal/965kJ; Protein 26.4g; Carbohydrate 16g, of which sugars 13.5g; Fat 7.2g, of which saturates 1g; Cholesterol 263mg; Calcium 226mg; Fibre 2.7g; Sodium 519mg.
Goan Prawn Curry Energy 171kcal/723kJ; Protein 21.9g; Carbohydrate 10g, of which sugars 7.4g; Fat 5.3g, of which saturates 2.5g; Cholesterol 227mg; Calcium 136mg; Fibre 1g; Sodium 344mg.

Prawn and Cauliflower Curry with Fenugreek and Star Anise

This is a basic fisherman's curry from the southern coast of Vietnam. Simple to make, it would usually be eaten with noodles, rice or chunks of baguette to mop up the deliciously fragrant, creamy sauce. Fenugreek seeds, which are much used in Indian cookery, have a distinctive curry aroma, brought out by dry frying.

Serves 4

450g/1lb raw tiger prawns (jumbo shrimp), shelled and deveined
juice of 1 lime

15ml/1 tbsp sesame or vegetable oil
1 red onion, roughly chopped
2 garlic cloves, roughly chopped
2 Thai chillies, seeded and chopped
1 cauliflower, broken into florets
5ml/1 tsp sugar
2 star anise, dry fried and ground
10ml/2 tsp fenugreek, dry fried and ground
450ml/¾ pint/2 cups coconut milk
salt and ground black pepper
1 bunch fresh coriander (cilantro), stalks removed, leaves chopped, to garnish

1 In a bowl, toss the prawns in the lime juice and set aside. Heat a wok or heavy pan and add the oil. Stir in the onion, garlic and chillies. As they brown, add the cauliflower. Stir-fry for 2–3 minutes.

2 Toss in the sugar and spices. Add the coconut milk, stirring to make sure it is thoroughly combined. Reduce the heat and simmer for 10–15 minutes, or until the liquid has reduced and thickened a little.

3 Add the prawns and lime juice and cook for 1–2 minutes, or until the prawns turn opaque. Season to taste, and sprinkle with coriander. Serve immediately.

> **Variation**
> Other popular combinations include prawns with butternut squash or pumpkin.

Whelks and Potatoes in Red Chilli Sauce

The South Pacific produces a wealth of shellfish, and local cooks have devised many recipes. One of these is the picante, a spicy stew of shellfish and potatoes. It is often very hot, but in this recipe the amount of chilli is subtle.

Serves 4

75ml/5 tbsp vegetable oil
1 large red onion, finely chopped
15ml/1 tbsp chilli sauce

500g/1¼lb white potatoes, peeled and cut into 2cm/¾in dice
2 fish or vegetable stock (bouillon) cubes dissolved in 500ml/17fl oz/generous 2 cups water
500g/1¼lb cooked whelks, cut into 1cm/½in pieces
salt
15ml/1 tbsp chopped parsley, to garnish
boiled rice and corn on the cob, to serve

1 Heat the oil and fry the onion over high heat for 3 minutes, then reduce the heat to medium and cook for a further 7 minutes, until starting to brown. Stir in the chilli sauce.

2 Add the potatoes and the stock to the pan, bring to the boil and cook for 20 minutes.

3 Add the whelks, season with salt if necessary (the stock may be salty enough) and simmer for a further 5 minutes, until the potatoes are tender and the whelks are heated through.

4 Transfer to a serving dish, sprinkle with the chopped parsley and serve with rice and corn on the cob.

> **Variation**
> You could use any shellfish that is available for this simple dish, instead of whelks. For example, you could use squid, prawns, oysters, clams, mussels or octopus. For a fresh flavour, try using a green chilli; remove the seeds and slice finely and add to the pan at the same time as the onion.

Prawn Curry Energy 232Kcal/971kJ; Protein 25g; Carbohydrate 13g, of which sugars 12g; Fat 10g, of which saturates 2g; Cholesterol 219mg; Calcium 167mg; Fibre 2.2g; Sodium 500mg.
Whelks Energy 362kcal/1514kJ; Protein 27.9g; Carbohydrate 28.2g, of which sugars 7.3g; Fat 16g, of which saturates 1.8g; Cholesterol 156mg; Calcium 138mg; Fibre 2.7g; Sodium 577mg.

Index